FLORIDA STATE
UNIVERSITY LIBRARIES

OCT 20 1993

TALLAHASSEE, FLORIDA

BORDERLANDS IN AFRICA

A MULTIDISCIPLINARY AND COMPARATIVE FOCUS ON NIGERIA AND WEST AFRICA

BORDERLANDS IN AFRICA

A MULTIDISCIPLINARY AND COMPARATIVE FOCUS ON NIGERIA AND WEST AFRICA

Edited by

A.I. ASIWAJU
Professor of History

and

P.O. ADENIYI
Professor of Geography

UNIVERSITY OF LAGOS PRESS — NIGERIA

DT
4765
B67
1989

© 1989 A.I. Asiwaju and P.O. Adeniyi

All rights reserved. No part of this publication may be reproduced, stored in
a retrieval system or transmitted in any form or by means, electronic,
photocopying, recording or otherwise without the prior permission of the
editors and the University of Lagos Press.

ISBN 978-2264-92-x (hardcover)
      978-2264-48-2 (paperback)

Printed by Civiletis International

Notes on Editors and Contributors

The Editors

Asiwaju, A.I.—Professor of History, Dean, Faculty of Arts (1983-85); research mainly in Comparative Borderlands Studies with particular reference to localised impact of international boundaries, transborder cooperation and regional integration in Africa; publications include *Western Yorubaland Under European Rule, 1889-1945: A Comparative Analysis of French and British Colonialism* (London: Longman 1976), *Borderlands Research: A Comparative Perspective* (The University of Texas at El Paso Centre for Inter-American and Border Studies, No. 6. Border Perspective Series. 1983); Ed. *Partitioned Africans: Ethnic Relations Across Africa's International Boundaries, 1884-1984* (Lagos University Press, 1984; C. Hurst & Co. Publishers, London and St. Martin's, New York, 1985) plus numerous book chapters and articles in internationally reputed journals including *The Journal of the Historical Society of Nigeria, Journal of African History (Cambridge University Press), Africa* (Quarterly Journal of the International African Institute in London), *African Studies Review* and *Comparative Education Review* (U.S.) *Bulletin de L'IFAN* (Dakar, Senegal) and *Presence Africaine* (Paris); Member of the International Board of Editors, *Journal of Boderlands Studies* (Las Cruces: New Mexico State University Press).

Adeniyi, P.O.,—Professor of Geography, University of Lagos, sometime Adjunct Professor of Geography, University of Waterloo, Canada; Research Interest in Remote Sensing; Consultant to U.N. Outer-Space Affairs Division, President of the Nigerian Remote Sensing Society; author of book chapters and articles in numerous international journals including *The Nigerian Geographical Journal* (Nigeria); Photogrametric, Engineering and Remote Sensing Journal (U.S.); *Applied Geography* (U.K.) and *Geojournal* (Germany); serves as member of the International Advisory Editorial Board for Geocarto International, (Singapore), *Photogrammetria,* and *The Nigerian Cartographer.* Presently functions as Co-ordinator and Principal Investigator in a Cooperative Research with the University of Waterloo, funded by the International Development Resource Centre (IDRC), Ottawa, Canada.

Contributors

Abass, O.—Professor of Computer Science and currently (1987) Dean of Faculty of Science, University of Lagos.

Adebekun, O.—Surveyor-General, Survey Division of the Federal Ministry of Works, Lagos, Nigeria. He has since the 1985 Seminar voluntarily retired from public service.

Adejuyigbe, O.—Professor of Geography, University of Ife. Research and publications mainly in the area of Internal Administrative Boundary Problems. Works include *Boundary Problems of Western Nigeria* (University of Ife Press, 1977) and several journal articles and chapters in books.

Aderibigbe, D.A.—Senior Lecturer, Department of Civil Engineering, University of Lagos. Research and publications in the area of materials science.

Adeyoyin, Felicia A.—Senior Lecturer in the Department of Curriculum Studies, Faculty of Education, University of Lagos. Several book chapters and journal articles on Social Studies.

Adigun, O.—Senior Lecturer, Department of Private and Property Law, Faculty of Law, University of Lagos.

Ajomo, M.A.—Professor of Law, Department of Jurisprudence and International Law, University of Lagos. Author of several works, mainly in the area of international law. Now Director, Institute of Advanced Legal Studies, University of Lagos.

Akintola-Arikawe, J.O.—Associate Professor of Geography, University of Lagos, with expertise and outstanding publication activities in the area of human geography.

Akintola-Bello, O.—Associate Professor, Department of Finance. Faculty of Business Administration, University of Lagos.

Aradeon, Susan B.—Senior Lecturer, Department of Architecture, University of Lagos.

Babatunde, E.D.—Lecturer in the Department of Sociology, University of Lagos. Research interest is in the area of cultural anthropology.

Balogun, O.Y.—Associate Professor of Geography, University of Lagos. Expertise is in cartography.

Brann, C.M.B.—Professor of Linguistics, University of Maiduguri, Maiduguri, Nigeria. Numerous publications on a wide range of linguistic problems. Chairman, Publications, Committee of the University of Maiduguri.

Ekoko, E. Formerly Senior Lecturer, Department of History, University of Ibadan, now Associate Professor, Nigeria Defence Academy, Kaduna. Research focus on Military and Strategic aspects of African History.

Ekpenyong, J.O.L.—Senior Lecturer, Department of Geography, University of Lagos. Expertise in Cartography; has a range of experience including a record of service at the World Bank.

Fakolade, A.—Lecturer, Department of Geography, University of Lagos.

James, I.—Formerly of the Department of History, University of Maiduguri, now (1987) Head of Department of History, University of Jos, Nigeria.

Johnson, M.A.—Senior Lecturer, Department of Modern European Languages, University of Lagos; expertise in French Literature.

King-Aribisala, K.—Lecturer in the Department of English, University of Lagos.

Malaka, S.L.O.—Senior Lecturer in Zoology, University of Lagos. Primary research focus is on the termites on which several illustrous publications have been recorded. Teaching interest in Animal Behaviour.

Martinez, O.J.—Professor of History and Director, Centre for Inter-American and Border Studies, The University of Texas at El Paso. Research focus is on Mexican history in the context of the U.S. and its relations with Mexico. Numerous publications include *Border Boom Town: Ciudad Juarez Since 1848* (University of Texas Press, 1978) and Ed. *Across Boundaries: Transborder Interaction in Comparative Perspective* (Texas Western Press, 1986).

Momoh, C.S.—Senior Lecturer in Philosophy, University of Lagos.

Nwuneli, M.L.—Senior Lecturer in the Department of English, University of Lagos. Expert in Afro-American Literature.

Owhotu, V.—Senior Lecturer, Department of Curriculum Studies Faculty of Education, University of Lagos. Research focus is on French language teaching in Nigeria and West Africa.

Sobowale, I.—Senior Lecturer in Mass Communication, Faculty of Social Sciences, University of Lagos. Research interest is in political communication and media performance. Publications include *Scientific Journalism* (Lagos: John West, 1981).

Stoddard, E.R.—Professor of Sociology and Anthropology, The University of Texas at El Paso; Pioneer in US-Mexico Borderlands Studies; Founder of the Association of Borderlands Scholars. Numerous journal articles, books and book chapters, the most outstanding work being *The Encyclopaedic Borderlands Sourcebook* which he co-edited with Richard L. Nostrand and Jonathan P. West (University of Oklahoma Press, 1982).

Strassoldo, R.—Professor of Sociology at the University of Trieste and formerly Director, Institute of International Sociology, Gorizia, Italy. Author of several incisive analyses of the European border impact including *Frontier Regions: An Analytical Study* (Strasbourg Council of Europe, 1973), *Temi di Sociolologia Delle Ed* (with Delli Zotti) *Cooperation and Conflict in Border Areas* (Milan: Franco Angeli 1982).

Ugonna, N.—Professor of Igbo Studies, Department of African Languages and Literature, University of Lagos.

Appendix

Keynote address by the Honourable Minister of Internal Affairs, Major-General M. Magoro, Opening Ceremonies, University of Lagos, Faculty of Arts Annual Seminar on Issues of Borderlands in Africa, University of Lagos, Lagos. March 27, 1985.

Preface

This book is the outcome of an experiment. It results from the proceedings of the first in the series of Annual Seminar of the Faculty of Arts, University of Lagos, held from 27 to 29 March 1985. The series are aimed at a multidisciplinary and comparative diagnosis and prescription in respect of specific societal problems. As a multidisciplinary, inter-university and international collaboration, the 1985 seminar focused on Africa's international boundaries with particular reference to the lands and local communities directly impacted by the borders. Unlike the more familiar works—mostly by experts in International Law, International Politics and Diplomatic History—which concentrates on the boundaries as lines of demarcation between sovereign states—the studies presented in this book focus on the boundaries in terms of their localised impact.

This emphasis on the spatial dimension is not only conducive to the use of multidisciplinary strategy as a tool of analysis, it also offers the opportunity for a focus on a neglected area of border research, which is of instant policy relevance. In Western Europe and North America, borderlands studies are essentially post-Second World War developments. This is especially the case in Europe where scholarly studies and policy analyses of 'frontier regions' (the alternative reference to 'borderlands', more frequently encountered in the European literature) have developed in scope and sophistication in view of the support they provide for transborder co-operation policy as a lately recognised prerequisite for wider regional integration.

After a decade or so of operation on the wrong assumptions that border problems are indistinguishable from the wider question of European Unity and that the former would automatically disappear once the latter is achieved, the European Economic Community (EEC) eventually came into agreement with the views, first articulated within the framework of the Council of Europe, that borders and borderlands constitute distinct entities, and that integration can take place at the level of the sovereign states without resolving the problem of conflicting relationships across nation-state boundaries. It was realized, in fact, the integration at the level of a continent or its sub-regions cannot be fully achieved without the special and deliberate effort for transborder co-operation specifically. In North America, as manifestly made clear on the U.S.-Mexico border, borderlands studies are essentially the intellectual wing of the transborder cooperation movements based on the intensive interaction between the peoples and the economies on both sides of the border.

One basic lesson to be learnt in the European and North American experiences is the closeness of the link that has been forged between organised research and policy formulation. In North America, the importance attached to border policy is reflected not only in the giant strides on border research as demonstrated in the large number of public-funded specialised institutions (programmes, centres, institutes etc.) located in all the universities on both sides of the U.S.-Mexico border. The creation in 1976 of the Association of Borderlands Scholars (ABS), the first of its kind anywhere, is a clear indication of the extent to which border studies as a specialised area of research endeavour have progressed. Although the core membership of the ABS is made up of mostly American experts focusing on the U.S.-Mexico border, there is a growing comparative interest in studies of borders and borderlands elsewhere in the world. This concern for a comparative perspective is manifested in the editorial policy and format of the Journal of Borderlands Studies, first published under the auspices of the ABS in 1985.

The biennial symposium of Mexican and American Universities, inaugurated in 1980 within the framework of the U.S.-Mexico Joint Commission on Cultural Co-operation, provides a common platform for both American and Mexican scholars of the border. Sponsored jointly by the Consortium of U.S. Research Program for Mexico (PROFMEX) and the Asociacion Nacional de Universidades Institutos de Ensenanza Superior (ANUIES), the Symposium focuses on themes of policy relevance and involves active participation of policy makers (national and local politicians and administrators, including diplomats) drawn from both sides of the border. The greater prominence of the U.S.-Mexico border, than other U.S. borders, is a final illustration of the marriage between border policy and research concerns in the North American region.

In Western Europe, the mutual link between government and research is even more explicit. A great deal of the developments in transborder co-operation endeavours, undertaken with an ever increasing vigour since the mid-1950s to compliment the wider regional integration activities, has been owed to the interaction between Council of Europe on the one hand and, on the other, specialised, research institutions and personnel on problems of 'frontier regions'.

Whether such programmes are housed by private organisations of individual border communities, such as the *Regio Basiliensi* astride the Swiss-French-German border in and around the tri-national urban conglomeration of Basel and the *Euregio* astride the German-Deutsche Border, or they are based in university institutions as are the cases of the Institute of International Sociology at Gorizia (affiliated to the University of Trieste in Italy), the University Institute of European Studies in Geneva and the Institute of European Studies of the Free University of Brussels, studies of European border regions directly address policy questions. Nothing illustrates the link between European border research and policy better than the series of Symposia on European Transborder Co-operation, organised by the Office of Regional and Local Authorities of the Council of Europe in 1973 and 1975. The European Outline Convention on Transborder Co-operation between Territorial Communities and Authorities, now ratified by all members of the Council of Europe, is a direct outcome of these symposia.

Africa today stands in dire need of the same effort aimed at the promotion and achievement of transborder co-operation to compliment the regional integration endeavours which have been the focus of attention. The history of these efforts must be viewed to include not only the case of defunct East African Common Market which has its genesis in the early colonial period of British East Africa, but also the Economic Community of West Africa (ECOWAS) inaugurated in 1975 and the African Common Market or Economic Community programmed for 2000 A.D. by the Organisation of African Unity's Lagos Plan of Action of 1980. The acceleration of these efforts since 1980 has been borne out of the correct conviction about regional integration as the only viable way towards the achievement of self-reliance and auto-determined development for the continent.

But imaginative as these endeavours have been, the chances for success are constantly put to flight in the face of the almost ubiquitous border wars or threats of war. Concern for security, fuelled by the political instability of most African States, has continued to promote the contradictory force of extremist nationalism which tends, characteristically, to sharpen rather than blunt the edges of state. This unhappy situation partly explains the complete lack of role for shared borders and adjacent borderlands in spite of their un rivalled qualifications as natural starting points for the prosecution of wider regional integration schemes for Africa. The omission is also conceptual: regional integration in Africa is pursued so exclusively within the framework of state-centric relationship, that the Lagos Plan of Action recognises no level of implementation lower than the individual member states of the Organization of African Unity.

Informed more by doctrines of international relations than by principles of transnational interaction, the on-going efforts at regional integration in Africa have thus continued to be deprived of the vitality of being rooted in the realities of cross-border geographical and historical interactions. Thus while a great deal has been achieved at the level of the interaction among the ruling elites, actual effects are yet to be produced on the ground. This failure is especially noticeable in border regions which, far more than other sub-national areas, offer unrivalled opportunities for international co-operative interaction.

It is the strongly felt need for organised knowledge, as prerequisite for transborder co-operation policy in Africa, that impelled us at the Faculty of Arts, University of Lagos, to consecrate the first in the series of our annual seminars on the preliminary exploration of the subject. Since little work of direct relevance has been undertaken, our ambition is necessarily a modest one: to provide an introduction to the subject. Hence the concentration on essentially elementary questions of definition of the field of study and the indication as to the nature and range of available material as well as research methodology and opportunities.

While the book, like the seminar that produced it, is preponderantly an affair of the Faculty of Arts, University of Lagos, there are substantial and enriching inputs from sister Faculties of Law, Social Sciences, Business Administration, Engineering, Environmental Design (now Environmental Sciences), Science and Education of the same institution. The invaluable papers by colleagues from other Nigerian universities clearly demonstrate the worth of inter-university co-operation on research within the nation. The indispensably fresh insight in the papers on the European and North American experiences illustrated the profit in a comparative analysis as well as in international interaction among experts. With the exception of the papers by Professor O. Abass of our Department of Computer Science on 'Transborder Data Flows' and by Dr. S.I.C. Malaka of our Department of Biological Sciences on 'Territorial Behaviour in Animals', which were commissioned thereafter to fill some of the identifiable gaps, all the contributions included in this book are based on actual presentations at the 1985 seminar.

The Keynote Address at the seminar was presented by the then Honourable Minister of Internal Affairs, Major General Mohammadu Magoro; the text is included as an Appendix to this book. Together with the paper by Mr. O. Adebekun, the then Director of Federal Survey Department, Federal Ministry of Works, Lagos, the Address is the evidence of the endeavour to relate the academic presentations to real policy concerns.

The book is in four main sections. Section I containing the five papers by O. Adejuyigbe, M.A. Ajomo, C.S. Momoh, A.I. Asiwaju and K. Ogundowole, is aimed at the elucidation of the spatial dimension of the basic concepts of 'border' and 'borderland'. The perspectives range from those of the geographer and the lawyer to those of the philosopher. Professor Adejuyigbe's raises no major controversies: it is essentially a matter-of-fact description of borderlands characteristics based on studies of both African and non-African situations. This global cast has the advantage of viewing the African within its proper world contexts. Professor Ajomo drew attention to the essentially historical relationship between borders and borderlands when he observed with characteristic precision: "Without boundaries there can be no borderlands." Thus while the concern of law is exclusively with 'boundaries', this cannot be properly viewed as irrelevant to borderlands concerns. It is, however, his "submission that the regime of borderlands is an entirely new development in international law." He argues for its full exploration in view of its prospects and potentials for a radical re-orientation of African states towards transborder co-operation and the promotion of continental and world peace. The paper by Dr. Ogundowole is, as titled, a philosophical speculation; that by Dr. Momoh is more empirically based. Asiwaju's essay concludes this section by drawing attention to policy implications of the spatial dimension of the definition of borderlands through a detailed discussion of manifestations in Nigeria's 'gateway' Local Government Areas.

Section II warns against one-sided approach to definition. Studies of borders especially demand a multilateral examination in view of the fact that lines drawn on the ground are no more than one of several manifestations of the same phenomenon of discrimination: race, ethnicity, language, sex, class and location. The need to probe the bio-psychological basis derives from the fact that an idea always begins in the mind before it manifests itself in other ways. The seven contributions included in this Section are aimed at drawing attention to the functional and comparative dimensions of meaning. Malaka's fascinating essay on "Territorial Behaviour in Animals" results from a strong desire for the knowledge of the origins. A proper reading of this contribution should, in addition to other merits, produce a desired humbling effect on the mind. The data and arguments recall those in Robert Ardrey's *The Territorial Imperative* and similarly remind us of the probability of the animal origins of property and nation. The lessons are also the same: the extreme danger in acts of aggression, and the self and group preservations, nourishment and development that result from mutual respect and co-operation between individuals and groups over claimed territory and property.

Babatunde discusses the periphery-centre antagonism as it manifests itself in relationship between the 'Urban Poor' and the 'Urban Rich' based on the two fascinating sets of comparative data, (Lagos and Chicago). Similarly based on data drawn from the two sides of the Northern Atlantic Ocean is Mrs. Nwuneli's discussion of "Black Aesthetics in Poetry". Mrs. King-Aribisala focuses on discrimination or borders based on sex. Miss Johnson's is an aggressive criticism of perspectives which limits discussion of the border phenomenon to only its spatial manifestations. Professor Ugonna's essay focuses on the wider subject of 'ethnic boundaries', and a case study of bridges that are encountered across them. Dr. D.A. Aderibigbe provides a specialised discussion of the concept of border in the world of matters and the factor of materials in intra-African and World conflicts as well as potentials for regional and global integration and development.

Section III is a sub-collection of thirteen diverse studies on Nigeria and the associated wider areas of the Economic Community of West African States (ECOWAS), each highlighting distinct factors or potentials in transborder relations in the sub-region. Balogun's is a useful discussion of the evolution of Nigeria's international boundaries. Although it goes over grounds which older works by J.C. Anene (1970) and J.R.V. Prescott (1971) have made familiar, the stress on the cartographic dimension offers a significant freshness. O. Adebekun updates the historical data by focusing on present-day problems regarding the boundary demarcation or re-demarcation; while Professor Brann's is a highly informative essay on the linguistic profiles of Nigeria's Northern and Eastern boundaries, Dr. Owhotu discusses the "conflict resolution" roles and potentials of the same factor in the wider area of the continent. Through an insightful emphasis on the architectural traditions, Susan Aradeon's essay compliments Brann's on the linguistic profile in a general effort to present a comprehensive picture of the indigenous cultural flow across the Nigeria-Niger border.

Adigun, Ekepenyong, Ekoko and James are explicit policy analyses. Adigun discusses the problem of citizenship and nationality when the definition in the Nigerian Constitution confronts such indigenous Nigerian communities with members on the other side of the national boundaries. Ekepenyong's focuses on the same problem with reference to shared natural and mineral resources. Ekoko's is an essay on the strategic history of Nigeria's western border and the lessons for present-day Nigeria. Ibrahim James' is a comprehensive historical analysis of the Lake Chad as an example of a coherent natural region split among several adjacent sovereign states with resultant conflicts as well as opportunity for co-operation, depending on the vision exercised by the political leadership of the inter-related states. The essay is an objective examination which points to the shortsightedness of the national governments, including the Federal Government of Nigeria, whose unilateral actions explain the poor performance—and, indeed, the failure—of the Lake Chad Basin Commission.

The remainder of Section III is made up of five contributions which concentrate on Nigeria in the wider context of the ECOWAS region. Fakolade's cast is in the mode of the rival relationships between cosmopolitanism and provincialism as dynamics for nationstate development. Akintola-Arikawe discusses the geographical aspect of the Law of the Sea as it affects the ECOWAS region. Akintola-Bello's is a speculative discussion of contraband across the boundaries of Nigeria and related West African countries, based on the familiar game theory in economic science. The papers by Abass and Sobowale—the one on the issue of Transborder Data Flows in Computer Science and the other on the role of Mass Communication as factor in the creation or resolution of border conflicts—are interrelated. Together with Peter Adeniyi's paper in Section IV below, devoted to the discussion of the use of remote-sensing techniques to collect and collate data for transborder planning and development, these papers constitute a familiar trio on mass communication, computer science, and remote sensing so critical in any meaningful discourse of transborder co-operative programming.

The fourth and final section is made up of the papers which discuss research strategies. Peter Adeniyi's paper draws attention to the collections and collation of such data as those relating to land use, natural and mineral resources, so important for regional planning and development across international boundaries. The use of this technique is a triumph over obstacles such as lack of roads and other forms of access across certain stretches of international boundaries (e.g., the inaccessible forest reserve on the Nigeria-Benin boundary in the area of Oyo State in Nigeria). Felicia Adeyoyin's paper is essentially advocacy of multidisciplinary approach to research. The historical accounts and descriptions of research programmes in Western Europe by Raimondo Strassoldo, and in the U.S.-Mexico borderlands by both Ellwyn Stoddard and Oscar J. Martinez are included in view of the lessons of experience that are there to be learnt from these older parts of the borderlands world. This Section is closed with a discussion of a specific research agenda on Nigeria's international boundaries. This research agenda has, at least in part, motivated the studies on Nigeria's International Boundaries subsequently undertaken by the National Institute for Policy and Strategic Studies, Kuru, Jos, Nigeria, with a substantial participation and contribution by experts based in the Faculty of Arts of University of Lagos.

Acknowledgements

These prefatory remarks must not be concluded without a word or two of appreciation and acknowledgement to those who have made both the original seminar and the book on its proceedings possible. In this regard, our indebtedness goes first and foremost to the Ford Foundation whose grant provided the bulk of the financial assistance both for the organisation of the seminar and, more particularly, for the publication of this book. It was the Ford Foundation grant that enabled us to invite such highly renowned 'limologists' as Dr. Raimondo Strassoldo, former Director of the Institute of International Sociology, Gorizia, Italy, and Consultant to Council of Europe as well as Dr. Oscar J. Martinez, Director of the Centre for Inter-American and Border Studies of the University of Texas at El Paso and Professor Ellwyn R. Stoddard, the founder and first President of the Association of Borderlands Scholars dedicated principally to the multidisciplinary study of the U.S.-Mexico borderlands.

The Federal Ministry of Internal Affairs, Lagos, not only offered a robust matching grant in support of the seminar; its manifest interest and participation secured for the meeting a most needed legitimisation. There is perhaps no better illustration of the Ministry's continuous interest in the project than the invaluable financial assistance it has offered for the book to be printed. The offer resolved the last of the obstacles that have stood in the way of this publication. The recognition of the policy significance of the seminar by the Federal Ministry of National Planning made it possible at all for our original proposal to have been recommended to the Ford Foundation.

It is perhaps needless to say that only the merits of the essays included need to be credited to the authors. Any defects of the overall presentation are our own responsibility. We sincerely apologise for all of them, visible and invisible. We seize this opportunity to express our regret for inability to include all the papers presented at the seminar, inclusions have been due less to the issue of the intrinsic merit of such papers than the constrains imposed by rising publication cost vis-a-vis highly limited funding resources.

Whether or not the individual participants have been so specifically featured, it is the solemn wish of the editors to present the book as the joint effort of all who participated in the University of Lagos, Faculty Arts, First Annual Seminar on Issues of Borderlands in Africa, 27-29 March, 1985. The book goes out in the fervent hope that it will stimulate both the scholarly study and policy analysis of African borderlands as linchpins for regional integration of the continent.

A.I. Asiwaju
P.O. Adeniyi
University of Lagos
25 January 1989

Foreword

It is my honour and privilege to be requested to write the foreword to this obviously important book.

The history of Nigeria, like that of any other nation-state, may be described as one of a continuous encounter with border problematics. We have here varying manifestations of all the categories. The spatial are evidently the most dramatic and, for a nation-state with a demand for a well-defined territorial framework, the most critical. We have a total of five international boundaries measuring, all together, about 4.775 kilometres of length: 770 running partly through swamps and riverbeds and partly on dry land with Benin Republic; 1,490 of mostly land border with Niger; 75 with Chad running entirely through lacustrine region; 1,680 of also partly land and partly reparian frontier line with Cameroun and 760 maritime along the Atlantic Ocean.

This external boundary system does not include the description of the continental shelf based on the emergent United Nation's Law of the Sea. The spatial dimension must also be reckoned to include considerations for the internal or intranational boundaries that define the 21 Constituent States of the Federation (excluding, the Federal Capital Territory of Abuja) and the 304 Local Government Areas including those of the Federal Capital Territory.

The functional categories of borders we have had to contend with as rapidly growing nation-state include those of the over 200 ethnic groups as well as the cleavages between religious camps, especially those between the adherents of the two world-wide monotheisms of Christianity and Islam. All these are in addition to the fissions between social classes, to say nothing of the new phenomenon of women versus the menfolk.

Readers with just a nodding acquaintance with our history as a nation should have no difficulty in appreciating the roles which these different categories of borders have played and are continuing to play as dynamic factors in the nation's growth and development. Witness, for example, the frequency of border incidents and related issues, as reported almost on a daily basis by the media, vis-a-vis the proximate countries. Relate this to the occasions which had compelled Government to order the expulsion of illegal aliens in 1983 and 1985 and the closure of the borders with special reference to the episode of 1984-1986. Recall the outbreak of the Civil War in 1967 and its prosecution to the end in 1970 'to keep Nigeria one' and save the Federation from forces of disintegration. Add the subsequent boundary disputes and clashes between several of the constituent States. This litany will be incomplete if reference is not made to 'the national question' and the treatment of ethnic minorities as well as the clashes of Muslims with Christians such as was sadly witnessed in Kaduna State in March 1987. In these and other ways and forms, the border poses challenges that severely put to test the managerial capability of those in charge of the machine of state.

One essence of the challenge is in the delicate balance that must be observed between the mutually contradictory demands for boundary maintenance and boundary eradication. On the one hand is the demand for boundaries which every social system, including—of course—the nation-state, makes in order to maintain its identity and ensure its orderly development vis-a-vis other rival systems. This obvious demand must be counter-checked, on the other hand, by the need to allow for fruitful interaction and avoid isolation. The task, then, is in determining when and how to 'open' as against when and how to 'close' the border. To make the point less abstract, we can state the policy question as it relates to our international boundaries as they must be made to function vis-a-vis our commitment to such regional integration schemes as the Economic Community of West African States (ECOWAS) and the Organisation of African Unity.

The problems posed call for knowledge in the type of organised form that is presented in this book. The special interest of the Ministry of Internal Affairs, in both the book and the Seminar that gave rise to it, derives from the Ministry's basic duty as an agency created by the state to ensure its maintenance from within. To fulfil this task, the Ministry not only houses the Departments of Customs and Excise and of Immigration Services, state apparatuses specially designed for border control and management. It also accommodates the Department of Prisons. This commitment to the system's maintenance necessarily links the Ministry with such other law-enforcement agencies as the Police, the State Security Services and the Armed Forces. There is perhaps no better illustration of this official commitment to system maintenance and, therefore, border control and management than the Ministry's prominent membership of the recently created National Boundary Commission, a multi-ministerial outfit aimed at a more effective management of our international and intra-national boundaries.

Borderlands in Africa provides an appropriate introduction to one of the most important and topical issues of our time both in Africa and elsewhere in a wider world, troubled and endangered by all kinds of invidious divisions. Its multidisciplinary and comparative canvas matches with a truly multidimensional and ubiquitous phenomenon. One major attraction about the book relates to the high calibre of the contributors which include the cream of expertise on the subject, that has ever been assembled anywhere. Professor Asiwaju, the leading editor and evidently the moving spirit behind the 1985 Seminar on which the book is based, is an internationally renowned authority on African boundary problems. There is no doubt, then, that the book has substantially expanded the existing frontiers of knowledge: reading it will surely benefit not just the scholar and the policy-maker but the general public as well.

J.N. Shagaya fss, psc, mni, Colonel
Hon. Minister of Internal Affairs
Ministry of Internal Affairs, Abuja
4 March 1988

Table of Contents

Notes on Editors and Contributors   v
Preface   ix
Acknowledgements   xv
Foreword   xvii
List of Figures   xxi
List of Tables   xxiii

SECTION I

BORDERS AND BORDERLANDS: THE SPATIAL ASPECT   25

1. Identification and Characteristics of Borderlands in Africa
   O. Adejuyigbe   27
2. Legal Perspective on Border Issues   *M.A. Ajomo*   37
3. Borderland as the Function of Space and Time   *E.K. Ogundowole*   45
4. A Critique of Borderland Theories   *C.S. Momoh*   51
5. Borderlands: Policy Implications of Definition for Nigeria's 'Gateway' State Administrations and Local Governments   *A.I. Asiwaju*   63

SECTION II

THE FUNCTIONAL BORDER   85

6. Territorial Behaviour in Animals   *S.L.O. Malaka*   87
7. Urban Marginality's Perception of Self   *E.D. Babatunde*   105
8. Bridges Across Africa's Ethnic Boundaries   *N. Ugonna*   117
9. Buchi Emecheta's *Destination Biafra*   *K. King-Aribisala*   129
10. The Black Aesthetic   *M.L. Nwuneli*   139
11. Border in French and French-African Literature   *M.A. Johnson*   151
12. Boundary Problems and the Policies of African Nations
    D.A. Aderibigbe   161

SECTION III
STUDIES AND POLICY IMPLICATIONS   178

13   The Process of Cartographic Definition of Nigerian Boundaries
     O.Y. Balogun   181

14   International and Interstate Boundaries in Nigeria   *O. Adebekun*   205

15   A Socio-Linguistic Profile of Nigeria's Northern and Eastern Borders
     C.M.B. Brann   213

16   Borderland 'Equilibrium' in Africa   *V. Owhotu*   247

17   Transborder Cultural Interaction   *S. Aradeon*   259

18   Nationality and Citizenship   *O. Adigun*   271

19   Borders in International Relations and Military Strategy
     A.E. Ekoko   279

20   Potentials of Nigerian Boundary Corridors as Sources of International
     Economic Conflict   *J.L.O. Ekpenyong*   293

21   Lake Chad as an Instrument of International Co-operation
     I. James   307

22   Off-Shore Boundaries and Jurisdictional Zones in Relation to
     ECOWAS Countries   *J.O. Akintola-Arikawe*   317

23   The Political Economy of Artificial
     Boundaries   *O. Akintola-Bello*   331

24   Transborder Data Flow and Action Plan for ECOWAS   *O. Abass*   339

25   The Role of Communication in Border Relations   *I. Sobowale*   345

26   Cosmopolitanism vs. Provincialism   *A. Fakolade*   353

SECTION IV
RESEARCH STRATEGIES AND A PROPOSED AGENDA   361

27   Some Questions and 'Sky' Solutions to Border Resource Management
     P.O. Adeniyi   363

28   Methodology of the Multi-disciplinary Problem   *F.A. Adeyoyin*   375

29   Border Studies: The State of the Art in Europe   *R. Strassoldo*   385

30   Research Activity on the U.S.-Mexico Borderlands
     O.J. Martinez   397

31   Developmental Stages of U.S.-Mexico Borderlands Studies
     E.R. Stoddard   403

32   The 'Area Study' Approach to Research on Nigeria's Borders
     A.I. Asiwaju   425

Appendix—Minister's Keynote Address   *Major General Magoro*   433

List of Figures

Chap. Num.	Figure Num.	Description
4	1	Minimal Borderland
	2	Zero Borderland
	3	Maximal Borderland
5	1	Border Administrative Units
6	1	Diagramatic schema of territorial and reproductive behaviour of the dragonfly *Libellula Saturata*
	2	A central nest of *Macrotermes natalensis* and surrounding *Cubitermes sankurensis*
	3	Illustration of trail laying and non-trail laying abdominal positions of *Amitermes evuncifer*
	4	Results obtained from the experiment on trail laying behaviour before and after food supply
	5	Bitterling male with mussel
	6	Diagram of lizard behaviour
12	1	Schematic of the analogy between open thermodynamic and social systems
	2	The S-Gyre of phase transformation in materials illustrating the universal structure of change
	3	Philosophical model of a system or global approach applied to the boundary problems and social systems
13	1	Niger to Lake Chad boundary in 1898 (straight lines and arc)
	2	The scheme of definition of Nigerian boundaries
	3	Nigeria without boundaries in 1885
	4	Nigerian boundaries by 1900
	5	Nigeria-Benin boundary from the coast to lat. 9°N
	6	Nigeria-Benin boundary after delimitation survey
	7	Nigeria-Benin boundary from lat. 9°N to the Niger in 1898
	8	Evolution of the Nigeria-Niger boundary
	9	Nigeria-Kamerun boundary in 1893
	10	Nigeria-Kamerun boundary from Yola to Lake Chad after delimitation survey
	11	The sharing of German Kamerun between Britain and France

Chap. Num.	Figure Num.	Description
15		Map of the Federal Republic of Cameroun showing the spread of Pidgin English
		Nigerian ethnic groups survey 1972
		A provisional language map of Nigeria
17	1	Zaria Mosque
	2	Sarkin Gobir Mosque (Nigeria)
	3	Moussadeye Mosque (Nigeria)
	4	Outer hall of the Filinge palace (Nigeria)
	5	Room for wife of billage head of Amori
	6	Merchant reception hall, Kouremaria (Niger)
20	1	Nigeria and its neighbours
	2	Ethnic groups and subgroups of Nigeria's borderlands
	3	Border administrative units
31	1	Evolution of social organization levels in the new world
	2	Cultural areas of North America
	3	Contemporary political-legal border between Mexico and the U.S.

List of Tables

Chap. Num.	Table Num.	Description
5	1	Nigeria's main 'gateway' states and local government areas
6	1	Courtship sequence in 3-spined stickleback
8	1	The sixteen configurations of divination
	2	16 Odu/Ogbara configurations of Ifa/Afa divination
12	1	Nigeria's import bill during the first six months of 1980
	2	World and United States reserves of 18 metals in 1980
	3	World production of 18 metals in 1980
15	1	List of language or dialect clusters
20	1	Ethnic groups or subgroups of Nigeria's borderlands
	2	Nigeria and Cameroun: crude oil exports
22	1	Basic off-shore jurisdictional zones recognized by the 1st (1958) and third (1982) Unclos and the main characteristics ascribed to them
	2	ECOWAS countries by type of location
	3	Existing claims to off-shore jurisdictional stage by ECOWAS countries
31	1	Typology of development stages in the field of U.S.-Mexico borderland studies

SECTION I
BORDERS AND BORDERLANDS:
THE SPATIAL ASPECT

Identification and Characteristics of Borderlands in Africa

by O. Adejuyigbe

This chapter discusses methods of identifying borderlands and examines their geographic characteristics within frameworks of political units. The discussion is divided into four sections. Firstly, there is a focus on the concept of borderlands; then, a review of different ways of identifying or delimiting borderlands area is undertaken; this is followed by an examination of the main geographic characteristics of borderlands; and finally, the characteristics are illustrated with examples from the borderlands of both intra-state political units and the sovereign states in Africa.

The Concept of Borderlands

A discussion of borderlands should first clarify the difference between them and frontiers. Such clarification is necessary because some writers use the two terms interchangeably whilst the differences noted by others are not clear. For example Kristof (1959, p. 270) stated that frontiers were borderlands, whilst De Blij (1967, p. 200) described the zone on either side of an international boundary suffering from the interruptive effects of the boundary as a frontier. House (1980, p. 458) described frontier zone as the territory flanking an international boundary and in which territorial effects might be concentrated. He later (1982 p. 55) described a borderland as the zone in which there is economic, social, cultural and political interaction between states. He also sated (1982 pp. 56 and 57) that within the borderland there may be a frontier zone for special privileges restrictions on the nationals of the states concerned.

The definition of frontier by House is different from its widely accepted definition as zone into which expansion takes place from one or more core areas (Kristof, 1959; De Blij 1967, p. 199; Whebell, 1968, p. 100; Adejuyigbe 1974, pp. 84-85). Expansion from a core areas into a frontier will continue until the people involved encounter either physical or human hindrances to their activities. Where the hindrances cannot be removed or overcome, the expansion will end and ultimately the limit or boundary of the political unit concerned will be fixed. The hindrances may be people from other core areas who were also expanding into the frontier from other sides. When the expansionists from different core areas meet within the frontier there may be mutual acceptance and co-operation on resource allocation. However, when some resources are inadequate for the needs of all sides attempts will be made by one or the other of the parties to claim exclusive rights over the location and exploitation of such resources. In the process boundaries will be delimited between the parties. This process implies that frontiers are zones within which boundaries are located, or occasionally, where no human hindrances are involved, the boundaries may be at the outer edge of the frontier. In either case frontiers are features of the period before boundaries are delimited or fixed.

From the above, borderland means land close to the border or boundary. This suggests that a boundary must be fixed before the associated borderlands can be identified. In other words borderland is a feature of the period after boundary delimitation. The implication of this is that it is inappropriate to identify a frontier within a borderland as House has done or even to use frontier and borderland interchangeably as some other scholars have also done. Consequently, it is suggested that whilst frontier continues to be used for the zone of expansion before boundary delimitation, borderland should be restricted to the post-boundary.

As explained in the preceding paragraph the term borderland should refer to a territory or zone close to the boundary of a political unit. This means that each of the political units separated by a particular boundary has its own borderland in relation to that boundary. In other words there are two borderlands are closely linked. This writer is of the view that an understanding of issues relating to borderlands requires a knowledge of the basis of delimiting the relevant boundaries and the sociopolitical situation in the political units concerned. The delimitation of the boundaries is a function of the basis or rationale for establishing the political units separated by the boundaries. The political units may be established on the basis of either of two principles, namely the territoriality and the cultural affinity. The territoriality principle is that political unit comprises members of the community and all the territory belong to them even if they are not the only people occupying such territory. On the other hand the cultural affinity principle is that all members of a community will be grouped in the same political unit even if they do not own all the territory occupied by them (Adejuyigbe, 1978).

Boundaries of political units constituted under the territoriality principle will, ideally, separate the territories of the different groups constituting the political units. If all the political units agree on the territoriality principle in delimiting their boundaries, borderland issues and problems will relate to the following:

(i) allocation of territories where there is conflict as to the first occupants and hence as to ownership,

(ii) rights over conquered territory especially where the land owners were not conquered by the conquering forces;

(iii) people occupying territories which do not belong to their own political unit and the conditions for such occupation;

(iv) territorial enclaves;

(v) where one political unit adopts the territoriality principle whilst its neighbour adopts cultural affinity, there may be serious borderland problems, particularly where members of the political unit insisting on cultural affinity occupy land belonging to citizens of that adopting the territoriality principle.

Even if the political units agree on the adoption of the cultural affinity principle borderland problems may arise in respect of the following:

(vi) the allocation of transitional areas where individuals have characteristics of the culture of the core areas of the political units;

(vii) unoccupied areas;

(viii) cultural enclaves;

(ix) rights of victors over defeated people who remain dominant in the conquered area;

(x) where citizens of political unit continue to expand after a boundary has been agreed and such migrants become dominant in a part of the adjacent political unit where they were not present or substantial before boundary delimitation.

Some of the borderland problems enumerated above are related to boundary delimitation and demarcation. Ideally such problems should be resolved by the time the boundary is demarcated. In reality, this does not happen with the result that many of such problems remain unsolved during demarcation hence they become problems in the borderlands and are most evident in the form of boundary disputes.

Identification of Borderlands

Borderlands may be identified in any of three ways:

by reference to the frontier which existed before boundary delimitation;

by reference to administrative units close to the boundary.

According to House (1980), many countries have treaties defining zones on either side of their international boundaries. The purpose of the zone may be give special customs privileges for residents, provide for investments and movements between the countries. It may also be for the purpose of creation of a demilitarized zone between belligerent states. Such areas are the borderlands of the countries concerned with reference to the particular boundaries. The width of the borderlands so delimited will be as specified in the treaties. For example, within the European Economic Community (EEC) the width of such zones is 20 kilometres, whilst the Italy-Yugoslavia treaty provided for a zone of up to 30 kilometres wide depending on changing needs. Also, according to House (1982, pp. 57-59) between 1961 and 1971 Mexico defined its borderland with the U.S.A. as a zone 20 kilometres in width and within which foreign manufacturing industries could be established with certain privileges and concessions. The U.S.A. also has statutory definition of its borderland with Mexico. The width of the borderland was about 240 kilometres (150 miles) up to 1965 when it was reduced to 40 kilometres (25 miles). Mexicans were allowed to move freely within the zone without special permission.

The definition of borderlands by treaty has the advantage of clarity. However, it should be appreciated that it is not always easy to determine all the points which are at the specified distances from the boundaries. Furthermore, there will be administrative difficulties especially when the zone cuts across a local government area or other important administrative units in any of the states. Additionally the overall effects of the boundary may extend beyond the stipulated zones.

The borderlands may also be identified on the basis of the frontier which existed before boundary delimitation and demarcation. For operational purposes, a frontier can be defined as defined as the zone where there is an overlap of the influence of the relevant core areas. In terms of territorial claims it will be the zone where there were conflicting claims over territory before boundary agreement. Culturally, the frontier is the zone where the elements of the two cultures are found especially where individuals possess traits of the cultures or there is in fact a competition for dominance between the cultures. In which every way the frontier is defined the tendency is that the final boundary is usually located within it. This means that usually there are sections of the former frontier within each of the political units separated by a boundary. Each political unit may describe its borderland with respect to the section of the frontier within it.

Definition of the borderlands with reference to the frontier has the advantage of realism in that is shows the borderlands as the transitional areas between the political units concerned. Following the definition of frontier by many scholars and their views that frontiers disappear when boundaries are fixed (Kristof 1959, p. 271; De Blij 1967, p. 200); (Adejuyigbe 1975, pp. 1-2) and the suggestion made earlier that borderlands are territories close to the boundary, it seems perfectly justified to define borderlands in terms of the frontier which existed before boundaries were delimited. However, it is to be noted that such frontiers were never clearly delimited. Indeed there may be no agreement on the cultural definition as different scholars may not agree on the indices to be used for the delimitation as shown by the attempt to delimit the U.S. borderlands which will cut across administrative units in the countries concerned.

The delimitation of the borderlands can also be based on the recognised local administrative areas within the political units. This can be justified on three grounds. First is that, usually local administrative areas are based on the spatially discrete communities in a political unit. The smallest of the communities may be a group of rural settlements which recognise the same central place and patronise the same social service centres such as markets and educational, health or religions centres. At other levels, the largest communities may be the ethnic nations or traditional sociopolitical units which had a history of independent political organization such as the traditional political units in many parts of Africa. Depending on the size of the political unit and of the communities, the latter may be given formal recognition by the government. Thus at the level of the traditional political units, village groups are recognised as a type of administrative unit even though the government of the modern state may not accord formal recognition to them. At the level of the sovereign states it is usual to give some recognition to the traditional political units even when they are not constituted into separate administrative units within the present set up. The implication of this is that there are appropriate recognised units for the identification of borderlands at both the local (intra-state) and international levels.

Another justification for the delimitation of borderlands on the basis of administrative units is that governments at whatever level usually refer matters pertaining to an area to the authorities of the administrative unit nearest to the affected area. The authorities are expected to assist in making investigations and rendering reports to headquarters. This practice means that matters affecting areas near a boundary will be referred to the headquarters of the administrative units closest to the relevant part of the boundary. Consequently, all administrative units adjacent to the boundary can be regarded as borderland units.

A third justification for adopting administrative units to identify borderlands is that data collected in respect of a political unit is usually published on the basis of administrative units. Such data include those on demographic characteristics, population movements, economic issues and other sociopolitical matters. This is particularly the case at the level of the sovereign state, but even at local or intra-state levels, some data are aggregated for village groups, etc. For example, it has been reported that in Nigeria the names shown for some rural settlements were in fact those for the groups of settlements of which the ones named were the focal points (Adejuyigbe & Arowolo 1972, p. 82). This means that census data and other information indicated against the named rural settlements are probably those of all those settlements in the group. The essence of this discussion is that the administrative units provide a good framework for collecting or analyzing data on borderlands.

If borderlands are to be delimited on the basis of administrative units there should be a set of criteria for such exercise. In this regard, two sets of criteria can be considered for adoption: namely the locational criterion or the characteristic or feature criterion. Administrative areas may be designated as borderland on the basis of their location with respect to the boundary. To this end, all units which abut directly on the external boundary will be designated as borderland units. The advantage of this is easy recognition. The disadvantage is that borderland characteristics and effects may go beyond those administrative units adjacent to the external boundary. For example, some units which are close but not adjacent to the external boundary may share borderland characteristics. Thus in Figure 1 the shaded administrative units may share borderland characteristics even though they do not abut on the external boundary.

A way out of the problem discussed in the preceding paragraph is to delimit the borderland on the basis of whether or not certain borderland characteristics or effects are to be found in particular administrative units. The characteristics are those of the transition zone or frontier area. The intensity or degree of such characteristics may depend on the purpose of study. For example Nostrand (1970) delimited the borderland of the U.S.A. with Mexico on the basis of counties with 50% Hispanic surnames; House (1982) adopted Counties with 35% for his delimitation of the same borderland. This lack of agreement on the cut-off point or even the particular characteristics to be used in the delimitation is a problem with this approach. But then, that problem is common to all attempts at statistical and quantitative methods of regional delimitation.

Borderland Characteristics

The characteristics of borderlands may be examined in terms of location, interaction patterns, and transitional features.

Location

The most evident feature of borderlands is their location with respect to the rest of their political units. The borderlands are usually the farthest from the core areas and the capitals in any particular direction except in the rare situation where the capital or core area is located at the boundary. This locational characteristic has important implications for the borderlands. The implications are largely due to the way governments function. The Governments and other administrative machinery of a political unit exist to cater for the interests of the population. For this reason government activities are concentrated in the areas where they will be of benefit to the greatest number of people. In particular the less ubiquitous facilities are concentrated in regional headquarters which are expected to service people in a number of local government areas. Such regional headquarters are located in the centres of population influence (CPI) of the areas they are to serve. Usually such CPIs are not at the extreme. This then means that usually borderland areas do not have in them regional facilities or the non-ubiquitous goods and services. Consequently, borderland populations have to travel to other parts of their political units to enjoy or have advantage of such services and facilities.

Interaction Patterns

There may be peaceful or conflicting interactions in borderland areas. The peaceful interaction characteristics of borderlands may be examined in two ways. First is the interaction with the core of their respective political units and second is the interaction between the two borderlands on either side of a particular boundary. The borderland-core interaction is a product of the locational characteristics. As the most distant part of their political units, borderlands areas tend to have less interaction with the core areas. In some cases where communications are difficult interaction between borderland population and the core areas may be highly restricted. In particular, visits by government officials may be virtually non-existent because such visits are usually to regional headquarters. Government functionaries do not visit borderlands with any regularity. Even when visits are made to every local government area, including those in the borderlands, places in the real borderlands are usually left out. Thus people in those areas, who cannot travel to the local government or regional headquarters, cannot meet or get to know government functionaries.

The restricted nature of borderland-core interactions means that borderlands are usually the last to be affected by cultural or technological innovations originating in the core of the political units. Thus borderland populations are usually regarded as conservative or backward by the other parts of their political units. Such an attitude may lead to feelings of alienation from the scheme of things by the borderland people.

On the other hand, however, the two borderlands on either side of a political unit are neighbours, hence there is considerable interaction between them. To appreciate this it has to be remembered that the boundary itself is a line with no appreciable width. The boundary is not marked in every section. Consequently, people who are operating close to it will not always be aware of its existence even though they may recognise that they belong to different political units. In effect such people will interact like any two neighbours. They will jointly patronise some social facilities like markets, and members of the communities will jointly visit each other like neighbours. Even at the official level the neighbouring functionaries will co-operate for certain purposes like maintenance of law and order or the like. This relationship will include inter-marriages and developments such as bilingualism of some people in the borderland areas.

The net effect of the inter-borderland relationships described in the preceding paragraph is that it may be difficult to determine the political identity of individuals and even whole communities in the borderlands. This in itself may affect the administration of such areas and may lead to conflict over territories between the two political units concerned.

Borderlands are areas of potential conflict over territory between adjacent political units. There are two possible sources of such conflicts: the local and the central sources. Conflicts may arise because of disputes between individuals over specific parcels of land. Each individual would turn to his government for support of his claims. The settlement of any such dispute would have to be at the level of the central governments of the two political units concerned. Therefore, if not carefully settled such local inter-personal disputes may involve international arbitration or the like. It is to be noted that if the disputes had been between two citizens of the same political unit the settlement might have gone to the court or other internal arbitration panels.

Territorial disputes may originate from any of the central governments. This is especially so where there are resources in which the governments are interested or where some areas are desired for military or other strategic reasons. In such cases the governments may want to insist on previous boundary agreements or even challenge the interpretation being given by the opposite side to the agreements. The involvement of the borderland population may be minimal especially where the boundary in question had been superimposed on the territory or social group of the borderland communities. Even then the impact of such disputes on the borderland population could be great in that troops may be dispatched to the area to protect the interests of the central governments. Even if no actual fighting takes place the deployment of troops to an otherwise peaceful area could have great psychological effects on the borderland population.

Where there is actual fighting over territory the first set of people to be affected will be those in the borderlands. In the first place each government may move sections or the entire population of its borderlands to safer areas within its own political unit. Such population movement will disrupt the social and economic life of the people concerned. Worse still during the fighting the property destroyed will be those of the borderland population. Therefore even if each person is able to come back to the same areas there will be great losses and it will take some time for the borderland population to settle back again. If the fighting should lead to the transfer of territory from one political unit to another it may mean a change of allegiance for those previously occupying the area of alternatively such people may not be willing or may not be allowed to settle in the transferred territory. A forced change of allegiance has adverse psychological impact whilst permanent displacement causes inconvenience and material losses from which some people may not be able to recover.

The interaction patterns discussed in the preceding paragraphs have implications for integration of borderland areas with the other parts of their political units. The peripheral location, lack of contact with government officials and relative disadvantage vis-a-vis other areas in the access to social services and other government opportunities may create disenchantment for borderland areas. However, since the adjacent areas are also borderlands, the disenchantment may not be expressed in desires to secede. At the same time the position makes it difficult for borderlands to be highly enthusiastic about the political unit concerned.

From the above it will be seen that the conflict situation in a borderland may lead to strong loyalist sentiments to the political unit. This is particularly the case where the government of the political unit has supported territorial and other claims of its borderland population against those of adjacent political units. In such cases the borderland population will resent any attempt to separate them from the core even though they may not enjoy much material advantage from the core.

It is possible to explain the attitudes of borderland populations in the non-conflict and conflict situations discussed in the two paragraphs above by the principle that the loyalty of the borderland population to their political units is a function of the interest of the core areas of those political units in promoting or protecting interests considered to be important by the borderland populations.

Transitional Characteristics

Borderlands are transitional zones—territorially, culturally and economically. The transition or change from one political unit to the other takes place at the boundary. However territorial-claims and land use interest of citizens of the different political units may cut across the boundary. For example it has been reported (De Blij 1967, p. 200) that in parts of the Portuguese-Spanish borderlands it is difficult to determine whether one is in Spain or in Portugal. The unsettled disputes over territorial claims between citizens of adjacent political units are to be found in the borderlands. For this reason the borderlands are the sections of a political unit which have potential of being transferred from one area of jurisdiction to the other.

Borderlands are also cultural transition zones. The interaction of people from different cultures at the borderlands leads to a mutual adoption of cultures. Individuals may speak the languages of the two cultures. Housing styles, religious ideas and other cultural traits may be mutually adopted. This cultural transition characteristic is to be expected since the borderlands were previously frontiers which, according to Kristof (1959, p. 273), are zones of transition between different spheres of life and which provide opportunities for mutual interpretation and sway.

Borderlands are economic transition zones. The products of the adjacent political units are exchanged at official and non-official exchange points (markets, e.g.) in the borderlands. This is a product of the inter-borderland interaction patterns. At the level of the sovereign states efforts are made to control such exchanges either by recognition of the borderlands as economic or trading zones where citizens of adjacent states may freely engage in economic activities or by creating special exchange or transfer border posts. However, it is generally realised that not all economic transactions pass through official border posts. Most sovereign states seem to accept or resign themselves to small-scale transactions through unofficial routes but make determined efforts to prevent large scale movements and transactions through such channels.

The transitional characteristics of borderlands make them the zones to be most affected by developments in adjacent states. In particular, during periods of stress or conflict in a particular state refugees find it easy to seek accommodation in the borderland areas of the adjacent state. Where the refugees are politically opposed to the government of their own state, a borderland may be subjected to military attacks from the opposing state. Whether or not refugees are engaged in anti-government activities their presence would mean greater pressure on the resources and facilities of borderland areas. This in turn would create hardship for the refugees and their hosts.

Characteristics of African Borderlands

The characteristics discussed above are common to both local and international borderlands all over the world. Consequently, they are applicable to African intra-state or international border situations. For example borderlands in Africa are remote from the capitals and other core-areas of their political units especially at the international level because the capital of many African States are located at the coast or at extreme corners of the countries, e.g. in Algeria, Sudan, Zaire, Nigeria, Ghana, Niger or Tanzania.

Inter-borderland interaction are highly pronounced especially where there are ethnic or traditional political ties between the people on either side of a boundary. Such interactions involve utilization of land for pastoral or arable purposes, attendance at markets and social ceremonies. Such interactions have been reported on the following borderlands: Ghana/Togo (Harrison-Church, 1951, p. 120) Nigeria/Republic Du Benin (Prescott, 1965, p. 63), Nigeria/Niger (Thom, 1970, pp. 169-204), Somali/Kenya (McEwen, 1971, p. 124); and Kenya/Tanzania (McEwen, 1971, pp. 148-149). These are only a few of many examples of borderlands in which inter-borderland interactions take place.

Boundary disputes are also to be found across borderlands in Africa as they are on the Sino-Soviet, Indo-China borderlands or those of Europe or South America. Although such disputes are not unique to African borderlands efforts should be made to find acceptable solutions to them. Those concerned with finding such solutions must bear in mind that the main point in boundary disputes is that the boundaries resulting from previous agreements are not acceptable. Consequently such disputes cannot be settled by reference to previous agreements but by studies which will examine the evolution of existing boundaries and the bases of the complaints about them. Suggestions for the solution of boundary disputes should be derived from such studies.

The studies suggested above will require detailed fieldwork on the history and patterns of land occupance in borderlands. Such studies should be undertaken by teams comprising geographers, historians, lawyers, anthropologists and possibly surveyors. The findings and recommendations of such teams on each boundary dispute should be submitted to national or appropriate sub-national government in the case of intra-state issues. In the case of international boundary disputes such findings and recommendations should be submitted to a committee of the O.A.U. which will act as an arbitration panel and whose decision will be final on each case studied.

Conclusion

Based on a review of the general characteristics of borderlands irrespective of their location, this paper comes to the conclusion that there are no features unique to borderlands in Africa. The remote locations, the interaction patterns, boundary disputes and transitional characteristics are common to borderlands all over the world. Consequently, it is to be realized that no matter the degree of inter-state boundary adjustments many of the problems and features of borderlands will remain in Africa. Even then, efforts should be make to resolve boundary disputes in borderland as these adversely affect the development process both locally and nationally. Scholars, government functionaries and policy makers should pay attention to the need to minimize the adverse effects of any particular characteristics of borderlands.

Bibliography

Adejuyigbe, Omolade, "Evolution of inter-community boundaries in Africa" *Cashiers De Geographie De Quebec* Vol. 18, No. 43, April 1974, pp. 83-105.

_____ *Boundary Problems in Western Nigeria: A Geographical Analysis,* (Ile-Ife: Univ. of Ife Press, 1975).

_____ "Principles of affinity and territoriality in the administration of inter-community borderlands" in Oguntoyinbo et al., *Resources and Development in Africa: Papers Submitted to the Reg. Conference of the Int. Geographical Union, Lagos, Nigeria* (Lagos: Federal Surveys, 1978), pp. 200-206.

Adejuyigbe, O. and Arowolo, O. "The Problems of Population Enumeration in the Rural Areas of Western Nigeria: The Example of Pars of Origbo Area in Ife Division" in Igun, A.A. and Acsadi, G.T. (eds), *Demographic Statistics in Nigeria*, (Ile-Ife: Demographic Research and Training Unit, 1972), pp. 77-93.

De Blij, H.J., *Systematic Political Geography*, (New York: John Wiley, 1967).

Harrison-Church, R.J., *Modern Colonization*, (London: Hutchinson Univ. Library, 1951).

House, J.W. "The frontier zone: a conceptual problem for policy makers", *International Political Science Review* Vol. I, No. 4, 1980, pp. 456-477.

_____ *Frontier on the Rio Grande: A Political Geography of Development and Social Deprivation*, (Oxford: Clarendon Press, 1982).

Kristof, L., "The nature of frontiers and boundaries", *Annals Ass. of American Geographers*, Vol. 49, 1959, pp. 269-282.

McEwen, A.C., *International Boundaries of East Africa*, (Oxford: Clarendon Press, 1971).

Nostrand, R.L., "The Hispanic-American borderland: delimitation of an American culture region" *Annals Ass. of American Geographers* Vol. 60, 1970, pp. 638-661.

Prescott, J.R.V., *The Geography of Frontiers and Boundaries*, (London: Hutchinson Univ. Library).

Thom, D.J. , "The Niger-Nigeria borderlands: a politico geographical analysis of boundary influence upon the Hausa", unpub. Ph.D. thesis, Dept. of Geography, Michigan State Univ., 1970.

Whebell, C.F., "Core areas in intra-state political organization" *Canadian Geographer* Vol. XII, 1968, pp. 99-112.

CHAPTER 2

Legal Perspective on Border Issues

by M.A. Ajomo

Some Preliminary Observations and Definitions

It is not unusual to start this type of discourse with some clarification of terms
or words used; for, in law, words may, at times, be attributed their technical rather
than their ordinary meaning depending on the context in which they are used. For
a start, the terminologies—boundary, frontier and border—have at times been used
interchangeably. Surprisingly, the ordinary meaning of each as given by the dictionary does not clearly bring out any distinctions. A boundary is an alignment or
an imaginary line which marks the legal termination of the territory of one state or
political unit which has an international status and role, and the commencement of
the territory of another state, or political unit.[1] In the case of sea and airspace boundaries, the termination of a state's territory adjacent to internal waters or the upper
atmosphere delineates the boundaries. A boundary is a line and not a zone, it has
not notional or actual width. A boundary marks a separation between territories or
states. What it separates are areas of administration or sovereignty.[2]

Frontier on the other hand, is used in common parlance as a synonym for international boundary; hence we speak of "crossing the frontier", "frontier posts" and
so on. Modern technical usage distinguishes the two terms. Boundary is linear
feature, frontier a zone; boundary is a legally prescribed or agreed separation of
jurisdiction, frontier is a zone of actual contact or separation, in the political,
geographical or economic sense.[3] "Border" is also used as a synonym for "boundary"; in contradistinction to "boundary", it has reference only to international
boundaries.

From the foregoing, it appears that the terms, frontier and border have closer
links with each other than for example, boundary. Yet, it is difficult, if not impossible, to discuss frontiers and borders on their own without boundaries. Borderland
is a word strange to international law. Boundary, frontier, have legal meanings;
borderland is probably a geographical terminology. However, this book is about
'borderlands', and we may as well adopt the definition contained in the guideline

provided by the editors. In their own words, borderlands are "those zones lying on both sides of a given binational boundary which enjoy functional interaction with one another as well as with each of the sovereign states or nations in contact. They are zones in which the cultures, politics and economic arrangements of the inter-related nation states interpenetrate and mingle".

Borderlands are effect of international relations and have from time, like boundaries, been veritable source of interminable disputes between nation states, especially in Africa. Since nation states are a *sine qua non* to the existence of boundaries and indeed, borderlands, it may well, therefore, be useful to look at the nation state, its origin, nature and status under contemporary international law and relations; for it is the nation state that is the concern of international law on issues touching on borderlands and not any entity with lesser attributes.

The Concept of the Nation State

The nation state is not an abstract entity, it is a portion of the globe inhabited by human beings delineated in a treaty or other written sources whilst the demarcation is the province of geography. It is for this reason that classical international law did not accept a vacant territory uninhabited by human beings as being capable of having the attributes of State. Rather, classical international law accepted the doctrines of territorium nullium by which a vacant portion of the globe, which is totally uninhabited, was said to belong to no one and thus was open to appropriation by any state either by symbolic taking or annexation[4] (which was then a permissible mode of territorial acquisition) or by actual occupation, an overt manifestation of sovereignty.[5]

The state as a person of international law must possess four qualifications:
  (i)   a permanent population;
 (ii)   a defined territory;
(iii)   government that controls the population; and most importantly,
(iv)   capacity to enter into relations with other states.

These conditions were laid down in the convention on Rights and Duties of States signed at Montevadio on 26 December, 1933 by the 7th International Conference of American States.[6] The Convention is commonly accepted as reflecting, in general terms, the requirements of statehood at customary international law. It has continued to serve as a point of reference whenever any entity appears on the international scene seeking recognition among the international community of nations.

The reason for the insistence on a territory as a condition for statehood is that one cannot contemplate a state as a kind of disembodied spirit. According to Oppenheim, "A state without territory is not possible....a wondering tribe, although it has a Government and is otherwise organized, is not a state until it has settled down in a territory of its own."[7] Thus the real meaning of the requirement of territory is that a state must have some portion of the earth's surface which its people inhabit and over which its government exercises authority.[8]

However, the concept of territory as an attribute of statehood does not necessarily include precise delimitation of the boundaries of that territory. International law insists on the need for territory as a pre-condition of statehood but not on the precise delineation of that territory. At least this was declared by the Germanic-Polish Mixed Arbitral Tribunal in the *Deutsche Continental GS-Gesellschaft v. Polish State.*[9] That attitude of international law might have accounted for the admission of Israel to the United Nations in May 1949, notwithstanding that its boundaries were then defined with precision.[10]

Forms of Border Disputes

Border disputes may be a territorial claim or a boundary claim. The actual difference between the two may be merely one of semantics as a claim to one may of necessity lead to adjustment in the other. A territorial claim is one in which one party challenges a boundary as an incidental to a much wider challenge to the way in which territory is allocated between itself and neighbouring state. The challenge to territorial allocation may be for a variety of reasons;

1) historical: where there is a claim to ancient sovereignty;
2) geographical: where it is claimed that the boundary should follow a natural feature;
3) ethnic or cultural: where it is claimed that a people or cultural group is split into two by a frontier;[11]
4) economic: where territory on one side of a boundary is felt to be essential to, or a concomitant of, occupation of territory on the other side;
5) military or strategic; where it is sought to rectify the boundary so as to make it more easily defensible in time of crisis or war.

Sometimes the dispute may reflect any one of the preceding groups based on the fact that the title of the pretended occupier to the challenged territory is 'bad in law' because there was no effective occupation, no valid cession, no treaty or agreement or whatever the mode of allocation may be. In all such instances, the boundary claimed is incidental to a claim to territory, which may be very extensive.[12]

What is more, the areas in dispute may be located between the disputants (e.g. Somali claim to Haud and Ogaden areas of Ethiopia); they may be contiguous to one of the parties (e.g. the conflicting claims in the Antarctica or the U.K.-Argentina dispute over the Falklands which developed into a full scale war in 1982 and has settled nothing even as of now); or they may be close to neither of the disputants (e.g. Norwegian claim over Eastern Greenland in 1919).[13] Some even go as far as to claim the whole territory of another state such as the Moroccan claim over Mauritania or the claim by Ethiopia and Somalia to the territory of Afars and Issas (now Djibouti) which they regarded as having been historically linked with the respective territories.[14] Examples can be multiplied.

It must be noted that it is the identification and acceptance of boundaries or borders by adjacent or contiguous sovereigns that has always been the source of interminable conflicts among nation states. With respect to Africa, the European partition with the Berlin Conference of 1884-1885 as a major milestone, sowed the seed of discord when it created arbitrary frontiers in Africa with little or no regard for pre-existing human and geographic patterns and so in the process separated ethnic or language groups who, before colonial rule, were culturally homogeneous communities.[15] In short, the historical phenomenon of European partition made African states successors to international boundaries carved out among the Europeans. The result is what we have today: shared populations and material resources that have become in Africa, according to a writer, "bones of contention and irritants for inter-sovereignty conflicts."[16] What then is the solution?

Utti Possidetis

The border problems in Latin America after the revolt of the Hispanic-American colonies against Spain in the 19th century was similar, in some respects, to that which prevail in post-colonial Africa. Newly emergent South American Republics had to make do with inherited colonial boundaries. To avoid inter-state strife and ensure some degree of stability in and among the republics, each of the new territories agreed to confine itself within the appropriate administrative division of the former Spanish Empire. It was first adopted in the constitutions of the revolted colonies, and later in their first treaties with one another. This doctrine they dignified by the term *utti possidetis* which was at first much less legal than political in its implications.[17]

From Berlin to the Organization of African Unity (OAU)

By the time the OAU came onto the international scene on 25 May 1963, the United Nations had been well established as a universal international organization committed to peace in the relations between nation states.[18] It ordains in Article 2(4) of its Charter that all disputes of whatever nature (including those over border or boundaries) must be settled by peaceful means in such a way that peace and security of the international community is not disturbed. it also prohibits the use of force "against the territorial integrity or political independence of any state". The United Nations thus introduced major changes in the international law of territorial acquisition in consonance with fundamental changes in international society.

The O.A.U., an offshoot of the United Nations and a regional organization within the meaning of Article 52 of the U.N. Charter, at is formation in 1963 at Addis Ababa, appreciated the problems of african international boundaries. It preempted claims to territorial regimes by accepting in principle that boundaries inherited from the colonial period are to be retained *faute demieux*. Like the UN, its mother organization, it stressed in Article III(3) and (4) of its charter "respect for the sovereignty and territorial integrity of each state...", and "peaceful settlement of disputes by negotiation, mediation, conciliation and arbitration."[19]

Utti possidetis was not expressly adopted, but it was appreciated by all that the total rejection of colonial boundaries would inevitably lead to chaos and strife. The point was strongly put by the Prime Minister of Ethiopia when in one of the plenary meetings, he said that "... if we are to redraw the map of Africa on the basis of religion, race or language, I fear that many States will case to exist. It is in the interest of all Africans today to respect the frontiers drawn on maps, even though they were drawn by the former colonialists".[20] However, at the Summit in Cairo in 1964, a resolution of the Heads of State and Government formally accepted the principle of *utti possidetis* in inter-African relations, although without using the terminology. The Resolution of the Heads of State:

1. Solemnly reaffirms the strict respect by all members States of the Organization for the principles laid down in paragraph 3 of Article III of the charter of the Organization of African Unity.
2. Solemnly declares that all member States pledge themselves to respect the borders existing on their achievement of national independence.[21]

The policy resolution is clear enough. To the meeting at Cairo, any process of realignment or redefinition of borders would, under prevailing circumstances, create confusion and threat to continental, if not global, peace.

Border, Borderlands and the Law

Observers may wonder why emphasis has been placed on boundaries rather than borderlands. The reason is obvious: the issues of law and fact attending to both are the same. These may at times be very complex. The role of politicians is inevitable for the existence of both of them; national territory and sovereignty are involved; a solution to boundary lines will be necessity usher in the peace and tranquillity necessary for the successful administration of borderlands. Without boundaries there can be no borderlands.

It is my submission that the regime of borderlands is an entirely new development in international law. Modern attitudes of African institutions have focused more on boundaries simpliciter and the need to maintain their *status quo* than confront the human problems that have to do with management of specific human species and environmental resources split by boundaries or borders between nation states. Perhaps, Africa may have to take cue from Europe in working out an appropriate trans-boundary co-operation policy for the continent. The Europeans, we must admit, seem to be setting the standard of civilized behaviour in international law and relations. They did so with human rights in 1950 when the Council of Europe converted the General Assembly Declaration on Human Rights of 1948 into a durable convention which was remained the first of its type in international law anywhere in the world.[22] The European Convention on Human Rights completely revolutionised the concept of the right of the individual in law and made a number of innovative provisions, the most radical being the one which gives an individual a right of action against members, contracting Parties to the Convention, as well as even against his home state.

Contrast this development with human rights in Africa. For example, we all know that Africa has one of the worst human rights records in the world; yet the need for a Charter on human rights, similar to that of the Europeans, had been under discussion since 1961.[23] It was not until 1981 (20 years later) that the Nairobi Conference of African Heads of State and Government adopted the Charter on Human and Peoples' Rights drawn up at Banjul.[24] Even then the rights have been so circumscribed with exceptions that the African individual may be better of without them.

It may well be that, like in human rights, African States will need to emulate the European and resolve to find a permanent and lasting solution to the problems of borderlands by the adoption of a convention similar to the one recently adopted by the Council of Europe at Madrid on May 21, 1980.[25] Under that Convention, the Contracting Parties, members of the Council of Europe, agreed to use it as a vehicle for trans-frontier co-operation between territorial communities or authorities within the jurisdiction of two or more Contracting Parties. There can be no doubt that a new universal principle of public International Law governing the regime of transborder frontiers is in the making.

Perhaps it will be too much an ambitious approach to advocate, at this stage, such a continent-wide arrangement such as Europe has just concluded. May be it is better to start with bilateral, localised, step by step administrative, economic and social co-operation between territorial communities or authorities across specific frontiers, leaving the wider continental co-operation on trans-frontier matters for the future. A model agreement of the sort envisaged here would be one similar in structure and in all material particulars to the frontier agreement popularly known as the "Maud Line" between Great Britain and Ethiopia in 1907, which permitted local inhabitants on either side of the line free gazing rights as well as free access to the wells on common basis.[26] Although the Agreement was abrogated on 29 September, 1947 and a new borderline drawn up with subsequent amendments in later years, the privileges to the border inhabitants in the original Accord of 1907, remained undisturbed.

Like charity, which must begin at home, the writer has advocated somewhere else the need for meaningful rapport between Nigeria and her neighbours East, West and North of the country, to ensure co-operation and better understanding so essential to the promotion of good neighbourliness.[27]

The recent reciprocal expulsion of aliens by Nigeria and Ghana and the apparent reluctance on the part of ECOWAS member states to put into effect the ECOWAS Protocol on free movement of persons within the sub-region is bound to make the establishment of transborder regimes somewhat difficult. That is not to say that the establishment of a belt of shared jurisdiction and co-operation on our state borders is going to be impossible. Is it not only recently, after a quadripartite summit in Lagos, that Nigeria, Ghana, Togo and Benin entered into three separate agreements covering matters of extradition, police co-operation and mutual administrative assistance in matters relating to customs, trade and immigration respectively?[28]

Given the political will, there is hardly anything impossible for the nation state to accomplish. After all, in this modern world of political, social and economic interdependence states do from time to time, shed part of their sovereignty either at the bilateral or multilateral levels in the interest of common objectives and goals. The establishment of a new regime of borderlands in inter-sovereign relations is one form of progressive development of international law, a contingency adequately provided for under Article 13 of the United Nations Charter.

Endnotes

1. Oppenheim, *International Law* (Lauterpacht ed., 1955), p. 53.
2. Allot, op. cit., p. 70.
3. See generally, E. Luard, *The International Regulation of Frontier Disputes*, (London, 1970).
4. On the right to title based on discover, historical association, symbolic annexation and the like, see Max Huber, sole arbitrator in the *Island of Palmas Case*, 2 RIAA 829.
5. On the actual occupation as a manifestation of sovereignty, see Schqarzenberger, A., *Manual of Int. Law*, 6th ed., pp. 96-99; *Island of Palmas Case* (The Netherlands v. U.S.) U.N. RIAA 829 (1928).
6. 165 LNTS 19; USTS 881; 28 AJIL, Supp. 75 (1934). For recent supplements to these requirements, see Harris, *Cases and Materials on International Law,* 3rd ed., p. 80.
7. Vol. 1 (Lauterpacht ed), p. 118.
8. On further elaboration, see A.O. Chukwurah, "Evidence of Acts of Possession in Disputes ever Territorial Sovereignty" Proceedings of the 6th Annual Conference of the Nigerian Society of International Law, Lagos. 1974.
9. Ann Dig. (1929-30), Case No. 5, p. 11.
10. Ian Brownlie, *Principles of Public International Law*, 2nd ed., p. 127. Starke, *Introduction to International Law*, 7th ed., p. 142; DJ. Harris, *Cases and Materials on International Law,* 3rd ed, 1983, pp. 176-77.
11. It is this type that is directly relevant to the subject of this book.
12. See for a more detailed analysis, Allot, op. cit., p. 75.
13. Legal Status of Eastern Greenland, PCIJ, Ser A/B, No. 53.
14. For the agreement between the British and the French Governments separating their spheres of influence, see BFSP, Vol. 100, p. 493.
15. See A. I. Asiwaju (ed) *Partitioned Africans: Ethnic Relation Across Africa's International Boundaries* (Lagos University Press, 1984). The better known examples include the division of the Masai between Kenya and Tanzania; the Ewe between Togo and Ghana and the Aja-Yoruba between Nigeria and the Republic of Benin.

16. Asiwaju, A.I., "The Human Face of Borders. African and Western European Experiences Compared" paper read at the 15th Annual Conference of the Nigerian Society of International Law, Calabar, March 28, 1985.

17. See D. P. O'Connel, *International Law,* 1965, Vol. 1, p. 491

18. UN: Charter, Articles 2, 3; The Charter was adopted on June 26, 1945 and it come into force on October 24, 1985; See U.N.C.--1.0. Docs, Vol. 15, p. 335.

19. The text of Charter of the Organization of African Unity is in 2 ILM 766 (1963); For an incisive analysis of the Charter and its origin, see T.O. Elias, "Charter of the Organization of African Unity" 49 AJIL 243 (1965); For the text of the separate Protocol on Mediation, Conciliation and Arbitration, see 3 ILM 1116 (1064). The Protocol is exhaustively discussed by Elias in 40 BYIL 336 (1964).

20. Zdenek Cervenka, *The Organization of African Unity and its Charter,* 1969, p. 14.

21. Ian Brownlie, *Basic Documents on African Affairs,* p. 361.

22. European Treaty Series, No 5: I European Yearbook, 317; 45 AJIL, Supp. (1951); BFSP, Vol. 156, p. 915.

23. In fact, Africa has over the years initiated developments in various aspects of international law but none materialized. See African Conference on International Law and African Problems, under the joint auspices of the NIIA and the Carnegie Endowment for International Peace (New York), Lagos, March 14-18, 1967.

24. Text in 21 ILM 59 (1982); OAU Doc. CAB/LEG 67/3/Rev. 5 of January 7-19, Banjul, 1981. The text takes the name Banjul after the site of the drafting of the document.

25. Council of Europe, European Treaty Series, No. 106, 1982; Noted in 20 ILM 315 (1981).

26. 3 Whiteman Digest, 662-668.

27. Ajomo, "The Nigerian/Cameroun Border Dispute: Implications at International Law" (1982) CL Rev. 144.

28. See *New Nigerian,* February 25, 1985, p. 13.

CHAPTER 3

Borderland as the Function of Space and Time: A Philosophical Insight Into the Issues of Borderland

by E. Kola Ogundowole

Borderland entails in itself and exhibits a conglomeration of material bodies. Each of such bodies possesses definite individual characteristics. Every material body possesses extent; it is either long, short, wide, narrow, high or low. This means that every material body entails a kind of motion. Every form of motion necessarily involves the displacement of bodies. Bodies, objects, exist in space: space therefore is a fundamental condition of the existence of material bodies and are displaced in space and time.

In materialist philosophy, space is conceived in objectively real form of the existence of material bodies, objects, in motion.[1] Borderland with its conglomeration of material bodies or objects occupies space. Space as a concept expresses the coexistence and separateness of object, bodies, their extent and the order of their disposition in relation to one another. Thereby creating material processes.

Material processes occur in a certain sequence, are distinguished by their duration and have differing phases or stages. This means that objects, material bodies, exist not only in space but they exist in time as well. Borderland is a kind of space that derives its meaning in time.

Thus, space and time are objectively forms of the existence of material bodies, objects, as well as of the borderland. Space and time characterise the sequence of the occurrence of material processes the separateness of the various stages of these processes, their development, duration, and limit, their boundary, borderland.

Dialectically, material bodies always and everywhere must exist in both space and time. Hence space and time are not merely organically interconnected with one another, but are the ultimate expression of the concept "borderland", boundary.

Etymologically, boundary means a border, a dividing line or limit. In philosophical sense, however, boundary is that which separates one object from another. Hence boundary may be *spatial, temporal* and *qualitative*. Every object entails in itself boundary. An extended object is separated from another similar object by that part of space which in relation to these objects is either neutral or otherwise exists amidst them as something they have in common. In terms of development, the existence of an object terminates in time, and the emergence, existence and development of a new object ensues, thereafter. In truth, every object is but the unity of certain definite variables. Borderland is the unity of various and varying concrete socio-cultural variables.

The definiteness of an object, by the force of which is that which it is and nothing else, Shushanashvilli calls "qualitative boundary".[2]

The boundary of an object is guaranteed only by the existence of other objects. This is so because boundary not only separates objects, but it is also the basis of their connection. It characterises that side of an object by which such object depends on other definite objects, that is to say, how it is conditioned by them. Borderland not only separates sovereign states, but also it is the basis of their connection, their immediate communication link. It expresses that feature of a sovereign state, by which it depends on other neighbouring sovereign state(s), that is, how a sovereign state is contained and conditioned by its neighbour(s).

The boundary of an object is at the same time the indicator of its limitedness in time, space and quality. This is true of a borderland; it is that which makes a sovereign state what it is at least, in time.

Some philosophers, particularly those with idealist leaning, deny the objective reality of space and time. These philosophers conceive space and time to be something that exists in the human consciousness. Thus, Kant in *Critique of Pure Reason*, regarded space and time as *a priori* forms of sensuous contemplation conditioned by the very nature of our consciousness. According to Ernst Mach (*Analysis of Sensations*) space and time are merely ordered systems of the series of our sensations. In Hegel's idealist dialectics, space and time are creations of the Absolute Idea that occur at certain stages of its development, and in such a manner that space appears first and was then followed by time.

Such notions of space and time are in conflict with human experience and the position of natural science which holds that the Earth, from which man conceived and formed the borderland, existed in space and developed in time for millions of years before man with consciousness and ideas ever emerged. As real forms of the existence of material bodies, space and time are characterised by a number of specific features. Some of these are that a) they are objective, they exist outside and independently of human consciousness; b) they are eternal, in as much as material bodies exist eternally; c) space and time are boundless and infinite.

It would be absurd therefore to conceive borderland space as existing only in human mind, as immaterial. The borderland not only exists objectively, independently of the wish of the people inhabiting the land mass, the material processes characteristic of the borderland exist eternally. However, the borderland is not boundless, limitless, and infinite.

The boundlessness of space implies that whichever direction we move or how far we go from an initial point, there will never be any boundary, limit beyond which we can go no further. It is in this sense that universal space is said to be not only boundless but also infinite.

Unlike the universal space, the borderland is not boundless; it is definite and limited, it is a dividing, and at the same time a uniting space between two or more sovereign states. Being a specific space in time, borderland exists only in material things, only through material things, and only thanks to them. Just as there can be no material body outside space and time, so there cannot or hardly can there ever be any space or time outside the material processes of any specific borderland area.

This concreteness, this non-boundlessness and relative limitedness of the borderland and its material possibilities is one of the roots of the restlessness associated with the life of peoples in borderland areas. One other factor that can influence the tranquillity or otherwise of the life of the borderland men is in conflict with the view held by Newton that space and time were objective, but that they existed independently of moving matter, were immutable, had no connection with each other and were absolute; borderland with its capacity and property of being a definite kind of space existing in concrete time cannot be said to be absolute. Such a view, as the German mathematician Hermann Weyl put it, is like regarding space as a "rentable apartment"[3] that could be occupied by any tenant or, if none were available, could remain empty. Borderland is never empty, or it would not be a borderland area of sovereign states.

Perhaps, one of the features, relevance, and importance of the non-Euclidean geometry to the discussion of borderland question is that it proves that the properties of space are not immutable and everywhere the same, but that they change depending on the properties of material bodies and on the physical processes occurring in these material bodies. This is applicable to borderland space. The diversity of properties in space of the borderland is an added source of the problems of interstate boundary disputes and the conflicts ensuing from them.

The traditional human attitude to space, before the overlay developed sovereign states and so before the formation of borderland was based on an idea of virtual infinity since there were no artificial delimitations of any kind. For sure, men long ago perceived a certain boundary separating, say, land from sea and so making apparent the limitedness of the early; nevertheless that boundary was an abstraction so remote from men's needs, as such it was naturally ignored in practical life.

But the extinction within a definite land area of a particular type of animal that provided successful hunters with sustenance at a moment in the history of our distant ancestor would have put an end to the idea of infinity in them.

Whether,

> in the early periods of human history, realisation of the aspects of finiteness was inseparably linked with a transition to new forms of virtual infinity,

that is,

> Discovery of the finiteness of some concrete form of natural resources gave rise to a need to pass to the use of other forms of relatively infinite resources[4]

as Ilya Novik claims, is not what is of interest to us here at the moment. Our interest and concern here is that the "realisation of the aspects of finiteness" of certain objects with utility value has contributed to the complicated situation and human relations at the borderland of sovereign states.

The awareness of the limitedness of natural material resources has considerably sharpened borderland conflicts and hardened the process of their resolution. In Africa the discovery or even the mere likeliness of discovering certain vital mineral resources often leads to armed conflicts, political disputes or outright attempts to occupy and seize parcels of land, or yet as it is in some cases efforts are made at a complete colonisation of neighbouring national groups. Such political and military adventures with solid economic greediness underlying them often result in restlessness and sufferings of the peoples inhabiting the borderland from either side of the sovereign states co-existing in conflict.

It should be stressed however that conflict and dispute are not necessary and unavoidable features of the borderland men. The borderland men may at times represent, consciously or unconsciously, a collective creative force. The spoken language of the people inhabiting the borderland area of sovereign states very often creates new trend in the languages spoken by these people. You may call it creole or broken language, if you like. It is in effect the transcendence of the limit of each of the spoken language that brings about the new trend out of such languages. At a close examination of the issues involved one would discover that the words that come together to form the new language-trend may be those that demand less energy or those that are more direct at expressing the ideas or objects of interaction.

It is also historical fact that what is being referred to nowadays as the ancient greek philosophy was developed and came to be not in the hinterland, the mainland, of Greece but on the tiny island of Iona which in a sense could be termed a borderland area between Europe and Asia Minor. This Island was in effect the melting point of various people, various races. In fact, it represented a complex web of cultures. The phenomenon of the emergence of the ancient Greek philosophy illustrates the fact that peoples of borderland areas have the ability to intermingle, intertwine not only in the sphere of economic activity, material activity, but also are capable of intermingling in the sphere of ideas e.g. like sharing common legends, language, objective knowledge, techniques of doing things. Dialectical mode of reasoning shows that when two objects or processes with different qualities particularly of opposing qualities meet there ensues a struggle, the struggle which as a law quite often brings about something new as the result of inherent conflicts.

Concerning the ideological implication and the effect of ideological orientation on the people inhabiting the borderland area especially of two countries exhibiting conflicting ideological orientation and practice, stimuli and responses entailed in inherent conflicts may be said to underlie the reason why peoples of borderland areas are capable of creating and exhibiting the feature of, or becoming agents of uncontrollable opinions, ideas that essentially may conflict with the aspiration, expectation of the larger community they represent severally. The Berlin wall is an example of efforts by peoples, their leaders, to control or contain such unwanted influences which could generate among the people on the either side of a borderland. But the Berlin wall is in truth a child's play when compared with the solid concrete walls in height, in width, and in length built by USA/South Korea during the years 1976-77 to physically divide Korea into two.[5] This wall was built to eternalize the separation of North Korea from South Korea. The concrete wall extends from the east coast of Korea to the west coast of the divided country. Each edge terminates at the ocean. In the capitalist countries (the so-called free world) and in most of the new states, the developing countries, people mainly are familiar only with the propaganda associated with the Berlin wall; whereas they know nothing or very little (and normally within a very limited circle) about the American-built Korean wall. The fact that within the USA itself and the capitalist world only the Berlin wall phenomenon is well known whereas silence is kept over the Korean wall is itself a characteristic feature of borderland politics. But, that despite the imposition of this kind of information flow, people within these countries still manage to know about the Korean wall, is itself a limit to hypocrisy in borderland politics and of the unsoundness of false propaganda regarding borderland issues. Information flow can hardly be suppressed successfully in the borderland area.

The Berlin wall, and the Korean wall are concrete instances of attempts by men to refrain their citizens or people under their influence from uncontrollable influences from their rivals, adversaries. But the advancement in the science and technology is making this much more difficult and may even make it to become impossible. Though the concrete wall in Korea may prevent even animals from crossing from North into South and vice versa, it cannot, however, prevent birds from flying to and fro either side. The wall cannot prevent even a missile thrown by ordinary hand let alone one dislodged by a gun or by even a highly sophisticated technological delivery system. So also the wall in Berlin cannot prevent the flow of wind and air.

The inability of people or political leaders to prevent or to control their people who inhabit borderland areas had also been witnessed in the incidence associated with the exploration of space and other planets by man. When the US astronauts led by Armstrong landed on the moon in July 1969, although TV systems in the USSR ran their normal programmes and closed at the usual time, in many capitalist countries TV programmes and operating hours were altered to allow for the coverage of the actual landing on the moon. Finland is one of those countries. As we all know Finland and the USSR have a common borderland. So people within the Soviet side of the boundary like their counterparts on the Finish side of it were known to have also stayed awake to watch the landing of the American astronauts on the moon on their own receiver sets but from Finland's transmitting station. Since it is easy and has become a common feature in the area that people on both sides watch programmes transmitted from either side of the borderland.

We can safely conclude therefore that the peoples of borderland areas not only exhibit confusion or that they are capable of doing so. They also have the possibility and capacity of fostering common understanding and friendly relations irrespective of whatever view or views their leaders share or discountenance. Whence, borderlands may be altered to the advantage of either side of states sharing a borderland, or in extreme circumstances a borderland may become a full fledge new sovereign state. Borderland being a sort of space endowed with material processes has the inherent dialectical potentiality to change. It is not immutable. Historically this may be said to have accounted for the disappearance of certain states and the emergence of empires in the past in Africa (foreign colonisation process not being taken into account here at the moment). In this sense, borderland is the function of space and time.

This "negation of the negation"—like characteristic feature of borderland space is still very active in our time and may still have to come into play for many generations to come until mankind can successfully resolve the intricate problems associated with the material bodies and processes underlying the need for the formation and preservation of borderland.

Endnotes

1. *Fundamentals of Marxist-Lenist Philosophy* trans. by Robert Daglish, (Moscow: Progress, 1974) p. 85.
2. G. Shushanashvilli, "Granitsa" (Boundary) *Filosofskaya Entseklopedja* Tom 1, (Moskva: Sovietskaya Entseklopedja, 1960) S. 402.
3. Quotes in *Fundamentals of Marxist-Leninist Philosophy,* p. 91.
4. Ilya Novik, *Society and Nature* (Moscow: Progress, 1981) p. 63.
5. For details see *Concrete Walls. Dividing Korea into North and South.* Pyongyang, (Foreign Languages Publishing House, 1984).

CHAPTER 4

A Critique of Borderland Theories

by Dr. C.S. Momoh

This chapter is divided into four parts. The first part deals with what I consider to be the importance and relevance of border and boundary studies. In the second part I draw a distinction in relation to frontiers, boundary and borderland. I hold the view that there are three types of borderlands: Minimal Borderlands, Zero Borderlands and Maximal Borderlands and that Nigerian Borderlands fall into the last category. In the third part, I see a parallel between the partitioning of Africa and the slave trade but point-out that Africans, like white men, have their own share of the bad and the good in human nature and experience. In the final part of the paper, I discuss theories of borderlands and conclude that boundaries are artificial and that they are now more of political and fiscal propositions than anything else.

Questions concerning boundaries, frontiers and borderlands have excited the perennial interests of scholars from almost all disciplines.

Nor should such an interest be surprising. After all the scholar is rooted in a particular community which definitely borders on other communities. The scholar is a citizen of a particular state which has boundaries and borderlands with other states. In the very unlikely situation of a scholar without community or without a state such a scholar is nevertheless a person and a neighbour.

Neighbourliness and the human anatomy seem to represent, on a personal level, the ultimate in boundary, borderland and frontier studies. Every joint in the human body, for instance, is the quintessence of a borderland in the sense that it is a contact zone for the peripheries of at least two parts of the body. A joint in the human body can be paraphrased also as a boundary in the sense in which Omolade Adejuyigbe understands it "as a point joining different parts of the body."[1]

Another important reason why it is not surprising that the scholar exhibits an abiding interest in borderland matters is the fact that he belongs to the privileged and elite group. This is the group which has much at stake in any state or society. A state which is constantly hostile to its neighbours leaves its borders in danger of external infiltration if not attack. Such a situation can spontaneously generate internal unrest and uneasiness amongst the general populace, a perfect setting that can trigger a stampede amongst the elites. It is also a setting that can upset the status quo.

The year 1985 is generally viewed as marking the centenary of the partitioning of Africa by the western European powers. For that reason, the theme of the seminar "Issues of borderlands in Africa" is very timely and apposite. But with specific reference to the prevailing internal and inter-national circumstances of Nigeria, the theme of the seminar cannot be more timely. Nigeria is faced with the threat, real or imagined, of the possibility of some fugitives procuring the services of a mercenary force to invade a country. Such a plan can succeed only with the covert or overt support of any of our neighbouring countries.

When I talk of boundaries, frontiers and borderlands, I do not, by any means, mean to foster the impression that the concepts are synonymous or that they can be used interchangeably. Fortunately, however, the images which the concepts conjure are interdigitated in the sense that they are 'tri'amese triplets; a boundary represents the determinate physical end of a frontier for the moment and a borderland represents the region or zone on both sides of given boundaries.

This characterization sounds a bit too dense and I think it is in order to explain the concepts a little more. I regard the borderland concept as the most ambiguous of the three and it should be taken first. The borderland concept is ambiguous and controversial in terms of its vivacity and extent and not in terms of its bald characterization; borderland is the inter-communal zone or zones bordering a boundary. In other words, how lively (confrontationally or cooperatively) will the contact zone of peripheries of a boundary be before it can be accepted as a borderland? If two communities on the opposites sides of a boundary are not culturally, ideologically or ethnically affiliated or homogeneous, does it make sense to talk meaningfully of a borderland in that zone? And the most important question of all: what is or should be the ideal spatial size or extent of a borderland?

It is obvious that where the people on both sides of a boundary have neither cultural nor ethnic affinity the space covered by the borderland will be very minimal, say 2-5 kilometres in diameter. We refer to this category as Minimal Borderland (Fig. 1). But where the people on the opposite sides of a boundary are diametrically opposed ideologically and even religiously, the borderland space will be zero. It is also likely to be a zone of friction and tension especially when the borderland residents are goaded from the centre. We classify this type as Zero Borderland.

The third category of borderlands is the Maximal Borderland. Here we are faced with an expansive area of contact—physical, economic or emotional—amongst borderland residents. The spatial limit and extent of a maximal borderland depends on the area occupied by residents on each side of the boundary. There is an enormous amount of cooperation between borderland residents irrespective of what the tariff of fiscal policies of the political sovereigns at the centre are. The existence of maximal borderland is a direct slap and pooh-pooh of the legality of boundaries.

Maximal borderlands easily develop in boundary areas where the borderland residents have ethnic, cultural, linguistic or even ancestral affinities. Where one boundary zone is inhabited by a people whose ethnic group is one of the major ethnic groups of country A and the same situation is duplicated on the boundary zone of country B, it is obvious that the extent of the borderland is the extent of the territorial habitat of both ethnic groups in both countries.

Professor Asiwaju explains that maximal borderlands "are rendered both wider and more complex by the fact of the familiar pattern of ethnic and cultural interlinks and interpenetrations associated with centuries, if not millennia, of intergroup relations in the African continent and its sub-region."[2] Asiwaju goes further to submit, with specific reference to the Nigeria-Benin borderland that "the western Yoruba sub-group astride the border share a sense of...community with the rest of the Yoruba culture area in the present-day Lagos, Ogun, Oyo, Kwara and Ondo states of Nigeria to the east and the more westerly sub-groups, such as the Jaluku, Mayibiri Ana and 'Fe and the middle latitudes of the Republic of Benin and Togo."[3] No wonder Nigeria's Chief Obafemi Awolowo keeps reiterating his belief that Nigeria's border is "somewhere in Togo". A Togolese leader, of course, can use the same criterion and say that Togo's border is somewhere in Nigeria.

On my own theory of Maximal Borderland, the borderland between Nigeria and Dahomey covers the area inhabited by the Yoruba people in both countries. The same reasoning applies to the Nigeria-Niger boundary where Asiwaju tells us that the "boundary split into two an observably coherent Hausa culture area in exactly the same way as our border with Benin has created a double image for each of the Aja, Yoruba and Borgu culture area".[4] The borderland between Nigeria and Niger, therefore, covers the area inhabited by the Hausa people in both countries.

In terms of effective patrol of boundaries, maximal borderlands have proved very difficult for the simple reason that the borderland citizens have not been directly co-opted into the scheme of things. The central authorities rely excessively on customs and immigration personnel and resources. To the borderland citizens, ethnic homogeneity and ancestral links are thicker than the political sovereignty and heterogeneity of the states. In other words, the Hausa man in Nigeria feels more closely knitted to the Hausa in Niger than he is to the Yoruba man in Nigeria while the latter feels more closely knitted to the Yoruba man in Dahomey than he is to the Hausa man in Nigeria.

The concepts of Minimal, Zero and Maximal Borderlands explicated above are models which hold in the absence of political, ideological or military interference. Thus the borderland of West and East Germany should clearly have been maximal but it is zero on account of political and ideological interference. The same situation holds for other borderlands like those of Iran and Iraq or North and South Korea.

For its own sake but also more specifically because of its connection to my concept of borderlands and the questions of supranationalism to come up later, I must discuss the traditional distinction between boundary and frontier.

It is now generally held that the frontier is no more in the original sense of the word because states had fully occupied lands which were once seen and known as Frontiers. Harm J. de Blij is a leading advocate of this view.[5] But it is important to point out that the original sense of frontier still persists not in the physical sense but in an ideological, economic, mental, religious, nostalgic or irredentist sense. Ayatollah Khomeini of Iran, for instance, knows the physical boundaries demarcating his state from its neighbours but he sees the whole Arab world as a frontier for the expansion of fundamentalist Islam. Capitalism as an economic doctrine sees the whole world as a frontier for expansion. The Yoruba man in the Republic of Benin sees the Yoruba states in Nigeria as frontiers of kinship if not of unity and irredentism.

Ladis K.D. Kristof discusses the nature of frontiers and boundaries in an article by that same title.[6] Etymologically and historically, "frontier" is that which is "in front". The word "frontier" carries the connotation of a dynamic concept in the sense of potentials for progress, march, movement, exploitation, development and

Figure 1. Minimal Borderland: No cultural or ethnic affinity between country A and country B. Borderland space is minimal.

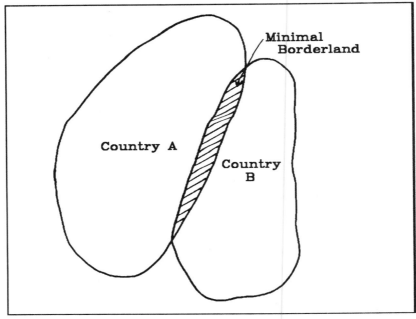

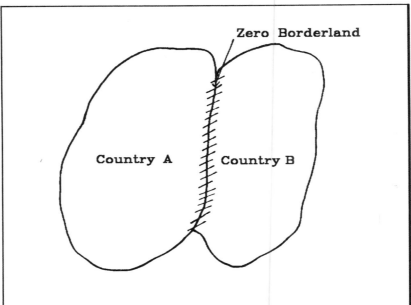

Figure 2. Zero Borderland: Borderland is conterminous with boundary. Country A and country B are ideologically or religiously opposed.

Figure 3. Maximal Borderland: Citizens of both country A and country B have ancestral ethnic and linguistic affinities and links spanning millenia.

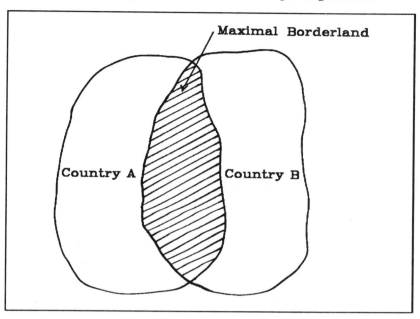

exploration of the unknown. Kristof traces the etymology of the word to Latin and French roots. The Latin word is "frons" and the french word is "front" meaning "forehead" of anything be it material or spiritual. The frontier never had the connotation of an area which is static and determinate in the sense in which a boundary marks the end of a political unit.

The term boundary, on the other hand, is appropriate to the modern day concept of the state. It is inner-oriented created and maintained, by the central government. For selfish reasons, states found it necessary to substitute a boundary for the frontier "not only because the enemy has to be kept out but because one's own citizens and resources have to be kept in."[7] "Few natural obstacles" according to Stephen B. Jones, "restrict the movement of persons, things, and even ideas completely as do the boundaries of some states.[8] Jones is right if what he has in mind are boundaries in what I have called minimum borderlands and zero borderlands. Otherwise as Kristof notes, American, Russian or Chinese or, as Asiwaju has also noted, African history shows that citizens of borderlands often develop their own interests "quite different from those of the respective central governments".[9]

For a state to exist and be recognised as such by others, it must have an area with well defined boundaries, over which the State exercises power and jurisdiction. Whether the state is as big as the Soviet Union or the United States of America in territorial extent or as small as Luxembourg or the Vatican City is not important. What is important is that a state has some territory with internationally recognized boundaries.

Omolade Adejuyigbe has already made the point that boundaries evolved from frontiers. He recognises seven stages of boundary evolution. (1) The expansion stage when communities step out of their homesteads; (2) Contact stage when expansion confronts natural or human hindrances; (3) Stabilisation stage when communities begin to consolidate territories that have been effectively occupied; (4) Allocation stage when communities begin to concede boundary and territorial limitations; (5) Delimitation stage which is the consultation period between communities about boundary lines; (6) Demarcation stage when the boundary line is finally and formally accepted and (7) Patrol stage when vigilance is mounted in boundary zones to ensure respect and compliance with the boundary demarcation.[10]

Of course no one is saying that every frontier must actually have gone systematically through the seven stages to evolve into a boundary. Nor does the patrol stage often come into play unless in climates of hostility, instability, threats and crisis in borderlands. Besides there are some countries where it makes sense to say that boundaries came before frontiers. In the United States and other new States, as Stephen Jones points out, "a framework of boundaries was laid down before the land was densely settled or even effectively controlled in many cases." In these circumstances "frontier" refers more to a locus of a way of life rather than a specific geographical location.[11]

All this notwithstanding, most political geographers will agree with Kristof that frontiers and boundaries are manifestations of sociopolitical forces. Consequently they are subjective and not objective. However, frontiers are the consequence of rather spontaneous solutions and movements while boundaries are fixed and "enforced through a more rational and centrally coordinated effort after a conscious choice is made among the several preferences and opportunities at hand."[12]

Talking of boundaries and frontiers being subjective seems a convenient point to discuss the traditional theories of borderlands or boundaries and the concomitant question of whether boundaries should be bonds or barriers. Before I do that, however, I think it is necessary to discuss a prior and antecedent question. This is called directly into focus on account of the theme of this seminar which is "Issues of borderlands in Africa."

I hold the view in African philosophy and, logically, that view has to be extended to the thesis of this paper—that there is nothing unique in Africa and about Africans. A fortiori, there is nothing unique in Europe and about Europeans. If history has taught anything, it is that there are patterns and paradigms of behaviour, actions, experience and though which man, irrespective of race, colour, religion or ideology has displayed, again and again, over time and space.

In other words, when we talk of Partitioned Africans, we can equally, intelligibly, historically and factually as well talk of partitioned Indians, partitioned Chinese, partitioned Americans, partitioned Germans, partitioned Asians, partitioned Russians, partitioned Europeans, partitioned British. This point is clearly appreciated in A.I. Asiwaju ed. *Partitioned* (Lagos University Press 1984); it comes out well in the concluding chapter on "The Global Perspective and Border Management Policy Options" but the editor himself. In fact we may decide to leave continents, nations and people aside and come nearer home to talk, following Plato, of a partitioned soul.

By partitioning, we mean the arbitrary separation of the linguistically, racially, religiously or culturally homogenous regions by international boundaries or the arbitrary grouping of linguistically, racially, religiously or culturally heterogenous areas within intranational boundaries. I doubt if there is any continent or state in the world which does not meet these two senses of partitioning, Africa, Europe,

America, Asia definitely contain instances of both.

Europeans colonized the Africans. Europeans enslaved the Africans. Europeans partitioned the Africans. They (the Europeans) did those same things on a larger and even more inhuman scale to themselves. They only came to Africa to visit and re-enact their experience on us. In contemporary memory, the white man partitioned Poland, Germany, Vietnam, China and Korea. Even now they are partitioning Great Britain and Canada. They have and they are still living by the sword. At the Berlin conference of 1885, European powers refined the grand rules for the partition of Africa. The Evil that men do, they say, lives after them. At the Paris treaties of 1919, Europeans repartitioned their own continent and, according to Stephen Jones, it is one of the ironies of history that the present map of Europe is essentially that established at Paris in 1919.[13]

When we talk of Europeans partitioning Africa what we are properly saying is that they had no business and certainly no right to slice up Africa into European spheres of control and latterly influence using unparalleled chicanery, deceit, outright lies and a self assigned right to determine the destinies of others. We do not mean to say that Africans had not partitioned themselves or that they would not have partitioned themselves.

I am not aware that the Fulani Jihadist refused to conquer peoples and annex lands whose language and ethnicity were different from theirs. The same thing applies to the Benin Empire, the Oyo Empire and the Ibadan Empire. Indeed in the words of Bolanle Awe, empires of the Western Sudan-Ghana, Mali and Songhai did not fare better.

Within each empire, says Bolanle Awe,

> there were more powerful forces making for division and the weakening of the imperial bonds....The empires were not homogeneous entities....They incorporated within their borders various ethnic groups of people at various stages of development and civilization....The process of imperial growth was often the extension by force under an able military leader of the imperium of a particular group over the rest of the surrounding country....[14]

Africans were and are still capable of conquering and partitioning people although they probably would have done it more humanly than the Europeans. We should not write about Africa and Africans as if the Europeans met a continent of innocent, noble and innocuous savages neatly packaged into linguistically or tribally homogenous units. I remember I always remind my students who think that christianity is the last word in religion that if the Yoruba had colonized the British instead of the other way round, the British today would have been mainly Ogun or Sango worshippers.

Europeans were steeped in the acts of partitioning, colonizing and enslaving within their own continental enclaves before they set their sails on African waters. An Auchi proverb says that a husband's cudgelling of his wife pales into spanking if he is known to have cudgelled his mother.

The same parallel holds for slavery and the slave trade. The white men did not think of themselves as mega-human beings who are unenslavable. On the contrary they had subjected themselves to millennia of slavery and slave trade before they came and pounced on Africans. In any case, if Europeans bough African slaves, African rulers and businessmen were the sellers. Slavery has been a universal institution for all time and, as I pointed out in a paper read at the Nigerian

Philosophical Association conference in 1975, man had always found excuses, strong or flimsy, to enslave his own brother.

David Brion Davis has shown that there was in fact, no break in slavery from antiquity until the era of the Atlantic Slave Trade.[15] Davis agrees that, to the white man, slavery "had long represented the ultimate limit of dehumanization, of treating and regarding a man as a thing."[16] What this means is that the tradition and culture of the white-man had conditioned his psyche and made him impervious to the sinful and inhuman aspects of slavery.

Owen Sherrard tells us that Roman slavery started in the household where Roman law gave the head of the family inconceivable and unlimited powers to manage the affairs of his household. The head of the family kept in his custody the right of his children. He could sell them away to be enslaved and he could condemn them to death.[17] In the 2nd century B.C. Rome was the greatest centre of slave trade and it is believed that about 600,000 slaves changed hands in the Delian market every month. The Roman slave was treated like an animal. Terror, torture and sadism were his lot. Vedius Pollio, for example, was said to have fed the meat of slaves to his pet fish. Slaves were often forced into deadly combat with animals.

Christian Europe master-minded the Atlantic slave trade claiming bible to be its authority. Their two greatest philosophers—Plato and Aristotle—had justified and rationalised slavery in their philosophical works. It is true that the same Europeans fought to end the human traffic but really for the same reason they started it—to swell their pockets.

Again nobody is creating the impression that Africans on their own knew nothing about slavery and slave trade. But there was an important difference. Hallen Fisher and Humphrey Fisher put it thus: "A survey of the position of slaves amongst various Liberian peoples reveals examples of the various benefits extended to slaves; the belief that upright slaves might hope for the same reward as did other people; the opportunity of some independent farming; the opportunity of some redress in cases of injustice; an arrangement by which a slave might himself change his master; the chance of freedom....or, on the master's death, the right of a slave equally to inherit with his master's own son; and permission granted in some societies to a slave to marry one of his deceased master's widows"[18]

In order to avoid any misunderstanding I want to reiterate my point which is that the white man introduced nothing new or unique to Africans and into Africa; be it the art of arbitrary partitioning of people and territories, slavery and slave trade, philosophy and religion, law and politics or technology and science. Africans had their own share of experience and knowledge of these things. The only difference is that the white man because of his insatiable greed for power and material wealth, broke through his own racial gates in search of new guinea pigs. Perhaps Africans, with time, should have done the same thing but it clearly would have been altruistically motivated.

I agree with Asiwaju and Kristof that boundaries, in Africa and elsewhere, are artificial creations.[19] Boundaries are supported and sustained by jural laws. "A boundary", says Kristof, "does not exist in nature or by itself. It always owes its existence to man."[20] More correctly and appropriately, boundaries always owe their substance and maintenance to the sovereign authorities. This point has to be emphasized because, as I have argued earlier, residents in maximal borderlands are oblivious of the boundaries. The Greeks could be cited as exemptions to this rule in the sense that they considered themselves to be surrounded by barbarians and so what they had at the peripheries of their boundaries were zero borderlands. Of course, it can also be argued that the average Chinese, Roman or Greek came to regard others as barbarians due to the effect of corporate propaganda or Plato's 'Big Lie'.

The traditional doctrine on boundaries is that there are two types of boundaries: natural and artificial. However, both types have a range of application which renders them vague. By and large it is safer to agree with Stephen Jones that ideas about boundaries are related to their geographical and historical milieu.[21] We are told, for instance, that it was the age of reason that produced the doctrine of 'natural boundaries'. According to Pounds, the origin was largely French and Philosophers of the Age of Reason appealed to it when they found it convenient.[22] Jan Broek has discussed the problems, limitations and vagueness inherent in the doctrine of natural boundaries.[23] Is 'natural' to be understood as physical, cultural, racial, linguistic or religious? Suppose a people raised within a boundary are culturally homogenous but religiously heterogenous? Or they are tribally heterogenous but religiously homogeneous? The Yoruba people of Nigeria, Benin and Togo are ethnically and linguistically homogeneous but religiously heterogenous. If they are to be raised within one nation, which of the principle(s) of natural boundaries do we apply?

Even the physical criteria of the doctrine of natural boundaries is not as simple as it looks. What we mean when we talk of a mountain, a river, a swampy land, desert or a thick forest acting as a natural line of demarcation for boundaries is that any of them can act as a physical impediment to check man's expansionist tendencies. It is not as if a people expanding their frontiers, found it convenient or advisable to push beyond a mountain and they did not. Or the two communities trying to establish a boundary between each other found other means of identification and they preferred mountains or rivers.

According to Omolade Adejuyigbe, people expanding their frontiers most of the time do everything in their power to get across or over physical barriers. It is when they fail that they settle for a physical and natural barrier as the limit of a boundary. Before then they might have succeeded in overcoming other barriers. This fact explains the presence of mountains, rivers, lakes, dense forest being encompassed within the boundary or territory of a nation or a people.[24] There are for example, many rivers and mountains in France, why the Rhine or the Pyrenees as natural boundary?

Once it is seen that the doctrine of natural boundaries is fraught with imprecision, vagueness and defects, the way is left open for the theory of artificial, subjective and political boundary to hold sway. For this is what all boundaries are: political, arbitrary, artificial and subjective on the will of the sovereign states. There have been numerous instances where politicians tried to make races, religions, cultures or languages to fit boundaries ostensibly demarcated on natural grounds. This only goes to reinforce the contention that boundaries are artificial creations by sovereign states. Many ingredients actually make up a boundary: the territory inside the boundary lines, the races, the culture, the religion and the language spoken by the people within the territory. For the doctrine of natural boundaries to be tenable all these parameters have to be harmoniously homogenous. The more states that answer to this homogeneity the more tenable the doctrine of natural boundaries becomes.

Even if we concede that some boundaries are not power-political in origin, in potentiality and actuality they are. For when the chips come down, according to

Lord Curzons, an enemy "has to conquer the approach to a boundary before he can use the passage."[25] The contractual concept of boundaries, the imperialist concept, the military concept, the power-political concept all come under the doctrine of artificial boundaries. In my own view, the doctrine of artificial boundary is primitive in that all other doctrines can be reduced to it.

Ideally boundaries should act as bonds between peoples rather than as barriers. Boundaries are a fact of modern sovereign states. The task for everyone is to see that boundaries act as bonds between races, nations and peoples and not as barriers. It will seem though that man has a gift for creating barriers. Even when physical boundaries between states are acting as bonds, man is tending to create transnational boundaries but this time ideological, religious or spiritual.

On the basis of religion, many Nigerians owe their allegiance first to Mecca or Rome. On the basis of ideology many Nigerians owe their allegiance first to Moscow, Washington or London. On the basis of spiritualism, occultism or mysticism many Nigerians owe their allegiance first to Germany, India or America.

This situation holds for many other countries in Africa. The physical colonization of Africa seems to be withering but neocolonialism is rearing its monstrous head not only economically but, more dangerously, ideologically, religiously and spiritually. What we are witnessing are creations of religious ideological and spiritual boundaries and associated borderlands which render meaningless the physical boundaries between nations. It is not for any African nation to check or ban these neocolonial movements. Rather Africa should come up with its own ideology to be promoted internally and externally. For once Africa should think of what to give to the world and I think that my doctrine of Moralism should be a good starting point.[26]

Of course, latest developments in weaponry have rendered otiose the notion of boundaries as faultless security propositions. Boundaries are more of economic and political propositions—the right of sovereign, economic, commercial and industrial barons to have exclusive territories for purposes of exercising political, economic and fiscal policies. Nigeria's boundaries, west, north or east are maximal borderlands. This dictates that the Federal Military Government has to create supplementary policies, in the words of Professor Asiwaju, "to allow cooperation between sovereign nation states at the level of the specific localities directly impacted by their shared boundaries".[27] Maximal borderland citizens have to be co-opted and taken into confidence by the adjoining sovereign states for the meaningful implementation of fiscal and economic policies.

Endnotes

1. Omelade Adejuyigbe, *Boundary Problems in Western Nigeria: A Geographical Analysis* (Ile-Ife: Univ. of Ife Press, 1975), p. 7.
2. A.I. Asiwaju, *Artificial Boundaries: Univ. of Lagos Inaugural Lecture, 1984* (Lagos: Lagos Univ. Press, 1984), p. 21.
3. Ibid.
4. Ibid., p. 26.
5. Harm J. de Blij, *Systematic Political Geography* (New York: John Wiley & Sons, Inc., 1967), p. 200.
6. Ladis K.O. Kristof, "The Nature of Frontiers and Boundaries", *Annals of the Association of American Geographers, (AAAG)* Vol. 49 (1959), p. 269.
7. Ibid., p. 273
8. Ibid.
9. Adejuyigbe, pp. 3-22.
10. *AAAG*, p. 275.

11. de Blij, p. 203

12. C.S. Momoh, "Modern Theories in African Philosophy" *Nigerian Journal of Philosophy* Vol. 1, (1981), p. 12.

13. *AAAG*, p. 275

14. Bolanle Awe, "Empires of the Western Sudan: Ghana, Mali Songhai," in *A Thousand Years of West African History,* J.F. Ajayi & Ian Espie eds. (Ikeja: Ibadan Univ. Press and Nelson, 1979), p. 58.

14a. See C.S. Momoh, "Ideas and the Trade in Blacks".

15. David Brion Davis, *The Problem of Slavery in Western Culture* (Ithaca: Cornell Univ. Press, 1966), p. 31.

16. Ibid., p. 453.

17. Owen A. Sherrard, *Freedom From Fear* (Greenwood Press, 1973), p. 43.

18. Allan Fisher and Humphrey Fisher, *Slavery and Muslim Society in Africa* (London: C. Hurst & Co., 1970), p. 16.

19. A.I. Asiwaju, ed., *Partitioned Africans: Ethnic Relations Across Africa's International Boundaries* (Lagos: Univ. of Lagos Press, 1984), p. 233.

20. *AAAG*, p. 278.

21. Stephen B. Jones, "Boundary Concepts in the Setting of Place and Time" *AAAG*, Vol. 49 (1959), p. 241.

22. Norman J.G. Pounds, "The Origin of the Idea of Natural Frontiers in France," *AAAG*, Vol. 41 (1951), p. 147.

23. Jan O.M. Broek, "The Problem of Natural Frontiers" in *Frontiers of the Future* (Berkeley & Los Angeles: Univ. of California Press, 1941), p. 9.

24. Adejuyigbe, p. 6.

25. Lord Curzon, *Frontiers* (London: Oxford Univ. Press, 1908), p. 53.

26. C.S. Momoh, "Moralism: The Best Philosophy for Nigeria" *Sunday Times,* June 20, 1982.

27. Asiwaju, *Artificial Boundaries,* p. 28.

CHAPTER 5

Borderlands: Policy Implications of Definition for Nigeria's 'Gateway' State Administrations and Local Governments*

By A.I. Asiwaju

The 'Gateway' States in Global Perspective

Eleven of the 19 constituent states of the Federal Republic of Nigeria abut direct-ly on one or another of the nation's international boundaries. They are, therefore, located at least in part within border regions defined as "sub-national areas whose economic and social life are directly and significantly affected by proximity to an international boundary." (Hansen, 1981: 19). This definition underscores the need to state that the concern of this paper is with areas along and across international, as distinct from internal administrative boundaries.

This clarification has become necessary in view of the confusion that may have been created by publications in some Nigerian newspapers (see Editorial of the *National Concord,* 24 May, 1984) which refer to boundaries between constituent Nigerian states of Cross River and Imo as "borders" in utter contradiction to the ordinary use of the term as a synonym for *international boundaries.* Thus even when similar problems are encountered, as has been the case on the Nigeria-Cameroun boundary, in the neighbourhood of Ikang in the Akamkpa Local Government Area of the Cross River State in the one case and, in the other, between the same Cross River State and neighbouring Imo within Nigeria, the fact of the international dimension of the one boundary and of the internal status of the other makes a fun-damental difference in the manner of management.

The identification of the eleven states (Lagos, Ogun, Oyo, Kwara, Sokoto, Kano, Kaduna, Borno, Gongola, Benue and Cross River) also emphasizes that the borders

---

*The original form of this paper was a memorandum submitted to the Local Government Review Commission set up by the Federal Military Government of Nigeria in June 1984. By the time of the publication of this book, two additional states have been created; Katsina out of the former Kaduna State and Akwam Ibom out of the former Cross River State. The addition of Akwam Ibom increases the number of border states to 12. Katsina simply replaces Kaduna as a border state.

in focus are the landward, as distinct from the coastal, international boundaries. This further limits the discussion in the paper by ruling out of its consideration not only the entire Bendel and Rivers State but also the oceanic fronts of Lagos and Cross River. Although in the case of Cross River and Rivers States vis-a-vis adjacent areas of Cameroun and Equatorial Guinea, there is evidence of considerable interaction and interconnection between local peoples and economies (Osuntokun, 1978), the extent does not appear to compare well enough with the situation in respect of the landward border regions.

There is yet no universally accepted or standard definition of the spatial dimension of a border-impacted area. The meanings of 'boundary regimes', 'border regions', 'borderlands', and 'frontier zones' as interchangeable references to the impacted areas vary not only in terms of the unit or level of analysis involved—that is whether the area is to be considered in the wider context of its own particular nation or its international setting. Interpretations also vary in accordance to perspectives which range from the strictly legalistic to the administrative socioeconomic categories.

When 'borderlands' are defined in terms of relation to their own nations, they respond to the classical interpretation of the area as one which 'stretches inward from the boundary and merges imperceptibly with the state' (Prescott, 1965: 33-34). In this sense, was cán legitimately think, talk and write in such exclusively one-sided particularistic and nationalistic terms as 'Nigerian' borderlands and limit our considerations uniquely to the Nigerian sides of the borders with the proximate sovereign Republics of Benin (formerly Dahomey), Niger, Chad and Cameroun. However, this periphery-centre emphasis has had to be compared with another emphasis based on the perspective of the 'periphery to periphery interchanges' across international boundaries (House, 1982: 55).

This parallel interpretation recognises functional links and interconnections between borderlands of any given pair of nation-states sharing a common border. The inter-peripheral transactions perspective allows or a more scientific definition of borderlands as 'zones of distance-decay into heartlands' of the sovereign states on both sides of the border. As can easily be illustrated with the works of Robin Mills on the Nigeria-Benin border (Mills, 1973: 45-49) and John House on the Rio Grande (House, 1982: 8-12), geographers as the main experts with a concern for the spatial dimension, have proceeded on the basis of this transnational model to devise strategies for measuring the 'distance-decay' impact of borders. Working under the same influence of the interpenetration between the U.S. and Mexico astride their common border, Ellwyn Stoddard (1982) has suggested the need for the two nations to recognise a "buffer zone" of 100 miles on each side within which the one state could carry out prescribed operations and institute stipulated services on the other's territory in the spirit of binational co-operation and subject always to sanctions of the sovereignty rights on the side of the border. Without making such direct policy suggestions, Mills has indicated a similar need for a zone of about 50 miles on each side of the Nigeria-Benin border. This would imply the inclusion of virtually the whole of Benin and even Togo within the border region!

By comparison to the nationalistic perspective, the transnational stance is unconventional and understandably far less known to existing scholarly literature and policy making tradition which, so far, have operated and are continuing to operate largely within the framework of the nineteenth-century European notions of sovereignty of states and sanctity of national boundaries. Nevertheless, the transnational model has been far more responsive to the realities of border regions and has won an increasing number of adherents among scholars and policy makers especially those of Western Europe and North America where the effect is now being felt in the increasing tempo for trans-boundary co-operation, planning and development. We must return to this comparative context later (see the discussion under "Generalisation" below).

Border regimes may be statutorily prescribed either by national authorities or international agreements. In Europe, the cradle of the modern nation-state system characterized by sharply defined and jealously guarded borders, legal instruments (Treaties, Protocols, Notes) which describe international boundary alignments often contain minutely regulated provisions and stipulations about zones on both sides within which local inhabitants could carry out specified trans-boundary activities and transactions (Boggs, 1940: 96-111). Similar provisions characterize the instruments in respect of a good number of international boundaries on the African continent (Brownlie, 1979 and MacEwen, 1971).

Alternatively, frontier zones may be a prescription of laws of particular nations for the purpose of special privileges or restrictions on foreigners or local residents. Examples include the strategically and economically motivate Mexican Free Zone defined in terms of a territorial band 12.5 miles or 20 kilometres along Mexico's side of the border with the United States. On the other side of the same border, the United States government itself operates parallel zones for the main purpose of controlling Mexican immigration: 150 miles (reduced to 25 miles in 1965) for 'White Card' permit holders who are entitled to visit U.S. cities across the border, and U.S. border cities for the 'green card' holders who commute to work there (House, 57-58). Similar in meaning to the statutorily defined region is the concept of borderlands as internal administrative divisions on one side of the border or in relation to adjacent administrative units of the neighbouring sovereign states.

The socioeconomic space generated by borders is, of course, immensely wider and far less easy to define than the statutory or the administrative dimension. With particular reference to the social aspect, this point will be easily appreciated once we bear in mind that the main concerns here are those of community characteristics and the problems arising out of the operation of networks of cultural (mostly ethnic) relationships that are inherently disrespectful of the concept of borders as barriers.

Anthropologists and sociologists of the U.S.-Mexico border, perhaps the best researched of all borders in the world, speak for many other parts of the world when they recognize the fact of a distinct border culture area characterised by an overlapping or interpenetration of the cultures, economies and institutions of the distinct nation-states legally separated by the binational boundary. In Africa, as elsewhere in the wider world of arbitrarily imposed borders (Asiwaju, 1984 [a] and [b]) the model of community has been particularly apt for an understanding of the predominantly ethnic context of transborder relations (Asiwaju, 1976, 1979, 1982, 1984 [b]). This conceptualization of border regions as areas of 'convergence and systemic linkages across boundaries (Loomis *et al* 1966; Stoddard, 1978 and 1982) rather than as a place where co-existing strangers in juxtaposition work independently of one another (Stoddard, 1978), further reinforces the transnational perspective of meaning as well as it supports trans-boundary co-operation policies.

The extensiveness and complexity of the economic space generated by borders have not been less dramatic. The point has been made so clear in studies of the mostly clandestine transactions across Nigeria's international boundaries (Mondjannagni, 1964; Mills, 1970; Thom, 1970; Collin, 1974; Igue, 1976). In the particular instance of the clandestine movement of the Nigerian cocoa into Benin Republic from 1968 to 1985, it has been demonstrated that, while the main activities were concentrated in locations of close proximity to the border, the entire networks of the operations covered much wider areas of Benin and Nigeria: purchases of the produce extended over the entire Nigerian 'Cocoa Belt' (i.e., the areas of present-day Ogun, Oyo and Ondo States) while sales in Benin involved the entire Republic from Parakou in the north to Cotonou, the nation's port which handled the re-exportation overseas (Igue, 1976).

A good illustration of the complexity involved in any effort to calculate the economic space generated by borders is provided by a recent Nigerian Television Authority story of a Nigeria-assembled automobile with a Lagos registration number, perhaps one of the several stolen daily in the Nigerian capital. The motor car, having been ostensibly smuggled into Benin or Togo (traditionally the destination for most goods so smuggled out of Nigeria through the western 'gateway' states of Lagos, Ogun, Oyo and Kwara), was being re-exported to Brazzaville, the Peoples Republic of Congo beyond the borders of Cameroun and Gabon, Nigeria's immediate eastern neighbours. The vehicle was detected when the foreign vessel carrying it was arrested by Nigerian security men during its passage (a re-passage for the motor car!) through Lagos.

The Nigerian Borderlands

This elastic and multiple nature of interpretation is significant. Quite apart from the hope that the foregoing discussion must have dispelled the obvious error in the general belief that border regions are marginal or peripheral and, therefore, non-priority areas of states, the need for a working definition of the concept of borderlands has been underscored. The discussion so far has perhaps made it clear that our bias is for the transnational or functional model of analysis. Thus while the specific attention is on the Nigerian borderlands in the first instance, the emphasis of the discussion is on the policy implications of the inherently binational orientation of social and economic life in the border regions. In other words the view adopted is that of the 'border region in the larger context of its own nation as well as its international setting' (Hansen, 1981: 19). The endeavour is to suggest a policy option that would reckon more than hitherto with the functional and essentially symbiotic relationship between the borderlands of Nigeria and those of the neighbouring sovereign states of Benin, Niger, Chad and Cameroun in adjacent localities.

Comparative studies have shown that the problems presented here are intrinsically not different from those encountered on borders elsewhere (Hansen, 1982; Asiwaju, 1983; Anderson, 1982). Consequently, the discussion of the Nigerian borderlands will be made to benefit fully from an awareness of developments in Europe and North America which represent areas of the world where problems similar to those of the Nigerian borders have been experience and where the type of policy being suggested here has been or is being tried with some measure of success. The Nigerian experience itself will be treated with considerable sensitivity for its implications for the rest of Africa where, as in the Western sub-region, most borders are like those of Nigeria splitting distinct culture areas and geographical entities, creating a situation of contexts between divergent (mostly Anglophone versus Francophone) traditions of state control; and giving rise to the need to harmonize conflicting interest of nation and locality.

For the reason of our choice of the transnational model of analysis, it is necessary as a preliminary step not only to draw up the full list of Nigerian borderlands a term that must now be understood to be referring to the nation's "Gateway" States and "Gateway" Local Government Areas (LGAs)—that is States and Local Government Areas whose boundaries abut on any of the nation's borders (see the Table and Map). We also required to check these against counterpart regional and local authorities in adjacent areas of the neighbouring independent state. In consideration of the factors of a more complete body of researched data, more direct personal knowledge and need to further reduce the area of discussion to manageable size, the Nigeria-Benin border will be the centre point of the presentation. For this purpose, the Beninese equivalents to Nigerian States and LGAs as stipulated in the 1979 Constitution (amended by Decree No. 1 of 1984) will be the 'provinces' and 'districts' as indicated in the Loi Fundamental of 1977 (*Journal Officiel de la Republique Populaire du Benin,* 19 Sept 1977) still operative.[1]

With particular reference to the Nigeria Benin case[2] then, our understanding of borderlands will be made to cover the relevant Nigerian 'Gateway' States of Lagos, Ogun, Oyo, Kwara and southern part of Sokoto on the one hand and, on the other, the Beninese counterpart provinces of Oueme, Zou and Borgou. Similarly, the Nigerian 'Gateway' LGAs are seen in terms of their binational links with the Districts in the adjacent areas of Benin. Accordingly, the following six main binational sets of local authorities are identified: Badagry LGA of Lagos State (Nigeria) and the Rural Districts of Iseme-Podji, Adjarra and Arrankou in the southern part of Oueme Province (Benin); the Egbado South LGA of Ogun State (Nigeria) and the Rural Districts of Ifonyin ('Ifangni' on Benin's maps) and Itakete (Sakete) in the central area of Oueme Province (Benin); the Egbado North LGA of Ogun State (Nigeria) and the Rural Districts of Ipobe (Pobe) and Ketu (Ketou) in the northern half of the Oueme Province (Benin); the Kajola and Ifedapo LGA's centred at Oke-Iho and Saki respectively, in Oyo State, (Nigeria) vis-a-vis the Rural Districts of Sabe (Save) and Ouesse in the Zou Province (Benin); and finally Borgu LGA of Kwara State and the adjacent Bagudo LGA in the southern extremity of Sokoto State (Nigeria) and practically all the eight Districts of the significantly identically labelled Borgu Province of Benin (see Map).

These local authorities across the Niger-Benin border are like sets of Siamese twins in every material particular of local geography, culture, language, history, politics and economy. This internal coherence has given rise to easily observed pattern of relationship whereby the inhabitants interact more with one another across the obviously artificial boundary than they do with other groups and subgroups in other parts of the nation-state in which they are statutorily located.

Since the details in support of this view have already appeared elsewhere (Asiwaju, 1970, 1976, 1979, 1984a and Stewart, 1984), summary statements will suffice.

It is common place knowledge, for example, that the Gun, who constitute the dominant element in the population of Badagry LGA of Lagos State, are in every way part of the same subgroup of the Aja-speaking peoples who similarly dominate the ethnographic and cultural landscape of the Rural Districts of Seme-Podji, Adjanfa and Avrankou as well as the Urban District of Porto Novo, Badagry and Porto Novo, the two main urban centres in the region, contain a comparable pocket of Yoruba who speak a closely related dialect, referred to by their Gun neighbours as 'Nago' or 'Anago', and are also bilingual in Gun. Both towns are located on the same stretch of the famous lagoon which, together with neighbouring Yewa (Nigeria) and

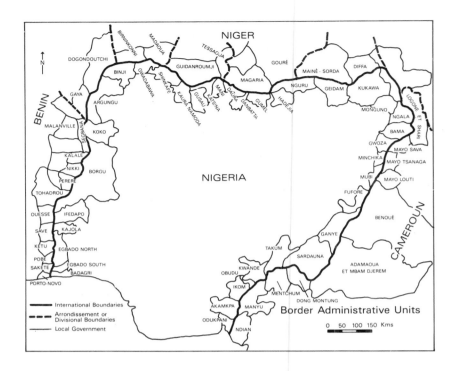

Oueme Benin rivers, serve the generality of the people from time immemorial both as means of communication and as sources of livelihood for the fishermen majority among them. The local markets, especially those of Badagry (Nigeria) Port Novo, Ajara (Adjara) and Topa (Cotonou), all in the Republic of Benin are commonly patronized by the Aja-speaking peoples regardless of the border.

The Gun, as we have noted elsewhere (Asiwaju, 1979), are a subgroup of the larger Aja culture complex which embraces not only the Fon of the area of the ancient kingdom of Dahomey and the Mahin to the north, all in the central and southern parts of present day Republic of Benin; it also includes the Ewe of southern Togo and Ghana. This socio-cultural setting explains the widely reported role of the Badagry-Porto Novo axis as the main 'gateway' into Nigeria for the ever increasing flood of undocumented immigrations and passages of goods from the mostly Aja culture areas of Benin, Togo and Ghana to the west, and vice versa. These modern developments operate within long established networks of relationships which clearly antedate the creation of Nigeria and Benin as modern states and of the border between them.

The essentials of what we have observed of the Gun subgroup of the Aja culture area across the Badagry-Porto Novo area of the border are replicated for specific Yoruba subgroups who constitute the main interlocking factors between (from south to north) the Egbado South, Egbado North, Kajola and Ifedapo LGA's in Ogun and Oyo States of Nigeria on the one hand and, on the other, the Rural Districts of Ifonyin, Itakete, Ipobe, Ketu and Sabe in the Oueme and Zou Provinces of the Republic of Benin.

The extent of the disregard which the Yoruba in the border regions have continued to show to the border as a dividing line is easily illustrated by the Ketu case (Asiwaju, 1970 and 1976). The Alaketu (ruler of Ketu, the ancestral city in Benin) has continued to be acknowledged as supreme authority by all Ketu and related people on both sides of the border. Adewori Adegbite, the Alaketu of Ketu (1937-1963), spoke for his people and the generality of the Yoruba when, in a reply to a question in 1960, he asserted that "we regard the boundary as dividing the British and the French, not the Yoruba" (Prescott, 1971). The persistence of this Ketu view is proved by an established tradition of cross-border visits among Yoruba Oba of which the most celebrated has been the visit of the Ooni of Ife—ruler of the ancient Yoruba town in Oyo State of Nigeria, widely customarily believed to be the ancestral home of all Yoruba—to the Alaketu of Ketu in January 1983.[3]

North of the Yoruba subgroups and similarly straddled by the Nigeria-Benin border was the area of the ancient Borgu (called Bariba by the Yoruba) Kingdom of Nikki split into two by the original Anglo-French line of partition so that Nikki (the capital was placed in today's Benin Republic while the rest of the traditional state—including Yashikera, Kaima, Okuta and Ilesa-Ibariba—was situated in what became the Nigerian side of the border. Nikki itself partakes of the same language, traditions of origin, political and social institutions and overall group consciousness with such other Borgu states centred on Busa and Illo on the Nigerian side of the border and Kandi (Kouande) west of Nikki on the Benin side. The 'Borgou' Province of Benin now embraces the part of the culture area in that country while the Nigerian share of it is contained mostly within the Borgu LGA of Kwara State with the rest, including Illo, placed in the Bagudo LGA of Sokoto State.

It must not be forgotten that the reason for the details about Nigeria-Benin borderlands is to show that the interlocking patterns and networks are not unique. Similar patterns of relationships are discernable on other borders of Nigeria and elsewhere. The Nigeria-Niger Boundary split into two an observably coherent Hausa culture area in exactly the same way as the border with Benin is known to have created the double image for each of the Aja Yoruba and Borgu culture areas. On both sides are the same Central Sudanese terrain and vegetation a predominantly Hausa society with pockets of the nomadic Fulani, the same Islamic culture of same farmers (planting mostly cereals and later groundnut for export), traders and craftsmen.

Aside generalities of a common geography, culture, history and economy, the borderlands in Northern Nigeria and Southern Niger share the areas of particular Hausa subgroups and traditional states. Thus, the areas of Argungu and Gwadabawa LGAs of Sokoto State and the adjacent local authorities embracing communities such as Dago Duchi, Mantakai and Filinguee in Niger approximate to the area of the traditional Hausa State of Kebbi with headquarters at Birnin Kebbi, now capital of the LGA of the same name west of Argungu, also in the Sokoto State. In the same manner, the Katsina and Mani LGAs in Kaduna State constitute the southern and metropolitan parts of Kasar Katsina (later Katsina Emirate) from which grew such southern 'Nigerian' townships as Maradi and Tassawa (Tassoua). The Daura LGA also in Kaduna State of Nigeria and Matameye, Magaria, Kwargwam, Botsotsunwa, Hawan Dawaki and so on in the adjacent local authorities of Niger were once integrated parts of the same traditional Kingdom (later Emirate) of Daura, customarily regarded by all Hausa states as their common ancestral base. Nothing illustrates better the 'Siamese Twin' relationship between the Nigerian and 'Nigerian' borderlands, as between the past and the present of this locality, than the especially binational locational characteristics of Birin Kuka in the Bamle Village area of Mani Local Government Area, one of the series of the border settlements with houses partly in Niger and partly in Nigeria.

The story is not different in Borno State vis-a-vis the adjacent areas of Chad and Niger. Here, as a colleague has so aptly remarked, it is common-place knowledge that Borno Emirate, which dominates the modern Nigerian State, was originally "an offshoot of the ancient Islamic Kingdom of Kanem, centred in the area north and north-east of Lake Chad and has had more in common with such states of the Chad depression as Kanem, Bagirmi and Waday (all in the modern Republic of Chad), historically, than with the rest of northern Nigeria" (Gina Porter, 1983). The Nguru, Geidam and western section of Kukawa LGAs of Borno State vis-a-vis the adjacent local authorities in Niger and the rest of the State's 'gateway' LGAs such as Monguno, Ngala, Bama and Gwoza, which front adjacent areas of Chad, are all interlaced not only by the fact of the same predominantly 'Sudan Savana' environment dominated by the Lake Chad. The commonly sparse population is predominantly Kanuri on both sides of the Nigerian border in relation to both Niger and Chad (Adefuye, 1984). The inherent difficulties in maintaining a divisive border superimposed in such a region of geographic, cultural and historical unity have been more than adequately demonstrated in what has now gone down into records as the Shugaba Affair[4] of 1981 (Asiwaju, 1984b, pp. 246-7).

Considering the several background studies that have been completed (quite a number published) on the Nigeria-Cameroun border (Anene, 1970; Adeleye, 1972; Njeuma, 1980; Bongfem Chem-Langhee, 1976; Fanso, 1983), it would appear unnecessary to repeat the details of such partitioned culture areas or traditional states and communities as Adamawa, Mandara, the Hingi and others in the Gongola State as well as the Ododop, the Ekoi and the Efik of the Cross River State vis-a-vis adjacent communities and local communities in Cameroun. The African continental dimensions of the whole phenomenon has been demonstrated in a recent collection of illustrative studies (Asiwaju, 1984b).

The interlocking relations between borderlands across Nigeria's—and indeed other African nations—boundaries have intricacies other than ordinarily suggested by the fact of the same specific lands and peoples across the lines. In Nigeria, the general applicability of the concept of borderlands as areas in which "the economic-social function of one state fades gently into that of its neighbour" (Mills, 1973; 44) is borne out by incontrovertible evidences of interpenetration of the national economies.

The Nigerian and neighbouring national borderlands at all points freely exchange each other's nation's goods and locally accept each other's nation's currency as legal tender: The Nigerian Naira is as acceptable in neighbouring borderlands of Benin, Niger, Chad and Cameroun as the West or Central African Franc is in the respective border regions (Gina Porter) are, like those similarly located in any of the other 'gateway' states and LGA's, freely patronized by traders coming across the borders from neighbouring sovereign states and vice versa. Reactions from Niger and Benin, recently reported in Nigerian news media, concerning the border closure in Nigeria have demonstrated that any change in the economy of one state quickly sends its ripple effects across the border into the neighbouring state where they are keenly felt. Similarly shared across the binational lines were such social amenities as health and medical institutions and agricultural services provided by government.

The improvement in mass communication, particularly the radio and increasingly the television (Ogun and Lagos States' television programmes are as regularly viewed in Benin as they are in Nigeria) have added innovative dimensions to the cross-border relations between Nigeria and her neighbours for which the borderlands were and are still the main channels.

It is made clear from the foregoing that our border regions are special localities. In contrast with other sub-national areas, the Nigeria, like most other borderlands, operate in greater association with neighbouring national frontier zones of 'foreign jurisdictions' than they do with regions and localities within their own nation. Quite apart from the fact of the primarily ethnological umbilical cords perpetuating the connection between Nigerian and neighbouring national borderlands, there is also the commonly acknowledged utter neglect of the border regions by successive Nigerian governments operating developmental policies that place priority on the core rather than the periphery of the state.

In a situation of virtual absence of reliable transportation system and other modernization influences that normally help socio-economic integration of parts with the whole, border communities are normally left to survive on their own steam, initiative and drive. Part and parcel of what has been dubbed as "the neglected rural majority" (Olatunbosun, 1975), border communities usually have little or no alternative to continuing in essentially traditional or folk life and the use of communication channels concerned largely with the maintenance of the various socio-economic, mostly ethnic and sub-ethnic ties. In the border regions, intra-group relations mean routine movements across an international boundary in manners that generally run contrary to the desires and the essentially border-maintenance interests of the nation-states concerned.

Policy Questions

In the context of the Nigerian local government policy objectives stipulated in the Constitution of 1979, as amended by the subsequent military administrations, borderland situations such as have been described pose rather peculiar and intriguing questions. Quite apart from the fundamental challenge to the national perspective, reflected both in the constitutional framework and even more so in the outlook and orientation of the leadership of a national army currently in control of government, the Nigerian border regions puzzle a local government system based on principles of local autonomy and initiatives as well as on high hopes about law-enforcement and developmental capabilities. The special complications of border regions arise from an unusual convergence of diverse jurisdictions and inherent internationalization of locality.

First are the problems that relate to convergence of laws and the multiplicity of control mechanisms. Not only are there laws of Nigeria and those of each of the four particular neighbouring sovereign nations. There are also the international laws governing trade, passages and other relations with each of them as well as the by-laws of the local and regional authorities in the immediate neighbourhood of each of our international boundaries. This convergence of diverse jurisdictions imply either an actual or a potential co-existence of generally ill-coordinated state control agencies including the Police, the Customs Enforcement Unit, Immigration and Intelligence Services both of Nigeria and the interrelating independent states.

The convergence of diverse jurisdictions impose constraints on vital aspects of the local government system envisaged by the Nigerian constitution. There is, for example, a conflict with provisions for local autonomy. The fact of simultaneous application of international, national and sub-national laws and multiplicity of control mechanisms is hardly compatible with operations that are expected to be based on "local wishes and initiatives". Yet these issues are so clearly stated in the *Federal Military Government Guidelines of 1976* (upheld by the present administration) regarding Local Government Reform, which require detailed local knowledge for the efficient performance of the new Local Government system.

This is not like repeating the complaint, usual of other Local Governments within the nation, to the effect of the erosion of their powers and initiative, by the supervisory state governments. In the border regions, local initiatives are whittled down not just by the interference of the supervisory Nigerian State Administration; the exercise of control by the national government through the operation of organs dedicated to state security produced important additional crippling effects. Finally, there is the problem posed by an overall nationalistic orientation of government, including the Local Government as prescribed in the Nigerian statutes and run by an equally nationalistic educated elite. Accordingly, actual operations ignore the transnational orientation of the various communities in borderland localities. This disharmony, if not outright antagonism, between local communities and government is a disadvantage which border regions do not share with other sub-national areas.

The convergence of diverse jurisdictions poses yet another operational difficulty to the Nigerian Local Government system. It terribly complicates the responsibility of Local Governments for law-enforcement within their stipulated areas. The Nigerian Constitution recognises only a centrally controlled national constabulary—the Nigeria Police Force. With reference to the needs of Local Governments, however, the projection was for units of the Force to be located in each of the LGAs (*Guidelines,* p. 15).

In consideration of the factor of local sensitivity, it was further envisaged that "most of the Police working in a Local Government area shall be conversant with its language(s) and social background". There would be a Police Committee made up (among others) of the Senior Police Officer in charge of the area, representatives of all the other law-enforcement agencies in the area plus the Chairman of the Local Government and at least a 'traditional leader'.

Impressive as this arrangement is, it runs into problems in a border-located LGA largely because of a lack of provisions for a binational dimension of operation. Peace-keeping and law-enforcement in a border region call for active collaboration between appropriate agencies on both sides of the border. The task of such agencies is rendered particularly difficult by the special attraction which border areas offer for activities normally regarded as clandestine within the context of the laws of the inter-relating nations. Border regions tend to protect such activities because of their considerable distance and remoteness from main centres of activities of the nation; proximity to a foreign jurisdiction constitutes the areas the areas into poles of attraction for those seeking asylum from national laws that have been breached or objectionable political regimes; the fact of too many laws and multiple controls can by itself tempt breaches; decades of neglect by the central authorities and the habitual gap between its interest and those of the local community has encouraged a vision of the central authority more as a thing to be avoided than embraced; finally, there is the almost irresistible temptation to engage in the usually highly profitable but usually clandestine border trade transactions based on the adjacency of two competitive market systems.

Nigerian borderlands, like most other borderlands, are sensitive areas of particular interest and concern for those charged with state security. However, the effectiveness of the relevant institutions ultimately depends on the extent to which the state authorities concerned can inspire local "community responsiveness and participation". So far, the opportunities are little explored. They are, indeed, ignored: Control is exercised from above, not rooted in local realities.

Border communities in Nigeria, as elsewhere in Africa, did not constitute decisive considerations for the definition and final demarcation of the borders in their neighbourhood. Indeed, most local communities were known to have resisted the new boundaries to the extent of their functions as dividing lines. In the colonial era when difference between the distinct colonial regimes began to be felt, border regions became a pole of attraction for communities who had to migrate from one side of the border to the other in protest against obnoxious governmental policies and administrative measures. A good number of settlements in Nigerian borderlands owe their foundation or growth to these protest migrations. Similar developments were known to have taken place all over West Africa (Asiwaju, 1976a; Ch. 6; Asiwaju, 1976b and 1977).

The absence of any policy innovation since independence has done much to perpetuate in many borderlands, a tradition of negative attitude to the border itself. The boundary-maintenance policy of the national government is inherently opposed to the border-free interests of the local communities. Law enforcement in such a situation is bound to have complexities unknown in sub-national areas outside border regions.

Finally, border regions complicate the officially envisioned role of the Nigerian Local Government as instruments of development and modernisation. The Nigerian LGAs, those in the border regions included, have been territorially defined in considerations for common interest of the community in the area [and] traditional association of the community" (Constitution, 1979: 7[2][b]).

As if to anticipate the criterion of 'traditional association' noted in the 1979 constitution, the *Guidelines* of 1976 stressed that "it is not the intention of Government to destroy the organic unity of the traditional Chiefdoms, Emirates or similar institutions". According to the *Guidelines,* "the traditional Emirates and Chiefdoms will remain, although their functions will be changed to accord with the present-day circumstances". For the avoidance of doubt, the Guidelines further defines "traditional institutions" as "those which have been accepted and derive their strength from over a history of many generations" (*Guidelines,* 1976: paragraph 18).

The Constitution affirms quite categorically: "It shall be the duty of a local government council within the State to participate in economic planning and development of the area" (Constitution 7[3]). In the Fourth Schedule of the Constitution, the functions of a Local Government are listed to reflect those which are exclusive concerns of the LGAs and others that allow for joint participation or concurrent action of government at both the Local and State Levels. To facilitate these functions LGAs are to be coordinated by the Ministry of Local Government in each state. The Ministry will, among other things, promote Local Government development plan, co-ordinate the work of designated town and country Development and Planning authorities, and encourage the development of associations of Local Government bodies so that these may discuss common problems and co-ordinate their approach (*Guidelines,* Table 2).

When placed within the context of the Nigeria 'gateway' LGAs, these ordinarily straight-forward definitions and provisions assume highly problematic postures. To start with, since 'locality' in the border region means an area astride an international boundary, Chiefdoms and Emirates such as exist also mean territorial units across the juridical line. Similarly, "traditional institutions" as institutions which have been accepted and derive their strength over a history of many generations are essentially those that are straddled by the border. For the Nigerian 'gateway' LGA's and their supervisory State Governments to function properly, there must be a close link with counterpart Local and Regional Authorities across each of the borders.

This policy imperative is all the more compelling in respect of the function of border-located regional and local authorities as developmental organs. Incidentally, whether in Nigeria or in the neighbouring countries, as the case of Benin easily shows, regional and local authorities are also commonly conceptualized as instruments for development. Indeed, before the *Loi Fundamental* of 1977 in Benin, regional administrative units (equivalents of Nigerian states) that thereafter came to be categorized as 'Provinces' were previously labelled 'Economic Regions' in emphasis of their being primarily conceived as units of development (Ayo, 1982).

In the border regions, however, the Nigerian State and, more particularly the relevant LGAs—viewed outside the context of the inter-relationships with counterpart units of administration across a given border—constitute what in the highly relevant "growth pole theory" literature may be called "incomplete development poles" (Hansen, 1981: 26-30). A similar view holds for adjacent regional and local authorities viewed solely within the context of their respective nations. The evidence of the Nigerian region supports the observation, based on a comparative analysis of the Western European and U.S.-Mexico borders, to the effect that "it is impossible for a local or regional authorities in a border area to implement a coherent regional development and planning policy without continual consultation with counterpart authorities on the other side of the border..." (Hansen, 1982).

This conclusion, is inevitable in view of the easily observed binational nature of the functions of the Nigerian LGAs with particular reference to those in the border regions. As the example of the Ogun State goes to show, such functions include management of markets, control of vermin, provision of community and recreation centres, parks, gardens and open spaces (including forest reserves), grazing (and hunting) grounds, control and keeping of animals.

Others are provisions of health facilities (health and maternity centres) and the administration of preventive medicine, and community health programmes; agricultural and animal extension services, rural and semi-urban water supply; fire services and similar emergency relief efforts, provision of roads; support for arts and culture; control of pollution and, one may add, general environmental protection as it relates to land use practices and such specific issues as game hunting and dry-season burning of bush both by hunters and nomadic cattle herders (Ogun State of Nigeria Local Government Edict, 1976: paragraphs 64 and 61, based directly on the Guidelines).

These functions embrace a range in which problems and solutions in situations of borderlands characteristically spill over the borders. Along and across Nigeria's international boundaries, the services and facilities such as have been provided exclusively for nationals on one side are known to have been regularly infiltrated by kinsmen from the other side of the border.[5] An illustration of the African continental dimension of this important phenomenon has been provided by the case of Zambia where the national government has had to complain about Mozambican and Mala-wian Chewa and Ngoni kinsmen who over-burden the medical, agricultural and educational facilities provided by the Government under its rural integration scheme for kinship groups on the Zambian sides of the boundaries with the neighbouring states (Phiri, 1980).

Proposals and Recommendations

The answer to the intricate policy questions, which border management raises, will be found only when and if we are prepared to undertake a radical revision of age-old policy instruments and supportive tradition of scholarship that are now fully realized to be in adequate, indeed irrelevant, to the realities of border regions. We refer specifically to diplomacy law and politics of International Relations—which so far represents the acceptable mode for treating relations between and among sovereign states, including of course, the relations across their common borders. Diplomacy requires that inter-relating sovereignties be treated as autonomous and primary units of analysis. However, the attendant view of a structural border bet-ween or among such sovereignties becomes a fiction in the context of the complex and numerous interconnections between geographically contiguous states. Borderlands situations call for an alternative policy option which will recognise the essentially dialectic position in which locality is internationalised and interna-tionality localized. Local Government in such a situation cannot and must not assume conventional forms and functions.

First, it must be realized that 'gateway' LGAs cannot function fully without cognisance taken of the international setting dictated by the presence of the border. There is need, therefore, for an officially sanctioned mechanism that will enable the affected LGAs to respond adequately to the realities of their intrinsic connection across an international boundary. What such a mechanism will achieve is formaliza-tion of the informal linkages at the level of the local communities, which have existed for as long as the boundaries and have indeed preceded them for centuries if not millennia. In other words, there is a situation in the border regions, which compels LGAs to function not just as LGAs but also as agents of international relations.

There is a call for a radical revision of the doctrine of National Self-Interest, basic to conventional diplomacy, in favour of an alternative emphasis on the doctrine of Mutual Necessity, based on the recognition of a symbiotic relationship (Stoddard, 1978). The nationalistic and essentially unilateral policies towards our neighbours on matters of local government reforms would not work in our border regions any more than they have done in most other parts of the world in which our type of border problems have been and are still being encountered. To give rise to the right type LGA at our borders, then, there is need not only for a direct mandate of our own national authorities. There is as well need for specific binational agreements that can bring about the commitment of all the nations concerned to adjust relevant laws and procedures within their systems, which may stand in the way of co-operation between the regional and local authorities in adjacent border regions.

Provided there is the will there is a very good chance for realizing a Nigerian transnational local government system. First is the opportunity of a federal type of constitution which ordinarily allows for a considerable measure of autonomy for regional and local authorities. While the local initiative and independence of action, so guaranteed by statute, are known to have been exercised by Nigerian States and more dramatically so by the 'Regions' in the era of Regional Government in Nigeria in respect of external borrowing of money and services from Europe and America and even consular representation in the U.K., the initiatives are not known to have been extended to Nigeria's immediate neighbours in the interest of a more effective control and development of our border regions. In any case, such initiative was never extended to local authorities within the regions or the succeeding states. The experience of prolonged military rule, compelled by irresponsibility and mismanagement of democratically elected governments, has itself contributed to the whittling down of the decentralisation and local initiative guaranteed by a federal constitution. However, the provisions themselves still remain and are available for use in favour of a transnational type of local government in the border regions, subject only to the preparedness of the national leadership to negotiate such a usage with proximate foreign Governments.

An equally important related opportunity is the generally good diplomatic relations with each of our four neighbours—Benin, Niger, Chad and Cameroun—and the fact of shared membership of several inter-governmental organisations (IGOs) most of which generally support the type of regional understanding envisaged by a transnational local government system. Indeed, a transnational L.G. system is the best test of the sincerity of such IGO's, it is the most effective demonstration of their relevance to border communities who, more than others, stand in need of the international integration efforts.

Quite apart from the series of bilateral agreements, particularly those providing for directly cognate binational institutions such as the Boundary Commission (with Benin, Niger and Cameroun), and the several functional organisations such as the Lake Chad Commission and the Niger Basic Development Authority, there are the larger continental and sub-continental bodies like the Organisation of African Unity (OAU) and the Economic Community of West African States (ECOWAS). Severally and individually, the various enabling treaties and protocols contain provisions that make for a sufficient umbrella under which a Nigerian transnational type of local government can be negotiated for the border regions.

The specific recommendation is for the creation of appropriate specialized organs. These can be done within the existing framework of either the OAU or ECOWAS. What one has in mind are institutions within one of these two IGOs, able to fulfil purposes and functions analogous to those of the Council of Europe and such institutions within it as the European Conference of Ministers Responsible for Regional Planning and more especially the Conference of Local and Regional Authorities of Europe (CLRAE).

Made up of representatives of 'districts' 'Cantons', 'Kreise', Lander, counties 'Departments', 'Provinces' or 'Regions', depending on the structures and categories of regional or local authorities in use in the nations concerned, the CLRAE is particularly useful as model of a body, the only such body anywhere in the world, which officially represents local and regional authorities across several international boundaries in their relations with international institutions, in this case those established by member states of the Council of Europe (Hansen, 1982). The OAU or ECOWAS equivalents, which this essay is asking Nigeria to initiate, may then be used to bring about an achievement similar to the European Outline Convention or Transfrontier Co-operation Between Territorial Communities or Authorities. The Convention open to the signatures of members of the Council of Europe at Madrid on 21 May 1980 and has since been ratified by all including centralist France. The convention cover a wide range of essentially local issues which, in border regions, require collaboration of adjacent local authorities of foreign jurisdictions for effective managements.

The recognition of distinct jurisdictional interests in border regions underscores the need not only for inter-governmental co-operation and co-ordination. It also stresses the need for a clear definition of functions and responsibilities. As to the issue of functions, which represents the easier aspects of the question, the salvation of the LGAs, especially those in the border regions, is in the preparedness of the higher levels of jurisdictions (State and Federal) to adhere strictly and judiciously to the definition of the LGA functions as so clearly stipulated in the 1976 *Guidelines.* Subsequent legislations including the Edict establishing the LGAs for each state and the constitution of the Federal Republic of Nigeria 1979 show faithful compliance with the *Guidelines.* Even when the various state governments in the discredited Second Republic created more LGAs, the statutory provisions about functions of strictly local importance were adhered to.

The problem, then, has not been so much that of enabling rules and regulations but that of practice. Under both the military and elected governments, but far more so under the former, the administration of the states interferes too much with the operation of the Local Governments. An important explanation for the Nigerian experience since 1979 is the policy of the Federal Military Government and that of the succeeding Civil Administration to the effect that "Local Government is primarily the responsibility of state governments (*Guidelines,* paragraph i). This policy has produced the effect of abandoning the LGAs to the mercy of their supervisory state governments who then use their powers not to 'supervise' but to 'control'. The local governments were rapidly degraded into 'local administrations', appendages of the supervisory state governments.

Since the Federal Government has constitutional responsibility to allocate funds directly to the LGAs, it ought to have been enabled, also constitutionally, to monitor the performance of the LGAs at least to the extent of the Federal funds committed to them. That the Federal Government rendered itself incapacitated in this respect must be considered an important explanation for the liberty which various state governments took to divert federally allocated local government funds into uses other than meant by the discharging federal government.

Before the Second Republic took off in 1979, strong views and opinions were registered in favour of the need for greater permanence of federal government interest in local government than suggested in the constitutional provisions of local government as 'third tier' of government. There were many important suggestions including the one for the creation of a 'National Council for Inter-Governmental Relationships' to be 'charged with review and co-ordination of the demands of local government...and ensure that the partnership between state and local government is kept in review in order to maintain appropriate balance" (Olagunju, 1979: p. 57).

Of similar import was the recommendation of a "National Council for Local Government which shall advise on the harmonisation of local government practices throughout the federation and establish local government manpower needs and relationships with other bodies within and outside Nigeria." (Nwokike, 1979: p. 213).

These recommendations for an institutionalized permanence of interest of the Federal in Local Government are supported by this paper in view of its focus on border regions where LGAs require some measure of international approval. This makes national-level institutions obviously important. The emphasis on the need for the federal government to be institutionally linked with the management of LGAs is not intended to dissolve the partnership of state with local government. Rather, the suggestion is to improve the chances for a balance that will give the LGA the psychological and material support vis-a-vis the state.

This balance must be achieved within the general framework of an approach which allows not only for a clear differentiation of roles but also proper co-ordination of the entire governmental machinery. In all these efforts, the local communities must be constantly involved. This means, in border regions, that their trans-boundary orientations would be taken into good account. Hence the compelling need for co-operation between authorities on both sides of the international boundaries.

The main import of the foregoing proposals and recommendations is that LGAs in border regions be enabled to play the role of 'gateway' into Nigeria: they must combine with their routine roles as LGs new functions as local agents for our external relations with our immediate neighbours. Accordingly the official or governmental presence in our borderlands must cease to be an affair solely of Customs Enforcement Unit, Immigration Services, Nigeria Police, State Security, Army or such other government screening institutions and coercion apparatuses. There must, of course, be control. But, equally importantly: There must be positive and accelerated pace in the modernisation process that alone will inspire the sense of a Nigerian belonging and loyalty among our border populations who have been everywhere subjected to abject neglect. To ask LGA's in our borderlands to play the role of 'gateway' in and out of the nation is to suggest that they must be models for the nation. The present realities are very far from this anticipated goal.

The sub-national areas covered by the 'gateway' LGA's have been among the most depressed socially and economically. In the colonial period when borders in Africa fell under more or less the same assumptions that influence thoughts in Europe where border areas were traditionally considered as 'disadvantage areas'[8] our borderlands were left out of whatever was done in the way of the development of infrastructure for social and economic development. Since European colonies were treated essentially as sub-systems of the respective Metropolitan countries in Europe, the same strategic consideration that generally led to the neglect of borders and border regions in Europe up to the end of the Second World War dictated more or less the same attitude to similar areas in the colonies. The same consideration of colonies as European national sub-systems also dictated the pattern of infrastructural development which oriented transportation solely to and from ports along the coast. In Nigeria, as in most West African countries with base along the Gulfs of Benin and Bonny (formerly Biafra) of the Atlantic Ocean, this has meant a South-North or North-South direction parallel to most of the borders. Thus, roads and railways, such as were constructed, and the traffic they generated avoid our Western and Eastern borders for example. Until recently, the same parallelism was noticed in respect of officially encouraged transportation system vis-a-vis the other borders.

The continuation of this tradition in the post-colonial era is indicated by the prevailing rarity of all-season cross-border transportation systems. Border regions normally have no schools, health or medical facilities and, of course, no industries were cited in them. The neglect of the colonial era has been continued in the era of independence, thanks to the adoption of an economic development strategy which, in spite of rhetoric about even development, has continued to emphasize 'centres' at the expense of the periphery. As periphery of the Nigerian state, the nation's border regions are among the most neglected of the traditionally recognized

"Neglected Rural Majority".

To achieve accelerated development of the border regions and reverse a disadvantage imposed by accident or history, we suggest a policy of Affirmative Actions of 'Compensatory Action' which will enable authorities to single out these areas for specially accelerated development. Our border regions must be treated as adversely impacted areas, deserving the sympathetic treatment of a nation of which they form a part and whose borders have for so long relegated them to backwaters of development. It is, therefore, strongly recommended that 'gateway' LGAs be covered by a special development fund by the Federal Government, in addition to the formula of Federal funding for all LGAs as was approved by the 1976-1979 reforms. The new 'gateway' roles and the national security considerations involved in the management of borderlands LGAs make such special 'Compensation Action' Fund extremely reasonable.

Finally, the extraordinary circumstances of 'gateway' LGAs indicate the need for specially sensitive leadership and personnel, capable of ensuring the necessary control and bringing about the desired developments. Both the political and administrative elites should show proof of interest in what may now be called 'micro diplomacy' and some measure of sensitivity for national security as well as for international harmony. They must be prepared to do original and innovative thinking, considering the specially dynamic nature of their environment which demands knowledge of planning techniques both within and across the national framework. They must be persons prepared for such innovative experiments like bilingual education in French (official language of our neighbours) and English in the local schools and negotiate for 'Nigerian Schools' in the non-Nigerian but closely related neighbourhoods.[9] Recruitment, training and advancement of LG personnel in 'Gateway' States must take into consideration the special requirements of their specifically 'gateway' LGAs as an integral part of our national security arrangements as well as agents for the promotion of mutual understanding between us and our neighbours.

Generalisation

We have, hopefully, made it sufficiently clear by now that the LGAs in the border regions are not like those in other locations of the nation. However, they are not so different from similarly located regional and local authorities elsewhere in the world. While studies have indicated important differences in local details and regional variation, borders and borderlands in one part of the world resemble those in other parts in all essentials of structure and function (Asiwaju, 1983b, 1984c). This explains our use of the comparative method which has enabled us to draw attention to areas of the wider world, western Europe and North America in particular, where similarity of problems has been matched with valuable lessons of experience in policy innovation that have produced encouraging results.

The transnational LGAs suggested will, when established, function exactly like the Metropolitan authorities in the U.S.-Mexican twin-cities along the U.S.-Mexico border, which maintain a relationship of very close cooperation in the management of several issues of policy including law-enforcement, control of air and water pollution and general environmental protection, fire service and related relief efforts in situations of disaster, public health, transportation and commuter labour (D'Antonio and Forms, 1965; Sloan and West, 1975 and 1977; Stoddard, 1981). However, the arrangements on the U.S.-Mexico border, productive as they are, suffer the

Table 1.   Nigeria's Main 'Gateway' States and Local Government Areas

States Serial No.	States in Alphabetical Order	LGA Serial No.	LGA Names	Relevant Foreign Jurisdictions
1	Akwa Ibom	1	Odukpani	Cameroun
2	Benue	2	Kwande	Cameroun
3	Borno	3	Nguru	Niger (Department of Zinder)
		4	Geidam	Niger (Department of Zinder)
		5	Kukawa	Niger/Chad
		6	Monguno	Chad
		7	Ngala	Chad
		8	Bama	Chad/Cameroun
		9	Gwoza	Cameroun
4	Cross River	10	Obudu	Cameroun
		11	Ikom	Cameroun
		12	Akamkpa	Cameroun
5	Gongola	13	Michica	Cameroun
		14	Mubi	Cameroun
		15	Fufori	Cameroun
		16	Ganya	Cameroun
		17	Sardauna	
		18	Wukari	
6	Katsina	19	Katsina	Niger (Dept. of Maradi & Zinder)
		20	Main	Niger (Dept. of Maradi & Zinder)
		21	Daura	Niger (Dept. of Maradi & Zinder)
7	Kano	22	Dambata	Niger (Department of Zinder)
		23	Gunel	Niger (Department of Zinder)
8	Kwara	24	Borgu	Benin (Nikki Dist. in Borgu Prov.)
9	Lagos	25	Badagry	Benin (Porto Novo Dist. in Queme Prov.)
10	Ogun	26	Egbado North	Benin (Ketu & Ipobe Dist.: Itakete
		27	Egbado South	Sokete Dist.-all in Quema Prov.)
11	Oyo	28	Kajola-Oke Iho	Benin (Sabe Dist. of Zou Prov.)
		29	Ifedapo-Saki	Benin (Sabe Dist. of Zou Prov.)
12	Sokoto	30	Koko	Benin (Malanville Dist. of Borgou Province)
		31	Argungu	Niger (Dept. of Dosso & Tahoua)
		32	Bagudo	Niger (Dept. of Dosso & Tahoua)
		33	Gwadabawa	Niger (Dept. of Dosso & Tahoua)
		34	Shinkafe	Niger (Dept. of Dosso & Tahoua)
		35	Kuara Namode	Niger (Dept. of Dosso & Tahoua)

disadvantage of being informal arrangements and, therefore, vulnerable to adverse sanctions of both State and Federal Governments on either side of the border.

It is this important disadvantage that recommends the pattern of developments in Western Europe as the model to be preferred. This model is characterized by a gradual but steady evolution from the informal relations at the level of the border communities to transnational regional and local authorities that enjoy the approval of the national governments working together in the concert provided by the Council of Europe. The solutions provided are to problems that are similar to those encountered in Africa, including Nigeria.

In both the European and African continents, borders arbitrarily split cultural and geographic entities and create sensitive management problems arising from conflicts between the boundary-maintenance policies of state and border-resisting tendencies of the local residents. The situation in most European border regions are very much like those of Nigeria where locality is internationalized. The similarities between African and European positions must ultimately be traced to the direct historical relationship between the two: borders in Africa are in very many and important respects extensions of the boundaries of former Metropolitan nation-states of Europe.

The lessons of the European experience, therefore, recommends itself to Africa, and the essence of that experience is in the steady realisation, since the end of the Second World War, of the need for active trans-boundary cooperation especially at the level of adjacent border jurisdictions. The new outlook overturns the hitherto exclusive use of diplomacy as the sole instrument for the management of relations between the sovereign nations. The suggestions and recommendations in this paper are, therefore, based not only on empirically proved needs of our own nation. They are also derived from the confidence that the policy innovation involved has been and is being tried with encouraging results in a known part of the real world where structures and functions are so similar to our own.[10]

Endnotes

1. Incidentally, Local Goverment reforms in the two countries were undertaken about the same time, though under substantially different circumstances. In each of the two cases, the reforms formed part of the larger move to fashion new Constitutions for the respective countries. The reforms were preceded by a series of preparatory seminars by experts, practitioners and general debates by the enlightened public. (The Nigerian story is contained in Walter I. Ofonagoro ed. *The Great Debate,* Daily Times Press, 1979, while the Benin experience has been subjected to a more scholarly analysis in Barthelemy Deguenon, "L'Adaptation des Structures Administrative Territoriales a L'Option Socialiste en Afrique Noire Francophone: L'Exemple du Benin et du Congo", These de Doctorat de Zeme Cycle, Cotonou, April, 1982 and S. Bamidele Ayo, "L'Administration Locale et Le Developpement Rural en Republique du Benin de 1960 d 1981", Doctorate de Zeme Cycle, Bordeaux, October, 1982.

2. This visit of the Benin traditional rulers to Nigeria took place in the same week of the incursion of Benin gendarmes into Koko Local Government Area of Sokoto State creating an atmosphere of diplomatic tension between Nigeria and Benin. This charged situation dictated the tenor of the speech made at the Installation Ceremony in Saki by Chief Bola Ige, then Governor of Oyo State. In the speech, the Governor charged the Benin traditional rulers in attendance to take message back to Benin Government that the incursion into the Nigerian territory further north represented a violation of the nation's integrity and could bring about terrible consequences for Benin. The visit of the traditional rulers demonstrates the cleavage between national and local community perspectives of border issues. Governor Ige's utterances clearly indicates the ignorance of the African political leadership elite about the non-nationalistic local perspective.

3. The Ooni's visit itself was a return of courtesy in respect of previous visits by the Alaketu of Ketu in 1981 and 1982, the one following the installation of the new Ooni and the other to attend the Converence of Yoruba Obas at Ibadan, at the invitation of the Ooni who presided as Chairman.

4. The Shugaba Affair is a reference to a highly publicised High Court Suit instituted by Alhaji Rahman Shugaba, then Majority Leader in the Borno State House of Assembly, against the Federal Government of Nigeria under the now discredited presidency of Alhaji Shehu Shagari. The suit was instituted to challenge the politically motivated deportation of the plaintiff on allegation that he was a Chadian, not a Nigerian Kanuri. The plaintiff's victory at the Borno State High Court Holden in Maiduguri, subsequently referred to a Court of Appeal for further adjudication, was nationally celebrated for the obvious reason of its wider implications for Nigerians most of whom belong to indigenous communities and culture areas which, like Shugaba's Kanuri, are split across the various international boundaries.

5. There are several services and facilities, provided by government for nationals on one side of Nigerian boundaries, which are equally utilized by kinsmen from adjacent areas of foreign jurisdiction. The Health Centre at Imeko and the schools at nearby Ilaro—all in the Egbado North Local Government Area of Ogun State are utilized by relations from Ketu and related settlements in neighbouring Benin Republic. It is not a one-way affair, as Nigerian Gun in Badagry Local Government Area of Lagos State (and other Nigerian) infiltrate medical services in Porto Novo, Benin Republic.

6. The European Outline Convention is a draft treaty with provisions which when ratified, bind signatory states to undertake a review of domestic laws and other discernible obstacles that may stand in the way of their border jurisdictions from entering into formal relationship with counterparts across their borders. The areas in which such local and regional authorities are strictly local and specifically stated. The Outline also contains draft model conventions suitable for adoption by the regional/local authorities themselves for purposes of cross-border co-operation which may range from information exchange through mutual consultation, active co-operation and harmonization of planning to real integrated development. The purpose of these draft model agreements is to standardize practice and ease eventual approval by the respective controlling national authorities (a copy of the convention is available with the present writer who can make it available to the Local Government Review Commission if it so desires.

7. In Western Europe, development of transboundary co-operation is at different levels of attainment. But perhaps the most spectacular achievements include the joint international airport at Malhouse in France, built with Swiss capital and run by a joint Franco-Swiss authority based in Basel. Particularly common are joint international actions to control water and air pollution and develop recreation facilities like parks. The Luxembourg-France-German Nature Park is a fitting illustration. A very instructive feature of the developments in Western Europe is critical role of the initiative exercised by the border populations themselves. There are several private organisations including the Regio Basiliensi based in the trinational city of Basel; the Euregio, created in 1970, which is an association of municipalities located in the German-Netherlands border region; the Conference of Upper Rhine Valley Planners whose activities cover the adjoining border areas of Western Germany, France, and Switzerland. The various partitioned culture areas of Africa, specifically analysed and listed in detail in the book on *Partitioned Africans,* have the same potentials of being similarly organised.

8. There is considerable literature on 'Location Theory' as it relates to border regions of Europe. For a   more   detailed   discussion,   seen   Hansen,   1981.

9. The concept of a 'Nigerian School' has been practically demonstrated in the experiment by Olatunde Lawrence, proprietor of Gaskiya College, Lagos, who in the early 1970s opened a branch of the 'Nigerian School' in Porto Novo, Benin (see P.O. Asiwaju, "College Gaskiya Porto Novo: A National School in a Non-National Environment" B.A. Ed. Essay, Unilag, 1984.

10. There is a deliberate exclusion of the militarized borders of the type maintained by communist/socialist states in central and Eastern Europe or that between the North and South Korea. This is because of the obvious inconsistency with our own type which fits more into the model of Western Europe and North America.

References

Adefuyw, A.I., 'The Kanuri factor in Nigeria-Chad relations', *Journal of the Historical Society of Nigeria* (JHSN) Vol. xii, No. 3 & 4 (1984), pp. 120-138.

Adeleye, R.A., *Power and Diplomacy in Northern Nigeria,* (London: Longman, 1969).

Anderson, M. (ed), "Frontier Regions in Western Europe" special issue of *West European Politics,* Vol. 5, No. 14, (1982).

Anene, J.C., *The International Boundaries of Nigeria,* (London: Longman, 1970).

Asiwaju, A.I., "The Alaketu of Ketu and the Onimeko of Meko: The Changing Status of Two Yoruba Rulers under French and British Colonial Rule" in Crowder, M. and Ikime, O. (eds) *West African Chiefs,* (Ife: Ife Univ. Press, 1970).

Asiwaju, A.I., *Western Yorubaland Under European Rule, 1889-1945: A Comparative Analysis of French and British Colonialism*, (London: Longman, 1976a).

———— 'Migrations as Revolt: The Example of the Ivory Coast and Upper Volta Before 1945', *Journal of African History*, Vol. xvii, No. 4, (1976b), pp. 577-594.

———— 'Migrations as an Expression of Revolt: The Example of French West Africa Up to 1945' *Tarikh*, Vol. 5, No. 3, (1977a).

———— 'The Socio-Economic Integration of the West African Sub-Region in the Historical Context: Focus on the Colonial Period', *Bulletin de l'FAN*, Dakar, Series B.T. 40, No. 1, (1978).

———— 'The Aja-Speaking Peoples in Nigeria: A Note on Their Origin, Settlement and Cultural Adapation up to 1945', *Africa* (International African Institute) Vol. 49, No. 1, (1979), pp. 15-18.

———— 'Border Populations as a neglected dimension in studies of African boundary problem: The Nigeria-Benin frontier case,' paper at an invitational seminar on Nigeria's international boundaris, Nigerian Institute of International Affairs, Lagos, April 7-9, 1982.

———— *Borderlands Research: A Comparative Perspective*, Border Perspectives Series No. 6, Center for Inter-American and Border Studies, Univ. of Texas at El Paso, November, 1983a.

'Centenary of African partition: whose celebration?' *West Africa*, Feb. 28, 1983b.

———— 'Artificial Boundaries ', Lagos Univ. Press Inaugural lecture series, 1984a.

———— *Partitioned Africans: Studies in Ethnic Relations Across Africa's International Boundaries, 1884-1984* (London: C. Hurst, 1984b).

———— 'Borderlands as Regions: Lessons of the European Transboundary Planning Experience for International Economic Integration Efforts in Africa', in Owosekun, A.A. (ed) *Towards an African Economic Community* (Ibadan: Nigeria Inst. of Social and Econ. Res., 1986).

Asiwaju, P.O., 'College Gaskiya, Porto Novo: a national school in a non-national environment', B.A. Educ. essay, 1984.

Ayo, S.M., 'L'administration locale et le developpement rural en Republic du Benin de 11960 a 1981', these de doctora de 3eme cycle, Bordeaux, October, 1982.

Buggs, S.W., *International Boundaries: A Study of Boundary Functions and Problems*, (New York: Columbia Univ. Press, 1940).

Brownlie, I., *African Boundaries: A Legal and Diplomatic Encyclopaedia*, (London: C. Hurst, 1979).

Chem-Langhee, B., 'The Kamerun Plebiscites, 1959-1981: perception and strategies', Ph.D. thesis, British Columbia, 1976.

Collins, J.D. 'Clandestine movement of groundnut across the Nigeria boundary', *Canadian Journal of African Studies*, x, 2, (1976), pp. 259-276.

Constitution of the Federal Republic of Nigeria 1979 (Government Printer).

D'Antonio, W.V. and Forme, W.H., *Influentials on Two Border Cities*, (Indiana: Notre Dame Univ. Press, 1965).

Deguenon, B., 'L'adaptation des structures administrative territoriales a l'option socialiste en Afrique noire francophone: l'example du Benin et du Congo', theses doctorat de 3eme cycle, Cotonou, 1982.

Eguntola, 'Ifonyi-Ile and Ifonyintedo: a case history of Yoruba "twin towns" on the Nigeria-Benin Border,' B.A. essay, 1984, Unilag.

Fanso, V.G., 'Trans-frontier relations and resistance to Cameroun-Nigeria colonial boundaries, 1916-1945', doctorat d'etat, Yaounde, 1983.

Fed. Republic of Nigeria: *Guidelines for Local Government Reform*, (Kaduna: GP, 1976).

Hansen, M., *The Border Economy: Regional Development in the Southwest*, (Austin: Univ. of Texas Press, 1981).

———— 'European transboundary co-operation and its relevance to the United States-Mexico border', seminar paper (mimeo) 1982.

Igue, J., 'Un aspect des exchanges entre le Dahomey et le Nigeria: le commerce du Cacao', *Bulletin de l'IFAN*, Dakar, T. 38 serie B, (1976), pp. 636-699.

Loomis, C.Z.K. and J.E. Gullahorn, *Linkages of Mexico and the United States*, (E. Lansing: Michigan State Univ. Experiment Station Bulletin No. 14, 1966).

McEwen, L.C., *The International Boundaries of East Africa*, (Oxford: OUP, 1971).

Mills, R.L., 'The development of a frontier zone and border landscape along the Dahomey-Nigeria boundary', *Journal of Tropical Geography*, Vol. 36 (1973), pp. 42-49.

Mondjannagni, A., 'Quelques aspects historiques, politiques, economiques et sociales del la frontiere Dahomey-Nigeria', *Etudes Dahomenes* Nouvelles Series, 1963, pp. 17-58.

Njeuma, M., *Fulani Hegemony in Yola (Old Adamawa, 1809-1902*, (Yaounde, 1978).

Nwokike, C.I., 'State and Local Government Relations' in Kumo and Aliyu (eds) *(Local Government Reform in Nigeria*, (Zaria: A.B.U., 1980).

Olagunju, O., 'Goverment at the Grass Roots', Kumo and Aliyu (eds), op. cit.

Olatunbosun, O., *The Silent Majority,* (Ibadan: NISER).

Osuntokun, A., *Equatorial Guinea-Nigerian Relations: The Diplomacy of Labour,* (Lagos, N.I.I.A, 1978).

Phiri, S.H., 'Some aspects of spatial interaction and reaction to governmental policies in border area: a study in the historical and political geography of rural development in the Zambia-Malawi and Zambia-Mozambique frontier zones (1870-1979)', Ph.D. thesis 1980, Liverpool.

Porter, R.,, 'Periodic rural markets and rural development in Bornu, northeast Nigeria', *Savanna,* 1983.

Prescott, J.R.V., *The Geography of Frontier and Boundaries,* (London: 1967).

_____ *The Evolution of Nigeria's International and Regional Boundaries,* (Vancouver: 1971).

Sloan, J.W. and West, J.P., 'Community integration and policies among elites in two border cities: los dos Laredos', *J. of Inter-American Studies and World Affairs,* Vol. 18, 1976, pp. 451-474.

_____ 'The role of informal policy making in U.S.-Mexico boder cities', *Social Science Quarterly,* Vol. 58, No. 2, 1977, pp. 270-282.

Steward, M.H., 'The Borgu people of Nigeria and Benin: the discriptive effects of partitions on traditional political and economic relations', *JHSN* xii, No. 3 & 4, 1984, pp. 95-114.

Stoddard, E.R., 'Functional alternatives to bi-national border development models: the case of the U.S.-Mexico region', paper presented to the annual meeting of the American Sociological Assoc., San Francisco, Sept., 1978.

_____ 'Local and regional incongruities in bi-national diplomacy: policy for the U.S.-Mexico border', *Policy Perspectives Journal,* Vol. 2, No. 1, (1982), pp. 111-136.

Thom, D.J., 'The Niger-Nigeria Borderlands: A politico-geographical analysis of boundary influence upon the Hausa', Ph.D. thesis, Michigan State University, 1970.

SECTION II
THE FUNCTIONAL
BORDER

CHAPTER 6

Territorial Behaviour in Animals

by S.L. Omo-Malaka

Go to the ant, O Sluggard,
Consider her ways, and be wise.
Without having my chief, officer or ruler
She prepares her food in summer,
and gathers her sustenance in harvest.
(Proverbs 6: 6-8) Revised Standard
Version of the Holy Bible

Introduction

The fact that man is part and parcel of the 'animal kingdom' cannot be argued. From the beginning man has continued to claim supremacy over all the other animals, to the level that man does not stop to learn from the behaviour of all the other lower animals. From the biblical quotation, however, it is clear that man has a lot to learn from the lower animals including even the ant. Evolutionarily, after all, insects existed on the earth before man!

This essay attempts a synthesis of mostly published information on territorial behaviour in animals other than man, a field in which lies this writer's own primary research and teaching focus. Ranging from invertebrates to vertebrates, from reptiles to mammals, and from the mouse and the rodent in the lower cadre of primates to the gorilla, man's closest 'cousin', existing studies of the territorial behaviour in animals from which we have drawn the examples used here demonstrate a unity of purpose: In all animals, territorial behaviour functions primarily to ensure the reproduction, nourishment, socialisation and protection of the young as well as the preservation and over-all welfare of the species and its individual adult members. Territoriality reduces, if not eliminates conflict and fighting between species members. At the same time, it maximises the times and the prospects for food production and other positive pursuits. Rather than the alternative of staying put to fight for scarce resources and be exposed to continuous fighting in an occupied space, all of which endanger the given species, most animals tend to move into new areas, much like in the tradition of migrations and colonisations in history or the story of man. Animals are extremely respectful of one another's territorial integrity: intruders are hardly aggressive, the inherent advantage of a home base being generally recognized and respected. Intrusions are normally met with stiff resistance on the part of the established occupant.

These and other traits and characteristics point to obvious interconnections with the domain of man. Accordingly, there is an abiding warning to researchers in the one and the other domain not to carry on their work in mutual isolation but, instead to embrace cooperation across disciplinary lines. The multidisciplinary cooperation between humanists and social scientists on the one hand and biological scientist on the other is especially important if we are to grasp with the correct breadth and depth of the problems that confront man in the management of his environment and particularly today's state-centric society. This chapter on territorial behaviour in animals should enhance our understanding of the same behaviour in man. For after all, as Robert Ardrey has so well argued in his book (*The Territorial Imperative,* New York, 1966), territoriality as the main delineating feature of 'property and nation' is a human trait that most probably owes its genesis to 'animal origin'.

Animals and Territory

Territory means an area in which a particular animal is aggressive and generally dominant with respect to other animals of the same species (Emlen, 1957). Lack (cited by Harris, 1964) refers to territory as an isolated area defended by one individual of a species, or by a breeding pair against intruders of the same species, and in which the owner of the territory makes itself conspicuous.

In short, a territory is a defended area. A restricted living area, occupied by certain reptiles and which is not normally defended against intruders of the same species, is termed a home range (not a territory). The essential difference between territory and home range is the absence of intra-specific fighting or intolerance in a home range. The difference between a home range and a territory depends on the behaviour of their owners. For example in an experiment, Evans (cited by Harris, 1964) was able to induce fighting and territorial behaviour in *Anolis carolinensis* during the winter (when the lizards are usually tolerant of each others presence) by injecting anterior pituitary hormone into them. It is well known that pituitary hormones are responsible for starting the physiological changes necessary to bring an animal into breeding condition. Thus an area considered to be a territory during the breeding season may become a home range at other times of the year.

Territorial behaviour or territoriality is the behaviour of an individual animal when it defends an area from other intruding individuals (Urbani, 1979). Therefore territoriality is rather antithetic to society in which more individuals live together in a restricted area at least for period of their life. There are, however, some territorial manifestations in social insects, although most of them are at the colony level rather than at the individual level.

It is important to note that among some gregarious lizards fighting is directed at establishing a dominance relationship between members of the same group. Such conditions naturally fall outside the definition of territorial behaviour, since other members of the same sex and species are tolerated in the living area, provided of course that they remain subservient to the dominant lizard (Harris, 1964).

In modifying Lack's definition, Harris (1964) defined a territory as an area over which a male asserts a dominant role towards all other members of the sex and species.

Territorial Behaviour in Insects

Generally, insects are credited to have accomplished many millions of years ago, certain phenomena such as chemical warfare, jet propulsion, sophisticated architectural engineering, cold light, air conditioning, and complex problems associated with aerodynamics, celestial navigation and communication (e.g. auditory, chemical, visual, tactile). According to Harris (1971) many things about termites are of interest to a variety of biologists, to protozoologists, to taxonomists, to geneticists, to biochemists and to students of ecology and animal behaviour/ethology.

Territoriality, although rare in invertebrates, are well exhibited in most insect groups. According to Chapman (1982), if male crickets are not confined to a small space in which fighting is frequent each insect tends to remain in a particular burrow on many successive nights. In and around the burrow it becomes dominant and so, a small territory is established. This has the effect of reducing the numbers of encounters between males, so that they sing the normal mating song more frequently at times appropriate to attract the females.

Territorial behaviour enables the males to be dispersed over a bigger area and this makes for maximum size and continuity of the acoustic field to which the female is attracted. Once the female is within the territories she is able to localise the position of a calling male more easily than if the males are all together in a confined space (Alexander, 1961).

Territorial behaviour also occurs in some dragon flies like *Plathemis, Perithemis* and *Libellula* (Atkin 1980, Chapman 1982). According to Chapman (1982), males fly over particular stretches of water, clashing with intruders so that individual territories are established. These may be very temporary, different territories being occupied on successive days, but often the boundaries are learned by the insects, so there is tendency for clashes to be avoided. In some cases, fighting has been replaced by ritualised behaviour involving sign stimuli. These behaviour patterns scare away intruders. For example, *Plathemis* species displays the bluish-white upper surface of its abdomen to intruding males, while *perithemis* species display their amber-coloured wings to scare away intruding males. Among other benefits territorial behaviour leads to dispersal of the species over a wide area (Longfield and Moore, cited by Chapman 1982).

Territoriality in Social Insects

Because of the opening statement (Prov. 6: 6-8) in this chapter, it is necessary to treat in some detail the various aspects of territorial behaviour in various groups of social insects. The fascination is in the lessons that there may be for man.

The two orders of insects whose members exhibit social life are isoptera (termites) and hymenoptera (ants, bees, and wasps). All termites are social. All ants are social. Not all bees and wasps are social. Just as there are solitary and social bees, so also there are solitary and social wasps. Termites are sometimes erroneously referred to as "white ants" although, as can be seen from the above grouping, they have no relationship with the true ant, except perhaps, that they are both social insect groups. Reference to termites, sometimes by experts, as social cock-roaches is consequent upon the high number of physiological and anatomical characters that they share. Both cockroaches and termites show a tendency toward aggregation, often due to pheromones (Luscher, 1970).

According to Boiullon (1970) the niche of a population of a termite in a given habitat is divided into territories or trophic fields centred around the nests, except in the families Kolotermitidae and Termispsidae. He stressed that in the study of

Figure 1. Diagrammatic schema of territorial and reproductive behaviour of the dragonfly (Libellula saturata) (Uhler). (Redrawn from D. L. Johnson, 1964, Master's thesis, San Diego State University, San Diego, Calif.)

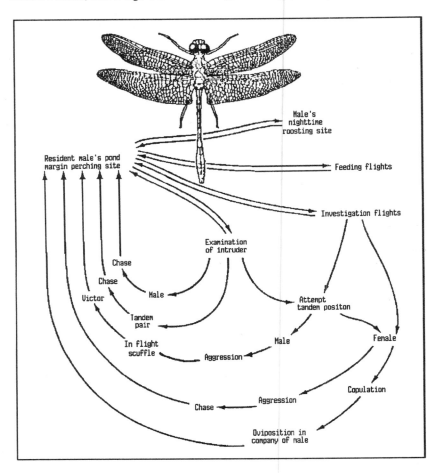

a niche, one must consider on one hand the conditioned nest and the society which inhabits it, and on the other hand, the trophic field and the workers which exploit it, accompanied by the soldiers. He also reported that the immediate environs of the nest can be connected with the nest and, for one reason or another, exclude the presence of other termites. He concluded that this is the case of the nest of *Macrotermes natalensis* in the region of Kinshasa (Congo) (see Figure 2).

According to Boiullon (1970) the territory is delimited by certain methods of constructions and markings, by the sternal gland and frontal gland secretions, or the excrement and the saliva, emitting odours which we are not certain are characteristic of a single society, a species or a group of species.

Josens (1972) in Lamto Savannah in Ivory Coast found that *Ancistrotermes cavithorax* and *Microtermes toumodiensis* completely overlap in distribution, and

Figure 2. A central nest of Macrotermes natalensis, surrounded by a zone avoided by Cubitermes sankurensis, whose nests are very numerous in the area. The distribution of the proximal nests of C. sankurensis is the natural arrangement; the others are regularly spaced but their distribution represents their true density. (From Boiullon, 1970).

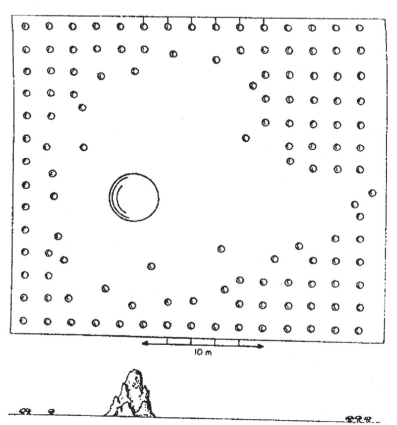

a fusion of two near colonies of the former apparently took place. Ernst (1960) reported a good example of such spatially mixed colonies in Tangayika (Tanzania) and found that 70% of the studied *Cubitermes* nests were mixed with at least one other termitidae.

According to Malaka (1973) who studied *Trinevitermes and Cubitermes* in Shagunu in the southern Guinea Savannah of Nigeria, 52% of all the termite mounds examined were occupied by their original termite colonies; 28.5% of the mounds had been invaded by insects or other animals which shared these mounds with the original termite occupants: different animals occupying separate parts of the mounds; 18% were either occupied by the insects which might have displaced the termites or were unoccupied. When mixed mounds occupied by ants and termites were broken open, for example, fighting immediately ensued between the two groups, the ants ending up feeding on the termites. Ernst (1960) found that in one instance, up to five species of termites have been observed living together. He also observed that fighting between different species occurred when the cells and the galleries of the nest were broken and the different populations came into contact.

Josens (1972), despite the good evidence he presented against spatial separation between termite colonies, proved the existence of competition between the two species *A. cavithorax* and *M. toumodiensis*. By distributing 9920 baits regularly in the field he found that 4544 were attacked by the two species in very similar proportions, but that only 40 baits were attacked by both species together; that 511 baits should theoretically have been exploited contemporarily by the two species during random foraging. Moreover, he found that, on all of the baits on which the two species were foraging together, there was also a soil wall to keep them entirely separate.

In other species, mostly in the higher termites, foraging territories seem to be well established. According to Malaka (1980)and, Maklaka and Leuthold (1986), so far, in *Amitermes evuncifer*, mostly workers (with some few accompanying soldiers) are involved in foraging/recruitment activities. It is common knowledge that in most social insects the worker caste act as scouts and recruiters of their nest mates (or confederates) to sources of food (or reward). The protective value of the soldier caste during foraging/recruitment exercise is exhibited by the accompanying soldier of *A. evuncifer*, whose recruitment activities are carried out by mostly the worker caste (Malaka, 1980). Malaka and Leuthold (1986) observed that, in *A. evuncifer*, both pheromonal trail and mechanical displays are implicated in recruitment to food source.

Malaka (1987) from his study from video pictures has demonstrated how trails are laid by *A. evuncifer*, during normal foraging activity (see Figure 3). The origin of trail pheromone in *A. evuncifer* is the sternal gland situated on the 5th abdominal sternite (Malaka, 1985).

The five different abdominal postures (e.g. T_1, T_2, T_3, T_4, T_5) exhibited by foragers of *A. evuncifer* are shown in Figure 3. In the first three postures, T_1, T_2, T_3, the worker termite exhibited varying degrees of contact with the abdomen dragging on the substrate which are believed to be associated with active trail-laying. In the last two abdominal position, T_4 and T_5, the termite exhibits non trail-laying positions. It was demonstrated that exploratory trails were laid at the beginning of a foraging expedition and that food, when detected, elicited strong trail-laying activity which facilitates recruitment to and from food source (Malaka, 1988) (see Figure 4).

Nel (1968), with various laboratory and field experiments, reported aggressive behaviour between individuals of *Hodotermes mossambicus* and *Trinervitermes trinervoides* in South Africa. He found that forced mixing of workers collected from different holes in the field resulted in intra specific fighting. He traced 12 different territories of *H. mossambicus,* averaging an area of about 93m² each. Observing routine fighting in experimentally induced situations, he concluded that *H. mossambicus* and *T. trinervoides* coexist in nature and that their method of avoiding interaction is through the development of a mechanism that prevents interspecific aggression.

It has been found (Urbani, 1979) that with a few exceptions represented by harvester species, termites never occupy a given area on which randomly foraging individuals may be encountered. Foraging activity is always made by groups in galleries or in trails, and all the members of these groups, both workers and soldiers

Figure 3. Illustration of the different trail laying (T₁, T₂, T₃) and non-trail laying (T₄, T₅) abdominal positions of Amitermes eruncifer. (From Malaka, 1988)

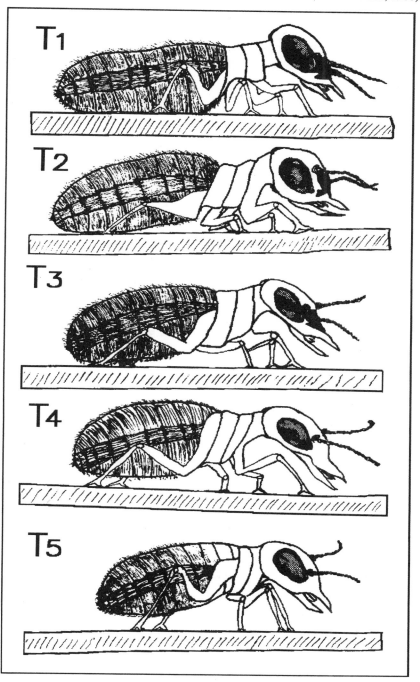

Figure 4. Illustration of the results obtained from the experiment on trail laying (TL) behaviour before and after food supply. (From Malaka, 1988)

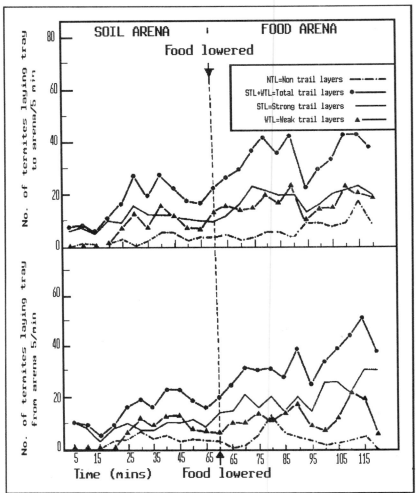

react fiercely to the presence of intruders. This is confirmed by the observations of Noirot (1959), of frequent fighting between 3 or 4 species inhabiting the same log and using different galleries in West Africa. Similar observations were made by Malaka (1983) Ella and Malaka, (1977).

Territoriality although rare in wasps, is much more frequent in socially primitive wasps than in the known eusocial species of the vespoid subfamilies: Polistinae, Polybiinae, and Vespinae. Lin (1963) reported a very strong territorial behaviour in the Sphecid cicada Killer wasp, *Sphecius spheciosus,* whose males defend a territory against intrusion by other males, other insects, and even thrown pebbles. There is some tendency to learn the boundaries between adjacent territories in order to reduce the amount of territorial conflicts. According to Lin (cited by Chapman, 1982), this behaviour enables males to spread over a wider area, thus increasing the chances of females finding mates, at the same time reducing interference of other males during mating.

True social wasps (e.g. *Vespa sp.*) may eventually compete and become aggressive against members of other species when particularly attractive food sources are limited (Kikuchi, cited by Urbani, 1979).

The neo-tropical polybiine *Myschocyttarus drewseni,* as well as species of Polistes, developed a highly specialised pattern of interspecific defence against the predation of ants; they smear the support of the nest with a secretion of the abdominal glands having a powerful repellent function (Hermann and Dirks, 1974; Jeane, 1970). According to Urbani (1979) up to eight species of wasps have been found on a single tree inhabited by a dolichoderine ant of the genus *Aczeta*. When disturbed, these wasp species usually retired into their nests leaving entirely to the ants the task of attacking eventual intruders.

It is obvious that wasps cannot defend a territory as large as the whole foraging area, since they may fly a considerable distance from the nest: the nest is regularly defended against intruders. This space seems to be more reduced in the subfamily Polistinae than in the Vespinae. The latter, moreover also extend their aggressive behaviour to the visited feeding places (Urbani, 1979). Bees are also similar to wasps in territorial behaviour to a larger extent. Male territoriality has been reported several times and in different groups of solitary bees (Linsley and Michener, as cited by Urbani, 1979).

Together with the phenomenon of male patrolling behaviour, at least some solitary bees show specialized nest defense mechanisms. This has been observed in several xylocopine bees whose females not only attack intruders, but also smear parts of the nest with a repellent secretion (Skaife, 1952; Michener, 1965). On the other hand defense of the nest entrance by different individuals devoted only to this task (usually young workers), seems to be a common feature in several social or semi-social halictine species, while such behaviour is apparently absent in the solitary members of the same family (Michener and Lange, 1958; Lin, 1964).

As could have been expected, it is only between members of the socially advanced family Apidae that nest defence and aggression of intruders became common and an easily observable phenomenon.

The European bumblebees (Bumbus Sp.) recognize intruders of the same species by the odour and the extraneous bees are attacked or stung sometimes to death. However, such purely olfactory barrier is easy of overcome and experimental mixing of colonies can be obtained.

Within the subfamily Apinae, both stingless bees of the tribe Meliponini and honeybees of the tribe Apini are known to fiercely attack man and other large mammals when approaching their nest (Wheeler, 1923; Lindauer, 1956; Howse, 1975). According to Wheeler (1923) a small swarm of *Trigona flaveola* observed in Guatemala ejected an irritating liquid from the mandibles that was capable of burning large portions of human skin.

The European honeybee *(Apis mellifera)* introduced into Japan, seems to have entirely replaced the native bee, *A. cerana,* by monopolizing food sources, direct fighting, and robbing or destroying the colonies of the latter. *Apis cerana* shows only two advantageous environmental adaptations, which are absent in the European bee: it can better survive in the cold climate of the mountains and it presents an escape reaction by abandoning the nest during the attacks of the hornet *Vespa mandarina* while the European bee is regularly killed during such attacks (Sakagami, 1969).

The African race of the honeybee *(Apis mellifera adansonii)* killed "at least 150 people and countless animals in Brazil" since its first accidental introduction into South America in 1957 (Gore, 1976), its higher vitality and aggressiveness dominated over the Italian *A. M. Ligustica* in hybrids between the two races (Kerr *et al,* 1970; Lavigne, 1972).

Koeniger (1975) observed that in Ceylon, colonies of *A. dorsata* (the giant Indian bee) in the jungle normally attack a man if he comes within a 20-m distance from the comb.

A single disturbed worker returns to the nest and alerts 50-5000 bees in one minute and these excited workers fly in search of intruders up to 3.2km distance from the colony site. A single alarm of this type may excite the bee population for several hours, but the whole population reacts quite nervously and attacks at the minimum disturbance at least for a couple of days more. However, there are *A. dorsata* colonies nesting in the villages that have become habituated to the presence of man and do not attack the inhabitants unless directly disturbed.

Other than these mechanical and chemical aggression mechanisms, other techniques are known for defending the nest and the food sources in honeybees. Domestic bees are known to mark the feeding places with a pheromone, which is more attractive to members of the same colony than to other workers (Kaltofen, 1951; Kalmus and Rabbands 1952; Butler, 1966, 1969).

According to Urbani (1979), *Apis dorsata* has been observed in Punjab to construct 3 to 4 nests hanging from the branches of a single tree and no more than a couple of metres part from each other without appreciable manifestations of hostility or interference between them.

Moreover, beekeepers regularly construct hives of domestic bees adjacent to each other without obtaining disturbance effects between different colonies. However, Kalmus (1941) observed that fighting for food occurs between domestic bees of different colonies when the food supply is limited.

Much has been accomplished on ant territoriality, more than on other social insects previously described since ants are probably the most common easily observable organisms in the world and since they usually have non motile nests and regularly wingless workers foraging on the ground.

Continuous variation of the foraging territory have been observed by Wilson *et al (1971) in Solenopsis invicta* and by Levieux (1971) and Levieux and Louis (1975) in three different species of African *Camponotus. C. acvapimensis* has about 12 m² foraging territory per nest and *C. congolensis* about 25m², but just 10% of the potential hunting area is exploited at a time, so that the whole potential area is of 400m² and 600m² for each species respectively. *Camponotus vividus* forages within 48-64km (30-40 ml) from the nest on the ground and up to 60m on trees above ground, but continuous variations of trails have been observed even within a one month period. Winged queens of *C. acvapimensis* found new colonies out of areas already settled by the species and since these same areas are preferentially occupied by other species, one can conclude that intra-specific competition is greater than interspecific competition.

Hangartner *et al* (1970) showed that *Pogonomyrmex badius* workers are able to distinguish the odour of their own nest material from that of other nests. Holldobler (1978) found that even trunk trails contain colony specific chemical cues that enable the ants to choose the trails leading to their own nest as opposed to those leading to a neighbouring colony. According to Holldobler (1976) trunk trails used by *Pogonomyrmex barbatus* and *P. rugosus* during foraging and homing have the effect of permitting the avoidance of aggressive confrontation between neighbouring colonies of the same species. The trails channel the mass foragers of hostile neighbouring nests into diverging directions, before each ant pursues its individual foraging exploration. This system partitions the foraging ground. Although foraging areas of conspecific colonies can overlap, aggressive interactions are usually less intense than at the core areas (i.e. trunk trails and nest yards), which normally do not overlap and are vigorously defended.

Fishes

Definite examples of territoriality are seen in many types of fishes, especially during the breeding season. Generally, a larger fish has a larger territory. In a lake, topography and vegetation determine size of territory. If there is considerable vegetation, for example, the territory is relatively small (Carpenter, 1958). In the cichlid *Hemichromis sp.* not all males are successful in establishing territories. Colour marking of successful males are associated with reproduction; unsuccessful males completely lack colour markings. However, when a territorial male of *Hemichromis* is removed, a formerly submissive male develops colour markings and takes over the abandoned territory. Thus only a certain number of territories can be established in an area, despite the abundance of territorial candidates (Baerends and Baerends-Van Roon, 1950).

Male Bitterling (fish) defend the area around the freshwater mussel against other males; to this mussel they attract a female (Boeseman, cited by Tinbergen, 1971).

Figure 5. Bitterling male with muscle (bivalve mollusc). (Redrawn from Tinbergen, 1971.)

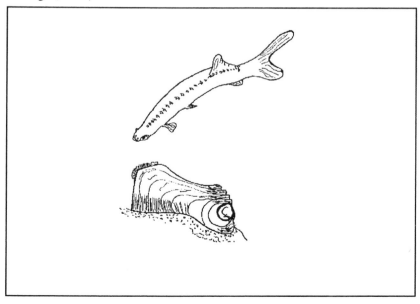

They induce her to lay her eggs in its mantle cavity, where they develop, leading a parasitic life.

Male 3-spined stickle back (fish) *Gasterosteus aculeatus* builds a territory (burrow) which it defends against other males which are normally red on the ventral surface (reproductive colour) during the breeding season. When the male stickle back meets another male in spring, it will by no means always fight. Whether it fights or not depends entirely on where it is. When in its own territory it attacks all trespassing rivals. When outside the territory, it will flee from the very same male which it, would attack when at its own territory. This can be nicely demonstrated in an aquarium, provided it is large enough to hold two territories. Outside the breeding season, stickle backs live in schools (Tinbergen, 1971).

Table 1. Courtship sequence in 3-spined stickleback. (After Tinbergen, 1971.)

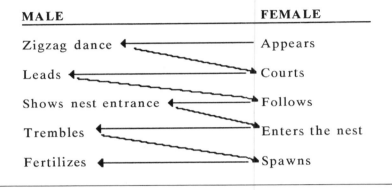

MALE	FEMALE
Zigzag dance	Appears
Leads	Courts
Shows nest entrance	Follows
Trembles	Enters the nest
Fertilizes	Spawns

Amphibians and Reptiles

Territoriality is seen in a variety of amphibians and reptiles, mostly during the breeding season. The male toad, *Bufo regularis,* for example marks its territory by croaking sounds which also attracts receptive females to their location. The male lizard, *Agama agama* establishes a territory and frightens any intruding male which normally possesses orange coloured head.

According to Harris (1964) the main function of a territory for *Agama agama* is to provide a mate, and, to provide the additional function of maintaining sexual bond. From available evidence, it is the female who makes a choice of a mate. Males who have recently established a new territory in uncolonized areas seldom have mates. A number of solitary males have been recorded on building sites in newly cleared bushland, but in all cases a female has appeared within a few weeks, and remained as the cock lizard's mate. In such cases the territory is established before the female lizard has appeared. It was found that the female stayed with the first male she met who did not possess a mate. Courtship and mating take place within the territory, not outside (Harris, 1964).

Although adult female lizards may stay in one territory throughout the breeding season, marking has shown that they wander beyond the confines of the territory during the off-breeding season and many settle in another territory at the onset of the next breeding season. This wandering phase and formation of new pairs clearly indicates that the sexual bond wanes at the end of the breeding season and has to

Figure 6. Diagram of lizard behaviour. (From Harris, 1964.)

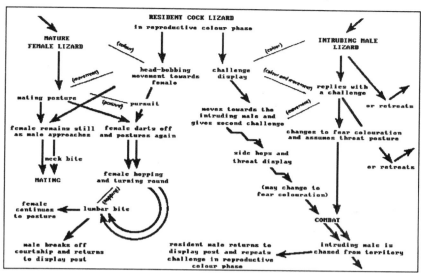

be re-established the following season.

In contrast, the cock lizards retain their territories and use them the following year (see Figure 6). The two main functions attributed by Howard (cited by Harris, 1964) to territory among passerine birds were: (a) the mate's acquisition of a mate, and (b) the provision of an adequate supply of food for rearing the young. Lack (cited by Harris, 1964) stated that territory is primarily of importance in pair-formation, and perhaps in maintenance of the pair.

Birds

Among birds, territorial behaviour is highly developed. The behaviour of the meadowlark may be considered as a general example. The male vocalizes in adopted area four weeks before the female arrives. The male chases another male intruder in the territory until it leaves the boundary.

The frequent encounters at the boundaries between mates, of adjacent territories typically involve vocalizations and various types of threatening postures. In most cases there is no actual combat between males; one male becomes submissive and backs off.

Some birds return to the same territory year after year. For example, a pair of European nutcrackers were observed returning to the same spot for ten years (Swanberg, 1950). Banding studies indicated that 70% of the robins that survived the winter returned to winter within 25 miles (40 km) of their birth-place (Farner, 1945).

In meadowlarks and a number of other species, courtship, nesting, and feeding occur within one territory. However, for some birds territories serve more specialized functions. For example courtship and mating territories are held by males of polygamous birds, such as prairie chickens and bowerbirds. Colonial water birds, such as penguins and gulls, establish nesting territories, which are sometimes only as large as a distance a sitting bird can jab with its beak. In all other situations no territoriality is exhibited. A few birds, for example, pomarine jaegers and seaside sparrows defend feeding territories that are separate from the nesting area. The size of the territory varies with the availability of food. In some cases, feeding areas are defended when food is scarce. A few birds, however, establish a winter territory separate from other territories associated with the mating season. The red headed woodpecker *(Melanerpes erythrocephalus)* defends stores of acorns in various cavities against both other woodpeckers and acorn-stealing blue jays (Kilham, 1958).

Mammals

Mammals also exhibit complex territorial behaviour, which takes on a variety of forms. Quasi-territoriality-home-ranges are developed by many mammals. As earlier stated, home ranges are not territories in the strict sense, because they are not defended areas. However, they are similar to territories in that the animals usually stay within the boundaries of a very definite area and are harder to defeat when attacked in this area than in others. The size of a home range varies considerably among mammals. Mice have ranges of a metre; some deer have ranges of several kilometres. There are two ranges among mountain goats; and these ranges change with the seasons: a summer range high in the mountains, and a winter range in the valley.

A special breeding area within a group of territory is established by males of an African antelope, known as the kob *(Adenota kob)*. The male fights to establish territory and then defends it against other males. It then attracts a female to the territory. A disturbance such as a lion or a passing automobile will cause the males to leave their territories temporarily without fighting; within 10 to 20 minutes they return to re-establish the order (Buechner, 1961).

A similar type of individual territory is established by pinnipeds (e.g. lions), and fur seals, which breed in harem groups. Males arrive at the breeding grounds (specific coastal islands) early in the spring and fight to establish territories which are only a few square kilometres each in area. Throughout the breeding season, males constantly vocalize and butt each other at the periphery of their territories. A female is welcomed into one of the territories along with other females. In the seals, females mate with the harem master, after the young conceived the last season are delivered. Females then go out to the sea and feed, returning periodically to nurse the young. Breeding areas appear very crowded and there are many males unable to establish a territory (Bartholomew, 1953).

Harem groups are also formed by males of the red deer during the sexual season. However, they are only maintained for a week or so. At the end of this period, the exhausted male—who has neither eaten nor slept very much during this period—retires to the uplands, the harem is then left for other males. During the remainder of the year, males live solitarily or in loosely organized groups. In contrast, females and young live in well organized matriarchal groups within summer and winter home ranges.

Territories within the larger confines of a colony are found among black-tailed prairie dogs, which live in complete system of burrows. The colony—called a prairie dog town—is subdivided into coteries, which typically consists of a male, several females, and their young. The territory which includes the coteries system of burrows, is defended against all other prairie dogs. Intra-coterie recognition is apparently facilitated by frequent contact between members of the groups: these consist of grooming, nuzzling, and climbing over one another (King, 1955).

In mammals chemical cues are also used to delineate territories. Male cats and dogs spray their strong smelling urine about their territories. Similar chemical cues can be used to mark trails: mule deer lay down a scent secreted by the interdigital glands located on their feet—which enables them to follow one another through wooded areas where vision is obscured.

The rhesus monkeys, which are primates, are very close to man in evolution. They live in clans of from 20 to 150 individuals. Within this clan, there is a strict linear hierarchy. The dominant male mates with the female at the height of oestrus and when food is concentrated in one area, eats before the others. The occurrence of dominance and submissive gestures is greatest when there is competition for food. Subordination in both males and females is expressed by adopting a posture of sexual presentation, the dominant animal then mounts the subordinates. Thus aggression and dominance are closely related to sexuality in these monkeys.

Summary

In conclusion, territoriality functions to reduce the amount of fighting between members of the groups. In addition, territorial behaviour tends to space individuals within an area; such spacing alleviates overcrowding and may force some animals to move into new areas.

This allows for equitable sharing of such vital resources as food and adequate shelter for the reproduction and up-bringing of the young. Too many bitterling eggs in a mussel (bivalve mollusc) will result in low ration for each. When many males would mate with one female instead of securing females of their own, this would be a waste of gem cells. Two broods of starlings (birds) may be fatal to both broods. Spacing out makes the individuals utilize the available opportunities/resources.

In the solitary wasps, for example, *(Sphecius spheciosus),* territorial behaviour enables males to spread over a wider area thus increasing the chances of a female finding males at the same time reducing interference of other males during mating. This behaviour fits much better one of the earlier definitions of territory for the vertebrates, than many of those described for their eusocial relatives/counterparts.

Although social insects defend their nests (all other animals do), outside the nest the area defended is reduced, and in most cases, seems to be related to the presence of food source.

Urbani (1979) recalls that the properties of constructing clusters of nests in partially favourable nest sites and of attacking disturbers of the nest, are largely the same for the feared Indian giant bee and for the house martin, and said that there is no ornithologist willing to define the latter as a territorial bird.

Territories of mammals and birds cannot be compared with those of social insects because the latter are not represented by defined surfaces but just by trails and points (Salman, cited by Urbani, 1979). To a minor extent, this also is the same for many vertebrates. Some ants (e.g. driver ant, *Atta, Pogononuyrmex* species) possess territorial behaviour similar to some extent, to those of vertebrates.

The use of the term territory must continue to be applied to social insects with modification. Schneiria (cited by Urbani, 1979). Defined territory for social insects, as "an area that is occupied.... for an appreciable length of time and from which other individuals of the same or closely related species are excluded for that time by virtue of disturbed reactions of the occupants to the entrance of invaders." Such definition is to some extent useful in ecological and behaviourial studies of both vertebrates and invertebrates. The perspective obviously enhances our understanding of the same trails in man.

Bibliography

Ardney, R., *The Territorial Imperative: A Personal Inquiry into the Animal Origin of Property and Nation* (New York: Dell, 1966).

Atkins, M.D., *Introduction to Insect Behaviour,* (New York: Macmillan, 1980) p. 237.

Alexander, R.D., "Aggressiveness, territoriality and sexual behaviour in field crickets" (Orthoptera: Gryllidea), *Behaviour,* (1961) 17, pp. 130-223.

Ampion, A. and Quennedy, A., (1981): "The abdominal epidermal glands of termites and their phylogenetic significance" in House, P.E. and Clement, J.L. (eds) *Biosystematic of Social Insects,* series of "The Systematic Association Special Volume 19, pp. 249-261.

Bartholomew, G.A., "The modification by temperature of the photoperiodic control of gonadal development in the lizard *xantusia vigilis*" *Copeia,* 1953, pp. 45-50.

Beuillon, A., "Termites of the Ethiopian Region" in Krishna, K. and Weesner, F.M., (eds) *Biology of Termites* Vol. II (New York: Acad. Press, 1970) pp. 154-273.

Butler, C.G., "Mandibular gland pheromone of worker honey bees" *Nature,* 1966, (London), pp. 212, 530.

Chapman, R.F., *The Insects: Structure and Function* (London: Hodder and Stoughton, 1982) 3rd Edit., p. 919.

Ernst, E., "Frende Termitenkolonien" *Cubitermes.* Nestern. Rev. Suisce Zool. 1960, 67, pp. 201-206.

Hangartner, W., Reichson, J., and Wilson, E.O., "Orientation to nest material by the ant *Pogonomyrmes badrus* (Latreille)" *Anim. Behav.* 18 (1970), pp. 331-334.

Harris, V.A., *The Life of the Rainbow Lizard* (London: Hutchinson, 1964) p. 174.

Herman, H.R.; Jr. and Dirks, T.F., "Sternal glands in polistine wasps: morphology and associated behaviour" *J. Ga. Entomol. Soc. 9,* (1974) pp. 1-8.

Holldolber, B., "Home range orientation and territoriality in harvesting ants" *Proc. Nat. Acad. Sci. U.S.A.* 71 (1974), pp. 3274-3277.

Holldolber, B., "Recruitment behaviour, home range orientation and territoriality in harvester ants, *Pogonomyrmex*" *Behav. Ecol. Sociobiol.* 1 (1976), pp. 3-44.

Holldolber, B., "Ethological Aspects of Chemical Communication in Ants" in *Advances in the Study of Behaviours 8* (New York: Acad. Press, 1978) pp. 75-115.

Howse, P.E., "Chemical defences of ants, termites and other insects: some outstanding questions" *Proc. Symp. Pheromones Defensive Secretions.* Soc. Insects, (1975) Dijon, pp. 23-40.

Jeane, R.L., "Chemical defense of brood by social wasp" *Science,* 108 (1970) pp. 1465-1466.

Josens, J., "Etude biologuque et econologique des termites (Isoptera) de la savane de Lamto Pakobo (Cote d'voire)", Ph.D. thesis Univ. Brussels, (1972), pp. 262.

Kalmus, H. and Ribbands, C.R., "The origin of the odours by which honey bees distinguish their companions" *Proc. R. Soc. Ser. B.* 140, (1952) pp. 50-59.

Kaltofen, R.S., "Eas Problem des Volksduftes bei der Honigbiene", *Z. Vergl. Physiol.* 33 (1951), pp. 462-475.

Kerr, W.E., Goncalves, L.S., Blota, L.F., and Maciel, H.B., "Biologia comparada entre abelhas *Apis mellifera adansonii* e suas hibridas", *An. Congr. Bras. Apic.* 1st Florianopolis, (1970), pp. 151-185.

Koeniger, N., "Observations on the alarm behaviour and colony defence of *Apis dorsata*", *Proc. Symp. Pheromones Defensive Secretions Soc. Insects,* Dijon, (1975), pp. 153-154.

Lack, D., "The behaviour of the robin. Part I: The life history, with special reference to agressive behaviour, sexual behaviours and territory. Part II: A partial analysis of aggressive and recognition behaviour. *Proc. Zod. Soc. Lond.* V. 109 A (1939), pp. 169-219.

Leviux, J., "Mise en evidence de la structure des nids et de l'implantation des zones de chasse de dena especies de *Camponotus* (Hym. Form) a l'aide de radio-isotopes", *Insectes Soc.* 18, (1971), pp. 29-48.

Lin, N., "Territorial behaviour in the cicada killer wasp, *Sphecius spheciosus* (Drury) (Hymenoptera: Sphecidae)", *Behaviour* 20 (1963), pp. 115-133.

Lin, N., "Increase parasitic pressure as a major factor in the evolution of social behaviour in halictine bees", *Insectes Soc.* 11 (1964), pp. 187-192.

Lindauer, M., "Uber die Verstandigung bei indischen Bienen", *Z. vergl. Physiol.* 38 (1956), pp. 521-577.

Malaka, S.L.O., "Observations on termites in Nigeria", *Nig. Field,* 38(1) (1973), pp. 22-40.

Malaka, S.L.O., "Foraging behaviour of *Amitermes evuncifer* Silvestri (Isoptera, Termitidae, Amitermitinae)", *J. Nat. Hist* 14 (1980), pp. 351-361.

Malaka, S.L.O., "Economic importance of termites: six case studies in Nigeria and Ghana", *Nig. Field* 47 (1983), pp. 4, 222-230.

Malaka, S.L.O., "Exploratory behaviour and feed retrieval habits of *Amitermes evuncifer* Silvestri (Isoptera, Termitidae, Termitinae)", Ph.D. thesis, Univ. of Lagos, (1985), p. 176.

Malaka, S.L.O. and Leuthold, R.H., "Mechanisms of recruitment for the retrieval of food in *Amitermes evuncifer* Silvestri (Isoptera, Termitidae, Termitinae)", *Ins. Sc. and Appl.* Pergamum Press, Oxford 7(6) (1986), pp. 707-721.

Malaka, S.L.O., "Establishment of foraging trail and qualification of trail pheromone by *Amitermes evuncifer* Silvestri (Iseptera; Termitidae; Termitinae)", *Ins. Sc. and Appl.* (in press).

Michener, C.D., "The life cycle and social organization in bees of the germs *Exoneura* and their parasite, *Inquilina* (Hymenepter, Xylocopinae)", *Univ. Kans. Sci. Bull.* 56 (1965), pp. 317-358.

Nel, J.J.C., "Aggressive behaviour of the harvester termite, *Hodotermes mossambicus* (Hagen) and *Trinervitermes trinervoides* (Sjostedt)", *Insectes Soc.* 15 (1968), pp. 145-156.

Sakagami, S.F., "Some interspecific relations between Japanese and European honey-bees", *J. Anim. Ecol.* 28 (1959), pp. 51-68.

Skaife, S.H., "The yellow-banded carpenter bee, *Mesotrichia caffra* Linn and its eymbiotic mite, *Diogamasus braunsi* Vitzthum." *J. Entomol. Soc. S. Afr.* 15: (1952), pp. 63-76.

Swanberg, (1950).

Tinbergen, N., *Social Behaviour in Animals* (Chapman & Hall, 1971) 4th Edition, p. 150.

Urbani, C.B., "Territoriality in Social Insects" in Hermann, H.R. (ed) *Social Insects* Vol. 1 (New York: Acad. Press, 1979) pp. 91-120.

Wheeler, W.M., *Social Life Among the Insects* (New York: Harcourt, 1923) p. 375.

Wilson, N.L., Diller, J.H., and Markin, G.P., "Foraging territories of imported fire ants", *Ann. Entomol. Soc. Am.* 64 (1971), pp. 660-665.

CHAPTER 7

Urban Marginality's Perception of Self: Preliminary Comparative Note on Ilubirin Apeja (Lagos) and 35-47th Street Southside Chicago

by E. D. Babatunde

In the Ghetto
Describe the Ghetto as best as you can,
The Dirty Streets, the Drunken man
The lifeless puppy found on the Curb
The crying baby that's never heard,
Broken windows, poverty-stricken homes,
Platform shoes, Natural Combs.
In the Ghetto, some encounter drugs, and
Some are beaten by merciless thugs,
So terrible these things seem to be, but
Still the Ghetto is home to me.

Donald Franklin

Definition of the Problem

In recent times, scholarly attention has been focused on the reactions of societies broken up or segmented by arbitrarily drawn borders. The new scholarly orientation differs from earlier attempts largely because rather than take the border areas as the periphery of states, borderlands are now presented as *sui generis*. They are regarded as areas of inter-digitation and overlap of cultures, economies and institutions of the nation-states separated by the borders. Consequently, any contemplated policy effectiveness on the part of the one state must (a) accommodate the input of the adjacent country, (b) make allowance for some flexibility on the part of border officials and (c) reckon with the opinion of the local communities. The focus of borderland scholars on territorial issues is understandable. Clear geographical boundaries between and within sovereign states are not only conspicuous, at least on paper; more importantly they carry dramatically grave political consequences.

But as many other boundaries exist as there are social systems. These include boundaries between sexes, religions and social classes. There are spatial as well as functional boundaries, but the one category does not occur in mutual exclusion of the other. As Strassoldo has argued:

> A more adequate approach to reality would point out that all systems, save perhaps purely conceptual ones, are both territorial and functional. All systems in fact are made up of some physical elements that occupy space and of some relationship between them, that is a function of their states, mutual position etc.... Predominantly functional systems, like a business corporation, a voluntary association, a political party, a church, a ministry, a service, are tied to space in several ways; their equipment oc-cupy space, sometimes it is built on the terrain and is not removable (Strassoldo, 1977).

In terms of the functional boundary analysis, the study of urban periphery or marginality becomes quite relevant. Its introduction as a borderland issue will widen the scope of research as the problems of the "periphery", "marginality", "frontier" will be seen as *species* in the *'genus'* of problems of marginality. The con-cept of borderlands will, therefore, accommodate not only the periphery located at the border, far from the centre, but also the periphery located within the centre itself. It is essential that "boundaries" as used here be understood as conceptual frameworks imposed by the observer or researcher. Strassoldo's rigorously ar-ticulated view on the concept of boundary and system will again serve as a cor-roboration. According to him:

> The concept of boundary is certainly central to the general theory of systems. The basic issue here is between a "nominalist" and a "realist" approach. The first assumes that the system is in the eye of the beholder rather than in the reality out there: that the definition of a particular system depends entirely on the subjective research interests of the observer; that at the bottom, systems "theory" is nothing else than a method, a calculus. This means that the boundaries we assign to the system are wholly conven-tional and arbitrary. There are no objective criteria to tell a system from its environment. The realist approach maintains that the systems do exist and function in reality, that they develop and maintain boundaries which can be objectively observed as sharp discontinuities in communication in-tensity and as absence of feedback loops (1979: 18).

Thus the consideration of urban marginality allows for the imposition of initially nominal boundaries which eventually acquire permanence due to learned behaviour and attitudes unique to the life-pattern of a slum and transmitted from generation to generation.

The comparative study of Ilubirin Apeja, a slum in metropolitan Lagos populated by Gun-speaking fishermen, and the Ghetto dwellers on the Southside of Chicago will reveal the unique views of urban marginality. Similarities include the fact that the majority of the people in both societies are low-income workers, relative to others within the individual social systems in question. They are homogeneous. Ilubirin Apeja fishermen are Gun while most dwellers of the 35-47th Street Southside are Americans of African descent. Both societies are located in metropolis regarded as the financial centres of their different nations. Both societies share the problem of being viewed as 'disorder' and, therefore, remodelled to meet with their larger metropolitan societies conceived as 'order' and 'civilisation'. Yet both societies have their own view about themselves.

Methodology

Immanual Wallerstein's view of the metropolis/periphery pattern of relationship, articulated in his work (*The Modern World System,* 1974), will provide a useful framework of analysis. An economic determinist, he saw the world simply as a system divided into the metropolis and the periphery regulated by economic relationship. The origin and substance of this system is made possible by the maintenance of a network of economic relationship which prefer functional to spatial boundaries. The subsystems on the periphery submit to instructions and regulations from the centre.

The one-way mechanistic orientation of the metropolis/periphery pattern of relationship should not prevent one from exploiting the contribution of the model to illuminate the marginality's relationship to the centre. The nation-state has its centre and its periphery. Its ideal pattern of expectation is that it is a closed system, in which tastes of people in the periphery are rigidly regulated from the centre.

Policies from the national centre were to be seen as applicable to all the subsystems irrespective of the peculiarities of their marginal locations. However, the periphery has views unique to self. Whether in relation to the urban area or on the national state, peripheries share certain characteristics. These include the facts that:

a) Majority of their members are low-income earners due to little or no skilled training.
b) The resultant limited access to factors of production leaves the people open to manipulation from the centre.
c) Marginalities have views of their own which often differ from those generated about them at the centre and which must be taken into consideration if policy were to produce effect.

How do marginalities generate views unique to them in the presence of a strong centre? Noam Chomsky's idea of dominant/muted patterns of relationship provides an answer. Chomsky maintained that all groups have internal divisions into those that are dominant and those that are muted. Dominant groups arrogate to themselves the power to speak for muted groups in all matters and in particular, on issues concerning muted groups. Dominant groups views on the muted are often far removed from views of muted groups about themselves. Muted groups generate their own views but because the conceptual plain on which verbalisation is possible has already been over-run by views of their own. To find expression they (muted group) ensure either that their own views displace those of the dominant groups, or the dominant group listens to views unique to the muted.

The Slum and the Culture of Poverty

Comparative parameters between Southside Chicago and Ilubirin Apeja pertain to those features characteristic of the concept of the culture of poverty. The culture of poverty is a way of behaviour that internalises those norms and values which make poverty endemic and transmissible from generation to generation. Poverty is determined by establishing a poverty line index. Basic natural needs such as food, shelter, health and expenses on procreation are costed on the average for a society. The basic cultural needs such as education, recreation, clothing and mobility expenses are costed on the average. Then the sum total of both natural and cultural needs becomes the poverty line index. Anybody whose income is below the index is poor.

Oscar Lewis who regarded the shanty-town context as the 'culture of poverty' characterised the individual poor as helpless, dependent, inferior, prone to resignation and fatalism. Peter Townsend (*The Concept of Poverty,* 1970) disagreed with the option of 'culture of poverty' and pointed at the difficulty in setting a common criterion for poverty. He suggested that a more realistic approach would be to set two standards, a national-relational standard and world-relational standard, since the level of wealth varies from country to country. Counter posed to the 'culture of poverty' orientation is Elliot Liebow's view of poverty as the result of situational constraints. In his *Tully Corner,* he noted that, given the right injection of economic inspiration, the poor will rise to a healthy standard of living and discard the tendency to live for the moment. Ulf Hanners, a Swedish anthropologist on low-income neighbourhoods, mainly of Blacks in Washington, D.C., synthesized the culture versus situation of poverty in his work, *Soulside: Inquiries into Ghetto Culture and Community* (1969). He argued that, although the situation constrained the Ghetto man to become a street corner bystander, his image could provide an alternative model, the 'successful' man to be emulated. This factor could inhibit change when the social constraints are removed.

More relevant to the West African situation, Kenneth Little's *West African Urbanisation* (1965: 45, 62) and J. Eades' *The Yoruba Today* (1980: 61, 77) show that the West African urban low-income dweller is removed in orientation and self-evaluation from the Ghetto dweller. Unlike the Ghetto dweller, he does not consider himself weak. He participates in matters of government and subscribes to organisations, such as thrift societies, aimed at removing him from the situation of dire economic constraint.

Controversial, though, the application of ideas of measurement may be, the reality of poverty does not need a treatise to establish. The poor have no need for the luxury of taking a vow of poverty. They are simply deprived. The researcher analyzed poverty but the poor live in it and know that the notion of poverty admits of no controversy. It will suffice to take the view of P. Townsend. He noted that:

> Individuals, families and groups in the population can be said to be in poverty when they lack the resources to obtain the types of diets, participate in the activities and have the living conditions and amenities which are customary, or at least widely encouraged and approved, in the societies to which they belong. Their resources are so seriously below those commanded by the average individual or family that they are, in effect, excluded from ordinary living patterns, customs and activities. (Quoted in Haralambos, 1980: 142)

In Ilubirin Apeja and Southside of Chicago from the 35th to 47th King Drive, certain existential or objective facts surface to illuminate the marginality's view of itself.

Empirical Data

Chicago, situated on the southwest shore of Lake Michigan, is the second most populous city (6,978,947 inhabitants) in America and has the third largest metropolitan area of some 224.2 square miles. It is regarded as the most influential city in the United States in terms of its strategic location and active domination of manufacturing, trade and finance. Its 3.8% of the American population is said to contribute 5.1% of the Gross National Product. It is a city of great contrasts: of the very wealthy and the very poor, a city whose cardinal points of north and south have been transformed into social and racial markers of distinctly bounded ethnic groups, arranged on the pattern of wealth and poverty respectively.

The Southside of Chicago from the 39th South King Drive to the 47th South King Drive form part of this comparative study. The effective boundary to the southern fringe of the Ghetto is the University of Chicago, situated in the Hyde Park, Kenwood section of the Southside of Chicago. *Webster's Reference Dictionary of English Language* defines the slum as a "Thickly populated, squalid part of a city, inhabited by the poorest or lowest class of people." Although this may be applicable to the area in question, the definition ignores an essential aspect of transformation and dynamism known in American urban study circles as the process of 're-gentrification.' It is not intended to pre-empt it here. The definition of the word "Ghetto" by the same dictionary is appropriate. It is said to be "A city area populated by people of a minority group usually due to financial or social restrictions imposed by the majority rule group...."

Inter Ghetto Relationship

An initial feature of urban settlement in Chicago is the ethnic factor. Germans, Italians, Mexicans, Irish, Polish, Puerto-Ricans and Americans of African descent, perhaps for reasons of security and mutual interest protection, settle in ethnic groupings. Exceptions to this rule abound especially among the wealthy who move into suburban, secure and wealthy neighbourhoods.

A paradigm useful to the notion of inter-Ghetto pattern of relationship is provided by the renown British anthropologist, Sir. E.E. Evans-Pritchard, in his work, *The Nuer.* He characterised them as an 'acephalus' society. The Nuer are said to have no centralised authority but operate on the principles of *Fusion* and *Fission*. Sections which fight among themselves competing for scarce resources group together to fight against a common external enemy.

A majority of the American Ghetto dwellers are unemployed and live on welfare (money paid to the unemployed) which at best guarantees *subsistence poverty*. The aid given by the government reflects costing of the basic necessities (Abel-Smith & Townsend, 1965; Haralambos, 1980; Liebow, 1967). Besides, welfare payments do not increase appreciably to absorb the level of inflation. This economic situation has a great impact on the family. Families tend to be large (six) on the average, compared to an average size of four in the wider society. Secondly, there is a high percentage of single-parent-and-children family groups. These tend to be matrifocal, that is, the mother stays with the family as the main source of support.

For children to qualify for welfare, the parent who is the breadwinner (presumed to be the father) must be dead, incapacitated or must have left the house. An unemployed father of five children prefers to leave the house, not by choice but out of necessity in order that his children will be catered for by the state. The mother becomes the breadwinner and her occupation is in looking after the family. Her payment for this is the welfare aid.

Cooperation areas include Church associations, recreation time and shopping offers. If the main suggestion of Oscar Lewis about urban marginality as being this-moment-oriented, weak and uninterested in secondary associations does not hold, his suggestion that they are fatalistic is relevant. The Ghetto has many churches but only two hospitals offering qualitative medical services. The nearest efficient hospital, The Michael Reese Mercy Catholic Hospital, on 29th Street, is at some distance away from the centre of the Ghetto. There are clinics and recreation centres to which mothers take their children or those of neighbours in the context of intra-Ghetto cooperation. Mothers also volunteer to look after other children in order to allow some mothers to play Bingo, a kind of gambling run by churches and private organisations for support.

A survey I conducted through the aid of 16-17 year old students on Citizens Educational Training Authority Programme for Youths (C.E.T.A.) in the summer of 1981 will illustrate the distribution of churches, schools, liquor stores, and restaurants. The comments of the students are included:

		Location	Condition
1.	*39th Street South King Drive (SKD)*		
	i Morning Star Baptist Church	3975 SKD	Very Clean
	ii Charlotte's Kitchen (restaurant)	397 SKD	(Beat up on all sides)
	iii Prayer Band Pentecostal Church	391 SKD	(In poor condition) Good from outside
	iv Toolsie New Keyhole	395 SKD	Poor Floor Needs Tile
	v Chop Suey Carry outs (Chinese restaurant)	3969 SKD	Good condition in and out
	vi New Parkview Barbar Shop	3951 SKD	Good condition in and out
	vii Ritzie's Lounge	3945 SKD	Just fair
	viii Oakwood Medical Clinic	3947 SKD	Fair was written and crossed out
2.	*39th Street Indiana—39th King Drive*		
	i Liquor Store—Rothschild	—	Poor condition. Good security
	ii Rowhouse Project-Housing	—	Over crowded. No recreation facilities, black poor live here. No clinic, no library.
	iii School: Wendell Philips High School	—	Good security (policemen) with guns in good condition
	iv Groceries: Snipe. Daddy and Sons	—	Good condition
	Loi's Grocery Store	—	Poor condition-good security
	L&L Supermarket	—	Good condition & security
	Bee Jays	—	Good condition & security
	v Fast Food Restaurants: King of the Sea	—	Poor, no security
	Afri Chicken Kingdom	—	Good condition but poor security
	Muse's Restaurant	—	Poor condition, good security
	Fish Shop	—	Poor condition & security
	Kemmy's	—	Poor condition & security
	vi Churches: Zion Grave Missionary Church		
	Baptist Church	—	Good security
	The Crusaders Church	—	Good security
	Church of God in Christ	—	Good security
3.	*41 Street Cottage-43rd Street Indiana/43rd Cottage-43rd Indiana*		
	i 1. Clinic—4301 S. King Drive Survey		
	2. Liquor Store—400E. 43rd Street		
	3. Restaurant—367E. 43rd Street		
	4. Liquor Store—355E. 43rd Street		
	5. Restaurant—362E. 43rd Street		
	6. Restaurant—354E. 43rd Street		

ii   1. Liquor Store—324E. 43rd Street
     2. Lounge—362E. 43rd Street
     3. Restaurant—320E. 43rd Street
     4. Liquor Store—204E. 43rd Street
     5. Liquor Store—4256S. Indiana
     6. Lounge—407E. 43rd Street

iii   1. Lounge—416E. 43rd Street
     2. Lounge—423E. 43rd Street
     3. Liquor—431E 43rd Street
     4. Recreation—Pool Hall—447E. 43 Street
     5. Lounge—456E. 43rd Street
     6. Clinic—507E. 43rd Street

iv   1. Liquor Store—526E. 43rd Street
     2. Liquor Store—558E. 43rd Street
     3. Clinic—646E. 43rd Street
     4. Library—4301S. Cottage Grove
     5. Liquor—4254S. Cottage Grove
     6. Recreation Centre—4301S. Cottage Grove

41st Street

1. Metropolitan Community Church
2. S&S Hotel 4142 South King Drive
3. Centre of New Horison 4150 South King Drive
4. 2 buildings, The Paul G. Stewart Apartments Phase III

401E. Bowen Avenue

5. First Steadfast Baptist Church 467E. Bowne Avenue
6. A corner store
7. 4120 Project (overcrowded skyscrapers for poor people)
8. 4140 Project
9. 729/727 Project
10. 730/732 Project
11. The Harris Temple NAOH Church of God—741 Cottage Grove
12. Mural—41st Cottage Grove
13. Holy Zion Healing Temple—4102 South Cottage Grove
14. Park on 41st Place

The survey of the selected streets in the Southside Ghetto is quite revealing about certain habits and attitudes. The services that are most needed to cope with the dire needs of the dwellers are in short supply. Hospitals are very few while clinics which provide generally non-qualitative medical services are on the average of one to a street. Churches are many, an average of three churches to the street. Liquor stores out number all other public service agencies. Lounge and restaurants also feature quite prominently. Recreation facilities are quite few and those available are not in good condition.

The presence or absence of good security is an important consideration for establishing business in the Ghetto. To their larger community, the Ghetto is unsafe and dangerous. If its type of civilization will prevail in the Ghetto, security will be ensured through the presence of powerful police machine. To their number is added the many security agents for every sky-scrapper, supermarket and shopping centre.

As a result it is the opinion of the larger society, that the Ghetto is a place where things do not work well and where people prey on one another, the Ghetto is almost permanently under police siege. The services are poor, liquor and drugs are freely available and churches are many. When things are at this stage, the process of re-gentrification commences.

Re-gentrification: Urban-Ghetto Relationship

Re-gentrification is one solution of the urban centre to deal with the marginal Ghetto dweller by gradually reclaiming the Ghetto from him. It is an unwritten policy whereby the conditions of existence are made harder for the Ghetto dwellers so that the process leading to decay may be accelerated. The combination of poor health services, unemployment, easy availability of beverages and drugs together with a harsh police presence drives the exceptional fairly well-to do Ghetto dweller to move out. As more people move out due to deteriorating conditions, real estate speculators reclaim the run-down areas and build expensive sky-scrappers which are beyond the means of the Ghetto dwellers. More of the Ghetto dwellers then move to suburban areas which by now are assuming a predominantly black constitution. The wealthy suburban dwellers then buy apartments in the condominiums or sky-scrappers. Meanwhile the now predominantly black suburb loses its rating and the reclaimed Ghetto now becomes the new focus of residential alteration.

Gradually, the services in the suburb deteriorate and a new Ghetto emerges. The movement to the reclaimed Ghetto then begins in earnest. It is this vicious cycle of reclamation that constitutes the process of re-gentrification, (re-establishing the gentry). As the influential *Encyclopedia Americana* noted:

> Chicago has shared with other metropolitan areas, the dilemma of decay
> in the central city, as middle-class neighbours have surrendered to the en-
> croaching slums and former inhabitants have fled to the newer suburban
> fringes. (1979 Edition, Vol. 6: 421)

It further noted *ad rem* that "Community development projects in Chicago have stressed selective demolition and the conservation and rehabilitation of proper-ty."(Vol. 6: 421).

In the context of Ghetto reality, the Ghetto is safe for the Ghetto dwellers. Those interviewed felt that the over-policing makes the Ghetto unsafe. Movement is restricted especially at night as Ghetto dwellers can be, and are often picked up for wandering.

If the Ghetto area makes its unique opinions known, it does so in one or more significant ways: In murals (drawing on walls) and in the intensity of its support for the Holy Angels School. The Holy Angels School, regarded as the Black Eton of Chicago is the largest black high school in America. Situated at the heart of the Ghetto on 607 Oakwood Boulevard off 39th Street King Drive, the School is run on very strict puritanical traditions aimed at the highest level of excellence able to command the respect of mainstream society. The resultant achievements stimulate middle class Black Americans, who would normally avoid the Ghetto, to patronise the school.

Murals are anonymous pictures and paintings on walls. In the Ghetto most of them are of African divinities such as Yemoja, Shango, Oya, Moremi, Olokun. The divinities are drawn on such a large scale and with artistic finesse which give an upliftment to the dilapidated state of the Ghetto area where they are often drawn. Messages vary from commentary or racial politics such as "let us go back to our ancestors" to the huge map of Africa drawn with Southern Africa painted in red upon which a huge question mark painted in white is super-imposed. Others show giant figures of black divinities towering over frail white equivalents.

These murals have more than aesthetic significance for the marginalized Ghetto dweller. The diminutive, unemployed American of African descent is over-awed by his weak position in the scheme of things. He is even confused about his past, blur-red by human deracinating brutality. He idealizes his past in African divinities who are believed to be great, majestic, attractive, powerful. In so doing, he achieves a measure of the satisfaction and solace at the level of symbolism which the political reality of this situation denies him. If he is weak, the divinities are strong. If he is marginal, the divinities are central. In the context of the Ghetto, after all, his posi-tion is central while that of the wider society is marginal. The context of relativity determines who is marginal at any time.

Ilubirin Apeja

Lagos, the capital of Nigeria is the economic, political and social centre of Nigeria. Ilubirin Apeja is a slum located by the lagoon off Okesuna Street, in the Idumagbo Local Government Area, of inner Lagos (precisely opposite the New Lagos State Incinerator Complex). As a homogeneous group, it is the an-thropologist's dream of a small, close knit group with common language, common descent, common major occupation and common primary traditional religion. It is made up of Gun-speaking migrants from the border villages of Ije water-side on the Nigerian-Benin boundary.

They are organised into compound families of husband and wives living in huts made of corrugated iron-sheets on raised platforms on water. The survey revealed, among other things, that the size of the average family is eight, that the fishing oc-cupation observed a rule of division of labour. Men do the fishing and women do the selling. The survey also reveals that the social organisation of the mother village, Ije water-side, was transplanted Ilubirin has a Bale (head of village) assisted by a group of twenty elders. Extended families or related compound families serve as politically articulate sub-groups within the village. Matters not resolved are transferred to the head of the mother-village Ije.

Although they compete among themselves to keep customers, they cooperate to bail arrested members of their community as well as assist the Catholic Church in running a school for them. Data gathering amongst them is still limited but an in-stance of group perception of its own needs will serve as a case in point to the unique views of marginality.

Ilubirin Apeja Catholic community went to great lengths to build a church and got the services of a priest. Thereafter the community impressed upon the priest that crossing the express way of the Lagos Third Mainland Bridge was so hazardous that the community suffers an average of a death per week since there are no overhead bridges. A Catholic school, christened "St. Anthony by the Lagoon", was establish-ed. Within the space of six months, it recorded an attendance of one hundred and sixty children between the ages of four and six. At the end of the year enrolment had tripled. The priest, thinking along the lines of the wider society, from which the migrant fishermen came insisted that it would be beneficial to start an experi-ment whereby the school children will be taught French and English at the elemen-tary level from the second year. The euphoria that greeted this renovation was short-lived and replaced by intense resentment.

In the priest's absence and without consulting him the Bale and the elders sacked the French teacher on the pretext that too many languages (Gun, Yoruba, English and French) will make the children sick. On more enquiry, it surfaced that the com-munity feared that eventually an attempt would be made to evict them because of the possible allegation that they are not Nigerians. To teach French in the school might confirm that they are foreigners. Rather than teach French, which would tend to alienate their children, they prefer English and Yoruba so as to identify with the immediate larger society. The priest had no option but to comply.

Conclusion

The Ghetto and the slum, 35th-47th Southside of Chicago and Ilubirin Apeja in Lagos as sub-units of the respective larger metropolitan systems have similar experiences. Situation constrains them within the marginal positions. The larger societies have ideas about them quite different to what the communities have about themselves. In Lagos, Ilubirin is looked at by some as a haven of outlaws; yet Ilubirin Apeja has a close-knit control mechanism aided by the special links of kinship relationship. Ilubirin Apeja is one of the many sources of Lagos fish for the inhabitants of Lagos who benefit from its cooperative services, yet the larger society regards them as squatters and an 'eye-sore' and sent bull-dozers on the 7th of March 1985 to destroy one quarter of the dwellings of the community. The larger society want to restructure the lagoon area to meet with its notion of order.

The Southside of Chicago provides comparable points of reference. The Ghetto is to the suburban dweller, drug-ridden and unsafe; a frontier which must be conquered and brought within the ambience of the metropolitan civilisation. This frontier dimensions is manifested in the vicious cycle of re-gentrification styled by *Encyclopedia Americana* as an urban policy of "selective demolition and reclamation". Perhaps Jack Turner's maxim, that frontier mentality remains even after an empire had reached its optional territorial extension, is corroborated by this phenomenon.

Re-gentrification is, perhaps, a case that allows for the processes of expansion and contraction of areas of influences.

But a unique point will be missed if it is not recognized that "those other areas to be colonised and civilized" have notions of civilizations of their own, unique to them. The findings of this emphasize the need for the authorities and leadership of mainstream societies to take cognisance of the feelings and responses of such of its members or citizenry located at the periphery, if they are to gain effective control of the borders that define the entire system. The research for this paper has been in two parts. While the findings on Chicago has been based on investigations carried out in the summers of 1978, 1979 and 1981 the research on Ilubirin Apeja has been undertaken as an extension of the writer's work in the community in his capacity as a Roman Catholic priest. I wish to express appreciation for the support received from Rev. Fr. George Clement of the Holy Angel's Mission in Chicago and to the Lagos Catholic Diocesan authorities for the Lagos sector of research.

Bibliography

Abel-Smith, B. and Townsend P., *The Poor and the Poorest* (London: Bell & Sons, 1965).

Asiwaju, A.I., "Artificial Boundaries", inaugural lecture, Univ. of Lagos, 1984.

Asiwaju, A.I., (ed) *Parititioned Africans* (London: Hurst, 1984).

Bacon, F., *Novum Organum,* Aphorisms.

Coates, K. and Silburn, R., *Poverty and the Forgotten Englishmen* (Hamondsworth: Penguin, 1970).

Eades, J., *The Yoruba Today* (Cambridge: C.U.P., 1980).

Evans-Pritchard, E.E., *The Nuer* (Oxford: Clarendon Press, 1940).

Hanners, U.M., *Soulside: Inquiries into Ghetto Culture and Community* (New York: Columbia Univ. Press, 1969).

Haralambos, M., *Sociology: Themes and Perspectives* (Slough: Univ. Tutorial Press).

Lewis, O., *The Children of Sanchez* (New York: Random House, 1961).

Little, K., *West African Urbanisation* (Cambridge: C.U.P., 1965).

Strassoldo, R., "The study of boundaries: a systems-oriented multidisciplinary bibliographical essay", *Jerusalem J. of International Rel.* Vol. 2, No. 3, (1977), pp. 81-100. "Boundaries in sociological theory: a reassessment", a paper presented at the International Conference on Boundaries, Regions and International Integration, Gorizia, Italy, (1977). I should acknowledge my indebtedness to Professor Asiwaju for drawing my attention to Strassoldo's works and for allowing me the use of his own copies of the essays.

Townsend, P., *The Concept of Poverty* (London: Heinemann, 1970).

Wallerstein, I., *The Modern World System* (New York: Academic Press).

CHAPTER 8

Bridges Across Africa's Ethnic Boundaries: The Example of the Afa and the Ifa Divination Systems of the Igbo and the Yoruba of Nigeria

by Nnabuenyi Ugonna

Divination is a convenient preoccupation of man. It is a kind of etiological mechanism used by overwhelmed man to explain events around him that he cannot understand. John Middleton, who asserts that all known peoples of the world have practised divination, describes it as an "attempt to discover events that do or will affect human beings for good or evil, but that are beyond their control and are believed to have a supernatural, mystical or other-than-human cause."[1]

There are perhaps as many systems of divination as there are peoples but each system basically distinguishes between the diviners or those who are presumed to bring messages, or interpret signs from the supernatural, and their clientele who consult them to find solutions to their human problems. Diviners, on their part, consist basically of mediums, or those who are transformed to serve the divinatory power as vehicles, and those who use mechanisms or objects and events considered to be signs of an external power to interpret phenomena. While the first kind claim possession by a divine power or an agent of a divine power—a god, a deity, a spirit, an angel or a saint—the second kind does not. The mediums, known variously as shamans, prophets, seers, avatars, etc., claim direct contact with their god or spirit and perform their divinatory role while possessed or in a trance but the divinatory interpreters base their interpretation on the general principle of causality. This presupposes that human fate is part of a wider cosmic pattern known to the divine maker and that certain signs which are part of the cosmic pattern reflect an individual's fate. These patterns that generate the signs may already exist in nature, for example, in the heavenly bodies (astrology), on the human body (chiromancy, neomancy, pedomancy, etc.) and in animals (haruspication, augury) or may be made by man, for example patterns made by stones thrown on the ground (geomancy) or by dice cast.

In this paper we examine the Afa system of divination among the Igbo and draw attention to the variants of the same system as practised by several other West

African peoples, particularly the Yoruba mostly in Nigeria but with culture area stretching into the Republic of Benin and Togo. We hope thereby, to be able to show that various subsystems are either derived one from another or are cognate and in this way demonstrate the cultural and linguistic unity of ancient Black Africa. Our hypothesis then is that in the distant past all that we see today as different systems of divination were one monolithic system but, as it diffused, the border phenomenon set in and created the differences we observe in the systems today.

By boundaries we do not merely mean the artificial boundaries drawn by European colonial powers in Africa to separate one African people from another or to divided same ethnic groups, but all barriers, (physical, political, linguistic and cultural) that separate one group of people from another thereby restricting social interaction and resulting in the development of splinter cultural systems.

In the past, distances were great, means of communication poor, physical barriers formidable and human memories unaided by writing. Thus, if a section of a community migrated to another area and settled, it was possible for them to forget the exact names of particular cultural items as applied in their former habitat and as means of communication were almost nonexistent, they could not ascertain readily the exact names of the items and so had to make do with whatever variant they remembered. Alternatively, settlers in new place would give the items new names altogether.

This is probably what happened with the divination system of West Africa variously known by the cognates Afa, Ifa, Eva, Eha, Iha and Eba. From where did it originate? Is it indigenous to Africa or was it borrowed from Asia? If it is indigenous to Africa, where exactly in Africa did it originate? Is its spread monogenetic, that is, developing at one point and spreading therefrom, or polygenetic, which means, developing simultaneously at several points?

Some scholars have stated that since the sixteen configurations of the West African divination system are similar to a geomantic system originating in the Near East and later adopted in medieval Europe and the Arab world, the possibility exists that the West African system, like the Malagassy one, is an adaptation of an imported cultural item.[2] It is tempting to make this suggestion; but considering the unique cultural characteristics of the West African systems of divination their being indigenous is more probable. The systems, therefore, ostensibly originated here in Africa. What is not as apparent is the third questions posed above, namely, where exactly in Africa did it originate?

As practically every scholar who has investigated the West African divination system has pointed out, the Yoruba, Igbo,[3] Edo, Igala, Idoma, Ewe, Fon[4] and Nupe[5] systems are related. Many commentators, following the example of Bascom[6] and Adimbola[7] appear to favour Yorubaland and ultimately Ife as the cradle of the West African divination systems.

Other cultural centres in Nigeria also lay claim to originating the divination system in the West African region. It has been claimed, for example, that Ifa cult was introduced into Yorubaland by one Setilu, a blind Nupe medicine man who, when he started practising divination, used sixteen small pebbles. His great success as diviner made muslims in his area jealous and they expelled him. He crossed the Niger southwards and went into Benin City from where he wandered into Owo and Ado and finally settled at Ile-Ife[8] where he became famous and had successful practice.

This account does not only raise the issue of a Northern origin of the divination but an Edo or Ado Ekiti origin as well. Indeed some scholars have mooted the idea of an Igbo and ultimately an Nri cradle of divination system in Africa.

Talbor as early as 1926 had argued that Afa of the Igbo "may have derived from the Yoruba Ifa or vice versa."[9] Shelton, agreeing with this verdict, suggest that "both systems may have derived from an aboriginal method."[10]

The Igbo claim to originating the Afa system could be looked at a little more closely. The Igbo, according to archaeological find by D.D. Hartle,[11] appear to have occupied the West African forest region much longer and therefore much earlier than any other group. They were inhabiting, it would appear, pockets of the SOuthern Nigerian forest areas as far as Ile-Ife and Ijebu. They spread, during an early migratory period, from their heartland, to Nsukka, Enugu and possibly as far as to Idoma in the North, to Ikwerre-Echee in the south and through Agbor and Benin to the Ile-Ife and Ijebu forests as mentioned above. When Oduduwa and his followers came to Yorubaland they met these Igbo in the forests of Ile-Ife and they periodically raided the Oduduwa intruders with masked warriors. What eventually happened is summarised in the Moremi legend. Eventually the two peoples fused. The same thing happened to the Igbo inhabiting the forests of the Edo country. Those Igbo who could not be assimilated into the Yoruba and Edo societies fled eastward and this gave rise to the Eze Chima legend.[12]

This legendary account of the migration of the forest peoples of Nigeria probably explains the affinity not only between the languages of Idoma, Igbo, Igala, Edo and Yoruba but their cultures. Indeed as Armstrong has demonstrated by using the controversial method of glottochronology, the Kwa languages of Idoma, Yoruba, Igbo, Edo and Igala etc., started branching off from the parent Proto-Kwa language about 6000 years ago.[13] This tends to show that the original inhabitants of the forest regions of West Africa were one people with a common language.

An early centre of cultural development in this forest area was the Anambra Valley. Here the Nri[14] fashioned out an indigenous civilization that had tremendous ritual influence all over the forest regions of southern Nigeria. They established a kingdom that spread its hegemony not through the force of arms but through ritual sanction. They codified Igbo religion and sent out religious missionaries in the form of *ndi dibia* (priest doctors). These *dibia* who combined the functions of priests, diviners and doctors were itinerant throughout the forest regions of Nigeria. They spread the Afa system of the Igbo and saw to it that Igbo customary law and religious norms were kept and maintained by Igbo communities. Relating the Igboukwu archaeological finds to the Nri civilising influence, Thurstan Shaw writes:

> The occurrence of grasshoppers and beetles in Igbo-Ukwu bronzes is suggestive of the ritual power believed to be possessed by the *Eze Nri* in controlling locusts and yam beetles. Every traditional Nri man has an *otonsi* staff.... Nri men carried such staffs when moving from one Igbo settlement to another in pursuance of their functions, and the staff served as a badge of office to ensure them a kind of inter-village diplomatic immunity.[15]

Any community that molested in any way any of the ambassadors of the Eze Nri or flouted the Eze's authority would be ritually isolated from other Igbo communities. Elaborate and costly sacrifices were performed to reintegrate such a community into the Igbo society.

It is reasonable to believe therefore that these ancient Nri, whose seers and visionaries codified Igbo religious laws, formulated the Afa system which their priests spread through the cult of Agwunsi into the Edo country and through Edo into Ado Ekiti and Ife from where it reached the Fon and Ewe and the rest of the world.

Writing about the origin of the Afa in the Nsukka area of Igboland, Shelton confesses that neither he nor his informants know, but he adds that in Oba a town near Nsukka, it is widely believed that Afa divination was introduced in the remote past by pygmy[16] *dibja* known as ndi 'nshie'[17] (Nshi, Nri, Nhi)." And throughout Igboland diviners will tell you that their practice had an Nri origin.

Besides these ethnological reasons for a putative Nri origin of the West African divination system, there are linguistic ones for suspecting that the system has an Igbo origin. A look at both Table 1 and Table 2 will show that the names of all the 16 configurations are cognate. It is significant that, although the words are signs with cryptic meanings which are jealously guarded by the diviners in each of the systems, a few of them have ordinary meanings in Igbo. If we take the first configuration, Obi, in the Igbo system, for example, it has the ordinary meaning of the Head of the extended family, a kind of king that rules the community. If we take the eighth Ogbara Afa called Okara, for instance, we see that as the eighth, it is in the half-way position, okara meaning half in Igbo. And finally, let us consider the last Odu, called Ofu in Igbo. If Abimbola's account of the reversal of the ranking of the sixteen principal Odu is accepted, then the last Odu, Ofu, is the first and ofu in Igbo means first, *onye ofu* (first person).

It is now perhaps easier to answer the last questions earlier posed, namely, whether the spread of divination method in West Africa was monogenetic or polygenetic. It is easy to accept that the spread was monogenetic as the linguistic correspondences among the systems are so close that they defy any polygenetic explanation. It is possible however that some of the systems developed from a Proto-Fa system but this does not rule out a monogenetic mode of spread.

Characteristic Features of the System

All the systems of divination in West Africa have similar features. They are occult. To become a member of the cult one has to be called--i.e. have vocation; and the call is to come not from humans but from the divination deity itself.

To illustrate the characteristic features of divination systems in West Africa let us look closely at the Ifa and Afa divination systems. The divination deity in the Ifa system is Ifa or Orunmila; in the Afa system he is Agwunsi. When Agwunsi wants a person to serve him in any capacity he calls the person (o waba onye ahu). Francis Arinze describes this phenomenon aptly:

> The clearest and indispensable sign of a vocation to be a *dibia* is possession of the spirit Agwu who is the special spirit of *ndi dibja,* the spirit of giddiness, rascality, discomposure, confusion and forgetfulness *(mmuo mkpasa uche)....* The possessed person has simply to choose between accepting or running mad or at least being a little insane.[18]

The candidate has to accept the call of Agwunsi and start the elaborate initiation process. Every male and female Igbo person is a potential candidate but not all those who are called eventually become diviners. Only a minority of the initiates into the Agwunsi cult ultimately become dibia. There are three categories of dibia in the Agwunsi society: (1) The *dibia aja* who can only offer sacrifices to the numerous

Table 1: The 16 configurations of divination
Position of the diviner is to the left of the page.

o=open, concave pod position, or single odu mark
x=closed, convex pod position, or double odu mark

	Yoruba	Benin	Igala	Idoma	W. Ibo	Ewe	Fon	Sikidy of Madagascar	Mauritania
oooo	ogbè	ógbí	èbi	ébì	ógbi	gbe	gbe	cavaiky	
xxxx	òyèkú	àkó	ákù	àkwú	àkwù	yeku	yeku	asembola	
xoox	íwòrí	òghòí	òghòlì	ògòlí	ògòlí	woli	ólí	alatsimay	zamer
oxxo	òdí	òdí	òdí	òjí	odí	di	dí	alikola	bwdna
ooxx	íròsùn	òrúhú	òlòrù	òlò	ùlúshù	loso	lóósò	soralahy	
xxoo	òwàrà	ògháé	ègálí	ègálí	oga	noli	nwelé	adabaray	
oxxx	òbàrà	òvbà	òbàtà	òblà	òbài	abla	abálà	alahijana	
xxxo	òkònròn	òká	òkàrà	òklà	ò'kàí	àklà	akáná	alikisy	
ooox	ògúndá	èghítá	èjítá	èjítá	èjíté	guda	gùdá	karija	
xooo	òsá	òhá	òrá	òlá	òshá	sa	sá	alakaosy	
xoxx	iká	èká	èká	èká	àká	ka	ká	alohomora	
xxox	otúrúppn	èehóxwà	àtúnúkpà	ètrúkpà	àtókpà	trukpe	trúkpè	alabiavo	
oxoo	òtuwa	ètúrè	òtúlá	òtre / òtlé	ètúlé	tula	túlà	alakavabo	
ooxo	irètè	ètè	ètè	ete	ete	lete	ètè	betsivongo	
oxox	òsè	òsè	òcé	òcé	òsé	tse	chè	adalo	
xoxo	òfún	òhú	òfú	òfú	òfú	fu	fú	alibotsy	

From Robert C. Armstrong in *The Historian in Tropical Africa*.

spirits of the Igbo; (2) The *dibia ogwu* or the medicine man who treats his patients of their various diseases with medicines; and (3) *dibia afa* or the diviner. It is possible for one person to combine two or all three of the functions.

To become a diviner one has to be apprenticed to a professional diviner and for many years the student diviner would be learning from his master the art and technique of divining, the mannerisms, the proverbs and other characteristic texts used during the afa consultation. The period of tutelage is not only long but demanding and often the unintelligent pupil falls by the wayside or graduates to become a third rate dibia afa. *"Ako bu afa"* (intelligence is divination), say the Igbo. The pupil has not only to memorise a great variety of patterns and their relevant texts but to interpret the signs speedily and make quick decisions as to which, of various possible interpretations, should apply in any given case. Before his final graduation the pupil diviner's eyes "are washed" ritually *(a saa or waa ya anya)* so that he can see in the dark, into the past, into the present and the future.

Despite his dexterity, the dibia afa must never falsify the signs. He is no more no less than an interpreter to the gods and should tell his clients what the Afa says. Any deliberate falsification of the facts might bring down upon his head the anger of his deity.

All the divination systems, as we have seen, have sixteen, principal configurations based on the magical number, 4, representing, in the Igbo case, the four market days of the Igbo week; viz Eke, Orie, Afo, Nkwo. The number 4 on its part is based

Table 2: Odu/Ogbara/configurations of Ifa/Ife divination

o=open, concave
x=closed, convex

	Wande Abimbola	Robert F. Armstrong		Robert G. Armstrong	M.A. On-wuejeogwu	Austin J. Shelton	Nnabuenyi Ugonna
	Yoruba				Igbo		
1.	Ògbè	ogbe	oooo	ógbi	Obi	Obi	Òbi
2.	Oyeku	Oyeku	xxxx	akwu̲	Akwu̲	Akwo	Akwu̲
3.	Ìwòrì	ìwòrì	xoox	ògòlì	Ogoli	Ogoli	Ogòlì
4.	Òdí	òdí	oxxo	òdí	odi or udi		Òdi
5.	Irosùn	ìrosùn	ooxx	ulushu	Ululu	Uhu	Ùrùhù
6.	Owórín	owara (oworin)	xxoo	ògáí/ògálí	Agali or Agbali	Egale	Ọgali
7.	Ọbàrà	ọbàrà	oxxx	ọbài	Ọbala	Ọbara	Ọbàrà
8.	Òkàràn	òkọnròn	xxxo	òkàí	Ọkala	Ọkara	Òkàrà
9.	Ogúndá	ògándá	ooox	ejite (ogbute)	Ijite or Ogute	Ijite/Mgwute /Ogute	ìjite
10.	Òsá	ọsá	xooo	oshá	Ọra	Oha	Ọha
11.	Ìká	ìká	xoxx	àká	Aka	Eka	Àka
12.	Òtúúrúpọ̀n	otúrúpọ̀n	xxox	Atunukpa	Eturukpa	Òtu̲ru̲kpà or tunukpa	
13.	Otúá	òtuwa	oxoo	etúlé	Otule	Oture	Ètule
14.	Ìretè	ìretè	ooxo	etè	Ete	Ete	Ète
15.	Òsé	òsé	oxox	òsé	Ose	Ose	Òse
16.	Òfún	òfún	xoxo	òfú	Ofu	Ohu	Òfu

on the magical number, 4, representing, in the Igbo case, the four market days of the Igbo week; viz Eke, Orie, Afo, Nkwo. The number 4 on its part is based on the binary principle of "open" and "closed", day and night, white and black, or +light and −light. Besides the 16 principal configurations (Oju Odu in Yoruba and Ogbaraukwu in Igbo), there are 240 minor ones, making a total of 256 configurations (Oju Odu in Yoruba and Ogbaraukwu in Igbo), there are 240 minor ones, making a total of 256 configuration. These configurations are formed from the possible combinations of the 16 basic configurations.

The sixteen basic configurations are obtained from a chance throw of one, two or four chaplets of 4 half-shells of certain West African seeds, for example, the seeds of the bush mango (ujuru, Irvingia gabonensis) or more commonly of the almond (*apipi,* Pterocapus osum).[19] The pattern that is formed when each chaplet is cast, based on whether the half-seeds *(mkpuruafa)* fall with their concave side facing upwards (open) or their convex side facing upwards (closed), gives name to the configuration. For example, if all the halfseeds in the chaplet are open when cast, the pattern formed is called Ogbe in Ifa and Obi in Afa, and if all the seeds are closed, the configuration is Oyeku in Yoruba Ifa and Akwu in Igbo Afa. (See Tables 1 and 2.) It is from these 16 configurations that we will discuss later.

Because of the increasing former border between the culture areas, different conception of these configurations have developed in different systems. For example, the Yoruba—because if their predilection for myths, personification and deification-have conceived Odu as divinities. Wande Abimbola has written of Orumila's promise to his children and his followers, before his final return to heaven, to send them "certain divinities who would perform some of the functions he used to perform when he was on earth."[20] But the Igbo on the other hand, in their unromantic, practical view of life, regard the Ogbara as spiritual forces used by Agwunsi, the divination deity, to make revelations to humanity through his priests.

Again increasing differentiations have affected the taxonomic analysis of the configurations. For example, the Yoruba classification of their 256 Odu is more irregular than the Igbo classification. After their 16 major Odu, they arrange their two hundred and forty minor Odu (omo Odu) into twelve groups, each known as Apola and each group bearing the names of twelve of the sixteen principal Odu. The number of Omo Odu in each of the Apola is irregular although altogether they add to 240.[21]

The Igbo classification of their 256 Ogbara on the other hand, is more regular. Their 16 major Configuration called Ogbaraukwu are as follows:

1. Òbinaàbọ	2. Àkwụnaàbọ̀	3. Ògòlìnaàbọ̀	4. Ōdinaàbọ̀
5. Uruhunaàbọ̀	6. Ọ̀galinaàbọ̀	7. Ọ̀bàranaàbọ̀	8. Ọ̀kàranaàbọ̀
9. Ịjitenaàbọ̀	10. Ọ̀hanaàbọ̀	11. Àkanaàbọ̀	12. Oturụkpànaàbọ̀
13. Ètulenaàbọ̀	14. 'Etenaàbọ̀	15. Òsenaàbọ̀	16. Ōfùnaàbọ̀

The naabo in the names signify that each of the Ogbaraukwu is a double configuration and this is achieved when the two ikpukpara (the Igbo divining chain or chaplet of half-seeds, normally thrown together, one held in the right hand and the other in the left, by the diviner[22]) show the same configuration.Thus, Obinaabo is when the eight half-seeds (mkpuruafa asato) are all open. In his description of the Nsukka method of casting mkpuruafa, Shelton states that 4 strings are cast thus; Strings No. 1 and No. 3 are cast simultaneously, No. 1 held in the right hand and No. 3 in the left, the strings being drawn toward the caster, raised upwards in a curve and cast straight outward so that the ends of the strings fall toward the suppliant. Then strings No. 2 and No. 4 are cast in a similar way.[23] The important thing to note here is that in all the methods of throwing the ikpukpara and decoding it, the signs are read, like Arabic, from right to left. Thus, if two strings of mkpuruafa are cast and they read as follows:

Left	Right
o	x
x	x
o	o
x	x

we will decode it as Oturukpa (the sign on the right) Ose (the sign on the left), written together to give us the Ogbaranta, Oturukpaose. Bearing this in mind, let us proceed to classify the minor configurations.

The 240 minor configurations in Afa are grouped into 16, each named after one of the 16 basic configurations and consisting of 15 Ogbaranta. Each division of Ogbaranta is called Ukwuogbara:

1. Ukwuọgbàra Ōbi   2. Ukwuọgbàra Ākwụ   3. Ukwuọgbàra Ògòlì
4. Ukwuọgbàra Odi   5. Ukwuọgbàra Urùhù   6. Ukwuọgbàra Ògalì
7. Ukwuọgbàra Ọbàrà   8. Ukwuọgbàra Ọkàrà   9. Ukwuọgbàra Ijite
10. Ukwuọgbàra Ọha   11. Ukwuọgbàra Aka   12. Ukwuọgbàra Ọturukpa
13. Ukwuọgbàra Etule   14. Ukwuọgbàra Ete   15. Ukwuọgbàra Osē
16. Ukwuọgbàra Ofu

Each Ukwuogbara as said above has 15 Ogbaranta. Thus Ukwuogbara Obi consists of the following Ogbaranta (minor configurations):

1. Ọbiakwau   2. Ọbiògòlì   3. Ọbiodí   4. Ọbiùrùhù
5. Ọbiogali   6. Ọbiọbàrà   7. Ōbiọkàrà   8. Ọbiijite
9. Ọbiọha   10. Ọbiàka   11. Ọbiọturukpà   12. Ọbietule
13. Obiète   14. Ọbiòse   15. Ọbiòfu

All the other 14 Ukwuogbara are formed in this way that is, by prefixing the name of the Ukwuogbara to the remaining 15 configurations. Thus Ukwuogbara Ogoli will consist of Ogoliobi, Ogoliakwu, Ogoliodi, etc., and Ukwuogbara Okara will comprise Okaraobi Okaraakwu, etc.

In all the divination systems, these configurations, although resulting from the casting of sacred divination seeds by a human agent, are nonetheless regarded as coded messages coming form the divination deity. At the mystical moment of throw the deity takes over control. It is perhaps a question of the hand being that of Esau and the voice being that of Jacob, for it is the diviner who casts the seeds by Agwunsi or Orunmila who causes the signification and he can do this only through the accredited hand of his dibia or babalawo.

Divination Poetry

Divination chants, songs, recitatives and narratives constitute oral texts of great literary merit as Abimbola's study of Ifa literary corpus has powerfully demonstrated. His work has shown us that divination texts—properly collected, transcribed, annotated, edited and published—could reflect in a unique way the totality of the world view of a cultural and linguistic group. They constitute great poetry of epic dimensions dealing with such recurrent themes as man's creation, man's state of innocence, fall and redemption. The Ifa literary corpus deals not only with a people's creation myths and legends of origin and migrations but with the totality of their social structure and the complexity of their literary tradition.

The sophistication of the Ifa priest poets is shown in their creation of Ese Ifa with its "eight-part structural pattern which distinguishes it from other forms of Yoruba oral literature".[24]

It is possible that Afa has an equivalent of the Ese Ifa but the few studies of Afa so far done have not documented this. The paucity of work yet done on Afa is perhaps due to the esoteric nature of Afa. This makes it almost impossible for a scholar to get any meaningful information on the subject. The dibia afa might chant a few poems for the curious scholar and mumble the manes of a few configurations. But when the enquirer starts to probe deeper the dibia afa immediately smells a rat and, like the tortoise whose shell he uses to store his Afa paraphernalia, withdraws into himself. He does not want to reveal his professional secrets to an outsider.

A number of studies in Afa are being carried out and one may expect that before long a more definitive account of Afa poetry may be given. Meanwhile all that can be said about the poetry of Afa is that each Afa session is a performance of oral literary texts comprising prose narratives, chants, songs, and recitatives partly in dialogue form, partly in epic style and partly rendered in the form of lyric. Some of these texts of Afa literary corpus are in the form of praise and some in the form of satire.

Before the literary session begins the stage is set. The diviner is the poet both in the classical sense of the *vates,* the seer, and in the more general sense of the artist, the rhapsodist, the social reformer and the healer. The client(s) or suppliant(s), is/are (a) participant(s) in the poetic drama. The stage is set in the diviner's consulting room, often secluded from the general area where the numerous clients of a dibia throng. The compound of a famous dibia afa is often crowded with suppliants who are normally arranged in the order of their arrival in a waiting room from where they are ushered in turn into the *iba afa* (afa theatre). The theatre is decorated to have a weird setting. There is on one side the Agwunsi altar called *Ibu Agwunsi* on which are arranged sculptured images of Agwu deity, his wives, children and other relations, his pets and spiritual forces.

When all these okika (nkwu, sculptures) are not in use they are stores away in the *akpa Agwunsi* (agwunsi's bag) also known as "the dibia bag which is very big and deep, with many partitions, and contains all kinds of things. Those who are not *ndi dibia* (i.e. ndi ofeke) must not look into the bag, hence the proverb: A choba a fu di n'akpa dibia; mana inyo anya n'akpa dibia bu nso mmuo (what ever you are looking for, you will find in the dibia's bag; but the spirits strictly forbid people to peep into the bag.)[25]

The setting for the performance will be complete when the *dibia afa* puts in their rightful place on the consulting platform the *udu arobinagu* (small pot, source of dibia's information), *egede,* or *igba Agwu* (a drum), *okiriko mbe* (tortoise shell), *mkpuruafa* (divination seeds), etc.[26]

Most of these items are highly symbolic of the power, speed, truthfulness, resourcefulness, legitimacy, antiquity, nobility and artistry of Agwunsi. After the stage is set, the diviner sits beside the altar usually on an animal skin spread on the floor. Then the clients are ushered in one after the other, individually or in groups as the case may be.

The client sits facing the diviner and the performance begins. He brings out his *okwa nzu* (wooden plate of powdery chalk), symbol of purity and unblemishedness and offers it. He beats the *egede* drum, the *okiriko mbe* (tortoise shell), blows the *ele* horn, or shakes the *oyo* and begins a chant in praise of his deity whose messenger he is. He pleads with Agwu to make truthful revelation and not play pranks on him.

Then the client presents his problem (izo afa). The first thing normally presented is an inquiry about the health of the extended family. The client asks, "Ndu m o dikwa? Ndu ezinaulo mo dikwa?" (What of my health? What of the health of my family?) Then the dibia starts casting his mkpuruafa to find out the answer. The first presentation, though innocuous enough, may be the heart of the matter. Let us assume that the suppliant's child is sick unto death and he expects the *dibia* to discover this through his afa and find a solution.

Sometimes it may happen that the signs he is getting are veering away from the stated problem and so he will keep on casting his seed until some kind of relevance is established. If after efforts he cannot find any correlation between the signs he is getting and the enquirer's problem, then he can either blame the enquirer for not coming with good intentions, his Agwunsi for playing pranks on him or himself for not being in the right frame of mind for divination that day. He could say that Agwu has gone on a journey and left his children to play pranks on him with the ikpukpara. He would then advise the suppliant to come back another day.

As the dibia afa gets these significations he chants appropriate texts or narrates appropriate anecdotes punctuating them with apt proverbs. These constitute the literary corpus of Ifa.

Onwue jeogwu had compiled the general themes dealt with respectively by the sixteen Ukwuogbara and they are as follows:

1. Ukwuogbara Obi—afa of action and motion
2. Ukwuogbara Akwu—of domestic relations
3. Ukwuogbara Ogoli—deal with death and misfortune
4. Ukwuogbara Odi—of lineages and human relations
5. Ukwuogbara Uruhu—afa of food
6. Ukwuogbara Agali—afa of conflicts
7. Ukwuogbara Obara—of commonsense and knowledge
8. Ukwuogbara Okara—deals with afa of events
9. Ukwuogbara Ijite—of emotions
10. Ukwuogbara Oha—afa of kinship
11. Ukwuogbara Aka—afa of the supernaturals
12. Ukwuogbara Aturukpa—of nobility and freedom
13. Ukwuogbara Eture—afa of peace
14. Ukwuogbara Ete—of human beings and animals
15. Ukwuogbara Ose—sacrifice and happiness
16. Ukwuogbara Ofu—afa of problems[27]

Social Uses of Divination

The Igbo ask the question: *'onye ka chi ya di mma o gawa igba afa?* (whose *chi* [fortune] is good and he goes to consult a diviner?), meaning that people consult diviners in critical cases.

There is, indeed, "little, if any evidence that divination reveals the actual truth," says Middleton,[28] and yet it persists. Three reasons given for this persistence are, (1) it gives confidence to people in trouble and uncertainty; (2) it enables individuals confirm their own suspicions; and (3) its statements even if guesses, will be correct by the law of chance, thus supporting the faith held in it.[29] It would then appear that divination persists because it has numerous social uses. On the personal level, it enables an overwhelmed individual to discover a solution to a problem he has been unable to solve. The individual transfers the responsibility of taking care of himself to another person and takes pleasure in being directed. As Park puts it "typically divination is called for in cases of illness and death, and in other life-crises" that "call for decision upon some plan of action which is not easily taken."[30]

Divination helps people "to satisfy their need to understand that which otherwise would remain forever unknown"[31] especially when we realise that we can only control what we know.

On the societal level divination seeks to achieve social harmony by restoring in the people a religious sense of equilibrium. It restores faith and sanity to the society by encouraging confessions, restitutions and sacrifices. Sacrifices are veritable means of social reintegration and through them a communion of the living, the dead, other spirits, and supernatural forces, is achieved.

Conclusion

The divination systems we have discussed are by no means the only divination systems we have in Nigeria of West Africa. As Abimbola has told us, Ifa "is not the only Yoruba God connected with divination."[32] Sango, Orisanla, and Osanyin, for example, have their own divination systems.[33]

In Igbo there are many other systems of divination, some no more that trials by ordeal or lie-detectors. There is, for example, the *Ntugbu* system in which two ore more contestants would take chickens to the Ntugbu shrine. These are tied onto stakes and it is held that the chicken of the persons who are in the wrong will die.

There used to be the Chukwu oracle at Arochukwu who spoke openly to people and gave solutions to their problems. There are those deities who are still consulted in the settlement of cases, especially land cases. Such deities are Igwekaala of Umunneoha, Agbala of Oka, Kamalu of Ozuzu, Ojukwu of Diobu and Ogwugwu of Okija, and so on. In these divination systems the deities act or talk directly and not through human intermediaries.

The divination systems we have examined are those in which a human agent interprets the wishes of the gods through signs he gets from the divination deity who is the god of health, a kind of Chukwu's Minister of Health. Incidentally, in the Igbo context, there are many famous dibia afa, accredited members of the Agwunsi cult who can communicate Agwunsi's directives to suppliants not by casting afa seeds in search of signs but by direct vision through the use of mirrors or water in basins, etc. Some diviners even use contraptions that make bird-like sounds in which the diviner is a kind of medium who sees in his mind's eye through the aid of reflectors, things that have happened, are happening or will happen to his clients and reveals the facts that are relevant to the inquiry.

Our study has sought to establish that the systems of divination in the West African region, especially the systems that use the half-shell casting method have basically diffused from one centre, either Ife, Nupe, Benin City, Ado Ekiti Or Nri in the case of the Nigerian region. They may have developed from one of the extant systems or from Proto-Fa. These systems called respectively Ifa by the Yoruba, Eba by the Nupe, Afa by the Igbo, Iha by the Edo Bini, Eva by the Isoko, etc., have similar characteristics as we have seen. We have posited that the differences that occur in them result from the issue of linguistic and cultural boundaries. Our efforts should therefore be directed toward narrowing these linguistic and cultural differences by emphasising the cultural similarities that unite us and playing down the differences that separate us knowing that originally we were one linguistic group.

Endnotes

1. John Middleton, "Divination," in *Encyclopedia Americana,* vol. 9, Americana Corporation, 1979, p. 196.

2. P. Morton-Williams, "The Mode of Divination", *Africa,* 1966, p. 407.

3. P.A. Talbot, *The Peoples of Southern Nigeria,* London, O.U.P., vol 2, 1926, p. 187.

4. Robert G. Armstrong, "The Use of Linguistic and ethnographic data in the study of Idoma and Yoruba History" in *The Historian in Tropical Africa: Studies presented and discussed at the Fourth International African Seminar at the University of Dakar, Senegal, 1961,* edited by J. Vansina, R. Mauny and L.V. Thomas, published for the I.A.I. by O.U.P., 1964.

5. S.F. Nadel, *Nupe Religion: Traditional Beliefs and the Influence of Islam in a West African Chiefdom,* New York, Schocken Books, 1970, p. 38. Austin J. Shelton, "The Meaning and Method of Afa Divination Among the Northern Nsukka Ibo", *American Anthropologist,* vol 67, No. 6. Part 1, December 1965, 1441-1455. *The Igbo-Igala Borderland: Religion and Social Control in Indienous African Colonialism,* Albany, State University of New York Press, 1971, p. 201.

6. W. Bascom, "Odu, Ifa, the Names of the Signs" *Africa* 1966, 408-421.

.7 Wande Abimbola, *Ifa: An Exposition of Ifa Literary Corpus*, Ibadan, O.U.P., 1976.

8. Samuel Johnson, *History of the Yoruba*, London, Routledge, 1921, p. 32-33.

9. Talbot, *The Peoples of Southern Nigeria*, p. 187.

10. Shelton, *The Igbo-Igala Borderland*, p. 201.

11. D. Hartle, "Archaeology in Eastern Nigeria", *West African Archaeological Newsletter*, No. 5; "Antiquities in Igbo Land", *African Notes*, Special Number, 1972.

12. Nnamdi Azikiwe, *My Odyssey: an authobiography*, London, Hursch and Co; 1970.

13. Armstrong, "The Use of Linguistic and Ethnographic Data," p. 10-12, p. 132.

14. M.A. Onwuejeogwu, *An Igbo Civilization: Nri Kingdom and Hegemony*, London, Benin City, Ethnographica Ltd. and Ethiope Publishing Corporation, 1981, p. 14-16.

15. Thurstan Shaw, *Unearthing Igbo-Ukwu: Archaeological discoveries in eastern Nigeria*, Ibadan Oxford University Press, 1977, p. 100.

16. The Nri collected all the midgets they came across in tehir surrounding communities and educated them as priest-doctors cum ambassadors. The Nri took these midgets (ankanri) on their religious and healing tours. They added a touch of the unusual and the other-worldliness to their missions.

17. Shelton, "The Meaning and method of Afa Divination", p. 1443.

18. Francis A. Arinze, *Sacrifice in Igbo Religion*, Ibadan University Press, 1970, p. 64.

19. Shelton, "The Meaning and Method of Afa Divination", p. 1442.

20. Abimbola, *Ifa: An Exposition*, p.26.

21. Ibid., p. 27-28.

22. M. Angulu Onwuejeogwu, "The Significance of Afa in Igbo Religious Philosophy: A Case Study of Nri", paper presented at International Congress on Igbo Religion, Nsukka, 1984, p. 23.

23. Shelton, "The Meaning and Method of Afa Divination", p. 1449.

24. Abimbola, *Ifa: An Exposition*, p. 43-63.

25. Arinze, *Sacrifice in Ibo Religion*, p. 65.

26. Ibid.

27. Onwuejeogwu, "The Significance of Afa", p. 32.

28. Middleton, "Divination", p. 197.

29. Ibid.

30. G.K. Park, "Divination and its social contexts", *Journal of the Royal Anthropological Institute*, XCIII, Part 2, July-December 1963, 195-209.

31. Shelton, *Igbo-Igala Borderland*, p. 202

32. Abimbola, *An Exposition of Ifa*, p. 10.

33. Ibid., p. 238.

CHAPTER 9

Buchi Emecheta's
"Destination Biafra"
A Case for a Border Perspective

by Karen King-Aribisala

In *Destination Biafra,* Buchi Emecheta castigates the Nigerian male on two counts. First, he is a figure confined by the boundaries of his own ethnic group. Second, he is a male chauvinist, viewing women as inferior. These boundaries of ethnicity and sex are seen ultimately to undermine the progress and independence of Nigeria, the black race, and "man" himself. For, as Raimondo Strassoldo observes, barriers and frontiers of any kind "hinder development."[1]

Tribal chauvinism ensures that Nigerian man is easily manipulated by foreign powers. In the colonial era, the British pit tribe against tribe in advancement of the policy of "divide and rule". When Nigeria finally achieves independence, Emecheta shows the British rigging the elections in favour of the Northern Hausa. Ethnic animosity is aroused. There is a coup and a counter-coup. Ibos are slaughtered in large numbers, and they decide to secede and form the state of Biafra. By implication, Britain and the Western powers continue to "divide and rule" even in the age of independence, exploiting the entire Nigerian nation for their own selfish interests.

Buchi Emecheta's male characters in *Destination Biafra* are also sexual chauvinists. They insist on regarding women as a relatively unimportant member of the society. Woman's sole function in life is to get married and have children.

Emecheta regards this male attitude as stultifying of human spiritual growth and progress. Accordingly, she advocates in her novel the need for a "border prospective." This is an outlook which is not entrammeled by the prejudices of any particular group, but which seeks to go beyond the limits of ethnic and sexual boundaries, towards the achievement of a "free" and independent society.

More than any other group of people, those who inhabit borderland areas are uniquely placed to realise this objective. Being on the border of a given "state", they are susceptible to influences from other contiguous areas. They are forced to weigh and balance issues. As one of Emecheta's characters observes, borderland peoples cannot afford to take sides. This means that their positions is at once vulnerable and a source of strength. Because they may be subjected to pressures from both sides of the border, their situation demands a certain flexibility in human relationships. More importantly:

> the proximity of the adjacent state makes national stereotypes less pervasive; transfrontier relationships highlight the common humanity emerging from national diversity.[2]

Significantly, Buchi Emecheta herself hails from the border area of Ibuza in the Midwest of Nigeria. In her foreword to *Destination Biafra*, she notes that:

> Records and stories have shown that Ibuza, Asaba and other smaller places along that border area suffered most (during the civil war).[3]

Yet, in spite of the atrocities meted out to borderland peoples, Emecheta writes in her account of the civil war, she has "tried very hard not to be bitter and to be impartial"[4] In short, she tries to recognise and internalise that common bond which links man with man.

Given this laudable objective, it is unfortunate that Emecheta sometimes betrays a narrowness of vision which is inconsistent with her proposed "borderland prospective". *Destination Biafra* sometimes appears no more than a piece of propaganda dedicated to promoting the cause of two groups with which Emecheta identifies—the Ibo and women. As such, much animosity is directed towards Yoruba and Hausa in particular, and all men in general.

However, there can be no denying that Emecheta does make an effort to go beyond the boundaries of ethnicity and sex. Clearly, she recognises the need for societies to strive, in the Forsterian sense, "to connect" the varieties of peoples, concepts and ideals within its confines. And it is for this very endeavour that she earns our admiration.

In *Destination Biafra*, Emecheta takes a fictional first step towards "true" freedom and independence. Towards a Nigeria which repudiates the imprisoning boundaries of tribe and sex. One which realises an all-encompassing perspective— the border perspective.

Throughout the novel, the main ethnic groups of the Yoruba, Ibo and Hausa, refuse to see each other in anything but uncomplimentary terms. Each ethnic group is viewed according to a tribal stereotype. Thus, the Yoruba party leader, Chief Oluremi Odumosu, responds to the news of the election of a Hausa Prime-minister with disgust. The leadership qualities of the new Prime-minister are not considered. A Yoruba chief hates the idea of being ruled by "gworo-eating wanderers from the North." The Hausa are, indeed, viewed by both Yoruba and Igbo as illiterates whose only mission in life is to pray to Allah. They are also considered to be loyal to the point of stupidity, which makes it easy for them to be dominated.

The Yoruba are regarded as cowards by the Igbo. Their only motivation in life is to make money. They are seen as ostentatious and given to corrupt practises. As for the Ibos, it is said that they eat human flesh. They are "ambition personified. Every beggar boy in Enugu or Owerri wants to be a doctor."[6] They are also considered to be extremely intelligent, but greedy and arrogant.

All of these male characters are not only confined by ethnic boundaries, but also by sexual ones. To the Nigerian male, whether he is Igbo, Yoruba or Hausa, woman is born to play a prescribed inferior role. She is to get married and to rear the produce of her union, that is all. Thus, when Abosi marries a girl who is virtually the same age as himself, he is subjected to ridicule. Even in age, the man must be older. Any hint of equality is frowned at. Emecheta observes that:

Many wondered why such a rich man who could have chosen any girl in Nigeria should go for a woman nearly the same age as himself; some cynics even said she was older. Yet they would have thought nothing of a man of seventy marrying a child of seventeen. To Nigerians, in marriage the male partner was superior and the female must be subservient, obedient, quiet to the point of passivity.[7]

Although Abosi does exercise a certain amount of independence of the expectations of his society by marrying a woman of his own age, he himself feels superior to women simply by virtue of being a man.

In the Northern region of the country, women are deemed to be too inferior to participate in the voting exercise. Indeed, the British Governor tries to advise Mallam Kano to allow the women in his area to vote, for the women in the south are all going to the polls. "It seems unfair to you Hausas." Mallam Kano shrugs his shoulders and tells the Governor to mind his own business.

As observed, these boundaries prevent the society from realising its full human potential. They nurture fear, insecurity, and inferiority and superiority complexes among the various groups. Furthermore, with specific regard to ethnicity, they facilitate British manipulation on the cultural, economic and political levels. This is so because each tribe actually believes in the aforementioned stereotypes.

In *Destination Biafra,* the Hausa feel threatened by the Yoruba and the Ibo. They see themselves as a vulnerable unit in an independent Nigeria, for they believe that their God-fearing ways ensure that they are easily set upon. Therefore, they place their fate in the hands of the British. They then proceed to play the Hausa role of a people who are easily dominated. And their sense of inferiority allows the eager British to capitalise on the interests of the entire nation.

British officials resolve to "show the Hausas that we are their friends, and that the country will be divided in such a way that they will be rulers of Nigeria." Thus, Governor Macdonald announces that the country's first Prime-minister is to be from the north. This declaration is made when only forty results out of a total of one hundred and ninety have been declared from the north.

Emecheta also points to the limiting nature of tribal boundaries, as evident in the desire for "ethnic balancing." When anything is planned, ethnic interests are seen to intrude, often to the detriment of the nation. It is interesting to note that this very pandering to ethnic balancing which contributed to the collapse of the civilian government, re-appears among the coup-plotters who vow to do away with tribalism. In the very organisation of the coup, tribal boundaries are considered in the decision as to who should kill who:

> It was agreed that the Yoruba soldiers were to take care of the corrupt eastern Ibo politicians, while the Ibo soldiers would see to the Yoruba West. That way, there was no danger of any of the politicians being spared or escaping. Nwokolo, from the Ibo minority in the mid-west was to take care of that feudal hangover, the Sardauna.[8]

Ironically, all of this ethnic balancing comes to nought. In spite of all the precautions, the coup still appears as an Igbo affair. When the Yoruba man who is supposed to kill the Igbo leaders arrives on the scene, he finds that one of them has gone to England for health reasons; and that his deputy is in hiding. Thus, one of the coup-makers' comments that "one would think we carried through this coup only to the advantage of the Igbo politicians."

Even during the civil war, Emecheta depicts the British and other Western powers playing one side against the other, a task which is facilitated by the fanatical tribal insularity of the ethnic groups. The British are portrayed as orchestrating Nigerians to fight each other so that they can draw on the country's rich oil reserves. The white character, Captain Alan Grey, strikes a deal with the leader of the Federal forces, Momoh. He agrees to obtain the military assistance of white mercenaries in return for oil. Alan advises Momoh:

> The best way may be to get a few white mercenaries to lead some black soldiers trained in England. We have many West Indians in London who look up to Nigeria as one of the most important black nations on earth. They wouldn't be fighting just for the money but because they want to see Nigeria great again. And because they're black, Abosi's soldiers would think they are Nigerians.[9]

The inference here is that whites are inspiring and training blacks to kill each other. Also, not only are black West Indians tricked into war, but so Biafrans, too. The latter are made to kill West Indians, believing them to be Nigerians. As for the Nigerians, they are "bought" to enrich Britain. In this manner, the whites exploit the divisions which they themselves created and nurtured in the black world through the processes of slavery and colonialism, to further entrench their dominance and control.

In an enlightened mood, the character Dr. Ozimba displays the awareness that the enslavement of his people to the ethnic stereotype has a debilitating effect on blacks:

> I believe in the advancement of the black race. I don't believe in tribalism, but we in Africa are being forced to acknowledge it because the foreign powers are using those very divisive groupings to tear us apart.[10]

Emecheta herself emphatically notes in her author's foreword that "I hope we Nigerians in particular and the black race in general will never allow ourselves to be so used."

Thus, by refusing to go beyond the boundaries of tribe, the men in *Destination Biafra* are made vulnerable, and are easily exploited and manipulated. They exist as tools in the hands of the Western powers. As a result, Nigerian independence has little meaning. The various ethnic groups so mistrust each other that, Emecheta suggests, they prefer to be guided by the British, rather than by a fellow Nigerian.

Ironically, the British themselves are seen to pursue a "border perspective" in their dealings with each other. They continually assert the need for what E.R. Stoddard has referred to as a "doctrine of mutual necessity, based on the recognition of an objective symbiotic relationship."[11] The British are a composite of Welsh, Scottish and Irish tribes. Like their Nigerian counterparts, they derogate each other on the basis of ethnicity. Thus, the Scots are supposed to be wily and untrustworthy. The English are said to be over-cautious, and the Irish are deemed to be stupid.

Emecheta even presents the scene of the Scottish Governor about to hand over the reins of government to Nigerians and wishing fervently that Whitehall had sent an Irishman to handle the issue. Then if he failed, "there would just be one more Irish joke to add to the thousands of others." However, when the occasion demands, the British are inclined to subsume their ethnic loyalties in the national interest. The Governor is Governor, not because he is a Scotsman, but because he is a man whose training and ability best qualifies him for his position.

Emecheta's British characters realise that those who occupy border regions are often more dynamic than their ethnically locked counterparts. This vitality derives from their very borderland position. As A.I. Asiwaju observes:

> The main challenge posed by border regions is in their attributes as sub-national areas where locality is internationalised. There is an inherent conflict between the national concern and local perspectives.[12]

This "inherent conflict" is seen by Emecheta's British characters to constitute strength, rather than weakness. The British, for example, are convinced that the borderland position of the Tivs, vis-a-vis the powers of the north, makes them a unique people. For they are able to appreciate and understand not only the localised fear of northern oppression, but also the need for a unified Nigeria.

Emecheta links ethnic and sexual chauvinism, implying that they are one and the same. The men in *Destination Biafra,* for instance, regard women as dependent and essentially subservient to men. Yet, they fail to realise that their ethnically blinkered attitude makes them, in turn, subservient to the British. In their relationship with the British, they act like stereotyped women. They are obedient to the British will and dictates. It is the British who decide which ethnic group should govern Nigeria, paying little regard to the leadership attributes of the individual.

Just as the British are seen to manipulate each ethnic group in accordance with a perceived tribal stereotype, so do the male characters of Emecheta seek to exploit woman. Again, this is in keeping with their narrow view of the female. In *Destination Biafra,* the woman in question is Debbie Ogedemgbe, the novel's heroine. Unfortunately for the men, however, Debbie is anything but the dependent, frail and subservient creature which the men believe her to be. She is an Oxford graduate who joins the Nigerian army as an active soldier. When hostilities come to a head between the Federal forces and the Biafran army, she is inveighed upon to go on a mission to see the Biafran leader, Abosi. Her purpose is to coax him to end the war. Since she herself believes in the concept of a "one Nigeria," she willingly accepts the proposition.

The sexual chauvinism of the Nigerian male is apparent when the leader of each ethnic group demands that Debbie should use her feminine wiles to end the war. Even her English boyfriend, Alan Grey, asks her to:

> Do your woman bit tonight...Abosi used to fancy you, I used to see the desire in his eyes when he talked to you at Government House in Lagos....
> Well, use that part of you to make him do what you say.[13]

Debbie slaps him. She is fighting "a personal war for her womanhood." Unlike her male counterparts, she cannot be used by Alan or the British. She refuses to play an inferior role to any man. She is an "independent soul." This trait is a sore point with her English boyfriend. Alan enjoys having an African girlfriend as a means of "going native." And he reflects that he is better off without her since she does not play the role of a humble, native woman.

Here, Emecheta emphasises the need to transcend sexual, and by implication, ethnic boundaries. For Debbie's independent stance ensures that she is not manipulate by anyone. Her sense of herself enables her to control situations. Indeed, she is forever turning the rule of the subservient female on its head, and becomes more powerful than the men as a result.

Some of the Nigerian soldiers, for example, believe Debbie to be inferior even when she is armed. They regard her with undisguised amusement, as if to say "whatever you do, however much you are armed and in command now, you are still a woman." The soldiers all eventually meet their deaths. Thereby, Emecheta warns of the dangers of a blinkered outlook. When people insist on seeing others in stereotype roles, they are at a disadvantage when faced with a nonconformist.

When Debbie finally confronts Abosi, he dismisses the mission and underrates its importance precisely because she is a woman. He, in turn, shamelessly tries to exploit her relationship with her English boyfriend, that he might acquire ammunition from the British. He appeals to her to travel to England and organise the transportation of weapons in Red Cross planes, instead of the supposed food and clothing. But she also "double-crosses" him. Contrary to what is expected of a woman, Debbie has a mind of her own. She decides that Abosi is misguided and selfish, and attempts to kill him. Here again, perceived stereotypes may be twisted by the role-player. Independence is asserted.

This is not to deny an inherent vulnerability of those who are courageous enough to free themselves from both ethnic and sexual boundaries. The leader of the first coup after independence, Brigadier Onyemere, is Igbo. He is convinced that the country fully supports his government. Events, however, prove otherwise. The officers spear heading the counter-coup which follows, find Onyemere in the company of his Yoruba friend, Oladapo. The latter is given the choice of becoming the next head of state, or dying with his Ibo friend. Oladapo places friendship above ethnic boundaries and both men are killed. Emecheta notes that "one of the early attempts to make friendship across tribes thus ended that evening." Yet, there is a sense that the "border perspective," one which, in this case, gives credence to friendship, rather than to tribal affinity, has triumphed, even is spite of their deaths.

Debbie, too in her attempt to cross sexual barriers, is placed in the position of the stereotyped vulnerable and fragile female. As her mother observes, Debbie wants:

> to be a man and wants men to know she wants to be like them, and still retain her womanhood.[14]

But she is brutally raped by soldiers. Superficially, it appears that Debbie has been forced to acknowledge the malesuperior/female-inferior divide. Men are more powerful than women. Women cannot rape men, but men can rape women. As Susan Brownmiller notes:

> Man's structural capacity to rape and woman's corresponding structural vulnerability are as basic to the physiology of both our sexes as the primal act of sex itself.[15]

When Lawal, one of the rapists, tells Debbie, "I am going to show you that you are nothing but a woman, an ordinary woman," there is a tendency to accept that Debbie (woman) is, indeed, the weaker vessel of male propaganda. This is especially so because "sexual assault is an invasion of bodily integrity and a violation of freedom and selfdetermination."[16] And it is precisely this that Debbie has been fighting to assert as a human being.

Yet, even in this rape, the strengths which may be derived from inherent vulnerabilities are apparent. Because Debbie is a woman, she is raped. Had she been a man, she would have been killed. Hence, she has the ability and the means to continue her struggle, Nigeria's struggle, for real independence.

It is here that the novel assumes symbolic significance. *Destination Biafra* refers to the means by which a Biafra can be realised. In keeping with her border per-

spective, Emecheta does not limit the use of the name Biafra only to that of the secessionist eastern states. The Biafra of her novel is much more. It signifies independence and freedom for all Nigerians.

When the coup is being planned, the soldiers decide to kill all the politicians,
who they see as servants of the British. They desire to give Nigeria "true" independence. This entails changing the name of the country, the argument being that
it was chosen by the British. They opt for the name Biafra. And one of the officers
comments:

> Our destination is "Biafra," since as far as I am concerned we're not yet
> independent. We sent away one set of masters, without realizing that they
> had left their stooges behind. Even the matches we use in our kitchens
> come from abroad.[17]

Biafra, then, represents the first step to Nigerian cultural independence. Biafra
is an ideal that all should "aim to achieve, a nation that has been detribalised, a nation where wealth will be equally distributed." Biafra stands for "freedom." The
realisation of this freedom is made especially difficult because the world is corrupt
and full of exploiters. Human nature is very hard to change. But the Biafra ideal of
freedom is what all peoples should strive to achieve.

The birth of any sense of independence is necessarily a painful one, and
Emecheta employs the artistic device of using two symbols of a baby to emphasize
how freedom may be realised. The first baby was born to Momoh, Nigeria's Head
of State, during the civil war. It is described as "a deformed piece of humanity," "a
giant frog more than any human." It is a monstrosity. The baby is born by means
of a caesarian section, and dies. Emecheta suggests that Nigeria, like the baby, has
been born through artificial means. Momoh's government has been thrust upon it.
As such, Nigeria's independence is superficial. It is not a natural evolution. This
point is underlined when the Head of State is seen reflecting on his wife's difficult
labour that he could not "order nature to act quickly. Neither was it a case of being
able to use the money from Nigeria's black gold."

Nigeria's independence should evolve as a natural process of birth. Moreover,
freedom cannot be bought. Any attempt to use a short-cut to arrive at an independent
state will result is a monstrous birth such as the bloody civil war. Thus, the Ghanian
novelist, Ayi Kwei Arman, points to the need for the African elite to take its time
in the journey towards "independence." Similarly, the Kenyan writer, Ngugi Wa
Thiong'o emphasises in his work the pain, labour, the back-breaking process which
accompanies the state of national independence.[18]

Emecheta's second symbolic baby—baby-Biafra—is a product of such pain. He
is born to a refugee who later dies, leaving him an orphan. Debbie, in the company
of other women, makes him her responsibility and ties him on her back as the group
try to make their way to the east. Soon, she feels tired with the weight of the child,
and one of the women asks her what kind of African woman she is. The incident
and the question have several implications.

The nation of Nigeria is symbolical orphaned, bereft of the parental guidance
of Britain since it achieved independence. Woman, in Debbie, exercises the option
of looking after the children, or being the caretaker of freedom. And here, freedom
is equated with responsibility, as is "true" independence.

Debbie's fatigue provokes the question, "What type of woman is Africa producing? That one can't even back a baby. How will you carry your own child when you
have one?" Some of the women comment sarcastically that she will probably push

her baby in a pram.

Emecheta suggests that Nigeria has two choices of achieving independence. It can either pander to the west—the pram—to carry it along, or it can employ its own people to steer it in the "right" direction. As we have seen, the men's enslavement to ethnic stereotypes leads them to dependence on the west.

The women in *Destination Biafra* assert traditional African guidelines as a means of realising independence. This is evident when the baby dies on Debbie's back. One of the women comments that Biafra, too, will die in its youth before it reaches maturity. By inference, Nigeria's freedom and independence is a necessary ordeal which must be experienced before any real sense of freedom can be realised. Also, the baby's death is seen as a communal responsibility. All of the women are griefstricken, just as if their own babies had died. This stresses the fact that the tragedy of Biafra should be viewed as the responsibility of all Nigerians. Biafra's death is actually seen in positive terms:

> On this issue, their common Africanness came to the fore, a child was the child of the community rather than just the biological parents.[19]

Boundaries of ethnicity, even of family, disappear in their common grief Emecheta points to the inherent value of African traditions in breaking down the impeding barriers of ethnicity.

As with E.M. Forester, she seeks "only to connect" the various elements of society that it might develop and grow.[20] Emecheta's objective of exposing the detrimental aspects of ethnic and sexual stereotypes is commendable. It is lamentable, therefore, that, at times, she also appears to be erecting borders in both of those areas. In spite of all intellectual intention to the contrary, she often seems to be making a special case for Ibo liberation and women's liberation.

The Ibos are presented as an exceptional people. More so than any other ethnic group. They are referred to as the Jews of Africa; God's chosen blacks who, because of their superior intellect and courage, are persecuted. They are in bondage, dreaming of the promised land of Ibo independence. And, Emecheta even provides them with a Moses in the person of Dr. Ozimba. All others are made to persecute the Ibos, orchestrating a genocide policy in which "it was said that over thirty thousand Ibos died in the first part of the troubles." They are continually referred to as sacrificed figures being led to the slaughter.

Emecheta's feelings are understandable. In the foreword of her novel, she mentions several of her relatives now dead as a result of the war. She is so full of bitterness that she entreats the Ibos never to forget the atrocities meted out to them, for only "a fool will forget." Oladele Taiwo hints at Emecheta's ethnicity in his work "Feminine Novelists of Modern Africa", but notes that this trait is limited to the foreword of *Destination Biafra*.[21] However, in the novel itself, there are many instances of Emecheta straying from her proposed "border perspective." Yet, in sum, she remains a writer who has tried to achieve a multifaceted and humane vision.

In the same foreword, Emecheta pays tribute to Obi Ebele for information about how "our people" organised their own militia in protection against the federal forces and the Biafran ones. She also thanks Wole Soyinka for his comments on the civil war in *The Man Died*. A work which reveals him as rising above his Yoruba ethnic group in order to see the civil war as one in which the human spirit suffered. She says that through his book, she realised that "some nonIbos suffered with us", and as such, she developed her central character with this in mind. A woman who is neither "Ibo, nor Yoruba, nor Hausa but simply a Nigerian." Clearly, Emecheta has made an artistic effort to transcend the boundaries of tribe in *Destination Biafra*, even though at times her sentiments lag behind her intellectual reasoning.

Similarly, with regard to sexual boundaries, Emecheta appears occasionally, to be championing the cause of women's liberation rather than a society which gains its strength from the equality of the sexes. There is a great deal of authorial comment and Debbie, the heroine, seems wooden. A vehicle for the transportation of Emecheta's ideas, rather than a fleshed-out character. Indeed, her stances and frequent outbursts of invective to the male characters are rather melodramatic and occasionally, ludicrous. When, for instance, at the novel's conclusion, Alan, her erstwhile boyfriend, begs her to marry him and leave the shamble which is war-ridden Nigeria, Debbie shouts, grenade in hand:

> I didn't mind your being my male concubine but Africa will never again stoop to being your wife; to meet you on an equal basis, like companions, yes, but never again to be your slave.[22]

Her sentiments are well-taken. Nigeria, should not be enslaved to the west on any count. But being a wife does not automatically mean slavery to a man. One can have a relationship within marriage which is based on sharing and respect for the qualities of each partner. Similarly, it is possible for Nigeria and Britain, Africa and Europe, to realise a relationship which is based on what one commentator has referred to as "mutual necessity." In this rather vitriolic outburst, Debbie is simply substituting one form of chauvinism for another. She tells Alan that he has been her male concubine all along. In other words, she has been exploiting him sexually—a fact which she herself is very much against, as is Emecheta.

Yet, in spite of those short-comings, *Destination Biafra* remains a courageous example of one who has overcome the stifling and confining borders of ethnicity and sex, in the realisation of a "border perspective." It is an outlook which ensures independence. In the words of Tom Mboya:

> Africa desires to be understood and to be recognised from the viewpoint and perspective of her own people. Africa is no longer willing to be referred to as British, French, Belgian.... Africa must create and assert her own personality.[23]

It is a personality, the independence of which can only be realised through the assumption of a "border perspective."

Endnotes

1. Raimondo Strassoldo, "Frontier Regions: An Analytical Study," in Second European Conference of Ministers Responsible for Regional Planning, 25-27 September, 1973. (Strasburg: Council of Europe, 1973), p. 23.
2. Ibid.
3. Buchi Emecheta, *Destination Biafra*, (London: Allison and Bushy Ltd., 1982), p. vii.
4. Ibid.
5. Ibid., p. 13.
6. Ibid., p. 7.
7. Ibid., p. 43.
8. Ibid., p. 61.
9. Ibid., pp. 200-201.
10. Ibid., p. 182.
11. E.R. Stoddard, "Functional Alternative to Bi-National Border Development Model: The Case of the U.S.-Mexico Border Region," Paper presented at the 1978 Meeting of the American Sociological Association, San Franciso, as cited in Asiwaju, *Artificial Boundaries* (Lagos University Press, 1984).

12. A.I. Asiwaju, "Artificial Boundaries," Inaugural Lecture, University of Lagos, 12 December, 1984, p. 30.
13. Buchi Emecheta, op. cit., p. 255.
14. Ibid., p. 161.
15. Susan Brownmiller, *Against Our Will, Women and Rape* (New York: Bantam Books Inc., 1976), p. 4.
16. Ibid., p. 248.
17. Buchi Emecheta, op. cit., p. 60.
18. See Ayi Kwei Armah, *The Beautyful Ones Are Not Yet Born* (London: Heinemann, 1969); and James Ngugi, *A Grain of Wheat* (London: Heinemann, 1968).
19. Buchi Emecheta, op. cit., p. 212.
20. See E.M. Forster, *Howards End* (Harmondsworth: Penguin Books Ltd., 1941).
21. Oladele Taiwo, *Feminine Novelists in Modern Africa* (London: Macmillan, 1984).
22. Buchi Emecheta, op. cit., p. 259.
23. Tom Mboya, "Address on African Freedom Day," in Langston Huges (ed.), *An African Treasury* (New York: Pyramid Books, 1961), p. 39.

CHAPTER 10

The Black Aesthetic: Comparisons Across the Atlantic Border

by Lynn Nwuneli

Is There a Black Aesthetic?

The subject of borderlands immediately becomes a philosophical question, when written literature is to be considered. The critic chooses his frame of reference—tribal, national or continental—according to what he hopes to accomplish, more aware than the politician that the borders he refers to, in terms of his own discipline, are arbitrary and artificial. Calling his field of study 'African Literature' emphasizes the relative un-importance of demarcations along national borders.

However, once one begins to generalize about the qualities of African literature and to formulate a black aesthetic—a theory of African sensibility with regards to shared concepts of beauty and function in literature—an interesting problem arises. Critics speak of black aesthetic particularly when attempting to articulate a theory of literature based wither on a study of oral tradition or on written works in relationship to the oral. Yet, 'black aesthetic' immediately implies a relationship with literature published outside the continent, and invites a comparative approach, particularly since the same term has been used for twenty years now in discussions of Afro-American literature.

In an article entitled "Black Aesthetic and African Literature" Theo Vincent[1] raises this question of whether there could be postulated a black aesthetic which includes literature of the black diaspora, but concludes that only 'fossils' of African culture could still remain outside the continent. In a literal sense this is probably true, although ethnologists have identified a number of African retentions in those areas of black American folk cultures most likely to contain the elusive African sensibility: religion, dance, music and verbal play. One still might be tempted to disregard this as irrelevant to a literature created predominantly by middle class writers, were there not several other perspectives from which to consider the question.

First, the research of Bernard Bell, Stephen Henderson and Berndt Ostendorf has found many links between black folk culture and literature, especially poetry,

in the U.S. with the Black Arts Movement of the 1960s the number of these connections drastically increases, poets consciously seeking to adopt their newly recognised tradition—part of their assertion of black identity and rejection of Western
history, culture and values.

One realized that however proud writers are to identify themselves with Africa
and to dissociate themselves from the old desire to assimilate into American culture,
calling themselves Afro-Americans does not make their culture thereby more
African. However, the politically motivated re-definition of self *against* the
American or Western tradition is of vast significance, for in a certain sense that is
what African writers and critics have also been engaged in, according to Bruce
King.[2]

The fact of shared historical experience is the final factor mediating against a
too-hasty rejection of the idea of a black aesthetic embracing the literature of
Africans and Afro-Americans. S.E. Ogude[3] asserts that the traumatic cultural and
psychological experience of the slave trade constitutes the shared racial memory of
black people; Franz Fanon says the same thing in *Black Faces, White Masks*. To
Ogude, this fact is central to the literatures and an emotional link between black people yet. Combined with continuing frustration on the international level with
Europe, and racism these as within the U.S., the sense of shared black experience
continues to exist, as witnessed to by numerous specialized conferences and events
such as FESTAC in 1977. Had American society actually permitted or encouraged
the full assimilation of black people, the concept of Afro-American literature would
have no more meaning than German-American literature has.

The fact that this is decidedly not so permits us to at least raise the possibility
of some or many congruencies between black aesthetics on both sides of the Atlantic
border. Furthermore, we suggest the possibility, at least in cultural and literary
terms of reference, of seeing Afro-Americans as a borderlands people, as even the
name suggests, representing an amalgam of two identities and ways of life. The militant Black Nationalism in the U.S. two decades ago is further evidence for the validity of this concept, for according to I.A. Asiwaju[4] borderlands constitute the areas
where the propaganda of a nation and its identity are weakest.

The Black Writer: Common Concerns on Both Sides of the Atlantic Border

The artistic dimension of black nationalism was represented at its most vocal in
the Black Arts Movement of the 1960s and early 1970s, during which time there was,
far more consciously even than during the Harlem Renaissance of the 1920s, a
widespread sense of formulating a separate, Black tradition of literature with techniques, themes, symbols, perspective, allusions, diction and goals sharply distinct
from those of 'mainstream' American literature. The intended audience, too, was
different than what had been assumed until then—not Americans in general with
special focus on white liberals, but a black audience with shared experiences to
which the style and messages of the literature were addressed.

One realizes that the century has been full of literary manifestos of one slant or
another, most of them with restricted interest and short-lived influence. In contrast,
the programmes and polemics by numerous critics in the 1960s, many collected in
Gayle's *The Black Aesthetic*,[5] did not exist in isolation from the literature. In all the
genres, but particularly drama and poetry, there was a vigorous response: a surge
of creativity by new writers and newly-inspired older writers which reflected the
black pride, communal values, consciousness-changing and revolutionary ideals of

the manifestos. Poetry, typically the least accessible genre to ordinary readers since early in the century, blossomed to change in the Afro-American community. Black poetry moved out of the recesses of its niche in academia into public forums: political rallies, broadsheets, cultural festivals, schools, the streets, parks, prisons and wherever else black people were to be found. Young radicals such as Don Lee performed their poetry dramatically even in bars to reach audiences cut off from the printed experience of literature, and long-established poets such as Pulitzer Prize-winner Gwendolyn Brooks followed him, adapting their work to the new mood and aesthetic.

The potentially fruitful relationship between literature and a relevant articulated aesthetic could not be more clearly illustrated than by the Black Arts Movement. From an African perspective this American experience holds particular interest in that it raises a number of questions also relevant to the situation here. The central function of an articulated aesthetic is to explicate and nurture a kind of literature representative of its specific audience in all the inter-related aspects included under the rough categories of style and content. Both the Afro-American and Anglophone African writer is aware of long-established literary traditions in English which will influence to some degree his own writing, yet into which he does not want to be so absorbed as to lose his own unique identity, voice, values and perspective.

The most pressing issue (though the choices of a writer need not be made con-sciously) is what he conceives of as his relationship with his audience, along with how narrow or broad that audience is to be. For the concerned black writer the ques-tion goes beyond whether his work is to be popular or 'high-brow', for the problems and situation of his own people are compelling when compared to the more comfor-table situation of the white society to which other literature in English is addressed. The African writer sees a society rapidly changing and being reshaped by outside and disintegrative cultural influences, a society of enormous educational and economic inequities which is far behind the foreign achievements and technology on which it heavily relies; a society too often with serious problems of leadership and vision. Similarly, the Afro-American writer sees a society divided not by tribe but by race, in which his own people as a whole are also educationally and economically disadvantaged by the effects of history and continued racism, a society in which the prevailing national ideology and myths often do not seem valid for his own people's experience and culture. Again, effective leadership and vision are problems.

In both African and Afro-American situation the people and their culture are likely to be randomly and detrimentally acted upon rather than shaping their own future, if leadership problems are not tackled by individuals with a broad awareness of group needs, having ideas about which values should be nurtured and which re-jected, and ideas of facilitating means as well as ends to be sought. Recognizing the shortcomings of existing leadership, knowing himself motivated by concern rather than self-interest, the black writer often feels a responsibility to address himself, his literature, to these issues and ends.

Literature in itself does not directly effect social change, but its greater power in this realm is to create awareness, alter a people's self-images, and shape values on the individual level. Literature need not be revolutionary in theme to have a far-reaching, though at first subtle, effect on the minds of its audience. All literature carries its own imposed perspective on existence and the identity of the individual within his world, so far as it has any relationship with reality—so far as literature supplies the mirroring effect which has been its most basic 'defense' through ages of literary criticism.

However penetrating his own vision, the black writer may still recognise a serious stumbling block in the way of his own assumption of leadership. The very education, economic position and experiences which are likely to have helped him to achieve an objective understanding of his people's situation are likely simultaneously to have alienated him to varying degrees from that situation. His very manner of thought and expressions differ from the people with whom he would communicate. Somehow he has to discover means of bridging the gap between himself and them, if he is not merely to speak to the relatively few people in his own position, or to be more appreciated by the 'other' culture (white or foreign) than by his own.

The rest of this article will focus on how Afro-American writers wrestled with these issues, and the solutions they found, with inherent implications for the similar search of African writers. Most emphasis will be given to one individual: dramatist, short-story writer, critic and poet Amiri Baraka (born LeRoi Jones), who was the crucial figure in creating the Black Arts Movement and articulating the aesthetic which is intrinsic in nearly all subsequent Afro-American literature. To be examined most closely are those poems of Baraka's in which he formulates aesthetic problems, prepares himself to be a fitting spokesman/leader for his people, and finally lays out for readers dramatically the principles behind his poetry and drama, and thereby the literary movement to which his work gives birth. It is here most fascinatingly that aesthetics and art can be seen to merge.

Baraka's Formulation of an Aesthetic

Goals and Difficulties

The often unsatisfactory relationship between black writers and the white literary establishment is captured with clarity and humour in Dudley Randall's "Black Poet, White Critic".

> A critic advises
> not to write on controversial subjects
> like freedom or murder,
> but to treat universal themes
> and timeless symbols
> like the white unicorn.
>
> *A white unicorn?* (Randall, p. 33)[6]

For most of its history until the 1960s Afro-American literature was predominantly protest literature, full of appeals to white society's sense of justice. White critic's 'responded' by ignoring the literature or terming it insignificant because of the nature of its racial material; black writers were advised to forget their race and be more universal. The absurdity of this is heightened by Randall's use of a unicorn to represent the 'universal'—a white symbol from fantasy. Black literature, the poem implies, must be just the opposite: controversial, disturbing, realistic and speaking to the needs of black people in the present, without concern for so-called 'universal' standards, or the opinions of white critics. Although other poets such as Margaret Danner and Melvin Tolson also exploited the question of what Afro-American literature is and should be in their poetry, it was Baraka's answer which influenced the outburst of poetry in the 1960s. It is in his second volume of poetry, *The Dead*

Lecturer,[7] that one can trace the initial stages of his formation of an aesthetic coinciding with his purgation of the 'double-consciousness' which Dubois calls an inseparable part of Afro-American experience: "This sense of always looking at one's self through the eyes of others...two souls, two thoughts, two unreconciled strivings"[8]–the artificial border of race, internalised.

The title "Balboa, The Entertainer" of the second poem in the volume indicates a duality in the role of poet difficult to reconcile. The poet is expected to be an explorer of new territory (Balboa) and simultaneously an entertainer, though much of experience is not pleasant enough to be material for entertainment.

> It cannot come
> except you make it
> from materials
> it is not
> caught from (the philosophers
> of need, of which
> I am lately
> one,
> will tell you. "The People,"
> (and not think themselves
> liable
> to the same
> trembling flesh). I say now, "The People,
> as some lesson repeated, now,
> the lights are off, to myself
> as a lover, or at the cold wind. (p. 10)

This first half of the poem expresses the poet's sense of the need to become a racial spokesman, conflicting with an awareness of his own limitations of knowledge, as a member of the middle class, and of love.

After facing up to some of his internalization of society's sickness, most movingly in "An Agony As Now", which gives an emotionally intense interpretation of Fanon's "Black Faces, White Masks" metaphor—"I am inside someone/who hate me." (p. 15)—the poet moves outside his private dilemma to make a more public statement of his changed separatist intentions and orientation:

Short Speech To My Friends
A political art, let it be
tenderness...
    I address
       /the society
       the image, of
       common utopia.
       /the perversity
       of separation, isolation
after so many years of trying to enter their kingdoms,
now they suffer in tears, these others, saxophones whining
through the wooden doors of their less than gracious homes.
The poor have become our creators. The black. The thoroughly
ignorant.
       Let the combination of morality and inhumanity begin. (p. 29)

Despite the declaration of readiness, the narrator's double-consciousness is obvious in the part of the passage concerning the reactions white people are likely to have to his newly politicised poetry, inspired by 'the poor' and their riots.

"I Substitute For the Dead Lecturer" (p. 59), he later writes. Most of this volume can be read as a 'killing off' of the reasonable, lyrical, bourgeois part of his identity, the spiritual death he is undergoing to be reborn a more fit spokesman and leader of an undivided revolutionary consciousness. In the concluding poem, self-estrangement still slows his assuming the role he has repeatedly declared necessary, as he confesses a continuing lack of control:

> "The Liar"
> .....   though I am a man
> who is loud
> on the birth
> of his ways. Publicly redefining
> each change in my soul, as if I had predicted
> them, (p. 79).

Essential Values of a Black Aesthetic

Following this is Baraka's largest, most important collection of poems, *Black Magic Poetry*,[9] which contains three books. The opening "Three Modes of History and Justice" in *Sabotage* gives a history of the black race "learning/America, as speech, and a common emptiness," interwoven with 'songs' as a contrasting motif. Only at the end does the poem's new group perception, *we*, return to the subjective *I*, as he thinks of the future when the harsh realities of racism and revolution will be gone, and "my songs will be softer and lightly weight the air." (p. 4)

The first major statement of a (romantic) aesthetic is given in "Gatsby's Theory of Aesthetics," (p. 41), where Baraka stresses poetry as 'result rather than form,' specifically aims at "reviving...meanings possibility and ubiquitousness." This prose poem is existentialist in its concept of meaning beyond the poem: "arbitrariness or self imposed meaning." Defining beauty as thus residing in effect rather that traditional form, *Sabotage* ends with "The Bronze Buckaroo," concerned with finding a contemporary art to replace conventional 'high' art: "the heavy pictures, unavailable solaces, emptying their churchy magic out":

> ...Poet clocks crouched in their Americas.
> Dreaming of poems, only the cold sky could bring. Not room poems or
> fireplace poems, or the great washed poetry of our dizzy middleclass.
> But something creeps and grabs them, rapes them on the pavement. (p. 44)

The complacencies of bourgeois poetry, withdrawn from the crises of the times, must give way to relevant, forceful, violent and effective poetry.

In *Target Study,* the second book of *Black Magic Poetry,* Baraka assumes a public role in "Numbers, Letters" in which he introduces himself in lines echoing Walt Whitman in *Song of Myself,* another poet who speaks for his nation and 'contains multitudes.' But the Whitmanesque lines are juxtaposed with a passage written in an entirely different diction, the black language of the urban streets. This voice demands answers and style meaningful to the urban poor:

>   say it straight to be
> understood straight, put it flat and real
> ....

> Say what you mean, dig
> it out put it down, and be strong
> about it. (p. 47)

This challenging voice represents a major value in the aesthetic we see Baraka formulating. The choice of a language is a choice of perception, and although the streetstyle remains only one of many in Baraka's poetry, subsequent Black Arts Movement poets were more fully to utilize urban black speech as an integral part of their separate tradition and community orientation.

The provinces of beauty and ugliness are clearly demarcated in the various poems, which cover nearly the entire range of tone and form, once white perceptions and images are rejected (c.f. "I don't love you," p. 55). "The blood in me, assumes a beautiful shape" (p. 50). Traditional connotations of 'white' are sabotaged:

> "the don'ts of this white hell" (p. 55)
> "Very very white." (p. 64)
> "white women and cars, the rotting artifacts
> of lost uncivilizations." (p. 69)

Eventually he drops the word 'white' entirely, calling his adversaries 'greys.' A new perception of beauty is associated with Baraka's move from Greenwich Village to Harlem: "new town, new black, new strength, new wealth." (p. 85)

> "Return of the Native"
> Harlem is vicious
> modernism, BangClash
> Vicious the way its made.
> Can you stand such beauty?
> So violent and transforming. (p. 108)

Target Study ends with two of Baraka's most famous poems, in which the essence of moral ugliness and beauty are juxtaposed. "Black Bourgeoisie," who "does not hate ofays/hates, instead, him self/him black self," (p. 111) and the rhetorically powerful oration written after the assassination of Black leader Malcolm X "A Poem for Black Hearts":

> For
> Malcolm's hands raised to bless us
> all black and strong in his image
> of ourselves, For Malcolm's words
> fire darts, the victor's tireless
> thrusts, words hung above the world
> change as it may, he said it, and
> for this he was killed, for saying,
> and feeling, and being change....(p. 112)

A good part of Black Aesthetic is formulated in this poem: the spiritual influence of black images and heroes, the capacity of words as weapon, the necessity of the committed life, and at the end a call for evolutionary change if manhood is not to be relinquished.

Art as Magic—Baraka's Fullest Articulation of an Aesthetic

After "SOS," a last urgent call for all black people to come together in unity, the central poem of the volume and source of the central metaphor of the Black Arts

Movement open the third book:

> Black Art
> Poems are bullshit unless they are
> teeth or trees or lemons piled
> on a step...
> ....We want 'poems that kill.'
> Assassin poems, Poems that shoot
> guns.....
>   Another negroleader
> on the steps of the white house one
> kneeling between the sheriff's things
> negotiating cooly for his people.
> Agggh...stumbles across the room...
> Put it on him, poem, Strip him naked
> to the world. Another bad poem cracking
> steel knuckles in a jewlady's mouth.
> Let there be no love poems written
> until love can exist freely and
> cleanly. Let Black People understand
> that they are the lovers and the sons
> of lovers and warriors and sons
> of warriors Are poems & poets &
> all the loveliness here in the world (p. 116)

Polemical, obscene, as hostile to the integrationist 'negroleader' as to 'jewlady' and 'wop', this poem not only advocated but is an exercise in juju (voodoo or hoodoo in the U.S.) or *Black Magic,* the second sense of the title referring to the magical power of word-spells to hurt or heal. Baraka is symbolically 'killing' the white and 'negro' enemies of black "virtue and love," those whose actions or self-centred passivity stand in the way of revolutionary change. The magical 'killing' has a psychological intention of terrifying the white reader while having a unifying and cathartic effect on the black reader or audience.

Black Art imagery is to be concrete; abstractions or meditative poetry in a crisis situation is 'bullshit.' The choice of language represents Baraka's alignment with the tough street-people who need not be convinced to reject the middle-class values they have never assimilated, as well as the orientation of black aesthetics to the oral skills of the people. This is "Another bad poem," the pun bringing together the conventional meanings of 'bad' with the black street-talk reversed meaning of 'strong and fine.' Black art, in other words, claims the right to invert conventional (white) aesthetic values, just as it intends to shake up society, in its quest for a world that will allow black people freely to love (and write lyrical poetry) again.

The last of Baraka's poems to be examined which utilizes the aesthetic theme offers a complete contrast in tone and imagery, for whereas "Black Art" advocates and is an example of art as a weapon, "Ka 'Ba" sings of the liberating and spiritual, life-giving qualities of genuine people's art:

> We are a beautiful people
> with african imaginations
> full of masks and dances and swelling chants
> with african eyes, and noses, and arms,

though we sprawl in grey chains in a place
full of winters, when what we want is sun.
We have been captured,
brothers, And we labour
to make gateway, into
the ancient image, into a new
correspondence with ourselves
and our black family. We need magic
now we need the spells, to raise up
return, destroy, and create. What will be
The sacred words? (p. 146)

The poet addresses himself to the space collective need for new non-European images, as a means of expressing the spiritual qualities of his 'black family'—all black
people, with Africa as the focal point, the "Ka 'Ba." Until the animating images are
created, Afro-Americans are mentally still slaves, seeing themselves through the
eyes, as DuBois says, and "revelation of the other world."[10] Forging life-giving images is a 'sacred' function of art.

Relevance of Baraka's Aesthetic to an African Context

For Baraka, as for Margaret Danner earlier, and for the many who followed him
right through his conversion to Islam, Africa became a central symbol of black affir-
mation and spiritual wholeness. But his experiences were American, and the themes
of his 1960s poetry relevant for the most part specifically to the Afro-American
situation then. One cannot expect to find essential aspects of black aesthetic in the
themes of his poetry, nor has Baraka (or his followers) stagnated into mere repetition
of the white-hate and black-pride themes, which like *negritude* in Francophone
literature, now appears to be a useful stage, but still only a stage of reorientation after
shrugging off the burden of double-consciousness.[11]

However, the poet's deliberate self-reorientation may suggest other, more currently useful parallels, depending upon what problems and needs the African writer
finds most pressing. He might trace a process of growing awareness, for example,
of the need for a politicised art, or for committing his art to the forging of a strong
national (as opposed to tribal) identity, or even a pan-African or unified Black
perspective. The work of South African poet Keorapetse Kgositsile, for many years
now resident in the U.S., is a perfect example of black consciousness breaking down
the artificial border between shared experiences of racism on both sides of the
Atlantic. Greater awareness of South African apartheid has been reflected in a
broader sense of identity in the black literature in many countries. Two final examples from numerous expressions of black unity can be found in Ola Balogun's
film *Black Goddess,* and (white) Brazilians novelist Antonio Olinto's *The Water
House,*[12] both affirming the links between West Africa and black Brazilians.

Most generally, the black aesthetic gives rise to works of art showing a concern
for those values most vital to preserve and foster among black people, the values
which have served best in the past and have the most to offer in the present against
the disintegrative lingering effects, for example, of colonialism, too rapid urbanisation, mass poverty, the uncontrolled influence of the *nouveau riche* mentality,
cynicism in public and private life.

Most of the Afro-American poets inspired by Baraka sought not only to address
the issues of their time and place, but to do so in ways that would reach the broadest

possible black audience, thus logically extending his ideal of a community-oriented art. In addition to finding public forums of all kinds for poetry readings, they wrote in such a way as to be easily understood. Poets willingly exchanged subtle complexity for clarity and dramatic effectiveness, agreeing with Baraka that the beauty of poetry in a crisis situation is in its results. Instead of literary tradition, their poetry is strongly grounded in oral tradition, owing much to sermons, oration, exhortation, and specifically black folk and urban forms such as toasts, raps, the dozens, and other oral put-downs. Equally influential have been the forms of black music: spirituals in earlier poets particularly, the blues following Langston Hughes' innovative example, and most of all, jazz.[13]

Were more of them concerned with broadening their audience, African poets might also turn to their own traditional oral and musical forms far more than they have so far. Any vital popular form ought to be capable of adaptation beyond its original situation and purpose, offering thereby a link understandable to a wider audience between traditional and contemporary experience, and facilitating a readier response than imported forms. One might consider the example too of Joy Nwosu Lo-Bamijoko's utilization of Igbo folk song styles for contemporary messages in her albums such as *Azania*. New popular forms are also capable of cross fertilization with other arts, as suggested by the far-reaching impact of Fela Anikulapo-Kuti's albums; the border drawn between song and poetry is often a artificial one, as the examples of ballads should remind us.

Fela's music raises another dimension of black aesthetic, namely that choices of language and diction also carry inherent cultural meaning, perspectives and values. Going beyond the obvious observation that the choice between writing in English or an African language is a choice of audience (and despite sporadic debate on the subject, ought to be a writer's own choice), one can focus more usefully on the existence of linguistic varieties of English and varieties of registers. Fela's use of street-language and what in the U.S. is called Black English. A people's unique language usage is a rich repository of their experience and world-view, which can be mined by writers on various levels. Frank Aig-Imoukhuede goes to one extreme in *Pidgin Stew and Sufferhead*,[14] showing how pungently and penetratingly pidgin can be used to express the common man's view of life and its ironies. Another mush discussed, extreme example is Gabriel Okara's *The Voice*,[15] in which the thought structures of Ijaw are strikingly transposed into English.

Beyond these extremes are many other options for the utilization of non-standard and 'nonliterary' language in literature, such as employing to varying degrees the structures of the 'Nigerian English' which linguists have long been documenting. That any given usage is not found in educated speech and writing is no argument against using it in literature for a calculated effect. Street-talk is also not the language of upper-class American blacks, yet contributes much of the distinctive vitality of black literature; Afro-American writers show that even obscenities can contribute a functional drop in register in order to dramatically enhance a particular theme.

It is worth pointing out that even individual words differ, if not in meaning, in connotations and emotional context in African usage, and their employment represents yet another dimension of the black aesthetic. Earlier, Baraka's use of words such as 'white' and 'bad' were discussed; in Nigerian usage there are many words whose meanings only partially overlap the standard denotation. Furthermore, a whole group of English words carry different, often more emotional connotations in African usage, for example: 'family', 'wife', 'ancestor', 'tradition', 'dance', 'medicine', and 'sacrifice'. Part of the African aesthetic is to be found hidden in the power of such key words which represent some of the deepest cultural values and attitudes.

The final aspect of Baraka's aesthetic relevant to an examination of African literature concern identifying, creating, and using symbols, myths, and heroes relevant for the intended audience. Symbols transmit and intensify meaning. They also carry beyond the world of literature their interpretation of reality in the mind of the individual who absorbs them, hence Baraka's search for symbols to liberate the minds of his audience from the prejudices inherent in much of white culture. He is only one of many who found a vital symbol in Malcolm X, probably the most written about person in Afro-American poetry, along with Nkrumah and jazz musician John Coltrane. Other poets reinterpret history, creating myths relevant to contemporary needs, for example Robert Hayden's "Middle Passage" and "Runagate Runagate," where the experience of resistance to slavery offers a mythical pattern for the continuing strength of black Americans in their present situation.

Myths are a resource for the African writer too obvious to examine closely here, other than indicating Soyinka as the most innovative reinterpreter of myths for contemporary social issues. It would be useful to compare the values and messages embodied in black myths on both sides of the Atlantic, for further insight into shared aspects of their aesthetics, both traditionally and in recent literature.

Leopold Senghor's use of Chaka as a symbol interpreted in relationship to the struggle for independence offers an African parallel to the American concern with heroes, as does Adams Fiberisima's operatic use of Jaja of Opobo and Femi Osofisan's *Who's Afraid of Tai Solarin?* One feels an urgent need for more such positive symbols to counter the self-cynicism revealed in frequently heard comments such as calling any bold rogue "a real Nigerian." A people's heroes incarnate their deepest self-image and cultural values.

Other symbols too are used to stress vital ideals, as the strike in Sembene's *God's Bit of Wood*[16]; or in the case of Soyinka's recurrent use of 'the road,' as a nexus of abhorred trends. Symbols may rise naturally from an environment, as with 'the river' in works of Delta writers, or may be deliberately created, as when Mamman Vatsa attempts to make Abuja a symbol of national unity in his volume *The Poetry of Abuja*.[17] An examination of the recurrent symbols, myths and heroes in black literature on both sides of the Atlantic, some representing similar values, others not, will reveal other aspects of overlap in the aesthetics of Africans and Afro-Americans.

Conclusion

As we have seen, an aesthetic can be discussed from two perspectives, either as being inherent in a people's culture and literature, or more narrowly, in terms of a conscious ideology formulating prescriptions for artists to follow. From the first perspective, an aesthetic is stable and can merely be extrapolated and described; from the second, it can be shaped and altered. The aesthetic of the Black Arts Movement was conceived of as rooted in the past traditions and art of Afro-Americans, but also certain traditions were down played for the sake of enhancing others interpreted as being more fruitful and relevant for the people's needs.

The original question of whether there is a black aesthetic valid on both sides of the Atlantic border is more complex than it may have appeared. In terms of merely describing the concepts of beauty and function in the two literatures, we have seen that there are areas of congruency, and areas of divergence where the cultures significantly differ. However, when one considers the ideological, prescriptive dimension of black aesthetics, it is clear that even where there is divergence, the possibility always exists of future convergence. One can assume that black writers and critics will continue to read their counterparts on the other side of the Atlantic with deep interest, learning from one another's experience and literary experiments, and thereby be receptive to mutual influence.

Endnotes

1. Theo Vincent, "Black Aesthetic and African Literature," *West African Journal of Modern Language*, No. 2, Sept. 1976, p. 19.
2. Bruce King, "Thoughts on African Literature," *NAJML*, Sept. 1976, p. 12.
3. S.E. Ogude, "Slavery and the African Imagination: A Critical Perspective," *Modern Language Association of Nigeria* Acts of the 6th Annual Conference, Univ. of Benin, April 1980, p. 36.
4. I.A. Asiwaju, "Artificial Boundaries" inaugural lecture delivered at Univ. of Lagos, 12 Dec. 1984, p. 7.
5. Addison Gayle, Jr. (ed), *The Black Aesthetic* (New York: Doubleday, 1971).
6. Dudley Randall (ed), *The Black Poets* (New York: Bantam, 1971), p. 33.
7. LeRoi Jones, (Amiri Baraka), *The Dead Lecturer* (New York: Grove Press, 1964).
8. W.E.B. Dubois, *The Souls of Black Folk* (Greenwich, Conn.: Fawcett, 1903/1961), p. 16.
9. Amiri Baraka, *Black Magic Poetry* (New York: Bobbs-Merrill, 1969).
10. Dubois, op. cit., p. 16.
11. For a discussion in greater detail on Baraka's influence on the aesthetic of other Afro-American poets see Lynn Nwuneli, "Dimensions of Baraka's Black Aesthetic Explored in Afro-American Poetry," unpublished paper.
12. Antonio Olinto, *The Water House* (Surrey: Thomas Nelson, 1982) trans. Dorothy Heapy.
13. See Stephen Henderson, *Understanding the New Black Poetry: Black Speech and Black Music as Poetic Reference* (New York: William Morrow, 1973) for a detailed account.
14. Frank Aig-Imoukhuede, *Pigeon Stew and Sufferhead* (Ibadan: Heinemann, 1982).
15. Gabriel Okara, *The Voice* (New York: African Pub. Co., 1970).
16. Ousmane Sembene, *God's Bits of Wood* (New York: Doubleday, 1970) trans. Francis Price.
17. Mamman J. Vatsa, *The Poetry of Abuja* (Lagos: Cross Continent Press, 1982).

Bibliography

Bell, Bernard W., *The Folk Roots of Contemporary Afro-American Poetry* (Detroit: Broadside Press, 1974).
Cartey, Wilfred, *Black Images* (No. 4, Teachers College Press, Columbia Univ., 1970).
Ostendorf, Berndt, *Black Literature in White America* (Sussex: Harvester Press, 1982).
Henderson, Stephen E., and Marcer Cook, *The Militant Black Writer in Africa and The United States* (Madison: Univ. of Wisconsin Press, 1969).

CHAPTER 11

Border in French and French-African Literature

by M.A. Johnson

Introduction

Contemporary education is characterised by compartmentalisation[1] which prevents specialists from perceiving the affiliation of various disciplines. It is assumed, for example, that the concept of border is alien to some sectors of the humanities, and only relevant to geography, history, political science and sociology.

The paper refutes the above assumption in the case of literature which cuts across disciplines, and whose artisans include people of non-literary vocations. By attempting to relate border to literature, the paper brings into focus the multidisciplinary character of the subject and consequently, the multifaceted interpretations to which it may be subjected. The paper is a general survey indicating a distinct ramification of the term border or boundary in literature, in the belief that this will enrich our understanding of the concept.

From the geographical perspective, borders and boundaries both denote lines of demarcation between areas or spheres of jurisdiction of defined authorities, be these individuals or groups. But while the former generally refers to lines of divide between sovereign entities, the latter may also apply to internal demarcations. In literature, both terms are often symbolic and are, therefore, synonymous and interchangeable. Moreover, emphasis is very often not on borders and boundaries per se (even when the action has to do with actual physical barriers), but on psychological response and mental adjustment to the impact of the phenomena.

Border and boundary symbolise moderation or sense of "limits" which man must exercise in his actions. They also represent barriers to human interactions and existence. These barriers may be conditions or attitudes. They may be in form of chauvinism between races, people of opposite sex, social classes and ethnic groups. They may also be in form of antisocial behaviour which makes an individual a misfit in the society. All these aspects are briefly illustrated in different sections of this study.

The Positive Image
Border, prohibition and Human Curiosity

Border should not be seen as a completely negative feature. In fact, its existence seems to have given a new dimension to the operation of the mind. The word immediately evokes related notions such as *the hidden, the forbidden* and *the inaccessible* in contrast to the commonplace which often lacks appeal.

The hidden exerts extraordinarily influence on human imagination; it creates excitement, it generates curiosity and also deepens appreciation. This is substantiated by some African and oriental ideals such as keeping a woman intact until marriage, discouraging undue exposure of her body and making her live in confinement to shield her from the covetous gaze of others.

The hidden is enticing, according to Jean Starobinski. Dissimulation, prohibition and absence constrain the mind to seek the inaccessible and invest all in its possession on such a quest.[2]

This observation is applicable to *La Princess de Cleves,* a 17th century novel narrated against a conducive historical background--the magnificent reign of Henry II of England, an epoch when dazzling appearance was the popular means of attracting people of distinction. In the novel, Madame de la Fayette added a new dimension to gallantry in the sense that the visual supplants the physical in the mechanism of inspiration and consummation of love. Thus, the clandestine love affair between the Princess and the Duke is tactfully sustained by periodic exposure of the object of desire to kindle emotion, and by creating pretexts for absence to intensify the pursuit of the loved one.

One of the interesting aspects of the novel is the psychological nature of conflict. For example the barrier between the princess and the duke is not social compatibility but a number of considerations which generated psychological conflicts. The obstacles include Madame de Cleves' marital status, her mortal upbringing, her mother's constant surveillance and notes of warning, and the duke's entanglement with other women of the royal court.

As earlier noted, curiosity gives birth to a spirit of adventure, which may positively contribute to knowledge. It also promotes tourism which is a way of breaking the monotony of existence. This tendency, however, needs to be curbed, for it may lead to misadventure, crime and disaster.

An example is found in Camus's *Misunderstanding* in which Martha's curiosity about Africa led to successive murder of her clients as she tried to raise funds for her journey to the distant continent. The dream of Martha who imagined that a trip to Africa would end her solitary existence in Czechoslovakia did not materialise, for she murdered her own brother who came in disguise, and she ended up taking the path of suicide.

A similar incident is found in Flaubert's *Madame Bovary* in which Emma, who wanted an exciting wedlock with an eminent person ended up marrying a mediocre shabby drop-out. Under the illusion that some love affairs would colour her drab existence and offer her occasional escape from her unsuitable marriage, she gave in to adultery and lived beyond her means in order to satisfy and retain her lovers. She eventually committed suicide after series of disappointments and mismanagement culminating in the imminent auction of her property. Emma's comportment is an example of hypertrophy of imagination, which Jules de Gautheir called "bovarism". Bovarism is the evasion of reality leading to illusion about self, others and the world.

Illusion was endangered and nurtured by Flaubert's twin perception of contrasting worlds and realities, which Albert Thibaudet appropriately described as binocular technique. Contrast in character depiction also provided a magnetic force of which the heroine became a victim. Emma was attracted to Leon and Rodolphe whose personality was in contrast to that of Charles her husband, and she became trapped in an attempt to have a glimpse of the opposite reality.

Although Emma was a 19th century portrait, her likes abound in contemporary society. In recent times people are developing a queer taste for the forbidden and the rare-to-find, the possession of which leads to an air of importance. Interest in the forbidden and preference for the distant are prominent features of the mentality of some Nigerians. For example, when champagne was banned in Nigeria, it became more cherished in some social gatherings, and the Mateus rose, which is similar in taste, immediately became a substitute. Similarly, the preference of some Nigerians for holidays outside Africa has not been altered by the imposition of a special levy of 100 naira for such travels.

Border and Human Freedom

As border denotes a limit to people's sphere of authority, it also connotes prudence and caution without which our world would perpetually be in a state of chaos.

Camus's stand on rebellion, which he described as a natural response to the absurdities of life, is attenuated by the concept of *"measure"* or limit. This concept clearly separates his philosophy from Sartre's existentialism. With Sartre, man's freedom is absolute with Camus, human freedom has a boundary. Whereas in Sartre's universe, it is possible to commit matricide with impunity as Orestes did in *The Flies,* in Camus's world whoever takes a life must lay down his own. Yanek the revolutionary who killed the Tsar of Russia in order to free the people from despotism, gave himself up for justice, his laudable intention notwithstanding.

Camus's condemnation of absolute freedom is unequivocal in *The Just Assassins* in which he contrasted Yanek's sense of moderation to Stepan's ruthlessness and nihilism. Unlike Stepan who would have destroyed Moscow in his plan to eliminate the head, Yanek refrained from throwing a bomb when the Tsar was in the company of some innocent children.

Absolute freedom leads to inordinate destruction the outcome of which is self-elimination as we find in Camus's *Caligula.* The protagonist of the play is an eccentric emperor who wanted to hold the moon in his hands and who though that he could destroy everything and still remain alive. His mental state show that he was no longer within the confines of rationally. He has crossed the border of humanity since his traumatic discovery of the finality of death, and has been trapped in the world of savagery. His monstrous desires led to the insurgence of Patricians who assassinated him to avert further disaster. Camus evoked this negative portrait in *The State of Siege* in his depiction of the Plague who dethroned the governor of Cadiz. The Plague's unlimited powers and delight in destruction would have annihilated Cadiz but for Diego who forced the tyrant to capitulate.

Border and Human Stability

Life is a challenge to do the best we can under varying conditions. It is an opportunity for us to develop the power of right action. But the opportunity is often compromised by the tendency to follow the course of least resistance.

History has recorded spectacular mass movement of people including emigration from France during the revolution and from some other European countries during the industrial revolution. Although the former is justified by political instability and the latter by population explosion which was matched with unemployment, such movements had devastating effects on the countries and regions concerned. Between 1821 and 1924 about 65 million people are estimated to have left Europe for other parts of the globe. But for restrictive measures at borders (demand for visa and passport), to curtail movement, emigration and immigration would be incomputable. The entire human race would have become a rolling stone.

While we would agree that man cannot achieve equilibrium without movement, we would want to stress that movement does not solve every human problem. It is implied in the teachings of naturalists that adaptability is a vital part of man's make up. From Claude Bernard's theories on intra-organic milieu, exponents of naturalism, Emile Zola in particular, held that man produces the environment which transforms him in return; and that human propensities are determined by the physical environment. Man is therefore expected to survive wherever there are human beings. The assertion is well demonstrated by Albert Camus in *The Plague,* a novel which narrates the experience of Rambert, a European journalist trapped in Oran following the outbreak of a plague.

Oran is a north African town which Camus described as ugly, dull, impassable, an embodiment of emptiness and boredom.[3] The social climate notwithstanding, Rambert survived in the town for an unknown period. Lack of option impelled him to make the best of his situation. His initial feeling of estrangement gave way to a sense of belonging and compassion for the infested. This won him acceptance and affection which made him reluctant to leave when the gates of Oran were at last reopened.

In many of his works, Camus placed deeper brotherhood above pretty nationalism, and one would expect Rambert's option to be for integration rather than for self-alienation. However, his choice must have been facilitated by the ethnic composition of Oran, the population being a mixture of blacks and Europeans from Spain, France, Italy, Greece and Malta.[4]

Man's natural ability to adjust is again demonstrated in Camara Lay's *Radiance of the King,* a novel which portrays a European seeking acceptance in an African society. Clarence made his way through series of obstacles. His accent was difficult, for it required purging himself of prejudices, casting aside his garment of pride and totally subjecting his body and soul. But he rose above all barriers and made the adjustments required for social integration.

The Negative Image

Border and Human Progress

From the complementary structure of the continents and the affinities in the climate, vegetation, mode of expression and ethnic make-up of some contiguous coasts, geographers advanced the theory of continental drift. They argued that the world was at first a single land mass and that it was fractured into continents with bodies of water in-between.

The above theory reveals that even the natural borders are relics of geographical accidents. When traced to their origin, natural borders attest to the unity of the earth and the natural connection of its peoples. They, therefore, project man-made borders as an extension of the gap which nature has created between men.

Border as a concept contradicts the principle of unity and the primary of oneness which have been the basis of reality since the redirection of physics by Albert Einstein and others. Borders are confines which frustrate man's effort to reach out for others and be touched. They limit man's mental expansion by concealing from his vision certain facets of knowledge and consequently falsifying his idea of knowledge which is the overall perception of the multiple relationships between people and thing, the apprehension of the natural connection of the part and the totality.[5]

Border confines and falsifies one's evaluation of the world as observed in Voltaire's *Candide*. Like Panglos, his master, Candide believed that "all is good" until travels and adventures exposed him to the gloomy sides of human existence. He witnessed war, shipwreck, racial discrimination, looting and human sacrifice. He experienced famine, earthquake and imprisonment and he met other people whose experiences were worse. After his travels round the world, his excessive optimism succumbed to a more reasonable philosophy of hard work.

Border is an enemy of progress when it serves no other purpose than to obstruct, for man cannot progress without access to his fellowmen, nor can communities advance if their intercourse is restricted to their immediate neighbourhood. Sentimental attachment to one's confines often results in total indifference to what other places have to offer. This tendency is nothing but "local patriotism". Local patriotism is a common feature in African literature in which the incentives for travels aborad are formal education and prospects of employment rather than for the deeper pleasure of discovering the world. Local patriots regard separation from their loved ones and displacement from their usual decor as a torment. Some characters in Camara Laye's *African Child* are good examples. When the protagonist was to travel to France for further studies, everybody in his house was in tears. His mother was inconsolable, as she only thought of the difficulty her son would encounter and not the advantages of the separation. Only his father, who knew that the journey was for a good purpose, gave him the moral support he needed.

Local patriots feel bored outside their habitual setting even when they are in another African country. For example, Climbie's fascination for Senegal and the excitement of being a student at Ecole Normale William Ponty in Dakar all evaporated after three years of sojourn in the Island of Goree. Two weeks before his departure, he had no other preoccupation but the home-coming. He and his alien comrades dragged the weight of their nostalgia through the streets of the Island. In Seydou Badian's *Sous L'orage,* villagers and urban dwellers are separated by a variety of prejudices and the two groups view one another with reciprocal antipathy. Villagers are repelled by the self-centredness and indifference of town's people while the latter, represented by Birama and Kany, are disgusted by the repellent odour, queer beliefs and animism of the former.

Local patriotism or refusal to see beyond one's geographical confines is a symptom of maladjustment which may create unsurmountable obstacles to mutual acceptance in the host/guest situation that people find themselves when they travel.

Border: Symbol of Alienation

Another example of maladjustment is self-sequestration, the erection of barriers between the self and others. Self-sequestration is very often rooted in a feeling of insecurity and the tendency to create imaginary enemies for oneself. It connotes separate existence which procures nothing but loneliness. An example may be drawn from *Reveries du promeneur solitaire,* Rousseau's meditation on himself and his society.

Rousseau's fervent belief in the precepts of nature led to some errors of commission and omission such as bringing up his five children with Therese Levasseur in an orphanage. His deviant social behaviour, quarrel-some nature, Bohemian life style and radical ideas about society incited sour criticisms which led to the rather hasty conclusion that ideas about society incited sour criticism which led to the rather hasty conclusion that society had contrived to bury him alive. Persecution mania deprived him of the friendship of his contemporaries, and eroded his being so profoundly, that he felt completely devoid of brotherhood, neighbourliness, friendship and other social ties:

> Me voici donc seul sur la terre, n'ayant plus de frere, de prochain, d'ami,
> de societe que moi-meme.[6]

But Rousseau was not devoid of lucidity. He was conscious of his bizarre nature. He knew that his impassability and distance from his fellowmen were unnatural and could only depict him as a monster.[7] *Reveries du promeneur solitaire* was not intended for self-exoneration or total condemnation of society. Like *Dialogues* and *Confessions,* the novel was meant to be Rousseau's self-evaluation and a search for his actual self.[8]

Neutral Consideration
Border in relation to Humanity and Animality

Border in its extended meaning is applicable to mental operations. Let us first of all consider the distinction between man and animal; In support of scientists, who claimed that men can think while animals cannot, Rene Descartes asserted that though is the only proof of human existence: "Je pense, donc je suis"[9] (I think, therefore, I am). But the philosopher did not dilate on the originality of thought, a major preoccupation among some modern writers, one of the most outstanding being Eugene Ionesco.

Ionesco's assessment of modern society is based on the Cartesian idea that only those who think are really living as Jean told Berenger in *Rhinoceros*.[10] The subject of the play is the contention that modern society is permeated by mass-thinking and social conformism otherwise known as "rhinoceritis", a label derived from the title of the play. Rhinoceritis is a contagious social malady with recognisable symptoms such as blind imitation, lack of originality in speech, preponderance of cliches and preconceived ideas in ones language, and herd instinct or sympathy for majority.

Ironically, logic is one of the recipes cleverly used for indicating the absence of rationally in human communication. Thus, the logician, one of those representing the intellectuals in the play, cam e out with propositions like:" A cat is mortal. Socrates is mortal. Therefore, Socrates is a cat".[11] The transmutation which Ionesco used as denouement is an open declaration that modern man has lost his thinking cap and has crossed the border of his natural domain as a thinking animal. *Rhinoceros* challenges man's superiority to animals. It is a pessimistic depiction of modern man who has lost his identify by becoming an object of manipulation. Even Berenger, the non-conformist, nearly lost his sanity in the end. He deeply regretted not becoming a rhinoceros like others, and it was for lack of alternative that he summed up courage to defend humanity.[12]

More than a century before *Rhinoceros* was written, man's status as a superior animal had been challenged. Alfred de Vigny demonstrated in a poem that man has descended below the level of animal as a result of inhuman dispositions. In "La Mort du Loup" (the death of a wolf, 1843) a male wolf trapped and killed by some ruthless hunters, demonstrated a courage and stoic resignation which the poet idealised in the following verse:

Seul le silence est grand, tout le reste est faiblesse.[13]

Vigny exalted the wolf to portry the superiority of the natural animal world to the so called civilized society in which people killing. The wolf's comportment gave heartless hunters some food for thought. It showed them how to face death with courage and dignity.

Between the Living and the Dead

As intelligence, thinking faculty and articulated language are recognised as boundaries between man and animal, so is freedom regarded as the border between the living and the dead.

Life and death are distinct conditions with different modes of operation. From the observation that "being is doing"[14] one tends to support Jean-paul Sartre's statement that transition from one condition to the other implies passage from a state of dynamism and freedom to one of idleness and complacency. Contrary to the African belief that the departed is busy seeking the interest of his or her survivors, Sartre's opinion is that the dead has no freedom of choice and cannot undertake any purposeful enterprise. With him death is a finality and this has been demonstrated in many of his books.

No Exit is a conversation between three dead characters—Ines, Estelle and Garcin, who saw themselves in terms of their past desires instead of their concret achievements. Sartre stressed the futility of their wish to repair their dented image when it was too late. Man's essence, he argued, is the aggregate of his actions when he is alive. After death, a line is drawn, and nothing else can be stated below except the sum total:

On meurt toujours trop tot ou trop tard.
Et cependant la vie est la terminee:
le trait est tire, il faut faire la somme.
Tu n'es rien d'autre que ta view.[15]

In Sarte's writings, we also find that people who are inactive or have been deprived of their freedom share the fate of the dead. An example is Frantz *(Altona)* the military officer who, after committing murder, was declared dead by his father in order to evade justice and avert a family scandal. The false declaration nullified his freedom. He could no longer function as a living being and he remained sequestered in the family house for the rest of his life.

Existentialists believe that man's essence is unchangeable, contrary to the theory of reincarnation which gives room for atonement, perfection and accomplishment of goals unattained. Sartre demonstrated in *Les Jeux sont faits* (The game is over) that opportunity for continued existence does not make a man what he is not.

In the play, Pierre and Eve extended their lease on life under article 140 which accords lovers, who did not meet when they were alive, the right to live again. But the gratification of their wish did not last, for many obvious reasons. First, they had no common goal. Pierre wished to bring his social struggle to fruition while Eve wanted to punish Andre her husband, who poisoned her in order to have another marriage of convenience with her sister. Secondly, they were not in love; their union was based on falsehood. Thirdly, they could not change their essence. Pierre gave priority to the workers struggle and this led to separation which revoked thie right to existence. Lastly, they were socially incompatible. Eve was a wealthy woman while Pierre was an ordinary worker.

As wife of the Secretary to the Militia, Eve belonged to the camp of the workers' enemy. Pierre's entanglement with her led to his rejection by his comrades who, out of indignation and disappointment, disregarded his profitable warnings. The workers were scattered like sheep without a sheperd. The militia triumphed and Pierre's action was abruptly terminated. He was shot again and Eve collapsed.

The failure of the characters mirror the idea of border from another angle, one of the barriers between them being their social class. Pierre and Eve belong to two distinct social classes: the proletariat and the bourgeoisie whose values and standards are direct opposites. In Sartre's writings, the bourgeoisie is often depicted as a groupf of conservative, unscrupulous capitalists who are enslaved by their own selfish interest. A typical example is Andre, the venomous opportunist who tried to repair his lost fortune by a marriage of convenience with his sister-in-law. The proletariat, on the other hand, is regarded as a victim of social injustice, the class to determine the future, and "the only class capable of effecting a radical change in society".[16]

Conclusion

Although literature depicts an imaginery universe of fictitious characters, it is essentially a reflection of real life and actual human experience as again supported by this study. This paper has shown that border is applicable to literature both in its restricted and extended connotations, although the bulk of the evidences seem to belong to the second category.

Some literary evidences show that borders are a symbol of alienation and barriers in man's path towards happiness and progress. Some other literary evidences indicate that borders help man to feel secure and uniue and that they promote curiosity, sense of discovery, sense of belonging and resourcefulness. The conclusions which may be drawn from all these are the following:

1. Although borders are sometimes necessary, they should not degenerate into prison walls which deprive the enclose the freedom to interact with the outer world.
2. For progress, meaningful existence and deeper understanding of the world, man must look beyond his geographical confines.
3. Man should not be self-reliant to the extent of seeing himself as an Island, for he is inextricably bound to his fellowmen.
4. On a moral level, border and boundary connote sense of moderation which man is expected to demonstrate in all his actions and desires.

Endnotes

1. A.I. Asiwaju, *Artificial boundaries* inaugural lecture, (Lagos: Univ. of Lagos Press, 1984) p. 12.
2. Jean Starobinski, *L'Oeil vivant* (Paris: Gallimard, 1961) p. 9.
3. Albert Camus, "Le Minotaure" in *Essais* (Paris: Gallimard, 1965) pp. 813-832.
4. Ibid., p. 848.
5. Paul Claudel, *Art poetique* (Paris: Mercure de France, 1907) p. 48.
6. Jean-Jacques Rousseau, *Reverie du promeneur solitaire* (Paris: Gallimard, 1965) p. 29.
7. Ibid., pp. 30 & 43.

8. Ibid., p. 29.

9. Rene Descartes, *Discours de la methode* (1537), part 3 where he further asserted that animals have no soul, no articulated language and no intelligence but instincts.

10. Eugene Ionesco, *Rhinoceros* (New York: Holt Rinehart and Winston, 1961) pp. 60-61.

11. Ibid., p. 61.

12. Ibid., p. 192.

13. Alfred de Vigny, *Les Destinees* in *Poesies choisies* (Paris: Larousse, 1864) pp. 91-94, Stanza 111.

14. Jean-Paul Sartre, *Being and Nothingness,* trans. by Hazel E. Barnes, (London: Methuen, 1957) p. 433.

15. Jean-Paul Sartre, *Huis clos* (Paris: Gallimard, 1947) p. 73.

16. Germaine Bree, *Sartre and Camus* (New York: Dell Pub. Co., 1972) p. 68.

CHAPTER 12

Boundary Problems and the Policies of African Nations: A Materials Engineering Approach

by D.A. Aderibigbe

Introduction

There is now a universal acceptance of the concept of boundaries associated with nation-states in Africa. However, within the last three decades, many scholars have tried to analyze the implications of these artificial boundaries in Africa, from considerations of diplomacy (especially international relations, law and politics) as well as the cultural, social and economic activities across such boundaries. Notable amongst such scholars are Anene,[1] Prescott,[2] McEwen[3] and Touval[4] whose works have been given a brief but critical appraisal by Asiwaju[5] in his edited book titled, "Partitioned Africans: Ethnic Relations across Africa's International boundaries, 1884-1984." The emphasis of Asiwaju in the book is on the role of the 'human factor' in Africa's international boundaries and he recognised the fact that the socio-cultural situations is an important factor which may involve "clandestine activities across the border; activities which have on occasions posed serious threats to state security and a more or less permanent challenge to the economy."

However, from a global perspective or what may be considered a systems approach, it appears that all the known analyses of the "issues of borderlands in Africa" have underplayed the role which *materials* have played and will continue to play in the overall stability and survival of African nations. Hitherto, the role of materials has been recognised, as basically that of commodities of trade across the boundaries. It is possible that this viewpoint is reinforced by the nature of the economy of most African nations which is dependent essentially on commercial trading across the boundaries (e.g. oil, inorganic minerals and agricultural products) in exchange for imported finished goods and the high level technology (such as, engineering, agriculture and medicine.)

However, it should be recognised that the nature of universal change will make it mandatory for a nation to progress through appropriate level of development and in such a situation, the type of economy based upon mercantile trading in basic raw materials across the boundaries of nation-states is bound to give way to an economy that will be sustained largely by internal processing and production of basic commodities. Thus, there will be a need t o re-appraise the nature of problems which may arise across the boundaries so that an appropriate combination of policies can be formulated by the relevant government to ensure the stability and economic buoyancy of the country. Already, signs of this gradual change are manifested in many African countries, such as Nigeria, Kenya, Ghana, Ivory Coast, and Senegambia, which are grappling with the problems associated with the transition from a trading to an industrializing country.

If we further recognize that materials have historically interacted with human behaviours and with man's intellectual and social structures to the extent that the concept of the 'Ages of Man' during evolution is based upon materials (for example, the Golden and Silver Ages of the Greeks; the Stone, Bronze and Iron Ages of the archaeologists), then, it is possible to share the viewpoint of Cyril Smith[6] that "because of the inconspicuous ubiquity of materials and the constancy of their individual properties they serve as a fine touchstone to reveal man's individual and social characteristics." In other words, if we can understand the nature of materials it is possible to understand the nature of man and correspondingly his society.

This, certainly, is a materialistic approach which is pertinent because our earth with its solar system is composed, according to Paul Twitchell,[7] only of matter, energy, space and time, it embraces both non-living and living matter including the human constitution. In this context, materialism should not be associated with the negative attributes of narrow-mindedness, self-interest, creature comfort and crass achievement. The materials engineer is that person who in the words of Morris Cohen[8] is "Committed to the study, or the production, or the application of materials"—whether metals, ceramics, polymers, or other classes of materials, "to serve the practical needs of the society."

It is against this professional bias that this paper is presented. The intention is to share observations on the similarities between the materials system and the human social system, with a view to adapting the well defined approach to solving boundary problems in materials systems to that of the "issues of borderlands (i.e. boundary problems) and the policies of African nations which is the topic for discussion in this paper.

In order to put the presentation in the proper perspective, I would first like to discuss some of the basic definitions and similarities between materials, man and the society. This will be followed by a discussion on methods for solving boundary (valued) problems in materials system. With this background, a philosophical model for tackling the problems of borderlands in African nations will be presented from a global perspective. Some of the present policies of some African nations will then be examined in the context of interactions in the boundary regions. Finally recommendations would be presented to effect a positive attitude to tackle the issues of border regions, so as to ensure peaceful co-existence and economic survival of African nations.

Basic Definitions and Similarities: Materials, Man and Society

In materials systems, the determination of the effect of the environment on the state of rest (i.e. equilibrium state) of a given system is assigned to the field of applied thermodynamics. Here, a system is defined as that portion of the universe (matter) under consideration. There are three types of thermodynamic systems:

(a) A *closed system* is a portion of the universe (matter) of fixed identity (e.g.

constant mass) enclosed within a well defined boundary, either material or imaginary, across which particles of matter do not pass. The boundary can move while heat and work may cross the boundary.

(b) An open system is a portion (or region) of the universe having a well defined boundary, material or imaginary, across which particles of matter may flow in addition to work and heat.

(c) In an *isolated* system, neither heat nor work may flow across the boundary.

The surrounding of a system is that region or space external to the system that is influenced by the changed occurring in the system. A system is specified by its instantaneous condition or *state*. The state on the other hand is specified by the *properties* of the system at a particular instant. The thermodynamic property of a system at any given state must be measurable at any instant without any knowledge of the previous history of the system. Some of these characteristic properties may include temperature, pressure, volume, composition as well as electric, magnetic and gravitational forces.

In drawing a parallel (or similarities) between the materials system and the human social system, one is bound to note the observation by Boulding[9] that "many objects in sociology, economics, biology and other sciences may be regarded as populations with the appropriate characteristics; a common feature of almost all systems of diverse nature, from crystal to human society, are subject to the laws of growth that can be presented in a unified and sufficiently rigorous form." In this respect, the classification of the human social system is analogous to that of the materials system and this is portrayed in the book written by the Russian trio— Blauberg, Sadovsky and Yudin—titled *Systems Theory: Philosophical and Methodological Problems* (Progress Publisher, Moscow, 1977). The basic difference is that instead of the isolated and closed systems of materials, the authors recognised 'absolutely closed' and 'relatively closed' systems after Bertalanffy[10] and Klir.[11] As a matter of fact, Bertalanffy believed that the general systems theory is "not limited to material systems but applies to any "whole" consisting of interacting "components". Thus, as shown in Figure 1, the materials system boundary and surroundings have their correspondence in the artificial boundaries and the environment, respectively, of African nations. As pointed out by Hall and Fagen, "the environment is the set of all objects, a change in whose attributes affects the system and also objects whose attributes are changed by the behaviour of the system."[12]

The Universal Structure of Change

The implication of the foregoing basic definitions is that any change in the condition or state of a system (either thermodynamic or social) may provide an opportunity for a new *phase*. In materials system a phase is defined as that portion within the system that is chemically homogeneous, physically distinct and mechanically separable. However, it is known that most materials of practical interest are composed of many phases and hence are heterogeneous. This is analogous to the heterogeneous nature of the social system within African nations. This concept of heterogeneity in a time-dependent physical universe highlights the dynamic nature of both the material and the human social system, and which is manifested in the universal structure of change.

This is illustrated in Figure 2 by the S-curve of a phase transformation in materials systems, such as during the hardening of steels. According to Cyril Smith,[6] the S-curve depicts "the beginning, growth and maturity of anything whatever." It

Figure 1. Schematic of the analogy between open thermodynamic and social systems.

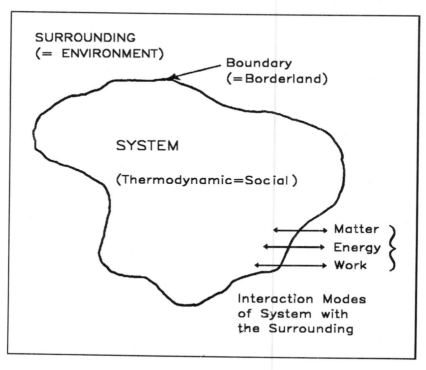

may therefore be used to illustrate, for example, "the beginnings of most branches of technology in the decorative arts, their industrial growth in response to a social demand, and their maturity in conflict and balance with other things. Both the beginning and the end depend on highly localized conditions and are unpredictable in detail". Thus, while the U.S.A. can be inferred to have reached 'maturity' in terms of the level of industrialization, Nigeria, Kenya and many other African nations (the so called industrializing nations) may be seen to be at the level of incipient growth on the S-curve.

The S-curve can also be used to demonstrate the nature of evolution in the social system. Here, one would like to agree with Morris Cohen[8] that "evolution does not flow along in a smooth, orderly manner. It actually works by trial-and-error, by adverse stepwise processes. Every little change that happens gets tested in competition with other little changes in the surroundings. Those phenomena or configurations or species which can take advantage of the existing conditions have a favourable chance to develop further; other variations which fail to compete do not flourish or lose out entirely. A given form (like the dinosaur) which succeeds prodigiously at some time and location may disappear with barely a trace if it cannot adapt rapidly enough to the changing environment. In fact, another species—slow to become established previously—may accommodate better to the new surroundings and thus emerge more prominently with the passage of time". Those who are devoted to studying phase transformation in materials systems are very familiar with

Figure 2. The S-curve of phase transformation in materials illustrating the universal structure of change.

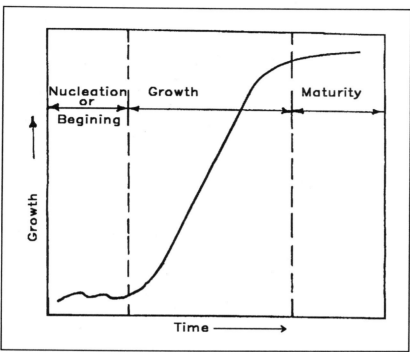

"structural changes involving nucleation and growth, leading to completely new states, only to find that slower processes often take over later in competition".

Cyril Smith[6] pointed out that we should be aware of "how the superposition of many small sequential S-curves themselves tend to add up to the giant S-curve of that new and larger structure which we call civilization." Thus, it is expected that the government of nations should be worried about the new combination of policies can be nucleated to prevent decay in the social system. This is more so because "the termination of one S-curve marks the limit of growth of one idea or policy; the continuation of the envelope marks the growth of a superstructure, incorporating, modifying, and sometimes eliminating, the previous stages within a larger organisation (such as the human social system)."

It is with this realization of the dynamic nature of change in all systems (material and social) that one would like to appeal to African nations to be conscious of the nature of changes around their borders so as to evolve meaningful policies for the survival of their nation-states. However, before we discuss how to go about achieving this, it will be necessary to examine the methodology of tackling boundary problems in materials system.

Boundary (Valued) Problems in Materials System

In a materials system, the transfer of matter and energy across the boundary is usually employed to change the state and phase of the system. The process by which matter is transported from one part of a system to another is called *diffusion*. This takes place as a result of random molecular motions which is also account for energy transfers, such as by thermal conduction and convection with the system.

However, in order to model the physical phenomena of mass and energy transfer, idealized systems are sometimes used to simulate as closely as possible the real systems. Thus, it is possible to assume that the material system is *isotropic* (i.e. the structure, diffusion and thermal properties in the neighbourhood of any point in the system are the same relative to all directions) or *anisotropic* (i.e. different properties in different directions.) Similarly, since practical materials are heterogenous in structure, it may be assumed that either the heterogeneity is as a result of particulates, in which discrete particles of one phase are dispersed in a continuum of another or it is a consequence of laminates, comprising layers of different properties sandwiched together. In either case the mathematical model of the system becomes very involved. Without going into details of the rigorous mathematical representation of physical science, which is well documented in the literature,[13-14] I will highlight the basic principles involved as they relate to boundary (valued) problems.

The general approach to predicting the behaviour or performance of the material system is to take advantage of the universal laws of conservation of both matter and energy. This is done by establishing a material and an energy balance across a defined elemental or control volume within the system. For example, the statement for the material balance of a component, A, being transported across the boundary of an elemental or control volume of the system will be of the form;

Rate of material output of A from control volume	−	Rate of material input of A from control volume	+	Rate of accumulation of A within control volume	=	Rate of degeneration of A within control volume

For the control volume, this statement will yield a differential equation in terms of the space- and time-dependent variables of the component in the system. Such an equation is generally called the material balance or *continuity* equation. The solution to this equation which is expected to predict the behaviour of the system is such that it must satisfy all the known initial and boundary conditions of the system. Thus an acceptable model of the material system must be that which satisfies the known conditions operating at the boundary of the system. For example, at the interface between two phases of different properties (P_1 & P_2, say) for component A, the boundary condition will be the application of the conservation principle such that: (a) the value of the properties are the same at the interface (i.e. $P_1 = P_2$ at the interface); (b) the flux of the diffusing species must be the same in the neighbourhood of the interface. In addition, if the values of the independent variables such as pressure and temperature at the interface are known, the they constitute the boundary conditions which must be satisfied.

It is noted that although the strength of the physical science lies in the prediction of the behaviour of materials systems given the initial and boundary conditions, yet one cannot use it to reconstruct historical events. This is why statistical methods are adopted to establish correlations, if any, amongst the identified variables of historical events. Thus, any proven theoretical or empirical correlation of the behaviour of the boundary of any system can always serve as input to specify the boundary conditions of the system which must be satisfied before the solution can be considered acceptable or optimal for the system.

If one applies this procedure to the behaviour of the human social system, it can be seen that for any given social system (i.e. with identifiable political and social structure), an acceptable combination of policies by the government must be that which must tend to satisfy the conditions operating at the boundary of the system. Such conditions are well known on the basis of historical facts or by prevailing circumstances, although in a qualitative sense. In practical systems (whether materials or social), the various boundary conditions are not mutually exclusive and this is why in adopting the global or systems approach the analyst must recognise the interaction effects amongst variables in the method adopted for the solution. For the human social system, this implies a multidisciplinary approach to evolving an optimal combination of policies for any nation state. However, this statement should not be seen as suggesting that a rigorous mathematical model can be formulated that will eliminate the problems of the issues of borderland in African nations. Instead, the attempt here is to increase our perspective on the multidisciplinary approach required to evolve meaningful policies in respect of behaviour across national boundaries, so that government can, in the words of Asiwaju,[5] "Convert them from hostility-oriented functions as lines of exclusion to more productive, more harmonious, and from the viewpoint of traditional African history, more defensible roles as line of mutual contact and inclusion."

A Philosophical Model for Obtaining Optimal Policies

In developing a philosophical model that will seek to guide African nations to evolve meaningful (or optimal) combination of policies for economic progress and the security of the systems (i.e. respective nations) it will be presumed that any given African nation, which constitutes a social system, has a well defined political and social structure. This is necessary to establish the availability of a functional government that can be charged with the responsibility of formulating policies. This social system (the nation) can therefore be said to be demarcated by the international boundaries, historically imposed by the colonialists. Such boundaries are now accepted realities and nobody can pretend that they do not exist. The description of the national social system is also applicable to intranational system, whereby within a given country, there exist internal boundaries amongst the states or regions which make up the country.

For the national social system, the primary objective can be described as the guarantee of maximum security and economic buoyancy of the nation. In order to achieve this objective, the independent variables at the disposal of nation-states, either within the boundary of the social system or external to it, are the human and material resources. However, it should be recognised that the government of nation-states usually harness the two independent but interactive variables through a number of dependent variables which are generally classified as the *policies* of nation-states. Such policies are manifested in the establishment of many social disciplines (both within and outside the system boundary), in the form of national policies related to both internal and foreign affairs (i.e. law, diplomacy and international relations), economy, industrialization, defence, educational and so on.

Although these policies are set by the central government, it is the contention here that since the implementation of such policies must necessarily spread to the border regions and beyond, then an acceptable (or optimal) combination of policies is that which satisfies the conditions at the boundaries. For this to happen, the combination of acceptable policies must be not in conflict with survival objectives of

Figure 3. Philosophical model of a system (or global) approach applied to the boundary problems of social systems.

Objective: Optimize the policies (economic, industrial, defence, foreign, etc.) such that the security and the Economic bouyancy of the system can be maximized.

Independent variables: Human and material resources.

Contraints: Effectiveness of policies at the boundary and financial resources.

Dependent variables: All policies (economic, industrial, defence, foreign, etc.).

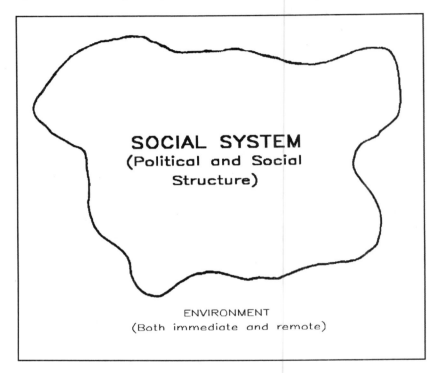

neighbouring nation-states (i.e. the environment of the system); it must be in harmony with the neighbouring systems objectives if there is an irreconcilable imbalance at the boundary region to the extent that the weaker nation is unable to adapt and cope with the policies of the stronger nation, then the universal law of change, which is aptly put by Herbert Spencer's phrase of "survival of the fittest", will operate. In this context, the surrounding or the environment of a social system should not be taken as referring only to contiguous or adjacent nation-states; it may also be very remote (or distant) but powerful nation-states. For example, the policies enacted by the nation-states of Britain, Germany, Japan, U.S.A. and U.S.S.R. may have a very devastating rippling effect on the economic survival of a developing or industrializing African nation such as Nigeria.

From the foregoing, the statement of the philosophical model which is illustrated in Figure 3 may be put as follows:

a given nation-state (i.e. social system) optimizes the national policies with respect to interactions between the human and material resources such that the nation will have the benefit of maximum security and economic buoyancy to sustain her continued development and growth within the constraints of financial resources and the effect of such policies along the borderland regions.

Such a philosophical model can only be effective if a multidisciplinary approach is adopted so that the cost-benefit aspect of each policy can be assessed in relation to the effect on the overall objective of the nation-state. This approach offers the possibility for nation-states to identify unnecessary policies whose effects may be negligible or diversionary. With this background, some of the policies or some African nations, in particular that of Nigeria, will now be examined. The primary focus will be on the economic and industrial, policies. These policies are so inter-related that they cannot be treated as mutually exclusive.

Economic and Industrial Policies

The discussion on the economic and industrial policies of some African countries will be presented against the observation by the American anthropologists, Fred Plog and Daniel Bates,[15] on the nature of "industrialism in a Global Society." After examining some of the complex manifestations of industrialization in a global sense, they came to the conclusion that:

> although wealth may be more concentrated causing differentiation between classes to increase, cultural and ethnic diversity has decreased, resulting in greater world-wide similarity *within* class lines. Industrialism draws people all over the world into one global system. Products are manufactured from raw materials grown or extracted on one continent, assembled on another continent, and sold on still another.

The evolution of this large-scale interdependence in the global industrial economy has created the multi-national corporations from the developed countries of America, Europe, Japan and USSR. The operating budget of these corporations exceed those of most African nations. As pointed out by Plog and Bates, "through expansion and diversification, global enterprises have insulated themselves from political and market pressures, creating what amounts to a privately run world economy." In essence, these multinational corporations operate beyond the reach of national governments and they play a dominant role in shaping the present and future of all nation-states. The magnitude of their presence in Africa can be assessed by trying to find out how many African nations are indebted to the International Monetary Fund (IMF) or are contemplating on borrowing money from it.

Economic Policy

In Nigeria, the 1985 Budget of the military government is very indicative of the economic policies to be embarked upon by the country. The primary objectives are five-fold: (1) to accelerate agricultural production, especially food and raw materials; (2) to reduce inflation; (3) to stimulate industrial production; (4) to achieve a healthy balance of payments position and (5) to increase and mobilize domestic and foreign capital.

In spite of the high debt-service ratio of 44% and the increasing rate of unemployment and the hardship of inflation, many Nigerians consider the policies as necessary burden to bear for the revival of the depressed economy. Of particular importance is the changing nature of the Nigerian economy as a consequence of the new policies: a move to change from traditional mercantile trading in oil, essential and non-essential commodities across the border, to that of internal production of essential agro-allied commodities and industrial products. This drastic change which is being forced on Nigerians because of the lapses of the previous government and by the nature of change, can be seen on the Universal S-curve (Fig. 2) to mark the point in time of incipient growth if only the nation will survive and adapt.

To achieve these objectives, the government needs to pay particular attention to the way the economic policies are implemented in the border areas, bearing in mind their effects on both immediate—and remote—surrounding nation-states. In this regard, the economic policies have to be backed by an appropriate combination of other policies (e.g. Industrial, Defence, Foreign, Educational, etc.) to guarantee the survival and the revamping of the Nigerian economy. In a situation where there is an imbalance in the nature of commercial activities across the artificial and porous borders with adjacent nations that view their economy with similar importance, it is noted that, "significant gains for one state would be more immediately felt as a significant loss for a neighbour. Retaliation would also be both possible and probable."[16] It is therefore recommended that African nations should "harmonize their economic policies including their prices" through regional organizations such as ECOWAS.

Industrial Policy

Closely related to the economic stability and self-reliance of a nation is the issue of industrialization within the context of a global economy. The government of every developing nation in Africa and elsewhere believes that there is need to industrialize in order to have a leverage that may guarantee both the security and the economic buoyancy of the nation. In order to appreciate the importance of this thinking, especially by African nations which are trying to industrialize, it will be necessary to find answers to some basic questions: What is industrialization? If not, what are the guidelines for a meaningful industrialization policy which would seek to guarantee the economic self-reliance and the security of such nation?

One useful and relevant definition of industrialization is that provided by Plog and Bates.[15] According to them, "Industrialization refers to the development of specialized productive units, utilizing concentrated forms of solar energy—fossil fuel—through highly mechanized procedures. These specialized units include not only the familiar one—the factories, warehouses and showrooms—but also the mechanized field of agro-industry that interconnects the specialized subsystems forming today's global economy." In essence, the definition recognizes the creative attribute of man to harness energy for manipulating materials to form productive units than can serve the needs of man. This, of course, is the basis of materials engineering.

In order to answer the second question of whether African nations do have any coordinated industrial policy, it will be necessary to appraise the performance of some key industries in some industrializing African countries.

The "oil boom" of the 1970s in Nigeria led to the initiation of a number of industrial activities which the policy makers then thought would transform the country into a rapidly developing industrial nation. For example, between 1972 and 1982, in the automobile sector, Nigeria established four main motor vehicle assembly plants: Peugeot Automobile Nigeria (PAN), Volkswagen of Nigeria (VON), Leyland Nigeria and Steyr Nigeria. Within the same period, Kenya, the second biggest African motor vehicle market after Nigeria, established three main assembly plants: Leyland Kenya. What is noticeable from the names of the various assembly plants is that they involve partnership by both Nigeria and Kenya with multinational automobile corporations.

If industrialization is taking place in a country under this type of partnership arrangement, it should be expected that the local content value of the assembled motor vehicle would increase with time to meet the expected target agreed upon by the African nation. In the case of Kenya, according to a report by Onyango Omotto in the March 1985 issue of the African Business Magazine, "the percentage of locally made parts and components was intended to rise from zero to 45 percent with five years." This objective has not been realised even after over ten years of assembly operation. However, it is reported that within certain assembly plants, the local content equivalent of 30 per cent was realized.

The situation in Nigeria is worse because considering the population of Nigeria, which is about six times that of Kenya, none of the motor vehicle assembly plants can boast of local content equivalent of up to 20 per cent. By 1983, with the depressed state of the Nigerian economy, which resulted in an acute shortage of imported spare parts and a general concern for why the local content input has been so low, the Volkswagen of Nigeria, managed to import Completely Knocked Down (CKD) parts to put three totally new models—Gold, Jetta and Santana—into the Nigerian market in addition to both the Beetle and the Passat TS models. In a country where there is a well-coordinated policy of industrialization, it should be obvious that changing the model of a motor vehicle when there is no noticeable form of industrial base will only preclude and destabilize any effort by the local entrepreneur to invest in local spare parts production that would increase the local content equivalent participation in the assembly. With the continuously increasing prices of assembled motor vehicles, it is doubtful whether Nigeria and Kenya are benefitting in full from the local motor vehicle assembly operations.

In the Iron and Steel sector, the predominant policy objectives of successive Nigerian governments have been:

(a) The optimal utilization of available local resources and endowments in manufacturing operations; and

(b) Import-substitution and the manufacture of essential constructional steel products.

To this extent, two integrated iron and steel plants in (Ajaokuta and Delta Steel Companies) and three Inland rolling mills at Kaduna, Jos and Oshogbo were planned to produce only long product constructional steels. The Delta Steel Company (DSC) is expected to feed the three inland rolling mills with billets for their production. The Ajaokuta plant is far from being completed. Similarly, the basic raw materials of iron ore for the DSC plant is presently being imported from Liberia and Brazil, while the Ajaokuta plant is expected to utilize the local ore reserves (at Itakpe and Agbaja) when it comes into full production. However, there is presently no visible effort in opening up the mines by the government establishment, the Associated Ore Mining Corporation, which is charged with the responsibility of processing the ore. In terms of the major energy source for the production of iron, the DSC plant utilizes the locally available natural gas at an unregulated very high cost, while the design of the Ajaokuta plant is based upon metallurgical coking coal which may have to be imported.

The lack of any coordinated and well defined policy by the government in respect of Research and Development work on locally available raw materials for the steel industry makes the future of the Nigerian Steel Industry very uncertain especially when it has to depend on the importation of basic raw materials including refractors and spare parts in a presently depressed economy. This situation is further compounded by the fact that the steel plants including those of the three rolling mills operate well below designed capacity. In spite of this, the total earnings from sales at DSC alone was 75.3 million niara in 1984. The low output from the DSC plants may be attributed to inadequate supply of electrical energy, raw materials, and spare parts. This situation forced the government to provide the three Inland rolling mills with import licence to purchase billets from outside Nigeria in 1984. Certainly, this is another example of uncoordinated industrial policy: whereby linkage industries have to share part of already scarce foreign exchange because the local basic industry cannot meet their demand.

In order to discuss the necessary guidelines for an effective industrial policy, I would like to use the metallurgical industry of which iron and steel is a part as an illustration.

Table 1 illustrates Nigeria's expenditure (import bills) on some basic materials during the first six months of 1980 and the three major suppliers. Of particular significance are the expenditures in foreign exchange on Aluminium (20.8m niara), Copper (12.5m niara) Refractory (8.72m niara), Zinc (6.52m niara) and Lead (0.74m niara), products. In the case of aluminium, Nigeria has no known deposits of bauxite of commercial significance and there is no aluminium reduction or smelter plants to produce primary products of ingots and billets. There are two privately owned flat rolling mills (divisions of multinational corporations) with a combined capacity of 20,000 metric tonnes, three extrusion plants with capacity of 6,000 metric tonnes and about 200 small scale finishing plants.

The top three suppliers of copper to Nigeria are Japan, Germany and Spain, while some African nations with copper production include Zaire, Zambia and Zimbabwe.

Nigeria has lead and zinc ore deposits whose existence has been known for long but, the extent of geological exploration has been limited and their industrial exploration is quite recent. The area in which the deposits are found, according to Onwugbolu's report,[17] extends in a narrow belt for about 400 km from Ogoja in Benue State and Adamawa in Gongola State to Bauchi State. However, there is no reliable estimate of the proven reserve, and the government has no coordinated effort to process what is known. Hence, the country has to depend upon importation of the products of these essential metals from outside her boundary.

The refractory industry is another area where Nigeria relies solely on importation to meet local demand. With more high temperature materials processing industries, such as the Glass, Cement, Petrochemicals and Steel industries coming on steam, the import bill of 8.72 million niara reported in Table 1 could be more than triple. In a recent report, Aderibigbe and Chukwuogo[18] have shown that there are at least fourteen known commercial clay deposits in Nigeria which have the potential for use as the fire-clay series of refractory products.

The vulnerability of Nigeria to the supplies of the essential metals and material products from outside her boundary is also revealed in Table 1 where it can be seen that out of the eleven basic materials listed, the United Kingdom is first, second and third in the supply of eight materials. Western Germany holds the same positions in six materials while Japan ranks the same in four materials. It is therefore not sur-

Table 1. Nigeria's import bill during the first six months of 1980

| Metal/materials | Expenditure Niara | Top 3 foreign suppliers with percent share in expenditure | | |
		No. 1	No. 2	No. 3
1. Pig iron	1,673,686	Japan: 84.83	UK: 13.83	—
2. Feromanganese	135,855	Japan: 27.51	Germany: 24.96	Spain: 16.39
3. Silver	855	UK: 100	—	—
4. Platinum	417,788	China: 61.36	France: 12.60	Germany: 11.46
5. Copper	12,561,844	Japan: 32.70	Germany: 31.72	Spain: 10.26
6. Nickle	727,927	Belgium: 43.58	UK: 29.86	Germany: 13.38
7. Aluminium	20,830,151	Switzerland: 22.50	UK: 22.05	Germany: 9.45
8. Lead	736,245	UK: 51.77	Netherlands:29.04	Canada: 17.25
9. Zinc	6,519,514	Belgium: 28.16	UK: 23.21	Canada:23.10
10. Tin	269,943	France: 29.75	Japan: 22.96	UK: 16.99
11. Refractrory bricks	8,723,846	Germany: 36.8	UK: 26.72	USA: 11.95

Table 2. World and United States reserves of 18 metals in 1980

| Metal | USA 10^3 ton | | Location of top 2 reserves | |
			No. 1	No. 2
1. Rhenium	3.5	1.3	USA	Chile
2. Gold	42.0	2.5	South Africa	USSR
3. Platinum	50.0	0.042	South Africa	USSR
4. Tantalum	67.0	—	Zaire	Nigeria
5. Silver	338.0	62	Canada	USA
6. Tungsten	2850.0	137	China	Canada
7. Cobalt	3,400.0	350	Zaire	Zambia
8. Columbium	3,800.0	—	Brazil	Canada
9. Molybdenum	10,850.0	5900	USA	Chile
10. Vanadium	17,400.0	115	South Africa	USSR
11. Nickel	19,800.0	2700	New Caledonia	Canada
12. Titanium	133,000.0	2000	Brazil	Australia
13. Copper	542,300.0	101,000	Chile	USA
14. Magnesium	2,685,000.0	10,000+	China	USSR
15. Chromium	3,700,000.0	—	South Africa	Zimbabwe
16. Manganese	5,500,000.0	—	USSR	South Africa
17. Aluminium	25,080,000.0	44,000	Guniea	Australia
18. Iron	105,000,000.0	5,800,000	USSR	Brazil

prising when policy decision in any of these three developed countries have serious rippling effects on the security and economy of Nigeria. The reality of this situation should be guiding factor in effecting meaningful combination of policies at this stage of industrial development (point of incipient growth in the S-curve) in Nigeria.

As a comparative study, let us perceive how the U.S.A., a country which is at the other extreme of the S-curve (i.e. post-industrial or maturity stage) looks at the issue of strategic materials. According to the report of a task group of experts[19] representing the Metal Properties Council Incorporation (MPC), Table 2 shows the estimated world and U.S. reserves for the eighteen metals of interest. Here, it is seen that the "domestic U.S. position indicates negligible reserves of tantalum, columbium, manganese, and chromium—all vital to tthe steel, aircraft, and defence

Table 3. World and production of 18 metals in 1980

	Metal	Production 10³ ton	Top 2 producers No. 1	No. 2
1.	Rhenium	0.011	USA	Chile
2.	Platinum	0.281	South Africa	USSR
3.	Tantalum	0.500	Canada	Brazil
4.	Gold	1.592	South Africa	USSR
5.	Columbium	12.250	Brazil	Canada
6.	Silver	14.150	Mexico	Canada
7.	Cobalt	29.800	Zaire	Zambia
8.	Vanadium	40.350	South Africa	USSR
9.	Tungsten	54.750	China	USSR
10.	Titanium	92.600	USSR	USA
11.	Molybdenum	120.500	USA	Chile
12.	Magnesium	352.000	USA	USSR
13.	Nickel	721.000	Canada	New Caledonia
14.	Copper	8,250.000	USA	Chile
15.	Chromium	10,000.000	South Africa	Philippines
16.	Aluminium	16,900.000	USA	USSR
17.	Manganese	25,300.000	USSR	South Africa
18.	Iron	791,600.000	USSR	Japan

industries in times of both war and peace." Table 3 illustrates the world production of the 18 metals. In world production, "the United States ranks first or second in six metals: aluminium, copper, magnesium, molybdenum, titanium and rhenium. The USSR now holds the favourable position of in nine metals: iron manganese, aluminium, magnesium, titanium, tungsten, vanadium, gold and platinum." After comparing the U.S. production and consumption of these metals, the team acknowledges that the "USSR and South Africa" are rich in mineral wealth. They control the world supply for six of the eighteen metals under study: platinum (99%), manganese (98%), vanadium (97%), chromium (96%) and iron ore (50%)." When the team analyzed the reliance of U.S on the imports of metals, bearing in mind the three major suppliers, they appreciated the importance of Canada as a source of supply: "It is the first supplier of six metals and second of three."

In the specific case of Tantalum, a metal in which Nigeria has the second largest reserve in the world, it is noted that Nigeria used to be a major exporter of columbium-tantalum in the western world. However, the high cost of tantalum carbide (TaC) used in steel cutting grades of carbide tools for improved hot hardness and greater resistance, has led to widespread substitution by carbide manufacturers. The new substitutes include: Columbium Carbide (CbC) and mixture of TaC and CbC or Hafnium Carbide (HfC) and CbC. For Nigeria, this development in foreign substitute for an essential raw material has significant implication: the high price and allocation problems of tantalum by Nigeria, resulted in substitution and loss of market. In essence, this type of development has a negative effect on the value added to the Nigerian economy as a whole, on the other hand it constitutes a major tribute to the ingenuity and creativity of the materials engineers.

From this type of analysis on strategic materials one develops an appreciation for the U.S. policies in respect of both Canada and South Africa. No matter how anybody looks at it, the U.S. policies of very good harmony with her neighbour, Canada, and lukewarm attitude to cries against apartheid in South Africa are understandable.

Apartheid policy are more in line with protecting the security and economic buoyancy of her country. African nations have a lot to learn from this example, especially the industrializing ones such as Nigeria. With the increasing yearning for industrialization, it should be realized that a country becomes tied up with the global economy of interdependence in the area of materials supply and demand which are essential for growth. In such a situation, both the industrial and foreign policies have to be synchronized in the interest of the security and growth of the economy. Thus, while it is normal to be horrified by the practice of apartheid in South Africa and to condemn the treatment mèted out to the Arabs by the Israelis, African nations should not become emotionally attached to the extent that these issues become diversionary factors with dominating influence on the national foreign policies. Within the context of universal change, whatever will be will be and there is no point in sharing in another nation's karmic debt.

The foregoing discussion is intended to demonstrate the extent of neglect which has been accorded the mineral mining industry of the Nigerian economy. In a changing economy, such as that from trading to internal production in Nigeria, priority has to be given to this sector to sustain any form of industrial growth within the economy. Even without having the relevant metallic-ore, such as is the case for aluminum and copper, it is possible for Nigeria to process some of the ores locally by establishing plants that would depend only on imported ores from friendly African countries. Nigeria is presently doing this for the Delta Steel Company and the three inland rolling mills. The government should encourage local entrepreneurs who would like to take the risk and establish similar plants for the copper sector. The issue of the aluminium smelter plant may be temporarily suspended because of the present depressed state of the economy, but it should not be totally abandoned.

The flat steel and the foundry projects are other areas of concern. There is no doubt that more than 50 per cent of current Nigerian steel demand is in the form of flat steel products for fabricating such industrial items as storage and process tanks, ships, trucks and rail-car bodies, welded pipes, enamelware, cans, and roofing sheets. However, from the material processing point of view, the production technique for the different grades of flat steel sheets are so varied that a single plant may have problems satisfying even one tenth of the market; this is quite opposite to the range of long steel products for bars, rods, angles and channels which are basically carbon steels without much variation in alloying additions. In this regard, the scale of the flat sheet plants should not be large.

There are many economically and technologically proven mini-mills in the world that can serve the purpose of producing specific grades of flat steel products and the local entrepreneur should be encouraged through appropriate incentives to invest in this area. The same thing applies to the foundry industry which thrives best when the scale is between small and medium because of the different grades, designs and sizes of the products. In the words of Chief Onwuka Kalu, at the recently concluded 4th National Seminar on Finance under the sponsorship of NAL Merchant Bank, "Nigeria is a country, that possesses all the potentials for a dynamic economy. High revenue-yielding resources, such as iron ore, tin, columbite, limestone, marble, kaolin, phosphate, uranium, manganese and so on, must not be allowed to remain dormant or under-utilized."

Within the framework of security and economic revival that would guarantee self-reliance in our social system, his following recommendations on industrial policy are therefore necessary guidelines:

(1) optimal utilization of local material and human resources;
(2) progressive substitution of raw materials and parts;
(3) exploitation of innovation potential;
(4) diversification—(a) development of mining and mineral processing industry, (b) development of natural gas, (c) development of petro-chemical raw material base, (d) capitalizing on the technological linkages of investment in steel, (e) agricultural raw materials for agro-allied industries,
(5) infra-structural requirement of power generations, transmission and distribution.

In addition, from the global perspective and bearing in mind the presence of nation-states outside the boundaries of Nigeria, both immediate and remote, these guidelines for industrial policy have to be synchronized with our policies so as to create harmony both within Nigeria and along her border and regions.

Summary and Recommendations

In summary, the effort in this presentation has been to examine the economic and industrial policies of some African nations and in particular Nigeria using a systems approach (global perspective) and bearing in mind the interacting independent variables of human and material resources. This has led to the development of a philosophical model which seeks, within a given social system, to maximize the security and economic buoyancy of the nation-state, within the constraints of financial resources and the effectiveness of different national policies at and beyond the borderland and regions of a nation. With this, the effect of the policies of other nation-states in the immediate and remote environment to a given nation-state can be assessed and appropriate measures taken to guarantee the attainment of national objectives. Emphasis has been placed on the role of the material resources especially as it related to industrialization in a changing economy.

In the case of Nigeria, the state of the security and economic buoyancy of the social system has been shown through consideration of some strategic materials to be very vulnerable to external manipulation, especially multinationals. The remedy has been demonstrated to be a re-orientation towards a well coordinated industrial policy backed by an appropriate science and technology policy all over the country.

Endnotes

.1 Anene, J.C., *The International Boundaries of Nigeria, 1885-1960: The Framework of an Emergent African Nation* (London: Longman, 1970).

2. Prescott, J.R.V., *The Evolution of Nigeria's International and Regional Boundaries, 1861-1971* (Vancouver, 1971).

3. McEwen, A.C., *International Boundaries of East Africa* (Oxford: OUP, 1971).

4. Touval, S., *The Boundary Politics of Independent Africa* (Boston: Harvard Univ. Press, 1972).

5. Asiwaju, A.I. (ed), *Partitioned Africans: Ethnic Relations Across Africa's International Boundaries, 1884-1984* (Lagos: Univ. of Lagos Press, 1984).

6. Smith, Cyril S., "Metallurgy as a human exprience: an essay on man's relationship to his materials in science and practice throughout history", *American Soc. for Metals* and TMS-AIME, 1977.

7. Twitchell, Paul, *The Far Country* (Illuminated Way Press, 1978), p. 197.

8. Cohen, Morris, "Materials, materialism, and search for meaning—essay," *Metallurgical Transaction.* Vol 14B, June 1983.

9. Boulding, K., "General systems theory: the skeleton of science," *General System,* VOL 1, 1956, pp. 11-17.

10. Bertalanffy, L. Von, Theoretische Biolgie, 2 Bd. Berlin, 1932-1942.
11. Klir, J., "The general system as a methodological tool", *General Systems*, Vol X, 1965, pp. 29-42.
12. Hall, A.D. and Fagen, R.E., "Definition of systems", *General Systems*, Vol 1, 1956, p. 19.
13. Szekely, J., and Themelis, N.J., *Rate Phenomena in Process Metallurgy* (New York: Wiley-Interscience, 1971).
14. Crank, J., *The Mathematics of Diffusion* 2nd ed., (Oxford: OUP, 1975).
15. Plog, F. and Bates, D.G., *Cultural Anthropology* (New York: Knopf, 1976), Chap. 20.
16. Collins, David, "Partitioned culture areas and smuggling: the Hausa and the groundnut trade across the Nigeria-Niger border from the mid-1930s to the mid-1970s" in *Partitioned Africans* ed. Asiwaju (Lagos: Univ. of Lagos Press, 1984).
17. Onwugbolu, C.A., "Overview of the non-ferrous industries in Nigeria", February 1985 meeting of the Industralization Committee of the Nigerian Society of Engineers.
18. Aderibigbe, D.A. and Chukwuogo, C.E.B., "Potential of some Nigerian clay deposits as refractory materials for the steel industry", proceedings of the 1984 Annual Conference of the Nigerian Society of Engineers, held at Kano, Dec. 6-8, 1984.
19. Stalker, KW, Clark, C.C., Ford, J.A., Richmond, F.M., and Stephens, J.R., "An index to identify strategic metal vulnerability", *Metal Progress*, October 1984, pp. 55-65.

SECTION III
STUDIES AND POLICY IMPLICATIONS

The Process of Cartographic Definition of Nigerian Boundaries

by Olayinka Y. Balogun

Introduction

On the subject of Nigerian boundaries, various scholars have chosen different focuses. Anene (1960), in his study of Nigerian International Boundaries, looks at the socio-political implication of and developments surrounding the boundaries. Prescott (1961) focuses on the course, causes and functions of Nigerian boundaries as well as the political circumstances leading to the delimitation of the boundaries. He also examines the impact of such boundaries on the indigenous frontiers, the people and their trades as well as the relationships among the three European Powers with territories around Nigeria. Brownlie's compendium of boundary treaties (Brownlie, 1979) gives the subject of African boundaries a legal touch, Brownlie's work has brought Hertslet's *"The Map of Africa by Treaty"* (1901) up-to-date and provided commentaries on the present position of boundaries of African countries. Mills (1970) considers the geographical implications of the boundary. This paper examines the cartographic processes that took place in the delimitation of Nigerian boundaries and describes the various boundary alignments which altered the shape and area of the country.

The importance of defining national boundaries literally on paper, cartographically on maps and physically on the ground cannot be over emphasized. Without these processes, especially the last one, adjacent territories may be constantly on the war path, making claims and counter claims especially when a party feels cheated after realizing the goodies that have fallen to the lot of the other party. In executing all these processes, the map is very important. In the allocation of territories and the literary description of their limits, the map is an obvious essential. This explains the situation whereby maps form an integral part of the document to be signed by concerned parties at every stage of the negotiations: both after detailed surveys and during the demarcation of the boundaries, the signed map is needed to show the course of the boundary in relation to the natural landmarks around it.

Stages of Definition of Nigerian Boundaries

Boundary definition provides limits of a property, thus defining the area where the owner can operate without being accused of transgression. Furthermore, from cartographic point of view, boundaries provide a unit or units of cartographic representation. Without boundaries of Nigeria, for example, it will be difficult to produce a true map of Nigeria and the portrayal of densities will be absolutely impossible.

Boundary definition comes in three stages which, according to Jones (1945, p. 57), are allocation, delimitation and demarcation. From cartographic point of view, one can slightly modify these stages as follows: Allocation and map-based description, ground-bases delimitation survey and mapping, and on-the-ground translation of the boundaries shown on the map (demarcation).

Allocation and Map-Based Description

A major milestone in the Scramble for Africa of the 19th century was the Berlin Conference of 1884-1885 at which rules were drawn up the application of which ultimately led to the partition of Africa and the resultant allocation of territories to various European countries. The European Powers did not quite understand what territories fell to them; they had not paid visits to most parts of the territories they were laying claims to. They were merely asking for areas enclosing places suspected or found to be endowed with minerals, raw materials, markets and marketable works of art by their explorers. At the time of the Conference in which British claims to the territory adjacent to the Gulf of Guinea were recognised, Lagos area was about the only part of Nigeria the British colonial administrators were familiar with. With respect to the other parts, they laid claims before acquiring them.

Two years after the Berlin Conference, Justus Perthe was able to publish a map of Africa titled "Spezial Karte von Africa" (special map of Africa). This German map later served as the map on which the description s of boundaries of most of the allocated territories were based. The map annexed to the convention of June 14, 1898 between Great Britain and France was composed of Sections IV and V of 1892 edition of Justus Perthe's map. On this map, all Nigerian boundaries except the section from 9°N to River Niger of the Western boundary were indicated. All the boundaries were depicted with straight lines and perfect arcs which were very easy to describe textually. The boundary that runs from Niger to Chad was the longest boundary line in Nigeria before the First World War. The following description illustrates how simply it could be done:

> From above Giri the boundary follows the midway of the Niger as far as the mouth of a dry water course, supposed to be Dalul Mauri. It then follows this water course until it meets the circumference of a circle drawn from the centre of the town of Sokoto, with a radius of 100 miles. It follows the northern arc of this circle until it intersects the 14th parallel for the second time. It then follows the 14th parallel for 70 miles; then descends due South to lat. 13° 20' N; then eastward along this parallel for a distance of 250 miles; then regains the 14th parallel, and follows it as far as meridian, passing 35' east of Kuka; and ultimately this meridian southward, until its intersection with the southern shore of Lake Chad". (Ravenstein, 1898, p. 73-5).

The frontier described above is illustrated in Figure 1. One can observe the use

Figure 1. Niger to Lake Chad boundary in 1898 (straight lines and arc).

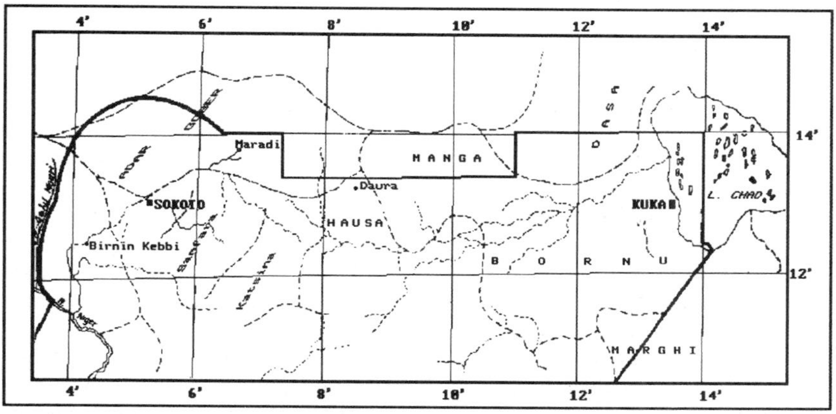

From Justus Perthe's Spezial Karte Von Afrika.

of perfect geometrical shapes: straight horizontal and vertical lines and arc described from Sokoto. The only section that was delineates with irregular line is the section of the boundary running along the Dalul Mauri river which had been surveyed
by Major Lang-Hyde of the Royal Engineers.

Where boundary courses followed natural linear features such as big rivers, or
crests of long ridges, map-based description could be as good as description based
on surveys. The only problems here are: (i) in order to place such natural boundary
lines on the map, their positions still had to be fixed, (ii) some so-called natural
boundary lines had in the past left boundary commissions utterly disappointed
because they could turn out to be ambiguous. For example, a boundary line defined
by a river or a lake could change with tide or seasons as in the case of Lake Chad
during the survey of the boundary from Yola to Chad in 1902; (iii) descriptions were
often bases on maps whose authenticity was still doubtful, most geographical
features wrongly located or named. Once its foundation, in form of the map, was
shaky, on-the-map descriptions often face the threat of absolute collapse. No
wonder then, descriptions not based on detailed on-the-ground surveys were only
to guide boundary commissioners in the delimitation survey work. Sometimes they
made the work of the surveyor more tedious especially when they had to be looking
for features mentioned in the description but which, in the real world, did not appear
close to the boundary on the ground.

As vague as map-based description of boundaries could be, at leat it could provide a frame within which colonial administration could go on. Allocation of territories and map-based descriptions of boundaries were usually included in treaties
which were procured between, and signed by concerned parties several years before
delimitation surveys. The process was a temporary measure pleasing to the European Powers who had, at least, gained some territories however small or amor-
phous, but grossly inconvenient for the indigens living around the boundaries. The
indigens initially did not know what had transpired at the Berlin Conference and carried on their normal duties without taking note of any artificial barrier which, of
course, was not visible. The extension of European reconnaissance influence and
colonial government to the boundary area introduced outlandish constraints which

caused frictions along the boundaries. This made the next stage of cartographic definition urgent.

Ground-based Delimitation Survey and Mapping

Delimitation simply means setting of the edge or the limit at which something ends. Map-based description is therefore a form of delimitation, even though it is not definite, not concrete and not realistic as in the case of delimitation survey and demarcation.

Ground-based delimitation is carried out in three stages: reconnaissance, survey and mapping. While map-based description was usually done on a map without necessarily taking people to the area around the frontier, delimitation reconnaissance, and survey actually took people to the boundary area. Reconnaissance involves visiting the boundary area, identifying the objects mentioned in the map-based description and observing the characteristics of such objects to see if they were permanent enough to be used in defining a boundary. The reconnaissance party looks for some other features that could be used as reference points in the boundary survey that will follow. All these activities often involve clearing obstacle such as trees, bushes and so on around the boundary and if possible establishing temporary beacons which make later survey work easier. During reconnaissance, a lot of alterations are often made to the boundary line defined by the textual description. In the case of Nigerian boundaries, for instance, compromises were often reached to re-unite villages or villagers and their farm-lands separated by the provisional boundary lines.

Delimitation survey methods and procedures were often specified in the treaty relating to territorial allocation. Survey is necessary in rendering the boundary line into mappable data. This aspect of boundary definition is cartographically more important than any other stage, including boundary demarcation. Without the delimitation survey, the boundary may be marked on the ground; this is simply a process partitioning and the frontier cannot be accurately represented on the map which usually accompanies the agreement signed by the two parties. On the other hand, if the delimitation is done on a map without proper survey, it will be difficult to mark the boundary accurately as map-based descriptions have demonstrated.

In the early years of colonial rule in Nigeria, boundary surveys provided the most accurate cartographic data for the mapping of the country, the area surrounding the boundary being surveyed accurately and in great detail. The practice with respect to Nigerian boundaries was to survey a strip about five kilometres wide on either side of the boundaries (Winterbotham, 1928, p. 178). In a country like Nigeria that was, in the early decades of the 20th century, yet to develop cartographic data base, provision of control data had to constitute a part of the boundary survey and took a considerable portion of the time spent on the whole survey. In most cases, the boundary commissions found it necessary to relate boundary lines to permanent structures such as the rulers' palaces in some big towns.

Up till the time the two Nigerian Protectorates were amalgamated and the Nigeria Survey Department was created, boundary commissioners were appointed by the Colonial Office on the recommendation of the War Office. The Commission were each usually made up of Military Officers who were very versed in precision survey, a doctor, an escort, an astronomer and sometimes, a geologist, a botanist and other researchers. The survey work itself was supervised by the Intelligence Division of the War Office (I.D.W.O.). The head of the British party must be a man who could combine "with technical qualifications an adequate amount of common sense to guide him in making, as he often has to do, decision on the spot which are not necessarily connected with survey" (Winterbotham, 1928, p. 186). The Commissioners from the other party too invariably included military officers.

The conduct of delimitation surveys was guided by relevant clauses in the agreement respecting the boundary in question. Where alterations in the agreement were made in favour of the British government during delimitation survey or where the boundary description in an agreement was conformed with, British Commissioners could use their discretion. Controversial issues, especially those that deviated adversely from the wordings of the agreement were referred to the Intelligence Division of the War Office and the Colonial Office for advice and directives. One would expect a similar procedure in the case of the other party.

Boundary surveys were usually conducted with a view to making maps of the boundary area which would accompany the agreement to be signed by both parties. Such maps provided permanent documents which, as later developments along the boundaries revealed, were more permanent than the objects, such as beacons and pillars, used in demarcation which often disappeared. The maps usually showed the course of the frontier and also the topography, drainage, geology and settlements within an area often kilometres around the boundary. Such maps were produced at different scales, the most common of which were 1:500,000, 1:250,000 and 1:200,000 depending on the length of the boundary in question. For instance, a scale of 1:200,000 may be alright for the northern boundary of Nigeria (River Niger to Chad) this scale will be too small for the Nigeria-Benin boundary.

A boundary line on a map is only valid so far as it can be identified on the ground. This is where textual description comes into the scene again. This time, it is not the narrative on the lines drawn on a map. Rather it is the description of survey points and courses on the ground most of which the map cannot include. For example the arc described in the Yola-Chad section of Nigeria's eastern boundary has its centre in Yola. At the scale used for the maps produced, Yola could only be shown in a very generalised manner. Textual description shows the exact point in Yola which served as the centre of the arc. Textual description based on surveys was done in steps using series of straight lines except where there was a river forming part of the boundary. The Nigeria-Benin boundary from the coast to the middle of River Niger, a distance of 696 kilometres, was described in sixty-five steps.

In the demarcation exercise that usually followed delimitation survey, the use of textual description in addition to maps had been found to be immensely helpful In fact, the Anglo-French agreement on Nigeria-Dahomey (Benin) boundary of 19 October 1906 included a clause which stated "in the event of any divergence being found between the line as described above and as indicated on maps, the description shall be held to be authoritative". (HMS Office, 1906, p. 12).

On-the-ground Translation of Boundaries Shown on the Map

Boundary surveys usually produce data for maps that show the boundary line as part of the treaty to be signed by interested parties. But nothing forestalls boundary disputes in so far as boundary demarcation or on-the-ground translation of the boundary has not been carried out. This involves the use of beacons, pillars, walls or other artificial features. These marks should usually be visible, inter-visible and difficult to remove. They show travellers, soldiers and so on when they have reached the boundary between two countries which, if the map is simply relied upon, be easily identified on the ground.

The demarcation of the boundary also involves surveys sometimes rigorous, if the marks left during the delimitation survey had been removed. Further surveys are necessary for the location of points whose coordinates were fixed during the delimitation survey, and for the location and alignment of pillars. Some clearing is done along the boundary for the proper maintenance of the boundary marks and to give room for the movement of immigration and customs officials, and the police who are posted there to prevent illegal crossing, smuggling of goods and evasion of justice.

The Scheme of Boundary Definition

The nature of political arrangements in and around Nigeria had a lot of bearing on the processes of delimitation and demarcation of her boundaries. First, in the early period of colonial rule there were three separate colonies by 1900, for example, these were three distinct entities: Colony, Southern Nigeria and Northern Nigeria. These colonies might have been collaborating in some ways being, as they were, all British territories; but they were administered separately and the question of boundary delimitation, though initially settled by the Colonial Office and the Geographical Section (General Staff) was resolved individually. Secondly, Nigeria is completely surrounded by non-British colonies such as Kamerouns (Germany), later French Camerouns, in the east: Niger (French) in the north, Chad (French) in the northeast and Dahomey (French) in the West.

The first explains the instalmental nature of the Nigerian boundary delimitation as a boundary survey would terminate at the limit of a colony that arranged for the delimitation. For example, the Nigeria-Benin boundary, in spite of tits relatively short length (692 kilometres) compared with the Nigeria-Niger boundary (1376 kilometres) was delimited in two sections: (i) the sea to 9 degrees North which was around the northern limit of Southern Nigeria; (ii) 9 °N to the middle of the River Niger which was in the sphere of influence of Northern Nigerian Government. The middle of the Niger forms a tripartite point for the boundaries of Nigeria, Niger, and the Republic of Benin. Other factors such as the length of a boundary, difficulty of terrain, exhaustion of supplies of boundary commissions, disagreement over the course of boundary and the presence of big rivers across the boundary course might also put a temporary stop to delimitation survey work even before territorial limit of the colony was reached.

The second political situation not only determined the nationalities of the commissioners but also how urgently the delimitation should be carried out. For instance, there was the tendency for Britain to be more prompt in delimiting and demarcating the boundaries of her colonies with the French Colonies than with the German Colonies. The reason can be found in Prescott's observation that Britain always found it easier to reach a compromise with Germany than with France on issues relating to their colonies in Africa (Prescott, 1961, p. 233).

The sum total of the political situation in and around Nigeria produced the boundary definition scheme illustrated in Figure 2. The figure shows the various sections of the Nigerian boundaries delimited by different commissions.

Development of Nigerian Boundaries

Figure 3 is a map of the area covered by Nigeria drawn in 1885. It show no boundaries apart from tribal frontiers. By 1900, all Nigerian boundaries had been defined

Figure 2. The scheme of definition of Nigerian boundaries.

1. Nigeria-Republic of Benin boundary
   a. The coast to Lat. 9°N
   b. Lat. 9°N to the Niger
2. Nigeria Niger Republic boundary (Niger to Chad)
3. Nigeria Kamerun boundary before World War I
   a. Rio del Rey Creek to Cross River Rapids
   b. Cross River to Yola arc
   c. Yola arc to Lake Chad
4. Nigeria Chad boundary
5. Nigeria Cameroun boundary

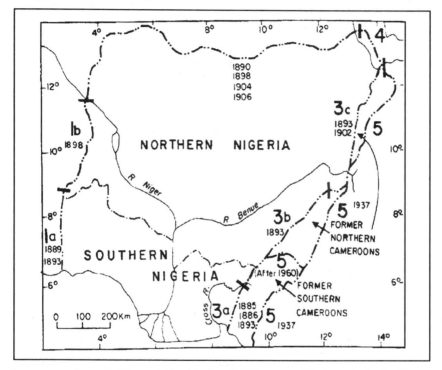

by treaty as shown in Figure 4. By this time (1900) some of the boundaries had been delimited as in the case of Nigeria-Republic of Benin boundary (the coast to Latitude 9°N in 1895-6 and Latitude 9°N to the Niger, 1900), Nigeria-Cameroun boundary from Sea to Cross River (1895). The Nigeria-Republic of Benin boundary had even been marked on the ground. The difference between a boundary that had only been defined by treaty and the one that had been delimitedT,&

Tthrough boundary surveys can be seen in the nature of the boundary line. The former is usually made up of straight lines and geometric curves while a delimited boundary line is usually irregular, having been made in conformity with the reality of the situation around the boundary. Most often, boundaries were made to coincide with river courses and crests of ridges all of which served as natural boundaries. They were also made to avoid, as much as possible, the division of settlements or separation of villages and their farmlands.

As Nigeria has common borders with four countries, the development of

Figure 3. Nigeria without boundaries in 1885.

Source: Thompson, J., "Niger and Central Sudan Sketches", Scittish Geog. Magazine, Vol. 2, 1886, p. 579.

Nigerian boundaries can be discussed in four section: (i) Nigeria-Benin (formerly Dahomey) Boundary, (ii) Nigeria-Niger Boundary, (iii) Nigeria-Cameroun Boundary and (iv) Nigeria-Chad Boundary.

Nigeria-Benin Boundary

The Nigeria-Benin was the earliest defined frontier in Nigeria. It was treated in two sections: the coast to latitude 9°North and latitude 9°North to the Niger.

Coast to Latitude 9°North

The section form the coast to latitude 9°North was first defined in a treaty signed on 18 August 1889 at which it was a straight line as shown in Figure 5. In the treaty, the line was simply described as follows:

> "On the Slave Coast, the line of demarcation between the spheres of influence of the powers shall be identified with the meridian which intersects the territory of Porto Novo at the Ajarra Creek, leaving Pokrah or Pokea to the English Colony of Lagos. It shall follow the above-mentioned meridian as far as the 9th degree of north latitude, where it shall stop." (Hertslet, *Map of Africa,* Vol.II No. 22b, pp. 729-733, as used in Anene, p. 184)

When the boundary was delimited in 1895-6 following an agreement signed in July 1893 on the conduct of the delimitation survey it was found that it could not follow

Figure 4. Nigeria boundaries by 1900

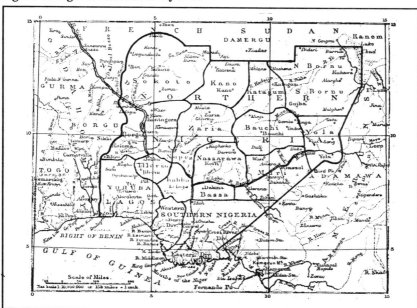

Source: Capt. C.H. Foulkes, "The New Anglo-French Frontier Between the Niger and Lake Chad," Scott. Geog. Mag. Vol 22, 1906.

the stated straight course without shattering many coherent villages and towns. Preference was given, instead, to convenience of using various sections of rivers such as Ajara, Amidu, Ibru, and largely, Okpara as mutual boundary. Figure 6 shows the new frontier as part of the Nigeria-Benin boundary. The boundary delimitation was accepted at the Anglo-French Convention of 14 June 1898 and the agreement was signed on 19 October 1906.

In 1912, an Anglo-French Commission was set up to demarcate the boundary and the protocol on this exercise was set up to demarcate the boundary and the protocol on this exercise was signed on 20 July 1912 by the British Commissioner, Major F.G. Guggisberg, who was then the Director of the Survey Department of Southern Nigeria, and Captain Forum, the French Commissioner. During demarcation, which was done with beacons numbered 1 to 142, some minor changes were made. These changes were necessitated by the fact that some survey marks and even some villages such as Ikotun, Ilore, Okoto and Ijalu could not be located. Some concessions and compensations were made in respect of some villages so as to ensure their road communications with other parts of the respective colonies in which they were located. The final agreement signed on the 18 February 1914 was silent about Article III in the agreement of 1905 which states as follows:

> The villages situated in proximity to the frontier shall retain the right to use the arable and pasture lands, springs and watering-places which they have heretofore used, even in the cases in which such arable and pasture lands, springs and watering-places are situated within the territory of the one Power, and the village within the territory of the other.(HMS Office, 1906, p. 13).

Figure 5. Nigeria-Benin boundary from the coast to lat. 9 °N

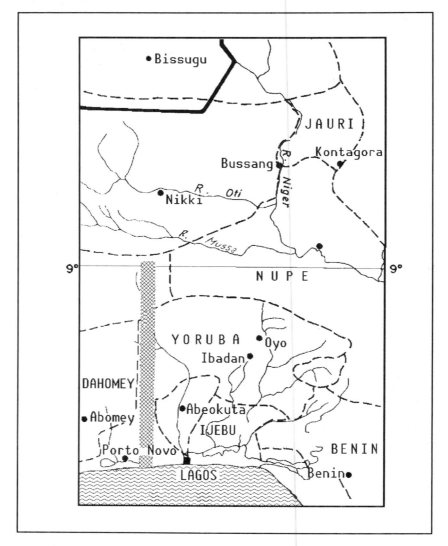

Latitude 9°N to River Niger

The second section of the Nigeria-Benin boundary, that is, from the point of intersection of River Okpara with Latitude 9°North to the middle of the Niger, was included in the Anglo-French Agreement of 14 June 1898. The section enjoyed the benefits of unusual pre-1900 familiarity of European Power with the territories they had shared by treaties. This section of the Nigerian boundary was therefore not described by one single straight line but by series of lines as shown in Figure 7.

The delimitation survey and mapping were carried out in 1900 and the demarcation was executed at the same time by cutting down trees alternatively along the

Figure 6. Nigeria-Benin boundary after delimitation survey.

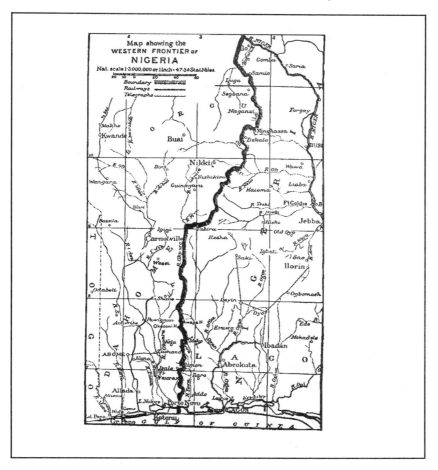

boundary (Brownlie, 1979, p. 188). A protocol was signed by the Boundary Commissioners on the 22 December 1900, but this section was again included in the 'exchange of notes' and agreement signed in Paris on the 19th October, 1906. The boundary agreed upon is shown as part of the Nigerian-Benin boundary in Figure 6.

The total length of the boundary line between the Republic of Benin and Nigeria was 696 kilometres (Hertslet, 1909) before final approval. The length as now apparent is fixed at 770 kilometres (Abiodun, 1982, p. 3).

Nigeria-Niger Boundary

The present Nigeria-Niger boundary runs from the tripartite point on the Niger river (i.e. the point at which the boundaries between Nigeria and Niger, Nigeria and Benin and Benin and Niger meet) to Lake Chad, a distance of about 1490 kilometres. The boundary defines the northern limit of Nigeria. The map-based description in

Figure 7. Nigeria-Benin boundary from Lat. 9°N to the Niger in 1898.

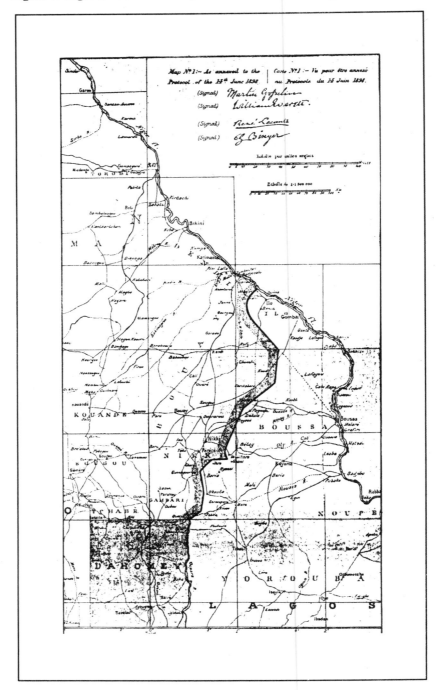

Figure 8. Evolution of the Nigeria-Niger boundary.

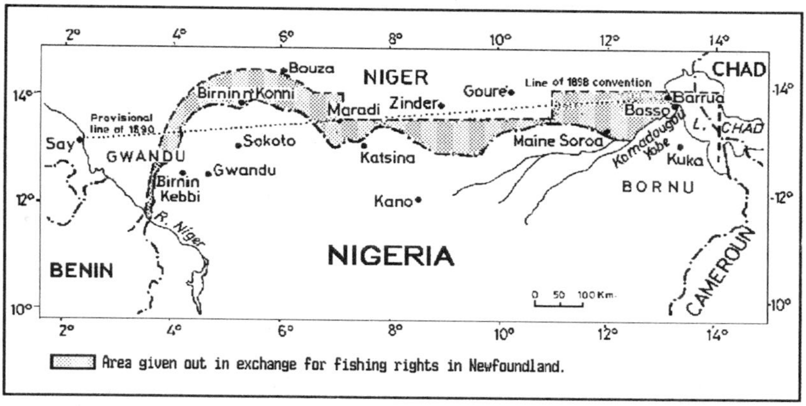

Adapted from Brownlie's African Boundaries: A Legal and Diplomatic Encyclopaedia, 1979.

the Anglo-French agreement of August 1890 put the boundary as a straight line running from Bay on the Niger to Barrua on the Western Shore of Lake Chad (see Fig. 8). A straight line is easy to draw on a map but a straight course is difficult to set out on the ground because of obstacles. Thus, this agreement merely denoted that the territory to the north belongedT,& Tto France while the one to the South was for Britain. The boundary therefore assumed several interpretations in the hands of the British and French cartographers (Foulkes, 1906, p. 565).

In June 1898, a second convention was signed. Even at this time, the country through which the new boundary line passed was hardly known. As a result, the new boundary, the starting point of which now moved down South of the Niger was defined in "geometric terms" (Elliot, 1904, p. 505) as described earlier (see Fig. 8).

From the above description, it is clear that this boundary was, in view of lack of knowledge about the country, a line of convenience which could easily be fixed by exact astronomical observation and charted on a map. It was therefore devoid of consideration of the importance of natural features and cultural groups in boundary delimitation. The reality of the situation started to rear its head when French West African troops frequently crossed the boundary, for lack of more suitable routes and water, to move from one part of their territory to the other. In response to a protest letter written by Brigadier F.D. Lugard, the High Commissioner of Northern Nigeria, Lt. Col. Peroz wrote as follows:

> Unfortunately, it is quite impossible for me to follow the advice which you tender referring to that of not holding or crossing the territories adjoining our mutual boundary. Perhaps you do not fully take into consideration that in such places as the delimitation of 1898 extends northwards, (to British advantage as far as all the country north of Sokoto and Bornu is concerned), such delimitation forces French territory back into a sterile country, where water is very scarce and where we cannot mark out to our own satisfaction a direction (lit road) which might suit us....I am convinced that the officers under your command do not have the same difficulties to face; thanks to the richness in provisions and water of the districts which fell to England's lot—None of these officers of yours will trouble

themselves to dispute our right to this desert land where with difficulty we keep the few dams of stagnant water, which, together, permits us retain in one, the several slices of the French so-called "Niger-Chad" territories, from the attacks of the Tornadoes (PRO, CO. 39254, 1901).

The tone of Peroz's letter indicates the type of animosity existing between Britain and France over boundaries of their colonies in Africa.

In 1904, France was delighted to be compensated for her renunciation of her fishing rights in Newfoundland by being given a region south of the 1898 boundary line that would ensure all-season route from Niger to Chad. This arrangement brought the map-based boundary line further south. But before then, delimitation survey under the leadership of Lt. Col. Elliot (British) and Captain Moll (French) had started on the 1898 line. The survey, though nullified and invalidated by Article VIII of the convention signed on 8 April 1904, had familiarized the British and the French with the political situation around the boundary. Both parties realised that the new line had cut through several districts but the best that could be done was to include a clause in the agreement that gave the people living near the boundary freedom to cross the frontier in order to settle in any territory they might choose. There was a provision for the fixing of the boundary line by a joint commission "when the political divisions of the country could be studied and the integrity of the lands belonging to the various tribes could be respected as far as possible (Foulkes, 1906, p. 567).

The realignment of the Nigeria-Niger boundary in 1904 did not go uncontested. For example, in a letter from the Resident of Sokoto Province, whose province had been considerably slashed, to the Higher Commissioner of Northern Nigeria, he stated:

It appears to me that the proposed cession of Damagaram is likely to be a serious blow to the Protectorate. It might be possible to offer an alternative tract of territory, perhaps equally valuable to France, but of which the loss would be less serious to Northern Nigeria. The Beibei district, from Junju (French) or Unguan Iliasu (British) to Nassarawa (British) seems to offer a possibility. It is a populous, prosperous district, in close touch with French towns of Junju and Karakara. (Northern Nigeria, 1907).

On the 2nd of May 1904, Lugard wrote as follows:

The large area of country ceded to French to the north of Sokoto gives them the district of Kiara, inhabited by the Asbenawa Camel herds, and hence deprives us of the last remnant of hold over these valuable breeders of transport animals and stock...It places upon me...the most difficult task of informing the Sultan of Sokoto whose dominion I recently pledged the good faith of England to protect...that promise is broken, and that a very considerable portion of his territory is to be ceded to France. Since the boundary is completely changed, it will, in my opinion, be necessary to have a new Boundary Commission. (Northern Nigeria, 1907, p. 7).

An Anglo-French Boundary Commission was, therefore, set up later in the year. The two teams met on the Niger in December 1904. The British Commissioner was Major O'Shee of Royal Engineers and France was represented by Captain Tilho. The two commissioners were experienced boundary surveyors, the former having accomplished the demarcation of the Rhodesia-Mozambique boundary, and the latter a member of the Commission that surveyed the former Niger-to-Chad boundary

Figure 9. Nigeria-Kamerun boundary in 1893, splitting Bornu, Adamawa and Marghi.

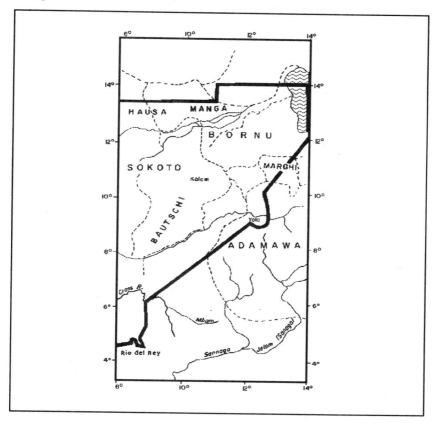

from 1902-1904. One important aspect of the delimitation survey was the agreement that the new frontier should be definitely fixed on the ground.

By 1908, the Commission had completed work on the delimitation survey and demarcation of the boundary. In all, one hundred and forty-eight beacons were established between 1906 and 1908. A description of the boundary was signed on Kano on the 25th February 1908. The protocol on this was signed after Exchange of Notes on 10 February 1910 while the final approval for Nigeria's Northern frontier was signed in 1911.

Nigeria-Cameroun Boundary

The eastern boundary of Nigeria up to the end of the First World War separate the British colonies of Southern Nigeria and Northern Nigeria from the German colony of Kamerun (Cameroun). Following the defeat of Germany in the Kamerun by the combined efforts of French and British Contingents, the territory was divided up between Britain and France, whose colonies flanked the German Kamerun (see Fig. 9) at a meeting in London on the 23 February 1916. Thus, initially there was a Nigeria-German Kamerun boundary; but after the war, there was created an

Anglo-French inter-Camerouns boundary. All these happenings around the eastern border created changing territorial extent of Nigeria and therefore caused modifications in the map of Nigeria.

Pre-War Nigeria-Kamerun Boundary

The Nigeria-Kamerun boundary, a length of about 1400 kilometres before the First World War was delimited in three stages: (1) the sea to Cross-River Rapids, (2) Cross-River to Yola, and (3) Yola to Lake Chad.

The first Anglo-German agreement in respect of this boundary was signed in 1885. The 1885 agreement only provided a map-based description from a point between Longitude 89° 42' and 8° 46' East at which 'Rio del Rey' entered the sea to the Cross River Rapids. This line was extended northeastwards to Yola by a convention of July-August, 1886. In an agreement signed on the 1st of July, 1890, a slight modification was made on the line from the coast to the Cross River following the discovery that there was no river named 'Rio del Rey'. Thus the starting point was adjusted to the head of the Rio del Rey Creek. Following the Berlin Convention of November 1893 between Britain and Germany an agreement was signed defining the Nigeria-Kamerun boundary from Yola to Lake Chad.

In all, the boundary between Nigeria and Kamerun by 1893 had been defined to a point on the southern shore of Lake Chad 35 minutes east of the meridian of the centre of the town of Kuka. The frontier was, but for the arc described from Yola, almost a straight diagonal line (see Fig. 9). The boundary line showed no consideration for physical features or the ethnic boundaries. The Kingdom of Borno was split into two. Similarly, Adamawa and Marghi were each divided between Great Britain and Germany. The populous city of Yola appeared to be the only place given special consideration: hence the arc described with a radius of about 46 kilometres from Yola.

The Sea to Cross River Rapids

The delimitation survey of the Anglo-German Nigeria-Kamerun boundary started in 1895 with the section between the sea and the Cross River 'Rapids'. This survey, conducted by Captain C.F. Close (British) and Lieut. Von Besser (German), was not conclusive and the final survey was not carried out until 1905 and demarcation until 1906. Generally, the delimitation of Nigeria-Kamerun boundary was very slow. As a result, the Germans were reported to have crossed the boundary frequently to take over important towns in the British territories. The West African Association of Liverpool had to show concern in 1900, imploring the British Government to settle the delimitation of the boundary quickly so as "to preserve the valuable tracts of land bearing produce and belonging to Southern Nigeria which are in danger of being absorbed by the German Colony of Cameroun." (PRO, Co 42159, 1900, p. 4).

Cross River to Yola Arc

The section from Cross River to Yola Arc remained a straight line on maps until after 1901. The delimitation survey by Lt. Col. G.E. Whitlock (British) and Obt. Von Stephen (German) did not start until August, 1907 and the demarcation until 1923. Following the completion of the delimitation survey in 1909, a protocol was signed on April 16, 1909. With respect to demarcation, the protocol was signed in 1913.

Yola Arc to Chad

On the 12th of December 1902, an agreement was signed on the procedure for the delimitation of the Section from Yola to Chad. Lt. Colonel Lewis Jackson was appointed the British Commissioner while his German counterpart was Captain Glauning. Some of the important measurements made by the Commission were the positions of Yola which was fixed by compromise as Latitude 9° 12′29.5″ North and Longitude 12° 26′54.3″ East and the Yola Arc measured to be 128 kilometres. The commission made rapid progress, rarely having any differences in their work up to Kukawa. However, northward to Lake Chad, a discrepancy had to be settled regarding the shore of the Lake. Article VI of the agreement of 12 December 1902 made it clear that the high water mark would be considered as the shore of Lake Chad. But according to Jackson's letter of 26th February 1904, to the Colonial Office (Northern Nigeria, 1909) the Germans attempted to use the low water mark which, if accepted, would have resulted in the loss to Nigeria of the towns of Dikwa, Uba and Bama. The best the commission could do in this case was to chart the boundary line along the Lake using the two water marks and return to Europe, as they did in May 1904, for settlement.

Another conference was fixed for March 1906 in London to settle the disagreement. At the end of the conference on 19th March, an agreement was signed that delimited the boundary from Yola to Lake Chad at as point with Latitude 13° 05′N and approximately Longitude 14° 05′E. Demarcation followed in the same year and was completed in 1907. The final approval of this boundary was not effected until 11 March 1913, almost a year before the First World War, which considerably modified the Nigeria-Kamerun boundary.

It does not require a very close look to notice that the boundary delimited (Fig. 10) deviates considerably from the straight line that existed before 1903 (Fig. 8). The

Figure 10. Nigeria-Kamerun boundary from Yola to Lake Chad after delimitation survey.

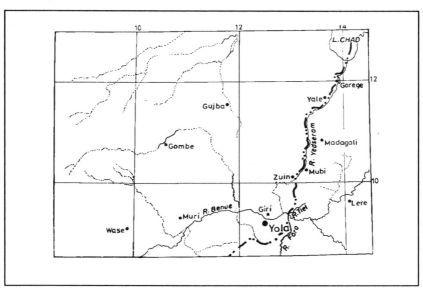

survey apparently brought the commissioners close to the reality of cultural frontiers. Lt. Col. Jackson was an advocate of the use of natural features to delimit boundaries. The need for exchanges of villages arose in order to avoid the division of settlements by boundary lines and to make use of natural boundary features. For example, Chikito was exchanged for Karua in order to use a natural boundary (River Faro). Also it was discovered that errors in fixing positions of places appearing on the late 19th century maps, such as Perthe's German maps on which the boundary definition was initially based, place some settlements under wrong rulers.

Whatever might be the perfection or imperfection of the new boundary line, late developments proved that it would not be the permanent frontier between Nigeria and Kamerun.

Post-War Nigeria-Camerouns Boundary

Germany lost badly during the First World War. By Article 119 of the Treaty of Peace she made with the Principal Allied and Associated Powers, she had to renounce her rights and titles over her overseas possessions. The German Kamerun, which was occupied by French and British Forces during the war, was consequently shared by France and Britain by the London Declaration of 1 July 1919. By the Treaty of Versailles, this decision was recognised by the League of Nations on the 22 July 1922 and the two powers were given mandates to administer the two divisions of the territory. This gave Britain more land to the east of the Nigeria-Kamerun boundary from the Coast to Chad except a section of the Yola Arc (see Fig. 11). The new British possessions were administered together with Nigeria and were known as Northern Cameroun and Southern Cameroun. The Norther Cameroun was separated at a segment of the Yola Arc. With effect from 26 June 1923, Southern Cameroun was regarded as part of the Southern Provinces of Nigeria while Northern Cameroun was regarded as part of the Northern Provinces of Nigeria.

The new possessions of France and Britain introduced a new frontier between the French sphere of influence and the British territory. The line agreed upon in July 1919 and by the Treaty of Versailles in July 1922 had to be delimited. The initial map-based description was done on a 1:300,000 Moisel's map of the Camerouns but the map attached to the agreement was on a smaller scale of 1:200,000. Article 2 of the 1919 Treaty emphasized the need to "lay down the frontier in accordance with natural features" (Colonial Office, 1926, p. 154). In 1930, the inter-Camerouns boundary was defined on the map in greater detail in a protocol that was signed on 9 January 1931. Proper delimitation survey, mapping and on-the-ground translation of the boundary line (demarcation) were embarked upon in late 1937. The project that was estimated to last six years would involve:

(a) A framework of astro-radio points along the boundary at intervals of approximately thirty miles;
(b) Preparation of topographical maps enhancing a strip 5-6.5 kilometres wide on either side of the boundary on a scale of 1:125,000 increased to 1:62,500 in special cases where more details were required.
(c) Demarcation of actual boundary line by pillars. The line was to follow natural features as far as possible, and monuments to be placed where the line meets of departs from them (on straight lines, monuments were to be placed at angle only).
(d) A line of instrumental levels to be run in the vicinity of the boundary, and to be tied to every astro-radio station.

Figure 11. The sharing of German Kamerun between Britain and France.

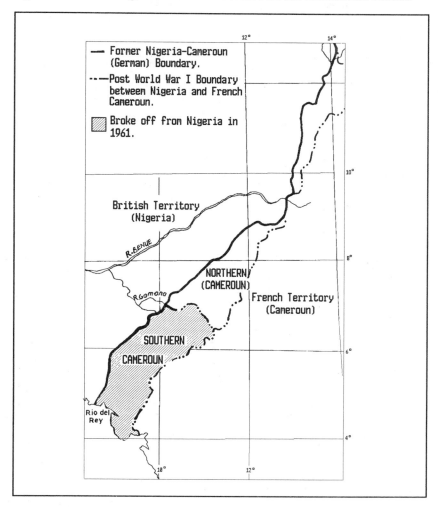

(e) Printing of map on a final scale of 1:100,000 (Nigeria Survey Department, 1937).

The Boundary Commission started work in November 1937 with a plan for the British party under the leadership of J.G.C. Allen, to carry out b,d,e above and half of the pillar installation in C while the French party would undertake the rest. By the end of that year, about two hundred kilometres of the 1600 kilometre boundary line had been mapped in detail from survey data obtained. However, the party could not go beyond Latitude 5° North before the Second World War broke out in 1939.

On 11th February 1961, Northern Camerouns decided in a plebiscite to joint the Northern Region of Independent Nigeria while Southern Cameroun was united with French Cameroun. Thus, the line separating Southern Cameroun as part of the

Eastern Region and Northern Cameroun as part of Northern Region became an international boundary.

Nigeria-Chad Boundary

In the agreement signed on May 29, 1906 between France and Britain over British and French possessions to the east of the Niger, the Nigeria-Chad boundary was defined simply as follows:

> "From this point (centre of the village of Bosso), it will run in a straight line to the point of intersection of the 13th parallel of north latitude with the meridian running 35' east of the centre of the town of Kukuwa, the meridian mentioned in the conventions of 14th June, 1898 and the 8th April, 1904" (HMS Office, 1906, p. 8).

The frontier is now described as a straight line from the Nigeria/Niger/Chad tripartite point (Latitude 13° 42'29" north and Longitude 13° 38' east) the Nigeria/Chad/Cameroun tripartite point (Latitude 13° 05' north and Longitude 14° 05' east).

Conclusion

One could observe intensive and extensive cartographic work in relation to the delineation of Nigerian boundaries in the early years of colonial rule. The efforts gradually got reduced not because all the boundaries initially allocated had been surveyed, accurately mapped and demarcated. In the early years of colonial rule, the enthusiasm was generated by the imagined and anticipated natural endowments of the territories. Gains from most parts of most territories did not justify this enthusiasm and European powers became less interested in boundary demarcation especially after the Second World War, than they were initially. Even to independent African nations, boundary demarcation and maintenance are not regarded as an urgent matter until some economic activities are going on near the boundary or a military incursion is reported. Thus, most villages near Nigerian boundaries have not felt the impact of the Nigerian government and the people living around the boundaries are sometimes closer to their brothers and sisters cut off on the other side than to the nationals of their country. The whole situation is like buying a plot of land that has not been demarcated by survey pillars or walls, and not visiting the plot of land regularly. One day, one would find that a large portion of the land (if not the whole of it) has been used by a more caring owner of the adjacent property.

The incidence of clashes experienced along the northern part of Nigeria-Benin boundary in April 1981, around Nigeria-Cameroun border in 1982, Nigerian-Chad boundary in 1983 has revived interest in boundary issues in Nigeria. General Yakubu Gowon's alleged action at the meeting he had with President Ahidjo of Cameroun at Moroua, Cameroun, in 1975 of giving away several square kilometres of Nigeria's territory to Cameroun (Ajomo, 1982, p. 138) shows that Nigeria had, in the past, not taken the issue of boundary definition as seriously as Britain did in the early decades of colonial administration in Nigeria.

Table 1 presents a summary of the progress of boundary definition in Nigeria. It appears as if Nigeria's eastern boundary, compromising the Nigeria/Cameroun and Nigeria/Chad borders, suffers the greatest neglect in respect of marking on the ground. The original boundary between Nigeria and German Kamerun had been demarcated with pillars by 1913, but with post-World War I developments, the only internationally valid sections of the demarcated boundary are a part of the Yola Arc

Table 1. Scheme of Definition of Nigerian Boundaries

Initial Treaties	Delimitation Surveys	Marking on Ground	Protocol Signed	Final Approval
1. Nigeria-Benin Republic (Anglo-French)				
a. The coast to Lat. 9°N—320 km				
Aug. 10, 1889,	1895-96	1895-96 trees	Oct. 12, 1896	Oct. 19, 1906
July 12, 1893		blazed-cairns	June 14, 1898	
[1] ..	1900	—	Jan. 20, 1900	
[2] ..	—	1912	July 20, 1912	
b. Lat 9°N to Niger—376 km				
		1900 trees blazed	Dec. 22, 1900	
[3] June 14, 1898	1900	& some cairns	& Jan. 1905	Oct. 19, 1906
2. Nigeria-Niger—1490km				
Aug. 1890	Nov. 1902-	—	Apr. 9, 1906	
June 14, 1898	Jan. 1904		May 29, 1906	
Apr. 8 1904				
May 29, 1906	1906, 1907		Feb. 25, 1908 &	May 17, 1911 &
			Feb. 19, 1901	July 1, 1911
3. Nigeria-Chad (Anglo-French)—75km				
[4] 1898, 1904, 1906	—	—	1906	
with Nigeria-Niger				
4. Nigeria-Kamerun (Anglo-Germany)				
a. Sea to Cross River rapids—224km				
Apr. 29/May 7,	1895, Dec. 1905	1906	1906	Mar. 11, 1913
1885, July 27/Aug.	May 1905			
2, 1886, July 1,				
1890 & April 14				
& Nov. 15, 1893				
b. Cross River-Yola Arc rapids—456km				
[5] Nov. 15, 1893	Aug '07-May 1909	1912 & 1913	Apr. 16, 1909	Mar. 11, 1913
c. Yola Arc-Lake Chad—560km				
Nov. 15, 1893	Aug. 10, 1903,	1906-1907	Feb. 12, 1907	
Dec. 2, 1902	Feb. '03-04 & '05	Mar. 11, 1907	Mar. 5, 1909	
5. Nigeria-Cameroon (Anglo-French)—1680km				
[6] Feb 23, 1916	1928		Jan. 9, 1931	—
July 10, 1919	1937-39			
July 22, 1922	(not completed)			

[1]Examination of frontier from confluence of river Iguidu and river Igiawun to road 200 metre north of   Ikoru.
[2]Resurvey/demarcation
[3]Not properly demarcated
[4]Not demarcated
[5]No more an international boundary
[6]Sea-R.Gamana was marked by an Anglo-German Commission (see 4a and b above)

and the section from Rio del Rey Creek to a point where the Gamana River crosses the old boundary (Fig. 11). This is even valid only if Cameroun would respect the protocol signed by Britain and Germany regarding this mutual boundary. The section from Gamana river to Kombon used to be a boundary between the Northern Cameroun and Southern Cameroun under British Trusteeship before 1961 and it had been surveyed. With the change in status, that is from a provincial boundary to an international boundary, it requires another survey that will be supervised by Nigeria and the Republic of Cameroun for it to be internationally accepted. From Gamana river eastward to Kombon and northward to the tripoint with Chad, the Nigeria-Cameroun boundary is yet to be demarcated.

The section of Nigeria-Benin boundary running from Latitude 9° North to the middle of the Niger has also not been fully demarcated with concrete pillars. The alternate cutting of trees along the boundary is not a permanent measure.

Because the Nigeria-Chad boundary falls on Lake Chad, there was no special attention given to its delimitation and demarcation. One would assume that the boundary had always been a straight line whose position shifted as the Lake Chad ends of the Nigeria-Niger and Nigeria-Cameroun boundaries changed. For example, the various conventions (1890, 1898, 1904 and 1906) respecting the Nigeria-Niger boundary also affected the Nigeria-Chad boundary. The end points of the line are now definite, as they are described by their coordinates.

From the foregoing, one could conclude that the Nigerian boundaries are defined enough for the cartographic representation of the territorial limits of the country. Various agreements signed by Great Britain and France on various sections of Nigerian boundaries can confirm this. It is however difficult for people to translate the line on a map onto the ground. Therefore, without proper demarcation with physical and conspicuously visible materials, even the people living around the boundary may not be aware of any boundary. Nigeria has set up joint boundary commissions with the Republic of Benin (since 1968) and the Republic of Cameroun (since 1970). These commissions have, however, concentrated on maritime boundaries. In respect of the Nigeria-Cameroun boundary, this was because of the oil exploration going on both sides of the frontier. Although some efforts at relocating, surveying and demarcating some portions of the Nigeria-Benin boundary have been reported (Abiodun, 1893, p. 5) one cannot be convinced that Nigeria had considered the adequate and proper demarcation of Nigerian boundaries as an urgent matter until the border clashes aforementioned.

It may be necessary for the Nigerian government to set up a permanent Boundary Commission with people from various relevant disciplines to look at the issues of Nigerian's international and intra-national borders. A detailed study of all agreements in respect of all boundaries, part and present, should be carried out. All the textual descriptions in such agreements should be translated on topographical maps of the boundary areas. Delimitation survey records should be checked with a view to reconciling survey tracts with the various demarcation pillars. The sections that have not been demarcated should quickly be surveyed for demarcation. All these are urgent and necessary if recent intensive search for mineral resources, especially petroleum, by various African countries, will not be allowed to promote temptations around the boundaries.

Bibliography

Abiodun, T.A., "Demarcation and survey of Nigeria's frontiers: an aspect of national security", paper presented at the XVIIIth Annual Conference of the Nigerian Institution of Surveyors, Owerri, Nigeria, April 1983.

Ajomo, M.A., "The Nigeria/Cameroun Border Dispute: Implications at International Law", *Nigerian Current Law Review*, April 1982, p. 133-144.

Anene, J.C., *The International Boundaries of Nigeria: 1885-1960* (London: Longman, 1970).

Brownlie, Ian, *African Boundaries, Legal and Diplomatic Encyclopaedia* (London: Hurst, 1979).

Colonial office correspondence relating to the territories of the Camerouns under British administration and their boundaries, AFRICAN (West) No. 1049, 1926.

Elliot, G.S., "The Anglo-French Niger-Chad Boundary Commission", *The Geographical Journal,* Vol. XXIV, No. 5, Nov. 1904, p. 505-522.

Foulkes, C.H., "The new Anglo-French frontier between the Niger and Lake Chad", *Scottish Geog. Mag,* Vol. 22, 1906, pp. 565-575.

Hertslet, E., *The Map of Africa by Treaty,* rd Edition, Vol. 1 Nos. 1-94,British Colonies, Protectorate and Possessions in Africa, 1909, London.

HMS Office, "Agreement between the United Kingdom and France Relative to the Frontier Between the British and French Possessions from the Gul of Guinea to the Niger", Treaty Series, No. 5, Oct. 19, 1906.

HMS Office, "Convention between the United Kingdom and France respecting the Delimitation of the Frontier between the British and French Possessions to the East of the Niger, Treaty Series, No. 24, 1906b, p. 10.

Jones, S.B., "Boundary Making" Carnegie Endowment for International Peace, Div. of Int. Law, No. 8, 1945, Washington, D.C.

Mills, L.R., "An Analysis of the Geographical Effects of the Dahomey-Nigeria Boundary" unpublished Ph.D. thesis, Univ. of Durham, 1970.

Nigeria Survey Department, *Annual Report of Nigeria Survey Department-1937.*

Northern Nigeria, Anglo-French Boundary: Correspondence (April 29, 1904-Oct. 11, 1906) Respecting adjustment of frontier under the Anglo-French convention of April 8, 1904, Colonial Office, London, October 1907.

Northern Nigeria, Correspondence (August 18, 1902-March 30, 1909) Respecting the Anglo-German Boundary (Yola-Chad) Delimitation, Colonial Office, London, May 1090.

Prescott, J.R.V., *The Evolution of Nigeria's International and Regional Boundaries, 1861-1971,* (Vancouver, 1971).

PRO, C039254, Letter from Lt. Col. Peroz to Brigadier Gen. F.D. Lugard, July 31, 1901.

Ravenstein, E.G., "The Anglo-French Boundaries in West Africa", *The Geog. J.,* Vol. XII, No. 1, July 1898, p. 73-75.

U.S. Department of State, "Dahomey-Nigeria Boundary" *International Boundary Study,* No. 91, Oct. 15, 1969.

Winterbotham, H. St. J.L., "The Demarcation of International Boundaries" Conference of Empire Survey Offices, Colonial Office, London, 1928, p. 173-186.

CHAPTER 14

International and Interstate Boundaries in Nigeria: Demarcation and Survey

by O. Adebekun

Introduction

Man's activities in exercise of his liberty and pursuits of his happiness have brought into sharp focus the issues of boundaries. He must exercise these rights within some framework. For example, he belongs to a particular culture group of people, and comes from a particular area of the world. The size of the culture group and the extent of the area the group of people occupies are definite limits within which these activities of man can take place. Borderlands are an offshoot of these definite limits. Boundaries are therefore the limits within which persons exercise some kind of authority. We do of course have landed properties and boundaries which are defined by their perimeter. There are community boundaries for example, i.e. some definite marks on the ground, which separate one community from the other. There are local government boundaries which delimit the areas of jurisdiction of one local government from those of the other, just as there are interstate boundaries which separate the land mass of the one state from that of another. An extension of these boundaries are international boundaries which delimit one country from another country.

In these days, international and interstate boundary issues have grown both in magnitude and in importance that it would be useful for peaceful co-existence to give some attention to them at a Seminar as has been arranged in this University at this time. There are many implications of international and interstate boundaries most prominent among which are political, economic and legal implications. These implications are interwoven into one another and closely inter-connected. Politically it is very necessary that the boundaries of a country are well defined as these determine the limits of areas over which the authorities of the country exercise sovereignty. All exercise of such authorities will have to be carried within the confines of the country and all persons except aliens in that country are legal citizens of that country. Legally, there should be allegiance to the authorities of the country situated within these boundaries by all its citizens. They are to be subject to the juridical and

fiscal laws and regulations of the country to which they belong and not those of
another country or contiguous neighbouring country. Economically, the fortunes of
the inhabitants of the country are tied up with those of the citizens of the country.

Nigeria's International Boundaries

Nigeria has four contiguous neighbouring countries namely People's Republic
of Benin (formerly Dahomey) to the west, Republic of Niger to the north, Republic
of Chad to the northeast, and the Republic of Cameroun to the east. The origin or
evolution of these boundaries is a matter of history about which it is not the intention
in this paper to dwell. It suffices to mention however that the international boundaries of Nigeria as known today have evolved from the series of treaties or under-
takings among the colonial powers made towards the end of last century or at the
beginning of this century. Whatever might have been the motivation and intention
of the colonial powers in making the treaties is not material to the purpose of this
paper. Nor is it considered critical how the colonial powers have arrived at the boundaries. What is important is that these boundaries of frontiers do exist, beyond
which the activities of the citizens of one country should not extend, if such activities are not to be carried out in another country. Of course we do know that to
the ordinary man in a country unless the boundaries have been demarcated, these
frontiers are generally not known, not withstanding that he knows that they exist.
A Nigerian is aware that it is his birth and existence within these borders in Nigeria,
for example, that distinguish him as a Nigerian. He is not a Beninoise on the other
side of the border, nor a Nigerian nor a Chadian, nor a Camerounian, not withstanding the similarities in the nature, cultural behavourial patterns of the peoples of
these contiguous neighbouring countries. As soon as he goes beyond the frontier
to the other side, whether by accident or by design, be begins, to breath 'new' air
notwithstanding that the chemical composition of air is the same all about the world.
If he is as dense as myself in languages, he is completely lost, as the official medium
of communication in the new place in which he has suddenly found himself is completely different from that to which he is used. On the ground, however, it is difficult
to know where the boundary is. Unless physically demarcated by a visible wall or
curtain or marks which are easily located and visible to all persons, to the ordinary
man, international boundary is an imaginary line, which delimits one country from
another. This is more so in the case of the inhabitants of the border areas, where
all along the extensive frontier, they are one and the same people, they have the same
mother-tongue, the customs and culture are the same, they intermarry. As these
boundaries are not demarcated on the ground, people without knowing, develop
their land across the frontiers. It is not impossible, I have observed, for someone
while having a rest in his house to have his head in his country while his feet are
in another country. More importantly, it is possible for a man in the border area to
have his house in one country and his farmland stretching across the border. Thus
while his residence is situated in one country, his means for living or daily activities
are in another country across the border. I have my doubt as to what anti-smuggling
preaching can mean to such persons.

Arbitrary and ridiculous as the international boundaries may seem, the reality
of life is that in Nigeria as well as in other countries in Africa the colonial international boundaries, treaties or understandings between the colonial powers, now
determine, and for ever will do so, the international boundaries between Nigeria and
contiguous neighbouring countries. This has to be accepted by all and sundry, willy

and nilly. In pre-independence era, the boundaries of the country were known by descriptions and accepted by colonial administrators and there would not appear to have been any border conflicts between Nigeria and its neighbouring countries. These same international boundaries of Nigeria were handed over by Britain at Independence. Unless one were to be mischievous, there should be no good reason to shift from the stance of what we took over from Britain.

Interstate Boundaries in Nigeria

Interstate boundaries in Nigeria are the frontiers between pairs of contiguous neighbouring states in the country. In this paper, it is assumed that the history of the present 21 State Structure and what constitutes each state in that structure is known. Of importance to mention however is that interstate boundaries in Nigeria have developed from the old provincial and divisional boundaries, backed up by the decrees of the government on the reports of the Irikefe Panel of 1975 on State Creation, and on the report of the Nasir Boundary Adjustment Commission of 1976.

As in the case of international boundaries, the main framework of interstate boundaries in Nigeria was inherited from the British. A visit to the National Archives in Ibadan, Kaduna and Enugu and a perusal through intelligence reports of the old district offices would vividly show how the framework has evolved. In the pre-independence era, there were, of course, community boundary clashes but it must not be forgotten that the rationale for the main framework of interstate boundaries was good governance, maintenance of law and order and a desire for bringing government to the people as closely as practicable. The measure of success achieved in the pre- and post-independence era is considered by the few number and seriousness of interstate border clashes which the country had witnessed, and which were far in between. It is only in recent years that these clashes have become more and more rampant and incessant. We have in the immediate past witnessed border clashes between the Cross River and Imo States, the Imo and Rivers States, the Benue and Plateau States, the Ondo and Oyo States, Ondo and Bendel States to mention a few. When for example the Cross River, Imo, Rivers, and Anambra States were in the former Eastern Region, there were no such clashes. The same could be said of Ondo, Bendel and Oyo States when they were all in the former Western Region. Nor were there incessant reported cases of inter-regional boundary clashes in the days of regional administration of the country.

Present day interstate border clashes have arisen as a result of old prejudices of the aggrieved communities under the old administrative machineries, a feeling of minority in recently created States and genuine fears of being adequately protected and provided for in the new arrangements, and inordinate desire to be able to control one's destiny by demanding to be constituted into a state, even when the resources available do not justify such a creation.

The ordinary man in the different states of the country is conscious of the state of which he is a citizen. He is also aware that there are interstate boundaries, but exactly where these are on the ground, he would not know. Unless there are definite marks on ground which delimit one state from a border, there is no way by which he can easily know that he is in or outside his state especially in areas remote from the urban areas, particularly in villages and settlements very close to the interstate boundaries.

The effect of knowing the boundary line is less serious here than in the case of international boundaries. The change from one state to another in Nigeria is less problematic than that between Nigeria and its contiguous neighbouring countries, as the entire Nigerian populace is limited by the same official language, same social welfare policy, legal system and have the same economic development aspirations.

Demarcation and Survey

We must distinguish between the technical terms "demarcation" and "survey", as used in surveying. Demarcate "means to place marks on the ground as to be able to see at a glance the separation of a property from another". Thus when a boundary is demarcated, survey marks are placed on the boundary so that the lines joining the survey marks, define such a boundary. Therefore as soon as a boundary is demarcated, it is easy to know on which side of the boundary a person is. Survey is the establishment or determination of the mathematical relationship of the survey marks to one another or to a fixed point either on the boundary or in an easily locatable position. This relationship is then drawn on a map or plan. By surveying the marks, it is possible to re-establish them in their correct positions if and when they are removed or obliterated or destroyed. The demarcation and survey of international and interstate boundaries is therefore panacea to the ills of poor definitions of such boundaries, and is consequently the last hope for the settlement of disputes arising from such poor definition.

Description

Available legal descriptions of international and interstate boundaries, since no survey marks and monument had been emplaced, and such marks surveyed, are generally not precise and therefore capable of more than one interpretation. Apart from the boundaries being arbitrary, the descriptions were based upon the maps which were available and used in delineating the boundaries before being described. Invariably no one had ever visited the field before the delineations of the boundaries on the maps were made. It is therefore not surprising that the descriptions of such boundaries were in general vague. In some cases they followed general natural features such as streams, deepest part of rivers, top of hills, bottom of valleys, along roads or footpaths which connect some towns, villages or settlements etc. In other cases, the descriptions are made in terms of general cardinal directions to well known features and approximate distances, these having been determined by rapid reconnaissance surveys carried out using magnetic compasses, and cyclometers or range finders or other approximate distance measuring techniques. Many interstate boundary descriptions for example had been prepared by the then young colonial administrative officers in the latter manner.

One relevant question which may be asked if these descriptions are to be used in the demarcation and survey of boundaries is to what extent have these descriptions been useful in carrying out the exercise? Let me say right away that these descriptions, no matter how vague or how general, are better than no descriptions at all. For example the treaties made in the early part of the century between the British and the French which provide for the description of the Nigeria/Cameroun international boundary from Yola to the sea were based upon available maps of the country at that time. Present day larger-scale maps are significantly much more accurate than those maps and are more detailed. Notwithstanding this, it may be found that the features which describe the boundaries in the older maps are not now indicated in the new maps. There have been phenomenal changes between the information as available on maps made in those days, and those made nowadays. Using these descriptions of delineation on present-day maps before proceeding to the field often present problems. There could have been nothing as good as actually demarcating and surveying the boundaries soon after the agreement and treaties had been made.

Boundary demarcation and survey is better carried out when there are no boundary conflicts, and emotional disruptions between countries/states. A Joint Boundary Commission of the states concerned comprising the technical experts of the countries/states concerned can then proceed to carry out its defined functions in an atmosphere of peace and mutual confidence using available descriptions. Where there are conflicting interpretations of the descriptions these are technically considered at the technical sessions of the Joint Commission and reconciled before the field operations of demarcation of the boundaries commence.

Status of Demarcation and Survey of International Boundaries

On the international scene, the international boundary between the People's Republic of Benin and the Federal Republic of Nigeria from the sea to the tripartite point on the Nigeria/Niger boundaries on the River Niger had been demarcated. The survey marks on the boundary are however so far apart in some areas that the inhabitants on either side of the boundaries do not know whether or not at any point in time, their activities are either in one country or in the other. Some efforts are now being directed to placing intermediate international boundary marks between pairs of non-invisible marks on the boundaries. In addition, the old boundary marks are now being replaced with more stable monuments which cannot easily be moved or obliterated. Only the southern end of the boundary has been surveyed. As soon as the work on the demarcation is completed, the survey of the entire boundary will be undertaken.

The international boundary between the Republic of Niger and Nigeria starting from the tripartite point on River Niger to the tripartite point on Lake Chad, has remained un-demarcated and unsurveyed. Nigeria has not had any border skirmishes with the Republic of Niger, but the issue cannot be left unattended until there are border conflicts between the two countries. The boundary is in the main along the Komadugu-Yobe River which from all indications is drying up. Besides, the River was being proposed for damming somewhere along its length. There is the danger that its course may alter as a result of such action. Now that its volume is receding, something should be done to demarcate and survey this boundary.

The Nigeria/Chad boundary is a straight line between the tripartite points with the Republic of Cameroun both on Lake Chad. The civil war in the Republic of Chad had frustrated all efforts to demarcate and survey this boundary in the past. This has been further compounded by the closure of all international boundaries by the Federal Military Government, since the take-over at the end of December 1983. [The boundaries were re-opened on 1 March 1986. Eds.] Border clashes between the Republic of Chad and Nigeria have been rampant in recent times particularly with regard to some islands on Lake Chad. The lake, it is understood, is drying up at a very rapid rate. It will be a step in the right direction to see that this international boundary is demarcated on the ground and surveyed to put to rest all uncertainties as to where the boundary really lies, and on which side some disputed islands are.

The Nigeria/Cameroun international boundary is in two sections; the first section is from the sea to Yola and the second is from Yola to the tripartite point with Chad. Neither of these two sections has been demarcated, although some work had been done in this regard in the Southern Sector. The stalemate in the delineation of the maritime boundary between the two countries is responsible for the apparent lull in the efforts to demarcate and survey these boundaries. Arrangements have been made to bring Cameroun to a conference table with a view to re-opening discussion on the demarcation and survey of these two sections of the international boundary.

This paragraph on the status of international boundary demarcation and survey will not be complete without mentioning the position about the maritime boundaries between the two countries. Presently no further work had been done on the delineation of the maritime boundary between Nigeria and the Republic of Cameroun beyond the 15 mile limit, because Nigeria has reservations about the delineation carried out by the joint experts of the two countries as approved by the constituted Heads of States of the two countries, while Cameroun maintained that what was approved by the two Heads of States was legal. A stalemate had been created since 1979 which has not been resolved.

The Nigeria/Benin maritime boundary delineation report had been prepared and is awaiting consideration by the respective governments of the two countries.

Status of Demarcation and Survey of Interstate Boundaries

Except when there were conflicts, very little attempt had been made in the past to demarcate and survey the old provincial and divisional boundaries which have formed the framework for the interstate boundaries of the nineteen states structure. Consequently not many of the interstate boundaries have been demarcated and surveyed. The demarcation and survey of the former Lagos-western boundary which is now Lagos/Ogun interstate boundary have been undertaken and completed. Other interstate boundaries demarcated include Isi-Uzo/Opokwu Section of the Anambra/Benue, Ajowa/Ayire Section Kwara/Ondo, Tudun Wade/Bora Section of Kano/Bauchi. There are many interstate boundary clashes which make it necessary that the demarcation and survey of interstate boundaries should be undertaken as a matter of policy. This will reduce tension arising from problems created by political and other economic activities.

Causes of Slow Action on Demarcation and Survey of Interstate and International Boundaries

In addition to the causes of slow rate of demarcating and surveying of international and interstate boundaries, which are obvious from the earlier submission in this paper, the arrangement for carrying out work on the boundaries would not appear to be totally satisfactory. In the case of international boundaries, the Joint Boundary Commissions are concerned with more than the single purpose of demarcating and surveying the international boundaries. The Nigeria/Cameroun International Commission and the Nigeria/Benin International Boundary Commission in addition to looking after the demarcation and survey of the boundary have in their ambit, co-operation and collaboration, and economic links between Nigeria on the one side, and Cameroun and Benin on the other side respectively. There is therefore a great deal of diversion from the Technical work of demarcating and surveying the boundaries. Once there is a break down in communication with regard to bilateral relations, there will be a corresponding break down in the technical work. This need not be so. The way out of this problem is to have the type of joint work of demarcating and surveying of international boundaries.

Another cause of slowness is the implication of international boundaries. It has to be realised and borne in mind that the era of looking for territories is past. International boundaries though not yet translated physically to the ground, have been agreed upon on paper. They can be indicated on maps and are therefore no longer negotiable. This is a lot of wasted effort in allowing political considerations to influence demarcation and survey of boundaries based upon well documented description of such boundaries. A purely technical solution to the problems of boundary demarcation and survey is advocated.

Internally, the problems are less serious. There must however be the political will to demarcate and survey interstate boundaries not only at the Federal Government level but also at the State government levels. Thus the necessary provisions for costs of the demarcation and survey of the interstate boundaries must be made by the Federal and State governments alike.

Demarcation and survey of all interstate boundaries had not been given the priority it demands in that it is only when there is a dispute that some attention is given to it. Once there is a respite, it is given very little or no attention. For the maintenance of everlasting peace and good governance, all interstate boundaries should be demarcated and surveyed as a matter of policy, from year to year until the exercise is over.

There is a very long time lag between the time that description of international and interstate boundaries were written and demarcation and survey. Due to human activities, the ground features as existed in the early part of this century and in terms of which the boundaries are described have changed significantly. This makes the work of the Technical experts who are to delineate them on present day maps which reflect only present day features difficult. The more the demarcation and survey of the boundaries is delayed, the more the problems which are created perhaps not only for present day experts but those of the future, and eventually for the future generations of Nigerians.

Field Instructions Procedures

It is not the intention of this paper to discuss field instructions for demarcation and survey of international and interstate boundaries because these are outside the scope of this paper. Yet, it is important that demarcation and survey of international and interstate boundaries must be such as will make it possible for all persons in the border areas to know the boundary and on which side of it they are at any point in time. Thus, the boundary survey marks, apart from being well built and unassailable, must be visibly emplaced. This will assist quite easily all law enforcement and security organisations in checking the illegal activities of smugglers and saboteurs and reduce incidents of crime or aggression from either side of the border.

Finally maps at suitable scales must be prepared to indicate the international and interstate boundary marks and which will serve as good reference for future visits to the marks.

References

Agreement between the United Kingdom and Germany respecting (a) the settlement of the Frontier between Nigeria and the Camerouns from Yola to the Sea and (b) the regulation of Navigation on the Cross River: Treaties Series No. 13, 1913.

Proclamations under the Nigeria (Constitution) Order-In-Council 1954-1958. First Schedule Part III Section 0.

Exchange of notes between the United Kingdom and France respecting the boundary between British and French Cameroun: Treaty Series No. 34 (1931).

Agreement between Britain and France relative to the Frontier between the British and French possessions from the Gulf of Guinea to the Niger 19th October 1906: Treaty Series No. 5 of 1907.

Agreement between the United Kingdom and France respecting the delimitation of the Frontier between the British and French possessions from the Gulf of Guinea to the Okpara River: Treaty Series No. 5, 1914.

Agreement between the United Kingdom and France on the demarcation of Borders between their respective possessions east of the River Niger signed in London 19th February, 1910.

Convention between Great Britain and France respecting the delimitation of the Frontier between British and French possessions from Yola to Chad. Signed in London 29th May, 1906.

Convention determining the boundaries between Cameroun and the French Congo signed on 18th April, 1908.

CHAPTER 15

A Socio-Linguistic Profile
of Nigeria's Northern and
Eastern Borders

by C.M.B. Brann

Introduction

The situation is presented on the triglottic configuration model, previously used in the description of Nigeria (Brann) and Cameroun (Tadadjeu), but now applied to the border groups.

At the level of autochthonous ethno-linguistic groups (chthonolects), Nigeria shares the Chadic sub-family deriving from the north with Niger (Western Chadic), Chad (Eastern Chadic) and Cameroun (Central Chadic), the largest ethno-linguistic fragmentation being on the Nigeria-Cameroun border. It shares Kanuri as the only Saharan language in Nigeria—but now its centre—with Niger, Chad and Cameroun; dialectal Arabic (Shuwa) with Chad and Cameroun in the northeastern corner, together with Kanuri. In the second belt (Borno and Gongola states), it shares Fulfulde—the only West Atlantic language in Nigeria—throughout the eastern border, north of the Benue; the fragmentation belt of the Adamawa language group in the area of that name in Nigeria and Cameroun; and finally it shares smaller Bantoid language groups on both sides of the Nigeria-Cameroun border—possibly originating in Cameroun itself. In addition to settled groups, nomads (Tuareg, Bororo), immigrants (Banana, Ngambai, Kabba) and migrant workers (Kaka) came into Nigeria from Niger, Chad, and Cameroun respectively.

At the level of lingua francas (demolects) for inter-ethnic communication, Hausa sweeps across the northern border into Niger, where it is also a major autochthonous (and national) language but serves as a lingua franca between the many Chadic-speaking minorities, more on the Nigerian than the Chadian or Camerounian side. Fulfulde as the lingua franca of Nigerian Adamawa is fast being replace by Hausa, whilst it remains the lingua franca of Camerounian Adamawa and Province du Nord (the former Fombina). Dialectical Arabic links the northeastern tip to its Chadian congeners, but is also the lingua franca of the Islamised minorities, as well as traditionally of the Kanembu-Kanuri. South of the Benue, it is Pidgin that serves as lingua franca on both sides of the Nigeria-Cameroun border.

At the level of exolects, or imported language, the northeastern borders were disputed by four colonial powers: the Arabs under Rabeh reinforced a prior Arab presence—Arabic being now considered a native, as well as an inter-ethnic language; the short-lived German colonisation, which disappeared without trace; and the lasting official use of French and English—French in Niger and Chad (which also elected Arabic as co-official), and French plus English in Cameroun. Whereas the borders north of the Benue are divided into English and Nigeria and French in Cameroun, south of the Benue English is officially used in Cameroun, in diglossia with Pidgin.

Phenomena of language maintenance, shift, separation (glossotomy) and spread are discussed with reference to demographic proportion of the ethno-linguistic groups on either side of the borders, and language use in various public domains—in relation to language policy, planning and development.

Whilst seizing the opportunity to present this essay within the framework of the Comparative Borderlands Research Project of University of Lagos, I must disclaim at the outset any completeness in the data presented here. On the one hand I have not had access to the *Atlas Linguistique du Cameroun* (ALCAM) which has a significant socio-linguistic element, for the simple reason that correspondence with that country functions badly. On the other hand though I benefitted greatly from the fine *Index of Nigerian Languages* of 1976 by the former Institute of Linguistics of Jos, I could not gain access to the detailed language map prepared by Professor Carl Hoffmann in the same year for the Federal Surveys. Professor Hoffmann's work, which must have taken many years, has no been available to the public, in spite of my repeated attempts to gain access to it. And concerning the *Index of Nigerian Languages,* it was precisely with regard to border languages, that the editors acknowledged weaknesses of location. The *Index* is at present being revised, but it may take some years before the results will be known. The National Language Centre in Lagos announced a year ago that it would commence on a nationwide language survey, but has so far lacked the means and direction to undertake such a gigantic task. [The Centre has since been merged into what is now Nigerian Educational Research and Development Council. Eds.] I have therefore had to limit myself to available written sources, including the 1972 *Nigerian Ethnic Groups Survey* by Ajato Gandonu, presently of Ahmadu Bello University, older materials and personal contacts. It was not, of course, possible within the space of two months, and with a full university schedule of lectures, to venture myself to the borders. That in itself would have been a year's work.

Within this limitation I can offer visible data in a conceptual framework—that of the triglottic configuration, which had been used both with various multilingual countries in Africa, and more specifically with Cameroun by Tadedjeu and Nigeria by myself. This framework will enable us to see the woods for the trees which, I am happy to say, have not yet all been axed to make way for industrialisation. For if the future promises Nigeria to get out of the wood, it may be for having sacrificed the trees within it. I am of course making metaphorical statements with reference to languages. The northern border region is characterised by wide open savanna plains, facilitating the movement of peoples on horseback or camel in former, and by motor vehicle and train in modern times. In addition there is the waterway of Lake Chad. The region has therefore favoured the incursion and spread of the Chadic-speaking peoples from the north and northeast, of which the Hausa are now the dominant representatives in historic times. The classical *Hausa bakwai* were established in what now is southern Niger and northern Nigeria, which thus forms one ethnic-linguistic block. Hausa, however, is more than an ethnic group in the making, being actually the most dynamic of all West African languages, in absorbing rapidly not only minority groups, but also members of major groups in the diaspora, as with the Fulbe and Kanuri, who settle among them (Kirk-Greene).

The two major groups of the northwest and the northeast both belong to the Saharan linguistic family, the Songhai and the Kanuri. The Songhai empire went down into what is now Niger and the northwestern border of present Nigeria, where peoples cross easily from one side to the other (cf. Prothero). The major group of the northeast, the Kanuri crossed Lake Chad in the 14th century, when they gradually overlaid and absorbed prior Chadicspeaking peoples, sometimes collectively called the 'So'. Kanuri is the only major Saharan language spoken in Nigeria, as well as in Niger and Chad in various dialects, though the bulk of the people of Kanem are now in Nigeria. However, whereas centuries ago the Kanuri absorbed Chadic-speaking peoples, it is now the opposition with respect to Hausa, which is fast becoming the lingua franca even of Kanuri cities, notably Maiduguri. Hausa is thus considered dynamic or aggressive, Kanuri post-dynamic or regressive.

In the northeastern corner of the Federation, the Kanuri live in symbiosis with the Shuwa, who are Sudanese Arabs and have lived in Chad for many centuries. They came with the Kanuri centuries ago, whilst more recent invasion by Rabeh brought fresh recruits to their numbers, where they are now centred on Dikwa in Nigeria, Ndjamena in Chad and Kusseri in Cameroun. Through the Shuwa, collo-quial or dialectal Arabic forms a lingua franca throughout the northeastern tip, through Chad and the Cameroun to the Sudan. In Chad, Arabic is now also an of-ficial language, as well as language of wider communication throughout the state.

The fourth major language group is the Fulbe (also referred to as the Fulani) whose gradual incursion as pastoralist, later agriculturalists and more recently scholar-missionaries and administrators, brought them from the northwest right across to the central northeast, where their language is still dominant throughout their former kingdom of Fombina (Abubakar, 1977), which is partly in Cameroun, and partly in Nigeria. Like the Kanuri, the Fulbe are the unique representatives of a language group—the West Atlantic—their origin being on the Senegal river.

The 19th century Jihad of the Fulbe came to Adamawa later than in the more cen-tral parts of the Sokoto Caliphate. It lasted from 1806 to 1851, the year in which Yola town was established. It was the largest of emirates, but also contained the smallest percentage of Fulbe, of whom some joined the jihadists from Borno.

Apart from the above major peoples, the northeast and centre east is inhabited by the same *Chadic-speaking peoples* as were there before the jihad. Whereas the *Kotoko* are almost all in Cameroun and speak the Shuwa as their second language, the *Mandara,* whose earlier capital Kirawa is in Nigeria, now have their capital, Mora, in Cameroun. Apart from their various dialects/languages, they speak Kanuri as their second language, having intermarried with them. The *Sukur,* whose origin lies in Psakali near Mokolo, live in the mountains. The *Highi* of Bazza-Michika are known as *Kapsigi* in Cameroun. Whilst they have Fulfulde language of the Fulbes as their second language on the Cameroun side, they have Hausa now as their second language on the Nigerian side. The same is true of the *Fali* of the border area east of Mubi, whence they are known as the Fali of Mubi. The *Bachama-Bata,* now known as *Bwatiye,* live in the Benue valley, between Garoua and Numan. To this language group also belong the Gude, equally divided by the border.

South of the Benue are a number of the *Adamawa language family,* which straddles the border of Nigeria and Cameroun, including the *Vere-Duru Group* with Vere,
Wom, Mumbake, Kotopo and Kutin, the *Nimbari Group* with Nyamnyam, the
Mbum Group with Laka and the *Sama Group* with Chamba (Dakka) and Dirim,
whilst the extensive (G)baya peoples are straddled by both the Nigeria-Cameroun
and the Cameroun-Central African Republic (CAR) borders, (i.e. they stretch right
across). These are on the sites quoted by the 1972 survey as being occupied by the
'Dakkakai', 'Liro' and 'Chamba'. On account of the situation across the Adamawa
mountains, it may be supposed that they are among the oldest settled peoples of
those parts. Apart from the *Chamba,* centred mainly in Nigeria and the *Gbaya,* centred mainly in Cameroun and CAR, these are minority peoples. On the Nigerian
side, these peoples are in the process of Hausanisation, whilst on the Cameroun
side, they have Fulfulde as their language of wider communication.

Southwards of this group are a number of Bantoid peoples, evidently related to
the vast family stretching across Africa, whom some linguist and anthropologists
suppose to have had their origin in Cameroun itself. The *Tiv,* a major people in
Nigeria spill over into Cameroun. To their linguistic group (the *Tiv-Batu Group*)
belong the Icheve, Evant, Bitare, Abon and Batu, of whom there are groups in both
Nigeria and Cameroun.

A previously widely spread people, the Jukun (Central Jukunoid, Jukun, Jibu
in Hoffmann) do not appear to spread into Cameroun. They have retreated from the
borders, their lands having been conquered by other peoples. To the Jukunoid
branch also belong the Yukuben and Kuteb (in Gandonu called Kutev and Zumperi),
who are sometimes cited as spilling over into Cameroun, sometimes not.

South of these is the *Mambila-Vute* group of languages, across the Mambila
Plateau and on both sides of the border: these are the Mambila themselves who, having Fulbe chiefs, still use Fulfulde as their second language, whilst the Kamkam,
Ndoro and Vute (Bute) tend to turn to Hausa on the Nigerian, and to Fulfulde on
the Camerounian side.

Classified under the Benue-Congo family, the *Cross-River Branch* comprises
peoples of the language groups living southwards of the above. Of these, straddling,
the border are the Bokyi, Kukele, Mbembe, Ikom, Korop (Ododop) and Efik, of
whom the last named is the largest group. They mostly share Pidgin as their lingua
franca.

Appellation and Localisation of Ethno-linguistic Groups: Who and Where?

The reason for the bewildering wealth of names for peoples and languages of
Nigeria is partly due to differences in classification by ethnographers and linguists.
Ethnographers, like Temple and Meek and their contemporary colleagues, work on
criteria of common descent, affinity and locality. Linguists have used criteria of lexical similarity and mutual intelligibility to determine the differences between speech
forms. Thus the *Nigerian Ethnic Groups Survey* of Gandonu lists 28 ethnic groups
along the northern and eastern borders of Nigeria (cf. Annex I...), whilst the *Index*
of Nigerian languages records some 56 languages for the same borders. Neither of
them records fluctuating or migrant populations, since both are concerned with
sedentary people and their languages; nor do they record any Margi.

North of the Benue. Thus along the northern border, the *Survey* lists 3 groups—
the Adar, Gobir and Asbin—which in the *Index* are subsumed under Hausa, since
they no longer speak their own languages, but have been assimilated; similarly the

Survey records *Manga* as a separate group, which the *Index* subsumes under Kanuri, as a dialect. The *Survey* does not mention either the *Mober,* of which it is not sure whether they are a Chadic-speaking or Kanuri-speaking people, or the *Buduma* on Lake Chad, who are Chadic-speaking. On the eastern frontier, the *Survey* also omits the *Affade,* related to Kotoko on the Cameroun-Chad side (Chadic). *Survey* mentions the *Gwoza,* where *Index* has Laamang, Dghwede. *Survey* records *Mandara,* where *Index* lists *Wandala* (381), *Glavda* (117), *Guduf* (124), *Ngoshe Ndhang* (294), not to mention *Sukur* and *Matakam*—all across the border. Both list *Fali* and *Higi,* but *Survey* uses *Cheke,* where *Index* has *Gude,* the commoner term for the same people/language (question of appellation). *Survey* presents *Turi* which could be *Tur,* a dialect of Laamang south, (i.e., of what *Survey* calls the Gwoza, from which it is separated on the map). *Survey* does not show *Nzanqi* at all, whilst *Batta* in *Survey* is well away from the border on its map, which spills over into Cameroun according to *Index* (question of localisation). Both mention the Fulbe as straddling the Benue: *Survey* as *Fulani, Index* as *Fulfulde.*

South of the Benue. Survey map shows *Yerre,* which is presumably is *Verre,* whereas *Index* shows several members of the Vere-Duru group as straddling the borders: *Vere* (377), *Wom* (383), *Leko* (253), *Mumbake* (282), *Kotopo* (219), *Kutin* (358). The *Index* also shows *Koma* (215) across the Camerounian border, as an unclassified Adamawa language, missing in *Survey.* Next, *Survey* shows in succession *Dakkakai, Luro* and *Chamba,* which could correspond to *Chamba Dakka* (61) and *Chamba Lekko* (62) of the *Index.* Perhaps there is confusion here with the *Dak-karkari* or *Lela of Sokoto State,* which *Survey* gives as *Dakarki.* Belonging to the Sama (Chamba) group. *Index* also mentions the *Dirim* (177), possibly another name for the *Dakka. Index* also shows the *Nyamnyam* (303) as straddling the border, not in *Survey.*

Next, the *Mambila-Vute* group (I.A.5.4 a.i. in Hoffmann) is subsumed under *Mambila* in *Survey,* whilst *Index* gives *Mambila* (256), *Kamkam* (193), Ndoro (2900—somewhat inland in location on *Survey* map), and *Mbute* (276).

Of the Tiv-Batu group (I.A.5.4.a.ii Hoffmann), *Survey* only records *Tiv,* but does not show its relation with the border, which it apparently straddles. Also belonging to the group, across the border, are the *Icheve* (142) known as *Mesaka* in Cameroun, *Evant* (in Cameroun known as *Assumbo*) (105), *Bitare* (49), *Abon* (2), and *Batu* (40).

Whilst, according to *Index,* no form of the *Jukun* language cluster straddles the border, *Survey* gives the related Jukunoid *Zumperi,* but also *Kutez,* which is given as *Kuteb* (Mbarike Zumper) (*Index:* p. 176), but not on the border. It would be interesting to ascertain whether the far-flung Jukun language is confined to the Nigerian side of the border with Cameroun.

Of the *Cross River* languages, *Index* lists *Obanliku* (305) as straddling the border but not *Survey* (unless it is there under another name), whilst *Bok(y)i* is identified both by *Survey* and *Index* (052); *Kukele* (225) is in *Index,* but not in *Survey; Mbembe* (273) in *Index,* is known as *Tigon* in *Survey* and is chiefly in Cameroun; *Ikom-Olulumo* (318) is shown as being on the border in *Index,* but not in *Survey; Korop* or *Odopop* (218) is listed in *Index,* but not shown in *Survey,* unless it is identical with Nidiri or Agara of the *Survey*—neither of which I have been able to identify in the *Index.* What is shown as *Anyang* in *Survey* is given as a language near Mamfe in *Ethnologue* and in the *Sociolinguistic Survey of Urban Centres in Cameroun* (Koenig). Of the *Ekoid* Bantu group (Hoffmann I.A.5.4.b.i.), *Ekoi* is shown as a unit on *Survey*, which would include *Bendeghe, Ejagham, Etung and Qua*, across the borders. Of the *Efik-Ibibio-Anaang* language cluster (I.A.5.3.b.ii, Hoffmann), *Efik*, (88) is shown both in *Survey* and *Index*. Apart from uncertainties in classification (e.g. Mober—a Chadic language Mbembe, Jukunoid or Delta Cross? Koma⁵Adamawa?), the chief uncertainties are in the location of the border language-groups, largely because of the inaccessibility of so many of them. This is stated quite frankly in the *Index*, which is being currently revised and is evident in the 1972 survey. Of the areas/languages of the borders, the *Index* is seeking information on: The Chamba Daka area; the Mober area on the border of Borno State and Niger; a number of border areas particularly along the Nigerian-Cameroun border which seem to be very sparsely inhabited and difficult areas of access, including the location of *Kaka* and *Kamkam*, mentioned as straddling the Nigeria-Cameroun border. Uncertainties in appellation of language groups arise mainly from accentuating one or the other *clan*, perhaps one in Nigeria and another across the border in Cameroun, both belonging, however to the same ethnos. Concerning appellation, it must be noted that in linguistic indexes, such as the one by SIL, the trend is to give the autonym, or self-appellation of the group, such as *Ejagham*, in lieu of *Ekoi*, *Kamwe*, instead of *Higi, Laamang*, instead of Gwoza etc. This trend can, of course, go too far—i.e. become disruptive of information, as when we would call the Germans against Deutsch or Dutch, etc. However, there is a dire need for the standardisation of ethnonyms and glossonyms, not only in Nigeria itself, but also as between Nigeria and her neighbours.

Definition of groups or languages. It has been seen that the chief differences between the *Survey* and the *Index* arose from a difference in definition and analysis. Since it had been announced in 1984 that there would be both revision of the *Index*, as well as a National Survey of languages in Nigeria, this might be the time to reconsider the criteria according to which speech forms are defined as languages, rather than dialects of the same language; language groups or clusters rather than a language, in an attempt to reduce the number of speech forms for a standardisation and inter-communication. In the case of speech forms spoken across international boundaries it would certainly be useful to consult with researchers from those areas, as with the *Atlas Linguistique du Cameroun*, which has been going now for a lustre. It will have to be decided whether purely formal criteria of lexis, or appreciation of intelligibility (whether reciprocal or non-reciprocal) should best be supplemented by attitude polls, to see which speech groups can be amalgamated, and which cannot. As a rare example, it may be recalled that recently the Bacama and Batta decided to join forces, and call their language Bwatiye, thus possibly saving their language from absorption by Hausa. At all events it will be essential for any overall survey to apply a centrally conceived plan and method, which is not always evident in the *Index*, which had to rely on the disparate collections of linguists and missionaries, with very different appreciations of ethno-linguistic forms and forces.

From the table of demographic distribution (Annex, III), we can see either the *dominance* of one language group in a country or its even distribution across the borders. (Figures in parenthesis are thousands; x⁵indeterminate; m⁵migrants). Thus the following language groups are predominant outside Nigeria: in Chad, the Banana, Gambai, Kotoko are predominant in its south, from where they came to Nigeria through the wedge of Cameroun. They come sporadically either as recent migrants or settlers, or are already wholly absorbed into Fulbe, Kanuri or Hausa society. Sudanese Arabs (in this country called Shuwa), however, are clearly predominant in Chad, from where they originally came, either as traders in the van of the Kanuri conquest, or more recently as soldiers in the army of Rabeh.

In Cameroun the Baya (140:5) are predominant though their largest concentration is in the Central African Republic.

The other prominent cross-border units are Kaka (25:m), who came into Nigeria as seasonal labourers; the Korop (Ododop) (13:x); the Matakam (136:3; the Mbute or Vute (21:1)—whilst most of the language groups on the Nigerian-Camerounian border predominate on the Nigerian side.

As between Nigeria and Chad the *Buduma* predominate (55:25) as well, of course as the Kanuri. However, the oldest Kanuri group, the *Kanembu,* predominate in Chad, whence they have come to Nigeria, as they did in the 19th century in large numbers with the court of the El-Kanemi dynasty. They have since totally assimilated to more recent speech forms of their cousins. Although it is known that there are large Hausa settlements in Chadian cities, available socio-linguistic descriptions (Barreteau, CONFEMEN and Sow) are strangely silent as to their numbers: are they looked upon perhaps as Trojan horses with regard to the big brother, Nigeria? At all events, they must constitute an indigenised, though not autochthonous minority. The Fulbe are equally ubiquitous, though less settled and form another link with Nigeria. It may be of interest to note the first census of Fort Lamy of 1911 (Works 1976:105), in which, out of 3148 persons, 669 were Arabs, 60 Fulbe, 86 Hausa, 606 Kanuri, 80 Kotoko and 205 Sara-Gambai.

As between Nigeria and Cameroun, most of the smaller groups predominate on the Nigerian side, such as the *Bitare* (46:4), the *Boki* (83:5), the *Dakka* (60:10), the *Chamba Leko* (160), the *Efik* (26:10), the *Fali* of Mubi (30:16), the *Glavda* (20:3), the *Gude* (40:18), the *Hiqi/Kapsiki* (180:41), the *Kukele* (26:x), the *Laamanq/Gwoza* (31:9), the *Mambila* (60:20), the *Southern Marqi* (x:y), the *Mumbake* (10:x), the *Ndoro* (10:1), the *Nzanqi* (14:8), the *Obanliku* (29:x), the *Sukur* (10:x), the *Tiv* (1400:x), and *Verre* (26:x). There are Hausa and Kanuri communities in the northern cities which retain their identities and may for that reason not be considered autochthonous in Cameroun, whilst the Fulbe (infra) are so considered.

In addition to language groups that show a predominance, there are some, both small and large, that are balanced as between the border countries. Thus the *Affade* are on both sides of the Nigeria-Cameroun border; the *Ejagham/Ekoi* are almost evenly divided (45:35), the *Adamawa Fulbe* are equally strong in Nigerian and Camerounian Adamawa. Though *Fulfulde* plays a dynamic role as lingua franca in the whole of the northern Cameroun, in Nigeria it is seen to be regressing, becoming a purely ethnic language, on account of the position of Hausa, which the Fulbe have helped to spread in Nigeria itself, but not in Cameroun. The *Kamkam* are equally divided, as are the *Kotopo, Shua* (100:64), *Wandala/Mandara* (19:24) and *Wom* (10:13).

The Demolects as Lingua Franca Across the Borders

Songhai. History tells us that the major languages in the Central Sudan were *Songhai, Hausa* and *Kanuri,* apart from Arabic, which will be considered under the exolects. Songhai-Zarma is reported to be spoken by 18% of the population of Niger by Tersis in Barreteau, 21% by Brauner (1985), 22% by Heine and 24% by *Ethnologue* (1984). If we take Brauner's figure of 21% as a mean, we still have a 'language nationale', but of limited range, being concentrated in the southwestern parts adjoining Sokoto state of Nigeria, which harbours some 50,000 Zarma-

Songhai speakers. One could say that Songhai, as an imperial language of wider communication, has dwindled to a medium ethnic language.

Hausa. In Niger, the number of Hausa speakers as a percentage of the population varies as between 38% in Tersis, 48% in Heine, 50% in *Ethnologue* and 51% in Brauner, but Heine gives in addition a total of first and second language speakers as 73% and Brauner as 85% of the population, characterising Hausa as the lingua franca of Niger, as it is of northern Nigeria, where the figures are quite comparable. Whilst until the 19th century Hausa was a relatively modest language by comparison with the imperial languages of Songhai and Borno, it was curiously enough the Fulbe who spread it first eastward during the 19th century, through their identification with the Hausa city states, and finally the British through its adoption as the co-official language of the northern provinces (except Borno) in the 20th century. Through its remarkable qualities of assimilation (which it shares with English), Hausa has become the lingua franca of the western Sudan, par excellence; has absorbed many of the minority languages of the north within living memory and is in successful competition both with Fulfulde and Kanuri in the northeastern parts of the country, in some parts right up to the Camerounian border and beyond. Though 24,000 first language speakers are recorded by *Ethnologue* for Cameroun, it serves as lingua franca in the northern cities, as between the various Nigerian ethnic groups in the diaspora, in such cities as Marwa (Muroua), Garwa (Garoua) whereas for the Camerounian groups *inter se,* Fulfulde serves still as the lingua franca, in addition to French. It is curious, though, that *Ethnologue* does not record any first language speakers of Hausa for Chad, where Hausawa (Hausa-speaking peoples) have lived in diaspora on the road to Mecca for centuries—possibly because they have identified with other peoples and have become bilingual (Works 1976).

Kanuri. Like Songhai, Kanuri has an imperial past, has gone through centuries of language and is now receding before Hausa. When the Sef dynasty came to Borno from beyond Lake Chad in the 14th century, that part was inhabited by Chadic-speaking peoples, probably the So, whom the Kanem people either pushed back, or totally absorbed. But some of the peoples peripheral to the empire, though they spoke Kanuri, retained consciousness of a separate ethnic identity, such as the Manga and the Mober on the borders of Niger, whilst the Buduma on Lake Chad, though they became Muslims at a later date, were never totally absorbed. Nor were the mountain peoples of the Mandara, even though dynastic marriages brought them within the cultural orbit of Borno, and spoke Kanuri as their second language. Since the 19th century jihad of Usman dan Fodio, the conquest of Katagum, the destruction of the capital Birni Ngazargamo by the Fulbe, the area covered by the Kanuri had been shrinking and the language has started to retract as a second language. This is exemplified by some Marghi, whose grandparents spoke Kanuri as their language, their parents Fulfulde and they themselves Hausa, whilst their children speak only Hausa and English, apart from Marghi. Or taking Maiduguri itself, which became the capital of El-Kanemi Shehus only in 1907, the Shehu Umar in the 1930's still forbade Hausa to be spoken at his court: Maiduguri was a city where only Kanuri and Arabic was spoken.

Early colonial administrators used interpreters in Arabic to speak to the Shehus, and were often posted with prior Sudanese experience. Even before the Second World War, emigrating Chadians, like the Sara-Ngambai or the Banana, learned Kanuri as their lingua franca, rather than Hausa. All this has changed in the last 40 years, especially since the opening of the region through roads, railways and air traffic, and more so since in 1967 Maiduguri became the capital of what was then known as the Northeastern State, bringing thousands of civil servants, junior staff, traders and craftsmen from the multilingual areas of Bauchi, Adamawa and Sardauna Provinces. As a result of the British administration, Arabic has been replaced by English as the high language, whilst Kanuri has been replaced by Hausa as lingua franca, following post-independence developments.

It would seem that Kanuri is suffering the same fate in Niger. Heine (1979) cites 8% first language speakers, but does not mention second language speakers; Tersis (1978) cites 6.5% whilst Brauner (1985) cites only 4%—even though Kanuri has been declared one of the 5 'national' languages. It is significant that the Manga are attempting their linguistic independence by having consented to have the scriptures translated into their dialect, whilst another translation is proceeding into Yerwa in Maiduguri itself. This is an example of international frontiers favouring the separate development of the same language: others will follow.

In northern Cameroun, the Kanuri there called *Borno* (in French *bornouan*) are both an indigenous minority of some 60,000 and a concentration of traders (in kola and hides) in cities like Marwa. There their lingua franca is Arabic rather than Fulfulde. Radio Garoua broadcasts in Fulfulde and Shuwa, but not in Kanuri.

In Chad, the original home of the Kanem, Kanembu as well as Kanuri one can only estimate the number of first language speakers around 200,000 in toto. Caprile in Barreteau, followed by Brauner, gives figures only for the whole family of Saharan language speakers, including the Tubu, whilst Sow omits Chad altogether from his book. Heine cites 13% first language speakers, which appears to be the figure given by Caprile as covering the entire Saharan family, and cannot therefore be adopted here. We have shown above that early in the century (1911), the Kanuri constituted 20% of the population of Fort Lamy, close to the Nigerian frontier including the Kanembu, while in 1950, Works cites no less than 23 Kanuri mosques out of a total of 36 for the same capital. In Chadian urban areas, like Fort Lamy, however, the Kanuri are highly Arabicised, the lingua franca of Ndjamena being Arabic at the colloquial and French at the official level, not Kanuri. In the state of Borno itself, the Kanuri live in symbiosis with the Shuwa, with whom they intermarry. But whilst the Kanuri nowadays easily adopt Arabic towards Chad, the converse does not seem any longer to be the case, showing the retreat of the language. This is also shown by the many Kanuri living in diaspora in the Hausa cities of Kano, Katsina, Sokoto, Zaria etc., where they have assimilated to Hausa within two generations, whilst maintaining the memory of their ethnic identity hence the large number in the 1963 census (Kirk-Greene, 1967). We thus speak of an Arabisation of the Kanuri in the Chad Basin, in Nigeria, Chad and Cameroun, and of a gradual Hausanisation westwards in Nigeria and Niger.

There has, however, been a conscious effort in recent years, both in Nigeria and Niger, to revive and standardize the language: Kanuri is broadcast from Zinder, and N'guigmi (Niger), Maiduguri plus booster stations and Njamena. In Borno, it is one of 3 state languages, with Hausa and English in Public Enlightenment, Broadcasting, Primary and Adult Education and in the recent Legislature. Indeed Borno was the only state of the Federation to introduce a Nigerian language for its legislative procedure other than one of the major three (i.e. Hausa, Igbo and Yoruba). And the use of Kanuri in the legislature was powerfully supported by the Manga members from the Niger border, who sometimes did not know Hausa, or did not want to be seen to know it. Since the Department of Languages & Linguistics of the University of Maiduguri is involved in this revival, and in the process of standardisation and modernisation, it will take some years to see whether or not the regression of the language is irreversible.

Fulfulde or Peul, the language of the Fulbe has had a converse development to that of Kanuri. Whereas the Kanuri have always been compact, the Fulbe have been and are still sporadic, from Senegal to Cameroun, arriving in Kanem-Borno as pastoralists in the 17th century. Since then they have lived as pastoralists and later as farmers among the Hausa, Kanuri and other northern Islamised peoples, without being absorbed, until the 19th century. The early 19th century saw their great day: through their religious leader, Usman dan Fodio, they spread throughout the Hausa states, most of which they annexed; and outflanked Borno on the east, by traversing what is now Nigeria, deep into Cameroun and into Central Africa. Linguistically, the outcome was the Fulbernisation of the northern kingdoms which became emirates under the sovereignty of the Sokoto Caliphate, somewhat like the Normans in England 800 years earlier. Like the Normans, the Fulbe were assimilated in turn by those they conquered, to the effect that nowadays none of the northern emirs, except those of Gombe and Yola, speaks Fulfulde.

As Kirk-Greene (1967) points out, the high figure for the Fulbe in the 1963 census (4.8 million, or 8.6% of the population) refers to ethnic identifiers, not to the number of first language speakers. It is, however, in Adamawa, far distant from Sokoto, that the Fulbe emirates of Fombina succeeded in maintaining the language and customs, against the influence both of the Kanuri and Shuwa in the north and the Hausa in the west—until recently. For 150 years Fulfulde was the daily administrative language of Fombina, which still influences the present states of Gongola and Bauchi and the Adamawa of Cameroun. On the Nigerian side, taking previous censuses (1952, 1963) into consideration, we can posit 25% as first and 75% as first and second language speakers, (i.e., some one and three million speakers respectively on the Cameroun side), the total population of the Federation being some 9 million, with 25% Muslims, it can be posited that there are some 2.25 million speakers of Fulfulde to whom half a million are first language speakers—not dissimilar to the situation in Nigeria.

The difference between the Nigerian and Camerounian situation is, however, that in Cameroun Fulfulde is the only predominant lingua franca of the north and appears to be maintaining its position, even in the presence of Kanuri (regressive) and Shuwa (stationary) and French (expanding slowly with western education). Whereas in Nigeria the main competitors are Hausa, to which Fulfulde began 'to yield on political and wide-contact grounds' (Kirk-Greene 1967:90) in the 1960's (i.e., after Independence) and English, which is gaining ground at the level of would-be universal primary education and adult literacy.

Taking the 1977/78 Sociolinguistic Survey of Cameroun Urban Centres (Koenig), it can be seen that in *Ngaoundere,* with a native Mbum population, Fulfulde was the first language of 44% and the second language of 58% of the stratified sample (N^5369). Hausa, on the other hand, was already the first language of 25% and the second language of 37% of the population. *Garoua,* further north, with a native population of Fulbe, Fulfulde was the first language of 56% and the second language of 72% of the urban population sample, whilst Hausa which had no first speakers was spoken as a second language by 20% of the sample. Yet further north, in *Maroua,* with a native population of Fulbe, Fulfulde was spoken by 73%

as first language, no Hausa being recorded. Whereas in *Kousseri,* near the Chadian border, (the place of Rabeh's defeat) with a native population of Kotoko and Shuwa, Fulfulde was the first language of 10% and the second language of 32%, whereas Shuwa was the first language of 24% and the second language of 85%, (i.e. most of the Kotoko population had been arabised). In the border town of Mokolo, with a native population of Mafa, Fulfulde was the first language of 33% and the second language of 60% of the sample, with no Hausa. In Banyo, native to the Wawa, Fulfulde was the first language of 54%, whilst Hausa was the first language of 15% and the second language of 38% of the population, with Vute also as 29% second language.

Finally in *Meiganga,* with native Gbaya, Fulfulde was the first language of 35%, but the second language of 77%, whilst Hausa was the first language of 20% and the second language of the adult sample population. Fulfulde is thus the main lingua franca of northern Cameroun. North and west of Maroua the number of Fulfulde second-language speakers lessens in favour of Shuwa, whilst in the Mandara mountains, the language of wider communication has been Mandara. In the border town of Mora, the 1977 survey records 24 residents speaking Wandala as first language and 7% as second language, Fulfulde being the principal second language for non-Mandara peoples in that town also.

In Niger, though Fulfulde is one of the 5 'National' languages, it is used as a lingua franca, being spoken by 12% of the population as first language. Fulfulde is used for adult, but little for primary education; Radio Niamey broadcasts in the language. Since many of the Fulbe are pastoralists, they cross freely into Nigeria since time immemorial. The dialect of Fulfulde spoken in Niger is based on that of Sokoto, which is now different from that of Adamawa. Whether both can be served by the same standardised language remains to be seen by linguists and educationalists alike. One could posit a standard high-Fulfulde covering the various dialects of Nigeria, Cameroun, Chad and Niger, which would then be in diglossia with the ones actually spoken on the ground, since they are bound to vary with the wide extent covered by the Fulbe in time and space.

Pidgin. The origin of pidgin English has been posited to be a direct lexical successor—by a process of relexification—to a pidgin of Portuguese, spoken by the traders on the Guinea Coast. It is therefore no accident that the concentration of the lingua franca is at present in Weskos, spoken in the southwest of Cameroun, (i.e., on the southeastern borders of Nigeria), as well as in large cities of Nigeria and Cameroun, with a heterogeneous ethnic population, especially where northerners and southerners are mixed. J.A. Kisob in the first issue of *Abbia* (1963) estimated that it was then spoken by some 75% of 'anglophone' West Cameroun Province, and by some 33% of the coastal provinces of the west, on which basis Carole Feral has estimated some 1.5 million pidgin speakers in Cameroun; this by now could easily be 2 million, making pidgin, the representative lingua franca of southern Cameroun, as against Fulfulde for northern Cameroun (cf. Map).

Whilst pidgin is, above all, an intergroup language in a very multi-ethnic and hence multilingual society, Feral points out that among the Bamileke it is also an *in-group language,* in as much as this 'ethnic group' has no one language in common, which is something of an anomaly. Kisob pleaded for making it a national lingua franca, and it certainly has a higher prestige in Cameroun than in Nigeria. Though even here pidginists aver that there is a growing number of first-language pidgin speakers. First language speakers of pidgin occur among the children of

**Map of the Federal Republic of Cameroun Showing the
Spread of Pidgin-English**

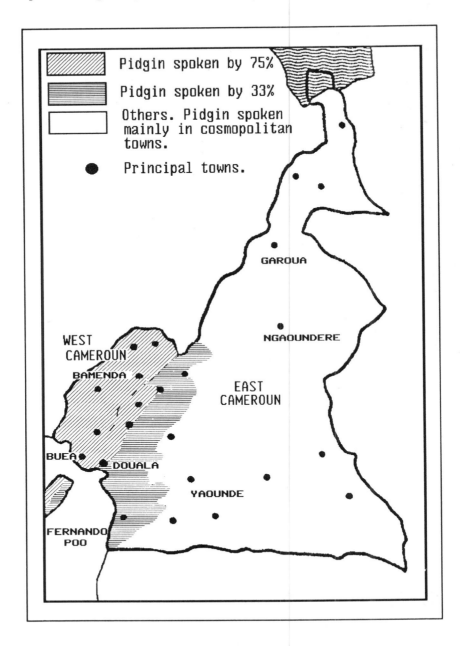

inter-ethnic marriages in Nigeria in the Sabon gari of the north, and also increasingly in towns of the littoral, such as Port Harcourt, Warri, Calabar and possibly Lagos. Unfortunately the Urban Language Survey of Edna Koenig did not take pidgin into account in the second language situation, whereas urban samples used by M.A. Adekunle in various Nigerian towns and by Carol Scotton in Lagos, clearly show its use in inter-ethnic situations.

It has nevertheless been reported that in Cameroun pidgin or Weskos acts as a significant code between anglophone and francophone Camerounians, (i.e. those in the former Trusteeship Territory of the southwest and the rest), especially in the south—in unofficial or commercial transactions. This use is also described by Carole Feral. The greater weight pidgin is given in Cameroun than in Nigeria, can also be seen by its repeated grammatical and lexical description, which is slowly being followed by Nigerian pidgin. Weskos is also used in some pulpits (portions of Scripture are translated into it), over some radio stations and partly in some southern newspapers—but so it is now over Radio Calabar and in *Lagos Weekend*. Thus, whereas in Nigeria it seems to be limited to 'joking relationships' and familiar or simple mercantile transactions, in Cameroun it has gained an additional domain, that of worship. In Nigeria, Christian worship is performed in over one hundred autochthonous languages, some identical to those in Niger and Cameroun, and there has therefore not been any need for pidgin in that domain. Precisely since Hausa was for some time associated with Islam, some middle belt peoples have preferred pidgin as an inter-ethnic language, which gives it an area of diffusion complementary to that of Hausa in Nigeria and to that of Fulfulde in Cameroun, (i.e., to the lower end of the Adamawa mountains).

Summarising, we can say that several lingua francas are competing for second or third language use on the borders of Nigeria. In the northwest, and north-centre, the position of Hausa is uniquely affirmed, whilst in the northeast, Kanuri exerts a traditional and Shuwa and increasing influence. On the central northeastern border Fulfulde is used in Adamawa, with Hausa increasing in influence down to the Mambila Plateau. On the southeastern border Weskos or pidgin is the intergroup lingua franca.

The Nationalisation of Lingua Francas

Whilst in Niger the term 'national' languages is used for the five languages (Hausa, Songhai, Fulfulde, Tamasheq and Kanuri), spoken respectively by 51/85, 21, 12, 10 and 4% of the population, (second slashed figure is for second language speakers), in Nigeria the term "major languages" is used for the big three Hausa, Yoruba and Igbo, spoken respectively by 21/40, 21/25 and 17/19% of the population. In Cameroun, attempts have been made to give special status to 'regional languages' like Fulfulde, Ewondo, Duala and Bassa, whereas in Chad the regional Arabic has been raised to national and official status, alongside French, in each case one of other of lingua francas so selected cross the Nigerian frontiers. Thus when considering a 'national' standard of the language(s), the question arises regarding a reference dialect as well as a standard orthography. Until the independencies of the 1960s, African languages were often written according to the International African Alphabet, promoted by the International African Institute under the directorship of Diedrich Westermann, or to the outdated orthographies of the metropolitan languages. Consider the spelling of Chad (British), Tchad (French); Cameroun (French), Cameroon (British) and Kamerun (German), of Hausa Maossa and Hausa of Fulbe, Peul and Ful, and so on. In the case of the standardisation of Hausa in Nigeria, Kananci was preferred and the Gaskiya *boko* script to the former *ajami,* based on Sakkwatanci. Will the Republic of Niger follow this example or will she prefer to follow the more modern spelling advocated by the UNESCO meetings on the harmonisation of African orthographies of Bamako and Younde? According to this proposal Hausa should be spelled *hawsa,* and analogy Garoua-Garwa, Maroua-Marwa, and so on.

Since it has often been seen that the nationalisation of a lingua franca, or language of wider communication, has led to its division into separate forms, it may be a good moment to ask whether international forms should be preferred to purely national ones. This would concern the standardisation of such languages as Kanuri, Fulfulde, Shuwa, Efik, to speak of the larger ones, but equally concerns Mandara/Wandala, Higi/Kapsiki, Bata/Bwatiye, Mambila, Ejagham/Ekoi, and other smaller languages. Was it really necessary to split Kanuri by two separate biblical translations into Manga and Yerwa; Kamwe be separate translations into Higi and Kapsiki; Mabmila by separate translations into Mambila and Yute? Since missionaries and linguists have been allowed to form their own policies for language development, they have almost always in the recent fifty years, *voted for glossotomy or particularisation, rather than for unification.* States have hardly been aware of the long-term implication of language development, in relation to bordering countries. This might be a good moment to reflect to what extent cross-border standardisation is desirable and feasible, as enhancing the communication value of individual ethno-linguistic groups. I do not presume to have an answer to the question, but merely wish to raise it, as of some importance in a seminar on border problems.

The Metalects of Exolects

Whilst the Western Sudan has been in contact with the Arab-speaking world for up to nine hundred years, and contacts have been continuous over the open desert and savanna, west coast contacts with Europe have been sporadic over only five hundred and continuous for some one hundred and fifty. It is therefore not surprising that Arabic has long been 'indigenised' in the forms of Sudanese, Chadian, and Nigerian (Shuwa) Arabic spoken as a first language by sizable population and by more as a second language. It is therefore perceived as an 'African' language.

This is only partly so with European languages, in so far as coastal contact have given rise to creolised populations, as for instance on Cape Verde, or to creole languages, as in Sierra Leone, where Krio is the first language of a representative coastal group and the second language of a large number of others going inland. English pidgin is, as we have seen, on the way to becoming as 'indigenous' as Sudanese Arabic. Whereas there are counterparts in the case of French in the Indian Ocean—e.g. on Mauritius, the Seychelles, and Rodrigues, it has always been denied by 'francophone' Africans that West Africa has a French pidgin—which would be the reason why anglophones and francophones in Cameroun hate to use the English variety for intergroup communication. That this is not quite true is shown by the growing importance of Ivorian Patois in Abidjan which must have parallels in other large cities of francophone Africa, including Niamey, Ndjamena, and possibly Yaounde: that remains to be investigated.

For the moment we are concerned with the non-indigenised metrolects, which are variously perceived as imposed, imported, foreign, received, assimilated, tamed (*langue apprivoiser* or naturalised, even 'nationalised') languages—according to temperament, mood or political opportunity. Whereas the *lingua francas* discussed above all (with the exception of pidgin) have an ethnic base, and are therefore marked and delimited by their ethnicity, the exolects are marked and delimited by purely external political factors (i.e., the Berlin Conference) and are to that extent perceived as being 'neutral', rather than 'natural'. It is a truism that the struggle for independence of African states would not have been as successful had it not been for the use of French in Francophone West and Equatorial Africa, or for English in Ghana and Nigeria: the protagonists of those struggles were also masters of the French and English language-teachers, journalists, poets, memorialist. The countries with which we are concerned were first divided into three spheres of influence—English, French and German—the international borders of which have been perpetuated towards Nigerian independence. The notable exception was the Cameroun Trusteeship Territory, whose northern British part chose to go with Nigeria, whilst the southern British part chose to go with the new Federal Republic. The only limitrophe country whose artificial borders have not settled down to this day is Chad, whose Arabo-Muslim-dominated north has not come to peace with the Franco-Christian dominated south. In the vast and sparsely populated Niger, successive governments seem to have settled into the francophone sphere, centred on Niamey, which was the birthplace of 'francophonie'—even though the period of glottophagy of the French administration was followed by a revaluation of indigenous major languages, such as Hausa, Songhai, Tamsheq, Kanuri and Fulfulde. In Chad, no indigenous language has been given a 'national' position, other than that Arabic which has been declared co-official with French, thus indigenising an exogenous language, and also polarising the north-south dichotomy.

In Cameroun though, both French and English became co-official and equal, though French, spread over four-fifths of the population/area, is more equal than English, as anyone knows who has been to Douala, Yaounde, or Garoua. It is an historic curiosity that the now defunct secessionist 'Biafra' is said to have concluded an agreement with France during the Nigerian Civil War, by which French would have become co-official with English in the enclave, which seems a not illogical conclusion (though I have heard this from a respectable source, I have not been able to authenticate this statement).

Trilingualism in Nigeria and Niger means the habitual use by significant parts of the society of the mother tongue or L1 (chthonolect = c), and indigenous lingua franca (demolect = d) and the 'received' language or L3 (metalect = m) = c+d+m). In Chad *trilingualism* means an indigenous language (c), Arabic and French (=c+2m); and also in Cameroun trilingualism means and indigenous language (c), a lingua franca (d) and French or English, or both (=c+d+2m), which really is tetraglossia. It is in fact Camerounian policy for every educated Camerounian to know both official languages, though this is much more frequent among the few anglophones than among the majority francophone elite.

We could refine these formulae by stating that in Nigeria trilingualism is c+H/P + E; in Niger it is c/d + H + F; in Chad it is C+A+F; in Cameroun it is c+Fu/P + P/E or c+Fu/p + F+E (tetraglossia): English is common to Nigeria and Cameroun; French is common to Chad, Niger and Cameroun, Fulfulde is used as lingua franca in Cameroun only; Hausa is common to Nigeria and Niger; pidgin is common to Nigeria and Cameroun.

It has often been stated in writing that the actual number of persons using the metalect in African countries is as low as 5, 10 or at most 15% of the population.

Can this be true a whole generation after Inpendence, with rising school enrolment ratio and rising literacy rates among children and adults? If by this percentage is meant persons who can fluently and pertinently express themselves in writing, I would agree; but if it means the percentage of persons habitually using the language, or being able to use it, it is doubtful. There is a continuum of competence and performance in the metalects (including also Arabic in Chad) from the mixed and pidginised to the educated varieties and metrolects. Surveys of language use will take into account the percentage of urbanised population in these four countries (five including Benin), where the exolects are mostly used, both in their metropolitan and indigenised varieties.

The language policies of France and Britain have often been contrasted in their attitude towards indigenous languages, Germany coming somewhere in between the two. It is true that in official/public education, French-administered schools have been wholly through the medium of French, but wherever religious groups (both Catholic and Protestant) managed to obtain control of schools, they have introduced the local African languages. This has been more obvious in the case of the Protestant schools (Presbyterians, Lutherans, Baptists, Methodists, Anglicans, and so on), but those of the Holy Ghost Fathers went the same way. The difference between the two colonial powers was that whereas the anticlerical French insisted on a majority control of schools, and were thus able to enforce their policy of 'straight-for-French' and the use of opprobrium (the symbol) for lapsing into the "vernacular" (a trick they learned at home from a Catholic order in Brittany, the Brethren of Ploemel who enforced French in schools there after the French Revolution), the thrifty British left most of their schools in the hands of religious orders, who followed an initial "vernacular" policy. This resulted in a larger number of linguistic studies on the languages of Nigeria than those of Cameroun, Chad, Benin or Niger, and their earlier standardisation for Scriptural translation, primers, or orthographies and in some cases pedagogical grammars. Hausa was in the unique position of being standardised and modernised as the co-official language of the northern region in the administration and legislature and orally also in the judiciary. However, after Independence, the 'vernaculars' had a reverse through the straight-for-English policy of the multilingual north, since the government saw in English an indirect means for nation-building (never acknowledged as such) by playing down ethnicity.

With the wave of authenticity of the late 60s, the festivals of culture, the international programmes of OAU and UNESCO there was a revival of interest in the indigenous languages in education in the anglophone countries (Ghana and Nigeria, though less in Sierra Leone), whilst the francophone countries tried to make up for the past century by quickly founding chairs for African languages (mainly in France), departments of applied and descriptive linguistics in the Universities in the francophone capitals (Dakar, Abidjan, Yaounde, Ouagadougou, Brazzaville, Naimey, Lome, Cotonou and so on) and adult literacy offices in the national ministries of education. Yet there is a great distance between fundamental and even applied linguistic research and its application in the educational sector. Whilst paying lip-service to the development of 'national' languages, the francophone countries have not, to any palpable extent, introduced them either as subjects or much as media into their educational systems, which continues to be purely in French— except in Cameroun where a policy of French-English bilingualism was laid down—rather than of developing the major languages.

Thus whereas the major languages of anglophone West Africa were standardised in the late 19th or early 20th century, following the rules of Lepsius or later of the International African Institute, the lingua francas of francophone countries are in the process of being standardised currently, following the principles of contemporary linguistic transcription, as put forward by UNESCO in its various commissions and meetings. Not only have these lingua francas, which are the same across the borders, been influenced by the vocabularies respectively of English and French, but also their standard forms tend to be based on the older or newer transcriptions. Thus Hausa is entrenched in its Kano dialect and Gaskyia script used by the Northern Nigeria Publishing Corporation, and is not likely to defer to the UNESCO orthography; Kanuri is also based principally in Nigeria; Fulfulde, though largely outside Nigeria, has found a strong basis in Adamawa on both sides of the Cameroun/Nigeria border and should now be standardised for publications in that form and orthography (in Roman script); Songhai would evidently be standardised in Niger, whilst Weskos/pidgin needs a standardised common form for the entire coast, if it is to be written at all: perhaps the Krio forms now being standardised in Sierra Leone could be used as a basis (cf. Todd).

The standardisation of local forms of the metrolects themselves is also being mooted: The *Inventaire du Francais en Afrique* (IFA) has recently come out with an initial collection of mostly common africanisms, from which it is proposed to select a pedagogical dictionary, sponsored by AUPELP and the *Agence de Cooperation Culturelle et Technique* in Paris. This would certainly aid the teaching of French in anglophone countries of West Africa also. On the other hand, both Ghana and Nigeria, which are not directly contiguous, each speak national Englishes, in the forms of Ghanaian and Nigerian English. It would be wiser to follow up the project of Ayo Banjo and Peter Young for a common dictionary of West African English, which, like IFA, could be descriptive in the first instance, and give rise to a pedagogical selection of acceptable forms, in the second. This is turn would help to stabilise the English used in Cameroun, which at present is much, and unfortunately, influenced by spoken pidgin, and would also help the teaching of English as a school subject in the francophone limitrophe states.

English and French thus continue as the major high languages of communication, though they are more exclusive in the written than in the oral code, as shown in the first two parts of the paper. In a predominantly oral and orate society, where the 'affecting presence' is so much more significant than written, telephonic or telegraphic communication, this means that in terms of social dynamics, the lingua francas are gaining ground everywhere, whilst the exolects can record gains only in the urban sector and through the written/printed word in proportion to the growth of real or functional literacy in the five limitrophe states. A measure of these language dynamics could be devised by quantifying sample repertoires (cf. the sample attempts of M.A. Adekunle) across the borders, in various domains of language use, both oral and written, active and receptive. To do this would require an international team of socio-linguists who would agree on common measures of performance and/or participation in communal, urban, regional and national affairs. This may show quite different, but possible complementary, language profiles for the indigenous lingua francas on the one hand, and the exogenous metalects, or link languages, on the other.

Conclusions

It has thus been shown that the present international boundaries, whilst dividing languages at the grass-root level (chthonolects), as well as at the level of languages of wider communication (demolects), have also set up linguistic boundaries through the exolects adopted on either side. The communication range of each of these is directly proportional to the demographic strength and concentration of the speech group concerned. The communication range of the smaller grass-root languages is small indeed, even if it is across the borders. Could frontiers be redrawn to accommodate these ethnic groups, so as to contain them within one polity? Would it be desirable on such a work of *linguistic irredentism*?

An answer to this is that the present boundaries are just as arbitrary as previous boundaries of empires and kingdoms, based on the principles of 'ejus regio, cujus lingua', (i.e., the Songhai, the Kanuri, the Fulbe, the Hausa) have in turn imposed *their* languages on smaller peoples, many of whom have been absorbed. Where is the famous realm of the So in the Chad Basin, the peoples of which have been entirely absorbed by the Kanuri, the Shuwa, the Fulbe, as the Jukun Kingdom of Kororofa has been by the Fulbe and Hausa, to such an extent that the Jukun language must have shrunk to a tenth of its former use.

Nor are the seemingly autochthonous peoples of the border so deeply rooted as it appears: most of them have wandered there within the past few centuries. Thus the *Batta,* we are told, derive from the region of Gobir, whence they wandered eastward in the 13th century toward the Chad Basin, entering their present habitat via Cameroun. Also it must be considered that the younger generation of the border peoples will wander into the cities, become bilingual, forget their language, leaving behind a vanishing generation of chthonophones.

Would it be proper to limit their ability to communicate widely by perpetuating the smaller of the languages, by standardisation across the borders? Already the ethnics of the smaller group shave to become bilingual, in order to communicate effectively. Would it not be better to standardise the *lingua francas* and develop *them,* rather than the chthonolects? Smaller groups can only survive ethnolinguistically if they group together with congeners and cognates, as did recently the Bacama and Bata, giving the Bwatiye a people of between 150,000 and 200,000. The Bwatiye Development Association, which has a membership from both Nigeria (the majority) and Cameroun, would be in a position to withstand absorption by Hausa, if it standardised the language fast enough and diffused it through the schools. For the smaller groups of under 100,000 speakers this may not be feasible, 100,000 being the figure taken by Nigerian broadcasting corporations for their language selections, as well as by publishers.

Development of the lingua francas is best made by language boards or committees. In former years the *Hausa Language Board* did yeoman service for the rising use in public affairs of the language in the Northern States of Nigeria. Though it has lain dormant for some years, there are signs of it revival. It will be in an excellent position to negotiate with educational and communication authorities in Niger, Chad, and Cameroun as to the forms preferred for use. Niger has everything to gain from Nigerian publishing in Hausa by the Northern Nigerian Publishing Corporation, and it is not likely at this juncture that the standards set by the Board in the 50s will now be changed in favour of UNESCO decisions taken in Bamako and Yaounde only a few years ago.

Similarly the Fulfulde and Kanuri Language Board, in Kano and Maiduguri respectively, would be revived and encouraged to standardise the languages across the borders of Niger, Chad and Cameroun, but also a development of the language in common. The alternative is a split of what used to be an international language, as with *Swahili* which is now being separately 'treated' for Scriptural translation into KiNgwana (the Zairois variety of the one hand) and KiMvita (the coastal variety on the other) thus creating two standards by the well-known process of glossotomy. Similarly Pidgin needs standardisation on a West African basis, if it is to play a role as a coastal inter-ethnic *creole*.

As for the exolects, there have been several recommendations by the inter-governmental pan-African (OAU) or West African (ECOWAS) Organisations, encouraging the development in education of the *plesiolect,* or neighbouring official language (cf. Treffgarne). Whilst this would at present be too onerous for Nigeria as a whole, border communities on either side might be encouraged to have special facilities in their plesiolect, in order to improve communication at all levels.

Nigerian Ethnic Groups Survey 1972

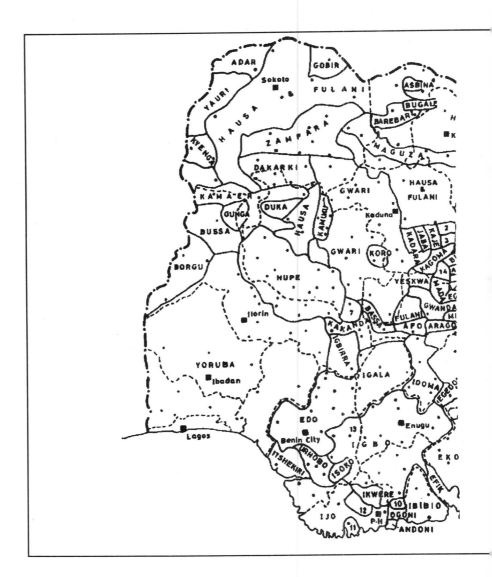

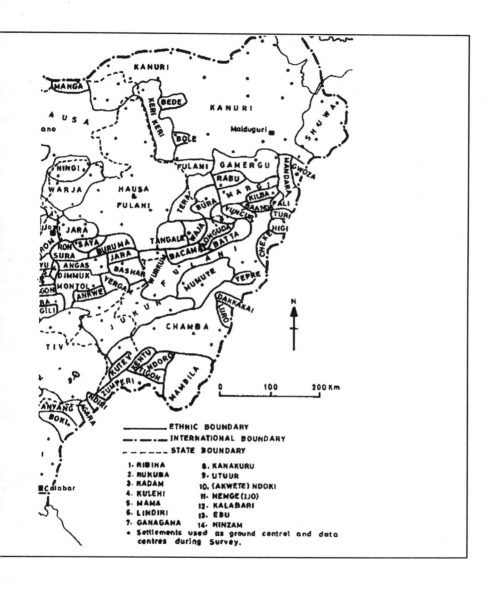

ETHNIC BOUNDARY
INTERNATIONAL BOUNDARY
STATE BOUNDARY

1. RIBINA   8. KANAKURU
2. RUKUBA   9. UTUUR
3. KADAM   10. (AKWETE) NDOKI
4. KULEHI   11. NEMGE (IJO)
5. MAMA   12. KALABARI
6. LINDIRI   13. EBU
7. GANAGANA   14. NINZAM

• Settlements used as ground control and data
    centres during Survey.

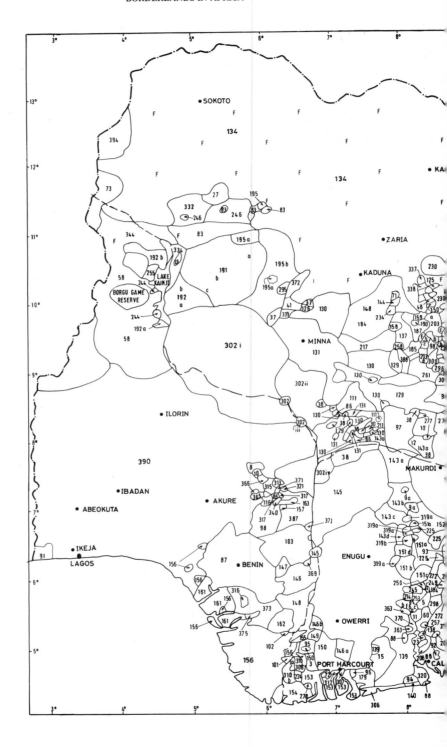

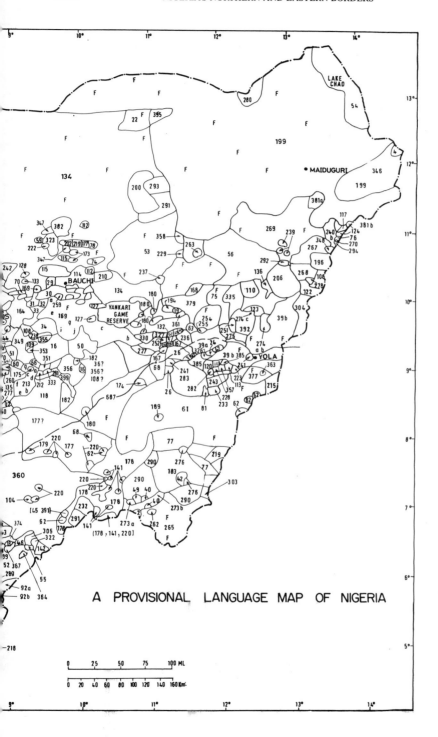

A PROVISIONAL LANGUAGE MAP OF NIGERIA

The List

It will be seen that each numbered entry in the list and on the map represents either a language or a dialect cluster. Each dialect cluster is marked by an asterisk. The members of the dialect cluster are then given in an indented list.

In the case of language clusters, there is no separate number given for the language cluster since each language or dialect cluster within the language cluster has its own separate number. The name of the language cluster occurs first with a double asterisk and then under this name the languages and dialect clusters are given in an indented list. Each dialect cluster has its dialect members further indented in the list.

1. Abanyom	54. Buduma	119. Gokana
2. Abon	55. Bumaji	120. Gongla
3. Abua	56. Bura	121. Gubi
4. Affade	57. Burak	122. Gude
5. Agoi	58. Busa	123. Gudu
6. *Agwagwune	59. *Buta-Ningi	124. Guduf
6a. Agwagwune	(59a) Buta	125. Gure-Kahugu
6b. Erei	(59b) Ningi	126. Gurmana
6c. Abini	60. Chakfem-Mushere	127. Guruntum-Mbaaru
6d. Adim	61. Chamba Daka	128. Gwa
6e. Abayongo	62. Chambe Leko	129. Gwandara
6f. Etono II	63. Cham-Mwana	**Gwari
7. Ake	64. Chara	130. Gwari-Matai
8. *Akoko North	65. Chawai	131. Gwari-Yamma
9. *Akpa-Yache	66. Chip	132. Gwomu
9a. Akpa	67. Chokobo	133. Gyema
9b. Yache	68. Chomo-Karim	134. Hausa
10. Akpes	69. Dadiya	135. Horom
11. Akpet-Ehom	70. Daffo-Batura	136. Hwana
12. Alago	71. Defaka	137. Hyam
13. Alege	72. Degema	138. Ibami
14. Amo	73. Dendi	139. Ibibio
15. Anaang	74. Deno	140. Ibino
16. Angas	75. Dera	141. Icen
17. Arum-Chessu	76. Dghwede	142. Icheve
18. Aten	77. Dirim	143. *Idoma
19. Awak	78. Dirya	143a. Idoma North
20. Ayu	79. Doka	143b. Idoma Central
21. Baatonun	80. Doko-Uyanga	143c. Idoma West
**Bade	81. Dong	143d. Idoma South
395. Duwai	82. Duguza	144. Idon
22. Bade	83. Duka	145. Igala
293. Ngizim	84. Dulbu	**Igbo
23. Bakpinka	85. Dungi	*146. Igbo
24. Bali	86. Ebira	146a. Eche
25. Bambuka	87. Edo (Bini)	146b. Egbema
26. Bandawa-Minda	88. Efik	147. Ika
27. Banga	89. Efutop	*148. Ukwuani-Aboh
28. Bangwinji	90. Eggon	149. Ogbah
**Barawa	91. Egun	150. Ikwere
*29. Geji	92. *Ejagham	*151. Izi-Ezaa-Ikwo-Mgbo
*30. Polci	92a. Bendeghe	151a. Izi
*31. Zeem	92b. Etung North	151b. Ezaa
*32. Dass	92c. Etung South	151c. Ikwo
*33. Zari	92d. Ejagham	151d. Mgbo
*34. Saya	92e. Ekin	152. Igede
(35) Barke	93. Ekajuk	**Ijo
36. Bashar	94. Ekit	153. Ijo Eastern
37. Bassa Kaduna	95. Ekpeye	(153a) Kalabari
38. Bassa-Kwomu	96. Eleme	(153b) Okrika
39. *Bata	97. Eloyi	(153c) Ibani
39a. Bacama	98. *Emai-Iuleha-Ora	(153d) Nkoro
39b. Bata	(99) Emane	154. Ijo Nembe
40. Batu	100. Engenni	*155. Ijo Biseni-Okordia
41. Baushi	101. Epie	156. Ijo Central
42. Baya	102. Eruwa	157. Ikpeshi
43. Bekwarra	103. Esan	158. Iku-Gora-Ankwa
44. Berom	104. Etulo	159. Ikulu
45. Bete	105. Evant	160. Irigwe
46. Bette-Bendi	106. Fali	161. Isekiri
47. Bile	F. Fulfulde	162. Isoko
48. Binawa	108. Fyam	163. *Ivbie North
49. Bitare	109. Fyer	164. Izarek
50. Boghom	110. Ga'anda	165. Jaku
51. Bokkos	111. Gade	166. Janji
52. Bokyi	112. Galambi	167. Janjo
53. Bole	113. Gengle	168. Jara
	114. Gera	169. *Jarawa
	115. Geruma	169a. Bankal
	116. Ghotuo	169b. Ligri
	117. Glavda	169c. Kanam
	118. Goemai	(169d) Bobar

169e. Gingwak
(169f) Duguri of Gar
169g. Duguri of Badara
169h. N.E. Duguri
169i. S.W. Duguri
169j. Bada
170. *Jera
170a. Buji
170b. Gusu
170c. Jere
170d. Ribina
171. Jidda-Abu
172. Jimbin
173. Jimi
174. Jiru-Kir
175. Jorto
176. Ju
**Jukun
177. Jukun of Wukari
178. Jukun of Takum and Donga
179. Jukun of Abinsi
180. Jukun of Kona
181. Jukun of Wurkum
182. Jukun of Wase
183. Jibu
184. Kadara
185. Kagona
186. Kaivi
187. Kaje
(188) Kaka
189. Kam
190. Kamantam
**Kambari
*191. Kambari I
191a. Kakihum
191b. Ibeto
191c. Salka
*192. Kambari II
192a. Auna
192b. Agara'iwa
(193) Kamkam
194. Kamo
195. *Kamuku
195a. Achipa
195b. Ucinda
196. Kamwe
197. Kana
198. *Kanufi-Kaningkon-Nindem
198a. Kanuf
198b. Kaningkon
198c. Nindem
199. Kanuri
200. Karekare
201. Karfa
202. Kariya
203. *Katab
203a. Katab
203b. Kagoro
203c. Ataka
203d. Sholio
203e. Kachichere
203f. Kafanchan
204. Kiballo
(205) Kila
206. Kilba
207. Kinuku
208. Kiong
209. Kir-Balar
210. Kirifi
211. Kitimi
212. Koenoem

List of language names corresponding to the numbers on the map (numbers enclosed in brackets are not shown on the map).

'· Dialect cluster   ** Language cluster

213. *Kofyar
213a. Kofyar
213b. Mernyang
213c. Doemak
213d. Kwagallak
213e. Bwol
213f. Gworam
213g. Jipal
214. Kohumono
215. Koma
216. Kono
217. Koro
218. Korop
219. Kotopo
220. Kpan
221. Kubi
222. *Kuda-Chamo
222a. Kuda
222b. Chamo
223. Kugama
224. Kugbo
225. Kukele
226. Kulere
227. Kulung
228. Kumba
229. Kupto
230. Kurama
231. Kushi
232. Kuteb
233. Kutin
234. Kuturmi
235. Kuzamani
236. Kwa
237. Kwami
238. *Kwanka
(238a) Kwanka
(238b) Boi
(238c) Bijim
(238b) Legeri
239. Kyibaku
240. *Laamang
240a. Laamang North
240b. Laamang South
241. Laka
242. *Lame
(242a) Bambaro
(242b) Gura
243. Lamja
244. Laru
245. Legbo
246. Lela
247. Lelau
248. Lemoro
249. Lenyima
250. Leyigha
251. Libo
252. Lo
253. Loka
254. Longuda
255. Lopa
256. Lotsu-Piri
257. Lubila
258. Lungu
259. Luri
260. Mabo-Barkul
261. Mada
262. Magu
263. Maha
264. Mama
265. Mambila
266. Mangas
**Margi
267. Margi Central
268. Margi South
269. Putai
270. Matakam
271. Mbe
272. Mbembe

273. *Mbembe (Tigong)
273a. Ashuku
273b. Nama
274. *Mboi
274a, b Mboi, Banga
274c. Handa
275. *Mbula-Bwazza
(275a) Mbula
(275b) Bwazza
276. Mbute
277. Migili
278. Mini
279. Miya
280. Mober
281. Montol
282. Mumbake
283. Mumuye
284. Mundat
285. Munga
286. Nandu-Tari
287. Naraguta
288. Nde-Nsele-Nta
288a. Nde
288b. Nsele
288c. Nta
289. *Ndoe
289a. Ekparabong
289b. Balep
290. Ndoro
291. Ngamo
292. Nggwahyi
293. See 22
294 Ngoshe Ndhang
295. Ngwoi
296. Ninzam
297. *Nkem-Nkum
297a. Nkem
297b. Nkum
298. Nkukoli
299. Nnam
300. *Numana-Nunku-Gwantu
(300a) Numana
(300b) Nunku
(300c) Gwantu
301. Nungu
302. Nupe
(i) Nupe Central
(ii) Ganagana
(iii) Kakanda
(iv) Bassa-Nge
(v) Eggan
303. Nyamnyam
304. Nzangi
305. *Obanliku
(305a) Basang
(305b) Bebi
(305c) Bishiri
(305d) Bisu
(305e) Busi
306. Obolo
307. Obulom
308. Odual
309. Odut
310. *Ogbia
310a. Kolo
310b. Oloibiri
310c. Anyama
311. Ogbogolo
312. Ogbronuagum
313. *Ogori-Magongo
313a. Ogori
313b. Magongo
314. Okobo
315. Okpamheri
316. Okpe
317. Okpe-Idesa-Oloma-Akuku
318. *Olulumo-Ikom
318a. Olulumo
318b. Ikom

319. *Oring
319a. Ufia
319b. Effium
319c. Okpoto
320. Oron
321. Ososo
322. Otank
323. Pa'a
324. Pai
325. Panyam
326. Passam
327. Pero
(328) Pidgin
329. Piti
330. Piya
331. Pongu
332. *Puku-Geeri-Keri-Wipsi
(332a) Puku-Nu
(332b) Geeri-Ni
(332c) Keri-Ni
(332d) Wipsi-Ni
333. Pyapun
334. Reshe
335. Roba
336. Rukuba
337. Rumaya
338. Rurama
339. Sanga
340. Sasaru-Enwan-Igwe
341. Sha
342. Shagawu
343. Shall-Zwall
(343a) Shall
(343b) Zwall
344. Shanga
345. Shani
346. Shuwa Arabic
347. Siri
348. Sukur
349. Sura
350. Surubu
351. Tal
352. Tala
353. Tambas
354. Tangale
355. Tapshin
356. Tarok
357. Teme
358. *Tera
(358a) Nyimatli
(358b) Pidlimdi
(359) Tita
360. Tiv
361. Tula
362. Turkwam
363. *Ubaghara
(363a) Biakpun
(363b) Ikun
(363c) Etono
(363d) Ugbem
(363e) Utuma
364. Ubang
365. Uhami-Iyayu
366. Ukaan
367. *Ukpe-Bayobiri
(367a) Ukpe
(367b) Bayobiri
368. Ukue-Ehuen
369. Ulukwumi
370. Umon
371. Uneme
372. Ura
373. Urhobo
374. *Utugwang
(374a) Utugwang
(374b) Okorogung
(374c) Okorotung
(374d) Afrike
(374e) Oboso
375. Uvbie
376. Uzekwe

377. Verre
378. Vimtim
379. Waja
380. Waka
381. *Wandala
381a. Gamargu
381b. Kirawa
382. Warji
383. Wom
384. Yala
385. Yandang
386. Yashi
387. Yekhee
388. Yeskwa
389. Yiwom
390. Yoruba
391. Yukuben
392. Yungur
393. Zangwal
394. Zarma
395. See 22

NB: initial number = *Index of Nigerian Languages 1976;* final = *1963 Federal Census.*

404 Affade
       Assumbo cf. Evant
       Bacama cf. Bata
       Bana cf. Fali
       Banana cf. Masa
 *21 Baatonun, Bariba, Barba
  39 Bat(t) a + Bacama, no Bwatiye (388)
       Baya cf. Gbaya
  49 Bitare, Yukutare
  52 Bokyi, Boku
  54 Buduma
 *58 Busa (239)
  61 Chamba Daka, Sama, Daka (162)
  62 Chamba Leko, Leko (253)
       choa cf. Shuwa
       Dama cf. Chamba
 *73 Dendi (260)
  77 Dirim, Dakka, Taram (264)
  88 Efik/Ibibio (004, 013)
 91* Egun, Gun
  92 Ejagham, Ekoi, Etung (1o4+1o5)
       Qua=Ekin
 1o5 Evant, Assumbo
 1o6 Fali, Bana, Baz(z) a (272)
 1o7 FULFULDE, Peul(h) (002)
  42 Gbaya, Baya (231, 281)
       Gamargu, cf. Wandala
       Gambai/Ngambai, Sara
 117 Glavda (288)
 112 Gude (293)
 124 Guduf (28o)
 134 HAUSA (003)
       Higi cf. Kamwe
 142 Icheve, Bacheve = Mesaka (113)
 188 Kaka (331)

 193 Kamkam, Bunu

 196 Kamwe = Higi = Kapsiki (3o7)
 199 KANURI (006), Manga, Mober?
       Kanembu?
       Kapsiki cf. Kamwe

215 Koma, Kuma (354)
218 Korop, Ododop, Durop
     Kotoko = Logone
219 Kotopo, Pere, (258)
225 Kukele (111)
232 Kuteb, Kutev, Zumper
233 Kutin (3671)
240 Laamang, Gwoza, Waha, Tur (3o6)
     Mafa = Matakam
265 Mambila (385)
     Mandara cf. Wandala
     Manga cf. Kanuri
268 Marghi (south)
     Masa = Banana (Chad)
270 Matakam, mafa (389)
273 Mbembe, Tigon (450)
     Mesaka cf. Icheve
276 Mbute, Bute, Vute
280 Mober, cf Kanuri ?
282 Mumbake (4o2)
29o Ndoro (4o8)
3o3 Nyamnyam, Suga
3o4 Nzangi, Njanji (414)
     Ododop cf. Korop
3o5 Obanliku
     Pere cf. Kotopo
328 Pidgin = Weskos (in CMN)
346 SHUA Arba, choa (437)
     Suga cf. Nyamnyam
     Taram cf. Dirim
348 Sukur (439)
     Tamacheq, Tuareg (Niger)
36o Tiv (008)
377 Vere (457)
                                  381a 381 b
381 Wandala, Mandara, Gamargu, Kirawa
     (386, 275)
     Weskos cf. Pidgin
383 Wom (467)
     Yamba cf. Kaka
39o* Yoruba (009)
391 Yukuben, Ayikiben
394* Zarma, Dyarma, Djerma (474)

(after Greenbers/Hoffman in Index in Nigerian languages, 1976: appendix I:169–9o)

I. NIGER=KORDOFANTAN　I.A.　NIGER=CONGO
　　I.A. 1.　WEST ATLANTIC　Northern Branch, Senegal Group　Fulfulde (1o7)
　　I.A. 5.　BENUE=CONGO I.A. 5.3　CROSS=RIVER
　a. Bendi sub-branch　　i.　Obanliku cl. (3o5) ii. Bokyi (52)
　b. Delta-Cross sub-branch　　i.　Upper Cross gr.
　　　　　　　　　　Mbembe c1. (273);　Olulumo-Ikom (318); Korop (Odedep) (218)
　　　　　　　　　　　　　　ii.　lower Cross gr (language cluster)
　　　　　　　　　　　　　　　　Efik (88)
　　　　　　　　　　　　I.A.5.4 BANTOID
　a. Non=Bantu i. Mambila-Vute gr. Mambila cl. (265); Kamkam (193); Ndoro (290);
　　　　　　　　　　　Vute (276)
　　　　　　　ii. Tiv-Batu gr. Tiv (36o); Icheve (142); Evant(1o5); Bitare(49); Batu(40)
　b. Bantu　　i. Ekoid Bantu gr. Ekoi cl. (92): Bendeghe)a); Etung(b); Ejagham(e)
　　　　　　　iv. Grassland Bantu　　　　　Kaka(188)
　　　　　　　　　　　I.A.6 ADAMAWA=UBANGIAN
I.A.6.1.a.x. Vere-Duru gr.: Vere(377); leko (62); Wem(383); Mumbake (282); Kotopo
　　　　　　　(219) Kutin (233)
　　　　　xi. Nimbari gr.　Nayamnyam(Suga) (3o3)
I.A.6.1.b　Sama group　Sama(Chamba) (61);　Dirim (77)
I.A.6.2　UBANGIAN ' Western group Baya(Gbaya) (42)
　　unclassified Niger-Congo language: Koma (215)
II. NIlO=SAHARAN　　　II.A　SONGHAI　Songhai cl : Zarma (djerma) 394); Dendi (73)
　　　　　　　　　　　II.B　SHARAN　Kanuri (199) (incl.Kanembu, Manga)
　　　　　　　　　　　II.E　CHAIR=NILE Sara gr.　Ngambai (Sara)
III AFRO=ASIATIC　　　III.A. SEMITIC　Shuwa Arabic (346)
　　　　　　　　　　　III.B CHADIC III.B.1 West Chadic
　III.B.1.1 Hausa group　Hausa (134)
　　　　　　　　　　　III.B.2　Central Chadic (Biu-Mandara) '
III.B.2.2 Bura gr. ii.eastern Kilba(Heba) (2o6); Margi (267)
III.B.2.3 Hiqi gr.　　Hisi (196) incl Kapsiki; Bana(Fali) 1o6)
III.B.2.4 Bata-Gude gr. b. Bata sub-group　i. North-Western Gudu (123)
　　　　　　　　　　　　　　　　　　　ii. North-Eastern Nzangi (3o4)
　　　　　　　　　　　　　　　　　　　iii. Southern Bata cl.incl Bacama (39)
III.B.2.6 laamang gr. laamang cluster (24o)
III.B.2.7 Mandara gr. Wandala (incl. Gamergu +Kirawa) 381); Glavda (117); Guduf(124)
III.B.2.8 Matakam gr. Matakam (Mofa) (27o)
III.B.2.9 Kotoko gr. Affade (4); Buduma (54)
III.B.2.5 Sukur gr.　Sukur (248)
　　　　　　　　　　　　　III.B.3　Eastern Chadic
III.B.3.2 Nancere gr. Kaba-lai　　　Masa gr. Masa (Banana)
comp.CMBB 14/3/85　　　　　　III.C. BERBER　Tamasheq

Annex III

Demography of Ethnic Identifiers = First language Speakers of Border language Groups of Nigeria. symbols: E= Ethnologue 1984; C= Census 1983; (2) = second language speakers

LANGUAGE	NIGERIA	NIGER	CHAD	CAMEROON	BENIN	TOTAL
AFFADE	+			+	195	E250
BAATONUN= Bar(i)ba	E55					
	c					
BANANA = MASA	+		E1o3	E1o3		E15o
BATA/RACAMA= BWAITYE	E 27+20			E3		E30+20=50
	C 141					
BAYA, GRAYA	C 5		CEN E700	E 140		E 845
BITARE	E 46			E 4		E 50
BOKYI, BOKI	E 83			E 4		E 87
	C – *					
BUDUMA	E 55		E 25			E 80
	C – *					
BUSSA, BOKO	E 50				E 50	E 100
	C 1o					
CHAMBA DAK(K)A, SAMA	E 60			E 1o		E 7o
Chamba leko	C 162 (+ leko)					
DENDI	C 1	C 21 +			E 21	E 42
DIRIM						E 22
EFIK	E 26					E 36
	C 166			E 1o		180₦
EJAGHAM, ETUNG, QUA	E 45			E 35		E 8o
	C 362 *					1oo ₦

LANGUAGE	NIGERIA	NIGER	CHAD	CAMEROON	BENIN	TOTAL
EVANT, ASSUMBO	E 3o			E 16		E 46
FAII, BANA, BAZA	C 51					
FULFULDE, PEUL(H)	c 48oo	E 7o9=15%		E 47o=7% E 5oo (1+2)		1ooo ℕ Adamawa Full
GAMRAI, SARA(H)	E +		E 6oo	E +		
GLAVRA	E 2o C 1o			E 3		E 23
GUDE	E 4o C 38			E 23		E 58
GUDUF	E +					
GUN, EGUN					E 173	E 173 +
HAUSA	C 12ooo	E 27oo=5o% ?		E 24	?	Wa 4o,ooo ℕ
ICHEVE, MESAKA	E 5			E 14		E 19
KAKA, YAMBA	+ (seasonal)			E 25		E 25+
KAMAKAM, BUNU	+			+		E 1
KAMWE, HIGI, KAPSIKI	E18o			E 41		E 221
KANURI, BORNO	C 4ooo	?		E 57		E 35oo
KOMA NDERA	E +			E ++		E 3
KOROP, ODODOP, DUROP	E +			E 13		E 1o +
KOTOPO, PERE, KUTIN	E +			E +,		E 19
LAAMANG, GWOZA, WAHA, TUR	E 31			E 9		R 4o
MAMRII(1)A	E 6o C 52 =			E 2o		E 8o
MANGA OF KANURI?	+			+		
MARG(H)I (SOUTH)	E 2			E 136		E 138
MATAKAM, MAFA	C 8					

LANGUAGE	NIGERIA	NIGER	CHAD	CAMEROON	BENIN	TOTAL
MEBMEB, TIGON(G)	E 3			E 36		E 39
MBUTE, VUTE, BUTE	E1 C−			E 21		E 22
MOBER	+	E 45				E 45 +
MUMRAKE	C 3 E 1o			E +		E 1o
NDORO	E 9 C 1o			E 1		E 1o
NYAMNYAM, Nimbari	E o, 12o *					
NZNAGI	E 14 C42 *			E 8		E 22
ORANLIKU	E 2o			E +		E 2o
PIDGIN	%			%/ (1) (2)		
SHUA	E 1oo –	E14oo		E 64		E 15oo
	C 156					
	E 1o					
SUKUR				?		E 1o
TAMASHEQ	+	E 250		+ Ageria 1o		E 26o
TIV	E 1ooo+ C14oo			E 'a few'		E 1500
VERE	E 16 C 38*	–		E 4		E 2o
WANDALA, MANDARA Gamargu, Kirawa					–	
WOM	E 19 C 11			E 24		E 43
	E 1o C 3			E 13		E 23*
ZARMA, DJERMA	E 5o C 44	E 13oo= 23%	–	–		E 1350
YORUBA	E 15 ooo –		–		2oo	E 15 ooo
	C 11 ooo					
KUKELE	C 26		–	E +	–	E 4o

Peoples on Nigeria.s boarders with Niger, Chad and Cameroon
extracted from A. Gandonu *Nigerian Ethnic Group Survey 1972*
(with compiler's notes; lingua francas are underlined)

I *Northern Border: east to west.* F=Fulfulde: H=Hausa; K=Kanuri; L=Language; S=Shua; P=Pidgin
1. Adar(awa). assimilated to Hausa(H); H monoglots; cross-border movement in Prothero
2. *Hausa*(wa). Ethnic group or language: cf. also Westermann, Salamone etc.
3. Fulani (autonymn Fulbe); live in symbiosis with H, having adopted their L in Sokoto/Kano. The House of dan Fodio itself no longer speaks *Fulfulde*.
4. Gibir(awa); H monoglots, one of the original 'Hausa Seven' (Hausa bakwai)
5. Asbin(awa); are these the Fulbe from Asbin or Air?
6. Manga: speak a dialect of Kanuri, but maintain ethnic identify. NT into Manga in progress.
7. *Kanuri* is one of 5 'national' LL of Niger. There are still many K monoglots,
    though in towns bilingual with H in Borno, or with S(huwa); in Kano and Hausa
    cities have become H monoglots.

II. *Eastern border, north to south:*
8. *Shuwa* (S) maintain their ethnicity, though living in symbiosis with K; many are K bilinguals; Into Chad as well as Cameroon, where S is also lingua franca, there being various dialects of Sudanese Arabic (cf. work of Kaye).
9. Gwoza, a location from name of ethnos, but many small L groups, cf. Laamang; in the plains they were bilingual with F, but are being Hausanized.
10. Mandara, collective term for peoples of the eponymous mountains, incl. Glavada, Gudur,
11. Fali = bana in Cameroon; Fali of Mubi. In Nigeria H=L2; in Cameroon F=L2.
12. Turi, could be Tur, a dialect of Maamang south, i.e. of the Gwoza peoples above.
13. Higi, their autonym is Kamwe; in Cameroon they are known as Kapsiki.
14. Cheke = Gude, also known as Mubi from place.
15. Fulani. (cf. 3) the dialect of Adamwa is somewhat different from that of Sokoto but is becoming the basis of a written standard.
16. Yerre, possibly a misprint for Verre.
17. Dakkahai. could this be Chamba Dakka?
18. Luro: could this be Chamba Leko?
19. Chamba (autonym Sama), includes here Daka, Leko, Mumbake, Wom.
    no Jukun-speaking peoples seem to reach the Cameroon border
20. Mambil (1)a: a group in the Mambila mountains: the Mambila-Vute gr. of linguists
    ruled by Fulbe chiefs, the people are bilingual in F.
21. Tigong = Mbembe
22. Zumperi, an opprobrious alteronym for the Kuteb (here Kutev). It is not clear whether the Yukuben-Kuteb group reaches into Cameroon. Related to Jukun and Chamba.
23. Ndiri; could this be a mistake for Ndoro, which are already on the map elsewhere?
24. Agara: who are they?
25. Anyang; not in Index or Ethnologue; but in Renaud and Cameroon Survey near Mamfe.
26. Roki.
27. Ekoi: Efik appelation for Ejagham, Etung, Bendeghe, Qua; bilingual with Efik and Pidgin
28. *Efik* ; influential L of the Ibibio gr. Gandonu points out Efut becoming Efik.

Bibliography

Abubakar, Sh'ad, *The Lamibe of Fombina* (Zaria: Ahmadu Bello Univ. Press and Ibadan: Oxford Univ. Press, 1977) p. 190.

Adekunle, M.A., Anene, J.C., "The Nigeria-Southern Cameroun boundary: an ethno-political analysis." *J. Hist. Soc. Nig.* 2/2 (Rec 1981) pp. 186-95.

_____ *The International Boundaries of Nigeria: The Framework of an Emergent African Nation* (London: Longman, 1970), pp. xxiii, 331.

Burreteau, Daniel (ed.) *Investa're des etudes linguistiques sur les pays d'Afrique noire d'expression francaise et sur Madagascar.* (Paris: Conseil International de la langue francaise, 1978) pp. 624, maps.

Brann, C.M.B. *Trilingualism in Language Planning for Education in Sub-Saharan Africa* (Paris: UNESCO, 1981) pp. 58, ed/81/WS 116.

_____ "Afro-Saxons and Afro-Romans: Language Policies in Africa *History of European Ideas* (Oxford, 5/3 1984) pp. 302-21.

Brauner, S. et al., Caprile, J., "le Tchad: description socio-linguistique" in *CONFEMEN* 1982 II: pp. 235-50.

Conference des Ministries de l'Education des pays d'Expression Francaise (CONFEMEN) Promotion et integration des langues nationales dans les systems educatifs: bilen et inventaire. 2 vols. (Quebec: CONFEMEN, 1982 & 1983).

Crabb, David W. *Ekoid Bantu Languages of Ogoja* (London: OUP & International African Institute, 1965) pp. xii, 108, maps.

Dieu, Michel & Patrick Renaud, "A propos d'une enquete de statistique du multilinguisme au Cameroun: quelques problems methodologiques" in Wald & Massey (eds.) *Plurilinguismes: normes, situations strategies* (Paris: I'Jarmattan, 1979), pp. 61-102.

_____ et al. *Atlas liguistique du Cameroun (AICAM)* ongoing linguistic and socio-linguisti survey (Yaounde: ONAREST).

Eguchi, P.K., "Notes on the Arabic-Fulfulde translational reading in Northern Cameroun" *Kyoto University African Studies* 9 (1975) pp. 177-250. Federal, Carole "de le cas du pidgin English Camerounais *West African Journal of Modern Languages* 3 (1978) pp. 154-65.

Grimes, Barbara F. (ed.) *Ethnologue: Languages of the World* 10th edit. (Dallax, Texas: Wycliffe Bible Translators, 1984) pp. xvi, 592, maps.

Fonlon, Bernard, "The language problem in Cameroun: a historical perspective" in D.R. Smock & N. Bentsi-Entchill (eds) *The Fear for National Integration in Africa* (New York: Free Press, 1975) pp. 189-205.

Hansford, K., et al, "An index of Nigerian languages" (Studies in Nigerian languages 5). Horsley Gree, UK, Summer Institute of linguistics, 1976, pp. 204, map.

Hoffmann, C., *A Grammar of the Margi Language* (London: OUP for Inter. African Inst., 1963) pp. xix, 287. (Introduction gives place of south Margi into Trusteeship Territory, now Cameroun.)

_____ "The languages of Nigeria by language family" in Hansford, pp. 169-90.

Irele, M., *Nigeria and Cameroun: An Annotated Bibliography* (Lagos: Libriservice, 1984) pp. viii, 67.

Ita, N.O., *Bibliography of Nigeria: A Survey of Anthropological Writings from the Earliest Times to 1966* (London: Cass, 1971) pp. xxxv, 271.

Kirk-Greene, A.H.M., "Tax and travel among the Mili-tribes of Northern Adamawa" *Africa* London 26/4, 1956, pp. 369-78.

_____ The linguistic statistics of Nortern Nigeria: a tentative presentation, *African Language Review 6*, 1967, pp. 71-101.

_____ *Adamawa Past and Present: An Historical Approach to the Development of a Northern Cameroun Province* (London: Dawsons of Pall Mall for the Int. African Inst., 1969) pp. xxi, 230, map.

Koenig, Edna & E. Chaa (eds) "Sociolinguistic survey of urban centres in Cameroun" working paper, 1975, pp. 10 & 5 (published since).

Meek, E.K., *A Sudanese Kingdom: An Ethnographical Study of the Jukun-speaking Peoples of Nigeria* (London: Tench, Trubner, 1931) s vols. (Bata I: pp 69-136; Chamba I: pp. 328-412; Mambila I: pp 532-82; Kamkam I: pp. 563-66; Margi I: pp. 213-52; Tigong (Mebmbe) II: pp. 551-89; Verre I: pp. 413-45).

Meyer Reinhold, "Die Rolle der lokalen Sprachen in nationalen Entwicklungs-prozess in Niger" (the role of local languages in nation-building in Niger) *Africa-Specktrum* (Hamburg) 3, 1977, pp. 263-73.

Nida, Eugene & Wilham Wonderly Gandonu, Ajato. "Nigeria's 250 ethnic groups: realities and assumptions," in R.E. Holloman & S.A. Arutimov (eds) *Perspectives on Ethnicity* (The Hague: Mouton, 1978) pp 243-70.

Gregersen, E.A., "Success and failures in the modernization of Hausa spelling" in J.A. Fishman (ed) *Advances in the Creation & Revision of Writing Systems* (The Hague: Mouton, 1977) pp. 420-40.

Laya, D., "Le Niger: description sociolinguistique" in *Sow 1977*, pp. 285-97.

Renaud, P., "La situation socio-linguistique du Cameroun" in Barreteau, 1978, pp. 473-92; also in CON-FEMEN II, pp. 95-116.

Salmone, F.A., Sow, I.A., (eds) *Langues et politiques de langue en Afrique noire: l'experience de i'UNESCO* (Paris: Nubia, 1977) p. 474.

Stenning, D.J., "Tnashumance, migratory drift, migration: patterns of pastoral Fulani nomadism" in S. & P. Ottenberg *Cultures & Societies of Africa* (New York: Random House, 1960), pp. 139-59.

Stumpf, R., *La politique linguistique au Cameroun de 1884-1960* (Bern: Peter Lang, 1979) pp 61 & 157.

Tadadjeu, M., "Language planning in Cameroun: toward a trilingual education system" in R.K. Herbert (ed) *Patterns in Language, Culture Society: Sub-Saharan Africa*. (Columbus, Ohio: Ohio State Univ. Dept. of Linguistics, 1975) pp. 53-75.

―――― *A Model for Functional Trilingual Education Planning in Africa* (Paris: UNESCO. Ed-80/WS/72) pp. 147 (English), pp. 113 (French).

Talbot, P.A., "Land of the Ekoi, southern Nigeria" *Geographical Journal* 36, 1910, pp. 637-56.

―――― "The Buduma of Lake Chad" *J.R.A.S.I.* 41, 1911, pp. 245-59.

―――― *The Peoples of Southern Nigeria: A Sketch of Their History, Ethnology and Languages, with an Abstract of the 1921 Census* (London: O.U.P., 1926). Reproduced Frank Cass, 1969, 4 vols.

Tersis, N., "Le Niger: description sociolinguistique" in Barreteau, 1978: Weladji, pp. 443-7. "The Cameroun-Nigeria border" *Abbia* (Younde) 27/28, June 2974, pp. 163-95, map.

Wente-Uka, R., "Zur sprachlichen stellung des Bana (Mandara Gebirge Nordwestkamerun)" (linguistic position of Bana in the Mandara mountains) *Africa u. Uebersee*, Hamburg, 57/1, 1973, pp. 1-15, bib.

White, S., *Dan Bana: The Memoirs of a Nigerian Official* (London: Cassell, 1966) pp. xvi, 268, map.

Works, J. jr., *Pilgrims in a Strange Land: Hausa Communities in Chad* (New York: Columbia Univ. Press, 1976) pp. xiv, 280.

Addenda:

Brauner, S. et al., *Verkehrs und National sprachen in Africa* (vehicular and national languages in Africa) (Berlin: Akademie-Verlag, 1985) p. 216, map.

Heine, Bernd., *Sprache, Gesellschaft and Kommunikation in Africa* (language, society and communication in Africa) (March: Weltforum, 1979) pp. 198, maps, diagrams.

Nida, E. & W. Wonderly, "Communication roles of languages in multilingual soceietes" in W. Whiteley (ed) *Language Use and Social Change: Problems of Multilingualism with Special Reference to Eastern Africa* (London: O.U.P. for Int. African Inst., 1971), pp. 57-74.

Salome, F.A. "Becoming Hausa: ethnic identity change and its implication for the study of ethnic pluralism and stratification" *Africa* London, 45/4, 1975, pp. 410-24.

CHAPTER 16

Borderland 'Equilibrium' in Africa: An Ethnolinguistic Perspective in Conflict Resolution

by Victor Owhotu

Introduction

Before opening discussion of the theme of this paper, we shall clarify certain key concepts with which the title is loaded, and by so doing we shall define pertinent conceptual and methodological bases of our position. The relevant segments of the title are:

Borderland 'Equilibrium'

'Equilibrium' is defined within the more desirable goal of peaceful coexistence between persons or Nation states; not through 'foul' (aggression, partition) but through 'fair' processes (negotiation and integration). The implicit question here is whether in fact, borderland equilibrium is a feasible goal to strive to achieve and, if so, whether the predisposing psychosocial (human) and political (state) behaviours are conducive to peaceful coexistence. It follows that a more functional, thus realistic, acception of 'equilibrium' would be not "a state of balance or equality between opposing forces" but a state of balance or adjustment of conflicting desires and interests."[1]

Ethnolinguistics

Through the medium of language we are able to look at something else: a collective consciousness, the mind, the will and culture of a people. The integration of two constituent terms ethnology and linguistics broadly defines the core value and problems in ethnolinguistics. Taken separately, ethnology falls within the branch of anthropology that deals with the characteristic and distinguishing features of various peoples and cultures. Linguistics as an expanded term on the other hand, can be defined as the scientific study of language and the relationship between various other convergent entities. These entities together reflect the psychological, sociological, neurological, and linguistic parameters of human verbal or non verbal communication. The emphasis is on the *problems of communication* between peoples who may have different exo-linguistic (English, French) and political orientations, but who within the context of basic traditions, and convergent indigenous cultural expressions may be more culturally motivated to seek satisfactory solutions to artificial boundary problems as has been typified in the case of Africa (Asiwaju: 1984).

Conflict and Communication

These will be defined here as the result of a breakdown of levels and purpose of communication between two or more groups for a variety of reasons which may be political, ethnic, racial, social, economic, ideological. In as much as conflict is basically *uncontrolled* levels and purposes in communication it can also be a vital tool in establishing the basis for identifying common values to which both parties could be committed and thereby maximizing the chances of peaceful relationships across borders. Our adopted working assumption therefore will be that "conflict and ineffective communications are causally related."[2]

The Origin of Boundary Conflicts in Africa

Boyd (1979), in a enlightening study of the origins of boundary conflict on the African continent, measures conflict along African borders first in terms of sets of statements of the causes of border conflict:

(a) that there is a direct linkage between disruptive, arbitrarily imposed boundaries, and conflict;

(b) that, for another school of thought, conflict "derives not so much from the specific impact of boundaries upon the lives of individuals or the environment as from the impact that the boundary situation has had upon the perceptions and views of African decision makers."[3]

This posits that the origin of boundaries can be traced to the advent of colonial powers and the attendant geographical and ethnological ignorance of the early colonial cartographers and diplomats. Hargreaves (1984) quoting *The Times* of August 6, 1890, reports that Lord Salisbury had acknowledged that colonial powers had been engaged in "drawing lines upon maps where no white man's feet have ever tread; we have been giving away mountains and rivers and lakes to each other..." without any knowledge of where these features were. Much of the documentation of the partition of Africa in Hargreaves' view would also support an "accidental rather than a conspiratorial theory of boundary demarcation in the period of the scramble for Africa."[4]

The merit of Boyd's study of the causes of border conflict was that it set out to test some hypotheses; the degree of correlation between seven independent variables (A^1A^7) and conflict occurrence, the dependent variable.

The A variables tested included A^1 Ethnic population over-hang, A^2 ethnic fragmentation; A^3 Domestic instability; A^4 Non-boundary conflict; A^5 Size-Status relationship (over a given country); A^6 Elite instability (within the country); and A^7 Salience of Ethnic Politics. Variables A^1, A^2, A^7 were in the direct relationship hypotheses category; that is, they were expected to yield high positive correlation between them and the occurrence of border conflict between African nation-states. In other words a positive rise in ethnic population overhang between two independent nation states, for example, will induce a corresponding rise in border tension and conflict; "When an ethnic group is bisected by an artificial border there will be domestic disruption."[5]

The results of data analysis showed that whereas all expectations would be for a strong positive relationship between population overhang between states and conflict, this yielded a weak positive correlation of .07. Furthermore, Elite instability (A[6]) Ethnic politics (A[7]) provided the strongest positive correlation of .54 and .31 respectively. What this mean, in effect, is that

i)   Ethnic population overhang theory which according to Boyd enjoys the greatest support in the traditional literature is not a reliable factor after all for explaining the stress and border strife Africa.

ii) Ethnic politics within states was shown by the study to be highly related to the levels of border conflicts especially where the divided ethnic group(s) were politically important at home;

iii) Perhaps the most significant finding relates to elite instability and increased border conflict (r=.54): "Turmoil at the elite level could lead to the development of boundary conflict."[6] No satisfactory explanation was however proffered beyond the fact the fact that change of government or instability increases the temptation for bordering states to foment boundary conflict.

Since this was a comprehensive study based on a thorough and systematic analysis of 32 Black African states its reliability clearly overshadows the results of single case studies that have invariably accorded universal validity to peculiar relations between ethno-culturally divided peoples, of which the much cited Horn of Africa (Somali-Ethiopia-Kenya) problems provide a rather unique perspective. The major point to note here is that generally ethnic affinity across border provides far less conflict between states than the political factor. This provides us with a first ethnolinguistic perspective in conflict resolution.

Another important study on policy and intra-Africa conflict behaviour was undertaken by McGowan and Johnson (1979). Code-named AFRICA project, "event data" or units of analysis were gathered for thirty-two African countries and their forty-three regimes. These "events" were classified into two types; verbal and physical actions. These categories cover any communique, utterance or "single action items of a non routine, extra ordinary, or news worthy character that in some clear sense are directed across a national boundary and have in most instances, a specific target".[7] Since this was quite an extensive study we shall be concerned here only with the relevance of the results of the study.

i)   The functional items (verbal and physical action) in the transborder foreign relations were such direct or implied events as 'deny', 'accuse', 'negative comment', 'demand', 'project', 'negative request', 'threaten', 'warn', 'reject' and so on.

ii) Non-verbal or physical functional items covered events such as 'Force', 'demonstrate', 'increase military capability,' 'aid opponent' (of the co-actor), 'reduced relationship' (break in diplomatic relations, reduction of embassy staff), 'size', 'expel', subvert.

iii) A scale for positive behaviour was also constructed on functional items such as 'negotiate', 'positive request', 'promise', 'agree', 'accept', 'support', 'increase relationship', 'reconcilation', disengagement', and 'communication'.[8]

One of the total calculated 'events' data representing behaviours of a given state vis-a-vis the other and vice-versa, there were 4802 occurrences within the early post-independence period of 1964-1966. The three major types were

a)   Neutral behaviour (N=584)

b) Conflict behaviour (N=885)
c) Cooperative behaviour (N=3333)

If, however, this statistic of cooperative behaviour painted a rosy picture of early post-independence intra-African relations, the picture of Africa today is a far cry from the early days. In other words, Libya-Chad, Somali-Ethiopia, Morocco-Saharaoui, Togo-Ghana, Senegal-Gambia, Nigeria-Chad, Nigeria-Cameroun would present a far bloomier behaviour graph than did the Africa Project. The crises in Zaire, the Nigerian civil war, Uganda-Tanzania conflict and military interventions were all to determine far less cooperative foreign policy acts between African States after 1966.

Secondly, and more relevant, there is the fact that much of the conflict arises from negative interaction with neighbouring or bordering states. The AFRICA project (1979) identified conflict in the case of almost all contiguous states either as a factor of border, or allegations of interference in the others' internal affairs. For non-contiguous states, conflict was based only on interference. The highest conflict acts for the period 1964-66 between contiguous states in rank order was recorded for [first figure represents total events, second figure represents total military clashes, coercion or subversion] Somalia-Ethiopia (69) (3), Somalia-Kenya (67) (8); Ethiopia-Somalia, (45) (5); Togo-Ghana (28) (3); Upper Volta-Ghana (28) (2); Zaire-Congo (24) (6); Uganda-Zaire (23) (1); Burundi-Rwanda (29); Zaire-Burundi (16); Ivory Coast-Ghana (16); Benin-Niger (15) (0); Chad-Sudan (12) (5). Within the two-year period there were 61 military incidents, subversive action and coercion, with the Horn of Africa accounting for the most serious and protracted case.

The concept of border is a dynamic and highly volatile issue since it is related directly to fundamental aspects of identity, sovereignty and jurisdiction, and self-preservation. As Shaw (1977) states:

> In international law a change in ownership of a particular territory involves also a change in sovereignty, in the legal authority governing the areas. This means that the nationality of the inhabitants is altered, as is the legal system under which they live, work and conduct their relations.[9]

While internally, and more so externally, territorial boundaries are instruments or factors of significant change or discontinuity in political and legal jurisdiction, what may not necessarily suffer from such 'artificial' discontinuities are the ideological, ethnic/cultural affinities between partitioned peoples. The classic example is that of Somalia-Ethiopia conflict. Such a psycho-ethnic disposition—unlike the limiting concept of national and national self interest—becomes a conscious, specific, well integrated dogma or doctrine of a mutually beneficial political nature, if carefully explored by contending parties.[10]

The harmonization of these two factors, therefore, should provide the second condition for an ethnolinguistic perspective of conflict resolution among contiguous nation-states.

Dynamics of Trans-border Communication

Since the basis of human communication in society is interaction, conflict was initially defined essentially as a breakdown in communication; trans-border communication thus becomes a conscious deliberate process from which can be derived infinite and complex systems of relationship established on well defined levels of interaction. Furthermore, such is the transcendence of this phenomenon in human

society that it is certainly justified to talk about the impossibility of not com-
municating. Communication theorists have been very much conscious of this.
Watzlawick, Beavin and Jackson (1967) describe this, among other things, as the
schizophrenic 'dilemma': "nonsense, silence, withdrawal, immobility (postural
silence) or any form of denial is itself a communication the impossibility of not com-
municating is a phenomenon of more than theoretical interest..."[11] This pragmatic
force which transcends the lives of individuals both intra-and inter-ethnic and
regulates to a great extent the core values of language, culture and ethnic ideology
of conformity and commitment, is bound to affect the behaviours of all co-actors
in any given communicative situation.

Structure of Communication

By structure is meant that macro component units of syntactics, semantics and
pragmatics that constitute the nature of discourse or behaviourial manifestations of
the intention to communicate positively or negatively, or ambiguously. Boyd's (1979)
repertoire of 'events items', discussed earlier, reflects some of the communicative
acts underlying African nations' inventions and relationship with the other; contiguous and non contiguous. Syntactics involves the actual problems of emission or
transmission of information between source T (utterance) and destination R (reception); comprising such intensive processes as encoding, and interpretative operation
as decoding. Semantics covers not only the expected positive decoding of transmitted message whether intra-individual or inter-state, but is also tied to varying levels
of cultural meaning of system of representation, especially intercultural fluency
which constitutes one of the most difficult tasks to master in approaching conflict
and communication within an ethnolinguistic perspective. The complexity of the
task has been variously treated in the literature on culture and communication;
Nivette (1976)[12] from the pedagogical view points, and Poyatos (1983)[13] from anthropological, interdisciplinary and systematic dimensions. Pragmatics as indicated
relates behaviour derived from predisposing factors of ethno-cultural values.

The problems therefore, in the nature of intercultural communication could be
better appreciated if the nature of interrelationships between syntactics, semantics
and pragmatics is clearly understood. As George (1962) states "In many ways it is
true to say that syntax is mathematic logic, semantics is philosophy (the problem
of meaning and knowing) and pragmatics (behaviour) is psychology, but these fields
are not really all distinct."[14]

Application to Ethnological Studies

The literature of the implications of these aspects of communication theory on
inter-personal and interstate relations is quite vast. For the purpose of this paper two
broad categories will be relevant to our position.

a) The axiomatic: general statements and assertions that stand to reason without
necessarily being backed up by proof or empirical data and
b) The hypothetico-anthropological: which is best summarized by what is known
as Linguistic Relativity, linguistic determinism or more popularly 'the Whort-
Sapir hypothesis, but whose premise of proof or validity has generated one of
the greatest debates in Linguistics.

The merits of the latter has been critically examined enough since the 1940s: and
the latest of which are Haugen (1977)[15]; Fishman (1977)[16]; Sampson (1980)[17] and

Stern (1983).[18] The profound interest, however, that this has generated has been monumental. Whether one was dealing with the axiomatic perspective or the hypothetico-anthropological, certain facts of life and their value or subjective concommitants have to be accepted as socially relevant since they serve to explain or rationalize culturally determined behaviour patterns and values of conformity and commitment to one's ethnolinguistic entity and derived affinities that constitute mental boundaries between likes and others, and even among likes. The concept and pragmatic implications of ethnolinguistic descriptions like 'Igbo-man/Igbo land', 'Yoruba land', 'Hausa-man/Hausa land' and so on reinforce the assumption of inter-ethnic boundaries in the eyes and minds of the other. On the other hand, 'Onitsha-man', 'Ijebu-man', 'ba-kano' may be equally potent pragmatic descriptions of intra-ethnic boundaries. It follows, therefore that one can justifiably argue that if the terms 'arbitrary', 'conspiratorial' 'fragmentation' can be used against the colonial partition it would certainly be because those preexisting ethnic, cultural, linguistic criteria of natural boundary demarcation had been violated.

The importance of this assumption has been emphasized by Maynard (1968) who describes the ethnolinguistic factor as the greatest road block to any form of (positive) human communication. He states further:

> Language is the most pervasive, ubiquitous and ethnocentric factor in our culture (and consequently) each culture is like a gigantic iceberg, carrying along beneath the surface of its observable differences its own assumptions, premises and biases.[19]

Maynard's axiom, quoted above, is well reflected in the recognition (in intercultural and international relations) of the importance of national cultures and the study of national character as a factor in diagnosing representative and characteristic collective behaviour, ethno-cultural particularities and the predictive value of such factors to international communication. While Mead (1968) claims some success with such statistical description and studies in the international relations of the U.S.A. through systematic empirical research (interviews with members of target culture; interview with members of other cultures who have lived very many years among the target culture, and intensive examination of cultural materials), she was to concede that world affairs are far more complicated today. As she has deposed, "many of the nations whose behaviour puzzles or bedevils the world today are so new that they cannot be said to either a national culture or national character."[20]

Although this was written in the early post-independence years and may have been true of colonially partitioned Africa, nation-states in Africa have come a long way in their effort to build national cultures. If the implementation phase of the 'Lagos Plan of Action of 1980, for example, has proved slow it is nonetheless true that FESTAC 77[21] came as the turning point in a partitioned peoples quest for cultural awareness and a global, national continental character. While Mead's statistical predictive study may have some relevance vis-a-vis the ethnocentric factor in inter-personal and intercultural communication a more global and more axiomatic position will be adopted here both for reasons of scope of this paper, the complex nature of international relations and problems of empirical methods. our ethnolinguistic 'working' assumptions are therefore three fold: One major and two subsidiary, derived from aspects already discussed:

1. Contiguous states with partitioned ethnolinguistic groups have the highest chances of positively managing and resolving conflicts.

2. The global wave of African Cultural awareness and identity provides potential reference points for conflict resolution of both contiguous and non-contiguous African nation states.[23]
3. The role of institutionalized fora in conflict control and resolution would be readily and positively serviced through an exploration of not only the less effective diplomatic type communication but through more intensively personalized and socialized communication.[24]

We shall now critically examine the bases of each of the three perspectives with regard to harmonizing incompatibilities and establishing communication.

Ethnological Bases of Conflict Management and Resolution

Where two or more nation states share a common, partitioned cultural group it should only take positive political will for all to arrive at lasting solution to the problem. Many studies have emphasized and demonstrated the natural, irrepressible attraction between splintered but ethnolinguistically homogeneous groups to reintegrate: The Berlin wall, the Palestinians; the Somali; and very recently the Israeli airlift of Ethiopian Jews (Falashas) from the drought stricken zone are but a few examples. The extent of the problem can be seen in a useful checklist of 'partitioned culture areas on the African continent provided by Asiwaju (1984).[25] We shall here look at a few representative cases for positive transborder communication based on the ethnolinguistic affinity factors. These are drawn from the East, the West, and the Horn of Africa.

Ethnic affinity and mobility across political boundaries have been well documented; Phiri's (1984) study of the Chewa and Ngoni before and after the colonial partition created the contiguous states of Zambia, Malawi and Mozambique shows that despite these separate nation states' political jurisdiction over their own land mass and citizens, "the medical, educational and agricultural services by the Government for the Ngoni and Chewa settlements located on the Zambian side of the boundaries have been made inadequate largely as a result of the use made of them by kinsmen crossing the boundaries from Malawi and Mozambique."[26] While such would be regarded as clandestine by the government concerned, the host splinter ethnic group would see such benefits to their kith and kin as both natural and welcome. Such patterns of trans-border mobility have been documented for almost all contiguous states with partitioned ethnolinguistically homogeneous groups.[26a] The Ghana-Togo conflict of the 1960s was political, between two political entities; not an Ewe-Ewe confrontation. The Gambia-Senegal border conflicts were more of a political nature, not against kith and kin. As Faith Renner has explained, longstanding proposals about Sene-gambian union, including the on-going experimentation with confederation, has continued to experience fundamental difficulties because of their political undertone. She must be adjudged as right that it is in the cultural (language is a core value of culture) field that the concept of Sene-Gambia would be easiest to realise and made acceptable to both countries."[27]

This is certainly not saying that inter-ethnic and intra-ethnic conflict did not mar or strain relations before colonialism. What is emphasized is that political partition sharpened sensibilities and reinforced centrifugal ethnolinguistic motivation in the partitioned cultures. And nowhere has it been so grimly demonstrated as in the 'Ethnic Overhang' factor in the Somali-Ethiopia-Kenya boundary conflicts. The Africa project (1964-66) showed that the Somalia-Ethiopia conflictual behaviour accounted for 4.60% of the total Intra-African conflict behaviour representing, in

those two years, a total of 226 conflict acts of which a total of 20 were 'military incidents, subversion, and coercion'. The basic ethnolinguistic perspective was vividly described by Samatar (1984) in relation to the Somali whom he qualified as a 'nation in search of a state'. His expose quoting Dr. Abdurashid Ali Sharmaarke the
Late President of the Somali Republic, is particularly poignant:

> Our misfortune is that our neighbouring countries, with whom, like the
> rest of Africa, we seek to promote constructive and harmonious relation-
> ship, are not our brothers.... We speak the same language. We share the
> same creed, the same culture and the same traditions. How can we regard
> our brothers as foreigners?[28]

The syntactic, semantic and pragmatic conditions for a highly integrative
transborder communication have never been so clearly identified, and breaking the
boundary predicament which remains unexploited is now a function of the *political
will* of the political opponents. The question of how best political will be can be
managed in conflict situations has a large share of the theoretical literature in International relations.

Within the African context, however, solutions to the problems are of utmost
necessity and the establishment of communication through convergent, linkage processes remains a prime objective. In order, therefore, to actualize the need to
establish communication between contiguous nation states in particular, two vital
points deserve due recognition; that

1. the most popular forms of communication are the least effective: talking,
   negotiating, voting and so on across the table.
2. the very considerable informal socialising processes that characterize ethnolinguistic affinity between otherwise inflexible political positions should be
   explored.

As Ager (1970) puts it, "the sustained interaction of delegates (of conflict zones) as
well as the variety of occasion on which they confront each other provides opportunities for the development of friendships across national boundaries that surpass
those of normal diplomatic intercourse (and communication)."[29]

This perspective on the informal should increase the probability of realising effective communication at the more formal level as the intensity of informal interaction is raised. Thereafter understanding and accepting the other's point of view
would be dictated far less by intransigent political attitudes and more by the will to
understand the other's position. It would therefore be wrong to see conflict across
contiguous states as a breakdown in ethno-cultural relations but in the divergent
political and diplomatic levels and intentions.

Pan-African Cultural Awareness and Conflict Resolution

The second 'working' assumption—a sub-category of the ethnological
perspective—is that of the Pan-African cultural awareness. Earlier expressions of
this awareness were 'Negritude' (Senghor), 'African High Command' (Nkrumah);
'Pan-African Lingua-Franca' (African Writers Conference, Rome 1960); and
FESTAC (Dakar 1964, Lagos 1977). These developments were directly related to
the revulsion of Africans vis-a-vis colonialism, and the colonial experience on the
one hand, and the post independence era of indirect threats of non-colonialism on
the other. The singular role of the FESTACs especially has been to break the border
predicament, albeit tentatively, thereby providing a general orientation and mobil-

isation towards a spiritual, cultural and ethnolinguistic communion. Not only have cultural links been renewed but the organisational and deliberate processes involved have made it of immense educational and philosophical value, FESTAC, being the most elaborate forum in this Pan-cultural revival and communications, has generated a lot of hope, and some reservations too. The true test, as Obiechina (1978) points out, is yet to come: "If it [FESTAC] does not create the *emotional* and *psychological* atmosphere for the emergence of a just, humane and *harmonious society* which has eluded Africans and African peoples and their countries up till now, then history, distanced and objectified, would not pronounce the Festival a success"[30] [our emphasis].

Continental Institutions and Conflict Resolution

The task of harmonizing this desired Pan African cultural goal with the grim realities of nationalism or the political will of African states—each to preserve its identity (social, economic, national)—should now devolve on existing continental and regional institutions like the Organisation of African Unity, the Economic Community for Africa and the Economic Community of West African States. For whatever they are worth the impetus of cultural awareness may well inform and condition the political attitudes of contending states. If Africa, in the policy statement of most African governments, is the centre-piece of foreign and intra-African relations then the strenuous mediating efforts—and appreciable results—made by Nigeria among others to resolve the Chadian conflict and the subsequent French and Libyan involvement, should be an indicator of the awareness and need for meaningful understanding and communication among African Nation states. The primary role and problems of ECOWAS' attempt at regional integration have been adequately treated by African scholars and critics from the economic, commercial, financial and nationalistic view points.[31] At each stage the role of effective communication has been clearly recognized and emphasized as the significant factor in regional integration and development. Furthermore, such core values as 'extended family', the Eagle and Kite principle, 'thy brother's keepers', cultural commitment and conformity which explain the dynamics of life traditional society in Africa, should find global expression in the communicative behaviour of African Nation states.

The need, therefore, for linguistic, cultural and educational reinforcement of relations between contiguous states in particular—given the ethnic hangover and conflict control and resolution perspective—is in our opinion long overdue. Continental institutions like the OAU and ECA should create effective agencies for the implementation of policy recommendations based on some salient features of border management approaches elsewhere. The cases of Sino-Soviet border conflict and the creation of permanent 'Friendly border', the rural development programmes in the case of the Chewa and Ngoni have been highlighted.[32] In both cases the human and ethnolinguistic realities of partitioned culture areas completely out-weighed political considerations. It follows that the human and psycho-cultural factors that bedevil the Somalia-Ethiopia conflict, among others, are in fact the only levels at which (if explored) the problem in the Horn can ever hope to be resolved.

The major role of the suggested agencies of continental organisations would be to seek greater 'rapprochement' between contiguous states through the maximal exploration of linguistic, educational and cultural relations between nation states. The parent organisations themselves (OAU, ECOWAS) linking up with the African cultural awareness orientation, should provide the motivating forces to break the political will of actors for positive transborder communication. The educational process of peoples have to deliberately de-emphasize the political boundaries and the complex problems of transborder communication that they have generated. It is in this regard that great awareness could be generated through the effective teaching of African languages and culture. Language planning across the borders is in a state of readiness; this has been clearly demonstrated by Tadadjeu's (1977) transborder language use profile of 33 African countries.[33] Furthermore, although the Festac Colloquia proceedings (1977) provide clear policy guidelines for African nations only in respect to the development of national languages as an indication of cultural awareness and national identify, transborder perspectives had not been duly considered. Cooperative transborder language projects and researches could be initiated under the aegis of a specialised agency, say, an "African Institute for Ethnolinguistic Studies and Trans-border Relations". Within the operations of such an institute emphasis will be on

a) contiguous or extensively used African languages for mass literacy and cons-cientization aimed at counteracting the obstruction posed by artificial boundaries and promoting Pan-African ideals, goals and aspirations.
b) Pan-cultural education, exchanges and visits and pen-friendship between the youths in contiguous states in particular.
c) the management and propagation of FESTAC studies, colloquia, and so on.
d) The instrumental role of English and French.

Conclusion

The structure of all human communication has been put down to syntactics (philosophy semantics and pragmatics (psychology, behaviour). The axiom has been underlined that it is impossible not to communicate for better or for worse. It has also been argued that no political artifact or devise (boundary, frontier) can stem the flow of man's instinctive communicative needs and the psycho-cultural problems that are generated. Since, also, language and its psycho-cultural concomittants will ever remain the most pervasive, irredentist and pragmatic factor in human society, the future and survival of cross-border communication in Africa and indeed in any other part of the world would depend on how skilfully those very factors of discord and conflict are explored, harnessed and managed. In other words if language and its ethno-cultural core values have determined societal progress and human civilization, it is no less true that the real source of man's problems in society is, indeed, linguistic.

Endnotes

1. *Webster's New World Dictionary of the American Language,* 1964.
2. Burton, J.W., *Conflict and Communication* (London: MacMillan, 1969).
3. Boyd B., "The Origin of Boundary Conflict in Africa" in Delancey, H.W. (ed) *Aspects of International Relations in Africa* (Bloomington: African Univ. program, Univ. of Indiana, 1979) pp. 159-189.
4. Hargreaves. J.D., "The Making of the Boundaries: Focus on West Africa", in Asiwaju, A.I. (ed) *Partitioned Africans: Ethnic Relations Across Africa's International Boundaries 1884-1984,* (London: C. Hurst and Company, and Lagos: Univ. of Lagos Press, 1984) pp. 19-27.
5. Boyd, B., op. cit.
6. Ibid.
7. McGowan P.J., Johnson, T.H., "The Africa Project and Comparative Study of African Foreign Policy" in Delancey, M. (ed) op. cit., pp. 190-241.

8. Ibid.

9. Shaw, M., *International Law* (London: Hodder and Stoughton, 1977) p. 204.

10. Boyd, B. op. cit.

11. Watzlawick, P., Beavin, J.H. Jackson, D.D., *Pragmatics of Human Communication* (New York: W. W. Norton, 1967) pp. 50-51.

12. Nivette, J. (ed) *The Teaching of Modern Languages in Various Countries: Selected Papers from the 5th AIMAV Seminar 27th August-1st September 1973, Brussels (AIMAV)* (Paris: Didier, 1976).

13. Poyatos F., *New Perspectives in Non-Verbal Communications* (Oxford: Pergamon Press, 1983-84).

14. George, F.H., *The Brain as a Computer* (Oxford: Pergamon Press, 1962) quoted in Walzlawick et al, op. cit., p. 22.

15. Haugen, E.: "Linguistic Relativity: Myths and Methods" in McCormack, W.C. and Wurm, S.A. (eds) *Language and Thought: Anthropological Issues,* (The Hague: Mouton Publishers, 1977) pp. 11-28.

16. Fishman, J.A., "The Sociology of Language: Yesterday, Today, and Tomorrow" in Cole, R. (ed) *Current Issues in Linguistic Theory* (Bloomington: Indiana Univ. Press, 1977) pp. 51-75.

17. Sampson, G., *Schools of Linguistics* (London: Hutchson, 1980).

18. Stern, H.H., *Fundamental Concepts of Language Teaching* (Oxford: Oxford Univ. Press, 1983) Chap. 10.

19. Maynard, H., "The Language of International Communications: Semantics and Linguistics" in Hoffman, A.S. *International Communication and the New Diplomacy* (Bloomington: Indiana Univ. Press, 1968) pp. 137-146.

20. Mead, M., "The Importance of National Cultures" in Hoffman, A.S., op. cit., pp. 89-105.

21. Appraisal, unpublished paper. See also FESTAC Colloquia Proceedings, Vol. 1, 1977.

22. Derived from related discussions in Boyd (1979) Mead (1968); Maynard (1968); and the concept of linguistic relativity (Hausen: 1977).

23. See Boyd, op. cit., McGowan, and Johnson (1979) op cit., and FESTAC Colloquia, op. cit.

24. See Burton, J.W., op. cit. and also Samantar, S.S., "The Somali Dilemma: A Nation in Search of a State", Southall, A., "Partitioned Alur" in Asiwaju, A.I. (ed) op. cit.

25. Asiwaju, A.I. "Partitioned Culture Areas: A Checklist" in Asiwaju (ed) op. cit., pp. 252-259.

26. Phiri, S.H., "National Integration, Rural Development and Frontier Communities" in Asiwaju, A.I. (ed) op. cit., pp. 105-125.

26a. Asiwaju, A.I. (ed), *Partitioned Africans: Ethnic Relations Across Africa's International Boundaries 1884-1984* (Lagos: Lagos Univ. Press, 1984) p. 275.

27. Renner, F.A., "Ethnic Affinity, Partition and Political Integration in SeneGambia" in Asiwaju, A.I. (ed), op. cit., pp. 71-85.

28. Samatar, S.S., op. cit.

29. Alger, C.F., "Non-resolution consequences of the United Nations and their aspects on international conflict" in Rosenbaum, N. (ed), op. cit., pp. 270-292.

30. Obiechina, E.N., "Doubts and Directions in Cultural Revival" in Kalu, O.U. (ed) *African Cultural Development* (Enugu: Fourth Dimension Pub., 1978) pp. 268-280.

31. See for example (i) Udokang, O. "Nigeria and ECOWAS: Economic and Political Implications of Regional Integration" pp. 17-80; (ii) Kumar A., "of West African States" pp. 45-56 in Akinyemi, A.B. (ed) (1978:80): *Nigeria and The World,* University Press; (iii) see also Diejomaoh, V.P. and Iyoha, M.A. (eds) *Industrialization in the Economic Community of West African States* (Lagos: Heinneman Educ. Bks. (Nig). Ltd., 1980).   32. See Phiri S., in Asiwaju A.I. (ed) op. cit.

33. Tadadjeu, M., "Cost-Benefit Analysis of Language/Education Planning in Sub-Saharan Africa" in Kotey, P.F.A., Der-Houssikian, H. (eds) *Language and Linguistic Problems in Africa: Proceedings of the VII Conference of African Linguistics, Florida 23-25 April 1976* (Columbia, SC: Hornbeam Press, 1977).

CHAPTER 17

Transborder Cultural Interaction: The Case of the Hausa Style Mosques Across Nigeria/Niger Boundary

by Susan B. Aradeon

Introduction

The mosques on both sides of the Nigerian/Niger border possess distinctively Hausa features. Hausa master masons exploit the Hausa arch to design mosques possessing a variety of spatial configuration rather than confining themselves to the low aisles found in most traditional mosques in West Africa. The distribution pattern of these arched mosques suggests that their design was closely linked to the prevailing prestige architectural style. Even though the prestige architecture in this geographical area is clearly identified with a particular ethnic group, it transcends both ethnic and national borders.

Mosque Architectural Styles Transcend Borders

Since Islam spreads rapidly over a large proportion of the world, one might expect to find that all mosques conform to a basic type transcending geographical regions and national borderlines. However, even though the liturgical requirements for mosque architecture were imported to all the nations where Islam is practised today, mosque architecture is noted for its distinct regional styles. The division of the Islamic world into regional as well as period architectural styles was made possible by the minimal liturgical requirements for a mosque, the rapid spread of Islam prior to the establishment of any preconceived mosque form, and the capacity of Islamic syncretism to assimilate local architectural technology and prestige architectural styles.[2]

Several regional mosque styles transcend the national borders in West Africa. The sahelian style is noted for its hypostyle halls supported on heavy piers arranged to create a lateral spatial configuration.[3] These mosques have large courtyards with massive pyramidal minarets. The famed Sankore Mosque in Timbuctoo exemplified this style. The dry savannah areas which have been exposed to Dyula influence constitute another style region. Dyula style mosques are noteworthy for their distinctive elevation revealing two conical forms projecting above the roof, one articulating the

mihrab and the other serving as the minaret. Conical forms also cap each of the but-
tresses which reinforce the walls.[4] Further east in the areas exposed to Hausa
culture, the mosque form consisted of a tall, massive minaret in the form of a splayed
cuboid which contrasted with the low splayed cuboid of the sanctuary. With Fulani
rule, the massive fortress tower/minarets were replaced by "step minarets", steps
rising to the level of the flat roof.[5] In the nineteenth and twentieth centuries, Hausa
mosques became distinguished by their spaciousness made possible by the incorporation of indigenous Hausa arches.[6]

The Hausa Style Mosques with Arches Generating Spacious Bays

Throughout West Africa, it is only in Hausaland that a traditional architectural
style has evolved possessing spacious arched and domed bays. The oldest recorded
arched mosque was commissioned in 1823 by the Gadado, a royal official in the
Sokoto Caliphate. As briefly described by Hugh Clapperton, this mosque appears
to represent a transition between the hypostyle mosques with a lateral, spatial configuration and the more spacious mosques supported on lofty arches. Seven rows
of arches created a rectangular sanctuary approximately 24.40m (80') wide.[7]

The Zaria Mosque (Fig. 1) designed between 1835-46 is the oldest and most impressive of the existing arched mosques. Arches which rise as pilasters from articulated piers support six domed bays. The two largest and most elaborate bays are
flanked on each side by two pairs of elongated bays whose structural systems contrast with the central, dominant bays. The arches supporting the central bays are entirely free of the walls relying on piers, including one massive freestanding partition
wall pier, for support. Although each bay is perceived as a separate unit, it is united
with the other bays because of the vistas perceptible between the piers and columns.
The lateral bays are each supported on one side wall and on those piers which also
support the central bays as well as on single piers at the end of each bay.

Several small, but important twentieth century mosques in Argungun were
designed by Gobirawa (Hausa) master masons exploiting the aesthetic potential of
the Hausa arch. Like master masons elsewhere in Hausaland, they were descen-
dants of slaves who had been professional master masons for the rulers.[8] Each of
their mosques is distinguished by a unique plan which emphasizes the special
qualities of the arch technology as distinguished from the beam technology. The arched space supplements the mihrab as a focal point of the mosque. These mosques
are especially relevant to the question of transborder cultural influences because
their master masons also designed mosques and palaces in Niger.

The Mallam Alu Mosque is the oldest documented Argungun mosque to exploit
the potential of arches to create large free spans. Sarkin Kebbi Samaila commissioned this mosque sometime after the arrival of the European in 1902 and before this
death in 1915.[9] Initially the Alu Mosque served as the principal mosque. It was
designed and built by Mohammadu Angu dan Galadima of the Yabo family of master
masons.[10]

The clarity and elegance of Angu's design solution is original and aesthetically
pleasing. Two rows of piers support three transverse arches which span a large central space opposite the mihrab. Additional space for worship extends from the piers
to the outer walls. Beams resting on corbels span the peripheral spaces on each side
of the central arcade. The arcade culminated in the mihrab. Thus spatially and
visually, the mihrab has become the focus of the architectural design. The central
transverse arches span 3.75m (12' 4") which is considerably larger than the standard

Figure 1. Zaria Mosque (Nigeria) Plan: Two central bays flanked by lateral bays. (After J.C. Moughtin, *Hausa Architecture* traced by O. Olugbemi.)

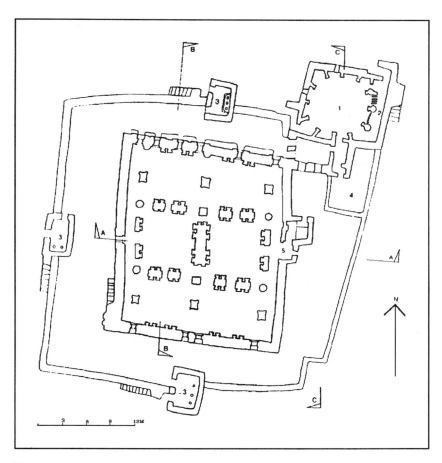

Illustration for "Prestige Architecture Transcends Borders: The Arched Mosques of the Hausa Master Masons" by Susan B. Aradeon, Department of Architecture University of Lagos.

1.80 (6') span possible with a lashed-palm wood beam.

Mohammadu Angu built the Sarkin Gobir Mosque which was commissioned by Sarkin Kebbi Mohammadu Sama before his 1920-34 reign. The special quality of the Sarkin Gobir Mosque (Fig. 2) derives from the use of a ribbed dome surrounded by an ambulatory spatial configuration. The dome covers a moderate space, approximately 5.00m (16' 5") square form pilaster-arch to pilaster-arch. The transverse arches spring from pilasters engaged to massive elongated piers. These piers are virtually freestanding partition walls. Pilaster-arches also rise from columns at the corners of the central space to provide supplementary support for the diagonal arches. These supplementary supports are rendered as massive battered columns. Their rounded contour encourages the viewer's eye to explore the ambulatory space. This structural system, a dome supported on arches which spring from massive piers

Figure 2. Sarkin Gobir Mosque (Nigeria): View from under the dome through huge partition wall/piers and a column to the ambulatory.

designed to generate a square domed space surrounded by an ambulatory, was adapted for use in the mosques commissioned by Djerma rulers in Niger.

Palaces and Mosques in Niger Designed and Constructed by Nigerian Master Masons

The colonial boundary lines severed the official political ties between the Hausa and Hausa/Fulani rulers in the present Sokoto State of Nigeria and their Djerma and Hausa counterparts to the northwest in Niger. Nonetheless, in the first decade of the twentieth century, the traditional rulers in Niger continued their custom of seeking architectural expertise from the Sarkin Kebbi in Argungun and the Sarkin Gwando in Gwando/Birnin Kebbi—to whom they owed fealty even though the Sarkin Zinder in Niger would have been able to send competent Hausa master masons.

Between the late twenties and the early sixties of this century, most of these prestigious architectural designs in Niger were significantly modified by the successors to the Gobirawa (Hausa) master masons residents in Nigeria who had carried out the original commissions. Many reception halls were designed by Umaru dan Bube who had worked under Mohammadu Ango of Yabo. Ango's father, Kaka, had been responsible for many of the earlier buildings designed at the request of Sarkin Kebbi and Ango had worked under him. Although Umaru settled in Amoren-Adowowi, his home village outside Gwandu, his architectural career flourished on the basis of the commissions be carried out annually in Niger.[12] His most beautiful design was for the outer hall of the Sarkin Filingue constructed between 1927-39 while his most decorative design was for the outer hall of the Sarkin Loba constructed in 1954.[13]

Umaru's elder brother, Gwani dan Bube, also carried out commissions in Niger. Gwani is credited with the 1942 design of a very small rectilinear storied ambulatory with central dome for the private room of Sarkin Tabla.[14] In 1961, Gwani also designed and built the Moussadeye Mosque.[15] Sources have variously credited the design of the Dosso Mosque and palace reception halls to either Umaru[16] or Gwani.[17] Further research is necessary to establish the architectural accomplishments of the two brothers and the nature of their professional relationship. Available evidence indicated that virtually all the existing buildings of architectural note in the Djerma and Arewa Hausa area from the Nigerian border north to Filingue were designed by these brothers.

The impressive Dosso Mosque (which has since been replaced by a tasteful modern structure) was designed as a hypostyle hall resting on articulated piers which support bays. In most of these bays, the tall, massive piers flowed into pilaster-arches which fanned out in eight directions generating flat-ceilinged quadripartite bays. Immediately in front of the mihrab, an extra large domed bay was designed as a *maqsura,* a sheltered area for the ruler. Massive piers screened off this bay forming an approximately 4.00m (13 ') square enclosure thereby creating an area which met at the apex. The lofty dome rose above the flat roof-line of the rest of the sanctuary articulating the basic cuboid form.

The Moussadeye Mosque, located north of Dosso on the untarred road to Filingue, was commissioned by Maigari Sirifi in 1961. Gwani dan Bube was sent for in Nigeria in order to carry out the commission. This mosque design follows the basic plan of the Dosso Mosque including the domed *maqsura* (Fig. 3) but with greatly reduced dimensions and inferior workmanship. Moreover, only some of the piers are linked by arches resulting in an awkward mixture of arches and beams supporting the ceiling.

Traditionally, palace architecture was more elaborate than mosque architecture. Many rulers have commissioned domed reception halls without redesigning the post and beam structure of the older mosque sanctuaries. Both entry halls for the Dosso palace are loftier and more elaborate than the *maqsura* of the adjacent central mosque. Like the *maqsura,* the inner hall relies on intersecting transverse and diagonal arches to support a moderately large space. However, the arches are supplemented by intermediate arches. They simultaneously embellish the dome and serve to reduce the span for the short infilling members laid from arch to form the skin of the dome.

That the incorporation of the dome form in palace design as a status symbol took precedence over its use in mosques is further underscored by the contrast between the *maqsura* and the outer reception hall of the Dosso palace which was reconstructed in the early fifties. As in the more refined Filingue hall (Fig. 4), the domed outer reception hall at Dosso is embellished with subsidiary ribs designed to create the impression that the dome rests on sets of five, rather than sets of three, intersecting arches. This *trompe l'oeil* effect lends a sense of grandeur to the space which is maximized by the addition of a rectilinear ambulatory visible through a succession of doorways and openings pierced in the dividing walls.

The design of reception halls embellished with subsidiary decorative ribs and enlarged with ambulatories is a feature of the Hausa architectural style imported to Niger by the Gobirawa master masons living in Sokoto State. Unfortunately, all of the quality traditional architecture in Gwando has been demolished and replaced by cement block structures with tin roofs. The only remaining architectural design in-

Figure 3.   Moussadeye Mosque (Nigeria): Umbrella arch configuration sup-porting masqsura dome.

Figure 4.   Outer Hall of the Filingue Palace (Niger): The diagonal arch in the centre of the photo is flanked by two subsidiary arches which have been given the girth and length of the three major transverse arches which intersect at the apex.

corporating the rectilinear domical space surrounded by an ambulatory is the enormous Council Chamber built for the Emir of Gwando in 1928 after his official residence had been transferred to Birnin Kebbi.[18]

The one remaining Nigerian example of the decorative arch style (Fig. 5) was built in 1958-9 by Umaru Bube as the room for the first wife of the village head of Amori, the village next to Umaru's home town. Although this room is for a much less important personage and function than the reception halls designed for the palaces of important chiefs, the patterning of the arches supplemented by purely decorative ribs is almost as elaborate as the patterning in the reception hall of the palace in Loba, a town on the road between Dosso and Filingue. The Loba dome differs only in the use of diagonal arches; however, it seems larger because it is surrounded by an ambulatory.

The Irrelevance of the Border to the Hausa Master Masons

Even after the Europeans created the boundaries that politically severed the Djerma and Hausa of Niger from the Hausa in Nigeria, these peoples disregarded the border in all those aspects of life not dealt with by their respective colonial governments. The taste for prestigious domed architecture and the selection of master masons with an identifiable style was not of prime concern to the colonialists although they must be credited for appreciating the qualities of Hausa architecture and exploiting them for official buildings and residences. Hence the patrons of the Hausa master masons maintained their pre-colonial sources of prestige architecture despite the national boundaries. Although master masons existed among the Hausa indigenous to Niger, especially at Zinder and Birnin Konni, the rulers in the area of Niger northwest of the present Sokoto State in Nigeria continued to commission Nigerian Hausa master masons indigenous to Sokoto State to design and build their prestigious palace rooms and mosques.

These Nigerians master masons travelled to Niger yearly in order to carry out architectural commissions. They brought their own masons and some labourers with them from Nigeria. Labourers were also hired at the site; so a few Niger Labourers acquired the status of master mason but actually very little technical expertise was transferred to Niger.

The routes taken by the master masons completely disregarded international border posts. They travelled by foot taking one to two weeks for the journey. Their routes were determined by the desire to minimize the walking distance and to spend the nights in hospitable villages. Thus, the route taken by Umaru dan Bube was as follows: Gwandu, Yeldu, Jantulu, Besheme, Kouremaria (on the main road in Niger between Dosso and Birnin Konni).[18] Over the years, Umaru carried out commissions in towns and villages along his routes (Fig. 6).

The traditional systems of remuneration for the services of master masons nullify foreign-exchange-related problems. In the wholly traditional system, secondary rulers owing obeisance to emirs can only receive the services of master masons delegated to them by their overlord. The construction of a lofty dome was a royal prerogative bestowed on a vassal as a symbol of the emir's delegation of authority to the vassal. In such cases, the emir financially supported his master masons while the vassal was responsible for their daily feeding and gifts of clothing and small livestock upon completion of the commissioned rooms. Over the years, the mason was responsible for yearly repairs at which time he received supplementary gifts. No predetermined fees were charged. In fact, the available evidence indicated that

Figure 5. Wife's Room, Village Head's Compound, Amori (Nigeria): Below the apex, the three transverse arches are intersected diagonally by purely decorative ribs.

Figure 6.   Merchant's Reception Hall, Kouremaria (Niger): Exterior view of a ribbed dome designed by Umaru in a town along his annual route from his home in Nigeria to his patrons in Niger.

the master masons were slaves prior to colonial rule.

The traditional type of socio-economic relationship persists across international borders even today. Sarkin Dogondoutchi, the ruler of a large Hausa town in Niger, owes traditional fealty to Sarkin Gwandu of Birnin Kebbi in Nigeria. Both the demolished traditional palace and the recently built modified traditional palace were designed and built by master masons working on behalf of and at the expense of the Sarkin Gwandu. Thus, although the work was carried out in Niger, the payments were made in the Gwandu emirate in Nigeria where the master mason were normally resident.[19]

Even after colonial rule had transformed the relationships between the master masons and those who commissioned prestige architecture, the traditional mode of payment in kind persisted. The royalty lost their prerogative to commission prestigious domed spaces. Private citizens could no longer be prevented from displaying their amassed wealth by commissioning lofty domes. Once the slaves were free, those who had been master masons were theoretically able to accept private commissions. In practice, however, the consent of the emir was sought for the most prestigious architectural designs because of the continued power of the emirs.[20] Nonetheless, both private citizens and traditional vassal rulers became free to commission architectural work on their own behalf provided they accepted responsibility for payment. In such cases the master masons were fed, given the traditional daily allotment of kola nuts and, upon completion, reimbursed in kind. The master mason would be paid with gowns and livestock including camels, sheep and goats which were herded home to Nigeria without any changing of currency. Nor would any customs duties be paid because the border was crossed where convenient without any long detours to the nearest customs post over one hundred kilometres away.

Conclusion

This exposition of a close affinity between the spacious architectural style of the mosque in Nigeria and Niger deceptively suggests that this transborder architectural style is dependent on the unifying force of Islam. The reality of Islam as a cultural element transcending both national and ethnic groups must not be disregarded. Yet in this instance, the introduction of a mosque style from one country and ethnic group to another cannot be said to be the direct result of Islamic proselytisation, nor of the introduction of a peculiarly Islamic style. Rather the mosque style relying on the Hausa arch and dome technology and the expertise of Nigerian master masons was transferred to Niger along with the prestige palace architecture introduced by these master masons. The Djerma rulers in Niger requested that master masons from Nigeria design their mosques because of their traditional ties to rulers resident in Nigeria and because of the perceived qualities of the Gobirawa architectural designs which were distinguished by the creative exploitation of the Hausa arch.

Endnotes

1. My gratitude goes to the University of Lagos for a Central Research Fund Grant for a project on Hausa architecture, to all the traditional rulers and their assistants including Ideal master masons who have so generously given of their time and knowledge in each of the places mentioned and to the officials of both the Sokoto State History Bureau and the Institute de Recherches en Sciences Humaines Niamey.

2. Grabar 1973, 104-138; Pretherbridge 1978, 208; Aradeon 1984.

3. Aradeon 1981.
4. Stevens 1968, 37; Prussin 1968.
5. Schacht 1954, 12-31.
6. Aradeon 1983.
7. Denham 1826, II, 323.
8. Saad 1981, 122; Sarkin Tambalwel. All undated references refer to interviews held in March 1984 at the residence of the informant or of his local ruler.
9. Mallam Isiu, Argungun.
10. Magini Machido and Magini Mohammadu Nomau of the Gobirawa family of master masons resident in Yabo provided the information on their family and on Umaru dan Bube's work with their family.
11. Zaroumeye Adamou (uncle of the present ruler), Dosso; Sarkin Dogondoutchi. Note that the British transferred the headquarters of the Gwando Emirate to Birnin Kebbi in 1906 (Hogben 1967, 227).
12. Gado Majidadi Adowowi, former assistant of Umaru dan Bube, Amoren-Adowowi.
13. Sarkin Loba.
14. Sarkin Albade Ismael, Tabla.
15. Moussadeye elders at the mosque.
16. Zaroumeye Adamou.
17. Mahman Sani, master mason who worked under both Gwani and Umaru, interview at Amoren-Adowowi.
18. Sarkin Magini Ibrahim, Birnin Kebbi.
19. Gado.
20. Sarkin Dogondoutchi.
21. Saad 1981, 363-64.

Bibliography

Aradeon, Susan B., "The Enduring Plan of the Sahelian Mosque," paper presented at the African Studies Association Annual Meeting, 1981, Bloomington, Indiana.

——— "Islam and the Rise of Hausa Architecture," Lecture I, Centre for Cultural Studies Lecture Series, 1981, University of Lagos. Typed.

——— "The Mosque as a Function of the History of Technology: The Nigerian Examples," paper presented at the Seminar on African Art in Historical Perspective, 1984, Centre for Cultural Studies, University of Lagos, December 11-15.

Denham, Major, Captain Clapperton and Doctor Oudney, Narrative or Travels and Discoveries in Northern and Central Africa, Vol. II, second edition (London: John Murray, 1826).

Godwin, Godfrey, Ottoman Turkey (London: Scorpion Pub. Ltd., 1977).

Grabar, Oleg, The Formation of Islamic Art (New York: Yale Univ. Press, 1973).

Hillenbrand, Robert, "Introduction" in Derek Hill and Lucien Golvin, Islamic Architecture in North Africa (London: Faber and Faber, 1976).

Hogben, S.J., An Introduction to the History of Northern Nigeria (Ibadan: Oxford Univ. Press, 1967).

Papadopoulo, Alexandre, Islam and Muslim Art trans. from French by Robert Erich Wolf (New York: Abrams, 1979).

Prussin, Labelle, "The Architecture of Islam in West Africa" African Arts, Vol. I, No. 2 (Winter-1968) pp. 32-35, 70-74.

Saad, Hamman Tukur, Between Myth and Reality: The Aesthetics of Traditional Architecture in Hausaland 2 vols. Arch. D. thesis, 1981, Univ. of Michigan, Ann Arbor.

Schacht, J., "Sur la diffusion des formes d'architecture religieuse musulmane a travers le Sahara" Travaux de l'Institute de Recherches Sahariennes 1954, 1958, Algiers, pp. 58-71.

Stevens, Phyllis, Aspects of Muslim Architecture in the Dyula Region of the Western Sudan (Legon: Inst. of African Studies, 1968).

CHAPTER 18

Nationality and Citizenship: The Legal Problematic of Transborder Ethnic Communities in Nigeria

by O. Adigun

Nationality and Citizenship: Some Definitions

In Black's Law Dictionary[1] Nationality is described as that quality of character which arises from the fact of a person belonging to a nation of state. Nationality determines the political status of the individual, especially with reference to allegiance, while domicile determines his civil status. Nationality arises by birth or naturalization. On the other hand, citizenship refers to one who under the constitution and laws, of say Nigeria, is a member of a political community, owing allegiance and being entitled to the enjoyment of all civil rights.[2] Nationality mainly deals with the international aspects of the membership of a state, while citizenship deals with the municipal perspective of the same issue.

There are, of course, contexts in which the two terms—nationality and citizenship—are interchangeable or synonymous one with the other especially if the nation and state coincide.[3] Nationality, for example, has both domestic and international dimensions. "As a concept within the domestic jurisdiction of a state, it serves to determine that the person upon whom it is conferred enjoys rights and is bound by obligations which the law of the state grants or imposes on its nationals. In its international aspect, it is the principal link between an individual and the subject of international law giving the individual the benefits of international law."[4] Thus, in matters relating to issues like treaty, rights and obligations, diplomatic action, immigration and deportation, nationality plays an essential role.

The concept of nationality is also capable of being used in relation to non-natural persons or objects. Corporations, ships and aircrafts possess a nationality of registration of the corporation or flag flown by the ship.[5] Sometimes some major corporations of the capitalist world are called multinationals denoting that their financial empire cut across the boundaries of many nations.

The word 'Nationality' could also refer to the subjects separate corporate sentiment of unity of members of a specific group forming a 'race' or 'nation'.[6] In this ethnic sense, the word refers to membership of an ethnic community. A 'native' of a place in Nigeria denotes the ethnic nationality of the person as opposed to 'native' of a place in Nigeria denotes the ethnic nationality of the person as opposed to 'natives' of other ethnic groups. To be a 'native' of a place or a specific group is not merely dependent on the accident of birth, but mainly on descent from a 'native' of the community.[7] In Allen V. Peliku[8], an Egba man was sold into slavery, rescued and taken to Sierra Leone, where he married the daughter of another rescued Egba and a son was born of the marriage. The parents afterwards returned to Abeokuta, bringing the son, then aged ten years. The Court held that the son, who was the plaintiff in the instant case, having been born in a British dominion is a British subject by common law of England; but he would also be a native of Egbaland according to Egba law. In the eye of the court, Mr. Allen possessed "dual nationalities"[9] by virtue of British and Egba laws.[10]

This ethnic conception of nationality was, however rejected by most modern African State's Constitutional definition which places emphasis on formal membership of the states. The effect is that members of ethnic groups indigenous to Nigeria could not acquire Nigerian Citizenship if they were placed in a different country by the act of the imperial partition which put the rest of the group in Nigeria. In the same vein, many non-natives acquired Nigerian citizenship on independence in 1960 because they were either British subject or they were British protected persons.[11]

We have dealt with the concept of Nationality in its different contexts to enable us appreciate the distinctions as well as the connections with the concept of citizenship. The status and rank of a citizen were first placed in their proper perspective with the genesis of constitutional government in the city states of Greece. The word citizen was first used to distinguish Greeks from "barbarians" who were the subject of autocrats like Egyptian Pharaoh. A distinction is drawn between a citizen in a democracy as opposed to a citizen in an oligarchy and the distinction between subjection and citizenship corresponds with the distinction between despotic and constitutional government.

Aristotle[12] had cause to speak on the qualities of a citizen. A person is not a citizen because he lives in a certain place, for resident aliens and slaves also share in the place. The attributes of the right to sue and be sued may not also denote a citizen.
In his view:

> He who has power to take part in the deliberative or judicial administrative or judicial administration of any state is said by us to be a citizen of that state; and, speaking generally, a state is a body of citizens sufficing for the purposes of life.[13]

So citizenship connotes a belonging to a political community and the status, rights and privileges and degree of freedom enjoyed by the citizen is dependent on the nature of the political rule.

The posture of the Greek city states as to citizenship differed from that of the Roman empire. To become a citizen of Rome was regarded as the high honour of the empire and it was possible for aliens to acquire the status. "The aspiring genius of Rome sacrificed vanity to ambition, and deemed it more prudent as well as honourable, to adopt virtue and merit for her own wheresoever they were found, among slaves or strangers, enemies or barbarians."[14]

Various philosophers have had cause to postulate on the various qualities of citizenship. In the view of Aquinas, a man can be said to be a citizen in two ways; first absolutely; secondly, in restricted sense. A man is citizen absolutely if he has all the rights of citizenship; for instance, the rights of debating or voting in the popular assemblies. On the other hand any man may be called citizen in a restricted sense if his claim is limited to residence only; such people are men of low status of children or old men who, in the view of Aquinas, are not fit to enjoy power in matters pertaining to the common welfare.[15]

Kant[16] listed three attributes of citizenship:

i) Constitutional Freedom is the right of every citizen to have to obey no other law than that to which he has given his consent or approval.

ii) Civil Equality, as the right of the citizen to recognize no one as a superior among the people in relation to himself; and

iii) Political Independence, that is, the right to owe his existence and continuance in society not to arbitrary will be another, but to his own rights and powers as a member of the commonwealth.

Political thought and his rights as a citizen are guaranteed by means of Bill of Rights of Fundamental Rights provisions in many Constitutions.[17] The citizen must truly be free from any coercion or intimidation by the government. In the protection of the citizen's rights, the law comes to the aid of the citizen to aid the preservation of the rights and rectify any injustice.

For the rights, duties, privileges and immunities afforded a citizen, the citizen is expected to reciprocate by sparing his time to attend to matters that affect his state. He must be willing to serve the state physically, for example, by bearing arms and weapons in the event of a threat to the security of the state and he can either be loyal or disloyal to the state. Because of the requirement that a citizen must have a mind of his own, the concept of citizenship cannot be extended to include abstract legal entities like corporations because it has no existence except in the contemplation of the law.[18]

Today, most countries extend its citizenship status to people, based either on the principles of descent (jus sanguinis) or the naturalization process. The latter enables qualified aliens who request for it to be conferred with the status of a citizen.[19] The principle of jus sanguinis—based on membership of a natural lineage and by extension of an ethnic group—establishes a connecting bridge between the concepts of 'nationality' and that of 'citizenship'.

The Implications of African Partition

In partitioning Africa, European power regarded the peoples as "stateless" persons. Thus no regard was paid to the homogeneity of the various community or their pre-existing states. There was no attempt to determine the nationality of the various people; the various treaties among the European powers led to territorial arrangements which arbitrarily divided several ethnic and kinship groups. In 1886 and 1893, the Anglo-German agreements partitioned the Adamawa people between British and German colonial territories. Also in 1890, the Anglo-French agreement partitioned Borno.[20] Lamenting his plight, the Emir of Yola was quoted as saying that the "Europeans had cut off the body and left him with only the head of his kingdom".[21] Furthermore, in the Hausa state of Kebbi, the capital—Birnin Kebbi—is in Nigeria, but its related settlements like Duchi and Mantaki are in Niger Republic. In the area of present-day Katsina State of Nigeria, the capital—Birnin Katsina—is in Nigeria, but people in closely related places like Tassawa and Maradi are found in the Niger Republic. The Cameroun-Nigerian border has divided the following people: Kanembu, Shuwa Arabs, Mandara, Wakna, Matakam, Gude, Adamawa, Chamba, Jibu, Ekoi, Ododop and Efik peoples. The Benin-Nigeria Border has separated Adja (Gun/Egun), Yoruba (Anago, Ketu, Sabe), Borgu (Bariba/Borgawa), Hausa and Fulani people. In some cases peoples like the Kanuri, Hausas, Shuwa Arabs are divided among three or four territories or states. The story is the same all over Africa.[22]

Citizenship Laws

Upon attainments of independence, most African nations had citizenship provisions inserted into their constitution. Laws were promulgated to determine who is a citizen of the respective states.[23]

In Nigeria, which we shall use as our reference country, as at 1st October 1960, the basic citizenship formula was contained in the Constitution of the same year. By virtue of Section 7(1) of the Constitution of the Federal Republic of Nigeria as amended by Decrees No. 1 of 1966 and No. 27 of 1967, every person born in the former Colony or Protectorate of Nigeria and was on the 30th day of September 1960, a citizen of the United Kingdom and Colonies or a British protected person, became a citizen of Nigeria on the 1st day of October 1960. However, the parents or grandparents must have been in the former colony or Protectorate of Nigeria.

The effect of these provisions is that if A is a Canadian and gave birth to B, his son, in the former Colony of Lagos and B married another Canadian C in Lagos and gave birth to D in Lagos, D is a Nigerian. In other words, by virtue of this provision, people who were not genealogically or culturally related to Nigeria became citizens. But those Yorubas born in Ketu o. Sabe in the adjacent Republic of Benin or the Hausa born in Southern *Nigerian* towns of Maradi and Matamaye will not qualify as Nigerians because the parents, even though sharing kinship ties with relations in Nigeria, were not citizens of United Kingdom and Colonies or British Protected persons. The misfortune of many in partitioned culture areas can be imagined as most of Nigeria's neighbouring states were under the influence of the French and this provision disqualified many persons that would normally be regarded as Nigerians.[24]

In Nigeria, marriage had no negative or positive effect on nationality or citizenship. A non-citizen of Nigeria married to a Nigerian man does not automatically acquire Nigerian citizenship. However, the woman can acquire the Nigerian citizenship by registration. The applicant must satisfy the President that she is of good character and had manifested an intention of desire to be domiciled in Nigeria and has taken the prescribed oath of allegiance.[25] Therefore, a Kanuri woman born to the group found in Chad Republic and married to a Nigerian man of Kanuri stock is not a Nigerian, unless she is so registered.

During the Constituent Assembly deliberations in 1978 on the citizenship chapter of the 1979 Constitution, there were some people who argued strenuously in favour of the extension of the citizenship of Nigeria by birth. By virtue of Section 23 of the 1979 Constitution, every person born in Nigeria before the date of independence, either of whose parents or any of whose grandparents belongs or belonged to a community indigenous to Nigerian provided that a person shall not become a citizen of Nigeria by virtue of section 23 if neither of his parents nor any of his grandparents was born n Nigeria. The protagonists of the section argued that some peoples' parents or grandparents were accidentally born outside Nigeria, for example, in Saudi Arabia and United Kingdom and that it would be unfair to deny them citizenship. Furthermore, a man from Mandara, which is a community indigenous to Nigeria, might have been born by a father who was born on the Cameroun side by grandparents who also lived on the Cameroun side. Although the man was born on the Nigerian side of the border and has since lived in Nigeria, he will not be regarded as a Nigerian. Nigerian citizenship can come to such a person only by way of naturalization. The argument is that a person, who like his parents and grandparents, was born outside Nigeria, is not a Nigerian properly so called and is not likely to fully identify himself with the country, its people, problems and progress.[26] But if the person is born outside Nigeria and any of his grandparents is a citizen of Nigeria, he can apply to be registered as a Nigerian citizen.[27]

It is generally recognized that the rights of a citizen are not available to an alien. The provisions of Section 25 of the 1979 Nigerian Constitution enables an alien, to become a Nigerian by naturalization. This process regulates that the person who desires naturalization must be of good character; show a clear intention of his desire to be domiciled in Nigeria,[28] and must have resided in Nigeria for a continuous period of at least 15 years immediately preceding the date of his application. An Efik man who is of a community indigenous to Cameroun or Bariba man of Nikki in Benin, will have to naturalize before he can become a Nigerian. But in reality, it is not so difficult. As these so called aliens share the same values and languages with their kith and kin on the Nigerian side, they easily assume nigerian names and sometimes get passports issued in their names. It is usually difficult to distinguish them from their people who are Nigerians by birth.

It is essential to determine the citizenship of a person as a lot of rights and privileges are dependent on citizenship. In the enjoyment of the fundamental rights, aliens and citizens alike have a right to life.[29] On the other hand only citizens enjoy some fundamental rights, like the right to private and family life,[30] freedom of movement,[31] and freedom from discrimination.[32] A citizen cannot be expelled or refused entry into Nigeria and in fact any executive order that purports to deprive the citizen of his rights will be rendered null and void.[33] This provision against the deportation of a citizen came up for consideration in the case of *Shugaba Abdulrahaman Darman v. The Federal Minister of Internal Affairs and others.* ÷×

The Shugaba Case Study

In Shugaba's case, the applicant was a member of the Great Nigeria People's Party (G.N.P.P.) and the majority leader in the Borno State House of Assembly. This is a state in the north-eastern part of Nigeria, which ha sboundaries with Niger, Chad and Cameroun. Common to Borno State and the adjacent foreign jurisdictions are a group of people called Bagarmi, a strain of the Kanuri. Shugaba was born in a Nigerian Kanuri village although his father was of the Bagarmi group born in Chikiwa in the Chad Republic. At the time of the father's birth, the Kanuri people saw themselves as one people and neither Chad nor Nigeria, as now constituted, was in existence. The father of Shugaba left his home-town when he was conscripted into a Sultan's army and finally settled in Maiduguri in 1911. Luckily for Shugaba, the father married the mother who is also a Kanuri stock in Maiduguri.

Up till the time when he was deported on the fateful January morning in 1980, no one doubted the fact that Shugaba is a Nigerian. He had joined Nigerian politics as far back as 1953, and for many years he was the Councillor representing his Constituency in various Local Governments. Even in 1979, he was elected to the then Borno House of Assembly on the platform of the GNPP. In accordance with Section

100 of the 1979 Constitution, only a citizen of Nigeria who had attained the age of 21 years can be elected into the House of Assembly. The reasonably inference is that the Federal Electoral Commission must have been convinced that Shugaba is a Nigerian before allowing him to contest in the election. To crown it all, as far back as 1968, he had been issued with Nigerian before allowing him to contest in the election. To crown it all, as far back as 1968, he had been issued a Nigerian passport which was renewed in 1978.

Despite all these incontrovertible evidence, the political foes of Shugaba declared him an alien and a political risk. He was consequently deported from the country. It was the case for the government that he was form the Chad Republic and so his passport was seized and he was dumped at the border with Chad. Whilst in Chad, he had no difficulty in moving from place to place, his typical Kanuri facial marks serving him as his natural passport which linked him to his kith and kin in Chad and Cameroun. He moved from Chad to Republic of Cameroun and from there he walked into Nigeria "as the Wasa road to Nigeria was open", that is, it was unpatrolled.

The case has some interesting perspectives to it. The man, who was Shugaba's host in Chad, had lived in Maiduguri. One of the defence witnesses testified to the effect that he is a Chadian citizen, had lived in Nigeria and had for upward of 29 years served in the Nigerian Army, and the Nigerian Police Force from whom he was collecting his pensions. When the immigration officer was asked to reveal the number of Nigerians that pass through his post everyday, he said they were so many that it was impossible to get them to fill departure cards and in fact many pass through the border more than once a day. It is evident that a sizeable number of the people who constantly crossed the frontiers are not Nigerians, properly so called, and "except in unusual circumstance when the frontiers are sealed, the people continue to move across the boundaries with little or no impediment."[35]

After an exhaustive review of the evidence before the court, the learned trial judge came to the inevitable conclusion that Shugaba is a Nigerian. The judge held that the deportation was unconstitutional and a breach of fundamental rights of the applicant Shugaba. When a man's right is infringed, he can come to court "for enforcing and securing the enforcement of his fundamental rights and for redress for violation of the same.[36] Where a deportation order is made against a citizen, such an order is ultra vires and constitutes a violation of his fundamental rights to personal liberty, privacy and freedom to move freely throughout Nigeria. The court further held that in accordance with Section 38 of the Constitution of Nigeria 1979, "…. no citizen (of Nigeria) shall be refused entry thereto or exit therefrom." and a passport is the only means of entering into Nigeria and exiting therefrom. The court therefore ordered the return of Shugaba's passport which was unlawfully impounded.[37]

The above is the predicament in which Shugaba found himself as he belongs to a borderland community. His plight can easily befall any other person in such borderland situation. Those who divided brothers and sisters realised what they were doing and merely concluded that "the troubles of boundaries cutting across tribes is not unusual and that with time the co-operation of the respective administration would produce a tolerable solution."[38]

The truth is that, as of now, no tolerable solution has been found to the problems occasioned by the arbitrary and unrealistic boundary fixtures. The affected communities continue with their old ties and the inter-trade between them is termed "smuggling". Customs points have arisen to artificially divide coherent trading areas, but the communities have resisted such division through a common recognition of the inter-dependency of their culture, language and morals.

It is generally agreed that the partition of Africa was for political bargaining among the European nations and this arbitrary breakdown of ethnic groups has constituted a grave and permanent factor of desertion. Some writers submit that the most realistic approach is to maintain the arbitrary boundaries based on geographical features rather than the interest of the people. Ajomo believes that a redivision on ethnic, racial or linguistic bases would lead to chaos and facilitate further foreign intervention to the detriment of all.[39] It is also believed that a readjustment in boundaries is difficult in view of its socio-economic implications.

As it is the countries fashioned out by Europeans in order to suit their needs, still serve as the satellites of the colonial states. The presence of France is still felt in all its former colonies and the economy of each of these countries is still tied to the French. The commonwealth of nations retains the Queen of England as its perpetual head and all African members remain loyal to Britain. Africa voiced the hope of his fellow neocolonialist servants when in rebuking Nkrumah he said:

> Nkrumah made a mockery of this organization (the Commonwealth) and under the mask of African Unity and non-alignment, proceeded to discredit the Commonwealth and to put difficulties in its way.... African Unity is a glorious ideal, but I know that this is impossible to achieve within our life-time... in spite of the Organization of African Unity, I will claim my citizenship of Ghana and of the Commonwealth in any part of the World[40]

The treaties, agreements, protocols and other legal instruments executed by the Europeans in respect of the arbitrary boundaries still remain[41] Asiwaju contends that it may now be argued that the leaders of independent Africa have been the inheritors of the imperialistic intentions and considerations which determined the attitude of the original partitioning European powers.[42] One must also agree that in view of the arbitrariness of the boundary lines, it is difficult to apply the Western legal definitions of 'citizens', 'aliens', 'nationals' to the people of the respective countries in Africa. The case of Alhaji Shugaba[43] demonstrates the fact that the Kanuri of Nigeria are not different from the Kanuri of Chad. The presence of the cross-border peoples should augur well for peace and healthy neighbourliness across the boundaries. This may well be the reason why it is unnecessary to disturb the boundaries as presently constituted.

On the other hand, some writers advocate a more positive approach to the problem of borderland people. The emphasis is on the need for bi-national co-operation and joint developmental programmes within the boundary localities.[44] This would facilitate healthy interaction and allow or an even development of the ethnic groups along the borders.

The third alternative postulates the emergence of a united Africa achieved through the breakdown of the existing frontiers. The various regional groupings like ECOWAS are designed to foster greater links in the socio-economic welfare of the people. However, we have to break down the political walls in order to achieve some measure of independence. It is the only way we can get out of the present economic bondage which ties the economy of all African nations to the apron of their past colonial overlords.

Endnotes

1. 5th Ed., p. 923.
2. Ibid., p. 221.
3. See Salmond, 'Citizenship and Allegiance' (1901) 17 L.Q.R. 270, 272.
4. Oppenheim, International Law (Lanterpacht) V.1 (1955 8th Ed.) p. 645.
5. See Boczek, Flags of Convenience, (1962), p. 102.
6. Weis, Nationality and Statelessness in International Law, (1956), p. 3.
7. *Habib v. Principal Immigration Officer* (1958) 3 F.S.C. 75, 79.
8. I.N.L.R. 116.
9. Dual nationality is not half one nationality and half another, but two complete nationalities. See *Inouye Kanao v. The King, 19 Hong Kong* L.R. 66.
10. See also, In re Sapara (1911) Ren. 605, 606.
11. See, Section 7 of the Nigerian Constitution, 1960.
12. See, generally, Aristotle, *Politics, Book III* translated by Benjamin Jowett, in Great Books of the Western World, Vol. 9 471 ff.
13. Aristotle, ibid., p. 472.
14. Gibbon, *The Decline and Fall of the Roman Empire*, Book 40, Great Ideas, Book 2., p. 218. At a period of its history, Roman citizenship could be purchased with money, see R.W. Leage, *Roman Private Law* 2nd Ed. (London: Macmillan, 1930) pp. 7-77.
15. Aquinas: Summa Theologica, Part 1 - 11, 105, in Book 20, Great Ideas et al.
16. Kant, Science of Right, 436 in Book 42 Great Ideas et al.
17. For example, the Bill of Rights in the United States Constitution, 17 and Chapter IV—Fundamental Rights, in the Constitution of the Federal Republic of Nigeria, 1979.
18. See, *Daimler Tyre Co. v. Continental Tyre Co.* (1915) 1 K.B. 896, 916.
19. The naturalized citizen "becomes a member of the society, possessing all the rights of a native citizen and standing in the view of the constitution on the footing of a native." Marshall C.J., in *Osborn v. Bank of the United States,* 9 Wheat. (SS, U.S.) 737, (1824).
20. See Barkindo, in Asiwaju (ed) *Partitioned Africa* (Lagos: Univ. of Lagos Press, 1985) p. 29.
21. A.H.M. Kirk-Greene, *Adamawa Past and Present* (Oxford Univ. Press, 1958) pp. 67-68.
22. See generally, Asiwaju (ed) *Partitioned Africa* op. cit., pp. 197, 256, etc.
23. See for example, Ghana Nationality and Citizenship Act, 1957; Nigerian Commonwealth Citizenship Act, 1963; Nigerian Citizenship Act, 1960 and 1961.
24. See further, *Nationality and Citizenship Laws of Nigeria,* A.V.J. Nylander (Univ. of Lagos, 1973).
25. See, Section 24(2) Constitution of the Federal Republic of Nigeria, 1979 and the Convention on the Nationality of Married Women, adopted by the General Assembly of the U.N. on 29th January 1957.
26. See, Proceedings of the Constituent Assembly, Vol. 3, pp. 24, 34-38 and Eweluka, Acquisition and Loss of Citizenship of Nigeria; (1982) N.C.L. Rev. p. 216.
27. See, Section 24(2) (h) 1979 Constitution.
28. Domicile is said to be "that legal relationship between a person and a territory subject to a distinctive legal system which invokes the system as his personal law...." Henderson v. Henderson (1967), p. 77 at 79. It is a combination of residence and intention.
29. Section 30(1) 1979 Constitution
30. Section 34 ibid.
31. Section 38 ibid.
32. Section 39 ibid.
33. Section 38 ibid. See the case cited in note 34.
34. (1981) 2 NCLR 459.
35. Asiwaju, *Partitioned Africa,* p. 246.
36. (1981) NCLR 459.
37. (1981) 2 NCLR 459, 520.
38. L.F. Nader, *A Tribal Survey of Mongalla Province* (Oxford: Oxford Univ. Press, 1937) quoted in Asiwaju *Partitioned Africa,* p. 57.
39. See further, Ajomo, M.A., "The Nigeria Cameroun Border Dispute—Implications at International Law", *Nigerian Current Law Review,* April 1982, p. 133.
40. *Africa, The Ghana Coup* (London: Frank Case, 1967) pp. 108, 111-112, quoted in Chinwaju, *The West and the Rest of Us Nok Publishers,* 1978 p. 360.
41. See generally, Brow i.e. African Boundaries, A legal and Diplomatic Encyclopedia, p. 6.
42. *Partitioned Africa,* (ed) Asiwaju, p. 245.
43. (1981) 2 NCLR 459.
44. See Asiwaju, op. cit.

CHAPTER 19

Borders in International Relations and Military Strategy: Focus on Nigeria's Western Boundary, 1898-1945

by A.E. Ekoko

The international boundaries of Nigeria, like those of all other independent African states were, by and large, the artificial creations of European imperialist powers. For whatever reasons a European power embarked upon the acquisition of a territory in Africa, in the form of a geographically defined entity called a colony or protectorate, the act automatically involved a 'defence obligation' on the metropole.

By 'defence obligation' is meant the legal, constitutional and military responsibilities which the metropole had to take upon itself to ensure the continued and inviolate existence of the colonial territory against other powers. Simply put, defence obligation involves the strategic and military mechanisms through which the territorial integrity of the colonial state is maintained with the context of the imperial system of the metropole. A colonial possession is, legally, a part of an empire in peace and war. The boundaries of a colonial state are, by definition, exclusive boundaries that demarcate one territoriality and one sovereignty from another. Therefore, Lord Curzon's dictum that 'Frontiers are indeed the razor's edge on which hang suspended the modern issues of war or peace, of life or death to nations'[1] equally apply to sovereign as well as colonial states. Indeed a European tradition existed that a war fought in Europe between imperial powers must be extended to their colonies.[2]

In this contribution we are concerned with the British perception of aggression on Nigeria via the western border and their responses to it from 1898, the year of the Fashoda crisis, through the First World War to the Second World War. It must be said that of all the four land boundaries of Nigeria the western boundary presented the colonial military strategist the most protracted problems in our period.

Britain and France were the dominant European powers on the West African Coast before the age of the Scramble. In large measure, the British nurtured dreams of a continuous territory between the Gold Coast Colony and Lagos in the 1870s and 1880s. But the project fell through.[3] The re-establishment of a French Protectorate in Porto Novo coupled with the dynamic French colonial policy in Western Sudan, and the sudden but dramatic German intrusion in Togoland ensure that the British dream of a continuous territory must remain unfulfilled.

Nevertheless the western boundary produced the most dramatic scenes in the evolution of Nigeria's international boundaries. The famous race to Nikki of 1894 between Major Lugard and Captain Decoeur, the protracted and delicate Niger crisis of 1897/8 in which troops of *Tirailleurs Senegalais* and British colonial forces stood face to face in Joseph Chamberlain's "chessboard" military policy were all functions of the western border.[4] The crisis revolved round the Anglo-French bid for the control of the navigable Niger. The idea was to make territorial, economic and strategic gains in this sub-region. Although the issues were resolved through 'defence by diplomacy' rather than 'defence by armed conflict' the nature of the crisis created in the minds of British colonial military strategists a "French invasion mentality" which they sought to contain by defensive and offensive war plans.

The Anglo-French Fashoda crisis of late 1898-99 had tremendous ramifications in West Africa. Significantly the cris galvanised the British war machinery to shift from coast-centric defence planning into transborder offensive posture. The Directorate of Military Intelligence (D.M.I.) of the War Office and the Colonial Office concerted to work out a regional war plan for West Africa. A small War Council was constituted to consider (a) the feasibility of immediate offensive action on the outbreak of war; and (b) the effective occupation of Dahomey, to be carried out as soon as possible.[5]

The War Council came out with a plan for a bi-frontal invasion of Dahomey with British troops in Nigeria. With Porto Novo as the main war objective, one British force from Jebba was to descend on Dahomey from the north, through Shaki, with the co-operation of Yoruba chiefs. Another force was to march, simultaneously with the first, on lower Dahomey from Lagos through Imeko or Meko. Two gunboats would be deployed to hold the Niger waterway against a possible French onslaught.

A *carte blanche* for the invasion of enemy territory was thus recommended; Willocks was to be informed that 'in the event of war with France, he should at once undertake offensive operations against Dahomey with a view to an effective occupation of that colony'. From a long term point of view, the recommendations of the 'War Council' of 1898 were the precursors of the more comprehensive plans which were nurtured at the D.M.I. at the turn of the century. The plans were significant because they were the beginning of offensive military planning in West Africa. Had the Fashoda crisis resulted in an Anglo-French war, Britain's overwhelming sea superiority would have guaranteed her West African possessions against a seaborne attack. And since French military policy during the crisis involved the concentration of almost all available troops at Dakar, the chances of a British occupation of Dahomey with troops from Nigeria would have been good.

But Fashoda soon passed into history and the attention of the British Empire was directed to the Boer War. Military policy and planning in West Africa in regard to land forces were however still carried on. Major Altham undertook the first after-crisis assessment of the military requirements of the West African Protectorates in a war with France. He observed that despite France's marked success in colonial imperialism in West Africa, she did not lack the zest of disappointment to spur her on to future designs; if she had an opportunity, she could make good what she felt was her rightful share in the territorial spoils. It could be recalled that as far as the navigable Niger was concerned France was not a 'satisfied power' in West Africa.

From the viewpoint of the strategic position of the western border of Nigeria, Altham did not regard the Niger as a possible avenue for French offensive action during a war, in view of the small number of French troops maintained in Dahomey. But as the future development of French military resources were to show, Altham's sanguine hope about the security of the British Niger crumbled with time.

By the turn of the 19th century British policy of "splendid isolation" was becoming unattractive. The Boer war had demonstrated the limitations of Britain's imperial war machine; Anglo-German negotiations had failed and the Anglo-Japanese alliance was signed as a consolation prize. But in 1901-2, as indeed for most of the last quarter of the 19th century, the worst combination Britain had any reason to dread was an alliance of France and Russia against her in war. The Admiralty and the War Office based their imperial defence policy on certain principles governing colonial defence. The most important of these principles was that "The maintenance of sea supremacy had been assumed as the basis of the system of Imperial Defence against attack from over the sea". In other words, it was the responsibility of the Royal Navy to defend any portion of the British empire against any maritime power, whereas land defence was a function of the imperial and colonial armies.

The relevance of this 'defence contract' to the West African sub-region generally and to Nigeria's western frontier specifically becomes readily obvious when we examine developments within Britain's newly re-organised War Office, the Committee of Imperial Defence, and the Directorate of Military Operations and Intelligence. These re-organisations were immediately reflected in the renewed interest in strategic and logistic planning which Lt. Col. E.A. Altham, head of the strategical section one of the DMOI, brought to bear on defence appreciation in his famous memorandum of 1901.[6] In a war in which the U.S. was neutral it was only in India and West Africa that the land possessions of Britain would be vulnerable to a Franco-Russian invasion. British colonies in West Africa must assume the offensive because a purely defensive strategy rarely leads to success in war. He advocated the strategy of Indirect Approach in which Britain would "Choose in overseas possessions suitable objectives for attack, and having captured them, can without anxiety, retain them in our grasp until the end of war."

For colonial Nigeria this strategy involved the assumption of military offensive against the French colony of Dahomey. Altham advocated the occupation of that territory, not because of its intrinsic strategic significance but because of "a political measure of the moment." Up to the outbreak of the First World War (or at least during the anti-French phase of British Colonial military planning) this principle of offensive warfare across Nigeria's western frontier dominated the strategic and military thought of the Directorate of Military Operations and Intelligence. Anglo-French military balance in the sub-region became a popular area of investigation among British Staff Officers. Evidence of increasing French military capability to initiate the offensive against British possessions began to emerge.

The commander-in-chief of the Imperial Army minuted with unconcealed anxiety of that "It would certainly seem as if we should experience great difficulty in keeping our West African possessions in the event of a war with France".[7] These circumstances forced the constitution of a West African War Conference at Winchester House, London, in July 1903 to reconsider British military strategy in the event of war with France.[8] The result of their deliberations and appreciations was code-named "Plan of Action July 1903". Now, 'Plan of Action' or 'Project of Attack' as the phrases came to be employed in colonial military terminology, generally implied war schemes involving offensive operations. We are beginning to notice that from 1903 crisis-inspired schemes of colonial conquests were beginning to give place to peacetime strategic calculations deigned to safeguard the colonial frontiers in a situation of a general war.

The Winchester House War Conference observed that in spite of growing French military capability in the sub-region, their ability to effectively invade Nigeria through the western frontier was seriously circumscribed because of garrison and internal security requirements of their vast Sudanese possessions. Only troops from Dahomey, and the Military Territories of the Niger and Chad could be available for the offensive against Nigeria through the northwestern frontier, with Say as the advance base. Say was within the French highly valued Goa-Dori-Say military triangle, the principal recruiting and settlement region for the *Senegalese Tirailleurs,* and their reservists.

An amphibious attack on the Niger could be launched from Say with considerable ease. The capture of Bajibo would provide the French with their desired objective on the navigable Niger. In the south, it was noted that the invasion and capture of the colony of Lagos and the disruption of communications with northern Nigeria would be attractive to the French as an alternative to their "Niger plan". These considerations conditioned British military strategists to design war plans that would enable them not only to maintain the western frontier but also to carry the war into the enemy's territory.

The Lagos Plan

Two plans of ware were considered by the Conference. The first, 'Nigeria Plan A' (N.P.A.), assumed that on the outbreak of war the whole field force should at once be concentrated at Lagos, with a view to the immediate capture of Cotonu and Porto Novo, and the seizure of the railway leading to the interior. The second, 'Nigeria Plan B' (N.P.B.) was radically different. Under it, the southern Nigeria contingent was to be sent to Bajibo on the Niger, as a reserve force, to meet a French advance from Say; or, if circumstances were favourable, to join in an advance westward from Bajibo with the occupation of Upper Dahomey in view.

Both plans of war had comparative advantages and disadvantages. Both assumed the seizure of Dahomey as the ultimate war aim. Between the two plans, however, the details of how the occupation should be effected differed considerably. The advantages of N.P.A. were that, politically, the immediate seizure of Dahomey was considered desirable. Dahomey was 'one of the most thriving of the French West African possessions' and its annexation, it was believed, would enhance the economic prosperity of Lagos colony. This is the first evidence of the desire for territorial acquisition in West Africa (as distinct from war-time occupation for peacetime negotiations) in the event of a European war. Occupation could score an initial success for Britain; Cotonu could be made an advance base for the capture of Upper Dahomey and for threatening the flank of any French plans on the Niger. The main disadvantage of N.P.A. was that while the capture of Dahomey would be easily effected, it failed to provide adequately for the containment of French invasion through the Niger with superior force.

The merits of N.P.B., which was initially defensive in character, was the considerable concentration it provided for against probable French main attack. If the anticipated French attack was not delivered or not threatened, then the capture of Dahomey could be executed in a north-south direction which was perhaps a more difficult approach. But plan 'B' gave the enemy the advantage of the military initiative, restricting British forces to a purely defensive initial role, thus injuring their prestige.

Between N.P.A. and N.P.B. the July Conference made no clear-cut recommendation. The decisive factor, it was noted, was the successful organisation and equipment of reservists. It was evident that in the event of a war with France, British troops available for the defence of the extensive western and northern frontiers of Nigeria would be asking the other colonies to furnish troops for the defence of Nigeria. Neither could reinforcements be quickly sent from England because of the standing objection of the Admiralty to undertake such tasks until the command of the sea had been attained. The establishment of the W.A.F.F. had not achieved military self-sufficiency in Nigeria by 1903. The Conference came to the painful conclusion that 'The local strategical position is... one of considerable weakness... and it is difficult to find an entirely satisfactory solution of the problem.'[9]

Nevertheless, the Inspector-General of the W.A.F.F. was requested to prepare a detailed plan for the capture of Cotonu. The 'Project of Attack' thus moved from policy formulation to policy execution. It took Brigadier-General Kemball a year to produce his 'Scheme for the Seizure of Porto Novo and Cotonu',[10] code-named 'No. 4 P.A.' (Number Four Plan of Action). In drawing up this plan, Kemball assumed that the decisive battles in the war would be fought in the region of Lagos and Lower Dahomey.

The general idea behind the plan was to secure the initiative, carry the war into the enemy's country and thus disorganize the French administration in Dahomey. The broad outline of the operations was that a southern Nigerian contingent would be employed to cut French communication system by an advance through Taketa, and by the occupation of Dagba. Troops from Lagos would then occupy Porto Novo and, subsequently, Cotonu. British rule would be established in Lower Dahomey and the southern Nigeria contingent would be set free to move north, either through Dahomey or by the frontier road through Imeko and Saki (Shaki).

Logistical and mobilisation details were worked out, the routes to be followed carefully mapped out and quantities of arms and ammunition ascertained. The Kemball plan was the most detailed war plan conceived with the sole aim of a British occupation and annexation of Dahomey before the First World War.

Planning in Northern Nigeria

In northern Nigeria the task of preparing the scheme for offensive operations fell to Morland, the commandant of the Northern Nigeria Regiment, and Lugard. The frontiers of northern Nigeria posed very serious strategical problems. Thus the Morland-Lugard scheme, drawn up in 1904, was unlike Kemball's, strictly defensive.[11] The Northern Nigeria Regiment was not strong enough to initiate offensive operations unaided.

During a period of international tension, the British forces in northern Nigeria were to regard a French concentration of troops at Say as pointing to either an advance down the Niger or a direct march on Sokoto and Kano. Their military strategy would be to concentrate all available forces to meet the enemy in the field; minor operations were to be discouraged. Jebba and Kano, it was believed, were the best points of British concentration. Garrisons in Ilorin, Borno, Kontagora and Ile would be hurried to Jebba while Kano was to be reinforced with troops from Katsina, Bauchi and Zaria. Particular attention would be given to Kano because of its commercial and politically central position; it would also serve as the 'great base of supplies and transport' during operations.

But the Inspector-General of W.A.F.F., Brig-General Kemball had serious reservations about the Morland-Lugard war plan. First, he pointed out that neither Ilo nor Sokoto had been looked upon as places to be garrisoned for political and strategic reasons. He wanted Lokoja, Zungeru and Yola to be regarded as 'obligatory' garrisons. Jebba was not the best place to concentrate the field force, because it left a very large country open to enemy occupation and the problems of the movement of supplies would almost be insurmountable. Yelwa, in his opinion, was a better point of concentration because of its geographical and strategic location above the Bussa rapids. From there Sokoto and Ilo could easily be supplied without exposing British territory to a French *coup de main*. In raising these objections Kemball was clearly anticipating a French move into Borgu and the Niger. His recommendations were approved by the Army Council and incorporated into the northern Nigeria scheme of defence and Project of Attack.[12]

It would be seen from the above that British military planning against France before the First World War was almost exclusively focused on the security of the western border of Nigeria. The reason for this is not far to seek. French military strength in Chad and Niger were negligible, and the two territories offered no great incentive to British Nigeria; the eastern frontier with German Cameroun did not enter into British putative strategic calculations because before 1905/06 there was no reason to foresee an Anglo-German war. In these years France, in alliance with Russia, posed the greatest threat to the British Empire, and French Dahomey offered British colonial military strategies the biggest prize war. That alone ranked Nigeria's western border higher than the rest.

However as things turned out, Britain was faced with strategic reorientation following the growth of the German Navy, and Germany's 'shock diplomacy' in Morocco. British diplomacy was able to aid strategic planning in West Africa, as elsewhere in the empire in minimising defence problems. From the Moroccan crisis of 1905-06 onwards the Anglo-French centre became a pseudo-Alliance; and consequently, the Cameroun replaced Dahomey as the colony which the WAFF would invade and capture in war. But one interesting point about this is that in the period of anti-German colonial war planning we do not find the type of enthusiasm and meticulous planning displayed for Dahomey in war plans of for the capture of the Cameroun.[13] The British in Nigeria wrote off German Cameroun as an easy plum to be picked up at their own convenience during a great war. They were proved wrong between 1914-16.

The Inter-War Years

The First World War ended with a cartographical revision of some colonial boundaries in West Africa in favour of France and Britain, the leading colonial power in the sub-region. The Camerouns and Togoland wee placed under the League of Nations Mandate System, itself a veiled type of imperialism backed by international legalism. In the colonial field, mutual rivalry which had characterised Anglo-French relation for centuries was beginning to give way to mutual co-operation.

Professor Asiwaju has ably demonstrated the desire for Anglo-French cooperation in Nigeria and Dahomey specially and across other borderlands in the west sub-region generally.[14] Perhaps the best example of this new spirit of mutual colonial co-operation is the Standing Order dated 25 April 1933 which W. Duncan, the British Commissioner for the Western Province of the Gold Coast gave the District Commissioner of Axim.

> I regard it as most important that Political Officers in the frontier districts should be in close touch with and maintain the most cordial relations with, representatives of neighbouring powers, in this case the French. You will therefore co-operate where possible with the French administrations across the Frontier. In these days when the interests of Great Britain and France in West Africa are more or less bound together in the common desire to further the development and prosperity of the peoples in their charge and when many problems of administration and development are common to both governments, the need for co-operation to both governments, I think, is sufficiently apparent.[15]

In fulfilment of this spirit France and Britain engaged to co-operate in such matters as smuggling, illegal migrations, tax evasion, trade and malaria control. Such problems could not but affect inter-colonial state relations especially along the Nigeria-Dahomey borderland with "strong historical, ethnological and cultural connections between ... peoples on both sides of the inter-colonial boundaries."[16] In such situations, Asiwaju argues, "movement of people across the new boundaries became inevitable and this often reduced the effectiveness of the boundaries as dividing lines ... (and) ... in certain cases ... the diplomatic agreements and protocols establishing the boundaries often had to include clauses which recognized such trans-frontier movements and endorsed their legality."[17]

During the inter-war years the tendency of blunting the sharp edges of colonial separateness and exclusiveness on the part of the civil administration of British and French West Africa was reflected in the strategic disposition of the British military. Co-operation in high diplomacy in Europe produced Anglo-French sub-systemic and sub-regional friendliness in West Africa. The rise of Hitler in 1933 and his demand for colonial retrocession so perturbed Anglo-French colonial susceptibilities that both were united against the German move.[18] A study which the British Chiefs of Staff undertook in 1937 on "The Defence Policy in the African Dependencies",[19] showed that in the foreseeable future France was not to be regarded as a potential enemy and that all British developments in West Africa would be secure against a French attack in a future war. But developments during the Second World War temporarily but seriously affected this growing optimism in sub-regional colonial co-operation in West Africa.

The Second World War and the Western Border of Nigeria

Ordinarily the Second World War was an armed conflict between two sets of European nation-states, the Allied and the Axis powers. Since France and Britain were in alliance against the Axis their colonial possessions were mutually guaranteed against hostile neighbourly attack. But the progress of war in Europe soon reversed this expectation. In June 1940 France suffered a crushing defeat in the hands of superior German forces and Generalship; she signed an Armistice with Germany on the 24th.[20]

When, by mid-June 1940, Britain was painfully aware that her ally would collapse sooner than later, her Chiefs of Staff drew up a plan for the defence of the French Colonial Empire and mandated territories against German and Italian invasion.[21] The government of the four British colonies were informed of the policy position as early as 18 June 1940; they were to prevent, as far as possible, African troops in adjacent French colonies from supporting the German cause. Conversely, French troopers were to be attracted to serve in neighbouring British colonies.[22] Military missions were sent across the frontiers to French colonies and solicit support for the Allied cause. It was in the midst of these activities that France fell and signed the armistice.

Obviously the effect of the collapse of metropolitan France on the Colonial Empire was, of course, a matter of great concern to Britain and of even more immediately anxiety to British West Africa. Throughout most of French West Africa the attempt by British military diplomacy to win over individual colonies to the Allied cause against Germany proved unsuccessful. Consequently, and following the appointment of M. Perre Boisson as the High Commissioner of all French West Africa by the Vichy Government of General Petain, the whole of French West Africa became Vichy-controlled territories. On the other hand, from August 1940 Chad, the Cameroun and other territories of French Equatorial Africa rallied to British-backed De Gaulle's Free French Movement. The French empire in Africa became a house divided against itself. At the end of 1940 therefore, Nigerians western border was exposed to potential enemy violations from Dahomey and Niger.

British open support for de Gaulle, who was publicly calling for the conquest of Vichy-controlled colonies, together with the military fiasco of *Operation Menace,* the Anglo-Free French futile bid to capture Dakar in September 1940, created grave strategic problems for Nigeria particularly along the western border. 1941 was a year of military anxiety in Nigeria eleven African's and two Europeans had died of an explosion of Lagos harbour on 4 June; sporadic violations of the frontier in Sokoto province were reported and the rumour went wild that the Germans would descend on Lagos in full force. In neighbouring Free French Chad, Italian war planes bombed various positions between June and October.

In May British authorities were contemplating trans-frontier subversion of the Vichy administration of Dahomey, by sending in agitators from Nigeria, promising the chiefs arms support and encouraging them to give the Vichy regime a lot of trouble.[23] Meanwhile Nigerians who lived on the northwestern borderland with Dahomey and Niger were clamouring for British military intervention in these Vichy-controlled territories to restore trade and normal family and inter-communal relations which the war had disrupted. In Badagry, members of the Local Council had suggested that British troops should "go into Dahomey at once to save their brothers from all the trouble they were experiencing"[24] The economic and social relations of the partitioned people of this frontier zone seem to transcend, at least from the African viewpoint, the hostilities that existed between Britain and Vichy France. Age-long and well-established economic inter-dependence and socio-cultural relations among Africans could not disappear just because the partitioning powers were at one another's throat. As one critically-minded young Nigerian, who refused to serve in British colonial army during the war, reportedly told Sir Bernard Bourdillon, the Governor of Nigeria,

> when you came to my country you told us that inter-tribal wars were wrong, and you even punished people for taking part in them. Now *you* are asking me to fight

in *your* inter-tribal wars.[25]

But African opinion in the border regions hardly had important impact on the strategic perception of the situation by the military. For example, in June 1941 the 'Military Appreciation' undertaken by the British Military Forces in West Africa showed that "Intensive air attacks on Lagos can easily be delivered from southern Dahomey but attacks from elsewhere, except on a small scale, cannot very easily be staged."[26] It was therefore contended that the defence of Lagos would be "of greater importance initially than that of Kano as it would be possible to divert friendly aircrafts and avoid landing at Kano."[27] By the end of 1941 the Nigerian government was seriously expecting a full-blown German invasion of the country through the northern and the northwestern boundary. They proceeded to draw up a railway time-table for the evacuation of all European nationals resident in Nigeria to Port Harcourt and Lagos for onward transportation to South Africa. This represented the height of strategic anxiety which the British in Nigeria passed through during the war.

In all reactions to the threatened and anticipated German and Vichy-French attacks, British colonial military authorities found the western border of Nigeria a profitable area of meaningful and rewarding counter-offensive. British sub-regional strategy pointed to the invasion and occupation of Vichy-controlled Dahomey as a counterpoise to the defence and security of Nigeria, valuable for the supply of strategic raw materials, minerals, food and manpower for Britain and the Western Alliance. Nigeria assumed greater significance in British war effort after the fall of her Far Eastern colonies to the Japanese in the winter of 1941-42.

Allied Planned Conquest of Dahomey

War intelligence and military appreciation by various staff officers of the Western Alliance were all agreed that some concerted effort was needed either to initiate the offensive or to prepare for a credible defence. A two-day Military Conference of the three colonial powers (Britain, Free French and Belgium) was held in Accra to recommend policy options.[28] The conference noted the problems which the sub-region faced especially the shortage of troops in all British possessions in view of the ongoing Ethiopian war but stressed the need to take the military initiative against enemy territory. Consequently, all the available Belgian Colonial Forces in the Congo were to be moved to the western boundary of Nigeria for the conquest of Dahomey.

Eventually, the Belgian Brigade Group, consisting of 9000 men including some 2500 carriers, was successfully transported to Nigeria and stationed in Lagos, Abeokuta and Imeko in readiness for offensive action.[29] The stage was thus set for on-the-spot preparation for the execution of the final plan.

The final war plan[30] provided for two operational zones: the Priority Operational Zone and the Subsidiary Operational Zone. The former covered the whole of southern Dahomey and southern Togo while the borderlands of Borgu and Sokoto Provinces along the western and northwestern boundaries constituted the latter. The general objectives of trans-frontier military activities in the Priority Zone was to provide continuous land communications between Nigeria and the Gold Coast, to prevent Vichy French troops from being moved from Dahomey-Togo towards Senegal and to seize the main aerodromes in southern Dahomey from which an attack could be launched on Nigeria.

In the Secondary Operational frontier zone the object was to eliminate enemy

garrisons on or close to the northern sector of the western frontier and the eastern
and central sections of the northern boundary of Nigeria. The trans-frontier military
object was to capture Zinder-Dosso Road as well as Birnin Konni and advance from
thence to Sokoto and Argungu. The aim was to concentrate two Brigade Groups in
the Sokoto-Dosso frontier zone facing Niamey in order to securely guard some 400
miles territories against possible Vichy and German attacks. But mutual suspicion
and the British insistence on the principle of "the undesirability of shedding French
blood by French men" ensured that military plans of the Secondary Operational
Zone never reached the stage of detailed preparations. The execution of the Priority
Operational Zone Project became the function of the Belgian Expeditionary Force
and British troops in Nigeria.

However, like all other war schemes which international crises had forced
British military establishments to draw up for the western border of Nigeria the 1942
war plan was never executed. Once the Allies and the Americans had invaded and
subdued North Africa in November and December 1942, the Vichy-controlled
possessions in Africa including Dahomey, rallied to the Free French Movement of
De Gaulle. With that the projected invasion of Dahomey from Nigeria became
unnecessary.

Yet the study of the invasion plan, drawn up to achieve certain geopolitical objectives, is pertinent and significant for this chapter in that it shows how knowledgeable
colonial military strategies were about minute cartographical details of the eastern
borderlands of Nigeria. The plan entailed a seven-phase movement of troops from
Imeko, Ketu, Abeokuta, and Ajilete, Igolo and Lagbe to various positions in
Dahomey indicating distances, topography, strategic positions, troops' disposition,
rivers and creeks. It was a detailed exercise in military map reading worthy of emula-
tion and improvement by the armed forces of independent Nigeria.

Lessons for Independent Nigeria

In present-day international relations, boundaries are the prevailing fashion and
are sanctioned by the very concept of territorial sovereignty. Boundaries mark the
furtherest territorial extent of a nation state. In Africa what were for the most part
remote frontier zones have become defined and defended, by diplomacy and
sometimes by force. Frontier relations are therefore governed by transborder co-
operation or conflict; co-operation in day-to-day inter-state peaceful co-existence,
and conflict, when diplomacy reaches its upper limit. Even regional organisations
such as Organisation of African Unity and the Economic Community of West
African States or such other international organisations like the River Niger Commission or the Lake Chad Basin Commission, tend to perpetuate the existing territorial status quo; but because they promote trans-boundary activities they reduce
the explosiveness of boundaries and their potentials as factors in international
conflict.

Since 1945 the world has witnessed wars, conflicts and disputes involving frontiers and territories. Some territorial wars have been fought "not so much to change
the map, as to define it". Nigeria and Cameroun were on the brink of such a war
in 1981. Frontier disputes are particularly endemic in areas, like Africa, where the
rise of new states is a very recent phenomenon in international relations. In the light
of this the OAU has pronounced against the revision of colonial boundaries; the continental Organisation is not prepared to question the illogicality of these boundaries.
The principle of the Roman law which says "as you possess, so you may possess'[31]

seems to be the OAU's imperative.

The status quo boundary policy of Nigeria since 1960 reinforces our contention that in order to "possess what we possess" Nigerian Armed Forces must constantly make staff plans for the defence of the boundaries ready to be set in motion when occasions call for them. The Nigerian Army specifically is duty-bound not only to have flawless, thorough, and practical knowledge of the border territories, but also it must ensure that the boundaries be meticulously demarcated and the survey beacons constantly monitored and properly maintained. We cannot afford a situation in which the Nigerian army in 1985 knows less of the cartography of our borderlands than the British colonial army knew during the Second World War. In the case of the eastern border where the demarcation process has not be properly completed; Nigeria should immediately re-activate the Nigeria-Cameroun Commission so that it can achieve the purpose for which is was established. The unsettled nature of the boundary, coupled with the economic potentials of the disputed borderlands, make it even more urgent for a dynamic military policy in the zone. The defence of national self-interests cannot be compromised on the altar of good neighbourliness.

It is perhaps in the Lake Chad region that Nigerian would encounter the greatest boundary problems in the nearest future. The four states of Niger, Chad, Cameroun and Nigeria share Lake Chad and are members of the Lake Chad Basin Commission established in 1964. One of the unfortunate inheritances of Nigeria is that she is surrounded by francophone states who still look up to France for ideological leadership and budgetary and economic survival. Francophone, as a neo-colonialist system, has cultural and defence/strategic dimensions. Friendliness towards Nigeria cannot be said to be one of its working principles. Indeed it is on record that in the late 1950s France persistently urged Britain to 'balkanise' Nigeria before granting independence to the "successor" state. The feeling was that an undivided independent Nigeria would threaten her erstwhile colonies, militarily and economically.

Camerounian and Chadian attitudes towards Lake Chad seem to suggest that both would wish Nigeria excluded from the Lake. Cameroun has dammed one of the rivers that supplies the lake with water, thus causing low water levels. Chad in spite of her internal problems, is noted to have unilaterally removed the survey pillars which demarcate the international boundaries from the bed of Lake Chad. Yet former President Shagari's Chadian policy, the so-called "Harmony II" computed to have cost Nigeria some 80 million American dollars, was an abysmal failure because our foreign policy was devoid of clear-cut objectives. It would appear that the much-quoted pronouncement about Africa being the centre-piece of Nigeria's foreign policy worked against the interests of Nigeria. Nigeria's sub-regional policy has been dominated by a "big-brother" mentality. We would like to hope that the re-definition of our foreign policy in terms of "three concentric circles" under the Buhari administration would enhance our policy actualization especially with regards to our borders.

One positive aspect of Nigeria's border policy that needs mention is the construction of trans-frontier highways across the three international boundaries. There are at least thirty trunk "F" or "A" roads leading from Nigeria to the neighbouring states. These cannot but play a major role in promoting inter-state understanding and co-operation. In times of crisis such roads could also prove militarily important. But the promotion of regional co-operation does not prevent our Armed Forces from carrying out constant strategic appreciations and the preparation of staff plans for the defence of our international boundaries in times of crisis. The history of the western border shows that cooperation alternates with crisis in trans-border relations. Nigeria must be prepared for both.

Nigeria maintains cordial relations with the Republic of Benin; there are two joint economic ventures between the two countries in the forms of the cement factory at Onigbolo and the Sugar refinery at Sabe (save) in Benin. The Papalanto-Ilaro-Pobe road was built to serve the frontier factory. In spite of these, however, the student of strategic studies looking at "Issues of Borderland in Africa" in historical perspective, with particular reference to Nigeria's western boundary, would still call for an active policy that should provide Nigeria with a credible striking military power whenever the border is violated. In this regard the proposed strategic Badagry-Sokoto highway, which is additionally expected to open up vast agricultural areas along the western borderland, is a welcome development because of its unintended military value. The defence of the western borderlands is the function of the 1st and 2nd Mechanised Divisions of the Nigerian Army with headquarters in Kaduna and Ibadan, respectively. Important towns along, or near the border, such as Badagry, Abeokuta, Shaki, Birnin-Kebbi, Argungu and Sokoto are properly garrisoned. What is required is the political will and leadership that can give the military a direction of purpose on border policy.

Endnotes

1. Lord Curzon, *The Romanes Lecture* (Oxford, 1907) cited by W.G. East, *The Geography Behind History* (London: Nelson, 1965) p. 98.
2. Andre Kaspi, "French War Aims in Africa, 1914-19" in Gifford, P. and Louis, W.R. (eds) *France and Britain in Africa, Imperial Rivalry and Colonial Rule* (New Haven, 1971) p. 376.
3. For details of these negotiations see J.D. Hargreaves, *Prelude to the Partition of West Africa*.
4. There are several works on these crises; but see J.C. Anene, *The International Boundaries of Nigeria (Ibadan History Series)* (London: Longman, 1970) Chpts. 5 & 6; C.S. Ukpabi, "The West African Frontier Force, 1897-1914, an instrument of imperial policy" unpublished Birmingham M.A. thesis, 1964 and A.E. Ekoko, "British Defence Policy in Western Africa, 1878-1914" unpublished Aberdeen Ph.D. thesis 1976.
5. C.O. 537/11. D.M.I. Plans for Attack, Report of 'War Council' 4 Nov. 1898.
6. Cabinet (AB) 3/1/1A, 'Military Needs of the Empire in a War with France and Russia', memo by E.A. Altham, August 1901.
7. C.O. 537/11, minute by C. and c- Lord Roberts, 14 Jan. 1903.
8. Ibid. Report of Conference Secret, July 1903.
9. Ibid.
10. C.O. 445/18, I.G. WAFF to C.O. 7 May 1904 and C.O. 537/11, 566 secret.
11. CAB 11/101 Part V ff.
12. Ibid.
13. For example, A.E. Ekoko "British Military Plans Against France in West Africa, 1898-1906", *Journal of Strategic Studies* Vol. 4 , No. 4-No. 3, Sept. 1981 and A.E. Ekoko "British War Plans Against Germany in West Africa, 1903-1914" *J.S.S.* Vol. 7, No. 4, 1984.
14. A.I. Asiwaju, *Western Yorubaland under European rule 1889-1945: A Comparative Analysis of French and British Colonialism* (London: Longman, 1976) and A.I. Asiwaju, 'Socio-economic integration of the West African Sub-Region in Historical Context' in Akinyemi, Falegan and Aluko (eds) *Readings and Documents on ECOWAS* (Lagos: NIIA/Macmillan, 1984) pp. 31-45.
15. A.I. Asiwaju, "Socio-Economic Integration..." op. cit., p. 31.
16. Ibid.
17. Ibid.
18. A.E. Ekoko, "British Attitudes Towards Germany's Colonial Irredentism in Africa in the Interwar Years", *Journal of Contemporary History* Vol. 14, No. 2, April 1979, pp. 287-308.
19. War Office (W.O.) 32/4140 memo.

20. R.T. Thomas, *Britain and Vichy* (London: Macmillan, 1979) p. 9.
21. CAB 21/1432; COS (40) 465; WP (40) 207 and A.E. Ekoko "Anglo-French Relations in West Africa During the Second World War" in S.O. Assein (ed) *Ekpoma Essays in Humanities* (forthcoming).
22. CAB 21/1432 Sec. of State of the Colonies to Governors. 18 June 1940.
23. F.O. 371/28246, Grey to Hankey, enclosed Hankey to Strang, 16 May 1941.
24. F.O. 371/28567.
25. B.H. Bourdillon, *The Future of the Colonial Empire* (London: S.C.M. Press, 1945) p. 69.
26. W.O. 32/9599, 19 Military Mission to War Office 13 June 1941.
27. Ibid.
28. W.O. 32/9599, Minutes of a Conference held at Hq. Military Forces in W. Africa, August, 1941.
29. W.O. 32/9599 Minutes.
30. The Plan is in W.O. 173/1287 and 1288.
31. Peter Lyon, "Regional Organisations and Frontier Disputes" in Evan Luard (ed) *The International Regulation of Frontier Disputes* (London: Thames & Hudson, 1970) p. 122.

CHAPTER 20

Potentials of Nigerian Boundary Corridors as Sources of International Economic Conflict

by J.L. Okon Ekpenyong

Introduction

As socio-economic conditions worsen generally around the world, and particularly in the West African Region, it is becoming increasingly necessary to examine more closely the effects which economic pressure may eventually have on the neighbouring countries of the region. This becomes even more urgent when considered against growing hostilities between governments and people who, for decades during the colonial occupation, had remained generally friendly and accommodating. Over the last decade, Ghana has had cause to send Nigerians out of its territories in 1969. Equatorial Guinea battered Nigerian workmen so inhumanely that the Nigerian government offered free passage to all her citizens willing to return home in 1975. In between these major escalations, innumerable minor skirmishes had been reported by Nigerian fishermen and tertiary workers since the early 1960s, and particularly during the period of Nigerian Civil War. In 1983 and again in 1985, Nigerian government sent away citizens of her both near and distant neighbours, a process that has continued, how be it, quietly to the present time. In almost all cases, the host countries including Nigeria, have claimed that their guests have invaded the economic fabric of their countries, they had robbed citizens of job opportunities and contributed to unemployment. Nigerians are said to have made their hosts a little nervous in the way they dominated both economic and social lives of the countries. For those Nigerians who were molested and harassed by neighbouring countries, their causes were often not taken up by the appropriate authorities. Too often, the acts which agents of the host countries perpetrated sounded so far-fetched that the Nigerian authorities did not take them seriously. One immediate reason for this lapse was that it was difficult to believe that in a region where the same ethnic groups are found on both sides of an international boundary, people would resort to extreme hostilities and inhumane treatment. Secondly, since the eradication of slave trade, mobility of population had become a conspicuous feature of West African life. Adegbola (1977) notes that such movements served to bind areas of West Africa more closely together because by the time of independence in 1960, almost every West

Figure 1. Nigeria and it's neighbours.

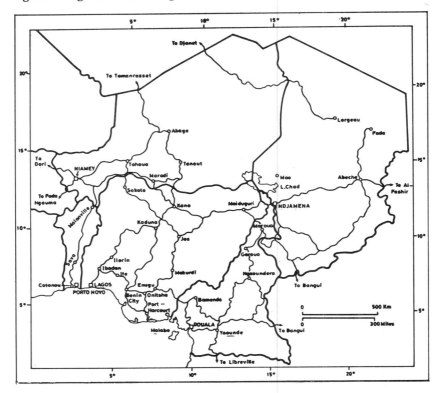

African country had sizable proportions of foreign born population within their territory. The diffusion of the Fulani across West Africa and their subsequent adaptation to new environments is well documented by Carter (1967), who notes that not only are the Fulanis represented throughout West Africa, they were also basically nomadic cattle herders; culturally, and socially distinct from the cultivators. However, since their migration to other parts of West Africa from Senegal, some have gradually lost their herds and mixed with cultivators in many locations.

Some Geographic Characteristics of Nigeria's Borderland

Ethnic Groups and Subgroups

The simple illustration of Fulani diffusion in migratory waves along the northern sector of the West African region, can be reconstructed for several other ethnic groups and subgroups. Indeed, Asiwaju (1984) has demonstrated the continent-wide spread of the phenomenon of part time culture areas. The Nigerian cases include several examples as may be shown in Table 1 and more graphically depicted in Figure 2.

Most of these ethnic groupings share deities, ancestral shrines, major rites, such as birth, manhood, maidenhood, womanhood, marriage, childbearing, manhood and burial customs. Some still share annual festivals and rituals which all members of the ethnic group have obligations to attend irrespective of location vis-a-vis an

Table 1

Boundary Corridor	Ethnic Groups or Subgroups
Benin-Nigeria	Yorubas, Gun or Aja, Egbado, Borgu (Yorubas)
Nigeri-Nigeria	Hausa, Admawa, Tazarawa, Manga, Moba, Kanembu/Kanuri
Chad-Nigeria	Kanembu/Kanuri/Baduma
Cameroun-Nigeria	Shuwa, Mandara, Wakura, Matakam, Kapsiki, Gude Vere, Chamba, Ndoro, Kentu Fungan, Tivi, Boki Mambila, Wum, Ekoi and Ododop

Figure 2. Ethnic groups and sub-groups of Nigeria's borderlands

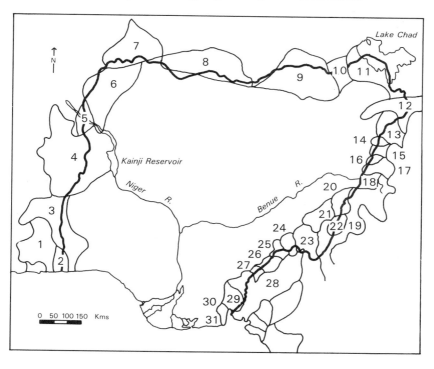

1 Kebu	12 Shuwa & Arabic Kanuri	22 Ndoro
2 Gun (Egun)	13 Mandara (Lamana)	23 Mambila
3 Voruba	14 Wakura (Kamwe)	24 Tiv Kuteb
4 Borgu	15 Fall (Matakam)	25 Yukebeo
5 Dendi	16 Kapsiki	26 Betcheve
6 Zarma	17 Nzangi (Gude)	27 Bokki
7 Adarawa	18 Yola/Laka/Koma	28 Ejagham
8 Tazarawa	19 Adamana (Chamba-	29 Efik
9 Manga	Daka)	30 Oron
10 Mober	20 Mundang (Vere)	31 Ekit
11 Kanembu (Buduma)	21 Jukun	

international boundary. Studies have shown that among several groups, it is commonplace for the traditional head of the group to live on one side of the border in the neighbouring country while portions of his 'subjects' live on the other side. There are occasions when a member of the group resident in a neighbouring country for decades had been invited to come and lead either the clan or the lineage as among the Turan and Ikurav-ya clans of the Tiv ethnic group astride the eastern border of Nigeria.

In spite of the seemingly low population density near the boundary corridors, the areas immediately behind them are densely populated, as is the case with the Cotonou-Porto Novo/Lagos-Badagry corridor. This is also correct of Kaduna-Zaria-Kano and Onitsha-Owerri-Eket which back up the respective sector of the Nigerian boundary. The result of all these is that the excessive pressure exerted by these areas of heavy population concentration on the available natural resources is passed on the seemingly lighter population in the border areas.

Economic Resource Base of the Region

Prior to independence in the region in 1960, the resource base of the area was mainly agricultural. Although there was strong indication of available non-renewable resources, it needed heavy investments and capital intensive programmes to develop and tap these resources. However, among the various resources commonly exploited without regard to the existing boundaries are farmlands, water, fisheries, fuel, wood, human resources, wild fruits, nuts, herbs for medicine, food, wild animals, traditional building materials, and in recent times, petroleum minerals. In addition to the above are traditional trading activities based on finished goods and agricultural products, handicrafts, artifacts and drugs.

Agricultural Activity and Sahel Drought

Although the region had remained mainly agrarian with the coastal region producing root and tree crops, while the Guinea Savanna hinterland produces grains, legumes, nuts and cotton, drier Savanna and Sahelian zones had been traditionally an area of what Monod (1975) describes as pastoral-nomadic economy. But the six-year drought, which reached its climax in 1973, hit every country in the region and changed agricultural patterns significantly. It was the semi-arid north, thereafter referred to as the Sahel, which was worst hit by the drought. It has been the most damaging drought since 1913. Thus, Robert McNamara (1975) noted that, due to this most devastating drought, Mali, Niger, Burkina Faso (Upper Volta), Mauritania, Senegal and Chad were unable to take advantage of the favourable world prices of their chief exports (groundnuts, cotton and livestock). Furthermore, he noted that the surge in petroleum prices was such that it had driven the cost of their essential fuel imports from 10% of their export earnings to 30% or 40%, at the time their food import requirements—literally to stave off mass starvation—have risen dramatically.

The impact of the drought and failure of agricultural production was so severe that waves of refugees from neighbouring countries more seriously affected by the drought and subsequent crop failure, started migrating into Nigeria. The distress of the area was not relieved by the floods that resulted from the rains which followed the drought of 1973. Legum (1975) has described the disaster caused by the flooding rains of August and early September of 1974. The floods compounded the problems created by the drought as transportation channels were disrupted with telling consequences on emergency food and medical supplies. The movement of population and cattle from the four poorest countries south of Sahelian region. Nigeria was, of course, the most prominent host country for the surging refugees.

However, the most sensitive issue in border relations to date is the well organised and integrated smuggling of agricultural crops such as groundnuts, into Niger, and cocoa shearbutter and timber into the Republic of Benin—to mention a few examples. This is encouraged partly by the lure of foreign currency (CFA) and the price differentials created by the gap in the prices offered producers in Nigeria and across the borders. Each season these agencies allow the Nigerian authorities to announce their commodities' prices before settling their own on the upper scale. Therefore Nigerian farmers located close enough, naturally prefer to sell their products across the borders for higher prices and more prompt payment.

Unproductive Human Resources

The bulk of population displaced as a result of the drought migrated into Nigeria which at that time (even though running out of food) was able to pay for imported food from oil proceeds. Needless to say that such mass movements did no sit well with the inhabitants of the host countries. As a matter of fact, Walker (1975) reports that when the vast herds moved into Senegal, they were met by angry Senegalese farmers whose own crops had also failed from the drought. It was estimated that Mauritania had lost 70% of its cattle population, Mali 55%, Niger 80% and Chad 70%. The strength of refugees moving south is best illustrated by figures for the town of Rosso on the Senegal which, in the space of six weeks, grew from 8,000 people to 40,000.

In Nigeria one could not obtain figures at the time, but it was obvious from the sheer presence of those of them who cared to come out into the streets begging for alms that Nigeria had received quite a sizable number of this people. They were found in every street corner in every sizable town in Nigeria. As the deteriorating condition persisted, the second wave of refugees hit Nigeria again, particularly as the civil war in Chad escalated. By 1982, Nigeria was obviously overloaded to the seams with citizens of its immediate and distant neighbours. But with economic conditions deteriorating in the country, it became clear that something had to be done: Government's response was the infamous mass expulsion of illegal aliens from Nigeria in January 1983. Bentsi-Inchill (1983), reporting the mass exodus, put the number at about 500,000 for Ghana and between 150,000 and 200,000 for Niger Republic in the first week. However, when the final reports came in a week later, the same correspondent, quoting official sources, put the figure for Ghana at 900,000 registered at the official transit points. The fact that such a large foreign population had settled in Nigeria placed a great burden on the already deteriorating food situation in the country and also generated a considerable contraband in finished products and local currencies.

Illegal Cross-Border Trade

It is said that illegal trade across Nigeria borders is as old as the borders themselves. It was nurtured by large profits and corrupt border officials, irrespective of rank and formation.* This, together with criminal activities by some aliens,

---

In recent times, all border posts are being manned by a combined team of representatives of the armed forces, customs, the police, immigration and security organisation.

prompted the military rulers to close the border in 1984. Such trade prevailed along the Lagos-Badagry-Cotonou corridor and Otta-Idiroko axis on the Western boundary with numerous intermediary routes and corridors in Oyo State. Along the northern boundary with Niger, there are Sokoto-Birnin-Koni, Katsina-Maradi, Katsina-Gazaoua, Kano-Nigeria and Damasak-Diffa corridors on the Maiduguri-Damasak road. Along the eastern flank, numerous cross-border routes exist in and around Yola Jato-Aka, Obudu, Agbokim, Ajasso, Ekang and Ikang as well as at Oron, Eket, and Ikot Abasi on the Atlantic front.

The trade involves the movement of imported finished goods which would ordinarily attract a considerable import duty across the border. Smuggling was largely to evade the payment of these duties into government coffers and, in return, buying manufactured products from Nigeria to sell across the borders. In this trade a tremendous amount of money exchange hands. The effects on Government are several. First, it generates absolutely no revenue to the government since no import duties are paid on the massive flow of cigarettes, spirit, machinery, munitions, textile materials, motor spare-parts, food items and so on into and out of the country. Secondly, the government faces a two-way loss since the currency of transaction is the Naira which is illegally taken outside the country with consequences for a corresponding reduction of the official value of our currency. At the same time this reduces drastically the amount of currency available in Nigeria for circulation and legitimate transactions. No one could give any figures in respect of such transaction, or say how much money changes hands at any of the numerous border markets. However, during several field investigations to Cotonou markets in 1982 and 1983, the writer witnessed the exchange of vast sums of money openly at Dantokpa, Cotonou's new market, by those whom one would assume were the licensed dealers because they operated in front of the market police post. These transactions involved Nigerian full-time traders, part-time traders like students and office workers, individual families and government officials who arrive in official government vehicles for shopping. The activities were done under the watchful eyes of the gendarmes and the Beninois police.

Water and Water Resources

One of the integrating elements in the environments like those of the West African region has been water, both in the form of rivers and in the form of rain. The pastoral nomads to the north migrate south as the dry season approaches and north again as the rainy season begins. They have been doing this for several centuries. However, the numerous rivers that traverse the area have helped as an integrating force by bringing a number of countries using the same body of water together. Prominent among these bodies of water are the Rivers Niger, Benue, Cross River and Lake Chad.

In addition to this, there is an often ignored but very important water way in what Webb (1958) describes as the largest system on the West African coasts. This stretches for about 258 kilometres from Cotonou in the Republic of Benin to the western edge of the Niger Delta in Nigeria. This lagoon system, like most others around the world, is sheltered from the open sea by a complex arrangement of sandy ridges interspersed with muddy hollows and backed by much narrower sub-parallel ridges. Although they have provided restricted transport across the borders even before the advent of the Europeans, these sheltered waters of the coastal lagoons and creeks have provided an important east-west route, extending from Lake Nokoue and Porto

Novo Lagoon in Benin Republic to the estuary of the Cross River in the Cross River State of Nigeria without venturing out to sea. Equally significant are the creeks and back waters that separate Nigeria from the Cameroun. At the height of colonial trade and commerce, foreign commercial companies operated efficiently organised fleets of river crafts which evacuated palm produce, rubber, copra and bananas from Nigerian and Camerounian buying points.

Although the local farmers and merchants have plied these routes in their dug-out canoes before the arrival of the Europeans, the Europeans merchant houses came to use these same routes in moving their goods to the numerous coastal bases by powered launches and stern wheelers. Within Nigeria, the volume of goods moved down the Niger-Benue systems to the Delta, the Cross River and Qua Iboe river ports and from Ndian (now Mundemba in the Cameroun) to Calabar, and to Lagos from Badagary and Okitipupa by water was considerable. The fleet, owned by the large commercial companies, operated from Benin and Cross River ports to well beyond the Nigerian frontier. The fleet included crew members from most of the neighbouring countries, and evacuated palm produce, timber, rubber, and copra from Nigerian hinterland while banana and other forest products came from the Cameroun. Although the use of the Niger was restricted beyond the falls at Bussa and Jebba, the construction of Kainji Dam and the insertion of locks made navigation beyond the rapids possible.

However, the numerous rivers named above, together with the various lakes, pools and the shallow waters of the continental shelf, have always provided fish and shrimps from which the local population derived a good part of the much needed protein. In addition, the inland waters such as Rivers Niger, Benue and Cross River, all rise from outside Nigeria and flow through a neighbouring territory before entering the country; they also provide alternative agricultural land on their flood plains. In all cases, they receive either a single flood, as is the case with Benue and the Cross River, of two floods annually, as is the case with the Niger. What this means is that it is possible to grow more crops in the year.

Fishing as a Source of Potential Conflict

The major areas of freshwater and marine fishing which could pose a threat to international peace include Lake Chad fisheries, marine coastal inshore and deep water sub-thermocline fisheries. The marine inshore fishery carries such species as *pentanemus quinquarius, polymenus quadrifilis, galeoides decadactlus cunoglossus* (soles), *luthanus dentatus* (snappers), *permadasys jubelini* (grunters), *arius sp.*, marine catfish, *sarotherodon tilapia* and *larimus peli* (croakers), and a host of others. Both the deep-water subthermocline and the inshore supra-thermocline sections include a wide variety of species. In addition to all these, there have been talks of profitable catches of tuna fish while at least four species of shrimps, *(penaeus duorarum nostalis, parapenopsis atlantica, parapenaeus longirostrus* and *panaeus kerethurus)* are commonly found in the coastal marine waters.

At the peak of its production, the Lake Chad fisheries is said to have contained close to 80 species including such better known *hydroeyon lineatus, adipofin, polyterus senegalus, tetrodan fahaka,* and *lates nilotecus.* The production by 1966 had reached 30,000 tonnes with an annual turnover of about ₦4,000,000. About 5,000 Kanuri, Hausa, Shua Arab, Kwatako, Buduma and Banana tribesmen in 18 villages, (Afunori, Mallam Fatori, Ajiri Metele Bongawa, Alagarno, Ali Meleri,

Dogoshi, Litilin Korimi, Cumnari, Difinowa, Bodoiri, Kirenowa, Jilliam, Botori Balabutobi, Manawagi and Wulgo) fish in the lake and its feeder streams. In 1972, the total volume of fish processed was put at 36,444 tonnes which yielded ₦300 million, and in 1977 the yield totalled 132,000 tons, in spite of close to 60% losses from insect infestation and spoilage. Fishing is the major occupation around the lake and all four countries—Cameroun, Chad, Niger and Nigeria—depend heavily on supplies from Lake Chad. In the case of Nigeria, it is estimated that 40% of its fresh fish is caught from Lake Chad. But Apanpa and Adebolu (1983) suggest 13,772.00 metric tonnes as the potential yield for the coastal fish species mentioned above, and about 3,500 metric tonnes for the shrimp on these waters. Esajere (1985) quotes Olaniyan as giving 600,000 metric tonnes of marine landings for both inshore and distant waters. Whatever the figures, it must be pointed out here that the devastating drought of 1973, which reduced the lake from a 25,000 km² expanse of water to a mere 6,000 km², also affected its fishery.

Nevertheless, the salient point here is that fishermen from all the countries have shared the fishing grounds together prior to Independence, with infrequent and minor incidence. In the last two decades, there have been allegations of very serious infractions and dehumanising treatments on all sides. Nigerian fishermen and fish dealers operating from both the waters of Lake Chad and the various fishing villages on the Nigeria-Cameroun border have reported repeated incidence of physical assaults, and often, incarceration without the due process of law. During discussions in 1981 with Nigerian fish dealers who operate out of Baga on Lake Chad, it was reported that Chadian gendarmes frequently, assaulted the fishermen and confiscated their catches which had been spread out to dry, or set up for smoking. Even the traders who had their wares paid for and packaged for transportation to markets had them seized.

Since Nigeria increased its territorial waters progressively from 5.00 kilometres in 1964 to 19 kms in 1967 and 48 kms in 1971 and the Economic Emergency Zone (E.E.Z.) to 320 kms in 1978, many foreign vessels—among them those of Cameroun, Italy and Togo-have been reportedly arrested for fishing illegally within Nigeria territorial waters. Most of the fishing vessels are accused of violating existing Nigerian Fisheries Regulation, especially the Fisheries Act of 1971, which prohibit poaching, over-exploitation of the marine resources, pollution, menace by foreign and indigenous trawlers exportation of shrimps at sea and piracy to mention just a few. The situation became so bad in recent past, that in February 1983, the General Manager of the indigenous fishing companies (Nigerian Coastline Fishing Company Limited) made an open conflagration in April 1983 when Nigerian and Chadian forces clashed. These unfortunate incidents were widely reported in the world press at the time. West Africa (1983) put the losses at 9 Nigerians and 75 Chadians troops, while 20 Nigerian and 32 Chadians were reported captured.

If the situation on the Chad border could be considered critical, that at the marine border with the Cameroun was graver still. On 16 May 1981 5 Nigerian soldiers on patrol duties at Ikang, a border customs post near Calabar were shot by the Cameroun gendarmes. These actions could be traced to the anxiety to protect two other resources in the area—fresh water and petroleum.

Chad and Niger Basin Commissions

The two main body of water that sustain lives in the area are River Niger and Lake Chad. The Niger basin comprises the inland swamps and lakes in Mali as well as such renown tributaries as Sokoto-Rima, Kaduna and the Benue Rivers. Chad receives its waters from rains and Chari, Logonne and Komadugu Yobe rivers. The River Niger Basin Commission and The Lake Chad Commission had been formed in an effort to monitor and regulate the management and use of the resources of the two basins.

During the inaugural Conference of Heads of State and Government of the Lake Chad Commission at N'djamena (Fort Lamy) from December 10-21, 1962, the participating nations agreed to recognise and respect the existing international boundaries on the lake. Even subsequent Chad Basin Conventions, among them that of 22 May 1964, upheld that decision. It is also interesting to note the membership composition of the two basins. The Niger Basin Commission includes Benin, Guinea, Mali Nigeria, Cameroun, Ivory Coast, Upper Volta and Niger while the Chad Basin Commission comprises Cameroun, Chad, Niger and Nigeria. Therefore, three of the neighbours are members of both commissions. But from all the events of the recent past, it would appear that only Benin and Niger maintain a reasonably peaceful relationship with Nigeria.

It is pertinent to draw attention to the potential danger posed by the inactivity and insensitivity of regulating commissions such as the Niger Basin and Lake Chad Commissions which fail to monitor the way member countries use and manage parts of rivers that flow through their sovereign territories. The Niger has a number of barrages and dams constructed at various points along its course, while it has been suggested in Nigeria that the barrage constructed at Lagbo on the Benue, 50 kilometres from Garoua, has contributed immensely to the considerably reduced volume of water in the river. It is alleged that the Cameroun officials did not consult with their Nigerian counterparts prior to its construction. Be it as it may, it is the effect of such damming that generates controversy. Several studies have shown that the construction of dams and barrages upstream tend to reduce not only the volume of water but, according to Oyebande *et al.* (1978), also the available area of fadama which the farmers had hitherto cultivated along the river valley. In many circumstances, the water available to neighbouring countries for irrigation has been drastically reduced. Some countries have gone to war in situations like this.

In April 1974, for example, both Syria and Iraq were alleged to have mobilised their troops at their common border in readiness for a military engagement over the dwindling waters of River Euphrates. The river could no longer support the irrigation farms in Iraq. Syria was suspected to have turned down the sluices at Tabqa Dam. Therefore, it is hoped that efforts will be made to monitor the developments and management along rivers and related water sources which we share with our neighbours.

Finally, one factor which has set all the countries in the region working feverishly is the exploitation of minerals, particularly fuel minerals. All the countries have watched Nigeria benefit fro the proceeds of petroleum resources. Therefore, it is not surprising that every country sharing common borders with Nigeria and beyond, is actively involved in the exploration, exploitation and refining of hydrocarbons,as shown in Fig.3.

Oil Exploitation as a Potential Source of Conflict

Nigeria became the first country in the region to discover oil in commercial quantities at Oloibiri in 1956, after the first two earlier attempts were aborted by the outbreak of the World Wars. In 1964 Tchad started exploration at Rig Rig by the

Figure 3. Border administrative units.

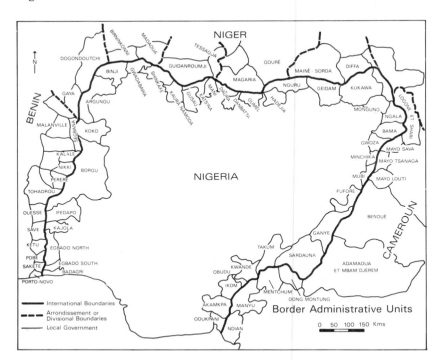

shores of Lake Chad and at Doba, about 270 kilometres southeast of N'djamena. But when the perennial civil war started again in 1974, *Conoco* suspended its operation. However, in a recent announcement, *Exxon* indicated that it was drilling an exploration well in the Southern Sahr area of Tchad. Cameroun has been pumping oil from Bakassi Peninsula on-shore and from several off-shore oilfields on the Atlantic Coast since 1977. The production and estimated recoverable reserves have encouraged *Sonara* to build a refinery at Limbe, while the construction of a planned gas liquefaction project was postponed in June 1982 due to downward revision of the reserves.

In Niger exploration started in 1968 and oil bearing formations had been located in the Erg region of Tin Touma, while the concessions blocked out by the government run into Lake Chad. In recent times, Nigeria has shifted its exploration activities to Gaji Gana in this very region. The Republic of Benin, where exploration started in 1964, made its first shipment in 1982, and has been producing at the rate of 250,000-500,000 tons per year. In all the cases where Nigerian neighbours are prospecting for oil, the oilfields are located near their common boundaries. But while the Beninnoise exchange information on their exploration activities with their Nigerian counterparts, others do not. And of all the countries concerned, only Nigeria and the Cameroun are exporting considerable quantity of oil as shown in Table 2.

A number of other minerals also straddle our shared boundaries or have been located very close to them. Limestone for the manufacture of cement is found to ex-

Figure 2. Crude oil exports in 000 barrels

	1979	1980	1981	1982
Cameroun	10,489.51	14,566.14	44,038.64	34,817.50
Nigeria	842,474.11	752,498.36	525,598.86	470,639.27

Sources: *Cameroun figures computed from Encyclopaedia Britannica Book of the Year, 1981-1985. Nigerian figures are obtained from Central Bank of Nigeria Annual Reports from 1980-1983.*

tend across the borders in Sokoto and Ogun States to neighbouring Niger and Benin respectively. Therefore, since the location of minerals does not respect international boundaries, those that occur at such locations in Africa have raised some vexing issues and created problems of boundary authentication. Most of the boundaries are said to be physically un-demarcated. This has created very serious but elusive problems between Nigeria and the Cameroun at the estuary of the Cross River and the off-shore oilfields where both countries are reportedly drilling from the opposite sides of the same oil-field. This has been compounded further by the Maroua Convention in 1975 between General Gowon and President Ahidjo, where—like European imperialist negotiators a century before—the two rulers used biro pens to re-draw the boundary over the sea where oil prospecting takes place.

The situation is also not altogether quiet between us and Benin vis-a-vis offshore fields or between us and each of Chad and Niger as further prospecting continues in the Chad Basin. It will get even more complicated should Equatorial Guinea start prospecting for off-shore petroleum in the Atlantic towards Nigeria and the Cameroun. Byogo Nguema Island, the major island of Equatorial Guinea, is barely 30 kilometres from the nearest Nigeria oil rig. Therefore, it is pertinent that all the countries in the immediate borders will find it fit sometime, somewhere and somehow, to sit down and work out a mutually acceptable boundary over their land and territorial waters. They may bear in mind the treacherous nature of the oil multinationals whose economic interests their conflicts serve, by heeding Anthony Sampsons' 1975 observation that Oilmen are like cats; you can never tell from the sound of them whether they are fighting or making love.

Conclusion

This study has attempted to show the pre-colonial unity in diversity which brought the various communities of the West African region together. This is best illustrated in the socioeconomic ties and environmental factors which continuously brought the people in close contact. However, the ripples from drought, poor harvest, spiralling population, massive unemployment and generally poor economic performance have brought tremendous pressures on the government and people of the region.

The nationals of the various countries seem to take the existing laws and statutes of others for granted. It is pertinent for the nationals of the various countries to note that every country in the area has very strict immigration and currency laws, which they enforce. Furthermore, it is clear from the discussions that friction and tension were nt as high, and border incursions and engagement by security forces as frequent when most countries in the region had good harvest, and were marginally rich or just marginally poor. Therefore, just as the entire countries in Third World view with some resentment and misgivings the wealth and general affluence of the developed countries, the less fortunate countries in the West African region will naturally look at the more fortunate and buoyant ones with some jealous bitterness and expectation. Since potentials for conflict in the area seem to increase as economic conditions deteriorate, it becomes necessary to set up more realistic economic policy and goals by all the countries in consultation with one another. There is a greater need now than ever before to evolve cross-border planning and development of resources for the mutual benefit of all. Joint industrial projects across the borders must be encouraged. Such developments, as the joint Niger-Benin cement factory at Onigbolo in Benin and Sugar in Sabe also in Benin help to stabilize the geopolitics of our border region. In addition, since currency has created a significant degree of strain between countries sharing borders together, official currency exchange bureaus should be set up at all border towns and posts, with the rules an regulations in the major languages on display.

Finally, the various governments should promote rapport between tertiary level administrators and counsellors. It has been found generally that official viewpoints and indeed accounts on events at the borders differ slightly from the perception of border people themselves. There is need to harmonize the gap between government and local community concerns. These efforts, aims at harmonising interests and concerns between government and the local communities on one side of the border and between governments on both sides of the borders, will go a long way in promoting cordial relationship at the borders and help to remove friction since issues of major concern can be ironed out more easily at this level before they can get out of hand.

Bibliography

Adegbola, O, "Some geographical aspects of the repatriation of Nigerian nationals from Ghana," *The Geographer*, Vol. 6, 1977, pp. 29-39.

Carter, Jean, "The Fulani in Bamenda," *Journal of Tropical Geography*, Vol. XXX, 1967.

Asiwaju, A.I., "The Aja speaking peoples of Nigeria, a note on their origins, settlement and cultural adaptation up to 1945," *Africa*, 49 (1), 1979, pp. 15-28.

_____ Asiwaju, A.I., *Partioned Africans*, (Lagos: Lagos Univ. Press, 1984).

Barbour, K.M., "A geographical analysis of boundaries in inter-tropical Africa," in K.M. Barbour and R.M. Prothero (eds.) *Essays on African Population*, (London: Routledge and Kegan Paul, 1961).

Monod, T. (ed.), *Pastoralism in Africa*, (Ibadan: OUP for Int. Institute, 1975).

McNamara, R.S., address to the Board of Governors, World Bank, Washington, D.C. 1974.

Legum, C., "African affairs," *Ency. Britannica Book of the Year, Special Report*, Chicago, 1975, 46-50.

Walker, M., The Sahel Drought, *Ency. Britannica Book of the Year, Special Report*, 1975, 66-67.

Sherman R. Harvey & Robbins G. Frances, "Agriculture and food supplies," *Ency. Britannica Book of the Year*, Chicago, 50-65, 68-69.

Bentsi-Enchill, Nii K., "The return to Ghana," *West Africa* No. 1417, 1983, 305-307.

Webb, J.E., The Lagoons of the Guinea, in the ecology of Lagos Lagoon, *Philosophical Transactions of the Royal Soceity of London*, Series B, Biological Sciences, No. 683, Vol. 241, 1958, pp. 307-419.

Apanpa, D. Alhaji and V.O. Adebolu, "Security in Nigerian waters with respect to the fisheries sector, *Nigerian Forum*, Vol. 3, 1983, 1054-1061.

Ekpenyong, J.L.O., "Geographical perspectives on the security of Nigerian waters," *Nigerian Forum*, Vol. 3, pp. 1043-1048.

Correspondent, "Nigeria-Chad, bombs and propaganda," *West Africa* No. 3434, June 6 1983, p. 1369.

Report, "Net gain along the shores," *Time, The Weekly Magazine*, March 14, 1977, p. 29.

Ibiabuo, J., *Daily Times*, Feb 14, 1983.

Maiduguru, Yaro, "Chad fisheries make big progress," *Daily Times*, Jan 1966.

Special correspondent, "Development of Lake Chad fisheries," *Daily Times*, Jan 1966.

Onita, C., "No fish in diminishing Lake Chad, once the home of fishes," *Daily Times,* April 1, 1980.

Esajere, A., "Fisheries and marine resouces," *Daily Times,* March 12, 1985.

Cushing, D., *Fisheries Resources of the Sea and their Management,* Science and Engineering Policy Series, (London: OUP, 1975).

Washington Post, Syrian Dams depr ves 3 million water, April 23, 1974, Washington. D.C.

Sampson, Anthony, *The Seven Sisters: The Great Oil Companies and the World they Shaped,* (New York: Viking, 1975).

Ward, P., "Strains along the border," *Ency. Britannica Book of the Year,* 1983, Chicago, 229-230.

CHAPTER 21

Lake Chad as an Instrument of International Co-operation

by Ibrahim James

Introduction

The Lake Chad Basin is today roughly shared by four African countries: Nigeria, Niger, Chad and Cameroun. The single most important geographical feature of the basin is Lake Chad itself. It is probably the eleventh largest Lake in the World today and covers an average of 22,000 square kilometres in surface area. The lake in its presents size and shape probably "represents the diminished minute remains of a former Lake of great extent and depth scholars now described as the Mega-Chad." The shore-line of the Mega Chad begins from the foothills of the Tibesti Mountains, some 700 milometres to the north of the present Lake Chad northern shoreline.[1]

This Lake basin is drained by innumerable rivers notably: the Chari, Logone, Komaduguyobe, Komadugu-Gana or Lesser Yobe Ebeji, the Yedseram, Ngadolu, Ngadda, Ebeji Mbuli, Botha El Beed, Taf-taf and Serbewel. Of the above rivers, the Chari-Lagone complex that flows from the Cameroun is responsible for 95 percent of all the water inflow into the Lake while the Ebeji, Kariya, Yedseram and the Komodugu are responsible for only 5% of the water in-flow. Hydrological studies reveal that the territorial distribution of the Lake's surface water is not constant; that it is subject to substantial fluctuations in water surface area and water level.[2] These fluctuations have probably been responsible for the sharp variations in the Lake's surface area which has ranged between 13,000 sq.km. and the present 23,000 sq. km. depending upon the yearly inflow from the Chari-Lagone complex, the Ebeji and the Komadugus.

One major problem has been with the gradual desiccation of the area, which has resulted in the permanent diminution of the lake. This is born out by hydrological studies which show that the Lake levels over 1870-1970 have, on the whole, been at a higher level than what prevails now and the Lake's surface water extent in 1962 was 30,000 km. which is twice the present areal extent of 15,000 km.[3] The actual natural geographical extent of the Lake covered a much wider area than both the present 23,000 sq. km. of water surface area and the present 427,200 sq. miles territorial coverage of the Chad Basin commission treaty area.[4]

Thus, though the largest natural lake in the world, the Lake Chad remains not only a hydrological puzzle, but as well an unpredictable and unreliable natural boundary. The Lake is a large hollow reservoir of water dotted by hundreds of innumerable islands and islets. Many of these islands and islets consist of floating rafts of vegetational growth and subsequent fragmentation and may be anchored by the roots of drift. Conservative estimates put the number of islands floating or submerged at between 1,000 and 2,000.[5]

The political boundaries of the four states of the Lake Chad Basin sub-region— Nigeria, Niger, Chad and Cameroun—straddle the hundreds of island and islets in a manner that makes any clear boundary demarcation well nigh impossible. This boundary problem is exacerbated by the inability of both the colonial powers of Britain, France and Germany and the succeeding independent states of Nigeria, Niger, Chad and Cameroun to count these islands, properly map and chart them "due to the Lake's constant changing level and the unstable character of its islands".[6] While the amoeba-like proclivity of this floating vegetational growth for multiple subdivisions particularly on the shallower Nigeria-Chadian boundary over the lake has been a constant source of conflict, the same hydrological puzzle represented by the Lake paradoxically provides the basis for co-operation.

Lake Chad remains an extraordinary integrative factor for the entire Chad Basin sub-region. This point is valid whether we look at the lake in its fullest or in its state of diminutions. The lake, all through history, has played roles more of a bridge than a barrier: in particular, the lake has been the major explanation of the intensive and extensive cross-cultural or inter-ethnic interactions that have characterised the history of geopolitics of the Megachad region. The droughts, especially the most recent ones, have especially dramatised this role of the lake as an important centre for ethnic and cultural fusion, economic interaction and ethnic and cultural diffusion.[7] This fusion and diffusion of diverse cultures in the bottom-land or the dried-bed of the Mega-Chad has been primarily as a result of human response to geographical, ecological and political changes taking place in the Lake Chad Basin sub-region.

The role of the Lake Chad as an important focus of diverse ethnic and cultural fusion and as farrago of diverse ideas has transformed it into a close human inter-link rather than a human divide in this region. It had provided a migratory corridor through which "influences, ideas and cultures were repeatedly received and transmitted between North Africa, the Nile Valley, Southern and Western Sudan for more than a thousand years."[8]

The migratory pattern has traditionally remained north-south and east-west in its main directions. Although a compensating counter—current of migrants-represented by the over-land pilgrimage to Mecca—was inaugurated by a group of Kanuris led by Sheikh Tylah in the later 17th century, nevertheless, the traditional north-south and east-west flows of migrants remained the dominant patterns until the attainment of political independence by the Chad Basin states in the 1960s.

Migrations

Since the achievement of political independence by the Lake Chad Basin States of Niger, Nigeria, Chad and Cameroun, the liberal attitude exhibited by the pre-colonial Chad Basin States of Kanem-Borgu, Bagirmi, Waddai, Damargrin Kotoko city states, Mandara and the colonial administrations of the British, French and German began to fade. With the post-1960 development of micro-nationalism, which ushered in the political independence of the colonial territories and the acceptance of the nation-state as their model, the concept of the exclusive boundary gained greater currency. The result has been the emergence of border issues and problems: closure, disputes, foreign investment laws, trade licensing, civil registrations and, above all, illegal immigrations aroused by droughts as well as by political instability in Chad.

But for the bulk of the ordinary population, the Lake Chad Basin is still perceived as a politico-geographical unit and the Lake itself is more of a link than a physical barrier. Thus, in spite of the restrictive measures—the border closure of 1984-1986, the Nigeria-Chad armed clashes of 1983, the Deportation of illegal Aliens of 1983 and 1985—transborder migrations of the ordinary population appears to have been on the increase in the Lake Chad Basin. In a region characterised by dramatic climatic changes as the Lake Chad Basin mass human migrations have frequently distorted geographical or political boundaries. Human migrations have resulted from mostly economically motivated movements of pastoralists, farmers, traders and fishermen in search of areas of optimum opportunities. There were also pilgrims, political and ethnic refugees in search of personal freedom and greater security. Lake Chad has been the traditional convergence point for the pastoralists: Tuareg, Toubou, Feda, Kanembu, Shuwa, Fulani and Wadai from Chad, Niger, northern Cameroun and northern Nigeria.

Pastoralist trans-humane patterns of movement across political boundaries in the Lake Chad basin would require more than the conventional wisdom of unilateral state action to contain. This is particularly so in a region "where the border line between the states remains a thin line across which movements on both sides have remained quite free, frequent and common".[9]

Any pragmatic and lasting solution must emanate from a coherent and collective sub-regional initiative. The earlier Lake Chad Basin member states adopt a much more realistic approach to the problem of international migratory movement in the Lake Chad Basin sub-region, the better for the region. For in modern time, as Jackson has so correctly asserted,

> migration is not only a test case in human relations but also a test case in international relations. These relations will never be satisfactory until in the ordering of migrations, the people concerned have not only arisen above erroneous, partial and narrow views, but have also absorbed what can be learnt from dispassionate attention to the demographic, economic and sociological problems involved.[10]

Border Problems

The international boundaries separating the four nations sharing the Lake Chad Basin emerged from an intractably interwoven tangle of conflicting British, French and German imperial interests and traditional between Borno on the one hand and her quasi-satellite states: Baghirmi, Kanem, Waddai, Damagarin and the Kotoko city states on the other.

Although the "Say-Barrua Line" provisional international boundary agreement of 1890 paved the way for the Franco-German boundary in respect of the eastern and southern shores of Lake Chad, it was the Anglo-French Convention of 1898[11] that created a boundary with a propensity for generating conflicts. Despite the concerted efforts made by the french and the British in working out definite guidelines for the final demarcation of the boundary in the Lake Chad Basin, boundary demarcation over the Lake's surface area gave rise to an elusive and unresolved problem to date. In general, these boundaries-defined in terms of latitudes, longitudes, geometric circles and straight lines—split several ethnic and cultural communities.

The inter-sovereignty boundaries drawn across the Lake Chad pose problems on account of factors making it difficult for the borders to function as the dividing lines that they were created to be. The difficulties arise at several levels. Firstly, the substantial fluctuations in surface area and water level, exacerbated by the unstable character of the floor and islands of the lake, make boundary demarcation and maintenance an extremely intimidating proposition. Secondly, there is the essentially anti-boundary phenomenon of cross-border ethnic relations of the Kauri, Buduma (the main group on the lake), the Sugarti and the Moba astride the Nigerian border with Chad; the Kauri again, Kanembu, Koyam, Manga, Shuwa Arabs, Fulani, Beriberi, Tuaregs and Tazarawa across the border with Niger; and, again, the Shuwa Arabs, Kotoko, Mandara, Matakan, Wakura, Kapsiki Guda, Wandela, Jibu, Matmeta, Vere, Chamba, Kontu, Fungon, Wum, Boki, Elor Adodop across the border with Cameroun.

Besides, there is the problem posed by a lack of researched and reliable data. Neither the colonial powers nor the independent states of Nigeria, Niger, Chad and Cameroun have been able to produce accurate up-to-date maps of these islands and the boundaries. This is borne out by the fact that during 1983 Nigeria-Chadian[12] border conflict "a platoon of Nigerian soldiers, which became a victim of ill-prepared maps, strayed into the Cameroun and was captured and detained for five days. Its release came only after a protracted negotiation with the Camerounian military authorities".[13] The colonial powers had tried to make of the Lake Chad and a natural barrier, through the imposition of artificial boundaries. However, economic, commercial, cultural, religious and racial links have converged to nullify the effects of these artificial boundaries. Lake Chad has come to be seen more as a great human link rather than as a natural barrier.

Consequently, a realistic approach to the critical problems posed by the international boundaries across the Lake Chad Basin lies in the functional alternative of peaceful trans-border co-operative relations. The search for this solution might not come through a shift of national boundaries but by means of actions taken across them. The failure of the military solution, demonstrated in the 1978 Nigeria-Chadian border conflict and 1983 border war, makes the functional-alternative argument more valid and urgent than ever.

The Functional Alternative—
The Formation of the Lake Chad Basin Commission

The functional alternative rests on the premise that the Lake's pre-independence role as a close human link rather than a human divide should constitute the basis for co-operation. Interaction among the four states of the Lake Chad Basin was to be organized around certain basic functional needs emanating from the Lake itself, notably fishing, agriculture, animal husbandry, transportation, water irrigation, recreation, conservation and trade. The governments of Nigeria, Niger, Chad and Cameroun were to transfer to appropriate bodies executive authority for the achievement of the specific ends of coordinating and integrating trans-lacustrine fisheries, agricultural, animal husbandry, irrigation activities and the transport systems. The successful performance of these functional activities by these borders would have the effect of turning the pre-existing cultural links into productive factors of international relations.

The functional alternative will naturally promote the basic human needs for physical security, economic and social well-being and cultural identify; it will as well bring these nations closely together through the building of a common interest in peace. This functional alternative would appear to have materialised in the signing of the "Convention and Statute Relating to the Development of the Chad Basin" by the Heads of States of Nigeria, Niger, Chad and Cameroun in 1964. This convention brought into existence the Lake Chad Basin Commission (LCBC) whose aims and objectives "are to promote and regulate the joint development of the resources of the Lake Chad area and to strengthen the idea of developing closer neighbourly relations for the purpose of the economic development for the mutual advantage of all member nations".[14]

Regrettably, the post-1960 development of micro-nationalism in all the treaty states has kept the governing elite and the nationalist leaders pre-occupied with the problem of safeguarding hard-won national sovereignty. The failure of the leadership in these countries to look beyond the national states has been demonstrated by their lack of the political will to co-operate in meaningful ways with the neighbouring states within the LCBC. Consequently, since the signing of the treaty establishing it, the Commission has not been able to forge realistic strategics beyond the usual summits by the Heads of State and the meetings of responsible ministers and technical experts.

By the Fourth Summit Meeting of the L.C.B.C., held in Lagos from the 21-22 April 1983, the Ministers and Technical Experts had held 27 sessions since the Commission's inception in 1964.[15] Yet at this Fourth Summit, Heads of the treaty-States expressed genuine concern for the lack of progress made so far by the LCBC. They, therefore, re-affirmed their wish to strengthen their co-operation in the LCBC through the pursuance of "true policy of socio-economic integration through a common and coherent development programme leading to the attainment of food, self-sufficiency in the conventional zone, its internal and international opening up and the training in rural economy."[15] The fact of this resolution is enough evidence that the LCBC has not lived up to expectation. Further more, it can be surmised that the adoption by this Lagos Summit of a New LCBC Plan of Action for 1982-1986 lends credence to the assertion that the 1970s for the LCBC have been years of apathy, inertia and indifference.

Leadership in all the treaty states became more and more inward-looking in the 1970s as the internal combustion elements in these states eventually got ignited and the leadership became more increasingly engaged in national unity, more so than in issues of international co-operation. The increased concern for national unity meant increased combined concern also for national boundary maintenance, not cross-border co-operation. The combined effects of political instability and the nagging problem of the post-1960 development of micro-nationalism have all conspired to frustrate the development of a functional co-operation and integration inaugurated by the pastoralists, fishermen, farmers, and traders in the Lake Chad from time immemorial.

The narrow inward-looking attitude adopted by the leadership of the member states is dramatised in their excessive pursuit of micro-political objectives to the detriment of macro-political goals even at the risk of contravening the provisions of the convention. The construction of dams on the Chari-Logone complex by the Cameroun Republic has, for example, been in flagrant disregard for provisions of the convention obliging signatory states to desist from land development and water utilization measures capable of affecting the general water level of the lake and its basin.[16] Considering the fact that the Chari-Logone complex is responsible for 95 percent of all water inflow into Lake Chad, there is no way the damming of the river system will not effect the general water level of the Lake and its basin.

Similarly, Nigeria's unilateral establishment of an autonomous statutory body known as the Chad Basin Development Authority (CBDA) through Decree No. 32 of August 1973 outside the framework of the LCBC was patently conflictual with the objectives of the LCBC as a supra-national organisation. The CBDA's South Chad Irrigation Project (SCIP) was meant to develop some 67,000 hectares of irrigable land out of 96,000 sq. km. of Nigeria's own treaty portion of the Lake Chad Bais at an estimated cost of 498 million naira.[17] Naturally, this is a gigantic project in terms of size, complexity and capital investment whose impact, when fully operational, could affect the general water system of the lake.

The negative effects of unilateral action by Cameroun through the construction of dams on the Chari-Logone complex might have robbed the Lake of an average yearly inflow of 40.32 milliard cubic metres of water.[18] Of similar, though less significant, effect is the action by Nigeria through the construction of the Tiga Dam on River Yobe, the on-going Alau Dam Project on River Ngadda, and the proposed Yedersam Dam on River Yedersam. Since these rivers have not been the principal sources of the Lake's water inflow,[19] the Nigerian Government action in damming them may not have produced the same degree of adverse effects as the Camerounian government's action on the Chari-Logone. Nevertheless, the Nigerian Government actions cannot be seen as any less adverse to the cause of the LCBC. Especially negative in this regard is Nigeria's unilateral response to the 1972-1973 devastating drought through the SCIP. Presumably, this might have triggered an avalanche of recrimination by her neighbours, thereby creating an atmosphere of mutual suspicion and mutual distrust.

Admittedly, of course, the persistent, perennial and substantial fluctuations in the Lake's surface area and water level may not have been entirely due to these man-made causes. The vagaries of nature are a well recognised explanation. Since the 1970s, Lake Chad has continued to recede at a very alarming rate to the chagrin of member states of the LCBC.[20] However, the fact of the natural factors does not rule out the relevance of micro-nationalism as a major explanation of the lack of coordinated development of the Lake Chad Basin as a coherent natural region and logical planning area in spite of the international boundaries drawn across the basin. The 1983 Lagos Summit of the LCBC, in a tacit acknowledgement of this fact, has instructed the Commission to "pursue studies on the evaluation, development and equitable utilization of water resources of the Basin"[21]. It is hoped that this new resolve for an equitable utilization of resources is based on a sincere determination on the part of the treaty to make a success of the LCBC.

The imperatives for regional integration confront the LCBC treaty states with no other viable alternative. This is now so in the fact of an intimidating combination of events and developments which underscore the inherent weakness of unilateral action: devastating drought and associated famine, desertification, epidemics and pestilence; the massive cross-border migration and the refugee problems issuing out of both the natural factors and the political instability as illustrated by the crisis in Chad. As Lake Chad continues to recede, thereby endangering not only the survival of human life but also that of the flora and the fauna, the national states whose boundaries tend to artificially divide the region are forced to recognise the value of joint action. The adverse effects both on the LCBC and the SCIP (i.e. Nigeria's South Chad Irrigation Project) show that the logic is more for common or cooperative planning, not a unilateral one. In fact, the current accelerated desiccation of the area, resulting the rapid diminution of Lake Chad, can be easily recognised as the generating impulse for coordinated action and the cooperation aimed at the protection of the eco-system around the Lake.

The Lagos summit of 1983 took cognizance of this imminent danger posed to the fauna and the flora of the region by the requesting "for the acceleration of procedures on the ratification of the Joint Agreement of Regulation on Fauna and flora signed in Enugu in 1967 of which presumably no action had been taken".[22] The 1983 Summit's commitment to a New Action Plan for 1982-1986 is indicative of a new resolve to forge a realistic, non rhetorical strategy for cooperation via the LCBC. The present crisis, precipitated by the vagaries of nature, is a catalyst to this new spirit of cooperation. Natural disasters have left nations in this sub-region with little or no options to cooperation; and Lake Chad forms the nexus or the focal point from which basic functional needs of the communities in the area derive: fisheries, agriculture, animal husbandry afforestation transportation and trade.

There are other important political and cultural variables that could facilitate the Lake Chad Basin regional integrative process. The landlocked states of Chad and Niger desperately need to secure transit rights across the territories of immediate neighbours such as Nigeria and the Cameroun. Conversely, as Nigeria and Cameroun lay the basic foundation for their industrialisation, both stand to benefit from Chad and Niger who possess the much needed strategic minerals such as Chromium, cobalt, titanium, uranium and platinum.

Tourism is another area in which Lake Chad could serve as a potential integrative agent but which has not been maximally and profitably explored. The tourist industry—a major foreign exchange earner for countries like Morocco, Tunisia, Kenya, Tanzania, Uganda, Egypt, Senegal and Gambia—could assist the ailing economies of Nigeria, Niger, Chad and the Cameroun. Lake Chad, which is the world's largest natural lake and the single most important geographical feature in this region, has tremendous potential as a tourist attraction centre. National and international interests in the Lake should not terminate in commercial fishing, communications, transportation, mineral extraction, national security and agricultural purposes alone but should extend to the recreational objectives as well. The prevailing consensus now is that of restoring to Lake Chad the capacity to continue to perform its traditional function of a close human link rather than a human divide.

As the sub-region gets industrialized and real economic development is achieved, nationals of treaty states of Niger, Nigeria, Chad and Cameroun would take to travelling for tourism rather than the current narrow employment-seeking objectives of present day cross-boundary migrations. With more development, nationals from LCBC treaty states would come to appreciate the importance of recreation in particular and of tourism in general, and would take advantage of the recreational facilities that Lake Chad might provide.

The future portends a trend towards possible increase in the inventory of potential parameters and variables for cooperation in the Lake Chad Basin. Leading among these is the issue of water and air pollution and the need for transborder cooperation in respect of control measures. With the discovery of oil by an international consortium led by the Continental Oil Company (CONOCO) in the Kanem area near Lake Chad[23] and the Nigerian National Petroleum Company (NNPC) at Gaji-Gana on the Nigerian side, Lake Chad could become a possible target of waste disposal by oil companies. Already, the Lake is the recipient of discharges from the shores bordering large settlements and from the inhabitants of the innumerable islands and islets dotted all over the lake. Moreover, there is the waste materials released into rivers Chari, Lagone, Ebeji, Yedersam, Ngadda and the Komodugus, which are eventually discharged into the lake. As oil exploration and prospecting expand towards the Lake itself, oil rigs on the Lake shores and shelves may yield products such as waste gases that will be discharged into the atmosphere. Moreover, any expanded use of the Lake for commercial transportation either of cargo or passenger traffic would also involve the discharge of rubbish and ballast from vessels. The immediate short-term need arising from the increase in commercial transportation on the Lake would be the coordination and integration of transport system of the treaty member states, while the wider problem of waste disposal and the threat of environmental pollution would have to be approached only from a common sub-regional platform such as is provided by the LCBC.

Conclusion

The current growing inter-dependence in the Lake Chad sub-region in the areas of security, ecology, economy, diplomacy and socio-cultural relations forms the basis for optimism. Apparently, Lake Chad alone possesses the potential of fostering greater sub-regional cooperation amongst the treaty member states as they become more and more emasculated and despondent before the devastating effects of natural disasters: drought, famine desertification, epidemics, rinderpest and so on. Conflicts and crisis over competition for the resources of the lake would continue to engage the attention of decision makers at national, regional and local levels of governments in Nigeria, Chad, Cameroun and Niger. Because Lake Chad presents multifaceted kinds of challenges, the Lake is a catalyst for cooperation. An inventory of the potential areas of conflict in the Lake is bound to focus, among other issues, on the Lake itself as a hydrological puzzle; the innumerable and ever multiplying islands and islets; the growing demographic pressures on the lake as a major water resource in a desert region; the near absolute dependence on the Chari-Logone river system; political instability and associated refugee movements.

The above problems cannot be confronted by the traditional nationalistic and unilateral search for improvements. The challenges of the Lake Chad sub-region transcends the microcosmic individual national frameworks. Thus, despite the resurgence of post-independence micro-nationalism expressed in the expulsion of foreign nationals, border closure, border conflicts, immigration restrictions and so on, integrative pressures are observable in the existing patterns of cross-border ethnic, culture and economic linkages. The prevalence of independent political, economic, social, culture, religious and institutional variables, that constitute vital leverage for the integrative process in the Lake Chad sub-region, creates the basis for optimism. The continued cooperation of Niger, Nigeria, Chad and Cameroun is demanded in order to confront he essentially shared regional problems of drought, famine, desert encroachment, rinderpest outbreak and so on. A common, collective sub-regional platform is as essential as the corporate existence of the individual states themselves.

Endnotes

1. Sikes, S.K., *Lake Chad* (London: Eyre Methuem, 1972) Preface xv. See also H.H. Lamb, *Climate: Present, Past and Future* (London: Methuem, 1978) p. 613.
2. Ibid, op. cit., preface xvi.
3. Lamb, op. cit., p. 613.
4. Nigerian Federal Ministry of Justice, Lagos, Nigeria's Treaties in Force, 1960-1968, p. 220.
. Sikes, S.K., *Lake Chad* (London: Eyre Methuem, 1972) Preface xvi.
6. Ibid.
7. Lamb, H.H., *Climate Present, Past and Future,* (London: Methuem, 1978) p. 613.
8. Works, J.A., *Pilgrims in a Strange Land: Hausa Communities in Chad* (New York: Columbia Univ. Press, 1976) pp. ix-x.
9. *West Africa,* 2 August, 1982.
10. Jackson J.A., *Migration: Sociological Studies* (Cambridge Univ. Press, 1969) p. 16.
11. Anglo-French Convention of June 14, 1898, No .241. See Herslet E., *Map of Africa by Treaty* Vol. II (HMSO, 1894).
12. These islands and islets were scenes of fierce-fighting during the 1983 Nigeria-Chadian Border Conflict. See *New Nigerian* (Kaduna) 16 May 1983.
13. *National Concord* (Lagos) 24 May 1983.
14. Fourth Summit Meeting of Lake Chad Basin Commission, Lagos, 21-22 April 1983. Final communique. See Federal Ministry of Water Resources, Water Resources Bulletin, Vol. 1, No. 7, p. 17.
15. Ibid.
16. Ibid.
17. Nigeria Federal Ministry of Justice, Nigeria's Treaties in Force 1960-1968 (Lagos), p. 220.
18. Federal Ministry of Water Resources, Water Resources Bulletin, Vol. 1, No. 6, p. 19.
19. The main source of water inflow into the lake other than the Chari-Logone Complex are the R. Ebeji, R. Yedseram, R. Ngada and the Komodugus.
20. *New Nigerian* (Kaduna) 16 January 1985.
21. Fourth Summit Meeting of Heads of State of LCBC Lagos, 21-22 April 1983. Final Communique.
22. Ibid.
23. CONOCO has spent a total of 30,000 CFA Francs on petroleum exploration in Chad between 1970-1980 it made 21 drillings and found 8 promising results in the Kanem area, 3 near Doba, 2 near Moundaou.

CHAPTER 22

Offshore Boundaries and Jurisdictional Zones in Relation to ECOWAS Countries: Existing Structural Diversities and New Opportunities for Cooperation

by J.A. Akintola-Arikawe

Aspects of Offshore Jurisdictional Space and Objective

The strategic, administrative and resource significance of ocean spaces adjacent to coastal countries was delineated by this writer in a restricted context some years ago (Akintola, 1979; 193-208). The issues involved have attracted even greater significance and wider dimensions since then and could be relevantly recalled here as a point of departure.

The water bodies of the earth which form over 70 per cent of the total area of our planet constitute a significant part of man's support system. For many centuries, coastal states have therefore made various forms of claim to exclusive control over zones of the ocean adjacent to their territories.

The specific motivations for such claims on the part of riparian states derive from diverse considerations. First, security reasons make it reasonable for coastal states to maintain a protective belt of territorial waters over which they have the same degree of sovereignty as they have over the land territories. Secondly, order on the sea is of particular importance to countries which depend on the sea for some of their wealth, whether through trade and commerce or by direct exploitation of valuable resources such as continental-shelf (and even deep-sea) fisheries.

Further, a most important contemporary reason derives from the fact that in recent decades, the mineral potential of offshore space had become widely recognized. The exploitation offshore of extensive deposits of hydrocarbons (which include crude petroleum, gas condensates and associated minerals) has brought unexpected and highly-prized economic strength to some states. The occurrence and exploitation of offshore petroleum resources signify more than any other single contemporary consideration, the incentive for partitioning the ocean and the rocks beneath it such that the coastal state has sovereign control over portions of the sea adjacent to its land territory.

Apart from petroleum, a variety of other minerals such as methane hydrate, copper, nickel, coal, iron ore, manganese nodules, cobalt as well as sand, gravel, lime shells, diamonds, gold, tin and other heavy minerals and sands are known to exist under the oceans (Dupuy, 1974; 137-139). while the hydrocarbons typically occur in the shallower continental-shelf areas adjacent to the continents, the poly-metallic nodules occur primarily in the deeper and more distant parts of the oceans (Kerr, 1980; 4).

In addition to such main considerations as the above, it has also been suggested that expansionist tendencies, especially on the part of erstwhile colonial states which have now become independent sovereign states initially led to continuous appropriation of offshore space, the only frontiers of expansion left on earth (de Blij, 1973-1974). Finally, problems of pollution and sanitation as well as the desire to combat smuggling and piracy (which might warrant the search for suspicious vessels even beyond the limits of a state's territorial waters) form part of the felt need for extending a coastal state's control into offshore areas.

It could be noted that claiming exclusive rights over offshore space is not a new phenomenon. When in the late sixteenth century, the Danes claimed territorial waters eight miles wide around Iceland, they did so to protect and preserve for their own exclusive exploitation one of the richest fishing grounds in the world. The two succeeding centuries witnessed various legal debates and conflicts from which eventually emerged many of the ideas that characterize the modern law of the sea. The debates over "The Free Sea" (Mare Liberum) advocated by the Dutch and the "The Closed Sea" (Mare Clausum) desired by the British (de Blij, 1973; 191: Kerr, 1980; 2) gradually produced appreciation for the need to extend the state's land-based sovereignty over adjacent portions of the sea. Thus, in modern times, it is recognized that the water body off the coast of a state can be generalized into various zonal categories. From 1958 up to the early 1980s there were (apart from internal waters)[1] four such zones: the territorial sea, the contiguous zone, the zone of diffusion, and the high seas, in that order from the coast outwards to the open ocean. Since 1981 when the Draft United Nations Convention on the Law of the Sea emerged, it has become formally possible to designate five such zones (using the same sequence): the territorial sea, the contiguous zone, the Exclusive Economic Zone, the Continental Shelf, and the High Seas.

While the *need* for territorial waters has ceased to be a subject of debate, there had never been, until the potential created by the U.N. Convention of 1981, complete agreement by all coastal states on *how wide* the territorial sea should be. From the eighteenth century debates on the width of the territorial sea came the cannon-shot rule which is believed to have yielded the notion that the zone should be three miles wide. The three-mile width which was adopted by Britain and the United States towards the end of the nineteenth century became, indeed, the most common claim during much of the nineteenth and the first half of the twentieth centuries. This relatively stable situation was possible because European colonial powers extended their domestic practices in this connection to their colonies in other parts of the world. However, with emergence to sovereign independence, the erstwhile colonial territories began to make claims they considered most appropriate to their particular situations. The result was an unprecedented level of diversity in the extent of territorial sea claimed by coastal states and a corresponding intensification of fishing disputes and related conflicts. For instance, 40 out of 62 states claimed the three-mile width in 1950 but by 1972, 56 of 111 states claimed the twelve-mile width and as many as eight countries claimed 200 miles (Prescott, 1975; 68).[2]

Although the width of the territorial sea (because of its status as a virtual extension of a country's land territory in terms of sovereign control) has attracted the greatest attention, the concepts, legal status and (particularly) the issues of width relating to the other offshore zones have also been traditionally shrouded in ambiguity and lack of precision, both in their own rights and as a result of their overlap with disputed or controversial territorial-sea limits. It is because of these problems that the Third United Nations Conference on the Law of Sea (UNCLOS III) which culminated in the new Convention (ratified in 1982) became necessary. The unprecedented duration of the Conference was warranted by the diversity of national positions on the issues at stake and the tenacious desire of the organizers to evolve a generally acceptable Convention which would provide uniform and legally recognized structural arrangements for all countries, including those in the West African sub-region.

While the basic motivation for this paper has indeed been the desire to elicit the implications of the new United Nations Convention on the Law of the sea for ECOWAS member countries and to propose an appropriate strategy for dealing with those implications, the stages through which the paper progresses to accomplish these basic objectives could be outlined as follows:

a) a brief review of the old U.N. Conference and Conventions on the law of the sea, especially as they relate to the spatial definitions of the various jurisdictional zones; and a synthesis of the main provisions of the new (1982) convention in respect of allowed widths and activities in the respective jurisdictional zones;

b) a concerted attempt to elicit the politico-legal and technical-research implications of the New Convention for ECOWAS countries, especially as regards the stupendous resource-development potentials inherent in the provisions relating to the jurisdictional zones; and

c) the presentation of a proposal involving the establishment of a regional organization through whose activities the latent opportunities of the new Convention could most fully be realised by ECOWAS member countries.

The United Nations Conferences and Conventions on the Law of the Sea

The long-felt desire to codify the existing international customary law led to an unsuccessful conference at the Hague in 1930 at which issues including law of the sea were discussed. With the formation of the International Law Commission (ILC) in 1949 and the passing of Resolution 1105 by the General Assembly of the United Nations in 1957 (calling for a conference to examine the law of the sea), the way was paved for the First United Nations Conference on the Law of the Sea (UNCLOS) held in Geneva from February 24 to April 28, 1958. That first UNCLOS produced four conventions: (a) the Convention on the Territorial Sea and the Contiguous Zone: (b) the Convention on the High seas; (c) the Convention on Fishing and conservation of the living resources of the High seas; and (d) the Convention on the Continental Shelf (Dean, 1958: Whiteman, 1958).

The second UNCLOS was held in Geneva in 1960 but narrowly failed to reach agreement on the two specific but related subjects discussed: the breadth of the territorial sea and fishery limits. Accordingly, no convention resulted from this conference.

Although the number of off-shore issues requiring international agreement increased after 1960, it was not until 1968 that a Seabed Committee of the United Nations addressed itself to some of the issues and in 1970, a General Assembly resolution called for a *Third Conference on the Law of the Sea* to start in 1973 (Kerr, 1980; 3). For various reasons, the third UNCLOS dragged on for about eight years until it adopted a Draft Convention at its resumed tenth session in Geneva on August 28, 1981.

It is important to point out some of the major differences between the main provisions of the first and third UNCLOS conventions. The points juxtaposed on Table 1 in respect of each jurisdictional zone of offshore space make such differences apparent, especially in relation to width/breadth and some other characteristics. It is worth recalling that the basic intent of the new (1982) convention is to bring orderly uniformity and equity into the structure and use of offshore space.

Of fundamental importance for the delimitation of the various jurisdictional zones have been the question of baselines from which the width of the territorial sea is measured. Normally, on a straight coastline, the baseline is the low-water mark. But many coastlines are of various degrees of sinuosity or indentation. From the famous fisheries case between Norway and England in the 1950s and the decision of the International Court of Justice therein, elaborate conditions have been installed to guide the use of straight baselines on indented coasts (See Dean, 1958; 617).

The real danger and fear of many law of the sea conferences is that a liberal use of straight baselines to enclose large bodies of sea water on the pretext that such water bodies are mere indentations (which could therefore be closed off as internal waters) would extend seawards the base from which the width of the territorial sea is measured and thereby, on the seaward margin, produce encroaching effects on areas which would have remained parts of the free high seas. It could be added that the first UNCLOS regarded the area beyond the twelve-mile limit as the high seas; while the third UNCLOS *generally* regards it as the area beyond the 200-mile limit.

The above overview is the background against which the structure of offshore jurisdictional space in ECOWAS countries must be viewed. The remaining parts of this paper are accordingly devoted to an examination in the light of the provisions of the new convention, of the pre-existing structure of offshore boundary claims among ECOWAS countries and the new opportunities presented for cooperation and collaborative endeavour.

Existing Structure of Offshore Boundary Claims Among ECOWAS Countries

The Economic Community of West African States (ECOWAS) was eventually formed among fourteen independent West African countries by signing the ECOWAS Treaty in Lagos on may 28, 1975. With the accession of Guinea Bissau and Cape Verde after their independence, the membership of the community has since risen to sixteen nations.[3] Of the sixteen countries, twelve are coastal, three are land-locked and one is insular or archipelagic (Table 2).

All of the three types of ECOWAS countries are affected by the new Convention on the Law of the Sea. Thirteen of them have coastal/jurisdictional waters in the Atlantic ocean; and the remaining three which are land-locked are required to be provided not only with access to the sea for normal purposes of commerce but also equitable shares in the surplus of the living resources of the exclusive economic zones of coastal member states (Articles 69 and 124-132 of the 1982 Convention).

It is not yet known (at the time of writing this chapter) how many ECOWAS countries have actually ratified the 1982 Draft Convention the law of the sea. The con-

Table 1. Basic off-shore jurisdictional zones recognised by the First (1958) and Third (1982) UNCLOS and the main characteristics ascribed to them

Designation of Jurisdictional Zone	Basic Provisions on Allowed Width and Other Characteristics	
	First UNCLOS 1952	Third UNCLOS 1982
1. Territorial Sea	Not more than 12 miles permitted; but states claiming 3 miles did not recognize widths greater than theirs; ILC left more definitive width to be fixed by a future international conference (Article3)	Breadths/widths up to 12 miles allowed all coastal states (Part II, Article 3). As in 1958, measurement is from baseline (which is normally low-water mark at the coast)
2. The contiguous zone	Width fixed at a maximum of 12 miles (Article 24)	Allowed width extended to miles; that is, 12 more miles seawards of territorial sea limit (Part II, Article 33).
3. Exclusive Economic Zone (EEZ)	Not provided for in the first UNCLOS	Zone where coastal state has sovereign rights relating to exploration, exploitation, conservation and management of living and non-living natural resources of the sea-bed, subsoil and superjacent waters, as well as other activities constituting economic use. Maximum width allowed for EEZ is 200 miles (Part V, Articles 56 and 57).
4. Continental shelf	Sea-bed and subsoil of submarine areas outside territorial sea limit to a depth of 200 metres or beyond to exploitable depths of the said areas (Article 2); superjacent waters and airspace excluded.	Sea-bed and subsoil of sub-marine areas beyond the territorial sea to the outer edge of the continental margin or to a 200-mile distance. Ancillary provisions recognize variations in submarine topography off different coasts (Part VI, Articles 76, 82).
5. The high sea	The High Seas exist outside areas of national jurisdiction; co-operation urged on all states in adopting conservation measures in the high seas area (Articles 1 and 2)	Beyond zones of national jurisdiction is the High Seas all states are granted numerous basic freedoms relating to the superjacent waters and airspace. But the sea-bed and ocean floor and subsoil beneath high sea waters (called "The Area" and otherwise designated "The Common heritage of mankind") are excluded from the freedoms. Administration

Table 1 continured.

of the resources of the "Area" is to be carried out by the "Enterprise" (an arm of the International Sea-Bed Authority) on behalf of all mankind (Part VII, Articles 86, 87, 136; Part XI Articles 133-191).

Notes: (a) All references to miles denote nautical miles. (b) All widths and breadths (distances in nautical miles) are measured from the baselines from which the territorial sea is measured.

Sources: Arthur Dean, "The Geneva Conference on the Law of the Sea: What was Accomplished," *American Journal of International Law,* Vol. 52, No. 4, Oct. 1958, pp. 607-628. Marjorie M; Whiteman, "Conference on the Law of the Sea: Convention on the Continental Shelf," *Amer. Journal of International Law,* Vol. 52, No. 4, Oct. 1958, pp. 629-659; U.N. *Third Conference on the Law of the Sea: Draft Convention on the Law at Sea,* Resumed Tenth Session, Geneva 3-28 Aug, 1981, A/CONF, 62/L. 78, 28 Aug. 1982, original: English; U.N. *Third U.N. Conference on the Law of the Sea: U.N.'s Convention on the Law of the Sea,* A/CONF.62/122, 7 October 1982 (82-30296).

Table 2. ECOWAS as countries by type and location

Type of Location	Number of Countries	Names of Countries (Alphabetical Order)
A. Coastal	12	Benin, Gambia, Ghana, Guinea Bissau, Ivory Coast, Liberia, Mauritania, Nigeria, Senegal, Sierra Leone, Togo
B. Land-locked	3	Borkina Fasso (Upper Volta), Mali, Niger
C. Archipellagic	1	Cape Verde

vention took an unusually long time (of 8 years) to emerge because of the need for varied negotiations that would make its provisions command a wide consensus within the international community. The chances are therefore high that ECOWAS member countries would ratify the convention if they have not already done so. But they would be doing so against the background of a truly diverse structure of claims to off-shore space which they had maintained up to 1981.

The available data on such claims cover 11 of the 13 coastal states for most of the basic off-shore jurisdiction zones: the territorial sea, the continental shelf, and the exclusive fishing (economic zone, see Table 3).

In respect of the territorial sea, the existing claims (up to 1981 at least) range from widths of 6 miles for Ivory Coast to 200 miles for Sierra Leone. On the whole, for the eleven countries with data and apart from Ivory Coat which claims the least width, four claim 12 miles, three (including Nigeria) claim 30 miles, one claims 50 miles, and the remaining two (Guinea and Sierra Leone) claim 130 and 200 miles respectively. It is also noteworthy that the issue of using straight baselines arises with three of ECOWAS countries (Guinea, Mauritania and Senegal).

Table 3. Existing claims to offshore jurisdictional stage by ECOWAS countries

S/S	Countries	Territorial Sea	Continental Shelf	Exclusive Fishing Zone
1.	Benin	12	100	12
2.	Gambia	50	?	18
3.	Ghana	30	cd	12
4.	Guinea	130	sb—	12
5.	Ivory Coast	6	200m	12
6.	Liberia	12	cd	—
7.	Mauritania	30	sb—	12
8.	Nigeria	30	csc	30 200 in 1978
9.	Senegal	12	sb; 200m	110
10.	Sierra Leone	200	csc	—
11.	Togo	12	—	12

Note: The codes on the table refer as follows: 'cd' indicates that state uses the same definition as tge (1958) convention on the continental shelf; 'sb' indicates that part of the territorial sea is measured from straight baselines; 'csc' indicates that state is signatory to the convetion on the continental shelf; the symbols ? — respectively indicate that the claim is unknown. Note als that the numerical values indicate width in nautical miles except where the addition of m signifies depth in meters.

Sources: Adaptations from J.R.V. Prescott, *The Political Geography of the Oceans,* (New York: John Wiley, 1975), pp. 226-228; Federal Republic of Nigeria, "Exclusive Economic Zone Decree 1978," *Laws of the Federal Republic of Nigeria, 1978* (Lagos: Fed. Gov. Press, 1979), pp. A259-A261.

The claims to continental shelf areas as shown on the table are not only incomplete; they also reflect the ambiguities in the convention on the continental shelf produced by the 1958 UNCLOS. Thus, while the Republic of Benin uses a distance (exploitability?) criterion and claims 100 miles for its continental shelf, two countries (Ivory Coast and Senegal) use the depth criterion and claim up to the 200 metre isobath for their continental shelf areas. And while four others either simply use the dual definition in the 1958 Convention (Ghana and Liberia) or were signatories to it (Nigeria and Sierra Leone), the remaining four have no specific information relating to the continental shelf.

The diversity in respect of the third jurisdictional zone, though less dramatic, is nevertheless remarkable. Of the nine countries with data, the majority (6) claim 12 miles and while Gambia claims 18 miles, Senegal's claim of 110 miles is by far the widest. In essence, Nigeria's claim of 30 miles up to 1978 amounted to no separated claim in respect of an EEZ since she claimed the same width for her territorial sea. (The same could also be said of Benin and Togo.) However, perhaps as a result of access to reliable information on the direction of consensus at the (then) seemingly endless UNCLOS III, Nigeria announced claims to a 200-mile wide EEZ in October 1978, the width now enshrined in the new convention.

Prior to the emergence of the new Draft Convention in 1981, the desirability of a uniform claim to off-shore jurisdictional space among ECOWAS countries had been discussed (Akintola, 1978). It now seems that the world-wide consensus on which the new convention is based would produce that uniformity. However, a truly meaningful adherence to the provisions of the convention through ratification implies a strong need for cooperation and collaborative endeavour on a wide range of legal and technical issues among ECOWAS countries.

The final part of this paper deals with the more apparent of such politico-legal and technical issues. The underlying thesis is that the wide opportunities provided for extended cooperation and collaboration by the new Convention among a group of already-cooperating states in a region should not only be recognized but should also be operationalized and institutionalised so as to provide a long-term basis for the exploration, determination, and scientific exploitation and preservation of the marine resources of the region to the mutual benefit of member states.

ECOWAS and the New Opportunities for Cooperation in Off-Shore Space

The very notion of an economic community embodies the commitment of all member states to cooperation in virtually all areas of economic activity and planning with a wide range of implications for the coordination of socio-economic and political policies. In any event, the fundamental purpose of economic integration is to bring relations among the cooperating countries as close as possible to what would obtain if those countries had been merely component parts of only one country. The implied all-embracing nature of cooperation in an economic community is even tellingly reflected in the Treaty of ECOWAS itself where its general aim is stated as that of promoting

> "cooperation and development in all fields of economic activity particularly in the fields of industry, transport, telecommunications, energy, agriculture, natural resources, commerce, monetary and financial questions and in Social and Cultural matters for the purpose of raising the standard of living of its peoples, of increasing and maintaining economic stability, of fostering closer relations among its members and of contributing to the progress and development of the African continent" (ECOWAS, 1975, Article 2 [1]).

Even in the light of this general treaty provision alone, specification of major issues for cooperation on the basis of the new Convention on the law of the sea amount essentially to providing content for an already-accepted principle.

The major issues on which formalized/institutionalized cooperation and collaboration are urged here could be grouped into two:
a) politico-legal, and
b) technical and scientific-research

Political-Legal Issues

The politico-legal issues have internal and external or bilateral dimensions. The internal dimension relates to the amendment of existing jurisdictional claims such that the claimed widths would become consistent with the provisions for the new convention. A necessary first step is for individual countries that have not ratified the convention to ratify it. Then, individual national laws should be made to reflect the widths provided for in the convention so that there would be in the whole ECOWAS region (as there should be in other coastal areas of the world), uniform and overlapping regimes of offshore jurisdictional space whose specific boundaries are set at 12 miles for the territorial area, 24 miles for the contiguous zone, 200 miles for the EEZ and 200 or 350 miles for the continental shelf, all from the baselines from which the width of the territorial seas are measured.

These internal matters of drafting and passing definitions expressing the respective widths into individual national laws should pose no difficulties once the political decision to carry them out has been taken.

In fact, the practice of legal upward adjustment of offshore jurisdictional boundaries is an exercise in which West African nations, like numerous other nations of the developing world, have considerable experience. For instance, Nigeria has increased her 3-mile territorial sea (of 1958 and 1964) to 12 miles in 1967 and then to 30 miles in 1971. Similarly, she increased her EEZ from 30 to 200 miles in 1978. Other member states of ECOWAS have effected similar upward changes at different times in the past (e.g., Gambia, three times; Ghana, two times; Guinea, once; Mauritania, three times; and Sierra Leone, twice; see Akintola, 1978; 199).

However, what is virtually unprecedented but warranted in many cases by the new convention is a downward adjustment, for instance in respect of territorial-sea widths, for countries whose existing claims exceed 12 miles. Similarly for the other jurisdictional zones. The further processes of delimiting the jurisdictional zones on maps and charts and physically marking or indicating their alignments in the Atlantic Ocean (demarcation) for purposes of functional guidance and enforcement could be done cheaper and more expeditiously on a regional or group basis established by ECOWAS acting as a single community.

Particularly related to the above and requiring at least external-bilateral (or preferably community-wide) arrangements by ECOWAS countries are the issues of *adjacency* on the other hand and that of the "opposite coast" on the other hand. The issue of adjacency concerns the alignment of the land-to-ocean boundary which sets off the off-shore jurisdictional zones of one coastal state from those of other coastal states adjacent or contiguous to them. Except where historical or special circumstances direct otherwise, the basic provision in respect of adjacent or opposite coats is to use "the median line every part of which is equidistant from the nearest points on the baselines from which the breadth of the territorial seas of each of the two states is measured" (Article 15). This would apply to the land-to-sea boundaries separating the off-shore jurisdiction zones of Nigeria and Benin, Benin and Togo, Togo and Ghana, Ghana and Ivory-Coast, Ivory Coast and Liberia, Liberia and Guinea, Guinea Bissau, Bissau and Senegal and Gambia on two fronts, and Senegal and mauritania. Of course, the community edge countries along the coast, Mauritania and Nigeria, would also have to work out their land-to-sea boundaries with the non-ECOWAS States on their flanks, Spanish Sahara on the one hand and Cameroun on the other.

The well-known border dispute between Cameroun and Nigeria vividly illustrates the type of unnecessary conflict which the ECOWAS-wide arrangement proposed here could pre-empt. (There is no space here to recall the dispute meaningfully; the reader may therefore wish to consult Ajomo's excellent paper on the subject (Ajomo, 1982; 133-144).

The most obvious opposite-coast situation in the West African sub-region involves Cape Verde whose archipelagic waters could affect the extent to which Mauritania, Senegal and Gambia could claim jurisdictional widths allowed in the new Convention. A community-wide arrangement which incorporates the principle of the median line provided in Article 15 should be capable of handling this type of situation and avoid unnecessary dissipation of national energies. The similar situation between Nigeria and Equatorial Guinea on the south-east could also be similarly handled within a bilateral arrangement.

Apart from the above issues belong more in the arena of legal arrangements and political decisions, there are others, which though intimately related, are more technical and related to scientific knowledge and research and on which ECOWAS countries could advantageously cooperate.

Technical and Scientific-Research Issues

The main technical issues relate to the use of research equipment and materials to carry out talks relating to the delimitation and functional demarcation of the limits of jurisdictional zones and even the drawing of straight baselines where necessary. Though mentioned earlier, inputs assumed by these tasks could now be more directly discussed.

The problem of using straight baselines to close off coastal indentations is probably the least complex, at least in the sense that the generally regular coastline of the ECOWAS region occasions very few instances of the need for straight baselines. nevertheless, such countries as Guinea, Mauritania and Senegal have used straight baselines from which the widths of all jurisdictional zones are measured, they are of fundamental importance. Joint ECOWAS arrangements in offshore jurisdictional matters should be such that member states requesting technical assistance in such seemingly internal matters as the establishment of straight baselines along their coasts should be able to do so freely. The need for such requests might arise from the difficulties associated with the various circumstances that could justify the use of straight baselines, the present of deep indentations reefs, fringing islands in the immediate vicinity of the coast, deltas, etc. (Articles 6-9 and 12). Practical work based on the appropriate type of expertise (which a member state may not possess) would be normally required to confront this type of task. The need for such practical tasks in relation to baselines and also in connection with delimitations of the territorial sea, the EEZ and the continental shelf is underscored by the specific requirements of the convention that the outer-limit lines (boundaries) and the lines of delimitation drawn in accordance with the articles governing each zone be shown on official charts of appropriately large scale(s) that a list of geographical coordinates of points specifying the geodetic datums could be substituted for such lines of delimitation: and that, in any event the coastal state should not only give due publicity to such charts or lists but must also deposit a copy with the United Nations Secretary-General (Articles 16, 75, 76 and 84).

It could be added that normal functional contexts within each of the jurisdictional zones as well as the needs for enforcement and control especially in relation to smuggling and piracy (Nigerian Institute of International Affairs, March/April, 1983) also underscore the desirability of functional demarcation by means of suitability waited and highly visible floats or other devices, and the procurement, use and maintenance of equipment and vessels for purposes of surveillance, patrol and related tasks. All these assume a wide array of technical requirements and different types of expertise which could be more cost-effectively organized under the auspices of a regional organization such as ECOWAS.   Most of the issues so far discussed in relation to jurisdictional limits appear relatively straight-forward as long as they remain tied to already-stated distances from the coast. One limit that does not fully conform to one stated width or distance is the continental shelf. Although the basic provision limits it to 200 miles, that limit could be exceeded (to 350 miles) where the physical continental shelf at the bottom of coastal-waters extends beyond 200 miles. Still other situations may require the use of the 2500-metre isobath and the thickness of sediments. These latter situations require reasonably accurate knowledge of submarine topography and stratigraphy in the areas concerned. They therefore call for research and specialized expertise.

The continental shelf off West Africa is characteristically narrow. An important implication of the narrowness is that the basic 200-mile width provided in the new convention could be uniformly adopted. Adopting that width would, in fact, include ocean depths which either correspond approximately to the implied geomorphic limits of the continental shelf (250-metre isobath) as is the case off eastern Nigeria, or considerably beyond (to depths of 3000 to 5000 metres), as off Lagos (Western Nigeria), Benin, Togo and particularly Ghana, Ivory Coast, and Liberia. Baselines established oceanwards of coastal islands from Sierra Leone to Guinea Bissau and even to Dakar (Senegal) would produce the same effect or accentuate it.

Besides, the basic purpose of providing for an EEZ as well as a continental-shelf area is to bring the living and mineral resources of these zones within the jurisdiction of the coastal state. Long years of dedicated research and exploration are clearly needed, in a region comprised of less developed countries, to plan and execute research, accumulate and interpret data and thereby be able to determine the types, characteristics, quantity and status of the resources available on the seabed and sub-soil as well as the superjacent waters of these two economic zones. The same considerations apply to the High seas where all nations can fish and, in conformity with the governing provisions, engage in research and other activities that are allowed and established as feasible in the "Area". The advantage of a regionally-based arrangement for collaborative research and other endeavour in these areas are therefore obvious. In fact, the convention explicitly allows for and strongly urges actualization of group or cooperative arrangements in these regards (e.g. Part VII, Section 2 on the Management and Conservation of the Living Resources of the High Seas).

The wide range of specialized expertise required to form the core of a regional organization for these purposes would include those of marine geologists, oceanographers, geographers, (especially geo-morphologists and cartographers), geologists and surveyors, fisheries experts and mineral engineers, marine conservationist/biologists, relevant international lawyers as well as others with established skills and research experience.

The Establishment of a West African Commission for Oceanographic and Marine Studies (ECOWAS): A Proposal

In view of the long-term nature and multifaceted legal, political, economic, strategic and scientific issues associated with the structural, resource and other dimensions of off-shore jurisdictional space in the West African sub-region, the establishment of a West African Commission for Oceanographic and Marine Studies (WACOMS) within the structure of ECOWAS is hereby proposed. It should not matter what the preferred name of such a commission turns out to be but its essential functions should embrace the following:

1. The continuous identification, referencing in bibliographic form, acquisition, and functional storage of relevant international, regional, national and other documents and resource materials or publications that could inform the commission or its agents o the various aspects of its responsibilities;
2. the design of a programme of research relating to and involving:
   (a) delimitation and functional demarcation of off-shore jurisdictional boundaries of the ECOWAS region;
   (b) the study of the superjacent waters of the Atlantic Ocean occurring in the

off-shore jurisdictional zones of West Africa as well as in the adjacent fishery resources as their species, geographical concentration, and peculiar depths of occurrences, breeding and reproduction cycles to harvestable status, applicable methods of exploitation (including equipments) and harvesting and conservation;

(c) the study of the seabed and subsoil of the Atlantic Ocean in the off-shore jurisdictional areas and beneath the High Seas ("the Area") adjacent to the ECOWAS region with emphasis on the topography and stratigraphy as well as living and mineral resources, the latter (resources) including appraisals featuring identification of organic species and mineral types, their geographic distributions and concentrations, feasible economic-exploitation status, and requirements or guidelines for actual optimum exploitation and conservation;

(d) The recruitment on a full-time and/or part-time bases of scientific personnel with appropriate expertise (as well as appropriate technical and other support staff) to carry out on a sustained bases the programme in 2 (a) and (b) above;

(e) the provision/procurement and maintenance of materials, equipment, crafts and vessels and other needs that might be required for the execution of the Commission's research programme and the dissemination of its results;

(f) the initiation and maintenance (to the extent necessary) of cooperation and collaboration with relevant institutions, commissions, bodies and agencies for the furtherance of the Commission's objective;

(g) the dissemination through appropriate channels of the results of the commission's research activities to all member states and relevant organizations or bodies, as such results emerge, and definitely through annual reports;

(h) the provision of advice to relevant organs of ECOWAS and member states on ascertained opportunities for the exploitation of particular resources, including whatever technical details of technology and internal-regional or international inputs or assistance that may be warranted; and

(i) that continuous review of the Commission's research programme to accommodate natural, technological, legal, scientific, economic and even political changes and developments that have significant bearings on its work;

3. the provision of technical advice that could help to resolve disagreements and conflicts relating to uses of off-shore space and resources arising between/among ECOWAS states and between an ECOWAS state and a third country, including issues relating to land-locked member states, whether in respect of access related matters or in connection with equitable shares of the "surplus" of the resources of Exclusive Economic Zones.

The establishment of the type of commission proposed would, of course, require the political, moral, legal and financial commitments of ECOWAS and its individual member states. Its status would be like that of the existing commissions of ECOWAS but its long-run benefits (deriving from its productive orientation) might even transcend those of the existing commissions. Luckily, formal obstacles to the adoption of the proposal for a West African Commission for Oceanographic and Marine Studies (WACOMS) should be minimal since the Treaty of ECOWAS has the flexibility to accommodate the proposal in its provision which states that "The Authority may from time to time establish other commissions as it deems necessary

(ECOWAS, 1975; Article 9, paragraph 2). In any event, the basic necessity and justification for a WACOMS is the multi-dimensional nature of the problems associated with off-shore jurisdictional space, the resource potentials involved, the low status of scientific knowledge relating to West African Oceanic waters and their resources, and the obvious and unnecessarily burdensome expenditure that effective unilateral arrangements would impose on any single member state.

Conclusion

This paper has essentially reviewed past and current international arrangements relating to off-shore jurisdictional boundaries and zones as well as the associated issues of resources development. In particular, the paper further covered not only the pattern of responses of West African countries to past law of the sea conventions but also and more importantly, elicited for ECOWAS countries the implications of the recent (1982) convention on the law of the sea. Especially in view of the potential economic benefits that could accrue to ECOWAS member countries and considering the impractically high expenditures and risks of conflicts that the needed applied research would impose on a member country that decides to go it alone, the establishment of a West African Commission for Oceanographic and Marine Studies (WACOMS) has been proposed.

Endnotes

1. Internal waters are regarded as part of a coastal state's land territory.
2. All references to miles in this paper denote nautical miles; one nautical mile equals 1852 metres or 1.852 km.
3. For a thorough-going account and analysis of the basic features of ECOWAS, including matters of formation, objectives, treaty provisions, trade status and other issues, see J. Ola Akintola-Arikawe, "The Economic Community of West African States (ECOWAS): Basic Features, Progress so far, Problems and Prospects", *The Nigerian Geographical Journal* Vol 25, Nos. 1 & 2, June & December, 1982, pp. 63-85. More comprehensive discussions are contained in A.S. Akinyemi, S.B. Falegan and L.A. Aluko (eds.) *Readings and Documentation on ECOWAS* (Lagos, 1983); Uka Ezenwe, *ECOWAS and the Economic Integration of West Africa*, (London, 1983).

Bibliography

Ajomo, M.A., "Protecting Nigeria's Four Sea Zones" *Nigerian Forum*, March/April (1963), pp. 1031-1037.

Ajomo, M.A., "The Nigerian/Cameroun Border Dispute: Implications at International Law", *Nigerian Current Law Review*, The Journal of the Nigerian Institute of Advanced Legal Studies, April 1982, pp. 133-144.

Akintola J.O., "Off-Shore Resource Zones and ECOWAS States: Need for Uniform Claims", Proceedings of the International Geographical Union: *Resources and Development in Africa*, edited by J.S. Oguntoyinbo, et al. (Lagos, Nigeria, 1978), Vol. II, pp. 222-227.

Akintola, J.C., "Nigeria's Territorial Sea: Evolution and Need for Expansion", *The Nigerian Geographical Journal*, Vol. 22, No. 2 (December, 1979), pp. 193-208; also in *Centrepoint* Vol. 2, 1, pp. 1-24.

Akintola-Arikawe, J.O., "The Economic Community of West African States (ECOWAS): basic features, progress so far, problems and prospects", *The Nigerian Geographical Journal*, Vol. 25, Nos. 1 & 2, (June & December, 1982), pp. 63-85.

Business Times (Nigeria) "UN Law of the Sea Conference Trying for a Conclusion", Tuesday, September 5, 1978, p. 5.

Dean, Arthur H., "The Geneva Conference on the Law of the Sea: What was Accomplished". *Amer. J. of International Law*, Vol. 52, No. 4, (October, 1958), pp. 607-628.

De Blij, H.J., *Systematic Political Geography* 2nd Edit. (New York: John Wiley, 1973).

Federal Republic of Nigeria, "Exclusive Economic Zone Decree 1978" *Laws of the Federal Republic of Nigeria, 1978.* (Lagos: Federal Government Press, 1979) pp. A259-A261.

Hedberg, Hollis D., "Ocean floor boundaries: the base-of-slope boundary zone formula gives the most acceptable jurisdictional limit for mineral resources", *Science,* 13 April 1979, Vol. 204, No. 4389, pp. 135-144.

Kerr, Adam J., (1980) "Mapping and Charting Marine Resources: Cartography and the Law of the Sea", Chairman, Commission on Oceanic Cartography, Canadian Hydrographic Service, Bedford Institute of Oceanography, P.O. Box 1006, Dartmouth, Nova Scotia, Canada, (mimeographed).

Nigerian Institute of International Affairs, *Nigerian Forum:* The issue of smuggling and coastal piracy in Nigeria, March/April, 1963.

Onitiri, H.M.A., "Towards a West African Economic Community" *The Nigerian J. of Econ. and Social Studies,* Vol. 5, No. 1, (1963), pp. 27-51.

Prescott, J.V.R., *The Political Geography of the Oceans* (New York: John Wiley, 1975).

Strahler, A.N. and A.H. Strahler, *Elements of Physical Geography,* 2nd Edit. (New York: John Wiley, 1979).

United Nations, *Third Conference on the Law of the Sea: Informal Composite Negotiating Text/Revision 2,* Nineth Session, New York, 3 March-4 April 1980, A/CONF.62/WP. 10/Rev. 2, 11 April 1980, Original: English.

United Nations, *Third Conference on the Law of the Sea: Draft Convention on the Law of the Sea,* Resumed Tenth Session, Geneva, 3-28 August 1981, A/OOBF.62/L.78, 28th August 1981, Original: English.

United Nations, *Third United Nations Conference on the Law of the Sea: United Batuibs Conventions on the Law of the Sea* A/OONF.62/122, 7 October 1982, Original: Arabic, Chinese, English, Russian, Spanish, (82-30296).

Whiteman, Margorie, "Conference on the Law of the Sea: Convention on the Continental Shelf" *Amer. J. of International Law,* Vol. 52, No. 4 (Oct. 1958), pp. 629-659.

CHAPTER 23

The Political Economy of Artificial Boundaries

by O. Akintola-Bello

The paper attempts an economic analysis of some of the problems that arise from the existence of artificial boundaries in Africa. The approach adopted is related to studies of the economics of criminal activity as, for example, in the paper by Becker (1968). Though the objective is to show how economic analysis can be used to formulate appropriate policy prescriptions for the control of such externalities as illegal trade across the border, the immigration of unauthorized aliens and criminals, the problem of tax evasion and, most importantly, the development of border regions, it is also the intention to demonstrate that because of the special characteristics of the border areas, routine economic analysis may be of limited value.

Hansen (1981) has shown for example that international trade theory is not well adapted for explaining the problems of border regions, for the "phenomena neglected in trade theory are in fact the key elements in any serious considerations of the problems of border regions". In much the same way, the economic methodology employed in the paper offers an insight into the understanding of some of the economic problems occasioned by the artificiality of boundaries; the policy implications for an economically rational solution lie in the realm of political economy. In other words, solutions lie beyond the realms of economics but in political and social arrangements which allow the internalisation of some of the international externalities.

The analysis of the problems of border regions is approached through an examination of two recent case studies on the problem and other anecdotal evidences. Collins on the Nigeria-Niger border (1976/1984) and Phiri on Zambia-Malawi-Mozambique borders (1984) provide examples of smuggling and tax evasion in cross-border movements which demonstrate that the type of economy prevailing within the border regions disobeys the national laws of the countries concerned. Moreover, the special characteristics of the border regions and the economic policies pursued by the government of the two neighbouring states, provide the necessary conditions for the existence of illegal-transactions in goods and currency and other negative externalities. The questions of interests are: What are the special features of the boundary regions? What economic conditions in the neighbouring states give rise to the clandestine movements of goods and people? What policy implications emerge from such an analytical framework, and what are its limitations? And finally, what other policy options exist?

The Artificiality of Boundaries

Asiwaju (1984) provides a working definition of artificial boundaries by emphasizing the exclusiveness or divisive functions assigned by man. According to him, "all boundaries are artificial as long as the purpose and ultimate function is to divide and separate lands and people within definable eco-systemic entities." Accordingly, all nation-state boundaries are artificial by these abstractions such as mathematically defined lines, circles of arcs or natural relief features such as rivers, lakes or mountains. As to the definition of borderlands, Hansen (1981) has made a useful offer. According to him, border regions (his own label for borderlands) are 'sub-national areas whose economic and social life is directly and significantly affected by proximity to an international boundary.' Therefore, these special regions of Africa created as a result of inter-colonial boundary negotiations of the era of the Scramble and Partition form the subject-matter of this analysis. However, despite the arbitrariness and the artificiality of the colonial boundaries, these boundaries have been accepted as legal definitions of the territorial frameworks of the post-colonial national-states. Moreover, the boundaries are "largely unpatrolled and unpatrollable and have little consensual or physical reality at the local level" (Collins, 1984). Consequently, they serve not as boundaries "but as an inter-state pathway, a conduit an incentive for the movement of goods and people, especially where there is economic disparity between the neighbouring states.

One important economic consequence of the existence of artificial boundaries is the cross-boundary movements and activities which are extra-legal, including especially the smuggling of goods. The identical, cultural environment prevailing on either side of the prescribed boundaries provides a general cover under which these clandestine cross-border takes place. These cross-border movements and activities often take place at the expense of the one or the other of the neighbouring states. These negative effects manifest themselves in the loss of revenues and foreign exchange earnings. These aspects of cross-border trade are well documented.

Economic Policies in Neighbouring States: A Case Study of the Clandestine Movement of Groundnuts Across the Nigeria-Niger Boundary

In spite of the existence of the boundaries, inhabitants of the various culture areas have maintained across the boundaries socio-economic relations. One factor which has also enhanced such relations, particularly in the economic sphere, is the economic policies pursued by the neighbouring states. Collins study of the Nigeria-Niger cross-border groundnut trade shows that 'the principal factors influencing a farmer's decision to cross the border to sell his groundnuts is the offer of a better price at markets on the other side'. The existence of price advantages or relative price differentials determines the direction and size of the cross-border groundnut flows. Another factor is the proximity of the buying stations. The buying stations were most heavily concentrated in the border areas of Magaria district in Niger. Collins argues that in spite of the intimidating presence of price patrols and enforcement procedures in particular areas, the relatively large prices differences will bring about relatively large movements of groundnuts across the border.

For example, in the 1969/70 groundnut buying season, the producer price for groundnuts at markets in Niger was estimated to be 20-50 percent higher than that offered at competing markets across the border in Nigeria. As a result, producers and middlemen buyers from Nigeria regularly brought donkey-loads of groundnuts to sell at Nigeria's border markets.

> These sellers from Nigeria would be paid the fixed price of 2,000 CFA Francs per 100 kilos of shelled groundnuts, ... with their newly-acquired franc notes, they would next go to one of the several money changers in the market and buy cheap Nigerian pounds.... These farmers would then return home to Nigeria having received at least $4 per 100 kilos of ground-nuts sold, instead of the $2.70 to $3.30 being offered for an equal weight across the border in Nigeria.

Similarly, there were middlemen buyers from Niger, financed by private groundnut-buying companies operating in Niger, coming to Nigeria to buy groundnuts and then returning to sell them at markets in Niger.

The active involvement of the government of Niger was a determinant of the existence of the relative price differential. The Niger governments's top priority was to maintain a competitive producer price vis-a-vis Nigeria. This position was dictated by two major factors, one of which is the economic importance of groundnut in Niger's economy. An average of 60 per cent of Niger's foreign earnings was derived from the export of groundnut crops. The second factor dictating Niger's competitive strategy derived from the structure of French foreign aid tied to the export of groundnuts. The offer of higher-than-world-market prices plus the guaranteed market for most of the groundnut exports by France influenced Niger's government incentive to manipulate cross-border groundnut movement.

The effect of the French price support for Niger's groundnuts was to offset Nigeria's natural competitive advantage resulting from lower transport costs to the European market. These factors culminated in the establishment of a government-owned groundnut marketing corporation along the lines of the marketing board system in Nigeria. And through government decrees, uniform producer prices were set annually. The Niger government explicitly used its producer price-setting powers to manipulate the movement of groundnuts across the southern boundary with Nigeria. However, the end-result of Niger's borders markets was not only to ensure the flow of groundnuts from Nigeria to Niger, but also to ensure that ground-nuts grown in Niger stayed in Niger.

On the other side of the border, Nigeria policy of maintaining artificially low producer prices from 1960 through the 70s contributed to Niger's success in manipulating the movement of groundnuts across its long and porous southern boundary with Nigeria. In any case, the earnings derived from groundnuts constituted a relatively minor proportion of total export earnings unlike in Niger, hence the relative indifference of the Marketing Board officials to cross-border groundnut movements and its impact on the Nigeria economy.

These factors provide explanation for Niger's successful competitive strategy for border area groundnuts. Nigeria's economic response to the outflow of groundnuts took the form of (i) increased police patrols along the border, (ii) and increase in producer price plus the elimination of all export and produce tax on crops and (iii) negotiation with Niger to establish a uniform producer price. The economic effects of these measures on Nigeria's economy and on the size and direction of cross-border flows are yet to materialise but these are continuing.

Border Economy and the Incentive to Smuggle

In the last two sections, the analysis has focused on the economic problems of the border regions and the influence of government policies on cross-border flows of goods and people. The existence of cross-border movements of goods have been explained in terms of relative price differential. Price advantage, it is argued, determines the direction of cross-border flows while the size of the price differential between competing border markets determines the magnitude of cross-border trade flows. It has also been that a relatively large price difference, even in the presence of intimidating police patrols will usually bring relatively large movements of across-the-border trade flows. Similarly, the existence of close kinship ties and government policies have also been adduced for the existence of cross-border movements. While these explanations have merits, they are in themselves inadequate for explaining the supply of illegal trade across the border. Yet an adequate understanding is necessary to enable the society identify the variables which can be manipulated in an effort to control illegal trade across the border. yet an adequate understanding is necessary to enable the society identify the variables which can be manipulated in an effort to control illegal trade flows. A model of the supply of illegal activities across the border is necessary.

To fully appreciate the supply of illegal activities across the border, one must look beyond the existence of profit and close kingship ties. The unpatrollable nature of the border regions affects the probability of being apprehended. Asides, the potential offender can be expected to respond to the expected utility of a two-state choice: the expected utility if caught and the expected utility if not apprehended. Added to this is the active involvement (though indirect) of government of at least one of the two neighbouring states in encouraging the incentive to engage in cross-border illegitimate activities. This factor affects the probability of detection with important policy implications.

The second important factor, often overlooked, is the nature of the economy of the border states. There are two forces at play here. One is that most border states are characterised by a situation where there is relative disparity in the state of economic development—a direct consequence of the artificiality of boundaries (for example, the existence of customs barriers, failure to take advantage of the complementarity of their natural resources). The existence of such factors always creates an incentive for the supply of cross-border clandestine movements. The second force has to do with the fact that the economies of most border regions are market-oriented economics where government restrictions upon economic activity are pervasive. The all-embracing nature of the regulation of economic activities by government almost always gives rise to a variety of forms of illegal income-generating activities such as bribery, corruption, smuggling and black markets. There is always competition for this illegal income. An example is import restriction and the allocation of import licenses for controlled consumer commodities. In fact, government officials themselves receive part of this illegal income.

Of immediate relevance to the problem of illegal trade flows across artificial boundaries is the people's perception of the economic system. If income distribution is viewed as the outcome of a lottery where wealthy individuals are successful (or lucky) illegal income seekers, whereas the poor are those precluded from or unsuccessful in illegal income generation, the market mechanism is bound to be suspect. Where it is difficult to associate rewards with social product, and where the market mechanism is suspect because it is perceived as a mechanism for rewarding the rich and well-connected, the inevitable temptation is to resort to greater illegal income-generating activity hence the amount of resources devoted to this form of economic activity is thereby increased. While the two factors have important policy implications this analysis will concentrate on the first: the incentive to smuggle or the supply of illegitimate activities across the border, while only the policy implications of the second factor will be explored in this paper.

The decision to engage in illegitimate activities is taken under uncertainty. This is because involvement in illegal trade does not automatically mean that he will be penalised. There are two choices open to the individual: (1) engage in legal trade, (2) engage in illegal trade. Assuming he chooses the second strategy his pay off will depend on whether or not he is caught. If not, he is clearly better off than under strategy 1 (assuming of course that the income from illegal trade exceeds that from legitimate activity). If he is, he is worse off. The choice confronting the individual is therefore a non-trivial one. To simplify the analysis, let us assume that the individual's utility function diminishes with increases in income, and has income as its only argument.

Marginal utility is assumed to be everywhere positive and strictly decreasing, so that the individual is risk averse. Now assume that the outcome is uncertain and that the rewards from illegal border trade and not being caught are different from those of being caught and punished. There are two possibilities: the offender is caught and punished (ii) the offender is not caught and therefore not punished.

The analysis starts off with the assumption that illegal cross border trade is a negative externality which must be controlled. The larger the volume of illegal cross-border trade the greater the cost imposed on the economy. The benefit to the offender also depends on the amount of time or resources devoted to it and the rewards of illegitimate activities. The expected utility from cross-border illegal activity exceeds the utility he could get by using his time and other resources as other activities. There must be a relationship between the probability of capture and punishment, the weight of the punishment and the income available from legal and in illegal activities, on the one hand, and the volume of illegal cross-border trade.

Let $V_C = f(P_i J_i U)$

Where V_C =Volume or magnitued of cross-border illegal trade flows.

   P=Probability of capture and punishment and $1-P$ is the probability of
      non-capture

   J=Punishment if convicted (monetary value)

   U=An umbrella term representing all other influences.

The individual will choose to maximise his expected utility from illegal activity:

$E(U) = pU(Y-J) + (i-P)(Y)$ (2)

   Y is the individual's income and is made up of (income from illegale activity) and Y_L income from legal activity

   U=untility function

   J=monetary equivalent of the punishment

Alternatively, if we let $Y_C + Y_L - J = R_a$ i.e. the return if caught and $R_b = Y_L$ as the return if not caught, the expected utility can be expressed as

$E(U) = pU(R_a) + (1-P)U(R_b)$ (3)

Where U(R) represents the utility of income function. Equations 2 or 3 says that the utility expected from engaging in illegal trade is equal to the sum of the utilities of the two states weighted by their probabilities.[1]

Assuming the objective is to discourage the volume or level of cross-border illegal activities, what is expected from the analysis is to manipulate one or more of the variables on which the supply of illegitimate activities depends. These variables are P, J, Y_C and Y_L. A priori, one expects that increases in P, J and Y_L would lower the level or the magnitude of cross-border illegal trades flows as would decreases in Y_C. An increase in P or J would reduce the utility expected from cross-border movement and hence the magnitude of cross-border movements[2] i.e.: The incomes from illegitimate transactions Y_C must exceed Y_L the legitimate income if there is to be any attraction in illegal trade to balance the penalty if caught. And If J, the monetary weight of punishment were to be less than the difference between Y_C, the reward from illegal activity and Y_L, the reward from legitimate activity, ie. J. $Y_C - Y_L$, there will be more cross-border illegal trade flows even if the probability of capture is 100 per cent (i.e. P=1) since the marginal differential reward from illegal trade flows across the boundary outweighs the value of punishment. In fact the expected value of the punishment, P^J, must be less than the marginal differential reward from illegal trade for an individual to participate in illegitimate activities.

The behaviourial model analyzed above will suggest that the focus of policy should be to increase the certainty of detection or the probability of being caught. When the probability of capture is increased, the magnitude of illegal trade flows can be reduced. The model's implications provide a rationale for the current view that heavy police patrols along the border may be the answer, rather than increased punishment. But the extent of policing the border depends on the amount of resources required. Policing a porous border would be enormously expensive, hence complete policing is costly. The cost of limitation of policing an arbitrary boundary places an effective limit on the attempts to forestall and detect cross-border illegal activities. The increase in resources devoted to policing a porous border will not necessarily manifest itself an increase in punishments, even though the probability of success of an illegitimate activity is decreasing function of the amount of expenditure undertaken by society to prevent and punish the crime. If the scale of policing and enforcement is correct, society should not be spending two naira to save itself one naira of damage. The relevant question then is whether the magnitude of cross-border illegal trade would fall by a naira if a naira more were spent on enforcement costs. There are other factors already analyzed which render in effect the policy of policing the border.

With the model's implication that illegal cross border trade may be a response to opportunity, the relative disparity in economic growth of the two border states suggest that one solution lies in creating better economic opportunities in the border states. This implies operating on Y_C and Y_L to reduce the gap between the two variables. Inter-governmental cooperation will be required to increase Y_L and reduce Y_C. Reduction of Y_C will in fact involve the redistribution of wealth between the border regions, as well as other measures aimed at developing the economy of the border regions. Current policies aimed at tinkering with the price mechanism—price harmonisation, and competitive producer price responses— would be effective if the barriers were not artificial and the borders can be effectively policed. Such measures are short-term measures, dictated by a more limited view of national self-interest.

Moreover, the all-embracing nature of government restrictions of economic activities in the border patrols and customs officials creates further distortions of the economies of the border regions.

Perhaps a more permanent solution lies in the creation of special development areas along the border regions with the active cooperation of the neighbouring states. The special Areas can be effectively managed by a Joint Commission that will be given the task of harnessing the complementary natural resources of the two borders states. The recent moves towards integration in Africa may provide an economic umbrella for the recognition of 'special development areas' across shared boundaries. The problems posed by the border areas and the issues analyzed in this paper poses further questions for research and policy analysis. For example, how can inter-governmental cooperation in the border regions increase Y_L and help reduce Y_C? How can wealth be redistributed between the 'zones' of overdevelopment in the border regions? Are customs barriers practicable between artificially separated neighbouring states sharing close kinship ties? Are increases in enforcement efforts and costs the solution to cross-border flow of goods and people? It is hoped that this analysis will yield some insight into the structure of the problem and raise relevant questions for further research.

Bibliography

A.I. Asiwaju (ed.), *Partitioned Africans: Ethnic Relations Across Africa's International Boundaries 1884-1984* (London: C. Hurst and Co. and Lagos: Univ. of Lagos Press, 1984).

G.S. Becker, "Crime and punishment: an economic approach", *Journal of Political Economy* 76, pp. 169-217.

D. Collins, "The clandestine movement of groundnuts across the Niger-Nigeria boundary" *The Canadian Journal of African Studies,* X, 2, 1976, pp. 259-276. Also reprinted in Asiwaju (ed), op. cit.

I. Ehrlich, "Participation in illegitimate activities: a theoretical and empirical investigation" *Journal of Political Economy,* 1973.

S.H. Phiri, National Integration, Rural Development and Frontier Communities: The Case of the Chewa and the Ngoni; Astride Zambian Boundaries with Malawi and Mozambique.

G.J. Stigler, "Optimum Enforcement of Laws" *Journal of Political Economy* 1970.

N. Hansen, *The Border Economy: Regional Development in the Southwest* (Austin: Univ. of Texas Press, 1981).

CHAPTER 24

Transborder Data Flow
and
Action Plan for ECOWAS

by Olayide Abass

Introduction

Telematics, which is the integration of digital computer technology with communication technology, has made it possible to transmit numbers, texts, voice and full colour video images as packets of data at ultra-high speeds. Progress in data communication and computer networks has made the telematics networks omnipresent. They can be used for processing and transmission of neutral, commercial, economic and environmental data.

With the use of telematics networks, distant data banks can be accessed interactively and at ultra high speeds. These new technologies have exponentially increased the capabilities of developed countries to acquire data about themselves as well as developing countries.

It is not only in the field of communication and data transmission that computers have affected our ways in life. Information has had impact on nearly all human enterprises. For a very long time, computers will continue to play dominant roles in the way we do business, organise our data, store and manipulate them However, just like nuclear fusion, computers have begun to create new social problems. One of these problems relates to what experts have come to regard as Transborder Data Flows (TDF).

Transborder data flows raise issues of privacy of an individual as well as security and sovereignty of nation. It has economic, social and legal dimensions. In order to underscore the importance of transborder data flows, it is necessary to briefly describe the types of information and data that are transmitted and/or accessed with telematics   networks.

Types of Data Flow

Neutral Data: This can be described as the data that do not affect its country's political or economic security. They are usually freely exchanged.

Examples are bibliographical information, scientific and technical literature.

Very many of international databases in agriculture, industry, energy, social indications and human resources fall into this category. By 1984, it was estimated that there were over 2000 on-line data bases on operation. Of this figure about 900 were bibliographical on-line data bases, a very small percentage of which was in the developing countries (Slatter, 1984).

Bibliographical data bases serve simply as store houses of human knowledge and experience. Progress of individuals or nations and the general advancement of human knowledge depend on accessibility to these data bases. It is therefore important that all nations of the world have access to them.

Commercial Data Flows: Commercial data flow relates to information exchanged in business transactions, banking, insurance, transportation, electronic funds transfer, electronic mails, airline passenger reservation system, and so on. There are over 1000 computer networks currently in existence that provide transborder data flow services i these areas. many of these networks are owned by multinational cooperations. They are used by the multinationals to exchange information between their headquarters and subsidiaries. Examples of such computer-communication network are SITA (Societe Internationale Telecommunications Aeronaitiques) and SWIFT (Society for World-wide Interbank Financial Telecommunications).

Commercial data are vital for running international business and corporate operations. The stock market in London is now linked by Computer network to that in the USA and Japan. It is possible to watch on a Computer Screen in London how stock prices change instantaneously in Tokyo.

Environmental Data Flow: These data relate to information about the natural resources of a country. Such data are obtained from terrestrial, aerial and oceanographic surveys, radar images and satellite remote sensing methods. Meterological and seismologically data are useful for predicting natural calamities and disasters; they are used for weather forecast. As more elaborately discussed elsewhere in this book, remote sensing data help in land use classification, mineral exploration, detection of cropping diseases; study of cropping pattern.

Economic Data Flow: This relates to exchange of information about technical and manufacturing processes. It also concerns international trade, international informatics products and data services. Even though there has been a world-wide economic recession, trade in informatics products has been on the increase. In 1984, it was estimated that the value of trade in informatics products amounted to U.S. $150 million, 50% of which was accounted for by trade in data services and data communication.

In Nigeria, we have been spending every year, since the inception of JAMB (Joint Admission and Matriculation Board), over 1,000,000 naira annually to process examination results externally. The production of 1983 election voter's list was done externally at a very huge cost by a British firm. Foreign oil firms operating in Nigeria do gather and process outside of the country large volume of data on oil reserves, exploration, development production and marketing activities. Processed data are held in data banks out of reach of anybody in this country.

The Issues Involved

Four most important issues clearly emerge from the four types of data flows that have been identified. These are related to both technological and economic question as well as to issues of sovereignty, national security and privacy of the individual.

Technology: The problem by neutral data flows is technological: namely that of standardization of equipment and protocols for data communications. For us to benefit in the sharing of accumulated experiences and human knowledge generated over the years, we must have very good, efficient and reliable communication facilities. These are the necessary infrastructures on which computer networks can strive.

Economics: Even though the concept of information as an economic quantity has been receiving attention of scholars (Emery, 1969), the impact of informatics on data communications has been in the need to refocus on information as a resource of the same importance as power and energy or any other type of precious natural resource. Besides, it is unique in the sense that through the process of instantaneous upgrading, informatics is inexhaustible unlike other natural resources. A country's ability to compete in international business is eminently enhanced if it has means to acquire information. Nigeria does not know how long her oil reserves will last, just as Ghana cannot foretell the capacity of her gold deposit. Yet these vital pieces of information are safely stores in some computer data banks somewhere in Europe or in the United States of America.

Sovereignty and National Security

By far the most bewildering problem caused by transborder data flow is associated with sovereignty and national security. Commercial and environmental data flows have political implications and raise issues of national security. The use of Computer networks and other modern data communication facilities have eliminated the artificial land boundaries between nations. They have turned the globe into an open book. According to Kirby, Chairman Australia Law Review Commission, ...informatics poses fundamental questions for the legal concept of sovereignty because a most valuable and potent force is suddenly release from physical adherence to a particular jurisdiction..." (Kirby, 1984). To illustrate this point, let us consider the operation of electronic message system: The electronic messages are generated in one country. They are switched to other countries. They are transmitted further to the countries. The messages are stored in other countries entirely. They involve persons and entities resident in another place (Fishman, 1981).

At present there are no agreed international regulations on such transactions. Such a transaction connecting several jurisdictions, therefore, raises a number of dangers. Countries may impose different incompatible municipal laws on transborder data flows that are difficult if not impossible to reconcile. Some countries may provide no laws. This may lead to such countries becoming "data havens" just as we now have tax haven countries. It may even lead to situations where transnational corporation may take over, provide laws and dictate to nations and consequently undermine the security of such nations.

Privacy Protection

In the USA and Western Europe, there are "data protection and data security" laws. These laws protect the privacy of the individual. They also give the individual right of access of most of the data about himself or herself. However with the transborder data flow such protection and right of access, central to the privacy legislation, may not be enforceable in a foreign state. The right to correction of false or outdated or irrelevant information may not be enforceable if the information is held beyond the jurisdiction of a single state. Thus has emerged a variety or range of new criminal phenomena—info-fraud, computer fraud, concerning intellectual property and other business transactions.

These and other social problems have lead many intergovernmental organisations and non-governmental international organisations in the last few years to focus attention on finding solutions to the problems that have arisen as a result of increased telematics networks.

Foremost among these organisations is Intergovernmental Bureau for Information (IBI). IBI has organised two international Conferences on transborder data flows. One was held in 1980 in Rome, and the other was held in 1984 at the same venue. The proceedings of these Conferences will provide very useful materials on the subject. Other organisations that have shown concern are the International Telecommunications Union (ITU), the Consultative Committee on Telephones and Telgraphs (CITT), United Nations Educational, Scientific and Cultural Organisations (UNESCO), the United Nations Centre for Transnational Corporations (UNCTC), the Organisation for Economic Co-operation and Development (OECD), the Economic Commission for Europe (ECE), the Commission of European Communities (CEC) and the United Nations Commission on International Trade Law (UNCITL).

Action Plan

From the contributions to the on-going debates on transborder data flows with reference to the nature, scope and variety of problems posed, it is very clear that no quick universal solutions can be obtained. The informatised countries of the North have proposed the principle of free flow of information. This, in effect, means that access to data should be unrestricted by any form of regulation; that a nation's access to data should only be restricted by that country's technological capacity. This position is obviously expected as it is the interest of their transnational corporations who, as pointed out earlier, dominate transactions in all the four types of data flows. It also facilitates the grip these corporations have on the economies of developing countries.

The challenge with particular reference to the Western African sub-region cannot be met within the narrow framework of the individual national states. The suggested action plan for West African Countries is, therefore, a regional approach. Luckily, there is already in place the necessary institutional base, the Economic Community for West African States (ECOWAS), for implementing this. ECOWAS should establish a body of experts that will look into the problems (technological, economic, national sovereignty and security etc.) posed by the TDF.

The body should, among others, include:

i) Informaticians (computer scientists) of the sub-region.
ii) International lawyers, with expertise in resolution of legal conflicts, copy right and intellectual property.
iii) Telecommunication experts.

The body should take a systems view of all the issues raised as well as other relevant issues and provide a regional framework for cooperation in resolving the issues. Ideally a convention should be prepared for signature and ratification by member states. in carrying out its assignment, the body should seek assistance from IBI, which has considerable experience on TDF issues. UNESCOs Intergovernmental Informatics Programme (IIP) is another body that can be contacted. Fortunately, nearly all members of ECOWAS are members of IBI and, of course, UNESCO.

This regional approach has been adopted in other parts of the world. For instance, Canada, and the USA started informatics talks in the fall of 1983; Grant Representatives of Latin American Countries who are members of IBI met in Buenos Aires in May 1984 on Transborder Data Flows and made the following declarations:

1. To recommend that Latin American national Authorities should undertake action leading to international cooperation, either by creating national organisations or by remission of special functions to already existing national organisations, in order to study and implement specific programmes on Transborder Data Flows.

2. To encourage harmonization of all international actions and policies on informatics, so that informatics may be rightly regarded as *Mankind Heritage,* having as a role the respect of nations' security and sovereignty and the respect of individual privacy.

3. To promote interchange and integration in the specific area of data transmission network technology, in order to achieve, within the framework of either regional organisations or of bilateral corporations, an independent and coherent development.

4. To fully support the programme on this subject, which is being developed by IBI: and to recommend to this organisation to undertake all necessary efforts leading to its implementation.

Similarly, Council of Europe has been working on TDF and associated issues since the 1970s (Early, 1984). A Convention drafted by a committee of experts was elaborated and opened for signature in January 1981. The process of signing and ratifying the convention is still on.

Two points are clearly demonstrated by now:

i) Other regions of the world have adopted approaches similar to the one proposed here and these similar approaches have produced useful results.

ii) The problems posed by TDF require urgent attention; they cannot be ignored because computers are here to stay. We should therefore start to tackle the problems now before they become more complex.

While individual member states of ECOWAS may initiate—as a first step—independent legislations on data protection and data security, harmonisation and integration and integration of control and development at the level of the entire subregion must be kept constantly in mind.

Bibliography

Emery J.C., *Organisation of Planning and Control Systems* (New York: Macmillan, 1979).

Fishman, Testimony of W.L. Fishman, United States Banking Sub-committee on International Finance and Monetary Policy, 9 Nov. 1981, pp. 10-11.

IBI (1980), Final Proceedings Rome, No. 8.

IBI (1984), TDF 260, Rome.

Kesler, V., "Legal Blueprint for Transborder Data Flow Cooperation" in Proceedings of 2nd World Conference on Transborder Data Flow Policies (1984). TDF 260 Rome 171-180.

Kirby, M.D., "The morning star of information law and the need for a greater sense of urgency" Proceedings of 2nd World Conference on Transborder Data Flow Policies (1984): TDF 260, Rome, pp. 81-101.
Slatter, A., "Prospects and implications of transborder data flows for developing countries" Proceeding of 2nd World Conference on Transborder Data Flow Policies (1984): TDF 260, Rome, pp. 112-121.

CHAPTER 25

The Role of Communication in Border Relations

by Idowu Sobowale

Human beings abhor encroachment on their spheres of influence, whether these be territorial, economic, political, social or even psychological will matter little. They often will resist disregard for what they "legitimately" consider their right. Such resistance can assume a violent proportion if what Imobighe calls 'Relative Attraction' (RA)[1] of the issue at stake is high and the Available Resources (AR) to defend it or fight for it is greater for the claim to their territory or to fight for it, people may choose open confrontation if the relative advantage is sufficiently high.

The desire to have more of what he has and to take that which belongs to his neighbour, if it is possible, leads man to infringe on the rights of others.

These conflicting, though fundamental, attitudes and behaviours, sometimes explain in part, why human beings, in their interpersonal, inter-communal, inter-ethnic, interstate and international relationships, lock horns in seemingly ceaseless conflicts.

Africa has had more than a fair share of border conflicts. Imobighe has listed conflicts which exclude intra-national disputes.[2] Any history book on any part of Africa is replete with accounts of border clashes which were waged by communities, ethnic groups and nations.[3] Indeed, the history of African states will seem incomplete without adequate accounts of the exploits of various communities of territorial supremacy.

Communication or the lack of it has always played a decisive role in creating conflicts. It has similarly played a major role in bringing about resolution of these conflicts. With such a vital role assigned to communication in creating and resolving conflicts, what then do we mean when we speak of communication as an instrument in conflict generation and conflict resolution?

The word "communication" is so ubiquitous that its meaning is always lost on those who use it. According to Wilbur Schramm, communication is shared meanings.[4] When codes employed in sending a given message evoke a dissimilar response from what the sender intends, then, communication has not taken place. For communication to take place, the same symbols must elicit similar responses in both the sender and the receiver of a message. Often, non-appreciation of this small but important aspect of communication is the cause of misunderstanding which sometimes results in conflicts. How often does communication affect border conflicts?

This paper now proceeds to discuss specific ways communication in general and mass communication in particular, through its various media, influences border conflicts and how it contributes to solving border problems. Apart from the traditional role of education, informing, and interpreting for people the circumstances/situations/events surrounding border disputes, the mass media, through which the business of communication is conducted these days, can act in five other ways to promote clashes or bring an end to such clashes.

The mass media can act as:

     i. distributing agents;
    ii. facilitating agents;
   iii. magnifying agents;
   iv. mitigating agents; and
    v. mediating agents.

Media as Distributing Agents

Perhaps the best known function of the mass media is that of information dissemination. News stories, including those of border conflicts, travel fast around the world as a result of the activities of five major international news agencies, mainly located in the industrialised countries of the world. These are Reuters, located in Britain; Associated Press (AP) and the United Press International (UPI), both in the United States of America; Agence France Passe (AFP), based in Paris; and TASS, based in the Soviet Union. There are a few continental as well as national news agencies such as Pan African News Agency (PANA), Press Trust of India (PTI), International Press Services (IPS), and News Agency of Nigeria (NAN). These lesser agencies enter into cooperation agreements with the five from the technologically more advanced nations of the world to facilitate dissemination of news across countries. Together, these news agencies of the world help to bring humanity into one compact world, "every part within easy reach of the other."

As these media distribute news of progress about peoples and nations they also distribute news of conflicts among the various groups and nations of the world. They tell us what individuals or groups of people are thinking and or thinking about; they tell us something about their feelings, attitudes and actions. Thus, they assist us to know of trouble spots throughout the world the same way they help us to know and appreciate the giant strides that people make across the world.

Perhaps what this knowledge function of the media does to human beings is to help them to assess situation, take positions for and against those situation, use information at their disposal to predict the environment in which they live and mobilise against eventualities.

The present writer has noted elsewhere that the mass media perform a significant role as carriers of information among the countries and within nations.[5] They assist people in contiguous geographical locations to monitor activities around their boundaries and to map out strategies for protecting their individual and national interests. The role of the mass media in this regard cannot be over-emphasised. For example, it was through the mass media that the Nigerian population learnt in 1981 that Camerounian gendarmes had invaded Ikang in Cross River State and killed five Nigerian soldiers. It was the mass media that informed Nigerians in 1982 that a

Camerounian "occupation army" threatened 16 Nigerian villages in Borno State.

The mass media alerted the nation to the danger posed to Nigerians by the "invasion" of the country by Chadian soldiers through the border between Chad and Nigeria in 1983. Through the activities of the media, particularly the press and television, Nigerians became aware of illegal routes through which Nigerian oil and other essential commodities were being smuggled to neighbouring Africa countries.[6]

Mass Media as Facilitating Agents

Although the myth of an all-persuasive effectiveness of the mass media was debunked more than three decades ago,[7] recent works in the field of mass communication research inform us that the mass media still play a dominant role in assisting members of the public to order their priorities.[8] Evidence exists to suggest that there is a strong correlation between what the media feature and what the people consider important enough to engage their attention. We also know that people expose themselves to mass media messages deliberately and choose what they want to read, listen to or watch purposively.[9]

This influence of the media, though limited, forcefully puts the mass media forward as the most powerful agency for placing border conflicts on national and international agenda. The emphasis and the slant placed on the conflict between two communities within a state, or between two states within a country, for example, Imo and Cross River States in Nigeria, whose proximate villages seem locked in perpetual border clashes, or between one country and another, as in the case of Ghana and Togo, Liberia and Sierra Leone; or Cameroun and Nigeria, to a great extent determines whether or not people will attach importance to that conflict and discuss it. It may mean all the difference between escalating that conflict or localising it. Hoffman puts it succinctly when he states that mass media "bring the world within instant sight and sound."[10] In other words, the media make events salient and relevant.[11]

As a result of the pervasive presence of the media everywhere, and their ability to force on our agenda of public issues the going-ons around and beyond us, people are inundated daily with reports of conflicts and the factors giving rise to them. Though the media may not be able to force people to engage in violent clashes with their neighbours, they can compel people to think about the possibilities of encroachment on their territorial rights, physical attack or other forms of harassment. Similarly, people can then begin to think about how to defend themselves and what they got. The Buhari/Idiagbon administration gave as a reason for keeping the Nigerian borders closed for 22 months in 1984/85, persistent reports of the smuggling of essential commodities from Nigeria to the neighbouring countries of Benin, Togo, Ghana, Chad, Niger and Cameroun. The Babangida administration that succeeded it also claimed to have removed up to 80 per cent of subsidy on oil because of the activities of those who were smuggling the country's major foreign exchange earner, oil, across Nigerian borders.[12] The media can also inspire those who think they stand to gain from a conflict to begin to exploit the feelings of a people; or those who think that their vital interests may be at stake may begin to make contingent plans to protect their national interests. Ghana has closed her borders with Togo and Burkina Faso several times on this account. Similarly, some of the painful economic steps Nigeria has taken in recent years were said to have been taken to safeguard her vital interests against encroachment by neighbours who traverse her rather porous borders. Such measures include the expulsion of aliens in 1983, the closure of her borders for 22 months from 24 April 1984 to 28 February 1986.[13]

Examples of this sort of repercussion abound elsewhere in the world. Although the U.S. is several thousand kilometres away from Southern Africa, yet it manipulates in that sub-region in her own national interest: The Soviet Union, too, cannot be said to be disinterested in the conflicts that rage between apartheid South Africa on the one hand and Namibia and the front-line states on the other. Britain and Argentina fought a bitter war over the Falkland Islands some years ago.

Mass Media as Magnifying Agents

Though the position stories are recorded in newspapers, the space allocated to them, the prominence they are given in the radio and television news bulletin, and the time devoted to them in the bulletin, the mass media grade events and persons they report. The stories journalists consider important are given prominence in their newspapers; they are carried under bold headlines, run over a fairly long space and featured on certain pages in the paper. Similarly, in the electronic media such stories will be included in the headline news and considerable air time will be devoted to them. They may even be accompanied by visuals in the case of television. The aspects of an event after focused by the cameraman and the angles from which the TV shots are taken say a lot about what the journalists thinks about the event.

By their nature, border conflicts fall in the category of news that will always receive prominence in the media probably because they bring out vividly, the tragedy in human relationships. And quite naturally, tragic events make good copy because they appeal to our sentiments and arouse our passions. The prominence the mass media gave to the "invasion" of the Nigerian border village of Ikang by the Camerounian gendarmes in 1981, in which five Nigerian soldiers were killed, the "occupation" of parts of Sokoto State by Beninoise soldiers in 1982 and the more recent incursion of Camerounian soldiers into Nigeria through Borno State in May of 1987, caused quite a stir in Nigeria. They raised worrisome questions about the capabilities of the Nigerian army to defend the country's territorial integrity and about the "big brother" posture of the country's rulers. The negative perception that these reports created compelled the Nigerian chief of Joint Staff, General Domkat Bali, to comment publicly on these events and to try to allay people's anxiety.[14] He charged that the media had magnified the skirmishes out of their significance.

It was the prominence given by the media to the "activities" of the citizens from the neighbouring states in Nigeria that probably necessitated the expulsion order issued to illegal aliens in Nigeria in 1983. Similarly, activities of the media have led to heightening of hostilities between Ghana and Togo, Ghana and Burkina Faso, Liberia and Guinea, Liberia and Sierra Leone,[15] Iran and Iraq, Morocco and the Saharawi Arab Democratic Republic and Ethiopia and Somali or even between Ethiopia and Eriteria (in the same country). The examples can be multiplied.

The way the message is couched and packaged says a lot not only about the judgement of journalists but also about how they want their audience to react to events and what the audience members eventually do with them. This has been so ever since journalism was started; people generally recognise it. What may not be so appreciated is the effect of sensationalism on the news and those who consume it.

The first likely effect of the media on border conflicts is perhaps to draw attention to the confrontation and those involved. This way, the media confer stays or prominence on both the "aggressor" and the "victim". It is possible that this kind of instant-celebrity-image may create a hero-image (out of aggressors) which some people exposed to the information may wish to emulate. For instance, it is reasonable to assume that the success that attended the Israeli Commandos rescue operation at the Entebe International Airport, Uganda, in 1977, motivated the ill-fated U.S. hostage-rescue mission to Teheran, Iran, in 1979.

By their coverage of conflicts, the media project the causes and courses of such clashes. Different attitudes can follow from repertorial activities of the media. In the first place, national and international sympathy and solidarity can be evoked in people who consume information about a border incident. They may feel that the aggressor state has been wronged and pushed beyond its tolerance limit. In the second place, it may provoke a feeling of revulsion and outrage against the aggressor state, more so if international opinion cannot justify the attack or encroachment. This is the case with Israel in her conflicts with the Palestinians in Lebanon and other occupied Arab lands; South Africa in its seemingly unjust incursions into neighbouring Angola, Mozambique and other African "front-line" states; and Libya and France in their interference in the Chadian conflicts.

Mass Media as Mitigating Agents

Just as the mass media act as facilitators of border conflicts so also do they act to mitigate their impact. The commonplace presence of the media and the immediacy of their information dissemination help to mitigate the effects of border conflicts just as they facilitate their occurrence. The same media that prodded the Nigerian government into expelling illegal aliens became the channel through which the inconveniences and hardships those aliens suffered both at the camps in Nigeria and in other places they had to transit before getting to their countries, were highlighted. The media picked the conscience of government functionaries to the extent that more humane measures such as improving conditions at the transit camp had to be taken.[16] While the media reflect the inflamed passions of Nigerians for revenge against neighbouring countries that infringed the country's territorial rights, they also, in their editorials and other comments, reminded the country of its obligations to find peaceful solutions in the spirit and interest of the OAU and good neighbourliness.[17]

The fast rate at which information travels around the world,[18] thanks to modern technology, makes it possible for diplomatic efforts to be made to diffuse some conflicts before they degenerate into warfare.

For instance, when a nation infringes the rights of another nation, the fast speed at which information moves around the world enables the aggrieved nation to bring its case before such bodies as the United Nations, the Organisation of African Unity and the World Court for adjudication. More importantly, such a country is able to bring its case before the court of world opinion for consideration. Before long the matter would have been taken up for discussion at various levels—national and international. The highly explosive misunderstanding between Nigeria and Cameroun in 1981 was resolved in this matter.

While the diplomatic process sometimes may be slow, it certainly helps to prevent or at least minimise the scope of border clashes through international mediation. Though the United Nations has not been able to come up with a resolution that is mutually agreeable to both the Israelis and the Arabs in the Middle East, it no doubt has played an important role in limiting the scope of hostilities in the subregion. The role of the OAU on the continent in this regard is no less commendable.

It has mediated about 42 border conflicts in Africa since 1963.[19]

In spite of the veracity and persistence of clashes between the Israelis and the Palestinians in Lebanon, a fourth Arab-Israeli war has so far been avoided. Regardless of the abhorrence of African and other nations to apartheid in South Africa, and despite the incessant incursion of South African forces into Angola and Mozambique, and its repressive hold on Namibia, a continental war which might have triggered a third world war has so far been averted. The United States and four other Western European countries formed what they called "the contact group" to help find an amicable solution to the independence problem in Namibia. Even though the group has been accused of insincerity of purpose, it has succeeded in delaying escalation of the armed struggle by liberation forces to free the territory from apartheid South Africa's rule. The OAU, on a number of occasions, put pressure on Libya, France, and other countries to get out of the conflicts in Chad. The continental organisation similarly influenced the events in Western Sahara by confining the crisis to Morocco and the Saharawi Arab Democratic Republic (SADR).

The same mass media that were instrumental in creating awareness of these conflicts the world over, facilitating support for the conflicts along interest lines, were also employed to lessen their impact and to find lasting solution to them.

Mass Media as Mediating Agents

The ability of the mass media to mitigate border crises is influenced by a number of factors such as the complexity of the relationships between the two contending parties, the degree of nationalistic fervour of those involved in the dispute and the acquisitive instincts of the combatants. Availability of information about a potential border conflict may not be able to prevent its blowing up into a major clash. Nevertheless, the media still play an important mediatory role even when the conflict has blossomed into a full-scale open confrontation.

By letting the world know of the existence of border clashes, they set in motion a complex nexus of mediation. The world is soon nudged into diplomatic activities that may eventually bring the situation under control and drag the combatants to the negotiating table.

Advances in technological development have contributed immensely to this achievement of the mass media in finding solutions, not only to boundary disputes but indeed to most national and international crises. The Lake Nyos gas leakage diaster in which thousands of Camerounians died on August 21, 1986 evoked a lot of sympathy from Nigerians and their government as well as others in neighbouring states. It became possible for these neighbours to render financial and material assistance to Cameroun. The role of the media in rallying international support cannot be overlooked. By instantly reporting the diaster they generated empathy which was translated into moral and material support for the government of Cameroun.

The role of the mass media in the U.S. in particular and in the world at large, in getting Israel and Egypt to negotiate their differences toward the latter part of the 70s cannot be ignored. On November 9, 1977, the late President Anwar Sadat of Egypt said, in answer to a reporter's question, that he was ready to go to any part of the world, including Israel, in search of peace. Walter Cronkite of the Columbia Broadcasting Service (CBS) picked on that and placed a phone call to Sadat during the prime time evening news the following day to confirm what he was reported to have said. President Sadat confirmed what was reported and before the whole world could recover from its disbelief of what had been heard, Sadat's historic trip to Tel Aviv had been arrange. A new impetus was this added to the Middle East peace efforts.

As has been noted elsewhere, the real challenge of the mass media for behaviourial scientists lies in their contradictions. As they can set individuals, groups or nations warring against each other so can they promote dialogue between them.

Perhaps it is necessary to note that the media can perform these functions in different cultures with differing degrees of effectiveness. Cultural differences and other relevant factors such as political climate of a country, the economic wellbeing of the nation, level of education among the population and the skill and orientation of the professional communicators, will of course, determine which events are covered by the media and which of the functions discussed above are emphasised.

Conclusion

In Africa, the mass media can, and ought to, serve as a bridge over the artificial boundaries created by the colonialists. They have a big responsibility to reverse the situation whereby sister African countries have to go through the capitals of their respective colonial lords to communicate with one another. The mass media also must redress the imbalance in information flow, not only between the North and the South but also within the South. The media in Africa carry more information about countries of Europe, America, Middle and Far East than they care to carry about sister African countries.[20] The current practice of relaying only negative information about sister African countries[21] is unacceptable and should change.

The media in Africa can, and should, bridge the gulf of artificial borders erected by those whose principal motive was to harness mineral resources for the development of their own countries. The establishment of the Pan African News Agency (PANA) is a right step in this direction.

African leaders should realise the important role of the mass media as interpreters of persons to persons, of actions to persons, of governments to persons and vice versa, of communities to communities and of governments to governments. In the context of borderlands, this role assumes a special significance as the mass media can aggravate or normalise relations between proximate communities much faster than is otherwise possible.

Governments and mass media operators must ensure that these powerful channels are used to facilitate communication between peoples of adjoining communities in order to increase the understanding and decrease tensions among them.

Endnotes

1. Imobighe, T.A., "Violences Across African State Borders" in Adeniran, Tunde and Alexander, Yonah (eds), *International Violence*, (New York: Praeger Pub., 1983) pp. 150-152.
2. Imobighe, Ibid, pp. 147-148.
3. Burns, Alan (Sir), *History of Nigeria*, (London: George Allen and Unwin Ltd., 1968); Fage, J.D.A., *History of West Africa: An Introductory Survey*, (London: Cambridge Univ. Press, 4th ed., 1969); Omu, Fred I.A., *Press and Politics in Nigeria 1880-1937*, (London: Longmans, 1978) pp. 100-171.
4. Schramm, Wilbur, *The Process and Effects of Mass Communication*, (Urbana, Ill.: Univ. of Illinois Press, 1974) pp. 8-18.
5. Sobowale, Idowu, "The Impact of the Mass Media on International Violence" in Adeniran, Tunde and Alexander, Yonah (eds), *International Violence*, (New York: Praeger Pub., 1983) pp. 221-230.
6. In each case when there had been a threat to the Nigerian border it was the press that alerted the people, possibly in some cases, the government, too.

7. Klapper, Joseph T., *The Effects of Mass Communication*, (New York: The Free Press, 1960).

8. McCombs, Maxwell E. and Shaw, Donald L., "The Agenda-Setting Function of the Media," *Public Opinion Quarterly*, 36 (1972) pp. 528-538.

9. McCombs, Maxwell and Becker, Lee B., *Using Mass Communication Theory*, (New Jersey: Prentice Hall Inc., 1979); Sobowale, Idowu, *Journalism as a Career*, (Lagos: John West Publications Ltd., 1985).

10. Hofman, Arthur S., *International Communication and New Diplomacy*, (Bloomington: Indiana Univ. Press, 1968) p. 4.

11. Cohen, B.C., *The Press, the Public and Foreign Polcicy*, (Princeton: Princeton Univ. Press, 1963).

12. Enahoro, Peter, "An Abuse and a Dilemma," *Africa Now* (Feb. 1983).

13. "Multitudes Move," *Africa* No. 138 (Feb. 1983) pp. 10-12, 17-19.

14. The National Television Authority (NTA) on May 29, 1987 carried an interview with the Chief of Joint Staff, Major General Domkat Bali, in which he tried to allay the fears of the public by charging the media with playing the border issues out of their significance.

15. Reports in a Sierra Leonian newspaper about Liberian President Doe's ill-treatment of his wife led to a strain in the relationships between the two countries and the closure of their borders.

16. "The Return to Ghana," *West Africa* (Feb. 7, 1983); Ghana Absorbs Its Own, " *West Africa* (Feb. 14, 1983).

17. "Cocoa Smuggling: Nigeria may lose ₦5 million to Benin Republic" *The Guardian*, Sunday, July 13, 1986, p. 1; "Cocoa Smuggling for Foreign Exchange," *Daily Times*, Tuesday June 3, 1986; "Colonial Borders that Split Families," *Daily Times*, Tuesday, Feb. 18, 1986; "Danger!" *Sunday Punch*, May 18, 1986; "Our Borders Still Porous," *Sunday Punch*, Oct. 27, 1985; "Smuggling continues unabated at Idi-Iroko" *Sunday Concord*, Oct. 27, 1985; "Border: ECOWAS Scribe Hails WMG," *National Concord*, Mar. 7, 1986.

18. Sobowale, Idowu, "Mass Media and Social Defence," a paper presented at the Fourth General Assembly of the Social Science Council of Nigeria, Ahmadu Bello University, Zaria, June 1-2, 1987.

19. Imobige, T.A., *International Violence*, op. cit.

20. Sobowale, Idowu, "Image of the World Through the Eyes of Five Nigerian Newspapers," paper presented at the 5th Biennial Conference of the African Council on Communication Education, Harare, Zimbabwe, Oct. 12-18, 1986.

21. A preliminary examination of the findings of a just concluded content analysis of how five Nigerian newspapers covered events in Africa between 1980 and 1984 shows that the Nigerian press is not at all different from the Western press in its negative portrayal of events in Africa.

CHAPTER 26

Cosmopolitanism vs. Provincialism: The Dialectic of Development of the Nation-State

by A. Fakolade

Introduction

The nation state is usually an assemblage of cultural communities and surges ahead through actions and considerations addressed to itself and by itself even in a world in which the cosmopolitan perspective is increasingly becoming the pervasive orthodoxy. Indeed, national unity or the confinement within a system of boundaries constituting the nation is strictly political, symbolised by a centra, 'independent' government, almost always bring together peoples of different cultural heritages (Belshaw, 1976: 96). Ostensibly, these nation states employ widely different and disparate methods and philosophies in handling issues of multiculturalism as well as that of aggregate national development effort. Such differences reflect the most fundamental differences in the indices of their qualitative development.

Development is a relative rather than an absolute term. In fact, Frank (1975) has put forward the conception of a dialectical unity between the development of development and the development of underdevelopment. Thus, the success of some nation states in improving the quality of life of their inhabitants is directly linked to the inability of some other nation states to bring about the same. Yet, these global perspectives are inextricably linked with local ones and are predicated on fundamentally the same principles and processes. The core region can have the same effect on the peripheral region as a developed country has on an underdeveloped country. The same is true of the city versus countryside. The relationship between ethnic groups within the nation state can exhibit the same effects.

A border, by whatever conception of the term, thus poses policy issues that can be described as a two-headed Janus looking in different directions. One is the direction of principle, of fundamental values, in so far as values are fundamental; the other is in the direction of the processes (and their institutions) by which the entity perpetuates its existence.

This paper examines the pragmatic need of the nation state to adopt a provincial perspective in dealing with issues of its survival and development as well as the profound imperative to relate to the more encompassing and cosmopolitan dimensions of contemporary reality, both at local, national and global levels. The process of development of the nation state is tied to an increasing capacity to evolve principles and processes to deal with these two conflicting exigencies, and yet to allow equity to flourish while being concerned for growth, to permit diversity and respect for local circumstances while craving for unity, and to make room for social justice and respect for the individual while committed to the preservation of law and order. This is the cardinal challenge of development. It is to the fundamental issues involved in that dialectic that this paper is addressed.

What is a Border?

Society is organised into discrete cells: The family, the neighbourhood, the village, the town, the region, the nation state, the supranational region and the world system. Such an atomistic organisation of society impels us to consider the basis for the shedding of affinities between territorial units, ponder the mediation of the relationships between one and another, and examine the logic of the domestication of our lives within the confines of particular units or cells.

The border, simply put, is the part or edge of a surface or area that forms its outer boundary. It is the divide between two contiguous territorial units. Available literature tends to associate borders with nation states and international boundaries almost exclusively. this need not be. Borders exist at various levels and with varying degrees of porosity. Some borders are a lot more permeable than others; people, ideas and goods cross some borders legitimately or otherwise much more readily than others. Some local borders may be more rigid and impermeable than national or international borders. The U.S.A.-Canada border for instance is a lot more permeable to the movement of people, goods, ideas and technology than most African regional or inter-state borders. In fact, other than for political purposes it may hardly be recognized when one crosses the U.S.A.-Canada border. But the U.S.A.-Mexico border is less porous than the U.S.A.-Canada border though certainly more porous than many African regional and inter-state borders.

The borders of African countries of the same imperial colonial descent are more permeable to each other than to those neighbouring countries of a different imperial colonial descent. Thus, the borders of Tangayika (Tanzania), Kenya and Uganda were certainly no more effective as political, cultural and even economic divides than provincial borders during the years immediately after their independence. Divergent philosophies and patterns of governance have pulled these nations apart and have been responsible for the stone-walling of the borders in recent times.

Before the concept of ECOWAS (Economic Community of West African States) and even still true to some extent, the border between Niger and Benin (formerly Dahomey) was less effective divides than the borders between Nigeria and Dahomey (Benin Republic) or those of Ghana and Togo at least in a political and economic sense. There were attempts by the governments and peoples of Libya and Upper Volta (Burkina Faso) to merge politically thereby rendering less significant their borders which are several hundred millimetres apart.

The point in all this is that we need to understand the concept of borders beyond the mere presence of a line of demarcation between two contiguous territories. We also need to understand that the border at the international level may be less functional as a separator of people, goods and ideas than the border within.

Thus, to understand the functions of a border as well as the policy issues and challengers it poses requires a conceptual location within the extant pattern and contingency of relationships between people of adjacent, even non-contiguous, territories. The permeability and hence the effectiveness of the border as a separator may derive from the mode of origin of the border. The degree of friendliness or antagonism in the cross-border relationships may be contingent on the nature of the border.

Borders have sometimes been demarcated along linguistic and cultural concepts. This was particularly the case in the division of the Austro-Hungarian Empire at the end of the First World War. When borders coincide with linguistic-cultural boundaries they tend to become stonewalls allowing only the barest movement of ideas across them. Such linguistic-cultural enclaves exhibits the profound effect of territorialism. Borders of such territories *exude* outward antagonism and *recruit* internal cooperation and concerted action quite effectively. Cultural rights denote inherent qualities of man vis-a-vis organised society and also reflects man's beliefs as to the nature of the society (UNESCO, 1977: 34). The assertion of cultural identity is a powerful force in the maintenance and reproduction of the society. However, in recent times there has been so much cultural inter-actions in the world that the reality of a culture in general is very difficult to define. Cultural variation diminishes with the advent of higher types of human technology and organisation (Wertheim, 1974: 60). Besides, there is a certain impermanence associated with cultural boundaries (Belshaw, 1976: 97). In fact, even talking of cultural boundaries there is a view that the future depends on the possibility of humankind transcending the limits of individual cultures.

The concept of legislated borders invokes a coercive authority on the demarcation of borders. Inhabitants of both sides of the border may have little or no input to the decision-making surrounding the fixing of such borders but are nonetheless required to respect the presence of such borders. The degree of quiet or turmoil associated with a legislated border depends on the dominance of the legislating authority and the equity involved in the process as perceived by the inhabitants of both sides of the border. As soon as that authority withers or disappears inchoate embitterment may come to the fore and the border may suddenly witness waves of antagonism. Many border disputes changes of constituent governments. But this awareness underscores the fact that legislation by itself, without seeking maximum agreement of the border communities, cannot resolve issues of legitimacy of such borders.

Contractual or negotiated borders constitute the last set of borders we want to examine. In contradistinction to the legislated, imperialist principle, contractual or negotiated borders derived from bilateral discussions without the threat of force. When borders are demarcated this way rarely do they become agitated spots. Such borders command respect and legitimacy from both sides. Borders of this type are few. Examples include many stretches of the U.S.A.-Canada borderline.

It could thus be seen that borders derive their existence from various concepts and modes. But whatever the basis of border demarcation, action over boundary fixation always takes place at the political level. Decisions are taken by policy-makers for the people themselves. Such decisions have profound effects on the social life and organisation of the people concerned. Border communities, in particular, experience the tempo of the relationship between two adjoining nation states and feel the pulse of underdevelopment of development of the economies of the adjoining nation states and feel the pulse of underdevelopment of development of the economies of the adjoining nation more profusely than the core communities of their home states. It is thus pertinent to examine the broader issue of development of the nation state from the policy options of a cosmopolitan or provincial perspective and to proffer scenario for the mediation of both perspectives. The next section is addressed to those issues.

The Cosmopolitan Perspective

One of the standard cliches in international politics today is that improvements in communication and transportation are creating an interdependent or integrated world. Price (1979: 18) notes that the various advances in the technology of transportation and communications are causing a global societal and economic integration. People are forced to cooperate in order to survive in this integrated world. This interdependence of societies is coupled with an interdependence of the problems which man is now facing. World problems cannot be considered in isolation; they are closely bound up with each other. Indeed, the UNESCO (1977: 9) posits that for contemporary thought he world forms an integrated whole, a unity of interrelated parts and that a global approach to world problems is manifestly the only approach which comes to terms with their real nature. International problems then, it seems, demand international solutions.

The single nation state on its own, rich or poor, could do relatively little to improve its own situation when confronted with fallout from the international system. Such fallouts include the enormous problems of dealing with the ever-rising number of refugees, the pervasive fear of the fleeting nature of world peace as reflected in the ding-dong over arms limitation talks, chronic inflation and unemployment at the same time, and the ever-growing exportation of smuggling and criminality across national boundaries. In another significant sense nothing has underlines the common dilemma of all mankind so clearly as the environmental crisis now unfolding (Brown, 1972: 15). Indeed the list of national problems which have only global solutions is increasing. These include the exploitation and management of ocean resource, the issue of environmental standards which will regulate pollution emission from various industries, inflation and economic recession. In fact, Brown (1972: 364) affirms that the most urgent item on our agenda in the years immediately ahead is the creation of a world without borders, one which recognises the common destiny of all mankind.

It is in this perspective that the view has been expressed that nationalism is too strong for the needs of the modern world and that it is rapidly becoming destructively dysfunctional in being inadequate to deal with the real issues confronting mankind (Belsaw, 1976: 125). Of course, national government is an artificial and deliberate concern. Its forms are set by constitution makers and organisers of bureaucracies. It is expected that the burgeoning human links will reduce the importance of artificially created political borders. Supranational arrangements and organisations, such as ECOWAS, OAU, EEC, OPEC, and the like, will increasingly substitute for the roles played by nation states. The movements of people, goods and ideas across international frontiers will increase in tempo, thus moving the world closer and closer to the concept of a global village or society.

Already, many of the most stimulating, and perhaps the most disgusting, developments in nation states will have their sources beyond the immediate borders. Indeed national unity itself can be dependent upon external relations. An interesting development in this regard is that members of the public who are obviously members of nation states are becoming rather more directly concerned about the way decisions taken outside their country affect them (Belshaw, 1976: 128).

The process of cultural homogeneity, or call it cultural invasion if you wish, is proceeding apace particularly in Africa and other developing countries. Television viewers in New York, Lagos, Accra and Banjul are increasingly being treated to the same programmes. As massive food imports become the order of the day, menus in most African countries get increasingly tied to the survival of international linkages and arrangements. Progressively social life and organisation in African countries is becoming a mirror, a poor match though it is, of that beyond their borders, particularly of Western societies. Indeed development has had the same effect in all societies; everyone has been enmeshed in a new web of dependence on commodities that flow from the same machines, factories, clinics, television studios, think tanks etc. (Illich, 1978: 21). It is this sense that Illich (1978: 21) asserts that most of the world's communities are facing exactly the same critical issue; people must remain ciphers in the conditioned crowd that surges toward greater dependence or they must find the courage that alone saves in a panic; to stand still and look around for another way out than the obvious marked exit.

The question then is: what integrity and functionality do the numerous African's national boundaries confer on their nation states as preserves of authentic and unique social-political arrangements? This may well be crux of the dialogue, as well as dilemma, of African development. Should policy seek to open up the borders of the nation states to all sorts of incoming ideas, peoples and goods? Should it discriminate in favour of some source regions? What is the system of values and ideas used in making the choice of source regions? Or, should policy seek to close the borders to all sorts of incoming influences? Can it do so? Who decides for whom? Around such issues are conjoined the dialectics of development of the (African) nation state. But before we examine the underling-matters in that dialectic we will devote the next section to an examination of the provincial imperative in the development of the nation state.

The Provincial Perspective

The awareness has been growing in some quarters that under-development is a product of the world capitalist system and an integral part of it. For instance, it has been argued that the luxury and affluence that exit today in the wet flow from the same process that resulted in poverty and misery in the Third World (Martin, 1976: 13). Thus, there can be no way of overcoming underdevelopment except by putting an end to the structures of dependent relationships. in this view, underdevelopment is not much an economic as it is a political problem. Rarely is cure constituted by more the same but a fundamental structural change. This awareness leads the discerning nation state to the realisation that it is alone in its effort to develop its own society; the metropolitan nation does not necessarily share the development aspirations of the peripheral nation state. In fact, the metropolitan nation may be committed in implicit and explicit ways to the continuing underdevelopment of the peripheral nation state.

This leads the peripheral nation state to resort to concepts of self-reliance and selective territorial closure as development strategy. The border then serves as a shedding point for ideas and strategies about appropriate social life and organisation between different societies. The requirements as well as the praxis of this new im-

perative may, however be ill-defined and not well understood. The admonition to
do it differently may itself be devoid of meaning unless the principles and processes
are well defined and articulated. In other words, territorialism or provincialism may
itself substitute for thought and action and may degenerate into an ideology of
resistance serving merely to protect inefficient or inequitable decision-making
within the nation state. This way well provide a launch-pad for different forms of
territorial chauvinism. And there are always no lack of arguments to justify any and
all actions taken by the nation state in the effort for self-preservation.

Territorial policies about national development manifest themselves in many
forms an encompasses such issues as agriculture defence, immigration and labour,
industrial development and overall national growth strategy. The urge to create its
own stamp and to respond to the authentic needs of its citizens is responsible for
Canada's determined commitment from about the mid-1970s to ensure maximum
Canadian content in its labour supply, training curricula and educational manpower,
for instance. It is on this same kind of premise that Nigeria introduced the In-
digenisation Decree and is pursing a programme of increased local content in the
nation's manufacturing. It is also to put a premium on the welfare of Nigerians and
to respond to problems of imported criminality that Nigeria declared 'war' on its
illegal aliens. For this same reason many African countries have put into operation
policies and programmes which are quite antagonistic to neighbouring states but
which are supposed to enhance the internal welfare of their nation states. One instance of such policies was the eviction of many Nigerians from Equatorial Guinea
in 1975.

When territorially chauvinistic policies emerge into the international scene from
any nation state they often provoke indignation and sometimes outright condemnation by other members of the international community.

However, such indignation progressively withers with time up to the point that
other nations surreptitiously and sometimes out-rightly adopt the same policies in
defence or propagation of their own territorial interests. Such chauvinism at the national level is usually at the root of developed patterns of chauvinism in the management and relations of the various units or cells within the nation state. A chauvinism
in the management and relations of the various units or cells within the nation state.
A chauvinistic nation state will almost have chauvinistic parts or regions and vice
versa. But once chauvinism of any sort (ethnic, religions, or regional) develops a
snow balling process chauvinism will become self-perpetuating; the attempt to right
one form of chauvinism creates a new pattern of chauvinism. In such settings, territorial boundaries may become stonewalls for the shedding of many kinds of affinities, such as those of religious, cultural, economic and political character, between contiguous parts of territorial system.

Yet, there is no denying the fact that the genesis of much growth is and has to
be internal. It is out of internal ideas and the internal exchange; of the fruits of productive activity that wealth, capital, the will to move and the expectation that change
is feasible will come. Indeed, most of the important values for development are particular and there is no substitute for eliciting them from the constituents themselves.
These values become the data whether it be for describing rocks, soils, animals,
people, or institutions and propel the development drive in any particular territorial
system.

The real issue about development of the nation state revolves around the resolution of this conflict of perspectives, that is, how to generate the necessary internal

dynamic for its development in the midst of a more encompassing cosmos. The next section is addressed to that issue and hence to the status and effects of accord borders of territorial systems.

The Dialectic of Development of Nation-State

An innate compulsion to defend one's property lies, of course, at the heart of the territorial principle. But just as close to its heart lies the recognition of the rights of the next animal (Ardrey, 1966: 218). The cardinal challenge of development of the nation state consists of the ability to prosecute the principles and processes of self-perpetuation without injuring the rights and interests of other nation states.

Contemporary evidence indicates that, far from the contrary, the process of development in one nation state, particularly the metropolitan nation, creates and perpetuates the conditions for the non-development of others, notably the peripheral states. Thus, the peripheral nation state must take fundamental decisions on matters relating to self-determination and the transactions with states beyond its borders. The same issues are reproduced within the borders.

Development does not take place at the same pace every where in the nation state. Some areas or regions develop much faster than others. The cumulative concentration of advantage and opportunity in such developed regions further widens the disparity between them and the lagging regions. How should policy respond to the observed disparities in development? Should policy hold on the developed regions while propping up the lagging regions? It is important to make a distinction between individual welfare, the welfare of every individual citizen, from that of the welfare of the region even the most developed regions. Debate and practice in this regard in Nigeria have centred on 'federal character' representation in matters of appointment, admission and distribution of the perquisites of development. A full-scale discussion of the substantive issues and processes are not pertinent here. It is however relevant to note that geographic borders and territories became decisive in matters relating to the individual advance of the citizenry. This raises serious questions about the equity and social justice of territorial organisation. In fact, how a territorial unit such as the nation state handles issues of multiculturalism and diversity is one of the most potent qualitative measure of its development. It raises issues about what premium is put on ensuring equity while being concerned with growth; what respect there is for diversity in the quest for unity, and what room there is for individual justice amidst a paramount concern for law and order.

At the local level, states or divisions manifest the principle of right to self-determination in the form of laws and processes that centre on-their own self-interest. Such states justifiably decide what problems or strategies in their development to accord the highest priority. In their zeal for self-preservation, however, policy-makers in such states may introduce discriminatory pricing of similar services for indigens and non-indigens. In such cases entitlement to select benefits and privileges are based on the source region or territorial origin of individuals. Canada and Britain are examples of nation states such as Kwara, Kaduna and Plateau in Nigeria do the same. This is a significant issue touching on territorial relationships and development policy. Should development policy take account of total flows of costs and benefits between territorial units and design a criss-cross of discriminatory policies in all directions? Surely accounting for such pricing will be enormously complex. This is not to talk of the fact that the lateral relationships that the peoples of such states really want to see evolve is very often different from the direction of policy.

Thus, there is a need to transcend the many divisions that territorial borders, of whatever scale, impose on human interaction. Dennis Goulet (1971) in dealing with development ethics advocates a system of mutual vulnerability. This vulnerability, he holds, has to be at all and different levels; between developed and the developing countries, between the rich and poor regions, between the city and countryside, and between rich and poor persons or groups. It is such a value premise and process that can ultimately enhance the individual liberty and welfare of human beings wherever they may be found. After all, development is about people; individuals and their institutions. It relates essentially to issues of the quality of life of the citizen, to the concept of the equality of persons, and to the equity or social justice of territorial organisation. The axis of measurement is relational rather than absolute.

Conclusion

World problems are inextricably bound up with one another. in fact, for contemporary thought the world forms an integrated whole, a unity of interrelated parts. The single nation state could do relatively little to improve its own situation when faced with fallout from the international system. Yet, the genesis of much development has to derive from an internal dynamic and original innovation.

The territorial organisation of space and the incidence of borders at different levels invokes an atomistic perspective of the many problems confronting mankind during the development process. The nature of the border conditions the pattern and the consequences of human interaction beyond it. Yet, there is a need to transcend the many divisions that territorial borders of whatever scale impose on human interaction. To do this effectively calls for a development ethic based on the concept of mutual vulnerability at all and different levels of human interaction.

Bibliography

Ardrey, R., *The Territorial Imperative: An Inquiry into the Animals Origins of Property and Nations* (New York: Dell, 1966).
Belshaw, C.S., *The Sorcerer's Apprentice: An Anthropology of Public Policy* (New York: Pergamon, 1976).
Brown, L.R., *World Without Borders* (New York: Random House, 1972).
Frank, A.G., *On Capitalist Underdevelopment* (Oxford: O.U.P., 1975).
Friedmann, J. and Weaver, C., *Territory and Function: The Evolution of Regional Planning* (Berkeley: Univ. of California Press, 1979).
Goulet, D., *The Cruel Choice: A New Concept in the Theory of Development* (New York: Atheneum, 1971).
Hall, E.T., *Beyond Culture* (New York: Anchor/Doubleday, 1976).
Hardin, G., "The Tragedy of the Commons", *Science* 162, (13), Dec. 1968, pp. 1243-8.
Hardin, G., *Exploring New Ethics for Survival: The Voyage of the Spaceship Beagle* (New York: Penguin, 1968).
Harvey, D., *Social Justice and the City* (London: Edward Arnold, 1973).
Illich, I., *The Right to Useful Unemployment and its Professional Enemies* (London: Marion Boyars, 1978).
Martin, R., "Who suffers whom? Notes on a Canadian policy towards the third world", *The Canadian Forum*, 56 (660), April 1976, pp. 12-19.
Price, T.J., "International transportation and integration: evidence from the El Paso/Juarez microcosm", *Int. Studies Notes* 6 (1), Spring 1979, pp. 18-21.
UNESCO, *Thinking Ahead: UNESCO and the Challenges of Today and Tomorrow* (Paris: UNESCO, 1977).
Wertheim, W.F., *Evolution and Revolution: The Rising Waves of Emancipation* (Harmondsworth: Penguin, 1974).

SECTION IV
RESEARCH STRATEGIES AND A PROPOSED AGENDA

Some Questions and 'Sky' Solutions to Border Resource Management

by Peter O. Adeniyi

An Overview of Some Fundamental Issues

The dialectics surrounding the issue of 'boundary', its demarcation and the associated border regions are borne out of the need to create a just world in which every human being has a chance of self fulfilment; a world in which all human beings realise that they are independent, and therefore, should share the world resources and create a more equitable distribution of labour and goods. Such a world can hardly be achieved without an 'ordered' spatial organization.

Indeed, every object has its own unique characteristics; but all objects relate to one another in various complex ways. An understanding of the composition and functional characteristics of the objects provide a basis for the classification of the objects into groups which, in turn, serve as prerequisites for the optimum functioning of the objects. Without classification, the objects would remain merely a bewildering multiplicity; the precise and unambiguous communication of ideas and concepts concerning these objects would be impossible. Thus, according to Shapiro (1969), the evolution of a body of *reliable knowledge* concerning any set of phenomenon through the process of accretion would be extremely difficult without classification.

The need for classification provided a basis for boundary demarcation; and the establishment of boundary leads to the existence of border regions. The grouping or the classification of people into nation-states has both a historical and psychological foundation. Psychologically, the practice rests in the fact that man is like other animals in his concern for territorial possession. Although the historical pervasiveness of human territoriality is certainly beyond the scope of this paper, the key controlling factor is human territorial behaviour is intrinsically associated with the availability and sharing of resources. Thus, prior to the development of agriculture, marginal and unpredictable food supplies in many parts of the world result in flexibility of group organisation. The absence of personal property and the need to be flexible regarding the location of food result in weak attachments to and the feeling of territorial ownership (Lee and Devore, 1968). But with the development of agriculture and the subsequent industrial and technological developments, human beings became territorially conscious (Barnes, 1970; Martin, 1972; Raynold, 1966 and 1972).

Consequently, people became attached to their land, resented its use by others. They became sensitive about where their land began and ended as well as resisted free and uncontrolled access by others. Accordingly, issues relating to defence became more and more critical where overlapping land use occurs (as in northern Nigeria).

This phenomenon is particularly entrenched in what is called "primary territory". "Primary territories" according to Altman (1975, p.112) "are owned and used exclusively by individuals or groups, *are clearly identified as theirs by others,* are controlled on a relatively permanent basis and are central to the day-to-day lives of the occupants" (emphasis mine). Examples of primary territories are a family home, a family farm and a nation's land. In effect, inability to control a primary territory successfully may have impacts on the psychological wellbeing of the people. Again the need to control leads to the establishment of boundaries which must be known and recognised by other neighbouring individuals or groups. It is, perhaps for these and other reasons that territoriality became the main basis for the organisation of human life. As argued by Edney (1976), territoriality functions to facilitate social processes such as planning, anticipating others behaviour, engaging in uninterrupted activities and having security.

It can therefore be added that it would be difficult to function well without a territory whose boundaries are well demarcated. The significance of boundary has for long been recognised as exemplified in the book of Deuteronomy of the Holy Bible (27.17) which states "cursed be he that removes his neighbour's landmark". In spite of the significance of boundaries, the fundamental concern has always been over the access, use and control of the resources within a territory.

In the light of the above discussion, it is pertinent to examine briefly the existing boundaries in Africa. The existing boundaries in Africa were established by the past colonial governments. While the boundaries have been criticised mostly for reasons of their irrationality and arbitrariness, it is pertinent to observe that much of the substance of such criticisms relates to the issue of allocation and development of resources. This is the main point made by such location theorists as Cristaller (1933) and Losch (1940). Both have argued, though with particular reference to the European situation, that international boundaries create artificial barriers and break up areas which otherwise could have been utilised as national planning regions. Such a development deprives border regions of being developed as complementary economic areas. The barrier functions of international boundaries reduce opportunities for economies of scale and free trade. The applicability of these arguments on European nation state boundaries to the modern state system in Africa has recently been noted by Asiwaju (1984a). Attention has been drawn especially to the adverse effects of partitioned culture areas and natural regions on planning and the imperative for transborder cooperation as a logical first step towards the realisation of wider regional integration. (Asiwaju, 1984b).

Given this situation, any interpretation or description of the colonial partition of Africa must be seen as an exercise in resource sharing which was done basically for the self fulfilment of the colonial governments. The partition was based on the imperialists knowledge of the resources in Africa as at that time. Temporal element in achieving their perceived objectives did not permit the consideration of cultural artifacts which, of course, was not central to their objectives. There is evidence that the knowledge of resources in Africa was better known by the colonial powers than the Africans themselves. Even today, the situation has not changed (Adeniyi, 1985a). Agreed that the contemporary needs of Africans may have been inhibited by the 'superimposed' international boundaries, some of the questions we should concern ourselves with are:

1) If African countries today are to be regrouped, do we have sufficiently accurate and accessible information for that exercise?
2) If we do (which I doubt) and we employ the data in regrouping the existing countries into new nation states (which would probably lead to the complete annexation of some of the existing countries), to what extent would such regrouping exercise be acceptable to all African governments?
3) If the regrouping is acceptable to all the governments, does that imply that border conflicts will cease to occur?
4) To what extent can the border conflicts in Africa and the resolution so far be interpreted to be an attempt at improving the lives of the border inhabitants?

Answers to these and related questions are beyond the scope of this paper. However, it is the opinion of the author that our hundred years of operation within sets of 'uncomfortable' territories can hardly be made comfortable by the creators of those territories who, through their 'growth of knowledge' are still able, today, to sustain the level of benefits they were deriving when the independent African countries were under their direct control. What is needed on the part of Africans and African governments is the acquisition of relevant knowledge on all aspects of border issues and supportive environment. The use of that knowledge for the formulation of beneficial policies and programmes must justify the urgency for the acquisition and analysis of relevant basic data. Without this knowledge and the future consequences will be compounded. This will happen because a smart person is always going to have the advantage of the other fellow. It is a phenomenon in nature. Rivers, for example, are known to have boundaries usually called river divide or watershed and their borders are marked by their flood plains. A 'powerful' river, through watershed regression diverts part of a neighbouring river system to its own basin leading to what is called river capture. This action, according to Wooldrige as quoted by Monkhouse is a normal incident in a veritable struggle for existence (Monkhouse, 1963).

In concluding this section, it is pertinent to note that:

1) Territoriality is a necessity for the proper functioning and organization of human activities.
2) The need for territoriality leads to the establishment of boundaries.
3) The fundamental reason for the establishment of boundaries is the control over access, use and management of potential and perceived resources.
4) An effective control and use of any resource requires the knowledge of the location, quantity, quality and the areal extent of the resources as well as their changing characteristics, and
5) The lack or the inadequacy as well as inaccessibility of the above information can have far reaching consequences on the socio-economic performance of any nation because it is on such facts that fundamental border policy issues and resource management problems can be resolved.

Although environmental system do not function according to political boundaries, the misuse and/or over use of any environmental components by any nation or groups of nations may have negative consequences on the ecology and the socio-economic activities of the neighbouring nations. This is particularly true for the border regions.

A solution to this must begin with an increased knowledge and accumulation of relevant information as used here, refers to data (about objects, things or areas) that have been organised and processed. In this context, knowledge (about the objects, things or areas) becomes ordered information. Thus, according to Nossin (1982), the progress in both the collection of data and the generation of information based on these data depends on the growth of knowledge.

In consideration of the above, an attempt is made in the next section to identify some of the basic data requirements for the management of border resources. The status of the identified data is generally assessed.

Basic Data Requirements and their Availability

Two categories of *basic* data set which are required for the proper management of border regions are:

1) Those required for the proper demarcation and/or adjustment of territorial boundaries;
2) Those that ate necessary for the proper management and monitoring of the resources within the border areas.

Boundary Demarcation and Boundary Adjustment

The fundamental data set needed for a proper demarcation of any international or intranational boundary as well as their adjustments should include the following:

i) Detailed land use information
ii) Land ownership information (cadastral information)
iii) Topographical information (land forms, drainage, vegetation, etc.)

The need for these basic data is dictated by the fact that land uses are direct indicators of the social and economic characteristics of the people. Land use itself is intricately associated and influenced by the characteristics and quality of the environment. Thus the placement of the boundary line requires accurate inventory of the spatial distribution of the human activities on the land.

However, accurate land use information is a rarity in Africa. For instance, no single agency in Nigeria has the sole responsibility for the acquisition of land use data; hence no comprehensive land use survey has been carried out in the country.

The collection of land use data, using the traditional field method, has not been successful. Some of the difficulties in mapping land use, using the field traverse method in Nigeria as well as in most of African countries, include (i) the lack of base maps at suitable scales; (ii) the inadequacy of the road network; (iii) the difficulty of movement and visibility in the forest areas and (iv) the high cost in terms of time and labour.

The land area owned by individuals or groups are equally important. Since all the land area owned by individuals or groups may not be under use, the information about the areal extent of such land area is vital to boundary demarcation and/or adjustment. This information can be obtained on cadastral maps. Like the land use information, no African country, except perhaps South Africa, has an up-to-date complete cadastral information. The factors which inhibit the conduct of land use survey are also responsible for the poor cadastral information (Adeniyi 1979). The situation is rather unfortunate that even most of the land owners themselves do not have readily accessible data on the areal extent of the land they possess. In a preliminary assessment of an on-going research on land use inventory in Nigeria by the author, only 18 farmers (i.e. 3.45%) of the 521 so far interviewed in Lagos, Ondo and Sokoto States were able to provide 'reasonable' information on the size of the land they possess. The provision of the 1978 Land Use Decree on the customary rights of occupancy where a land owner need to provide *a sketch or diagram* of the land he possessed at his own discretion seems to be at variance with the need to properly demarcate the boundaries (1978 Land Use Decree Section 36-3).

The establishment of a good land registration system is a basic investment of major importance to a nation in that: (i) it provides security to owners and all persons who have interest in the land; (ii) following from (i), it stimulates investments in the land; (iii) it reduces cases of disputes and litigation thereby leading to better human relation; (iv) it helps in many areas of public administration; and (v) it provides valuable information for agrarian reforms as well as a means to check the fragmentation of land. These advantages tally with the functions of primary territory.

Given the facts that most human needs for food, clothing, shelter, energy and amenities come from the land and the fact that the use of the land represents the sum total of the attitudinal and perceptual responses of individuals in institutions, land use and cadastral information are critical to any beneficial boundary demarcation and/or adjustment. The failure of the various attempts to resolve the persistent conflict in the border areas of the Lake Chad area is mainly caused by the lack of information to be used in the demarcation or adjustment of the boundary.

Another important data requirement is topographical information. Such information can be obtained on topographical maps. Topographical maps serve as a basis for (thematic) land resource and socio-economic mapping. Topographical mapping was started by the colonial governments. Field triangulation was the initial method of survey. The mapping activities were essentially carried out in the coastal areas, areas with high relief, areas settled by Europeans and areas identified by the colonists to possess high resource potential. By 1949, reconnaissance maps at scale 1:200,000 or 1:250,000 has been completed for 43% of Africa. Only the Nile Valley, some coastal areas, small area of South Africa, Kenya, Madagascar, Dakar and Abidjan were mapped at scales larger than 1:75,000. Generally 30 to 40 per cent of the (then) French West African countries, part of Liberia, Zaire, and Western Nigeria has also been mapped by 1949. Other countries were either slightly mapped or not mapped at all (Adeniyi, 1985a).

Today most African countries have not got complete topographical coverage of their country. Even in Nigeria not all the 1:50,000 topographical maps covering the country have been published. Some of the published ones are several years out of date. The production of topographical maps after the colonial period has not increased substantially.

The problems of obtaining these fundamental data requirements are caused partly by the inadequate recognition of their contribution to resource development and this again leads to poor financial allocation to the government establishments charged with the responsibility of acquiring data.

Border Region

The same sets of data requirement for boundary demarcation or adjustment are also needed for the proper management of the border regions. The additional information includes information about the natural qualities of the land including its surface and subsurface characteristics, its vegetation and the location of economic minerals. In this context, information is required about the soil, geologic, hydrologic, climate and vegetation. These and the information on current use and tenure are necessary for the decision on how the resources within a particular border area will be used now or in the future. The acquisition of the above information is particularly necessary where the boundary cut across international boundary or is used for its demarcation. In such a situation the use of the river for domestic water supply or for irrigation by either of the nations may lead to negative impact on the ecology or the socio-economic system of the other nation. In such areas, accurate background information is necessary as well as monitoring capability. A typical example is the establishment of a dam by the Cameroun government on the Chari-Logone drainage complex in the Lake Chad area. Since this complex supplies nearly 95% of the water inflow to Lake Chad, the damming of the river has enhanced the harsh climatic situation in the area and this, in turn, has affected the human activities in the area.

The difficulty of identifying the previous boundary on the ground has led to the joint agreement by the government of Niger, Chad, Cameroun and Nigeria to cooperate over the utilization of the Lake Chad area. This effort has not materialised and it is doubtful whether it will ever work unless the basic element of territoriality and how it functions are duly recognized.

Given the dearth of relevant data and considering the constraints associated with the acquisition of the basic data noted above, fast and cost-effective method of data acquisition should be sought. Since we need information to make beneficial decisions, we therefore need the survey and the survey methods that produce them. In the next section, a new survey method is discussed.

'Sky' Solution on the Acquisition of Information for the Proper Management of Borderland Areas

There are few alternatives to ground (in situ) truth, but it is uneconomical to obtain all the required environmental information in the field. The environment itself has placed several 'temporal' obstacles in the way of human trespassers; diplomacy compounds the situation. Thus, this section examines, in a general form, the application of remote sensing technology as an alternative solution to the acquisition of basic information for boundary demarcation and borderland resource management.

Remote sensing is defined as the measurement or acquisition of information of some property of an object of phenomenon by a recording device that is not in physical or intimate contact with the object or phenomenon under study. A common remote sensor is the camera/film combination. Most of the sensors have different platforms (air or space platforms); hence the use of the term 'sky'. The three commonly used products of remote sensing are aerial photographs, satellite (Landsat) and radar photographs. These forms of remote sensing products have the following general characteristics:

a) A broader view and more selective ability to detect variations in environmental conditions;

b) A capability for recording more permanently the patterns detected;

c) A better recall system so that patterns at different points in time might be considered with greater accuracy and in greater detail;

d) Unlike maps which are generalised and symbolised; remotely sensed imagery can show every terrain element as of the time of acquisition hence they possess the capability to play back the past (Barret and Curtis, 1976).

These characteristics make them suitable for the acquisition of basic data for proper understanding and management of border regions. This is not to say that their application is limited to border studies. In fact, remote sensing is well suited for multi-disciplinary data acquisition. A single remote sensing product can be used by different specialists to acquire data relevant to their needs.

Each of the three remotely sensed products has specific relative advantages. Aerial photography has relative higher spatial resolution and they are generally acquired within the visible portion of the electromagnetic spectrum (just like the human eye); hence the images acquired are familiar to human eye. However, their acquisition depends on good weather condition and it can be acquired during the day. Because of their relative higher spatial resolution, nearly all objects can be detected from large scale aerial photographs. It was for this inherent characteristic that aerial photography was regarded as confidential material by the colonial governments. According to Palgen (1979) it was in fact the concerted intent of the colonial powers to keep the African photographic data bases in their own hands. This secrecy is still largely maintained by several African countries even up to the extent that their citizens are usually denied access to them.

However, aerial photographs have for long been used for topographic mapping. The need for resource information has led to their use for soil, water, vegetation, geologic, agricultural, land use, cadastral and wetland surveys as well as urban and regional surveys, including human and animal population estimation. Inaccessible areas can be studied with relative ease. These forms of information are directly relevant to the study of border regions. When the photographs are available for different periods, they can be used to study both cultural and environmental changes. If a boundary is established at a point in time and the photograph of the boundary is taken the boundary can be rediscovered years after its establishment even if the land marks have changed or the artificial beacons have been removed or washed away.

In Nigeria, aerial photography has, over the last three decades, been used largely for topographic mapping. The slow development of photogrammetry (the art and science of making accurate planimetric and height measurements on aerial photographs for the purpose of making general maps—topographic maps) is due to lack of personnel and inadequate local educational programmes and facilities. With the exception of photogeology and the application in forestry, the use of aerial photography for other resource surveys is scanty.

Another important new development in remote sensing with greater potential for border studies is satellite imagery. With particular reference to the acquisition of resource data, satellite imagery (Landsat) has characteristics which include:

1) Broad synoptic overview of very large areas (about 34,000 km² per Landsat scene). Only 50 frames cover the whole of Nigeria.

2) Repetitive coverage with a periodicity of once in every 18 days over the same tracks on earth.

3) Multi-spectral capability; and

4) Data availability in both digital and analog form.

These characteristics and the fact that there is no restriction on its acquisition make Landsat data extremely suitable for the acquisition of information on border area. Landsat is not constrained by boundaries; hence regional data over border regions on both sides of any boundary can be acquired and analyzed. Because of the possibility of computer manipulation of the data, various enhancement can be applied to aid the acquisition of desired data. The greatest advantage of Landsat which is relevant to border studies is its monitoring capability. Changes in environmental system and cultural activities can be monitored nearly on a real time basis. Natural hazards can, to some extent, be predicted, and impacts of hazard can also be assessed rapidly. Crop area and crop yield estimate are some of the areas where Landsat data have been successfully applied. These and many other application areas are directly vital to the assessment and management of border regions.

The major constraint is that Africa, again excluding South Africa, has no ground receiving station. This precludes our ability to obtain real time information. Also, the technology is until quite recently, regarded as esoteric hence its application in Africa has lagged behind even those of other developing countries. Most of the applications of Landsat data have been carried out by foreign consultants hence the knowledge of the resources of the area concerned and the knowledge of how remote sensing has been employed are gained by the expatriates (Adeniyi, 1985a; Larin-Alabi, 1978). Also writing on the factors which influence the effective utilization of Landsat related inventory in West Africa, Hall (1982) argued that project products such as inventory maps and analysis prepared by foreign consultants can be successfully employed in resource development plans only it the techniques used and the resulting data are thoroughly understood by the host country's scientists and planners. Thus, in spite of the potential of satellite data, the lack of local experts has led to the false belief of the neutrality of basic data collection in resource management.

One of the major constraints of acquiring timely environmental resource information over large areas through passive remote sensing systems (e.g. photography) is caused by the inability of these systems to overcome the problem of atmospheric attenuations. This problem which is more pronounced in the humid tropical regions, is further compounded by the dependence of passive sensing systems on solar energy. A solution to this problem is a system which generates its own energy and which is less affected by atmospheric attenuation. Radar is such a system.

Radar is an active remote sensing system which generates its own energy to illuminate the earth's surface. It operates entirely independently of solar energy; thus radar can function both day and night, and it can acquire information about objects without significant interference from adverse atmospheric conditions.

Radar systems may or may not produce images. A common form of non-imaging radar is the type used to measure vehicle speeds usually termed Doppler radar systems. Another type of radar is the plan position indicator radar (PPI). PPI systems are commonly used for weather forecasting, air traffic control and navigational application. These forms of non-imaging radars are directly utilisable for monitoring purposes especially in the border areas.

The most common imaging radar systems are the side-looking airborne radars (SLAR). SLAR systems produce continuous strips of imagery of large areas of the ground located adjacent to the aircraft flight path. SLAR was initially developed for military reconnaissance but it later became a research instrument for natural resources surveys in late 1960s.

SLAR has been found to be very useful for regional reconnaissance surveys (Adeniyi, 1985b). According to Nunnally (1969) radar "provides a means of delimiting varying associations of physical and cultural phenomena through the outlining imagery variations in tone, texture, pattern and shape. It can be demonstrated that image patterns delimited on radar are visually correlated with known, observable variations in physical and cultural phenomena. Although the small-scale and limited resolutions of the radar prohibit interpretation of fine detail, enough information can be interpreted to basically categorize landscape regions. The value of the approach is that valuable regional categories can be quickly established and characterised...". Besides integrated landscape approach which is useful for broad categorization of border regions, radar has been found useful for the mapping of regional settlement patterns, vegetation, terrain analysis and terrain traffic-ability and the mapping of linear features (Adeniyi, 1985c).

Another important area in which radar can be used for border studies is the comparative analysis of the terrain on both sides of international boundaries. Because radar obtains terrain information on the sides of the aircraft flight path up to range of 100 to 150 km, the flight path can be planned parallel to the boundary such that the radar can acquire terrain information over 50 km on both sides of the boundary without flying over the air space of the adjacent territory. This facility removes the usual constraint associated with field data collection or the use of aerial photography which can only be employed within each territorial boundary. This facility provides a unique opportunity to obtain rapid terrain and cultural information on both sides of the given international boundary.

Remote Sensing and Border Monitoring

Border areas are sensitive regions not only in terms of movement of people and goods but also in terms of security. Thus border areas require adequate monitoring. The concept of monitoring concerns the purposeful gathering of information on the characteristics of a region in order to provide the potential for a more effective understanding and strategic management of a regions than would have been possible without such information (Hynes, 1974). Monitoring is, therefore, conceived as a set of interconnected activities which include, among other things, data collection, storage, retrieval, analysis, and evaluation. It is an intelligence activity. Intelligence as used here refers to the process of gathering a myriad of facts and bits of information, making a coherent pattern of them and drawing inferences from that pattern.

As noted by Avery (1977), intelligence in international affairs (including issues of international boundaries) is foreknowledge is a powerful peacetime tool for making advance predictions of a hostile nation's reaction to varying political, economic and military crisis. Of course, in times of all-out-war, a superior intelligence system may hold the balance of power and the key to ultimate victory. An example is the skilful photo reconnaissance work by British interpreters during World War II, which led to the destruction of launching sites for the German V-Bombs (Avery, 1977).

A strong monitoring capability can also inhibit the outbreak of hostilities if the aggressors know that their actions are fully seen, analyzed and understood. In other words, the aggressors have been denied the singular advantage of a surprise. The point being made here is that an established monitoring capability based on the technology of remote sensing can help assure the avoidance of border clashes and/or early victory when clashes occur by supplying up-to-date information on enemy forces, terrain factors, communication systems, weaponry installations, weather conditions and other environmental and cultural information.

The necessary monitoring information cannot be obtained through the traditional field surveys without difficulty. Such surveys are in fact limited to one's own side of the territorial boundary. From the general characteristics of remote sensing discussed above, essential monitoring information in the border regions can be obtained through the acquisition and interpretation of remotely sensed imagery.

With respect to resource and environmental changes, land use and land use intensity, settlement patterns and all grades of transportation routes, river regimes and flow, deforestation and overgrazing (and their impacts on micro-climate and illegal exploitation of resources) are possible to be detected through remote sensing techniques. If such changes continue undetected, they may lead to permanent damage with severe socio-economic consequences.

In terms of military and security, remote sensors, according to Avery (1977) can be used to detect and monitor the following:

1) Military targets with retaliatory power such as missile-launching sites, anti-aircraft emplacements, bomber basis and military airfields, shipyards and submarine bases, military posts and troops concentrations, supply trucks and conveyors.

2) Armament storage areas and industries producing war materials which may include ammunition dumps and supply depots, armament manufacturing plants, shipyard facilities, aircraft factories, petroleum oil and lubricants refineries and storage areas, chemical production plants, food production plants and water supplies etc.

3) Transportation/communication networks such as highways, rail, roads, bridges, tunnels and ferries, shipping lanes, radio and radar installations, telephone lines and underground cables, power transmission lines and transformers etc.

The fact that these military and industrial features can be detected through remote sensors make border location unfavourable to certain industrial development. Yet, by the fact of location and security reasons, certain borders require development. Although the discussion above may seem to be irrelevant, contemporary world development does not justify such conclusion. The growing concern for peace and development brings along the need for security. Peace cannot be achieved without security. Security demands for timely and accurate information. Environmental and cultural changes are occurring at a rate faster than conventional measurements can monitor. Ability to plan the use of resources to benefit the inhabitants of a place depends largely on their knowledge of the place and the means they devise to obtain the needed information. Remote sensing offers a unique opportunity to obtain several basic information necessary for the understanding of border areas. Our usual dependence on outsiders to help us collect needed information for national purposes is at variance with the principle of contemporary economic development. Perhaps, the reason given by the Canadian government for participating in the Landsat programme may provide us some food for thought.

Morley states "I don't mind confessing that one of the reasons the Canadian government approved our proposed ERTS programme so quickly was that some of our lawyers became very exercised about sovereignty implications. The attitude was we can't have the Americans knowing more about our natural resources than we do." (Morley, 1977). With respect to Africa, and Nigeria in particular, attempts should be made to acquire more information about ourselves, to improve our knowledge of our own country, to show us more glaringly the unequal and negative impact of our development and policies to date and to further improve our capacity or plan our future. Remote sensing provides one of the ways by which this can be achieved.

Conclusion

An attempt has been made in this paper to raise some fundamental questions about boundary demarcation/adjustment and the associated border areas. Some suggestions are also offered. While the questions raised and the solutions suggested are not fully treated, certain points stand out clearly. These points include:

1) That territoriality is a basic necessity for the proper organization and functioning of human activities;
2) That the need for territoriality demands for the establishment of an unambiguous boundary;
3) That the fundamental reason for the establishment of boundaries is to have control over access, use, and the management of potential and perceived resources within the territory;
4) That an effective control and use of any resource requires the knowledge of location, quantity, quality, areal extent of the resources and their changing characteristics;
5) That the lack or the inadequacy as well as the inaccessibility of the above information has contributed to the partial or total failure of nearly all attempts to settle boundary disputes as well as all projects established within the borderland areas.
6) That the traditional belief about the neutrality of data in decision making and the continuing dependence on the traditional data collection techniques can no longer help us in resolving several of the border problems.
7) That the issue of borderland areas in Africa requires active research efforts and governmental support.
8) That one of the research areas is the development and the application of remote sensing technology especially in the area of resource inventory and management as well as in the areas of military intelligence service.

As argued by Fossi (1977), knowledge and its technological applications have political significance and dimension which we ignore at our peril if we cling blindly to belief in the neutrality of data and their collection.

Bibliography

Adeniyi, P.O., "Some fundamental issues in land and land use planning in Nigeria," *The Nigerian Geographical Journal,* (1979) Vol. 22, No. 1, pp. 59-79.

_____ "Remote Sensing, Resource Development and Education in Africa" in *Education and Training in Contemporary Cartography,* D.R.F. Taylor (ed) (Chichester: John Wiley, 1985a) pp. 189-225.

_____ "Resource inventory of Ondo State based on regional interpretation of radar mosaics" Proceedings of the American Society of Photogrammetry (ASP) Conference, Washington, D.C., March 10-15, 1985b, pp. 755-766.

_____ "Imaging radar system" paper presented to the Second UN, WMO, ESA, FAO International Training Course on Remote Sensing Applications to Operational Agro-Meterology and Hydrology, 16th April-2nd May, 1985c, Nairobi, Kenya.

Adney, J.J., "Human territories: comment on functional properties" *Environment and Behaviour,* (1976) 8(1), pp. 31-48.

Altman, I., *The Environment and Social Behaviour: Privacy, Personal Space, Territory and Crowding* (Monterey, Calif: Books/Cole, 1975).

Altman, I. and Chemers, M.M., *Culture and Environment* (Monterey, Calif Books/Cole, 1980).

Asiwaju, A.I., *Artificial Boundaries* (Lagos: Lagos Univ. Press Inaugural Lecture Series, 1984a).

_____*Partitioned Africans: Ethnic Relations Across Africa's International Boundaries, 1884-1984* (Lagos: Lagos Univ. Press, 1984b).

Avery, T.E. *Interpretation of Aerial Photographs* (Minneapolis, Minn: Burgess Pub. Co., 1977).

Barnes, F., "The Biology of Pre-Neolithic Man" in S.S. Boyden (ed) *The Impact of Civilization on the Biology of Man* (Canberra: Australian National Univ. Press, 1970) pp. 1-18.

Barret, E.C. and L.F. Curtis, *Introduction to Environmental Remote Sensing* (New York: Hasted Press, Wiley, 1976).

Christaller, W., *The Sentralen Urte in Suddentschland* (Jena: Gustar Fischer, 1933) as cited in N.M. Hansen, *Border Economy: Regional Development in Southwest (U.S.A.)* (Austin: 1981) Ch. 2.

Fossi, G., "New Elements for Decision-Making" in J.J. Nossin (ed) *Surveys for Development: Multi-disciplinary Approach* (Amsterdam: Elsevier Scientific, 1977).

Hall, L., "Factors in the Effective Utilization of a Landsat Related Inventory in West Africa" NASA Conference Publication (1982), pp. 22-61.

Haynes, P.A., "Towards a Concept of Monitoring" *Town Planning Review,* (1976) 47, No. 1, p. 5029.

Larin-Alabi, F.B., "Problems of Remote Sensing in the Tropics: An Appraisal of the Nigerian Situation with Regard to Forestry Resources" in Collings and Genderen (eds) *Remote Sensing Applications in Developing Countries* (Remote Sensing Society, 1978) pp. 57-61.

Lee, R.B. and Devore, I. (eds) *Man the Hunter* (Chicago: Aldine, 1968).

Losch, A., *Die Raumliche Ordnung der Wirtschaft* (Jena: Guster Fischer, 1940) as cited in Hansen *op. cit.*

Martin, R., "Concepts of Human Territoriality" in P.J. Ucko (ed) Man, Settlement and Urbanism (London: Duckworth, 1972) pp. 427-445.

Monkhouse, F.J., Principles of Physical Geography (Warwick, London: Univ. of London Press, 1963).

CHAPTER 28

A Methodology of the Multi-disciplinary Problem: Borderlands and Socio-cultural Interactions

by F.A. Adeyoyin

Introduction

This paper examines borderlands as regions lying along and across the boundary separating one country from another. Hansen (1981) regarded such regions as "sub-national areas whose economic and social life are directly and significantly affected by proximity to an international boundary". Williams (1976), writing about the region noted that "beyond the town or district there is a wider territory, (here identified as borderlands) usually called a region". However defined and demarcated, he further noted, regional consciousness is a reality.

Borderlands are remarkable for their regional affinity as expressed in a common outlook: "a common subculture, customs, speech and work". No one can fail to notice the interaction of place, folks and work, the blending of the physical landscape and the works of man, a synthesis of earth and man endowed with a kind of personality that possesses cohesion of sentiment and social unity. In short borderlands are discussed in this paper as a living reality. Because of their "artificial", "porous" and "multidimensional nature", borderlands provide researchers the opportunity to explore human problems, which are inherently complex, from a multidisciplinary perspective, the richness of which takes cognizance of that complexity.

The Problem

The problem investigated in this paper was posited as follows: Given the nature of borderlands and their attendant multidimensional characteristics, what should be the appropriate methodology for the study of borderland communities? The approach adopted for this investigation is the social studies approach which cuts across demarcation between disciplines and suggests a holistic approach using the participatory integrative methodology to the investigation of human problems.

The Issue of Borderlands

The issue of borderlands had been with us for as long as human memory can fathom. They are areas taken for granted by their very nature and by their very location and situation. Because they are Zones lying along binational boundaries, they enjoy specific working relationships with one another and with each of the adjoining countries with which they come in contact. They are also adversely affected by factors of development which are greatly reflected in their infra-structural and socio-economic advancement or the lack of it. When in 1952, this writer visited the Nigeria-Benin border in what is now Borgu Local Government area of Kwara State of Nigeria, she beheld the Baribas on both sides of the border, a mere twenty eight kilometres away from her homeland. She saw them as simple folks filtering across the border demonstrating a blending of subculture; customs, work and dress. Little could she imagine that such simple folks neglected, as it were, by the main cultures could one day form part of a national and international conference such as this. All the fascination provided at the time was the cherished cheese (warakashi), cold pap (eko kolobo) and fresh milk that the Bariba sell, which formed (and still does) their main means of livelihood and which the visitor very mush wished to obtain fresh and cheap.

The Problems and Prospects of the Borderlands

The best person to discuss the problems of the border man, as it were, is probably the border man himself. Anyone who had been brought up in any of the eleven border regional states of Nigeria will have a series of stories to tell, a freeman today and a bond the next. Borderlanders are victims of political, religious, socio-economic, hence psychological changes. The Minister of Internal Affairs, Brigadier Muhammed Magoro, speaking to airport correspondents on the nature of borderlands in December 1984, remarked that Nigeria's borders are porous because of the absence of natural demarcations. He remarked that the nation's border situations is unlike Europe and other Western countries where border demarcation were naturally established. In line with the "porous" nature most of us here listened to a brilliantly presented inaugural lecture titled "Artificial Boundaries" (Asiwaju 1984) which added a second dimension to the nature of borderlands.

The present paper examines not only the porous and artificial nature of borderlands but also adds the psychological angle which reflects the mental predisposition of borderlanders towards a situation where man attempts to divide a culturally homogenous group of people into separate entities. The reasons are not only political and economic impositions by the main culture over the subculture but also a reflection of supremacy of the imperialistic bureaucratic majority over the colonised underprivileged minority. The results further reflect sufferings, economic paralysis, social ostracism and psychological subjugation of the oppressed by the oppressor, the strong by the weak, the centre man over the frontier man. Any attempt to curb the effects by the weaker is regarded as smuggling, economic sabotage, and so on which are easily countered by the arms of the law.

Borderlanders face multidimensional problems. In Nigeria there are many examples of victims of borderlands due to the creation of states in 1967 and 1976 into the twelve and nineteen state structure respectively. For instance the man living at Ote formerly in Western region, suddenly finds himself one day living partly in Oyo and partly in Kwara State. Because his farmlands are on either side of the main signpost which welcomes the visitor to, and bids him goodbye from Kwara, he finds himself farming in Oyo and Kwara States, worshipping in Kwara, with friends and relations on both sides of the "artificial" boundary separating Oyo from Kwara. A division which to him never existed and still never exists, it nevertheless obliges him to respond to two sets of relations decreed respectively at Ibadan demanding his income tax at home and from Ilorin also demanding his income tax on his farmlands. The peaceful settler suddenly finds himself torn apart at the slightest border conflict. So-called friends turned open enemies, eager to take over his fertile farmlands. Schools which had welcomed his children because of his useful contributions to the community now regard the same children as aliens with restricted differential higher school fees.

Examples can be multiplied of the problems of interstate borderlands within the same nation-state. In the northern part of Nigeria, the case of Uba can be sited. When Nigeria had the twelve state structure, Uba was a town in the then North East State. When that state was divided into Bauchi, Borno and Gongola States, the Trunk "A" road running through the centre of Una was used to form part of the "visible" boundary separating Borno from Gongola. Thus the people of a town which used to be one suddenly woke up to find that by crossing a main road they became "alien" in another area of jurisdiction. During the Second Republic ruthless politicians emphasised and capitalized on the divisive aspect of the artificial boundary in order to create social unrest and gain cheap popularity and political victory. Another aspect however which must not be overlooked in this issue is the rivalry which ensued and which expanded the frontier of development in the areas. Each side tried to outdo the other in the provision of basic facilities for its people. This is particularly true in Bauchi and Plateau States where the state capitals and other developments points are glaring examples.

In the Nigeria-Benin border areas along Okuto, Gbawojo, Igolo, Idiroko and Seme border-towns, simple folks are known to filter daily across borders bringing into Nigeria tomato puree, fresh and roasted fish, cloths, stockfish, liquor, jewellery, fruits and several food items. They exchange these through the medium of the naira for detergents, provisions, cocoa seeds and food. At the end of each day's activities, business had been successfully transacted bringing pleasures to the borderlanders on both sides of the boundary by the simple fact of crossing "artificial" boundaries. The next day Nigeria's military men take over power in order to curb the excesses of former political leaders, bring sanity to society and revamp an ailing economy. To do this effectively, Nigeria's boundaries are declared officially closed. Life for the border man is disrupted. Everything comes to a standstill. How long will this impasse last remained uncertain.

From these few examples it is quite clear that most of the African nationals have their kith and kin spread over international boundaries of neighbouring states. Asiwaju Jr. (1984) remarked for instance that there is a strong connection between the Western Yorubas and Eguns in Nigeria and the Yoruba and the Eguns in the Eastern and Northern part of the Republic of Benin. The same connection could be established between the Ejagbam of Cross River State of Nigeria and Western Cameroun while the Fulani nomads and the Hausa of Northern Nigeria are closely related to the Fulani and the Hausa in Niger, Chad and Cameroun. These variously related peoples, especially the illiterates, (unlike the educated in both countries, who recognize the implication of international borders) interact freely, e.g., trading, (usually regarded as smuggling) in cocoa, for example, across the Nigeria-Benin frontiers and groundnuts across the Nigeria-Niger frontiers. To these people who live astride national boundaries, all said and done about economic sabotage and smuggling or border closures constitute meaningless governmental policies.

The complexity of the reality of the borderline becomes aggravating when one thinks that because of the artificial demarcation of the boundary originated by European powers, the pen put on paper thousands of kilometres away was dividing lines separating people from the same home and dictating according to Boggs (1940).

> As a result of this border-play which the borderlander is not party to, he has now been made to feel different. Asiwaju Jr. (1984) in "A study of College Gaskiya—a Nigerian school in a non-national cultural environment" remarked that during his several trips across the Nigeria-Benin border, sharp and contrasting ways of life between the educated elites of the Republic of Benin and Nigerian elites were recognized. He observed that both elites on either side had schooled in two different and distinct alien cultures and had gained a new social place and a new culture, and thus were not inclined to work within the context of indigenous culture.

In the educative process, the fact is recognized that the French rigidity and assimilation policy, for instance, did not allow the development of the mother tongue which included Fom, Egun and Yoruba in Dahomey. French, being regarded as the unrivalled language of instruction from the preparatory or nursery school to the University, was used. Similarly, one became aware that the British policy of toleration encouraged not only the development of the mother tongue but placed it on the school curriculum thereby making it recognized as a medium of instruction. By implication therefore, while the Beninoise educated Yoruba is vast in French he is completely illiterate in Yoruba orthography. He demonstrates his expertise of French, not only language-wise but in his general comportment as bearers of French culture, a situation that nauseates his counterparts on the other side of the artificial boundary who are not only well versed in English but deeply learned in local languages" (Asiwaju Jr. 1984, p.8).

From the foregoing discussions it must have been established that border regions are a living reality demonstrating an inner coherence and unity peculiarly their own.

Basic Assumptions

The basic assumptions from which this study derives are that border regions as socio-cultural systems are a living reality. They are part of the society and are characterized by an inner coherence and unity which is essential to their nature. Vico and Montesquieu (1968) identified within them meaningfully interrelated complex of traits, not a haphazard assortment. Burke and Maistre (1968) stressed the idea that a society is like an organism the parts of which are in a natural balance that should not be disturbed by arbitrary innovations derived from abstract reasoning". Similarly this writer is of the opinion that border regions, by virtue of their nature and characteristics, have attained certain harmony of character which is distinct to them. Their study, therefore, requires a systematic analysis, integrating the interplay of knowledge and experience to bring out their richness and quality of life as wholes not in parts.

Suggested Methodology

It is on this premise that social scientists in general and social studies educators in particular make their claims that the proper study of man, where ever he exists on the surface of the earth, requires an integrative participatory approach. Hence the methodology suggested in this paper for the study of borderlands is that which views man as an essential actor with specific problems related to his environment and which must be appropriately diagnosed and solved to demonstrate man's mastery over, and contributions to, his environment.

Musa (1985) referred to this type of study as participatory research identified as "research which is based on the democratic interaction between the researchers and those among whom the research is conducted". This democratic interaction is premised, as it has been established earlier in this paper, on "the political participation of the exploited and oppressed classes in society in conducting research on the causes of their exploitation. It has its roots in the anti-imperialist struggles which have taken place and are continuing to take place in the colonies and neo-colonies of the world". In this context, the experience of the Chinese Communist Party in the early 1940s under the leadership of Mao Tse-Tung is relevant. Central to Chairman Mao's conception of development was the question of education through participation for the vast masses of the people so that they could become fully conscious of their own development potential.

Talking about development, Nyerere (1973, p.60) observed that "People can not be developed; they can only develop themselves". Hence to improve the lot of borderlanders and thus aid the development of borderland regions there must be an awakening of critical consciousness of borderland communities. The catalytic process of freeing the creative forces of the impoverished and exploited of any given society and enabling those forces to come to grips with the problem of underdevelopment would necessitate the involvement of the hitherto "researched" people in the study of their own environment.

To achieve these objectives therefore, participatory research is advocated. Hopefully this will lead to pragmatic reforms. Such reforms will not only involve the borderlanders in this research process and thus offer a learning opportunity to them and us the researchers; but which will also incorporate the government officials and political leaders at all levels in the common inquiry. In this way, there comes a merger of interests between the borderlanders and researchers on the one hand and administrators on the other. Participatory research, as suggested in this paper, not only fosters cooperation between and amongst the researcher, borderland communities and the authorities, but also leads to the establishment of development projects. The best that can be attained for borderland regions is in the area of development projects where efforts will be directed at developing each border region. This is where the interplay of knowledge and experience, referred to earlier on and stressed by social studies, becomes significant.

In order to embark on practical research that will provide an adequate understanding of the complex reality of borderlands and provide a view of human behaviour such that each individual is seen as active agent in his environments rather than passive objects functioning only to the tune of "unrealistic" government policies, many fields of knowledge such as is incorporated in integrative education, must be employed. Williams (1976) making a claim for integrative education observed that school subjects have tended to become preserves belonging to specialist teachers, a situation which has resulted in the creation of artificial barriers between disciplines, which in turn has tended to make teachers feel unqualified or not free to trespass upon the dominions of other teachers. The specific values of each subject have been pressed to the neglect of values common to several or all. He went on to remark that the school course has come to resemble the hundred yards course, each subject following a tract marked off from the others by a ledge that the "specialism has certain strengths, it is urged that the common ground of subjects, the seedbed of sound learning, should not be neglected".

This is a strong case for the social studies integrative approach to the study of man. Social Studies makes no claim on early specialization but rather a broad based education which enables the individual to perceive a given aspect in its multiple dimensions. Its approach cuts across the barriers in subject areas. Its stronghold is a wealth of knowledge derived from many sources ranging from the humanities, to the social and physical sciences and law. Its strength is participation in experience to be felt and lived through as concrete experiences not as abstract reasoning. The process reveals a systematic progression from the known to the unknown, the familiar to the distant approached wholly not partially (Adeyoyin in Aina et al., 1982). Any approach at a proper study of the borderland regions must take cognizance of these aspects in order to preserve their inner coherence, unity and harmony of character in a natural balance.

Recommendation

As follow-up to this seminar, and in an attempt, therefore, to help the border regions to develop themselves, the following recommendations are made:

i) That the participants in this seminar as participant/observers be grouped according to their regional interest.

ii) That each group demonstrates the interplay of knowledge "expertise" and experience in their composition.

iii) That development projects be set up in each region whereby the researchers and members of a research constituency enlist the support of the binational authorities in order to bring about a change in some identified behaviour and thus ensure the "take off" in the border region's state of development, and

iv) that such participatory research projects form the basis of subsequent annual seminars.

Bibliography

Adeyoyin, F.A., "Social Studies: An Overview" in Aina, N.F., et al. (ed) *Social Studies: A Book on Methodology* (Ibadan: Evans Brothers, 1982).

Asiwaju, A.I., "The Alaketu of Ketu and the Onimoko of Meko: the changing status of two Yoruba rulers under French and British Colonial rule" in Crowder, M. and Ikume, O., (eds) *West African Chiefs* (Ife: Univ. of Ife Press, 1970).

_____*Western Yorubaland Under European Rule, 1889-1945: A Comparative Analysis of French and British Colonialism* (London: Longman, 1976).

_____"Migrations as revolt: the example of the Ivory Coast and Upper Volta before 1945" *Journal of African History* XVII, 4, pp. 577-594.

_____"The Aja-speaking peoples in Nigeria: a note on their origin settlement and cultural adaptation up to 1945", *Africa* (Int. African Inst., London) Vol. 49, No. 1, (1979), pp. 15-28.

_____*Borderlands Research: A Comparative Perspective*, Border Perspectives Series No. 6, Centre for Inter-American and Border Studies. University of Texas at El Paso (CIABS UTEP) November 1983.

_____"Borderlands as regions: lessons of the European trans-boundary planning experience for international economic integration efforts in Africa", paper presented at the International Seminar on the Economic Community of West African States and Lagos Plan of Action, NISEB, Univ. of Ibadan, Dec. 12-16, 1983.

_____"Artificial boundaries" inaugural lecture delivered at the University of Lagos, Dec. 12.

Asiwaju, P.O., "College Gaskiya, Porto Novo: a national school in a non-national environment", B.A. education essay, Univ. of Lagos.

Boggs, S.W., *International Boundaries: A Study of Boundary Functions and Problems* (New York: Columbia Univ. Press, 1940).

Burke and de Maistre, "Cultural integration" in *Integration International Encyclopedia of the Social Sciences* Vol. 7, (London: Collier and Macmillan, 1968), p. 372.

Hall, B., Gillette, A. and Tandon Rajesh (eds), "Creating Knowledge: A Monopoly?" Participatory research in development. Publishers, Society for Participatory Research in Asia New Delhi Participatory Research Series No. 1 (1982).

Hansen, N., *Border Economy: Regional Development in the Southwest* (Texas: Univ. of Texas Press, 1981).

Mao Tse-Tung, "Some questions concerning methods of leadership" in *Selected Works of Mao Tse-Tung* Vol. 3, (Peking: Foreign Languages Press, 1967), p. 290.

Musa, M.B., "Demystification of knowledge creation: a critical reconsideration of research for human centred development", *Lagos Education Review* (1985).

Nyerere, J.K., *Freedom and Development* Dar-es-Salaam (Oxford: O.U.P., 1973), p. 60.

Pope, Alexander, "The Study of Man" in S.G. Wesley (ed) *The Social Studies Curriculum Proposals for the Future* (Fairlawn, NJ: Scott, Foresman, 1963).

Vico and Montesquieu, "Cultural Integration" in *Integration: International Encyclopedia of the Social Sciences* Vol. 7, (London: Macmillan, 1968), pp. 372-386.

Williams, M., (ed), *Geography and the Integrated Curriculum* (London: Heineman, 1976).

CHAPTER 29

Border Studies:
The State of the Art in Europe

by Raimondo Strassoldo

Traditional Border Studies

Europe is a densely, thickly settled region, with an old written history and a large number of centres of study and research. Every inch of its territory, every local community, however small, almost every human group has been the object of more or less extensive, recent and "scientific" literature. Border communities are no exceptions. In most of them one finds a vast storage of knowledge on local history and geography—civil libraries, museums, cultural institutions, academies, individual scholars. The border, being *one of* the defining features of such communities, most of this literature can be considered as "border studies" or, it can be re-analyzed in such a framework.[1]

Then there are those studies where the border is *the* focus of analysis. This can be of two sorts. One is mainly "academic", descriptive/interpretative, and usually carried out in the context of "regional geography". Borderlands are places where the "anthropic" realities and, in particular, social, political and economic institutions, make a peculiar imprint on the physical landscape (Whyttlessey). Moreover, in these places it is easy to carry out comparative studies. Thus within regional geography one finds a sizable spate of analyses of border regions.[2]

The second type of traditional, explicit border studies is characterized by its focus on disputed, conflictual borders of nation-states, its legal-military-political approach, and often its policy-orientation. Such studies are often instigated by institutions dealing with foreign and military policy, and are motivated by the search of the "just" or "natural" boundaries, by the effort to legitimize some of them or to lay claim to some others. The literature of this type is large; some such studies are unabashedly ideological or instrumental,others are more objective and scholarly; some are quite local, particularistic, others have broader views and more universalistic, (i.e. generalizing, aspirations). Political geography and geopolitics are the disciplines in which border problems are more extensively and systematically treated.

In sum, "traditional" border studies are characterized by a legal and geographical theoretical approach, by the focus on conflict, (i.e. on disputed borders, and by a statist ideological orientation).[3]

Modern Border Studies

Since the mid-sixties, a wholly different sort of border studies have developed in Europe. They are characterized by a new emphasis on the socio-economic aspects; focused on integrative, rather than conflictual processes, and on the problems of border people, instead of the nation states; and are instigated by local authorities and European organizations, rather than by national governments. Even more than the traditional ones, however these studies are policy-orientated.

The distinction between "traditional" and "modern" (or, perhaps better, between "old-fashioned" and "contemporary"), like most such dichotomies, is more logical than ontological. Descriptive studies of state boundaries and their adjoining areas are still being done, although political geography suffered along period of neglect, and regional geography, as the systematic description of regional differentiations, has long lost its centrality among the geographic disciplines. On the other hand, in older literature one can find some examples of strikingly modern approaches; (e.g. the "theorie des frontieres" put forth eighty years ago by the Belgian sociologist and social reformer, Guillaume De Greef), and the "social principle" of boundary-making suggested shortly afterwards by the geographer, L.W. Lyde. The former suggested that the general social processes of differentiation of the internal structures of social systems are paralleled by corresponding processes at their boundaries, which tend to "fray" at the same time as the processes—sometimes indicated as "ecological expansion" (i.e. the widening of social systems) bestow a crucial role on border areas as the "growth poles" the junction and saturation between societies.[4] Lyde, in discussing the criteria for the best way to draw boundaries between societies, criticized the widely prevailing "separation" principle, according to which boundaries should be drawn along the lines of minimum contact, (i.e. in less populated and active places); on the contrary, he maintained, they should be drawn across thickly settled areas and towns, in order to "force" the neighbouring powers to cooperate in the management. This is roughly akin to the "buffer-state" and the "condominium" principles; but makes sense only in a pacifist and integrationist perspective.[5]

There are no direct links between such speculations and modern border studies in Europe, which arise from two different, albeit intertwined, socio-political developments. One is the post-war drive for European unity, the second is the reawakening of localism and regionalism. The new Europe was envisioned by many as the "Europe of the peoples", not of the State-Nations. The emphasis on economic integration, the "Common Market", was meant as one of the instruments and avenues of socio-cultural-political integration; but there were others. One was the establishing of a tissue of direct communication and cooperation between local communities, across state boundaries. This was taken up as special province by the Council of Europe. It was on its lap that representatives of local communities from the whole of the Western part of the continent met and organized themselves as Council of European Local and Regional Authorities to exchange views, compare problems, think out common solutions. And it was soon clear that the communities and regions, more struck by European divisions and more eagerly pressing for its integration, were those located in the borderlands. Their "cahiers de doleances" began to show typical patterns. Border regions emerged as a distinctive type of regions, characterized usually by:

a) problems of ethnic and linguistic minorities;
b) economic problems due to the peripheral location with respect to their national core areas and to the dependency of borderland economies on the vagaries of boundary policies and international relations;
c) cultural and psychological problems, due to often ambiguous relationships both with the centres and the communities across the boundaries; and
d) planning and environmental problems.

Border areas are the ones where the physical infrastructure of the neighbouring systems have to be harmonized; they are often real "bridges" across nations. But marginal areas are also the ones in which the mainstream societies tend to dump their wastes, and locate obnoxious plants. As "pollution knows no frontier", there are problems of coordinated environmental control.[6]

Local authorities in borderlands, of course, did no limit themselves to the presentation of problems. They were long busy in trying to meet them, to set up cross-border organizations. Such activities were quite informal and in fact, illegal in most European countries, where all "foreign" relations are direct responsibility of the central states; only a few of them allowed some, very limited, competence to local and regional authorities in this field (notably in the federal states like Switzerland, Germany and Austria). Much of the cross-border "transactions" were therefore of a spontaneous, "private" type; a growing need was felt to recognize themselves as a pressure group to force the states, first, to proceed faster on the road of European integration and, second, to devolve on frontier regions more power to deal with their peculiar problems.

The potential of frontier regions as a special force toward continental integration was quickly perceived both by Europeans activists and theorists and by the Council of Europe. But the potential of European organizations in protecting and furthering their interests was equally well perceived by the representatives of border regions. This alliance seemed particularly felicitous to those who envisioned a federalist, bottom-up, regionalist, model of a united Europe, as a collection of local and regional authorities.[7] A colder reception was given to the issue by those who had other ideas about Europe. Thus, for the economy-oriented technocrats of the Common Market, the problems of border regions are simply wither a) problems of imperfect integration, which will wither away as the union progresses; or b) problems of economic and spatial marginality, to be redressed by policies of regional re-equilibrium.

The issues of "frontier regions" (as borderlands are usually called in Euro-Franglais)[8] were presented in ever more numerous and important forums. What formerly were simple "log rolls", passionately spelled out by mayors and other political leaders, grew into more and more systematic and detailed studies, especially in the issues of planning and of "frontier workers".[9] They were instigated by both local authorities and sectional interests (such as the Chambers of Commerce) and by European organizations. But also some centres of academic research grew interested in the subject. These literature constitutes what we have called the modern border studies in Europe.[10]

They can be classified and analyzed in a number of ways. Some are local (case studies), some are more general. Some (few) are more empirical, others more conceptual, theoretical and speculative. Some are more descriptive, others heavily normative.

It is not easy to pronounce judgement on over-all quality. We feel that they could be much better, if concerned parties could invest in them even a smallPP fraction of what is spent on other fields. We also feel that the most rigorous and useful are the juridical studies. Economic and sociological research on European borderlands with a focus on the effects of the border, its problem and their solutions is almost nil.[11]

This posits a problem in the sociology of science (or sociology of knowledge). Why is empirical, broadly social, research on borders so woefully underdeveloped in Europe? One possible answer lies in the general underdevelopment of the concerned disciplines, and in the generally lower status of empirical research, relative to the situation in other cultures (we are thinking especially of the U.S.). A second explanation is that the "frontier region movement" is concerned not so much with the detailed description and analysis of the problems, but with their potential as political issues, with their instrumentality in furthering the interests of local communities and of European unity. The common attitude is "we know enough; what we need is to act". While this is understandable, it is hardly conducive to research. The shortcomings easily manifest in a society where more and more the decisions, even political ones, are rested on rational basis inspired by an objective knowledge of the real world. The peril is that European border studies end up by feeding only on themselves.[12]

The Diversity of European Borderlands

The special features of "modern" European border studies can thus be traced back to the prospects for integration which are rather peculiar to this subcontinent.

Here however it should be pointed out that European borderlands are of many different species, in correspondence to different geographical and political contexts.[13]

Central Axis. Most of the "frontier regions" literature basically refers to the common borders of the Netherlands, Belgium, France and West Germany. This is, politically and economically, the core area of integrating Europe; and the local and regional communities in this area (essentially along the Rhine axis) have been the pioneers in the field of cross-border organizations and the driving force of what we have called the "frontier regions movement".[14]

Other "internal frontier regions". To this nucleus we can add the borderlands between France and Italy, also both original members of the European Communities, and those between the newer members. The situation here is, however, very diversified. The borderland between Germany and Denmark has been the seat of intense cross-border cooperative exchanges for a long time. On the other hand, the boundary between the Irish Republic and Ulster is one of the few officially disputed ones in the world, and the borderland in which one of the most active and bloody conflict still rages. The France-Spain boundary has two faces: the officially long-standing peaceful and cooperative relations, owing also to the presence of the same ethnic groups on both sides (Basques and Catalans); and the tensions and conflicts generated by the militant separatist groups. Then there are the borderlands between Spain and Portugal, about which little is known to the present writer; more light will be undoubtedly thrown in the near future, since Spain has volunteered to host the next European Conference of Frontier Regions.[15]

All these interior frontier regions of the European Community are placed in a perspective of ever closer and "more prefect" integration (economic, political, cultural etc.) of the bordering countries.

But then there are other border situation, where the neighbouring countries belong to different political contexts, and have no immediate perspectives of formal "merging", although they may already be highly integrated in a number of aspects; and, finally, borders along countries of widely different socio-political orientation and structure. Such borderlands can be grouped as follows:

Nordic Countries Norway, Sweden, Denmark and Finland have common borders, both territorial and maritime. They belong to different political alignments (Norway and Denmark belong to the NATO, Sweden is non-aligned, Finland has "special relations" with the USSR), but also have many historical cultural, economic and other things in common. They entertain a variety of good-neighbour policies, and numerous nuclei of "trans-frontier co-operations" can be detected, beginning in the far North, cross-border home of the nomadic Lapp pastoralists, and ending in the south, where the main problem is the management of common transport infrastructure in the Skagerrak and the Oresund. What characterizes these activities is their matter-of-factness, their lack of political rhetoric. This may have to do with national characters; or the lack for perspective or urges for degrees of political integration and union, beyond the present ones, which are already high enough, and apparently quite satisfactory for everyone concerned. These borderlands are object of excellent socio-geographical studies.[16]

The Alpine Arc. Two of the countries in this section, Switzerland and Austria, do not belong formally, either as a rational choice or because of external constraint, to the European society, economy, and culture. To the Alpine arc belongs also part of Yugoslavia, a socialist, one-party country. Of course, France and Italy also have Alpine borders. In this whole area, borderland cooperation is prompted by many factors—the presence of recognized national and ethnic minority groups (Italian vestiges in France, French Occidents and Franco-Provencals in Italy, Germans and Slovenes in Italy, Slovenes in Austria, Italians in Yugoslavia, etc.) common history and culture (Switzerland being a four-nationality country; large sections of the Eastern Alps being former provinces of the Hapsburg empire, etc.); common socio-economic problems, connected with the Alpine environment, and, finally, the need of a common management of transport infrastructure across the rugged Alpine ranges. Despite the different internal and foreign political reactions of their respective countries, border regions along the Alpine arc have along tradition of cooperation and trans-border organization.[17]

Maritime-peripheral region. Europe is a continent rich in islands and peninsulas, and these regions display some features in common with borderlands; essentially, their being peripheral with respect to national (and European) core areas. French Brittany and Sud-ouest, Italian mezzogiorno, Ireland, Cornwall and Scotland, and now some Iberic regions, belong in this category, in some context lumped together with other types of border regions (indeed the open sea is a certain type of border).

Regions along the "Iron Curtain". Europe harbours, along with the more open ones, also the most hermetically closed and "ugliest" of all boundaries: that between Western and Eastern Germany[18] the primacy being contested only by the frontier between North and South Korea. Also the Czechoslovakian borders with Western Germany and Austria are extremely tight. These borderlands are literally "with their backs to the wall" and have therefore special disadvantages. They are granted special assistance both by the concerned governments and the European

Community.

Eastern Europe. Little is known to the present writer about the borderland situation in Eastern Europe. The impression is that basic conditions for the development of "frontier regions" in the Western sense are lacking. There are, for example, no autonomy of local community and social forces in prospects for a freely-chosen trans-national integration. Being forced to live in a supranational, coercive and economic context, Eastern countries are extremely jealous of their national identity, and of what little sovereignty they are left with.

A further characteristic, probably hindering trans-frontier cooperation, is that most Eastern Nation-states are, in a sense, very young, uncertain of their identity, and occupying partly new and disputed territories. It may be interesting to stress here that most Eastern European boundaries are much more "recent" and "artificial" than the African ones. Most Eastern countries harbour large minorities of different national and ethnic groups, and, when they have managed to form homogenous units, this has usually been done through extensive and painful population transfers, ruthless policies of assimilation and suppression of diversity, and substantial relocations of boundaries. All this has left heritage of ethnic-national problems which embitters, although usually only in a latent form, relations between the "brethren" in the Socialist camp. In other words the impression is that in Eastern countries border problems are still of the "old-fashioned: type, connected with nationalism, and territorial claims, and rife with potential conflicts. This is quite clear in the case of Hungarians in Rumania (Transylvania) and in the case of Bulgaria's claims over Macedonia belonging to Yugoslavia and its suppression policies towards the Turkish minority.[19]

The Common Peculiarity of European Borders: "Openness" vs. "Porosity"

Beneath the variety of European border situation one finds, however, one common trait: all of them (with some very minor exception) are tightly controlled by the Central Governments. They may be more or less open or closed; by they are not "porous", if by this term is meant the spontaneous state of permeability, the inability of the states to regulate themT,&
Teffectively. Smuggling is certainly not unknown, especially in the case of light weight, easily concealable, high-value wares (e.g. drugs and currency); and illegal movement of persons, clandestine migration, is also present. But in comparison to the enormous amount of legal cross-border exchanges, the above do seem to amount to a tiny fraction, and also in absolute numbers there seems to be nothing to compare to some border situations in other parts of the world.

This hypothesizes peculiarity seems attributable to a number of reason. One is the relative homogeneity between bordering countries; differentials in prices, wages, opportunities, standards of living, etc. are not as high among European countries as, for instance, the U.S.-Mexico case, where the richest and one of the poorest countries in the world meet or, as has been noted by Professor Asiwaju, the most spectacular land border between the First and the Third World.[20]

A second factor is probably the stronger grip of the State system on their citizens. Most of the European peoples have live under some sort of Central State for centuries, and are generally very state-conscious, law-abiding loyal citizens. There are (or rather were) cases of smuggling traditions, and even of a smuggling folk cultures, in some European border communities, especially in some remote mountain areas, or in some busy harbours like Naples (harbours, like airports, are a special type of border-place). But in general, again, it can be maintained that these are marginal phenomena.

This factor is linked with two others. A stronger state tradition means usually a stronger State machinery for the control of boundaries. In fact, customs guards and border polices are among the oldest State and military institutions; they are part and parcel of the European history and literature (Take just two examples; the *Three Musketeers* saga and Bizet's *Carmen*). In general, State services are in Europe highly organized and respected, deeply rooted in the consciousness as well as in the territories - "hard" in contrast with what G. Myrdal called the "softness" of many newer States. The administration of borders, their management and regulation, is firmly in the hands of central States; the technical machinery is, in general, quite effective.

Finally there is the geographical factor. Illegal border crossing is easier in places of high population density (because of the anonymity of urban crowds); or sparsely settled, remote, forested or busy, or otherwise rugged terrain. Many European boundaries, however, run through intensely cultivated and settled areas. All vehicular routes are controlled by border police, and strangers walking in the fields near boundary lines are liable to be quickly spotted and reported by the law abiding rural folks.

As we have said, however, the main reason of the relatively low (illegal) "porosity" of European borders is their high (legal) "openness" and the high homogeneity of neighbouring countries. Where, in Europe, there were important elements of differentiation (of political economic systems) and a low level of openness, as with the Eastern countries, the amount of clandestine passages could be quite high, so much as to require the well-known physical sealing of the borders with walls, barbed wire and mine fields.

Three Models of Border Situations

What we have in mind in the above is, obviously, a comparison between African, the American and European border situation. It seems to us that they correspond to three general models or ideal-types, which can be arranged in a comparative-evolutionary scale, referring to three different stages of societal development. They can ce labelled, respectively, the Nation-Building, The Coexistence, and the Integration models.

Nation-building. Nation-states of more recent origin have the paramount problem of internal integration, which also means a "hardening" of their boundaries. In order to function effectively, a system must, among other things, be able to control its relations with the environment; for a socio-political system, this means the ability to selectively filter inputs and outputs; (i.e. to control ever more finely its boundaries). Autonomy, self-sufficiency and sovereignty mean, first of all, the control over the inflow and outflow of persons, goods, energies, ideas. National "unity" and "homogeneity" entail differentiation from other societies. All this has clear implication for border areas. Once homogeneous areas are split by state boundaries, the fractions tend to develop along divergent paths, nurture different loyalties, languages, values, economies. This, of course, often means disintegration of older local unities, laceration of communities, and often intersocietal tensions and conflicts. African borders seem all too often to belong to this type.[21]

Co-Existence. In this case, the neighbouring nation-states may have already achieved some satisfactory degree of "systemness", (i.e. of internal integration).

They have no major problem of national identity. Their "functional" (cultural, political, economic etc.) boundaries, as well as their territorial ones, are un-disputed. Because of their contiguity they have in any case what the economists call "externalities", (i.e. relations arising out of sheer spatial contact). They can choose a policy of "closure" (avoidance, dissociation, separation), and therefore inhibit all human "commerce" in the border areas; in some cases, they lay waste a strip of ter-rain ("no man's land"); in others, they build fences and walls, This co-existence may nevertheless be called peaceful, even if it is the peace of lifelessness. Relations bet-ween the two systems are carried out exclusively centre-to-centre. In this case, there is not much scope for border studies; other that those illustrating the marginaliza-tion of such areas.

In most cases, however, contiguous societies entertain some level of "neighbourliness"; people living in border areas areT,& Tallowed some interaction across the boundary. The differences between the neighbouring societies, in fact, stimulates exchanges of many types. This is particularly so in the economic sphere, since the differences in price, quality and types of goods and services naturally pro-motes exchanges; but also cultural, political and generally social diversity has some effect of this kind.

Most commonly, borders between co-existing societies alternate closed segments (where passage is prohibited) and open ones, where passage is permitted in a regulated mode. Such alternation may occur also in time, and/or with reference to particular types of exchanges.

State policies in border areas may reflect predominantly the goals and interest of the society as a whole, as conceived by the central powers, or may take into ac-count, to some extent, the interests of the border populations. The latter may even be granted some special statutes and facilities (for instance, easier passages, economic franchises and import permits, access to trans-border facilities). This, in effect, amounts to drawing "lesser" internal, functional and spatial boundaries around affected border regions.

The "peaceful co-existence" model seems by far the most common the world over. Most neighbouring states do allow some interaction at the borders, and do have some special arrangements to regulate them; many of them also have some kind of special policies for border areas and people. Because of its universality, and pro-bable prevalence also in the future[16], this model seems also the most interesting for scientific research and policy suggestions. The US-Mexico border seems a perfect instance of this model.

Integration. In this case, the neighbouring systems are steered towards ever higher degree of integration, of mutual interpenetration, of merging. States are will-ing to "devolve" their powers and surrender their sovereignties to higher and wider levels of societal organization. At their borders, what were walls and barriers evolve into doors, bridges and junctions; and these, in turn, may evolve into the new centres of the overall supra-system.

All this was very common in the past and is very well documented in history. Many frontier outposts developed into the core area of new civilizations. Buffer states—like Belgium and Switzerland—become continental and world centres. This is the kind of process sociologists like De Greef had in mind when they theorized about frontiers and boundaries.

The Integrative Context of European Borders

Transnational integration is another name for what other sociologists used to call "ecological expansion" or "epigenesis of political communities", (i.e. the widening of societal horizons to bring about the growth of larger societies through the absorption of lesser ones, the spreading of organized, large-scale, ever more "civilized", and "modern" societies) (Etzioni). It seemed obvious, to classic social theorists, that this process would progress until the whole of mankind would from a single, unitary, integrated world society.

This is not the place to discuss this enormous issue.[22] World society does seem to be growing, but at a pace much slower than one hoped for (or feared), with growing dis-equilibria, and in forms often unexpected. New divisive and disintegrative forces have arisen, and the prospects for terminal catastrophes seem much closer than those for planetary integration. "Regional" unions at continental level are progressing at a disappointingly sluggish pace, if at all. The main drive seems to be, the world over, towards the strengthening and internal integration of state societies, and the hardening of boundaries between them.

The area where (sub-) continental regional union seems to have progressed more steadily, even though, for some, exasperatingly slowly, is Western Europe. There may well be other comparable cases, where the neighbouring countries are at a reasonably similar and advanced level of civilization, are wide-open to each other, and the levels of de-facto interpenetration and integration are even higher than in Europe; the US-Canada border cases comes immediately to mind. But there may be many more, in Latin America or elsewhere.

What is unique to Western Europe is that continental unity has become a widely shared value, a political ideology. The sociological spread and moral intensity of this ideology is certainly still limited, much too limited in our views; but we believe that it is stronger, in both relative and absolute terms, than in any other continent.

What is important in this "Europeanist" ideology is that, in its fullest expressions, it presupposes the "withering away", the overcoming of the nation-states. Europe, is, it seems to us, one of the few places in the world where the Nation State model of political organisation has lost much of its moral fascination in the heart of men, and where it is subject to manifold ideological attacks.

It was in Western Europe that nation-states were first invented, and it is only natural that here they first matured and, hopefully, decayed.

Of course the state machinery is there, stronger than ever; the "Welfare State" is still bloating and extending, and practical, utilitarian nationalism is rampant. But state-nationalism, as the paramount social philosophy and moral force of the XIX Century has, we submit, grossly weakened. One of the main successor ideologies is European Unionism.

Again, the issue cannot be adequately dealt with here. We just want to emphasize that on the subject of regional integration Europe is ahead the situation in other continents such as, for example, North America is respect of the US-Canada case. We know of no socially and politically legitimate movement for the merging of those two states: as far as we know, nationalism is rampant there as in most other place in the world. We know of no US-Canada border local authorities battling in the interest of their communities by claiming the more perfect union between the two countries; we know of no "frontier region movements" as pressure groups for the merging of US and Canada.

In general, movements for trans and supra-national integration are quite weak in the world outside western Europe, for a number of reasons. One of them is that, apparently in historical experience, the processes of "ecological expansion" and of integration of societies were always accompanied by the force of arms. It appears that political communities grow and unite only through wars of the threat thereof, and of course war has become a less and less socially acceptable mode of inter-societal interaction. Thus, while some other forms of integration (communication, economy, etc.) may be progressing, legal-political integration is not. The formal in-ternational system has been generally "frozen" in the form shaped by the last World War; with the only difference that former colonies became new states, in the mould of the classic European model, and in the bounds traced by European colonial powers. Even in the most obvious cases of "ecological expansion" by war, as in the cases of Laos and Kampuchea in the Indo-Chinese peninsula, the forms have been respected. The world over, state boundaries (National Frontiers) are still utterly sacred and one of the main political concerns is to demarcate, sharpen, strengthen and harden them.

Only in Europe one hears of the need for "de-functionalizing", "Devaluing", overcoming, withering away of the boundaries, one hears of the Nation-state as an "obsolete" mode of societal organization, of the need to "efface" it towards higher levels (European union) and lower levels (local and regional communities); of fron-tier regions as "laboratories" for the experimentation of such new models of political organization, as points of saturation of old, painful wounds, of foci and spearheads of integrative processes; of borderland communities as miniature ex-emplars of the new, united Europe.

Admittedly, these feelings are still in the buds; they need much care and cultiva-tion. But they are, we believe, the most advanced one can find the world over.

They have been grown out of the ashes of terrible wars, the Great European Civil war, 1915-1945, during which some European Nation States transmogrified into militaristic, totalitarian monsters, and it took the efforts of the whole world to destroy them. The drive for European Union is nourished by the memories of this tragedy and the determination that is should never, never happen again; and that the merging of European Nations is a common political system was the best safeguard.

History does not repeat itself. We hope that trans-national unions, in other con-tinents, will be grounded on other bases than the immense heaps of rubble and cor-pses we had in Europe. But we also hope that the European experience, in the field of overcoming state-nationalism and alleviating the problems of border people, can be of some inspiration also elsewhere, so that European horrors will not be replicated.

Conclusion: Some Principles of the Theory of Borders

It is in this spirit that we should like to end this sketch of the European experience by recalling some of the principles that can be distilled from the European literature, both "traditional" and modern, on border problems.[23]

a) The first is that *all boundaries are artificial.* They are human impositions on the continuous tissue of nature. Boundaries can be old or recent, accepted or disputed, already impressed on the landscape or cutting through still homogeneous landscape and so on. African boundaries, for instance, are in no way more artificial than European or other boundaries.

b) The second is that *boundaries are essential part of every system (or thing).* Nothing can exist (i.e., "stand-out") unless it is somehow bounded, differentiated from its background or environment. To make boundaries "wither away" is tantamount to a wish to dissolve the system into non-existence. Boundary-maintaining is one of the basic functions of all living systems, from macromolecules to international communities. *Boundaries are needed to protect diversity.*

c) *Most systems have two kinds of boundaries:* Spatial and functional, and there are relations between them.

d) *Spatial boundaries have ambiguous features:* they divide and unite, bind the interior and link it with the exterior, are barriers and junctions, walls and doors, organs of defence and of attack and so on. Frontier areas (borderlands) can be managed so as to maximize either of such functions. They can be militarized, as bulwarks against neighbours, or made into areas of peaceful interchange.

e) There are three main kinds of border situations: the "frontier" (open, expansive, dynamic, attractive, rich); the *"periphery"* (closed, static, stagnant, repulsive, poor); and the *"bridge"* (open, active, attractive, rich). In the modern world, all space has been partitioned among nation-states, and there is no more place for "classic" frontiers; they have been metaphorized in economic and symbolic terms. Periphery is the standard situation in closed, centralized societal systems, unless effective policies of regional equilibria are implemented. Bridges occur at the point of junction between any two societal, partly-open systems.

f) *Borderlands are usually different from core* (central, interior) *areas, and have some commonalities with "sister" borderlands across the boundary.* This arises from a great variety of factors. One of them is that usually boundaries cut across homogeneous cultural areas, and create minorities. The second is their distance (spatial, social, etc.) from the respective cores. A third is the dependency of their economies on the border policy decision made at the centre. A fourth is the similarity of functions (e.g. military or economic). A fifth is the occurrence of economic integrations (e.g. cross-border commerce, industrial plants, etc.). A sixth is their physical contiguity (need for joint infrastructural planning, environmental management, etc.) and so forth.

g) *Spatial justice require that border people be not handicapped, in their daily lives, by their location.* Governments should take into account the disadvantages (as well as the advantages), of living in the borderlands, and adopt adequate special policies to redress the imbalances. This usually means granting border regions a number of special statuses and aids.

h) *Daily lives of local communities in border areas often require interaction and cooperation with people across the border.* Local authorities should be granted the autonomous powers to do so, and even enter into legal obligations and formal organizations with their counterparts across the border. *Neighbouring relations between border communities are not international relations.* An experiment in this direction has been made within the Council of Europe with the "outline convention on trans-frontier cooperation", signed by many states.[19]

i) *Relations between border people should be manages so as to maintain a sense of friendliness and common humanity,* because borderlands are one of the potential or actual "foyers" of trans-national integration, and thus of pan-human solidarity.

Endnotes

1. The present author has done something of the sort for his own border region, Friuli: see e.g. R. Strassoldo, B. Cattarinussi (eds), *Friuli, la prova del terremoto*, (Milano: Angeli, 1978): R. Strassoldo, *Friuli-Venezia Giulia, a border region*, in VV.AA., *Regionalismus in Europa*, (Munchen: Intereg, 1981): R. Strassoldo, "Regionalismus and Ethnicity—The Case of Friuli," *Int. Political Science Review*, 6, 2, 1985.

2. A good example of such studies is F. Lentacker, *La frontiere Franco-Belge, Etude geographique des effects d'une frontiere internationale sur la vie des relations*, (Lille, 1974). Extensive bibliographies can be found in the already classic books by Prescott, The Geography of Frontiers and Boundaries, (Chicago: Aldine, 1965) and of P. Guichonnet and C. Raffestin, *Geographie des frontieres*, (Paris: Puf, 1974).

3. The references here could be legion, covering the whole of political-geography literature, and many international-law studies. A study trying to develop an interdisciplinary approach to a "science of boundaries" (or limology, from lat. limes=limit) is H. Dorion, *La Frontiere Quebec-Terreneuve*, (Quebec: Presses de l'Universite Laval, 1963). There are also historical and comparative studies of border disputes, like S. Tagil, *Studying Boundary Conflicts: A Theoretical Framework*, (Stockholm: Esselte, 1977). A case study employing a sociological, comparative, anthropological and historical approach is that of F. Gross, *Ethnics in a Borderland, An Inquiry into the Nature of Ethnicity and Reduction of Ethnic Tensions in a One-time Genocide Area*, (Westport, CT and London: Greenwood Press, 1978).

4. G. DeGreef, *Theorie des frontieres et des classes*, (Brussells: Larciere, 1908).

5. L.W. Lyde, *Some Frontiers of Tomorrow—An Aspiration for Europe*, (London: Black, 1915).

6. The environmental issue has grown as one of the most burning ones in trans-frontier affairs. A larger and larger part of transfrontier contacts and organizations revolve around it, and also official international organizations, like the EEC and most notably the OCDE, have been active and effective in this field. See e.g. OCDE, *Problems in Transfrontier Pollution*, (Paris: OCDE, 1974). A very good overview of the issue (without scholarly apparatus of references, however) has been presented at the Borken Conference (1984) by J.M. Woehrling, director of the European Affairs at the French Ministry for the Environment.

7. The best "manifestoes" of such a doctrine issue from the European Cultural Centre and the European University Institute of Geneva, both animated by Denis de Rougemont. His thought, synthetising federalist, regionalist and environmentalist theories (along with many others) has been sumamrized in *L'avenir est notre affaire*, (Paris: Stock, 1977) and has enjoyed a wide popularity, having been translated into six languages. It has also been the object of seminars and ensuing "satellite" publications, like G. De Puymege (ed) *Autour de "L'avenir est notre affaire"* (Lusanne, Charles Veillon, 1984).

8. The terminological issues are rather thorny and pprobably insoluble, due to the interference of several linguistic traditions, even within what is officially English. Many authors have discussed the differences between "borders" "boundaries" and "frontiers" and the several, sometimes contrasting, connotations of each term. It seems that "international English", under the American influence, prefers the terms border and borderland, while the English used in continental Europe more often uses the term "fontier regions" under the influence of French, where there are almost no alternatives to "region frontiere" or "region frontaliere" (the terms *limite, borne* are much rarer).

9. The leading expert here isw C. Ricq of the Geneva Institutes mentioned above and Geneva University, author of several highly valuable studies on the subject; the latest one having been presented at the Borken conference. See also his full-scale book, *Les travailleurs frontaliers in Europe* (Paris: Anthropos, 1981).

10. Pioneer in this field, in addition to the Geneva centre, has been the University of Bruxelles, which in 1969 organized a seminar whose proceedings where published a year later under the editorship of P. Romus with the title *Les regions frontalieres a l'Heure du Marche Commun* (Bruxelles: Presses Universitaires, 1970). In 1972 the Gorizia seminar took place; the proceedings were edited by the present writer in a multi-lingual book with the title *Boundaries and Regions: The Peace and Growth Potential of Border Regions* (Trieste: Lint, 1973). Among the later ones, we can mention the 2nd Gorizia Conference, held in 1979, with two books of proceedings in English, R. Strassoldo, G. Delli Zotti (eds), *Cooperation and Conflict in Border Areas* (Milano: Angeli, 1982); and B. De Marchi, A.M. Boileau, *Boundaries and Minorities in Western Europe* (Milano: Angeli, 1982). An important seminar was held at the European University Institute in Florence 1981; the proceedings have been edited by M. Anderson, of the Univ. of Edinburgh, and published by Frank Cass, London, first as a special issue of the "Journal of West European Politics" 5, 4, Oct. 1982, and then as a free-standing volume.

11. A pioneer effort by R. Gubert on the Italian-Yugoslav border, *La situazione confinaria* (Trieste: Lint, 1972) has been left without noticeable followers. Many surveys and other types of sociological analyses have been conducted in many other border areas, but usually with less theoretical and systematic ambitions. No comparative research has been done, to our knowledge.

12. This is the sensation one sometimes gathers in the perusal of papers presented at the various "frontier reegions" conferences, specially those of a more "political" character, and the materials gathered by the Council of Europe. These are often collections of official records and press releases of official meetings of local authorities; it is often difficult to understand what the sociological and behavioural substance is, beneath the rhetoric.

13. The most scrupulous analyst of European cross-border organizations is V. von Malchus, author of a cumulative row of papers on the topic. See e.g. his *Partnerschaft an Europaishen Grenze, Integration Durch grenzuberschreitende Zusammenarbeit* (Bonn: Inst. fur Europaishen Politik, 1975); idem, "Bilanz und Perspektiven der Institutionelle Entwicklung grenzuberschreiteder Zusammenarbeit in Europa" paper presented at the 3rd Meeting of European Frontier Regions, Borken (W. Germany) 1984.

14. Most of the regions in this borderland have an umbrella joint organization, called Association of the European Frontier Regions (ARFE), which is heavily German. Also the official name is German, according to the charter (Arbeitsgemeinschaft Europaisher Grenzregionen, AGEG).

15. The preceeding ones have been held, under the auspices of the Council of Europe, in Strasburg (1972) and in Innsbruck (1975) and, as mentioned, in Borken (1984).

16. For inst. see T. Lunden, *Individual Spatial Behaviour in a Boundary Area* (in Swedish with English summary) (Inst. of Geography, Univ. of Stockholm, 1973).

17. The meetings and the literature on border cooperation in the Alpine Arc are numerous. A very large-scale meeting was held in Milan in 1973; its proceedings have been published in three volumes (in Italian) as *Le Alpi e l'Europa* (Bari: Laterza, 1975). A second meeting on the same scale has been held in Lugano, March 1985. Individual transfrontier regions in this area are very active; among the best organized seem the "Community of the Central Alps" (ARGE ALP) joining German Bavaria, Austrian Tyrol and Vorarlberg, Italian South Tyrol, Trentino, Veneto and Lombardy. At the estern extreme of the arc we find the Community of the Regions of ALPE-ADRIA, with the Italian regions of Friuli-Venezia Giulia and Beneto, Austrian Styria, Carinthia, Low-Austria and Salzburg, and the Yugoslav republics of Slovenia and Croatia. Memberships in such organizations are somewhat confusing, since multiple memberships are allowed. There are differences between "full" member and "observer" status, and all can be easily altered from session to session. These organizations are usually very productive in glossy brochures and planning documents.

18. German planning departments are richly documented about the plight of such areas. They have also been the object of a study by D. Shears, *The Ugly Frontier* (London: Chatto and Windus, 1970).

19. One example of such border-ethnic problem study is P.R. Magocsi, *The Shaping of a National Identity, Sub-Carpathian Rus, 1848-1948* (Boston: Harvard Univ. Press, 1978). A collection of studies of the Eastern situation, with a focus on the problems of ethnic and national minorities, can be found in AA.VV., *Regionalismus in Europa* (Munchen: Intereg, 1981), cit. A socio-economic study of the effects of Poland's post-war boundaries has been done by A. Kruszewski, *The Oder-Neisse Boundary and Poland's Modernization* (New York: Praeger, 1972).

20. A.I. Asiwaju, *Borderlands Research: A Comparative Perspective* (El Paso: Center for Inter-American and Border Studies, Univ. of Texas at El Paso, 1983).

21. The literature on African boundaries has recently been enriched by the study edited by Prof. Asiwaju, *Partitioned Africans, Ethnic Relations Across Africa's International Boundaries, 1884-1984* (London: Hurst and Univ. of Lagos Press, 1984).

22. Suffice it to refer to the literature on international politics (or, better, the "interior politics of the Planet Earth"), international relations and international sociology, variously called. I have tried to explore such issues in several other papers and books, and especiallyu in *Temi di sociologia delle relazioni internazionali* (Gorizia: ISIG, 1979), where extensive references can also be found.

23. The following principles are a distillation of several writings of the present author, in turn based on rather extensive, multidisciplinary readings on the general issues of boundaries. The most detailed and complete study can be found on the book cited above, Chapter 3 ("La teoria dei confini"); the most synthetic and "philosophic" one to date is *Boundaries in Sociological Theory, A Reassessment*, in R. Strassoldo, G. Delli Zotti (eds), *op. cit.*

CHAPTER 30

Research Activity on the U.S.-Mexico Borderlands: Trends and Challenges

by Oscar J. Martinez

The purpose of this presentation is to provide some information regarding research in the field of U.S.-Mexico Borderlands Studies, to discuss some of the problems faced by border specialists, and to suggest strategies that might be followed in the future to improve our understanding of the region. I will focus some attention on research activity at the University of Texas at El Paso, an institution where many faculties have long been involved in Borderlands Studies. Hopefully the information to be presented will be helpful for drawing useful comparisons between what African border scholars and institutions with interests in border research have encountered in their work, and what their counterparts in the United States have faced as they have sought to develop Borderlands Studies as a recognized field of academic inquiry.

The Development of U.S.-Mexico Borderlands Studies as a Research Field

Awareness of the U.S.-Mexico border area as a distinct region deserving serious attention from researchers began in the 1920s when Herbert Bolton, a prominent American historian, promoted the teaching and research of the history of the "Spanish Borderlands", i.e., the Southwestern United States. Bolton pioneered numerous studies on Spanish exploration and colonization of the region. His students continued that tradition, building an impressive body of borderland historical literature.

Since Bolton's time, other historians have done considerable work on borderlands history, emphasizing in particular events of the 19th and early 20th centuries, when Mexico and the United States clashed repeatedly over numerous boundary-related issues. Most of this research focuses on the borderlands in the context of the relations between the two countries.

Historians continued to dominate the field of Borderland Studies until the 1960s when members of other disciplines became interested in the rapid population growth and economic development that was taking place along the border. Studies focusing on such topics as demographic trends, migration, urbanization, industrialization, trans-boundary relation, ethnic relations, and environmental concerns began to appear with regularity.

By the 1970s, there were enough American and Mexican scholars engaged in borderlands research to merit the creation of professional association, which became known as the Association for Borderland Scholars. The principal force behind the effort to establish this group was Professor Ellwyn R. Stoddard, who has presented a more direct first hand experience in the paper that is also included in this book.

The work of borderlands researchers, which was once seen as marginal by mainstream scholars in Mexico and the United States, is now well accepted and respected. Universities, foundations, and government agencies have made more resources available to promote the study of the region, and this has encouraged younger scholars to focus their energies on the borderlands. Thus, compared to previous years, the field of U.S.-Mexico Borderlands Studies finds itself in a very favourable situation, and the future looks promising as well.

Problems and Challenges Faced by Border Researchers

As a group, borderlands scholars have made impressive gains regarding their standing in the profession, but as individual researchers they continue to confront some unique difficulties in carrying out their work. Financial support for borderlands research is still relatively limited, although this varies from discipline to discipline. For scholars who doe interdisciplinary work, it is often difficult to obtain support because many funding sources are accustomed to thinking along single disciplinary lines. No funding source has a programme that applies specifically to the U.S.-Mexico Borderlands, or to the study of binational zones in general.

Apart from funding considerations, borderlands researchers encounter certain problems not faced by non-border investigations.[1] For example, in getting background information on a topic, the binational borderlands researcher finds few studies that treat both sides of the boundary. This is explained by the practice followed by most scholars of stopping their investigations at the border, wither because the other side is outside their own geographic limit, or because they lack the tools to do research in another language, or they know little about the neighbouring country. The consequence of this situation is that many studies are incomplete, or their perspectives reflect parochialism and ethnocentrism.[2]

A related problem is the difficulty in finding source material. Research is much easier on the U.S. side, because the published literature and the primary documentation is far more abundant than on the Mexican side, and the facilities are much better. The Mexican side lacks resources to maintain and make available basic research materials, although in recent years some progress has been made through the efforts of the Centro de Estudios Fronterizos del Norte de Mexico and various universities. On any given topic pertaining to the Mexican borderlands, the chances are that the researcher will have much better luck getting information in Mexico City, where research facilities are better developed than in the border region itself.

Investigators who use statistical or mapping data are frustrated by the lack of uniformity and comparability in the data that are available. There is little coordination by the two sides in the conceptualization of the data gathering process and in the presentation of the information. Consequently researchers can only present a part of the reality of the border. In a few cases some semi-meaningful statistical comparisons can be made between the two sides, but assembling and presenting the data can be very laborious and frustrating.

Obtaining access to data is often a problem, especially on the Mexican side. This can often be overcome to some extent by working cooperatively with Mexican scholars who are closer to the data sources and who know their own country's bureaucracy much better. This consideration as well as other advantages flowing from transborder academic cooperation have led a number of U.S. and Mexican institutions to undertake joint border projects. One example is the biennial border research conference sponsored by PROFMEX (Consortium of U.S. Research Programmes on Mexico) and ANUIES (Consortium of Mexican Universities). Another is the on-going 12-volume Border Atlas project, which involves the participation of an equal number of Mexican and American scholars. The Border Atlas is under the direction of the University of California at Los Angeles.

A final problem that is very appropriate to mention is that it is very rare indeed to find published studies on the U.S.-Mexico borderlands that take into account how that research relates to work done in other border regions of the world. Little attempt has been made to draw comparisons between the U.S.-Mexico borderlands and other binational zones. If this approach were followed by even a handful of scholars, perhaps we could begin to generalize about the functioning of borders in the modern world. In the relative absence of such research, we in the United States and Mexico will continue to examine our borderlands through parochial lenses, in isolation from other parts of the world.[3]

We may cite some examples to illustrate how the shortcomings in the way border research is conducted diminishes our understanding the region.

It is widely accepted that intense social, economic, and cultural interdependence makes the borderland a distinct area, yet that distinctiveness is difficult to describe in precise terms for lack of binational research. An example of a topic that needs to be treated in a trans-boundary framework is the condition of the Mexican population in the region. Existing studies on Chicanos (People of Mexican descent who live on the U.S. side) incorporate little information about the impact of the Mexican side on their lives. Similarly, studies of the Mexican border population have failed to establish links with conditions on the U.S. side. There is no question that the relationship between these two groups is a significant one, but the nature of those ties remains largely unexplored.

A related question that begs for more research is the extent of the cultural and economic differences between the U.S. borderlands and the U.S. interior, and the Mexican borderlands and the Mexican interior. Writers typically mention linguistic, cultural and economic characteristics that illustrate differences between each periphery and its corresponding centre, but in depth, systematic analysis is lacking. What is it precisely that sets the border zones apart from the core areas? How far do the unique features of the border areas extend inward? What differences does all this make in the lives of the people?

It is often said that the interests of the border population (on both sides) clash with those of the central governments. This is particularly evident in key policy areas such as immigration and trade. While the generalization about conflicting interests may be correct in principle, we do not know the degree of that divergence or precisely what characteristics it assumes. Unquestionably for the U.S. government the border area is an irritant; to a lesser extent that is also true for the Mexican government. For the border population, policies formulated in Washington, D.C. and in Mexico City often produce major headaches because of disruption caused in the normal flow of goods and people across the boundary. To understand the phenomenon of conflicting interests we need to address basic questions such as the following: How fundamental is the clash between the interests of border people and those of interior populations? Does each government have a clear and consistent policy toward the border? How are decisions that affect or are directly aimed at the border made? What role do border people play in the formulation of those decisions?

Promoting Borderlands Research in the University:
The Case of the University of Texas at El Paso

Having given some background on the development of the U.S.-Mexican Borderlands Studies and having mentioned some of the problems encountered by investigators in this field, we should now turn to the unique challenges that have faces scholars who have attempted to develop Borderland Studies as a recognized and supported research field in their own institutions. We will focus on the University of Texas at El Paso not only because it is the writer's own university, but also because it is recognized as the institution with the most sustained borderlands research activity dating back many years. Aspects of what has transpired at UTEP may be found in other American universities as well, but the effort to institutionalize Borderlands Studies research in a university setting is best revealed in the UTEP case.

It took a long time before Borderlands Studies gained the support from local administrators, that was necessary to establish it as an important field on our campus. It then took additional effort to persuade state authorities to fund the programme we developed at a respectable level. Simply put, there existed a lack of recognition of UTEP's uniqueness as a border university possessing ideal advantages for conducting borderlands research. The University's remoteness from the state capital and weak ties with influentials and decision makers did not help our cause. The relative lack of institutional support, however, did not deter UTEP borderlands scholars from carrying on their work, and over the years they compiled a very respectable research record. Recently our fortune has changed, and now we have some basic institutional support that we lacked in the past.

The Centre for Inter-American and Border Studies, which the writer directs, is the entity that coordinates and supports borderlands research on campus. Support is offered to our faculty through administrative services and through small research grants. Our scholars can also publish their research findings through the Centre's Publication Programme, which includes the publication of research papers, reports, and monographs. Books are published in cooperation with Texas Western Press, which is located on the campus. A special part of the Publications Programme is our newspaper series, which allows researchers to disseminate findings and ideas to the public at large.

The most active component of our Publications Programme is our research papers series, which is divided as follows: (1) the Border Issues and Public Policy series, and (2) the Border Perspectives series. The first series focuses on policy questions that are important to the people of the borderlands, and the second series allows for humanistic, philosophic, theoretical, and other non-policy oriented interpretations. Since 1982 the Centre has published some 30 research papers, and they have been circulated throughout the United States and abroad. In 1984 the Centre cosponsored publication with Texas Western Press of a book on border resource needs and issues, and in 1985 we will cosponsor publications of a book on contemporary Mexico and another on transborder relationships in comparative perspective. The Centre was also instrumental to the publication in 1984 of a book in Spanish on Chicano short stories.

In developing our publication programme, we began by publishing the work of our own scholars, but lately most of our authors have been from other universities. Recruitment of manuscripts has been aided considerably by our close ties to the Association for Borderlands Scholars. Over the last two years our Centre has been in charge of organizing the annual meeting, and that has pus us in close touch with many researchers, and has given us an opportunity to expose them to our publications programme. Consequently we have published a number of the best papers presented at the meetings.

As already stated, the Centre for Inter-American and Border Studies is the lead border programme at our University, but there are other entities that complement our activities. Mention has already been made of Texas Western Press, which has been publishing books and monographs since the early 1960's on a wide variety of borderlands topics. The Chicano Studies Programme coordinates teaching and research activities having to do with the Chicano population. The Institute of Oral History, an entity of the history department, maintains a collection of some 700 tape-recorded interviews representing a cross-section of border society. Perhaps half of the interviews are in English, and the other half in Spanish. The majority are transcribed, making it easy for researchers to utilize the materials. In the School of Business, the Bureau of Business and Economic Research collects and disseminates data on business and economic conditions along the border. Statistical information and scholarly articles are published by the Bureau in its *El Paso Business and Economic Review.* Finally, the library maintains an outstanding collection of published and unpublished materials on northern Mexico, the border region, and the American Southwest. Known as the Southwest and Border Studies Collection, it is housed in the Department of Special Collections and Archives, which is situated on the top floor of a new, spacious building which overlooks Ciudad Juarez, El Paso's twin-sister city on the other side of the border.

The combination of these support programmes and the active participation in border-related research of some 30 faculty members make UTEP a leader in U.S.-Mexico Borderlands Studies. Yet it is only one of many universities in the Untied States promoting this field. Other institutions with significant border-related programmes include the University of Texas at Austin, Pan American University, New Mexico State University, University of New Mexico, University of Arizona, San Diego State University, University of California at San Diego, and the University of California at Los Angeles (UCLA). UCLA deserves special mention because of its on-going Border Atlas publication project, which will produce about a dozen volumes focused on varying aspects of the border region. On the Mexican side of the border, the Centro de Estudios Fronterizos del Norte de Mexico carries on an impressive research agenda as well as a publication and teaching programme.

Summary and Conclusion

Today the field of U.S.-Mexico Borderlands Studies commands considerable visibility in the United States and Mexico because of the growing importance of the borderlands for both nations. The number of scholars investigating borderlands issues has increased dramatically in recent years, with a corresponding expansion of the published literature.[4] Universities throughout the borderlands and beyond have established programmes to promote teaching and research in this field.

Yet despite the advances recorded, much remains to be done by researchers to provide a satisfactory understanding of the nature of the area. Most of the available studies fail to treat the borderlands in a binational framework, and only a few published sources draw comparisons between the U.S.-Mexico borderlands and other border regions in the world. It is encouraging that a number of researchers are now attempting binational studies but, apart from the work of Anthony I. Asiwaju with Roger Gravil,[5] and perhaps a few others who have escaped detection, very little comparative work is being done. It is hoped that as borderlands scholars from different countries come together in conferences like this one, it will serve to stimulate research that is global in its conceptualization. That strategy is essential to the further development of Borderlands Studies in the United States and Mexico, in Africa, or anywhere else in the world.

Endnotes

1. For a more detailed discussion of this subject, see Paul Ganster, "Difficulties Encountered in Binational Border Research" (in the forthcoming volume resulting from the 1983 border conference held in Tijuana, Mexico, to be published by PROFMEX [Consortium of US Programmes on Mexico] and ANUIES [Consortium of Mexican Universities]).

2. Interestingly, the question of imbalance in resource material has also been reported as a major methodological problem in African research experience. (See A.I. Asiwaju, *Western Yorubaland Under European Rule 1889-1945: A Comparative Analysis of French and British Colonialism* (London: 1976), p. 6. This pattern is fortunately changing in the case of the U.S.-Mexico, as revealed in the descriptions of a number of on-going borderlands research projects. See the *International Inventory of Current Mexico-Related Research* Vol. 4, (San Diego: The Centre for US-Mexican Studies, Univ. of Calif., 1984), items 428, 436, 439, 441, 442, 451, 457, 459, 468, 475, 477, 478, 479, 487, 494, 503, 512, and 513.

3. One American researcher who does engage in comparative borderlands research (comparing conditions along the US-Mexico border with those found in European border zones) is Niles Hansen, from the Univ. of Texas at Austin. See his *The Border Economy: Regional Development in the Southwest* (Austin: Univ. of Texas Press, 1981). *Across Boundaries: Transborder Interaction in Comparative Perspective* (El Paso: Texas Western Press, 1986) also examines the US-Mexico border in a comparative framework. For a relevant critique of US-Mexico border scholars, see A.I. Asiwaju, *Borderlands Research: A Comparative Perspective* (El Paso: Centre for Inter-American and Border Studies, Univ. of Texas, Border Perspectives Paper No. 6, Nov. 1983).

4. Cesar Sepulveda and Albert E. Utton, (eds), *The U.S.-Mexico Border Region: Anticipating Resource Needs and Issues to the Year 2000* (El Paso: Texas Western Press, 1984); Jerry Ladman, (ed), *Contemporary Mexico: Crisis and Change* (El Paso: Texas Western Press, 1985); Oscar J. Martinez, (ed), *Across Boundaries: Transborder Interaction in Comparative Perspective* (El Paso: Texas Western Press, 1986); Ricardo Aguilar, et al., *Palabra Nueva: Cuentos Chicanos* (El Paso: Texas Western Press, 1984).

5. A.I. Asiwaju with a contribution by Roger Gravil, "Border Impact: Notes on a Comparative Study of the Nigerian, U.S.-Mexico and Western European International Boundaries", mimeograph, Lagos, 1985.

CHAPTER 31

Developmental Stages of U.S.-Mexico Borderlands Studies: Implication for the Study of African Borders[1]

by Ellwyn R. Stoddard

Introduction

Unlike traditional academic *disciplines* such as political science, sociology of history, border studies as a specialized *field of inquiry* must draw upon those scholars willing to venture outside the narrow confines of traditional academic boundaries to make their professional contribution. These scholars then must skilfully balance their own discipline's demands for "mainstream conformity" and at the same time pursue controversial and innovative investigations in the peripheral border studies field. Yet, preparatory training for research in broad multidisciplinary frameworks is not readily attainable, even in the most liberal of academic disciplines.[2] So border scholars, without a formal regiment for training neophyte investigators, must learn much from trial and error. Those scholars initially attracted to border studies because of its exotic issues and complex methodologies are often disenchanted when they must also deal with the strains of professional marginality which accompanies those who chose a speciality field outside the accepted limits of their disciplinary boundaries.

The milieu of the U.S.-Mexico border region, one of the leading areas of the world within which this emergent field has evolved, has a pre-history and historical legacy. Its study should assist our understanding of the obstacles and challenges of evolving a professional border studies field. This essay will trace the evolutionary development and stages on the U.S.-Mexico border in order to see if they parallel those through which an emergent border studies focus on West African boundaries might also traverse.

A Prehistoric View of the U.S. Mexico Border Region

Today, the regions surrounding the 2,000 mile border between the U.S. and Mexico is comprised of a sparsely settled semi-arid desert area.[3] But some thousands of years ago, this American southwest region was very different. About 10, 000 B.C. it was a wet and marshy area, the water supplied from melted glaciers distributed

by seasonal monsoon rains. Dense semi-tropical foliage grew in abundance, allowing giant herbivores such as the elephant-like Mammoth to feed and live here.
Smaller plant-eating animals were stalked by sabre-toothed tigers, the oversized dire
wolf, and the deadliest of all huntsman. These hunters, known as Clovis, followed
the herds of shorthorn bison and lived among dog-sized horses, giant sloths and
camels, now all extinct in this region when the marshes dried up over the many centuries. When the water was no longer available in abundance, the plants became less
plentiful. The larger animals could no longer survive, and with their passing the
human hunters were forced to wander to other regions after the herds of bison, deer
and elk. But a few isolated sedentary clans remained in the arid southwest, adapting
to their grim conditions and living in pueblos, cliff-dwellings or in river hamlets
along the river valleys. Indian corn became a secure winter food supply and modern
archaeologists have discovered their use of pottery and tools suitable for their hostile
environment.[4]

About 1000 A.D. nomadic Athapaskan-speaking Indians from Alaska arrived in
the southwest. They not only hunted, but they live by raiding the meagre stores of
the agricultural settlements. Thus continue the cycles of conquest and adaptation in
the Borderlands. Meanwhile, in northern Mexico, the Casas Grandes regional
trading centre flourished and had reached its zenith.[5] For all of these early culture
areas, the U.S.-Mexico border did not exist and did not restrict their trade or mobility. Only mountain ranges or broad desert sands modified their migration patterns.
Any land was "owned" by the group currently using it and the herd animals available
belonged to those who had mastered the hunting skills. Territorial integrity was a
concept which was foreign to prehistoric man and remained that way even after the
capricious nation-state borders had been artificially determined and established.

European Conquerors and the Border Region

Chronologically, the first persistent European conquest and colonization of the
Western Hemisphere began with Columbus landing in the Caribbean islands. From
there, the Spanish explorers spread out into South America, Meso-America and the
southwest. Figure 1 shows that at the time the Spanish arrived, only a few indigenous cultures had developed the societal complexity to be called "state
societies." For the most part, New World cultures existed in vaguely defined culture
areas separated from other culture areas by uninhabited lands. Topographical
characteristics were often the determinants of culture area limits. Among such
characteristics were impassable mountains or large lakes and rivers.

As early as 1540, Coronado led his expedition into the southwest in quest of
precious metals. Much territory was claimed from these exploratory ventures in the
hopes of future treasures which might yet be discovered, but the land was not valued
per se. As other European powers gained a foothold in the New World, the northern
boundary of Spanish-claimed territory shifted to the south.[6] Only a direct Russian
threat from Alaskan-based explorations forced the Spanish Crown to build a chain
of missions along the southern California coastline. But on the Louisiana frontier,
economic pressures forced Spain to retreat and consolidate her missions and
presidios as token strength for vast land claims. Ultimately, emergent independent
states broke away from their Iberian masters leaving only the dependent settlements
of northern New Mexico allied with Mexico.

The nineteenth century in the New World began with many colonies seeking
"Independence". More realistically, independence was merely the substitution of

Figure 1. Evolution of social organization levels in the New World
Source: Sanders and Price (1968:50)

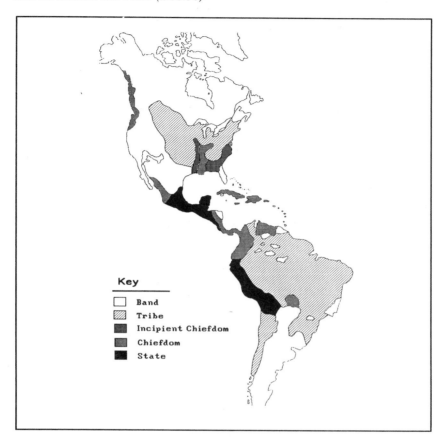

Key

- ☐ Band
- ▨ Tribe
- ▦ Incipient Chiefdom
- ▨ Chiefdom
- ■ State

New World elites for the former Old World monarchs. The existing feudal system, which had been transferred to America from fifteenth century Europe, did not change markedly as the newborn nations of South and Meso-America emerged as autonomous states. Mexico, which declared its independence in 1823, tried to control its elongated territory to the south and the north but within two decades had lost the Republics of Texas and California. In 1846, an American military action claimed the last northern stronghold—northern New Mexico. Following the signing of the peace treaty of Guadalupe Hidalgo (1848), the international border between the two countries was established in 1853. Although provisions were made to protect Spanish and Mexican land claims, the shift from the old Napoleonic Codes to the individual ownership system of British common law created conflicts and problems in claim legitimation. Though General Santa Ana, the undisputed ruler of Mexico, had encouraged the migration of Anglos to the Texas territory from 1823-1830, the official halting of further immigration did not stop the hordes of Western European immigrants who ere land-hungry, fleeing the poverty of Europe and seeking a better life for themselves and their families. These Anglo settlers had little compassion for the nomadic native peoples of America since their nomadic lifestyle and an absence of agricultural skills, according to strict Christian theology, meant that they had not honoured their stewardship over the land. Failing to subdue the land, they had lost their claim to it by Divine mandate.[7]

In summary, the Spanish feudal system used Spanish overseers and native labourers to do the menial work. In colonization, they sought a *land-with-people* over which they could rule. Therefore, in America's southwest they were generally unsuccessful in coping with the great expanse of arid desert and the nomadic Indian groups who roamed over it. On the other hand, the Anglo newcomers sought permanent *land-without-people* and as they secured their homesteads, they forced the hunting and gathering Indians to move elsewhere. Thus, both of these European conquerors maintained an air of inherent racial superiority over the indigenous inhabitants, but their colonization pattern differed markedly concerning the value of land ownership and the role of indigenous peoples in the development of the New World nations.

Establishment of the Political U.S. Mexico Border

Except for minor changes, the border as established in 1853 by the Joint Border Commission has become the official legal boundary between Mexico and the United States. But in a symbolic way, the wealth and power of Mexico's neighbour has perpetuated the belief that "gringos (Americans) stole nearly one-fifth of Mexico from its rightful owners." This smouldering resentment is a factor which underlies all border relations and diplomatic discussions. On the other hand, the U.S. continues to treat Mexicans as indigenous peoples who are inferior to those of European stock. This is evidenced by the severity with which border regulations are enforced on the southern border with Mexico as compared with how these are carried out on the Canadian border.

U.S. border cities have acquired their large population recently. For the first decades of this century, most border cities were small and underdeveloped. With the growth of agricultural enterprises, industries, and the railroads linking the border with the rest of the country, U.S. border communities have increased dramatically in population, while still remaining the poorest urban centres in all of the U.S.A.[8] And during those years when preservation of the integrity of our southern border was not a high priority for the federal officials and legislators, border cities in the U.S. and in Mexico grew in tandem, as twin cities.

The usual pattern was the location of an industry on the U.S. side which requires agricultural commodities or transformation industries. The capital would come from the U.S. and the labour would be supplied from the Mexican side. This symbiotic relationship grew along with the border community's population. Border jurisdictions knew that informal liaisons provided a coordinated effort to solve local border problems and that international agreements at the federal level only threatened border culture with severe dislocations. Traditional patterns of border cooperation and border movement of goods, services and people had been established over the decades. Now, when federal regulations were introduced to be enforced along the border, token compliance usually placated upper echelon bureaucrats and functionaries while functionally avoiding compliance as required. Official reports and statistics were submitted to support compliance which did not occur.

In time, two levels of border controls were operative—one the structural or formal negotiations which proceeded through official channels, and the functional of

Figure 2. Cultural areas of North America
Source: After Castile (1979:3)

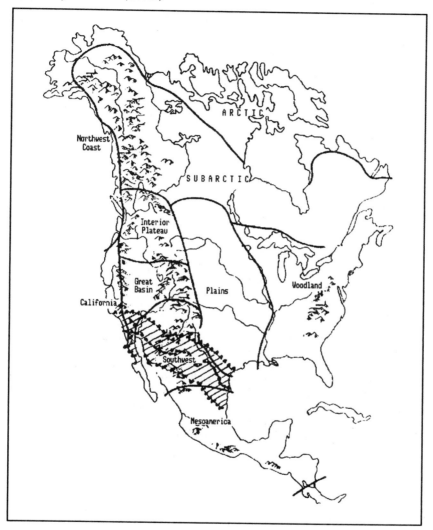

informal relationships which were unofficially maintained by local border functionaries. Federal mandates in conflict with local traditions and customs were first
ignored, then circumvented to the extent possible. If pressed by higher authorities
for compliance, they were altered in such a way as to fit in with existing border standards and patterns of behaviour.[9] In this way local border culture, consisting of a
single cultural entity extending across the political-legal boundary has been able to
survive against coercive codes and legislative mandates made by decision-makers
far from the border and without benefit of border input. Currently, the problem of
illegal Mexican migration to the U.S. is an institutionalized practice from a

Figure 3. Contemporary political-legal border between Mexico and U.S.

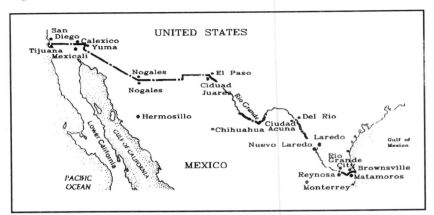

Borderlands perspective rather than a sudden burst of criminal law-breaking activity.[10]

Figure 2 shows some of the ancient *culture areas* throughout North America and Mexico with the modern Borderlands region superimposed upon it. As the vague culture areas emerge as zone or *frontiers,* the territorial demarcation of areal limits are more precisely designated.[11] When international diplomats agree on borders by means of arbitrary lines on a map without regard for topographical features and natural culture areas, it is no wonder that local border residents are often non-supportive of existing national borders such as appear in Figure 3. Although the formal boundaries are more precisely drawn on the national maps of national territoriality, the informal networks along a given border are the channels through which most day-to-day border activity is handled. But earlier students of the border region were not as aware of these intricacies as are contemporary Borderlands Scholars. So in order for us to trace the stages of development through which the field of border scholarship has moved, we must go back to the beginning of New World history and its European origins and work up to the present-time. The six temporal stages outlined in Table 1 will serve as a general guide for indicating major shifts in the field and its researchers.

Archival/Impressionist Stages (1492-1880s)

From the earliest era of Spanish Conquest of the New World, church friars dutifully recorded their operations, not only to document future financial requests, but to maintain doctrinal purity in an age of potential heresy. Las Casas, an early critic of Spanish *encomenderos* and military brutality, gives a far different notion of Spanish-Indian relations than later reports issued by the Spanish Crown. Following the Cortez victory among the mainland Aztecs, Sahagun[12] recorded many personal interviews in the indigenous Nahuatl language which captured pre-European Empires and their social and cultural systems. The Spanish missions, used to change nomadic Indian groups to a sedentary life and servile roles for Spanish overlords, preserved their letters. Many reflected extreme intolerance with indigenous populations even through the 18th century.[13] In some cases, a friar's account provided the only reputable information available about Spain's American empire. Their impact

Table 1. Typology of developmental stages in the field of U.S.-Mexico borderland studies

Stage of Development (Temporary Period)	Major Data Resources & Theoretical Perspective	Study Focus & Use of Analytical Concepts	Impact of Findings; Policy Implications
Archival/Impression-1st Stages (1492-1880s)	Explorer/military/church diaries, records; personal travelogues and ethnocentric perceptions	European management of indigenous peoples. Mostly anecdotal narratives.	Ligitimation of evolutionary development of cultures and justification for conquest or control of the land
Early Empiricism (1880s-WWI)	Native cultures--on-site description; Europeans--historical events & "Great Man" (hero) accounts	Data accumulation & limited diagnostic summaries	Heirarchial ordering of native and European cultures; sedentary superior over hunting/gathering
Research in Border Region (WWI-Post WWII)	Holistic ethnographies of native cultures, psychocultural interpretations; pre-historic man data	Comparative ethnologies; technological matrix of cultural evolutionary phase of development	Assimilation of non-English peoples and changing of native Americans; filling pre-history voids, supplemented by archaelogical finds
Border Issues & Resolution (Post WWII-1969)	Demographic, economic, political & cultural problems; border *structural* line between nations	Current issues, informal trans-border interaction as deviant; border region a comparative laboratory	Border solutions via international relations and diplomacy; political appeals to respective national leaders
Border Reconceptualization (1970-1982)	Empirical studies, often multidisciplinary; intra-national comparisons; border as symbiotic social system	Symbiotic linkages & *functional* border networks; border survival, adjust to to non-border mandates	Informal border networks functional, not deviancy; centralist policies not always applicable to local issues and problems; regional solutions?
Synthesis of World Border Studies (1983-present)	Multi-national data; border comparisons of developed-developing, developing-developing nation borders; world-wide coordination of border scholarship	Formal-informal border systems; national-local resolution; con-tiguous & "treaty" borders; multi-disciplinary & standardized border concepts	Acceptance of border networks for resolving border issues; shift from doctrine of national sovereignty to relevance of *structural* & *functional* frameworks in distinct border locations

was forceful. Fray De Niza's description of the Seven Cities of Cibola, unfounded as it was, prompted the Coronado expedition throughout the southwest.[14] Other reports were also influential.

Military leaders or explores issued reports or kept diaries. Bernal Diaz de Castillo[15] kept one account of Hernando Cortez campaign against the Aztecs. The names of Castaneda, Jarmillo, Beltran de Guzman, Coronado, the little known Melchor Diaz[16] and the brutal De Soto[17] all wrote on indigenous peoples and of their travels in stage lands. New World policies of expansionism or retrenchment were based largely upon these fragmentary, and unverifiable, accounts. Though early religious descriptions of pre-Columbian cultures are tainted by religious biases, they are still the most complete and earliest ethnologies of the region.[18]

Old World travellers often penned informative travelogues of their visits to the American frontier during the latter eighteenth century and the early nineteenth century.[19] Some Anglo American narratives were also written during that same era.[20] During the latter decades of the nineteenth century, many of these exuded racist comments which mourned the adulteration of the superior Teutonic or Anglo heritage.[21] But this was a common derivative effect of the smothering evolutionary theories, the ideology which dominated that period. Some writers subtly couched their views of racial superiority in condescending descriptions of "the noble savage" and his "quaint customs."[22] But this period of archival accumulation is still a valuable asset for background information, and especially useful to document the ethnocentrism of Europeans in their perception of the New World as of non-European peoples and lands elsewhere.

Early Empiricism (1880s-World War I).

There was no clean and perceptible break between the earlier impressionist writers and the more objective field observations written by travellers through the area. For example, Lumholz' descriptive narrative of the Tarahumars of northern Mexico is still the point of departure for modern anthropologists who wish to study that isolated culture.[23] Pioneering work by solitary scholars began a pattern of fieldwork, and data accumulation which would continue for some decades. An early pioneer couple, Adolph and Fanny Bandelier[24] worked among the Pueblos of New Mexico, effectively describing it as a culture area. During the first half of the twentieth century, many of the culture areas of the American southwest would become modern laboratories for examining pre-historic cultures and the dynamics of change accompanying European conquest.[25] The work of historians and ethnographers were scarcely discernible one from another because of the general scope and similarity of training each received; thus, historians claim Hodge and anthropologists revere Kroeber's consolidation of field research among the Indian ethnic groups in California.[26]

As increasing numbers of Anglo colonists moved westward to the California territory, the southwest became an exciting region for those recording these events. Individual chroniclers pursued their interest in recording particular events or periods. The practice of maintaining personal diaries, and the aforementioned archival records of mining, presidios, missions, early trade, and land ownership were only a few of the resources which could be used to reconstruct early events of a specific theme or period.[27] Just as the diaries of sea captains had provided some of the most insightful narratives concerning the era of conquest. Issues covered range from relations between Anglo invaders and the Mexican to events such as the Alamo and the

War with Mexico[28] including the record trek of the Mormon Battalion from Kansas to San Diego.[29]

A leading historian of that period, Herbert Bolton, discussed the northern frontier of Spanish influence. In his published volume, *The Spanish Borderlands,* which described the southern lands from Florida to the Pacific coast,[30] he had coined a word which would subsequently be applied in a more limited way to the final binational boundary between the modern states of Mexico and the U.S. Other individual historians made significant contributions as they focused on frontier life and events, institutions and immigrant adaptations to the harsh realities of the 'untamed' west.

A significant team effort of that period was the historians, archivists and writers under the direction of Herbert Howe Bancroft who methodically took each of the southwestern states and complied a thorough history of its development under the control of European immigrants. The monumental seven-volume set, which resulted from this effort, has the unique distinction of providing simultaneous accounts of events and perceptions as recorded by mainstream chroniclers and dissident writers.[31] But team projects were rare. Indeed, most of the scholarly work was done by individuals devoted to an issue. Such individual researchers collected materials and complied them into a readable account for others to become informed on a particular subject. An age of scholarly objectivity had emerged, although some impressionists continued to issue their publications and it was as important to know something of the book's author as to know about the subject being investigated.[32]

Scholarly Research in the Border Region (World War I-Post World War II)

This temporal stage was characterized by greater scholarly activity and sophisticated studies of peoples, events and institutions which happened to be located within the Borderlands. No noticeable preoccupation with the existence and impact of the border seemed to dominate the research of that period. Culture area studies by anthropological teams from eastern American Universities were common through northern Mexico and the American southwest. In fact, these continued right up through the World War II years.[33] Moreover, during the years of the Great Depression (1930s), the U.S. department of Agriculture initiated a series of field researches on rural life in America. Often referred to as "community studies," these focused on the Europeans and their adaptations to rural living in various regions of the country. These studies were usually done by rural sociologists, sometimes in concert with agricultural economists, or cultural anthropologists in sites which happened to be located within the southern Borderlands.[34] But these seldom perceived the border as a major factor in affecting the quality of life of rural residents nor as an obstacle to effect adaptation to the frontier environment. Even the classical work of Spicer,[35] which articulated the superimposition of Spanish and Anglo culture on prehistoric peoples of the border region did not focus particularly on the border as a major variable in his analysis.

Disciplinary boundaries were not as rigid during that period. Many scholars were generalists, being involved in political science, economics and sociology as their field(s) of expertise. Historians-turned geographers began to focus on the spatial features of border life, and to identify the cultural landscapes as a background for their historical interpretations.[36] Cultural geography branched out into political geography, describing the border interaction and its barrier effect.[37] From sociology, geographers borrowed the "central place theory" concept and began to explain the spatial patterns of the sparsely populated, semi-arid regions of northern Mexico and southwestern U.S. Comparative land-use studies became common along the border during the final years of this phase. Gradually, more teams were engaged in a single research project, some of which were inter-disciplinary in composition. But the greatest amount of border research completed in this stage was peripheral to the border and was mostly intra-disciplinary or at best, interdisciplinary in scope. Really multidisciplinary designs were still to wait.

Border Issues and Their Resolution (Post WW II-1969)

This stage reflected the increased pragmatism which was common to all research efforts of the post-War era. Thus, border studies began to focus on specific issues which gradually introduced the critical *role of the border itself* in the creation and amelioration of existing problems. The border was conceived as a political-legal demarcation line between two autonomous nations, a barrier to each through which the flow of people, goods and services was limited and monitored. The cultures which lay in juxtaposition to the bi-national border were the periphery of each na-tional system. "Leakage" through the barrier was seen as dysfunctional to both na-tional systems. This international relations model recognized only formalized trans-border interaction, and perceived that border problems had to be clarified and solv-ed within the diplomatic channels common to the federal governments of both na-tion involved. Because the border was perceived as a clean line of demarcation, it was a perfect comparative laboratory in which to examine the impact of cultural values on each side of the boundary line as they adapted to common problems of agriculture, quality of life, and border propinquity. Within this setting, the present writer, as a future Borderlands scholar was initiated into the growing field with its problems and policy issues.[38]

In 1954, a departure from former field projects involving southwest research was experienced at Michigan State University. Charles P. Loomis, with a substantial research grant from the Carnegie Foundation, assembled a team of established scholars to coordinate their expertise in studies of border life.[39] They represented anthropology, demography, medical personnel, political science and sociology; and after having researched their respective areas, these were brought together and com-bined into a single multidisciplinary report of border activity. The impact of this project was two-fold: it legitimated scientific research on the border area, while strengthening the *structural* model of national borders. The approach has the effect of masking the operations of complex informal networks operative along the entire length of the U.S.-Mexico border for nearly two decades. Similar team efforts at the University of Arizona's business research bureau and at Notre Dame, Indiana, sought to integrate the work of colleagues without seeing a need to develop a broader framework which permit multidisciplinary scholarship to flourish.

Border Re-conceptualization (1970-1982)

Having been a participant and active researcher in the Michigan State border project, this writer's relocation to the University of Texas at El Paso in 1965 made him a natural "clearinghouse" for colleagues doing border-related research. Some seasonal scholars, some aspiring Ph.D. candidates doing dissertation research, and ultimately border scholars from other countries began to inquire by letter or formal visit as to other scholars working on similar problems or the availability of published summaries of prior research in a specific area or on a given issue. At that juncture, only a sub-group within geography, the Conference of Latin American Geographers (CLAG), provided a formal professional vehicle for scholars interested in border studies to exchange views and become familiar with contemporary border research. In sociology, anthropology, political science and economics, some individual researchers were focusing on border problems but no coordinated effort to accumulate research findings was available.[40] Personally, I had become involved with border research as a necessary adjunct to my studies of *Mexican Americans*.[41] Informal contact with John A. Price (Department of Anthropology at San Diego State University) and Charles R. Gildersleeve (Departments of Geography at Oklahoma and Omaha, Nebraska), and Felix D. Almaraz, Jr. (Department of History at the University of Texas at El Paso and San Antonio) others in far away locations and in unfamiliar disciplines produced a growing resource of published material and expertise which was largely confined to *intra*disciplinary cooperation. To provided more *inter*disciplinary contacts and at the same time to provide a benchmark regarding the current status of borderland studies in some of the more active disciplines, five scholars were recruited to present "status of borderlands studies" surveys in a 1972 professional meeting. These represented political science, history, geography, economics, sociology and anthropology. Each summarized what had been published and what research was lacking to guide future scholarship. Updated versions of these manuscripts were then published as a special journal symposium.[42] As a beginning effort to formalize a professional association for border scholars, a publication was issues listing all known active researchers, their publication, interests and future research priorities.[43] Then, to replace the informal system of colleague communications, a formal organization was established in the Spring of 1976, complete with a newsletter, *Frontera*, and a paid-up membership of 50 people. The Association of Borderlands Scholars (A.B.S.) grew rapidly as isolated border scholars requested membership. As its firs president, I launched a project to assemble the most knowledgeable scholars in all disciplines relevant to the multidisciplinary investigation of the U.S.-Mexico Borderlands and published an encyclopedic reference work, the *Borderlands Sourcebook*.[44] A second project, the *Border Atlas,* outlines in 1977, did not materialize although another version is now nearing completion outside the ABS auspices.[45] The newsletter was to have become a refereed journal, an outlet for broad borderlands materials rejected by the non-specialized organs. [The dream for a professional journal was ultimately filfilled spring 1986 when the first issue of the *Journal of Borderlands Studies* was published—Editors]

In the early 1970s, a decade prior to the publication of the *Sourcebook,* an ideological impasse developed while I was accumulating lists of names on border scholars. What constituted the border? What made a border scholar different from a scholar doing research in the Borderlands? The traditional political-legal notion of contemporary structural bi-national border was not a framework in which scholars from more that a half-dozen disciplines could identify. Clearly, this field was in need of clarification and its time had come. In an effort to perform this function, I had written a short introductory essay on border studies together with the lists of border scholars and their research and publications. Rejecting the *structural* political-legal boundary model of border reality, a more comprehensive *functional* orientation had been adopted.

The border was seen as an accumulation of disciplinary *overlays,* each defining the border differently by area, period of time and its nature. The term Borderlands

(with an "s") came to be the symbol for allowing such diverse scholars as the ar-
chaeologist, colonial historian, contemporary demographer and desert botanist to
contribute their efforts at understanding the Borderlands phenomena without
restricting them to the simplistic "international diplomacy" framework. As scattered data were accumulated from scholars in a wide range of disciplines, each participant found it necessary to broaden his scope to include other disciplinary
variables. This new *multidisciplinary* approach became the basis for the contents
of the *Borderlands Sourcebook*.

The U.S.-Mexico Borderlands was conceptualized as one system (i.e. a *single
culture* spanning the national boundary) which had been created from an interpretation of cultural, economic, social, political and kinship linkages so necessary for
successful articulation of border activity on a day-to-day basis. This distinct border
culture also revealed the vast number of informal transborder networks which tied
border institutions together in a highly interdependent symbiotic relationship.[46] By
the end of the decade, other scholars, quite independently were conceptualizing the
Borderlands in similar terms.[47] Not only was the ABS organization been successful
in giving its individual border scholars a sense of *community,* some *visibility* and
legitimacy, but its influence encouraged others to promote the "field" of
Borderlands Studies as a potentially rewarding area for future research and scholarship. With more that 300 members, it has sustained the borderlands scholar as he
fights the war for legitimacy within his respective discipline.

This period of re-conceptualization of the nature of the Borderlands as well as
the adoption of a multidisciplinary orientation ended with some comparative border
studies of an *intra-* national character. The most obvious comparison was to differentiate between the workings and policy applications on the Canadian-U.S.
border with the southern U.S.-Mexico Borderlands.[48] Even though a number of
foreign scholars visited El Paso, the direction of scholarship was to explain U.S.-
Mexico border phenomena from concepts developed elsewhere or to acquaint
visiting scholars with the range and breadth of research being conducted in our
region. Otto Verkoren (University of Utrecht-Holland) contacted me to make informal arrangements for his geography graduate students to do research and receive
some direction from seasoned scholars in the El Paso-Ciudad Juarez area, which
later became somewhat formalized through the University of Texas at El Paso. Hans
Briner (Regio Basilienses-Switzerland) and scholars from Australia, South Africa,
Britain and Germany, in addition to the great number from Canada and Mexico interested in border concerns, shared information which gave an international flavour
to subsequent research efforts on the U.S.-Mexico border. But the broadening
aspects of comparative studies of international borders around the World were to
come later for me, and from a very unlikely location—Africa!

Synthesis of World Border Studies (1983-Present)

My own perspective of multi-continental comparisons of borders and border
processes was radically changed during the late Spring of 1983. Prior to that time
I had used contemporary studies of African border problems as illustrative
materials showing the process of changing culture areas to frontiers, and frontiers
to more formal nation-state borders.[49] Some papers and publications comparing
European and U.S. borders by Niles Hansen[50] had made me realize that a total grasp
of my own regional speciality would not be possible without knowing how border
processes develop in borderlands elsewhere throughout the World, but I had not

realistically pursued the active study of non-U.S. borders. Then, arriving at the El Paso International airport on a reconnaissance tour of border studies centres in America came Professor Anthony I. Asiwaju, University of Lagos, from Nigeria. Arriving in a blinding snowstorm which had altered local airport flights and had closed down the University of Texas at El Paso at noon, Professor Asiwaju was quite reluctant to make contact with Professor Oscar J. Martinez, director of the Centre for Inter-American and Border Studies at UTEP. But making a call and finding Martinez in, he came to the campus where he also spent some fascinating hours in my office. We exchanged information on our border experiences as well as our acceptance by more constrained "disciplinary colleagues." We compared notes on the conceptual format used to study on the Yorubaland colonial experience,[51] he departed until Summer when h returned with his family to conduct a comparative analysis of the Nigerian border and the U.S.-Mexico Borderlands.[52] This was followed by an international symposium on comparative border problem-solving held in the Spring of 1984. Many leading Borderlands scholars from different regions came together to present their views and to examine what was unique or common to the many border regions under investigation. I then submitted some requests for research funding for on-site studies of the Nigerian borders[53] which partly because of rapidly changing political-military condition and partly because of my own unrealistic perception on modern African nation-state development. The specific reference here is to the closure of the Nigerian land borders in April 1984 and the extreme sensitivity surrounding border research in Africa.

Upon arriving at the present Seminar on Border Issues in Africa in Lagos, my extended discussions with Raimondo Strassoldo (Institute of International Sociology, Gorizia, Italy), also invited to the seminar, piqued my curiosity in as much as the *functional* models which had been developed for explaining border activity along the Nigerian borders and on the U.S.-Mexico border did not seem to be as relevant to conditions at the Italian-Yugoslavia boundary. It is a comparison which I hope to actively pursue in the next year or two.

Many of the U.S.-Mexico Borderlands researchers will become increasingly immersed in comparative border studies. These will show the unique character of each of our regions while dealing with those problems which are common to most other borders. We will become increasingly integrated with border scholars from other countries and other continents. Some of the most important contacts will be those excellent scholars whose work at the Nigerian Seminar was so well researched and complied under less than ideal conditions.[54] Although unprepared as I was for the level of scholarship exhibited by the participants, my perspectives on the utility of comparative border studies have broadened considerably and have added some new skills which I hope to apply in my own work in the near future.

From limited observations with West African colleagues, it appears that Borderlands research in that region will not have to pass through some of the stages noted in the development of U.S.-Mexico Borderlands studies. Because Nigerian academicians have retained their broad perspective of indigenous societies as well as the academic specialization which accompanies technological revolutions, they need not incorporate the ideological pitfalls experienced in the development of the U.S.-Mexico Borderlands field. Moreover, ready as they are for some professional integration, as Association of West African Borderlands Scholars or its equivalent is imminent. Whether it is modeled after the Association of Borderlands Scholars which has focused principally upon the U.S.-Mexico region, or modifies its professional operation to meet different conditions which exist in developing nations is immaterial. That there be continuous contact and exchange of research results, new conceptual treatments and accurate descriptions of successful policies found on other borders *is* a requisite for this surge of Borderlands interest and activity to continue over time. Perhaps, then, all of us might learn more rapidly because we continually learn from each other.

The impact of Borderlands research on national leaders and domestic decision-makers may not be now of great magnitude and may not be immediately apparent. As scholars, we are painfully aware that our scientific frameworks for investigating border life is not the one used by national bureaucracies in maintaining national sovereignty and territorial integrity. Therefore, certain catch phrases which are mutually exchanged within the scholarly circles must be used with care. For example, I have used somewhat casually the politically sensitive concept of "artificial boundaries," which was recently used as the focus for an insightful analysis by Asiwaju.[55] Yet, as Asiwaju himself powerfully argued, it is not the border which is artificial, but the separating or divisive functions assigned by man. A more precise label would have been an "artificially determined border" which would be far less threatening to insecure national leaders who feel that a porous border is a problem of *centralized control*. The border is real, whatever our inclinations about its establishment or maintenance; and as long as powerful political leaders *feel* that the border is real and should be maintained, their decisions and policies will be *real in their consequences* regardless of local reluctance to adhere to border restriction. If Borderlands scholars are to have impact among policy makers, we must be more cautious in our selection and use of concepts and less threatening to those not used to our scholarly challenges within the open forum of ideas.

Some scholarly criticisms of the *structural* or international relations approach to problem-solving along borders may carry an implicit assumption that the current border *location is the problem!* Yet, if the U.S.-Mexico boundary had been drawn according to national and local views of the 1850s, it would be dysfunctional today because of technological advances, changes in social institutions, the demographic growth patterns and unequal political and economic development on a nation and regional basis. The century-old European partitioning of Africa[56] is no less subject to these constant changes in people, products and technology. Thus, the role of Borderlands scholarship is not much an ideological harangue over existing borders *per se* but rather as Asiwaju has attempted to do (Asiwaju, 1984b, 24-36), the construction of workable alternatives. To offer a pragmatic operational replacement for a current system of national boundaries requires an intricate knowledge of *all* existing vested interests and the maintenance power of the processes which hold present boundaries in place. Another role for Borderlands scholars is to offer the decision-maker an alternative perspective, such as the functional approach to borders which accepts the network of informal border linkages as positive channels and utilizes them instead of considering them lapses in border control.[57] Another function is to have an accurate knowledge of the workings of these border networks which will allow the people and institutions in the Borderlands to cope with their disjunctive situation.

Endnotes

1. Revised and expanded paper commissioned for the Seminar on Issues of Borderlands in Africa (March 1985) University of Lagos, Lagos, Nigeria.
2. Stoddard and McConville (1978) and Stoddard (1982a:21-30) discuss these hazards.
3. Some exceptions are lands along the Rio Grande and the western California coast.
4. Additional surveys; Heizer (1978) for California; Lekson (1983) for Arizona, New Mexico; Fewkes (1902) on West Texas; Hester and Eaton (1983) Middle & Lower Rio Grande regions. Noteworthy cultures of antiquity of this region are the Hohokam (Haury, 1976), Mogollon and Anasazi (Martin and Plog, 1973).
5. Early Athapaskan migrations see Gunnerson (1956); contemporary Alaskans, see Simeone (1982). Di Peso's (1974) volumes record Casas Grandes restoration project.
6. Nostrand (1983) gives graphical account of receding Spanish northern frontier.
7. Court decisions rationized the taking of indians lands utilizing this philosophical justification. For actual cases refer to Deloria (1972).
8. Beginning the twentieth century with insignificant border populations, urban border cities have exploded with population increases of 150-250% over two short decades on the Mexican side (Stoddard, 1984b). In the U.S., the U.S. Commerce department monitors more than 300 urban complexes throughout the nation and has found that the poorest 5 SMSAs in the nation lie along the southern U.S.-Mexico border (Stoddard, 1978a).
9. Stoddard (1982b, 1984a) describes the simultaneous functioning of formal and informal border systems within various institutional contexts.
10. Illegal immigration as an institutionalized migration pattern has been empirically substantiated by border researchers (Stoddard, 1976a, 1976b; Stoddard et al., 1979).
11. Kroeber (1953:5-6) outlines the methodological difficulties in delineating vague culture areas, and their demise as more clearly defined frontiers emerge.
12. See Las Casas (1542) and Sahagun (1932).
13. In 1773 Fray Serra wrote about California missions (Tibesar, 1955), Fray Lopez about Texas (Lopez, 1940) and Fray Senan on colonization policies in California (Simpson, 1962). These all reflect anti-indian sentiment.
14. Arteaga y S. (1932).
15. An interesting comparison of two accounts of the Conquest of Mexico, one by Bernal Diaz del Castillo, shows the impact of personal bias on many of the earliest written accounts of the New World conquest and its indigenous peoples; see Iglesia (1940).
16. See Arteaga y S. (1932), Donaghue (1929). Melchor Diaz researched by Ives (1936).
17. DeSoto proudly wrote in his journal how he purposeely attached and destroyed Florida villages, allowing wounded to escape to spread word of the terrible conquering Spanish (Collier, 1947: 113).
18. Early contact with indigenous cultures includes the Jesuit Father Neumann among the Tarahumaras (Christelow, 1939), Father Kino among the Pima and Papago (Bolton, 1932, 1936), Fray Sedelmeyr with the Maricopa and Yuma, Fray Serra in Alta California (Tibesar, 1955) Fathers Rodriguez, Lopez and Espejo in New Mexico (Mecham, 1926a, 1926b) and the legendary "beautiful woman in blue"—Mother Maria de Agreda—among the Humanos of East Texas (Bolton, 1912).
19. Earliest southwest travelogues include that of the French sea captain Pages (1791), Captain Shaler (1808) and British Captain Beechey (1831).
20. The trader, Josiah Webb (1931), describes Santa Fe in 1844; U.S. Attorney for New Mexico Davis (1857) comments on customs and manners of that frontier region; and the Boston socialite, Richard Dana (1840), recalls his days as a sailor and his initial reactions to California.
21. For one example, see Blackmar (1891). A more thorough survey of Anglo perceptions of the southwest during the nineteenth century see Noggle (1959).
22. One who became enthralled and wrote, without malice, in a somewhat condescendding manner was Lummis (1925) as he adopted the southwest as his own.
23. Lumholtz' comprehensive two-volume work (1902) or earlier article (1894).
24. Bandelier (1890-1892). Hodge (1932) describes the unique contribution of Bandelier's pioneering efforts and methods.
25. Classic ethnographies from Columbia University, University of Chicago and other professional anthropologists are the magnificent reservoir of raw data for subsequent culture studies in America (Stoddard, 1975c: 41-42, 45-57).
26. Hodge (1910); Kroeber (1925)
27. Bibliographic surveys of historian contributions to border studies can be found in Almaraz (1975, 1983), Vigil (1983), Simmons (1983) and Meier (1983).

28. Casteneda (1949) illustrates the strains between General Santa Ana and General Scott; General San-chez Lamego (1968) gives a Mexican perspective to the Alamo.
29. Bourke (1891), Crook (1946); diary of an Englishman on the 2,500 mile trek of the Mormon Battalion through borderlands found in Gracy and Rugeley (1965).
30. Bolton (1920). See also Bolton (1908, 1912); and frontier missions (1917).
31. Bancroft (1884-1890).
32. Prescott's (1936) volume, the *Conquest of Mexico,* written before the turn of the century, is considered by non-discriminating historians to be a classic and accurate reference, has been revealed as "romantic art" when comparing his original sources and impressionistic narrative (Levin, 1959, Humphreys, 1959).
33. Surveyed in Stoddard (1975c: 41-47).
34. Ibid., pp. 40-41.
35. Spicer (1962).
36. Gildersleeve (1975: 23-26) notes how Carl O. Sauer's work as a historian merges with cultural an-thropology and comparative geography of the 1930s. He suggests that work by geographers Richard Nostrand (1970) and Donald Meinig (1972) has overlapped Stoddard's comparative sociology approach in discussing the context of border problems in multidisciplinary formats.
37. Boggs and Bowman (1940) or Prescott (1965) are still cited extensively.
38. My B.S. in International Relations, with M.S. and Ph.D. minor in Political Science, led me to accept the structural framework without question. My earliest publication followed this trend (1969). But even before this publication was in print, I had painfully altered my theoretical orientation to fit my research findings from numerous on-site border projects. The result was a shift to a functionalist perspective (Stoddard, 1982a).
39. Short histories of the project include Loomis et al. (1966) and Loomis (1974). Major projects resulting from it include Cumberland (1960), Beegle et al. (1960), D'Antonio and Form (1965) and others sum-marized elsewhere (Gildersleeve, 1975: 24-26; Stoddard, 1969, 1975c: 35-36).
40. See summaries by Bath (1975) and Taylor (1975).
41. Stoddard (1973), in which the border figured prominantly in the self-identity and stereotypes bestowed upon Mexican Americans.
42. Stoddard (1975a). The original historian, Dr. Oscar J. Martinez, left to complete research in Mexico City, and Dr. Felix D. Almaraz, Jr. consented to do the published summary of the "status of borderlands studies: history."
43. *U.S.-Mexico Borderlands Studies: An Inventory of Scholars, Appraisal of Funding Resources and Research Prospects* (Stoddard, 1974).
44. Stoddard et al. (1983). A descriptive account of getting an encyclopedic multidisciplinary volume pulished is found in Stoddard (1982c).
45. The original *Atlas* was to have been demographic and spatial maps, charts and graphics to accompany available empirical data. The current *Atlas* project nearing completion at UCLA is a collection of scholarly discussions on a major area of interest, with more than a dozen volumes already outlined.
46. Selected studies showing these information networks between border twin cities include D'Antonio and Form (1965), Price (1968, 1973), Dillman (1969), Sloan and West (1976, 1977), Stoddard and West (1977), West (1978), Ladman (1979), Stoddard et al. (1979), Alvarez (1979) and Stoddard (1982b, 1984a).
47. Whiteford (1979), Alvarez (1984), Asiwaju (1984a, 1984b).
48. Price (1983), Duchacek (1984) and others.
49. As an anthropologist, I was acquainted with the stone age Berbers of North Africa, the Igbo and Hausa of West Africa, the Bunyoro Kingdom and Baganda of the central region, and Bushmen and iKung of the Kalijari desert. But I was only superficially informed on modern Africa and the strains produced from tribal and nation-state loyalties. I also used articles by Zartman)1965) and Starr and Most (1976) on African frontiers, but only to illustrate the processes of changing culture areas to frontiers, to borders.
50. Hansen (1978, 1983).
51. Asiwaju (1976).
52. Asiwaju (1983).
53. Scheduled for the summer months of 1984 if funded.
54. In Nigeria, higher education has grown from a single colonial university at Ibadan to about two dozen regional colleges. Buildings, including libraries, for new colleges were built with oil profits, but since the collapse of the world oil market, there is little money to continue current journals, obtain new books, buy or repair typewriters, obtain photocopying equipment or computers, or to build up large data collections. Most scholars depend largely on personal libraries or the libraries of colleagues, mostly stocked with books printed in Europe.

55. See the inaugural address of Asiwaju (1984b).

56. An edited volume (Asiwaju, 1984a) of eight boundary case studies from various locations in Africa, and some commentary chapters.

57. As noted, borders are both permeable membranes and impermeable barriers, depending upon the emphasis placed on their functions at a given time. Moreover, such peripheral regions lying juxtaposition to two nations must serve as a "differential converter" through which national antagonisms and ethnocentric opinions must be dispersed or neutralized. In effect, the systems of informal border linkages are the most important channel through which political myths, entertained by national leaders, are converted to a reality which allows local border coordination and cooperation and gives rise to positive feelings between the two nations. Changing conditions require rapid adjustments, which are less difficult informally than when more formalized mechanisms are radically altered.

Bibliography

Almaraz, Felix D. Jr. 1983 "Texas History" in E.R. Stoddard et al. (eds) *Borderlands Sourcebook* Norman: Univ. of Oklahoma Press.

_____ 1975 "The status of borderlands studies: history" *Social Science Journal* 12/13, Oct 1975/Jan 1976: 9-18.

Alvarez, Robert R. 1984 "The border as social system: the California case" *New Scholar* 9 (no. 1 & 2): 119-133.

_____ 1979 "Familia: migration and adaptation in Alta and Baja California 1800-1975" unpublished Ph.D. dissertation, Stanford Univ.

Arteaga y S., Armando 1932 "Fray Marcos de niza y el descubrimiento de Nuevo Mexico" *Hispanic American Historical Rev.* 12, Nov: 481-489.

Asiwaju, Anthony I. 1984a (ed) *Partitioned Africans: Ethnic Relations Across Africa's International Boundaries 1884-1984* (Lagos: Univ. of Lagos Press).

_____ 1984b *Artificial Boundaries: An Inaugural Lecture* (Lagos: Univ. Lagos Press).

_____ 1983 "Borderlands research: a comparative perspective" *Border Perspectives No. 6* (November), Univ. of Texas at El Paso, Center for Inter-American and Border Studies.

_____ 1976 *Western Yorubaland under European Rule 1889-1945* (London: Longman).

Bancroft, Hubert H. 1884-1890 *History of California, Mexico, Northern Mexican States and Texas, New Mexico and Arizona* (7 Vol.) (San Francisco: Bancroft Co.).

Bandelier, Adolphe F. 1890-1892 *Final Report of Investigations Among the Indians of the Southwestern United States 1880-1885* (Cambridge: Arch. Inst. of America, American Series NO 3 & 4).

Bath, C. Richard 1975 "The status of borderlands studies: political science" *Social Science J* 12/13, Oct 75/Jan 76: 55-69.

Beechey, F.W. 1831 *Narrative of a Voyage to the Pacific and Bering's Strait* Vol I & II (London: np).

Beegle, J. Allan, Harold F. Goldsmith and Charles P. Loomis 1960 "Demographic characteristics of the United States-Mexico border" *Rural Sociology* 25 March: 107-162.

Blackmar, Frank W. 1891 *Spanish Institutions of the Southwest* (Baltimore: Johns-Hopkins Univ. Press).

Boggs, S. Whittemore and Isaiah Bowman 1904 *International Boundaries: A Study of Boundary Functions and Problems* (New York: COlumbia Univ. Press).

Bolton, Herbert E. 1936 *Rim of Christendom: A Biography of Eusebio Francisco Kino, Pacific Coast Pioneer* (New York: Macmillan).

_____ 1932 *Padre on Horseback: A Sketch of Eusebio Francisco Kino* (San Francisco: Sonora Press).

_____ 1921 *The Spanish Borderlands: A Chronicle of Old Florida and the Southwest* (New Haven: Yale Univ. Press).

_____ 1917 "The mission as a frontier institution in the Spanish-American colonies" *American Historical Review* 33 October: 42-61.

_____ 1912 "The Spanish occupation of Texas 1519-1960;; *Southwestern Historical Quarterly* 16 July: 1-28.

_____ 1908 (ed) *Spanish Exploration in the Southwest 1542-1706* (New York: Barnes and Noble, reprinted 1952).

Bourke, John C. 1891 *On the Border with Crook* (New York: Scribners).

Castaneda, Carlos E. 1949 "Relations of General Scott with Santa Ana" *Hispanic American Historical Review* 29 Nov: 455-473.

Castile, George Pierre 1979 *North American Indians: An Introduction to the Chichimeca* (New York: McGraw-Hill).

Christelow, Allan 1939 "Father Joseph Neumann, Jesuit Missionary to the Tarahumaras" *Hispanic American Hist. Review* 19 Nov: 423-442.

Coller, John 1947 *Indians of the Americas: The Long Hope* (New York: New American Library Mentor).

Crook, General George 1946 *General George Crook: His Autobiography* (Norman: Univ. Oklahoma Press).

Cumberland, Charles C. 1960 "The United States-Mexican border: a selective guide to the literature of the region" *Rural Sociology* 25 June: 1-236.

Dana, Richard Henry 1840 *Two Years Before the Mast* (New York: np).

D'Antonio, William V. and William H. Form 1965 *Influentials in Two Border Cities* (Notre Dame: Univ. of Notre Dame Press).

Davis, William W.H. 1857 *El Gringo or, New Mexico and Her People* (New York: np).

Deloria, Vine Jr. 1972 (ed) *Of Utmost Good Faith* (New York: Bantam).

Dillman, C. Daniel 1969 "Border town symbiosis along the lower Rio Grande as exemplified by the twin cities, Brownsville (Texas) and Matamoros (Tamaulipas)" *Revista Geografica* 71 Dec.: pp. 93-113.

Di Peso, Charles C. 1974 *Casas Grandes: A Fallen Trading Center of the Gran Chicimeca* Vol. I-III (Flagstaff: Northand Press).

Donaghue, David 1929 "The Routes of the Coronado Expedition in Texas" *Southwestern Historical Quarterly* 32 (January): 181-192.

Dcuhacek, Ivo D. 1984 "Transborder Overlaps between Three Federal Systems: From Gulf of Mexico to the Arctic Ocean" paper presented to Western Social Science Association (April) San Diego, California.

Fewkes, Walter J. 1902 "The Pueblo Settlements near El Paso" *American Anthropologist* 4 (January-March): 57-76.

Gildersleeve, Charles R. 1975 "The Status of Borderlands Studies: Geography" *Social Science Journal* 12/13 (October 1975/January 1976): 19-28.

Gracy, David B. II and Helen J.H. Rugeley 1965 (Eds) "From the Mississippi to the Pacific: An Englishman in the Mormon Battalion" *Arizona and the West* 7 (Summer): 127-160.

Gunnerson, Dolores A. 1956 "The Southern Athabascans: Their Arrival in the Southwest" *El Palacio* 63: 346-365.

Hansen, Niles 1983 "European Transboundary Cooperation and its Relevance to the United States-Mexico Border" *Journal of the American Institute of Planners* 49 (Summer): 336-343.

_____ 1982 "Economic Growth Patterns in the Texas Borderlands" *Natural Resources Journal* 22 (October): 805-821.

_____ 1978 "Alien Migration: Mexican Workers in the United States and European 'Guest Workers' " *Texas Business Review* 42 (June): 107-111.

Haury, Emil W. 1976 *The Hohokam: Desert Farmers and Craftsmen* (Tucson: University of Arizona Press).

Heizer, Robert F. 1978 (ed) *California. Handbook of North American Indians* Vol. 8. (Washington, D.C.: Smithsonian Institution).

Hester, Thomas R. and Jack D. Eaton 1983 "Middle-Lower Rio Grande Archaeology" : pp. 70-74 in E. R. Stoddard et al. (eds) *Borderlands Sourcebook* (Norman: University of Oklahoma Press.)

Hodge, Frederick W. 1932 "Biographical Sketch and Bibliography of Adolphe Francis Alphonse Bandelier" *New Mexico Historical Review* 7 (October): 353-370.

_____ 1910 (ed) *Handbook of American Indians North of Mexico* (2 Vol.) (Washington, D.C.: Bureau of American Ethnology) reprinted, 1959.

Humphreys, R. A. 1959 "William Hickling Prescott: The Man and the Historian" *Hispanic American Historical Review* 39 (February): 1-19.

Iglesia, Ramon 1940 "Two Articles on the Same Topic: Bernal Diaz del Castillo and Popularism in Spanish Historiography and Bernal Diaz del Castillo's Criticism of the History of the Conquest of Mexico by Francisco Lopez de Gomara" *Hispanic American Historical Review* 20 (November): 517-550.

Ives, Ronald L. 1936 "Melchor Diaz—The Forgotten Explorer" *Hispanic American Historical Review* 16 (February): 86-90.

Kroeber, Alfred L. 1953 *Cultural and Natural Areas of Native North America* (Berkeley: University of California Press).

_____ 1925 (ed) *Handbook of the Indians of California* (Washington, D.C.: Government Printing Office, Bureau of American Ethnology, Publication No. 78).

Ladman, Jerry R. 1979 "The Economic Interdependence of Contiguous Border Cities: The Twin City Multiplier" *Annals of Regional Science* 13 (March): 23-29.

Las Casas, Bartolome de 1542 "La Brevisema Relacion de la Destruccion de las Indias" (Reprinted pp. 36-39 in J. F. Bannon (ed) *Indian Labor in the Spanish Indies* (Boston: D. C. Heath. 1966).

Lekson, Stephen H. 1983 "Southwestern Archaeology" pp. 66-69 in E. R. Stoddard et al. (eds) *Borderlands Sourcebook* (Norman: University of Oklahoma Press).

Levin, David 1959 "History as Romantic Art: Structure, Characterization and Style in The Conquest of Mexico" *Hispanic American Historical Review* 39 (February): 20-45.

Loomis, Charles P. 1974 "History and Results of the Michigan State University Carnegie Corporation Project" paper presented to Southwestern Sociological Association (March) Dallas, Texas.

Loomis, Charles P., Zona K. Loomis and Jeanne E. Gullahorn 1966 *Linkages of Mexico and the United States* (East Lansing: Michigan State University, Experiment Station Bulletin No. 14).

Lopex, Fray Jose Francisco 1940 "The Texas Missions in 1785" *Mid-America* (January).

Lummis, Charles F. 1925 *Land of Poco Tiempo* (New York: Charles Scribner's Sons) originally published 1893.

Lumholtz, Carl 1902 *Unknown Mexico* (2 Vol.) (New York: Charles Scribner's Sons) reprinted, Glorieta Press.

_____ 1894 "The American Cave Dwellers: The Tarahumari" *American Geographical Society Bulletin* 26 (No. 3).

Martin, Paul S. and Fred Plog 1973 *The Archaeology of Arizona: A Study of the Wouthwest Region* (Garden City: Doubleday/Natural History Press).

Mecham, Lloyd 1926a "Supplementary Documents relating to the Chamuscado Rodriguez Expedition" *Southwestern Historical Quarterly* 29 (January): 224-231.

_____ 1926b "Antonio de Espejo and his Journey to New Mexico" *Southwestern Historical Quarterly* 30 (October): 114-138.

Meier, Matt S. 1983 "California History" pp. 49-52 in E. R. Stoddard et al. (eds) *Borderlands Sourcebook* (Norman: University of Oklahoma Press).

Meinig, D. W. 1971 *Southwest: Three Peoples in Geographical Change 1600-1970* (New York: Oxford University Press).

Noggle, Burl 1959 "Anglo Observers of the Southwest Borderland 1825-1890: The Rise of a Concept" *Arizona and the West* 1 (Summer): 105-131.

Nostrand, Richard L. 1983 "A Changing Culture Region" pp. 6-15 in E. R. Stoddard et al. (eds) *Borderlands Sourcebook* (Norman: University of Oklahoma Press).

_____ 1970 "The Hispanic-American Borderland: Delimation of an American Culture Area" *Annals, Association of American Geographers* 60 (December): 638-661.

Pages, Pierre Marie Francois de 1791 Travels Around the World in the Years 1767-1771. np

Prescott, J.R.V. 1965 *The Geography of Frontiers and Boundaries* (Chicago: Aldine Publishing Co.)

Prescott, William H. 1936 *History of the Conquest of Mexico* (New York: Modern Library).

Price, John A. 1983 "Mexican and Canadian Border Comparisons" pp. 20-23 in E. R. Stoddard et al. (eds) *Borderlands Sourcebook* (Norman: University of Oklahoma Press).

_____ 1973 *Tijuana: Urbanization in a Border Culture* (Notre Dame: University of Notre Dame Press).

_____ 1968 "Tijuana: A Study of Symbiosis" *New Mexico Quarterly* 38 (No. 3): 8-18.

Sahagun, Fray Bernardino de 1932 *A History of Ancient Mexico* (Vol. I-III) (Nashville: Fisk Univ Press).

Sanchez Lamego, General Miguel A. 1968 *The Seige and Taking of the Alamo* (Santa Fe: The Press of the Territorain).

Sanders, William T. and Barbara J. Price 1968 *Mexoamerica: The Evolution of a Civilization* (New York: Random House).

Shaler, William 1808 Journal of a Voyage Between China and the North-Western Coast of America. np.

Simeone, William E. 1982 *A History of Alaskan Athapaskans* (Anchorage: Alaska Pacific University Press, Alaska Historical Commission).

Simmons, Marc 1983 "New Mexico-Colorado History" pp. 42-45 in E. R. Stoddard et al. (eds) *Borderlands Sourcebook* (Norman: University of Oklahoma Press).

Simpson, Lesley Byrd 1962 (ed) *The Letters of Jose Senan, O.F.M.* (Ventura: Ventura County Historical Society).

Sloan, John W. and Jonathan P. West 1976 "Community Integration and Policies among Elites in Two Border Cities: Los Dos Laredo" *J. of Inter-Amer. Studies and World Affairs* 18 (November): 451-474.

_____ 1977 "The Role of Informal Policy-Making in U.S. Cities" *Social Science Quarterly* 58 (September): 270-282.

Spicer, Edward H. 1962 *Cycles of Conquest: The Impact of Spain, Mexico and the U.S. on the Indians of the Southwest 1533-1960* (Tucson: University of Arizona Press).

Starr, Harvey and Benjamin A. Most 1976 "The Substance and Study of Borders in International Relations Research" *International Studies Quarterly* 20 (December): 581-620.

Stoddard, Ellwyn R. 1984a *Functional Dimensions of Informal Border Networks* (El Paso: University of Texas at El Paso, Center for Inter-American and Border Studies), Border Perspectives No. 8 (January).

_____ 1984b "Northern Mexican Migration and the U.S.-Mexico Border Region" *New Scholar* 9 (No. 1 & 2): 51-72.

_____ 1983 "Overview" pp. 3-5 in E. R. Stoddard et al. (eds) *Borderlands Sourcebook* (Norman: University of Oklahoma Press).

_____ 1982a "Perils of Multidisciplinary Rresearch in Borderlands Studies: A Professional Dilemma for 'General' Scholars" *The Borderland Journal* 6 (Fall): 11-40.

_____ 1982b "Local and Regional Incongruities in Bi-National Diplomacy: Policy for the U.S.-Mexico Border" *Policy Perspectives* 2 (No. 1): 111-136.

_____ 1982c "Multidisciplinary Research Funding: A 'catch 22' Enigma" *American Sociologist* 17 (November): 210-216.

_____ 1978a *Patterns of Poverty along the U.S.-Mexico Border* (El Paso: Organization of U.S. Border Cities, University of Texas at El Paso Center for Inter-American Studies).

_____ 1978b"Functional Alternatives to Bi-National Border Development Models: The Case of the U.S.-Mexico Border" paper presented to American Sociological Association (September) San Francisco, California.

_____ 1976a "Illigal Mexican Labor in the Borderlands: Institutionalized Support of an Unlawful Practice" *Pacific Sociological Review* 19 (April): 175-210.

_____ 1976b "A Conceptual Analysis of the 'Alien Invasion': Institutionalized Support of Illegal Mexican Aliens in the U.S." *International Migration Review* 10 (Summer): 157-189.

_____ 1975a (Ed) "The Status of Borderlands Studies: A Multidisciplinary Symposium" *Social Science Journal* 12/13 (October 1975/January 1976) : 1-112.

_____ 1975b "The Status of Borderlands Studies: An Introduction" *Social Science Journal* 12/13 (October 1975/January 1976): 3-8.

_____ 1975c "The Status of Borderlands Studies: Sociology and Anthropology" *Social Science Journal* 12/13 (October 1975/January 1976): 29-54.

_____ 1974 *U.S.-Mexico Borderlands Studies: An Inventory of Scholars, Appraisal of Funding Resources and Research Projects* (El Paso: University of Texas at El Paso, Center for Inter-American Studies).

_____ 1973 *Mexican Americans* (New York: Random House, reprinted, Univ. Press of America, 1981).

_____ 1969 "The U.S.-Mexican Border: A Comparative Research Laboratory" *Journal of Inter-American Studies* 11 (July): 477-488.

Stoddard, Ellwyn R., Oscar J. Martinez and Miguel A. Martinez Lasso 1979 *El Paso-Ciudad Juarez Relations and the 'Tortilla Curtain:' A Study of Local Adaptation to Federal Border Policies* (El Paso: El Paso Council of the Arts and Humanities, the Univ. of Texas at El Paso).

Stoddard, Ellwyn R. and J. Lawrence McConville 1978 "The Effectiveness of Sociology in Training and Rewarding Scholars in a Multidisciplinary/Multicultural Field" *Western Sociological Review* 9 (Fall): 67-75.

Stoddard, Ellwyn R., Richard L. Nostrand and Jonathan P. West 1983 (eds) *Borderlands Sourcebook* (Norman: University of Oklahoma Press).

Stoddard, Ellwyn R. and Jonathan P. West 1977 *The Impact of Mexico's Peso Devaluation on Selected U.S. Border Cities* (Tucson: SW Borderland Consultants, Economic Development Administration, Organization of U.S. Border Cities).

Taylor, James R. 1975 "The Status of Borderlands Studies: Economics" *Social Science Journal* 12/13 (October 1975/January 1976): 69-76.

Tibesar, Antonine 1955 (ed) Writings of Junipero Serra (Vol. I). Washington, D.C.: np

Vigil, Ralph H. 1983 "Colonial Institutions" pp. 36-41 in E. R. Stoddard et al. (eds) *Borderlands Sourcebook* (Norman: University of Oklahoma Press).

Webb, James Josiah 1931 Adventures in the Santa Fe Trade. Glendale, California: np

West, Jonathan P. 1978 "Informal Policy Making along the Arizona-Mexico International Border" *Arizona Review* 27 (February): 1-8.

Whiteford, Linda 1979 "The Borderlands as an Extended Community" pp. 127-137 in F. Camara and R. Van Kemper (eds) *Migration Across Frontiers: Mexico and the United States* (Albany: State University of New York, Institute for Meso-american Studies).

Zartman, William I. 1965 "The Politics of Boundaries in North and West Africa" *Journal of Modern African Studies* 3 (August): 155-173.

CHAPTER **32**

The 'Area Study' Approach to Research on Nigeria's Borders: A Proposed Programme*

by A.I. Asiwaju

Prefatory Remarks

Since Anene and Prescott completed their independent, though mutually complimentary, studies on the evolution of Nigeria's international boundaries in 1960,[1] there have been quite a few follow-up analyses of the performance of the boundaries in terms of their localized impacts.[2] In all these endeavours, however, concern for policy has been more implicit than explicit. There are even no systematic studies, known to the present writer, on such vibrant border institutions as the Customs Preventive and Immigration Services. In spite of their importance as the very basis on which the nation-state rests, our borders receive attention only when they are crossed by gendarmes of our understandably jealous neighbours to violate our territorial integrity, sometimes killing Nigeria's own men or when our nationals, declared 'wanted' by the police, escaped through the same border networks used in normal times for smuggling and related clandestine activities. Since January 1983, when undocumented immigration became a serious offence in Nigeria, the borders have been given the notoriety by the news media as nest not only for smuggles but also for forces aiding and abetting the officially unwanted "Alien Invasion" of the nation. The need for a systematic research aimed at improving knowledge of the situation has received little or no attention.

---

*This proposal was originally written and circulated in November 1983 to a large number of establishments—The Federal Ministries of Internal Affairs, External Affairs and Defence; Universities and Polytechnics in the Nigerian 'Gateway' states; the Nigerian Institute of International Affairs and the National Institute for Policy and Strategic Studies. It formed part of the basis of the writer's inaugural lecture (Artificial Boundaries) in December 1984 and the core of concern for the Seminar on Issues of Borderlands in Africa in May 1985. The Border Research Project, floated in August 1985 by the National Institute for Policy and Strategic Studies, probably derived its inspiration from the proposal. However, the permanence of the research programme, which it advocates, is still to be realised.

The concept of 'Area Study' is proposed as an aggressive instrument of analysis. It is to combine the best in two research traditions: viz: the policy concern of the type which has motivated United States of America to support programmes focusing on regions of the world considered of strategic importance to the American nation,[3] and the models of painstaking local studies of the type which has produced the excellent scholarly histories of British Indirect Rule in Nigeria.[4] Unlike these distinguished Nigerian predecessors, however, the Borderlands Studies to be undertaken will hold themselves obliged to offer policy advice. History can no longer afford to look on when junior sister disciplines in the social sciences with which it is in daily interaction, discharge the responsibility of public service.

Defined in terms of the culture areas through which our borders have been drawn, the following borderlands are proposed for detailed study:

   i) Nigeria-Benin.
   ii) Nigeria-Niger.
  iii) Nigeria-Chad.
  iv) Nigeria-Cameroun.
   v) Nigeria-Equatorial Guinea.

Each of these will be further sub-divided into cultural and geographical units for detailed analysis. Thus, in addition to the focus on the factor of divided ethnic groups and culture areas, there will also be emphasis on shared natural regions such as the Lake Chad Basin, the Niger and Benue River systems and the Atlantic seaboard. The suggestion in the proposal is for experts in all related academic disciplines to take charge of their specific fields within the area in which their institutions are located. Such institutions will include all universities and university-level teaching and research institutions in the 11 out of 19 states of the Federation, with at least one boundary conterminous with a section of the nation's borders. In other words, all 'gateway' states must be focused.

Borders are, like war, too serious an affair to be left only to army generals; similarly its study cannot be left to any specific disciplinary bias. The scholar has a particular responsibility to conduct dispassionate research into the various levels concerned with border relations: viz. the national governments, the sub-national authorities (State/Local Administrations) and the local communities. Most border problems arise from conflicts within (usually between interacting governments) or between these different levels of relations (usually between the national and the local communities). The main policy challenge is in establishing a harmony between the levels. There must be genuine co-operation capable of leading ultimately to coordinated planning and development at all levels. The fact of universality of these problems justifies the comparative perspective suggested in this proposal.[5]

Description of Project

The objects of study are the two zones lying along a given binational boundary or border but in functional interaction with each other as well as with each of their own particular sovereign states. Functionally, this is an overlapping zone in which the cultures, economies and politics of the inter-related nation-states interpenetrate and interface. These zones, spawned through the interaction of the sovereign states sharing the common border, are referred to as borderlands; and for the purpose of this design, borderlands are viewed as distinct regions and *milieu* for most aspects.

The project is designed strictly as a collaborative effort. Not only is it expected to involve a multidisciplinary team of experts of appropriate research orientation and interests in the related disciplines of the Humanities, Social Sciences, Law, Environmental Sciences, Education and Medicine (especially Community Health) within the University of Lagos.[6] It is ultimately planned to embrace the collaboration of similar experts in sister institutions located within and across Nigerian borderlands, particularly in such other Nigerian border states as Ogun, Oyo, Kwara, Sokoto, Katsina, Kano Borno, Gongola, Benue, Cross River and the adjacent subnational authorities in the neighbouring nation-states of Benin, Niger, Chad, Cameroun and Equatorial Guinea.

The focus on the Nigerian borders as an area of primary concern will take adequate cognizance of the wider West African and African continental settings. A very important corollary to studies of the borderlands is a series of purposive country studies of Nigeria's four landward francophone plus one maritime Spanish-speaking neighbours in terms of the basic national characteristics and the extent of relationship to Nigeria features across the common borders.

The project will begin with a focus on Nigeria's International Boundaries and will concentrate on the use of Nigerian resource persons and institutions while establishing appropriate links with counterparts in the neighbouring countries.

The levels of analysis will range from local, regional, state, national, binational to international perspectives.

The multidisciplinary, interuniversity, binational, international and comparative character as well as the specialized focus on borders and borderlands easily distinguish this research proposal from the programmes in the more specialized governmental institutions such as the Institute of International Affairs in Lagos (focusing on orthodox diplomacy) or the Nigerian Institute of Policy and Strategic Studies at Kuru, devoted strictly to policy and strategic considerations. But the obvious relevance to the work of these institutions should form the basis of working relationships.

The proposal is modelled on a blend between two traditions of border research programmes. On the one hand is the practical private type exemplified by the 'Regio Basiliensi', a project of practical study for the actual development of Basel, a trinational urban agglomeration straddling the common border between Switzerland, Western Germany and France. Then, there is the University of California Consortium on Mexico and the United States (UC Mexus), based in Los Angeles, which co-ordinates the University's nine-campus programmes related to Mexico and the U.S. with priority attention on the inter-connected borderlands. Location and operation of the proposed programme within a university environment allows for a Liberalism that is crucial for a full release of ideas.

The University of Lagos is especially suitable as the coordinating centre for the project for the following three major considerations:

a) The availability of resource persons of demonstrated experience and/or potentialities for the kind of project proposed.

b) The laboratory advantage of Lagos City and State in terms of both the border and regional locational characteristics. Lagos State is bounded in the West by the southernmoust section of the Nigeria-Benin international boundary and in the north and west by the neighbouring Nigerian state of Ogun; it thus represents the majority of the Nigerian states (11 out of 21) which share a borderlands situation. The city of Lagos has, since the advent of trans-Atlantic trade, acquired the status of a regional centre with hinterlands always extending across what late became the Nigeria-Benin international boundary;

c) The relative ease of communication with other Nigerian and related borderlands.

Need and Objective

This design is dictated by the need to update policy and the imperative for an institutionalized programme specializing in a comprehensive research on a subject of critical importance for international peace.

International boundaries or borders are effects of international relations, characterized more by a sense of conflict than harmony. It is common knowledge that nearly all major international crisis of the era of nation-states, including the two World Wars, have hinged on border adjustment or maintenance. The Ethio-Somali conflict in the Horn of Africa, the Moroccan-Polisario war in the Maghrib and the Namibian Liberation Movement in Southern Africa are as directly or indirectly related to border questions as the crisis in the Middle East—to cite just a few of the several relevant contemporary illustrations.

In Nigeria, the last few years have shown that we are not an exception in the world of troubled borders. First was the incursion into Sokoto State in the border area around Illo by Beninese *gendarmes* in 1981. This was followed in 1982 by the cold-blooded massacre of five Nigerian soldiers on routine patrol of the Ikang sector of the Nigeria-Cameroun border in the Cross River State by Cameroun *gendarmes*. This brought to a head a series and process of tension and conflict that had been in evidence along this border, for over a decade. Finally, there was the exchange of artillery fire between detachment for the Nigerian Army and counterparts in crisis-riddled Chad between April and June 1983, following a Chadian military incursion into the Nigerian side of the Lake Chad.

This orientation towards tension, conflict and crisis had dictated the framework for research and policy formulation. In Africa, as in Europe and other parts of the wider world of nation-states and borders, there is the heritage of an exclusively state concern in scholarly tradition and policy studies; investigations about borders by both scholars and policy makers have been and are continuing to be handled more often than not within the narrow perspective of diplomacy or International Relations. Accordingly, the sub-disciplines of choice have been International Law, International Politics, Diplomatic History and Political Geography in that order of importance in the existing literature.

In these studies, which focus on International Relations, the units of analysis are the sovereign states; the border is treated outside the context of its local or regional setting; the usually human and developmental concerns of the dependent borderlands or frontier zones, including the generally binational situated border communities, are at best marginalized or, at worse, analytically excluded. Diplomatic concerns have soft spots for boundary maintenance and hold transborder co-operation possibilities and efforts in suspect.

The place and pertinence of the diplomatic framework must be recognized. However, the inadequacy of this exclusively state-oriented, conflict-stance and essentially single-minded approach to research and policy formulation on a subject, which constitutes a pivot for international and world peace, has been systematically exposed by studies based on the recognition of borderlands (i.e., the zones on both sides of international boundaries) as distinct regions and the use of the multidisciplinary instrument for its study. This alternative research orientation and strategy has been to dictate a new emphasis in policy advice. In this new approach, the traditional—though erroneous—notion of national structures lying in juxtaposition of a common boundary is abandoned. Instead, borderlands are viewed as an overlapping zone of national and cultural diversity, a region of cultural and economic interpenetration in which the socio-economic functions and influences of the state on the side of the boundary fades gently into the area of its neighbour.[7]

Rather than continue to view borders in conflict and tension terms, the new approach emphasises the more positive issues of transborder co-operation, planning and development. Borderlands are viewed in terms of its human needs and material developmental possibilities. Contrary to the disposition of the traditional diplomatic approach by which the often distantly based national governments monopolized control, the new strategy allows borderlands problems which are mostly local to be so studied and resolved. It is realized, for example, that it is impossible for a local or regional development and planning policy without adequate consultation with the counterpart body on the other side of the border. In such a circumstance, the old ideology of national self interest is being strongly persuaded to yield place to an emergent doctrine of mutual necessity and functional relationship between peoples and governments on both sides of a border;[8] international boundaries should be maintained, but encouragement is given for them to function less as lines of division and exclusion than as points of contact and mutual inclusion.

In Europe, the cradle of nation-states and borders, this new approach to study and actual development has become quite noticeable. Transborder informal linkages, inspired by the fact of shared human and material resources straddling several of the European borders, have been accorded formalized and legalized status in recent years through processes which have now resulted in the statutory endorsement, by all member states of the Council of Europe, of the now famous *European Outline Convention on Transborder Co-operation Between Territorial Communities or Authorities*.[9] This European approach has been strongly recommended to the governments of the United States of American and Mexico as the most appropriate solution to the problem of actual and potential conflicts along their common border.[10]

An important goal of the present research design is to attempt the comparative study of the informal linkages operating within and across African and specifically, Nigerian borderlands and explore their policy potentials.

Projects to be Accomplished

These will include:

The compilation of a comprehensive bibliography and acquisition of specialized and rare items of literature, including maps to be pooled into a special Borderlands Research Collection in the University of Lagos Library. The emphasis will be on materials relating to Nigeria and immediate West and Central African neighbours.

Collection and processing of mappable data and the production of a standard Nigerian Borderlands Atlas along the model currently being pursued on the U.S.-Mexico border by the *U.C. Mexus*.

Research interests should include border demography, ethnography, and local history and patterns of informal linkages; demarcation of borderlands as planning regions; transborder planning and socioeconomic development; small-scale industrial development inspired by the models of the *Maquiladores* or the twin-plants along the U.S.-Mexico border based on the advantage of cheap labour from a neighbouring country; feasibility surveys for legitimate cross-border trade and investment; integrated transportation and rural development; environmental impact studies; spheres of binational conflicts (differences between the neighbouring nations in their systems of formal education, legislation, official languages and administrative traditions); sensitive policy issues such as immigration, smuggling and border-induced crimes and criminal behaviour and law enforcement generally; the comparative perspectives at the binational and international levels.

Projects may be pursued by individual researchers; but teamwork of interdisciplinary and multidisciplinary character will be specially favoured.

The modes of operation will include seminars, workshops, symposia, lectures on a regular basis.

The project is designed to generate policy information and public enlightenment through the publication and circulation of a newsletter and a journal for the benefit of policy institutions, scholars, private businesses and the general reader. Project activities will produce occasional series of publications including books and monographs. Features on the borderlands, suitable for the television, radio and printed media, will be commissioned to generate public enlightenment on the subject.

Duration of Project

Boundaries define the spatial limits and the territorial framework for the nation-state. Knowledge of their nature, character and functions are obligatory. Such a knowledge must be kept under constant review and made to depend on organized research on a permanent basis. What is planned, then, is a systematic and permanent programme of research, subject only to a periodic review and evaluation.

Estimated Cost and Suggested Sources of Funding

The implementation of this proposal will involve:
a) the establishment of a specialized documentation centre or research collection;
b) the creation of a distinct research fund to support individual and collaborative proposals within the project;
c) provisions for a modest administrative machinery to control, co-ordinate and monitor works within the framework of the project as well as to solicit for continuous funding. In addition to University of Lagos as coordinating centre, zonal control centres are envisaged for each of the remaining 10 borderlands states of the federation. Lagos, Kano, Maiduguri, Borno States and Calabar (Cross River State) centres will function as liaison offices for the neighbouring republics of Benin, Niger, Chad and Cameroun respectively.

The required fund may be derived from a variety of sources ranging from government to private business; but for reasons of preponderance of interest, most if not all the initial grant, must come from the Federal Government, particularly the research resources of the concerned Ministries of Internal Affairs, External Affairs (Africa Division), Defence, and Special Duties, (concerned with state security). External aids could come from such an agency as the Ford Foundation in the absence of alternative indigenous African Foundations. Finally, private business, especially those coordinated by the Nigerian and West African Chambers of Commerce are an important sector of the project's clientele and should be expected to give support as appropriate.

Endnotes

1. J.C. Anene, *The International Boundaries of Nigeria, 1885-1960 (London: Longman, 1970) and J.R.V. Prescott, The Evolution of the Regional and International Boundaries of Nigeria* (Vancouver, 1971).

2. See, e.g. A.I. Asiwaju, *Western Yorubaland Under European Rule 1889-1945* (London: Longman, 1976); A. Mandjannagni, "Queslques Aspects Historiques, Economiques, et Politiques de la frontieres Nigeria-Dahomey", *Etudes Dahomeenes,* 1, 1963-64; R.L. Mills, 'An analysis of the geographical effects of the Dahomey-Nigeria boundary' Ph.D. thesis, Durham, 1970; D.J. Thom, 'The Niger-Nigeria borderlands: a politico-geographical analysis of boundary influence upon the Hausa' Ph.D. thesis, Michigan State Univ., 1970.

3. For a note on the American 'Area Studies' strategy see L.J. Monoz, 'The dual mandate of modern European languages', *West African Journal of Education.*

4. See e.g., O. Ikime, *The Niger Delta Rivaly* (London: Longman, 1969); A.E. Afigbo, *The Warrant Chiefs* (London: Longman, 1972); J.A. Atanda, *The New Oyo Empire* (London: LOngmand, 1973) and P.A. Igbafe, *Benin Under British Administration* (London: Longman, 1979).

5. For a note on the global perspective, see A.J. Asiwaju, "Borderlands Research: A Comparative Perspective", *Border Perspectives Monograph Seies No. 6,* (El Paso: Centre for Inter-American and Border Studies, Univ. of Texas at El Paso, 1983).

6. The papers contributed to the present seminar from the various faculties demonstrate the potentials within the university.

7. For a description of the border as an area of cultural interface and inter-retration, see L.R. Mills, "The development of a frontier zone and border landscape along tthe Dahomey-Nigeria boundary" *The Journal of Tropical Geography* Vol. 36, June 1973, p. 44.

7a. For a relevant and more elaborate analysis of the border as a factor in international interaction, see H. Starr and B.A. Most, "The substance and study of borders in research, *International Studies Quarterly* 20, 4, Dec. 1976.

8. E.R. Stoddard, 'Functional alternatives to binational border development models: the case of the U.S.-Mexico border', paper presented to American Sociological Association, San Francisco, September 1978.

9. Council of Europe, Strasburg: European Treaty Series, No. 106.

10. Niles Hansen, "European transboundary cooperation and its relevance to the United States-Mexico border" seminar paper, 1982.

APPENDIX

Key-Note Address Delivered by
the Minister of Internal Affairs,
Major-General Mohammed Magoro psc, fss,
During the Seminar on "Issues on Borderlands in Africa",
Organised by the Faculty of Arts, University of Lagos,
from 27th to 30th March 1985

The Vice-Chancellor,
The Dean of Faculty of Arts,
Distinguished Ladies and Gentlemen.

I feel greatly honoured to be invited to deliver the Key-note Address for this Seminar whose topic is very dear to this Administration. As you are aware, the Ministry of Internal Affairs is responsible for, among other things, Immigration and Emigration, Customs and Excise matters. These are issues that are closely associated with our borderlands.

The topic of this Seminar which is "Borderlands in Africa" could not have come up at a more opportune time than now. This is because this country has just ratified three protocols with three other countries in the West Africa sub-region namely, Benin, Togo and Ghana, in order to enhance the objectives of ECOWAS. The primary aim of the protocols is to enhance security in the sub-region by checking on the influx of illegal aliens as well as on illegal trade. I hardly need to point out the fact that smuggling contributed immensely to the present economic malaise of this country. We are all living witnesses to the efforts already being made by this Administration to tackle the rather intractable problems associated with the borderlands namely, the influx of illegal aliens and the menace of smugglers and currency traffickers.

The problems of the borderlands in Africa are quite enormous. It is perhaps necessary at this point to flash our minds back to the root cause of the problems associated with our borderlands today. The problems, as you are all aware, stem from the fact that all the African boundaries are a product of artificial creation. The boundaries shared by African countries today are the results of what has been referred to by the historians as 'Carve Up' mentality that emanated from the Scramble for Africa and the resultant infamous Berlin Conference of 1884-1885 during which Africa was literally shared among the European countries. The reasons for the 'Scramble' and the subsequent partition of Africa which made most of the boundaries arbitrary and difficult to identify, are various but the most outstanding one is economic. After the daring adventures of early European explorers and the discovery of lucrative trade along the African coasts and the hinterland, the attention of all Europe became focused on Africa. As time rolled by, however, the emphasis gradually shifted from ordinary trade in materials and slaves, to competition for raw materials from Africa. The raw materials where needed to sustain the famous industrial revolution in Europe. It thus became fashionable for every European country to own a Colony in Africa.

The possession of colonies in Africa seemed to assure the competing European powers of permanent foreign market both for the disposal of their factory products and for the supply of the much needed raw materials for their home industries. The European countries thus gained both economically and politically from their partition of Africa. After the partition and subsequent imposition of European influence and cultures, some valuable cultural preserves of the African countries then referred to as either colonies or protectorates, began to get polluted by the so called 'European influence'. If one may ask, what therefore did Africa gain from European intervention? The answer has several sides but our main concern here is that the partitioning of Africa in 1884-85 did not take into consideration the cultural or ethnic affinities among the African people. Some Yorubas were for example left in Benin Republic while some are in Nigeria. Some Fulanis are in Cameroun and Niger while others are in Nigeria. Some parts of the former Sardauna Province in Nigeria is today in the Camerouns. Nigeria, Cameroun, Gambia, Senegal and indeed all African countries, are classic examples of the 'Carve Up' mentality that was part of the 'Scramble for Africa'.

The artificiality of the boundaries of a country like Gambia is appreciated when we note how it stretches like a finger into Senegal. What is said here does not in any way suggest that boundary problems are peculiar to Africa. The problems of the Middle East and the Gulf War all have to do with boundary disputes, but we must admit that the African experience in boundary matters is unique and more problematic. One of the main effects of all the Scramble, all the partitioning and all the 'Carve Up' is today the unmarked and the confusing boundaries that are shared by the African countries. The European intervention in the African political and social set up which culminated in the Scramble and Partition of Africa, is thus in the main responsible for most of the problems of our borderlands namely boundary disputes, smuggling across the borders and influx of illegal aliens. A classical example of this artificial boundary with its manifest problems is at Idiroko in Ogun State where it is not easy to know when one crosses the boundary between Nigeria and Benin Republic. The same experience obtains around Gaboru Ngala in Borno State, where the boundary with Cameroun is not easily identifiable. In each of these two places, the obvious problem of the unmarked borders is compounded by the cultural and socioeconomic affinity between the people at each side of the boundaries. This development has created intractable problems for the Immigration and Customs officials in terms of who-is-who at the borders.

The situation at these borders is such that sometimes a man who dies at one side of the border, is a maternal or paternal relation of another man who lives on the other side of the border. The critical question then arises; would you tell the man whose brother had died on the other side of the border, that he would need a visa to cross over to mourn his dead relation? Would such a person be able to appreciate the rationale for asking him to obtain one at each of such or similar occasions? One fact that is easily appreciated about our borders is that there are no major social barriers such as differences in language that exist among the inhabitants of the different sides of the borders. This is why even though the people who live at the two sides of the borders belong to different countries, they go to the same markets, and attend the same churches and mosques. They shared cultures of the people at both sides of the borders, make it almost impossible to differentiate the nationals of one country from those of the other. This, in fact, is the starting point of our problems in controlling the influx of illegal aliens and the activities of smugglers at our borders.

One of the far-reaching measures by this administration in an attempt to deal decisively with the problems created by the illegal aliens and smugglers at the borders, is to bring the Department of Customs and Excise to the Federal Ministry of Internal Affairs. The main advantage of this re-alignment is that there will be a unity of purpose and minimization of government bureaucracy. This you will no doubt agree, will go a long way in ensuring optimum surveillance and utilization of scarce resources by the Security Agents at our borders.

The border problem in our own context is a very intriguing one. Our borders are among the most porous ones, one can come across in the whole world. It is because of the lack of natural barriers at our borders as already stated, that the citizens of West African Sub-region stream into Nigeria in search of social and economic opportunities. In the course of this, many of them engage in criminal activities. We are all living witnesses to the fact that when in February 1983, a total of 1,705,500 illegal aliens had to leave the country on the orders of the Federal Government, the crime rate, especially the incidence of armed robbery, came down appreciably. It saddens one to recall that the apparent advantage realized from the expulsion of the illegal aliens in 1983, was rather short-lived because those aliens capitalized on our porous borders with its numerous footpath, to sneak back into the country in large numbers. The chase for illegal aliens in this country, which was further intensified on the inception of this administration, has thus become a deep sore whose cure requires a very intensive treatment. This is why, even with the closure of the borders and the presence of the security agents, the smugglers are still active to some extent and the illegal aliens keep making desperate efforts.

In spite of the die-hard posture adopted by the smugglers and the illegal aliens, I wish to assure you that this administration is determined to deal decisively with the phenomenon of smuggling and to minimize the menace of illegal aliens. There will be no truce in the war against them.

I wish to say that many proposed solutions, some of them radical, have been made for the elusive problems associated with our borderlands. The most radical of these is a suggestion that our vast borders should be fenced or walled using an 'incremental, piece-meal' or what is best described as 'a step-by-step approach'. This approach envisages that the borders could be completely fenced or walled if we start work on them. Some other suggestions touch on the total policing of our borders. One is tempted to ask if the Berlin Wall could be scaled, how feasible are these proposals? It is the belief of this administration that the total and effective participation of every Nigerian is the only answer to the problems of smugglers and illegal aliens. I, however, feel reassured that one of the aims of this very important and thought-provoking seminar is a 'conscious search for policy alternatives if not innovations' on matters concerning our borderlands. I assure you that the policy options you are bound to come up with, will be given adequate attention and the innovative ideas associated with them, carefully examined and whenever possible, resources permitting, they will be given a trial. Since this seminar has attracted an assemblage of reputable academicians, who are experts in their different disciplines, I have no doubt in my mind, that you will come out with suggestions that would serve as a credible springboard for the solution of the problems associated with borderlands, not only in Nigeria but also in Africa.

Notes

Notes

Notes

Notes

Notes

Notes

Notes

Notes